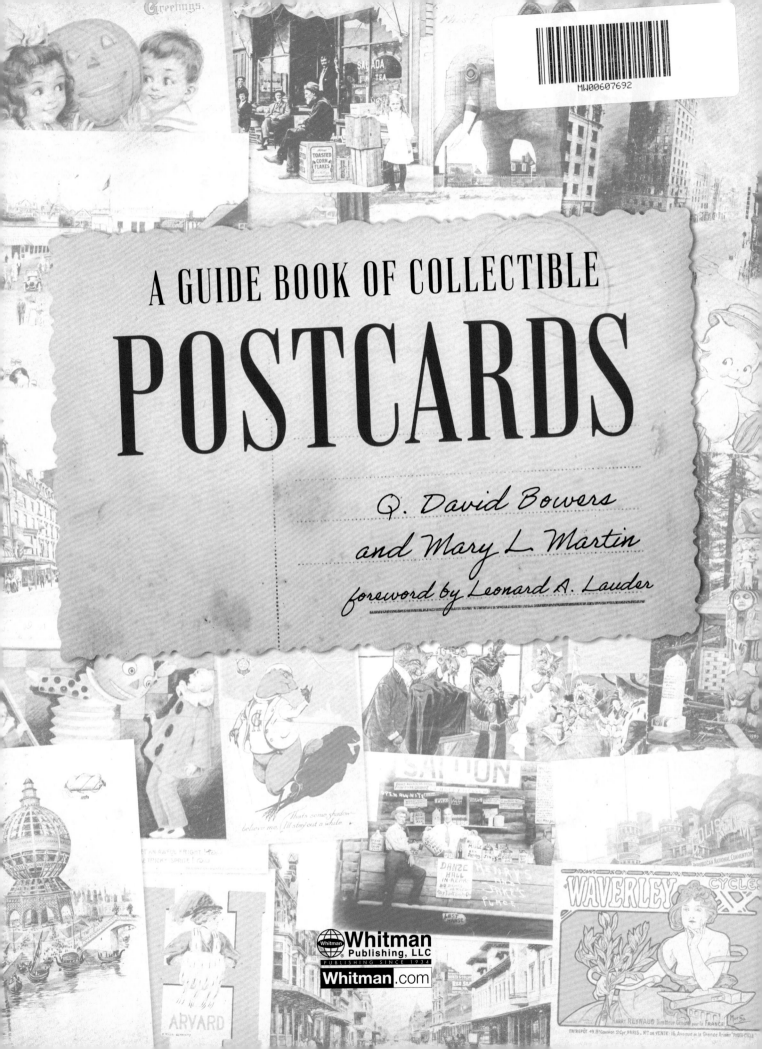

A GUIDE BOOK OF COLLECTIBLE

POSTCARDS

Q. David Bowers

and Mary L. Martin

foreword by Leonard A. Lauder

Whitman
Publishing, LLC
PUBLISHING SINCE 1934

Whitman.com

A Guide Book of Collectible Postcards

© 2020 Whitman Publishing, LLC
1974 Chandalar Drive • Suite D • Pelham, AL 35124
ISBN: 0794847374
Printed in the United States

Correspondence concerning this book may be directed to Whitman Publishing, Attn: Collectible Postcards, at the address above.

Whitman Publishing is a leading publisher of hobby reference books, supplies, and storage and display products that help you build, appreciate, and share great collections. To browse our complete catalog, visit Whitman Publishing online at www.Whitman.com.

If you enjoy this book, we invite you to learn more about America's history by starting a new postcard collection and reading as much as possible.

If your historical and collecting interests cross over to coins, tokens, medals, and paper currency, you can join the American Numismatic Association (ANA), the nation's largest hobby group for collectors of money-related material culture. Learn about numismatics and make new friends in the hobby. Explore the ANA at www.Money.org.

WHITMAN®

TABLE OF CONTENTS

Table of Contents continues on next page.

FOREWORD

Postcard collectors are passionate people. Ever since I was a charter member of the Metropolitan Postcard Club of New York City, which I joined as a teenager, I have had inspiring conversations with fellow collectors about their unwavering searches for the perfect cards to build their collections—whether a small group on a very specific theme or a wider selection on many topics. My own passion began when I was a young boy, and I spent my first allowance on cards depicting the Empire State Building, purchased at the Woolworth's on the ground floor of that very building. A few years later, the striking pastel-colored and crisply designed cards of Art Deco hotels in Miami Beach reignited my interest and as a teenager I joined the Metropolitan Postcard Club of New York City, where I began to exchange cards with other members. Postcards were my "gateway" collection—I soon branched off into film and propaganda posters, filling all available storage spaces in our New York City apartment—including the bathtub!—and later I began my art collection.

My passion for postcards returned with a vengeance after I had completed college, served in the U.S. Navy, got married, started a family, and took on a role at the Estée Lauder Company. Traveling for business in the 1960s, I came across turn-of-the-century cards in astounding numbers at flea markets and antique stores in London and I began to haunt postcard shops in Paris. I remember vividly one shopping day in London when I became enthralled by the swirling lines and rich, brilliant colors of a group of Japanese Art Nouveau postcards. Another time I found photographic cards depicting the German Revolution of 1918 and 1919, selling for pennies, and was drawn in by the way they brought to life an event I had learned about in history books. I felt like I had come upon a treasure. Like a kid in a candy store, I began to seek out more and more such finds; they not only brought back my childhood enthusiasm for postcards but also linked to my adult interests in history, design, and art. I earnestly began to compile a collection that I considered to be destined for a museum.

But I knew that passion was not enough. I needed to learn about the postcard—the most important communication form of the early twentieth century and a significant force in artistic and visual culture. I bought many books and consumed them avidly. I also relied on the dealers and collectors that I encountered at postcard fairs and in shops throughout the world. What incredible knowledge and history can be found within the postcard community! I remember many an afternoon at shows, filled with stimulating conversations with fellow dealers and collectors as we combed through boxes and boxes of postcards. Their understanding of the medium's history and their ability to discuss artists, series, publishers, variations, and even individual cards so often inspired my own collecting, and spurred my desire to know more and more about postcards.

This new reference, *A Guide Book of Collectible Postcards*, comes from two of the most knowledgeable postcard champions I know, my dear friends Mary L. Martin and Q. David Bowers. It puts their years of experience and

wisdom together for a wide audience. I have known Mary since she was a child—postcards are in her blood. Her parents, Mary and Bill, were leaders in the renaissance of postcard collecting during the last third of the twentieth century. They were always dedicated to postcard promotion and education. Mary grew up among all of us who benefitted from their work and passion, became a leader in the field in her own right, and has passed on the love of postcards to her son, Joe Russell. For decades, Mary has maintained the family tradition of postcard excellence. Her Havre de Grace inventory is unparalleled, but her role in the postcard world is far bigger than just being an excellent dealer. She brings together the best dealers at her shows, fosters a sense of camaraderie in the community, promotes collecting among the young, and spreads learning through publications of all kinds.

Mary's frequent partner in these publications, Q. David Bowers, is an enthusiastic collector in his own right and has tirelessly sought to link his passion for historical objects with his scholarly pursuits. Also bit by the postcard bug when he was just a boy, David has been enormously influential in generating awareness of the postcard. His work on the medium represents just one of his fields of expertise, which include coins and musical instruments as well as theater and cinema. David's voluminous publications represent much more than his passion for collecting, speaking to his generosity as a person who has made it a priority to share his valuable experience and the knowledge he has acquired over many years both in the trenches and in the libraries.

Together, Mary and Dave have raised the bar for the serious recognition of the postcard as one of the most important forms of mass media in history. David's book on the postcards of Czech artist Alfons Mucha, which he wrote with Mary's mother, is a classic. My own well-thumbed copy helped me complete my collection of Mucha postcards (which today are in the Museum of Fine Arts in Boston, the home to my collection), with knowledge and confidence. The version he published in 2016, updated with Mary, has proven equally valuable to the new generation of collectors that they bring into the field through their tireless work. Mary's sorely missed magazine, Postcard World, to which David was a frequent contributor, shed light on so many important moments of postcard history. Now, this invaluable *Guide Book of Collectible Postcards* brings to life the history of the postcard, from production and circulation to the postcard's rightful place today in many important private and public collections. For those of you who will not have the pleasure of sitting at a postcard show talking shop with Mary and David, this book makes available the extraordinary knowledge they have amassed through lifetimes dedicated to the postcard. We postcard collectors, historians, and scholars alike are indebted to them.

Leonard A. Lauder
New York City

PREFACE

Like many hobbyists, I've read Q. David Bowers's books since I was a young collector. For more than fifteen years I've also had the honor of being his publisher, adding many new works to his extensive oeuvre. As for Mary L. Martin, I've known *of* her for almost as long—Dave sings the praises of Mary's parents, and of Mary herself, as experts in the field of postcards. It was an honor to finally meet her in person a few years ago, at her shop in Havre de Grace, Maryland, as the three of us discussed their latest collaboration, the *Guide Book of Collectible Postcards*.

Early in the planning process for this book, Dave shared some letters written between himself and a well-known postcard collector: Andreas Brown, president of the famous salon-like Gotham Book Mart (West 47th Street in Midtown Manhattan's Diamond District). Dave had invited Brown's feedback on a manuscript he was preparing on the postcards of Alphonse Mucha. Their letters back and forth are a fascinating exploration of grading, rarity, market values, buying and selling—every aspect of the postcard hobby, "an interesting field of interesting people collecting interesting things," as Dave put it in one letter.

Those letters illustrate that Dave Bowers is neither a newcomer to the hobby, nor a dilettante. They were written in 1980. Dave's coauthor on the Mucha book was Mary L. Martin the elder—mother of his current collaborator.

Collectors of coins, paper money, medals, and tokens have known Dave Bowers as a prolific researcher and writer since the 1960s. Some also know he's written authoritative references on other interests, such as automatic music machines and early silent-film history. Over the years as Dave's publisher at Whitman Publishing, I've often been asked, "How does he write so many books?"

First of all, as Isaac Asimov and other productive authors have said, "A writer writes"—and Dave has been doing this for more than fifty years. But what he does is multi-faceted and immersive, more than the simple (but important) physical act of sitting down at a desk and putting pen to paper.

The cornerstone of his system is the Bowers archives. Long before the Internet, Dave was compiling a personal library and research center of books, newspapers, magazine clippings and snippets, and other resources—anything and everything relating to his scholarly interests. He read and studied decades' worth of old periodicals and made note of everything relating to, for example, postcards, collecting in the Golden Age, the intricacies of printing and distribution, Post Office procedures, and more.

As technology has advanced, so has the Bowers research machine. Historical images that he earlier had to clip, photograph, or photocopy can now be scanned and saved digitally in high resolution. Instead of having to

travel to faraway museums and archives, email and the Internet put him in a hundred places at once, with instant communications.

This touches on another important factor in how Dave Bowers works: collaboration. "To have a friend, you must be a friend," as the saying goes. Over a career that has spanned decades, he has built a reputation as a researcher who generously shares information instead of jealously guarding it. In return, other scholars share their own specialized insight—and Dave absorbs and synthesizes it as only he can, to then give to you, his reader.

Another element of the Bowers method is a constant and never-resting spirit of inquiry that spans genres, disciplines, and fields. Dave is as curious a student of current events as he is of the past. His book subjects run up and down the Dewey Decimal System. The hobby community is fortunate that postcards captured his imagination early on, and have never let go.

For the *Guide Book of Collectible Postcards*, the foundation of the manuscript was the knowledge Dave Bowers has been gathering over many decades as an active collector and historian. His partner in building on that foundation needs no introduction to postcard collectors. Mary Martin is the owner and operator of the biggest postcard dealerships and shows in the United States (quite possibly the world?), and an accomplished researcher and prolific author in the field. She has authored, coauthored, or edited some fifty books on the subject of postcards. When I visited her Maryland shop in 2018, her inventory numbered in the millions of cards, dating back to the Golden Age.

Mary collaborated on the outline of the *Guide Book*, reviewed Dave's research, provided hundreds of high-quality scanned images, and, along with her son, Joe Russell, marshaled her extensive knowledge and experience to provide valuations for the 1,200-plus cards illustrated, plus values for hundreds of card types, varieties, and topics.

As famous collector Leonard Lauder observed in his foreword to the 2016 Bowers/Martin book *The Postcards of Alphonse Mucha*, "Postcard collectors value the hunt." Every hunter benefits from a good guide, and the current volume leads the way.

Not simply a useful reference, the *Guide Book of Collectible Postcards* will appeal to multiple and diverse audiences. Students of art, history, advertising, and related fields will find it interesting and informative. Fans of Art Nouveau, American comics, and vintage photography will enjoy a gallery of outstanding works. Active hobbyists will benefit from the valuation charts, detailed catalogs, and check lists. These resources give a blueprint to follow while building your collection, as well as a guide to valuing and analyzing cards you already possess. The bibliography, glossary, appendices, and indexes add to the book's already impressive utility.

These diverse and well-crafted facets—educational and artistic, collector-oriented, market-savvy, and historical—combine to make *Guide Book of Collectible Postcards* a delightful and valuable addition to every bookshelf.

Dennis Tucker
Publisher, Whitman Publishing

INTRODUCTION

W elcome to *A Guide Book of Collectible Postcards*. For well over a century collecting postcards has been one of our country's most dynamic, most widely enjoyed hobbies. In the following chapters you will find details about production, distribution, and collection of postcards used in America and desired today by collectors—including cards printed in the United States and elsewhere.

Collecting postcards has been a popular passion in America since the late nineteenth century. Visitors to the World's Columbian Exposition in Chicago in 1893 were eager buyers of cards lithographed in color and depicting various attractions. This launched the hobby. Today collecting postcards is one of America's favorite pastimes.

Among collectibles, postcards are among the most egalitarian, for want of a better word. With a very modest budget you can build a definitive display of many specialties. On the other hand, there are classic rarities that sell in the hundreds of dollars, or even more.

Reading this book is equivalent to spending a few days immersed in a postcard convention or show. Hundreds of cards are illustrated, described in detail, and have estimated values. In addition, detailed information and more values are found in various specialized chapters.

In the United States, postal cards (as they were first called) were made by the Post Office Department in the second half of the nineteenth century. These had the postage of 1¢ imprinted on them. In time the souvenir postcard made its debut and required the addition of a 1¢ stamp to mail, giving them the nickname of "penny postcards." These form the focus of most collections today. *Post card* and *postal card*, as two words, and *postcard*, one word, are the three main spellings used on the cards themselves. Collectors and historians usually use one, *postcard*.

Although countless postcards were printed domestically from the last decade of the nineteenth century to the onset of the World War in 1914, some of the most beautiful postcards with American subjects were printed in Germany, where the art of colorful lithography was at a high level. Beautiful cards were also printed in England, and smaller quantities came from France.

In 1976 Clarkson N. Potter published *Picture Postcards in the United States 1893–1918*, by George and Dorothy Miller. The title reflects the era of early pictorial postcards starting with those for the World's Columbian Exposition held in Chicago in 1893, including a suite of colorfully lithographed cards showing the fair's various buildings. Color cards of the early era used artwork as well as colorized black-and-white photographs. The Miller book brings down the curtain with 1918, the year after the United States entered the World

Charlotte on Lake Ontario — The Coney Island of Central New York

769. · REVERE BEACH, MASS., WONDERLAND PARK.

love to all from Mary

War, although the importation of lithographed postcards from Germany ended before then. We have used the Miller timeframe for what we call the Golden Age of postcards, a term in popular use by others as well.

Since the publication of *Picture Postcards in the United States 1893–1918*, dozens of other postcard books have been published—most specializing in views of a particular city or area, or postcards displaying the work of specific artists. The *Encyclopedia of Antique Postcards*, by Susan Brown Nicholson, published in 1992, has been a particularly useful guide for many collectors. *The Postcard Age*, 2012, by Linda Klich, curator of the Leonard A. Lauder postcard collection, offers many images, as do two other books based on Lauder's holdings.

In the mid-twentieth century some collectors suggested that *deltiology* be used to describe the hobby and that participants be called *deltiologists*. This never caught on in conversation (though the terms are sometimes seen in print), and today "postcard collecting" and "postcard collectors" are always heard at meetings and shows. In contrast, coin collectors often call themselves numismatists, and stamp collectors are philatelists. Less well known, mycologists study mushrooms and vexillographers study flags. The endings for those two words are adaptations of the Greek *logica*, or *knowledge*.

During the Golden Age most scenic cards were made from black-and-white photographs with color added by lithography (the case with nearly all imports) or in many instances by hand-tinting (mostly by domestic shops, such as that of Frank Swallow). Many motifs were produced in America and Europe by talented artists who created holiday greetings, humorous scenes, images of beautiful women, and other topics. After 1918 art-type cards were mostly replaced by folded greeting cards housed in envelopes. These allowed for extensive art and for messages and sentiments that could not be read by postmen. Accordingly, most printed postcards after the Golden Age are scenic or advertise products, services, or events.

In the early twentieth century the quality of cards printed in America increased dramatically. The Detroit Publishing Company, Curt Teich, and others produced many cards that rivaled imports. In the 1930s Curt Teich pioneered the "linen" card—a card printed on regular stock but with a slightly rough surface fancifully like the feel of linen. Nearly all of these were made in color. From the 1930s onward "chrome" (from *chromatic* or color) cards have been made from color photographs. Chapters 23 and 24 are devoted to these.

In the pages that follow we have collected more facts and figures about postcard creation and collection than have ever before been contained in one convenient volume.

A world of information awaits you.
Enjoy the book!

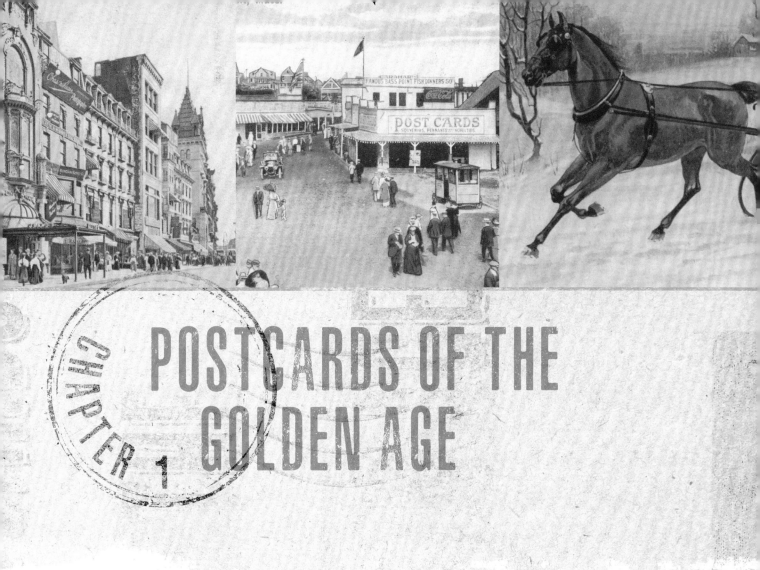

POSTCARDS OF THE GOLDEN AGE

CHAPTER 1

This chapter tells of the rise of postcards with scenes, art, and other images that are so avidly collected today. The Golden Age issues, particularly those of the early twentieth century, are among the most beautiful ever produced.

The 1890s

Beginning in 1873 the Post Office Department provided postal cards (as they were designated) for use in mailing advertising, notices, and other information, but these were strictly business and not recreational or scenic. On June 1, 1878, the General Postal Union (which suggested regulations for member countries, including the United States) fixed the maximum dimensions of a postcard as 3.5 by 5.5 inches. Early cards are sometimes called pioneer cards.

Front and back of a United States postal card of the 1880s. There were many different variations produced. Today these are widely sought by stamp collectors (philatelists), but there is minimal interest among postcard collectors. EF to Mint: $5–$8; discontinued post office, $10+

1

The first scenic postcards printed in quantity for distribution in America were issued for the 1893 World's Columbian Exposition. Postcards of that decade include high-quality lithographed cards imported from Europe and domestic cards in color and black and white. The black-and-white cards were mostly made by newspapers and printing plants, not by established postcard companies. Views printed in America in the late nineteenth century, such as the hundreds of scenes published by the *Brooklyn Eagle*, were usually local or regional and of indifferent printing quality.

Toward the end of the 1890s many colorful scenic cards made in Germany depicted American scenes. Early cards had plain or undivided backs that, per postal regulations, could not include messages. The backs were reserved for addresses and, sometimes, the name of the printer or publisher.

The Postal Act of May 19, 1898, provided for the extensive private production of postcards to measure 3.25 by 5.5 inches, although this size rule was often ignored. Messages could only be written on the front. The back was reserved "exclusively for the address." These cards were used until 1907 by law and sometimes later when printers continued the old backs.

Series No. 7, Design No. 7, in Charles W. Goldsmith's series of color postcards issued for the World's Columbian Exposition in 1893. Front and back view. Cards from the fair marked the beginning of popularity of color postcards for tourists and collectors. EF to Mint: $5–$10

A panorama of Coney Island in 1897, as published on a pioneer postcard by H.A. Rost Printing and Publishing Co., New York City. EF to Mint: $15–$20

Into the 1900s

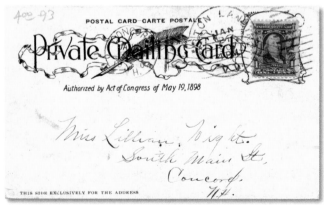

Messages, not allowed on the back, had to be written on the front, as seen here on a postcard of the Lick Observatory, Mount Hamilton, California (Edward H. Mitchell, No. 59). EF to Mint: $3–$5

Collecting in the Early 1900s

Domestically printed postcards from the 1890s through the first several years of the twentieth century were mostly black and white, although there were many

A color postcard from the turn of the century depicting Mount Washington in New Hampshire and sold by Chisholm Brothers, Portland, Maine. This and related "Greetings from" cards were printed in Germany, the American version of the "Gruss aus" cards of the same style published in Germany and depicting scenes from that region. EF to Mint: $2–$4

A circa-1905 Mount Washington card published in Germany and distributed by Chisholm. EF to Mint: $2–$4

A Detroit Publishing Company postcard of Keith's Theatre in Boston. Printed in Detroit and copyrighted in 1906. During the first decade of the twentieth century the firm issued thousands of scenes. EF to Mint: $2–$4

exceptions. Quality varied widely. Within a few years high-quality color cards, mostly imported from Germany and England, became wildly popular, joined in 1899 by color cards of the Detroit Publishing Company, which were serially numbered beginning with 1 during 1899 and the next few years. Beginning in 1906, and continuing for years afterward, Detroit issued many cards with the copyright date of 1906 and some in color from black-and-white images copyrighted in 1900. Collecting postcards became a nationwide fad—some called it a craze—starting in the early years of the twentieth century, far out-rivaling the collecting of stamps and coins. Unlike the case for the latter two hobbies, a hobbyist could form a fine collection of postcards for very little cost. The rush was on and collecting cards became widespread. From that time, postcards have remained popular subjects in the media. Today news and advertisements for postcard shows and related events are published widely, various postcard clubs are active, and

periodicals specializing in antiques and collectibles take special notice of postcard events. The popularity of the Internet has introduced countless new enthusiasts.

In the meantime, since the late 1890s many postcards were made by amateur and professional photographers who printed images on glossy stock. Today these are called Real Photo Postcards, abbreviated in print as RPPC. At shows these are usually called real photos. (RPPC is mainly used in written communications. If pronounced it is by the letters.) Many of them memorialized events, disasters, and other short-lived incidents and occasions.

After March 1, 1907, the law specified that messages could be written on the backs of cards. Cards of the new style, called "divided back" by collectors, had a vertical line, to the left of which a message could be written, with the address to the right. "Undivided back" cards remained in many inventories of shops, and some printers kept using undivided backs for a few years. Accordingly, it is not unusual to find undivided-back cards with postmarks of a few years past 1907.

The following are selected articles from the early years of the collecting passion in America.

The Day, August 7, 1905, published in New London, Connecticut, included this:

Printed with an undivided back, this card depicting the Prospect Hotel on Surf Avenue, Coney Island, New York, was converted in 1909 by the user, who drew a vertical line and added a message to the left of it. EF to Mint: $6–$8

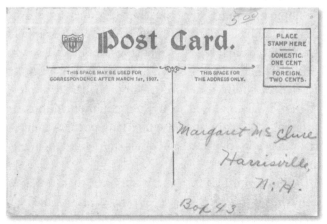

This transitional back was printed in 1906 or early 1907 and advises of the possibility of adding a message on the back beginning on March 1, 1907. EF to Mint: $4–$6

An evidence of the prevalence of the fad for collecting souvenir postal cards was shown Sunday when the excursion from Providence was in here for a short stay. A postal clerk who was captured for the excursionists for the time being had an opportunity to sell 400 one-cent stamps. 4,000 of the penny stamps were sent to Plum Island to be used by members of the 13th Heavy Artillery of New York, now encamped there, and a local news dealer bought 1,000 of the one-cent stamps for the same use.

In New Brunswick, Canada, the *St. John Sun* newspaper conducted the Each and All Club and printed correspondence, mostly from the United States, in its news columns. The November 17, 1906, edition had this in the "Correspondence and Postcard Exchange" column:

I received a postal the other day from New Hampshire of Lover's Walk, Canobie Lake Park, but no name was written on it. Will you please ask the girl who sent it to send me her name and address? Of course, I know you do not know the person, but would like you to put it on our page.

A.L.B., Philadelphia.

I am a young married woman, having been married eight years, but have no children. I am a musician, having been a teacher of piano for years. I also do some embroidery, but music is my great talent, also I am very fond of cooking. I would like to have my name enrolled in the postcard exchange. I will return them by return mail. I would like them from anywhere and all kinds except comics.

Mrs. G.R.F., West Lynn, Massachusetts.

I am trying to get the Capitol building of each state, and I will exchange cards with any of the girls, as I work at a stationery store, and we handle cards from all over the United States. I am interested in elocution and photography, and if I can be of any service, kindly let me know and I will be glad to help.

Charlotte M.B., Philadelphia.

"Post Cards" sign on a souvenir shop at Bass Point, Nahant, Massachusetts, a favorite summertime recreation spot for residents of Boston and nearby areas. (Essinger & Cook, Bass Point, circa 1910s.) Cards were all the craze and every amusement park offered them for sale. EF to Mint: $10–$15

Interior of the Provincetown Advocate Post Card Shop, with postcards on the wall to the right. EF to Mint: $15–$25

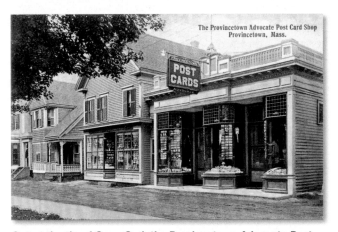

Out at the tip of Cape Cod, the Provincetown Advocate Post Card Shop, Provincetown, Massachusetts, offered a large selection of postcards for sale, including German imports and Curt Teich Co. cards with the imprint of the *Provincetown Advocate*, this being a local newspaper. (Circa 1910s.) EF to Mint: $15–$25

The main counter in the Provincetown shop. EF to Mint: $15–$25

The *Pittsburgh Press*, December 6, 1906, printed this under "Fads of the Day" (excerpts):

The postal card fad is one of the greatest crazes that have ever arisen. It is literally universal, for in every out-of-the-way corner of the world it is possible to procure a photograph of the place on a postcard. One would suppose, to judge from the crowd surrounding the postcard counters that Americans were the largest investors to this habit, but the fad over here is not to be compared with that in European countries, where the cards are actually shipped by the bushel. . . . The trouble with people who have the collecting habit is that they are apt to forget that other people are not as interested in their hobby as they are themselves, and are only bored when forced to look through albums and catalogues galore. This does not prevent one from enjoying one's own collection, or in comparing it with that of others interested in the same subjects. . . . As a pastime for young and old, and in many cases as an educational factor, a good collection of some interesting kind is profitable and should be encouraged.

Again in the *Pittsburgh Press*, January 3, 1907, under "Uses of Postcards":

Postcards have become so popular and fascinating in their variety that many people have made interesting collections that are a source of entertainment to their friends. There are postcards made of wood, leather, aluminum, and of photographic prints and blue-prints besides the ordinary paper ones. Aside from its intrinsic value, each is characteristic of the sender. Many have most clever and amusing brevities scrawled across them. . . .

The *Lewiston Evening Journal*, Lewiston, Maine, February 7, 1908, printed this article by Sam E. Conner:

A thousand picture postal cards are mailed in Lewiston every day.

"It's just a passing fad." So they said when the souvenir postcard first made its appearance. That was some time ago. In the months and years which have elapsed since then the collection of postcards has long since passed the fad stage. Today it is just as much a pastime as the collection of stamps and coins. Instead of a passing fancy it has come to be a business, in which thousands of persons are securing a living.

Many a person has raised his voice in protest against the cards. They are killing the art of letter writing, so these opponents of the small bits of cardboard say. The same protest was raised against the typewriter and the stenographer. But the two latter came and stayed. So far the souvenir cards have stayed and give no indication of leaving. . . .

Here in Lewiston and Auburn scores of people average to send fifty to seventy-five cards a week to distant friends and relatives. I know one man whose duties take him away from home and around the state a great deal, who averages to send ten cards from each place he visits. His wife and his sisters both have the card collecting habit. . . .

This postcard business is comparatively new in America. Up to four or five years ago it is doubtful if more than a hundred shops in the United States had them for sale. Today there is scarcely a village or town so small that it hasn't a postcard shop and its own particular set of cards. Some, no doubt, suppose the postcard idea originated in America. It did not. The sending of postcards has been in vogue in Europe some time before the United States took it up.

The Americans at first did not seem to take kindly to the idea. A few stores put in assortments of cards. They sold slowly. Just as hope that it would catch on with the American public was about dead, came a revolution of public feeling, and the postcard craze was on. That was about four or five years ago. Since then it has grown by leaps.

A Lovers' Walk postcard from Canobie Park, similar to that received by *St. John Sun* reader **A.L.B.** of Philadelphia (see page 4). EF to Mint: $3–$5

"Smallest News & Post Card Stand in New Orleans, La. 103 Royal Street, Size 4x4." At the top in the image the sign reads, "Wallace Magazines and Periodicals." Under magnification these magazine covers can be seen: *Sporting Life, Smart Set, Everybody's Magazine, Scientific American, Puck, The Saturday Evening Post, Harper's Weekly, Leslie's Weekly, Women's Home Companion, Judge, The Standard & Vanity Fair, Judge's Library, New York Dramatic Mirror, The Billboard,* and *Collier's.* (No publisher; circa 1908.) EF to Mint: $30–$45

Then there wasn't a card manufactured in this country. Everything was imported, mostly from Germany. Today there are many establishments in this country where the postcards are made, as well as many where albums for holding them are manufactured. Now, as in the beginning, the best cards come from Germany. It is said that the Americans have not the machinery for making the best cards. . . .

In the past two or three years postcards have been superseding the old fashioned valentine. Today they are to be had with all the beautiful sentiments and heart-shaped designs dear to the valentine maker of yore. These postcard valentines are not taking the place of the high priced tokens, but of those sold for five and ten cents. The change, too, is for the better, the postcard valentine being superior in every way to the old time brand… Like nearly everything which comes to America the picture postcard has got into politics. Postcard ballots have long been in vogue in this country. Since the postcard came, candidates have used them to advance their cause. They have been used to make the faces of candidates familiar to those whom they desire to represent.…

The New York City Post Office averages to handle 100,000 cards per day. It is figured that in New York City alone during 1906, at the lowest point, $700,000 was spent on picture postcards. It may be said that the picture postcard is a fad, that it will follow the fate of the picture advertising card of twenty years ago.[1] The figures of its growth and the present great interest would indicate differently. Besides, the postcards are different from those cards of other days. The advertising card of a quarter of a century ago told of the wonderful curative powers of patent medicines, the great things which hair restorers would do. Some of them are clever, even artistic in design. The postcard is different. It may not last, but at this time there is no sign of a decrease in its popularity. Instead the reverse is true.

"Postal Carditis"

In March 1906 *American Illustrated Magazine* printed "Postal Carditis and Allied Manias," by John Walker Harrington. The article epitomizes the old saying: you are either a collector or you are not. Harrington found the acquisition of postcards in quantity rather strange. Excerpts:

Postal Carditis and allied collecting manias are working havoc among inhabitants of the United States. The germs of these maladies brought to this country in the baggage of tourists and immigrants escaped quarantine regulations and were propagated with amazing rapidity. There is now no hamlet so remote which has not succumbed to

Looks after the artistic health of the community

A cartoon from "Postal Carditis."

A picture of the City Hall

Another cartoon from "Postal Carditis."

the ravages of the microbe postale Universelle… Unless such manifestations are checked, millions of persons of now normal lives and irreproachable habits will become victims of faddy degeneration of the brain.

By far the worst development of the prevailing pests is Postal Carditis, which affects the heart, paralyzes the reasoning faculties, and abnormally increases the nerve. It had its origin in Germany twenty years ago, but did not assume dangerous proportions there until 1897. Sporadic cases of it were observed in the United States, and the year 1900 saw the malady rapidly spread from one center of infection to another. It seems only yesterday that the postal cards were on view almost entirely at hotels which were patronized exclusively by foreigners, or in little dingy shops on Third Avenue, or on the remote East Side. A population which had only recently come from outré mer purchased them to send to friends and relatives in Europe.

Advertisements appeared in the Sunday newspapers, setting forth that certain Germans had for sale the rights of a "novelty." So as opium was introduced into China by way of Hong Kong, virulent forms of the post card pest found their way to the United States by way of Munich and Berlin. Shrewd speculators imported these bits of pasteboard by the millions. Germany, where the output is constantly becoming more artistic, sends large consignments; England furnishes tons of the heavily humorous variety; France inflicts the piquantly flavored ones, while the United States grinds out half-tone views, comics, and the high art variety, good, bad, worse, and indifferent.

With ingenuity worthy of a better cause, dealers have abetted this form of insanity by inventing new and diabolical designs of postal cards, as well as albums, racks, and other means of preserving them. A favorite device is the album. From small beginnings the pasteboard souvenir industry has fattened upon epistolary sloth and collecting manias until there are extant in this country today 150,000 varieties of picture postal cards. Bookstores which formerly did a thriving trade in literature are now devoted almost entirely to their sale. There were in Atlantic City last season ten establishments where nothing else was sold, and Chicago, Boston, Pittsburgh, and New York have emporiums where postals constitute the entire stock.

In West Bethel, Maine, the Whitten & Dennison partnership was full-speed into the postcard craze. Probably ordering from other sources, they offered greeting cards, standard cards with imprints for a particular town, and "Glossy Views" (actually a medium-quality black-and-white printed card with a glossy surface) from customers' own negatives. The Wholesalers Post Card Club was another aspect of business. (Whitten & Dennison. Postmarked 1908.) EF to Mint: $15–$25

On the back of this RPPC (full card and detail shown), Lela R. writes to a postcard-exchange friend, Miss Marie Babbe of Spencer, Indiana: "Thanks for the picture of your church. It is very pretty. I will send you a picture of my church as soon as I can get one. The picture on the other side is myself. Brother Irving took the picture. Would be glad to get yours sometime. Bye bye. With Love. Lela R. Reader, Ill." (Postmarked May 20, 1912.) This card with a pretty girl and with the person and location identified, plus an interesting message, is worth more than a related card would sell for without such information. EF to Mint: $4–$6

Goodman's Book Store in Manchester, New Hampshire, had a large stock of postcards for sale near the front door. This view dates from about 1907. In this image, view cards are closest, and art cards are behind them. EF to Mint: $30–$45

The American Athens [Philadelphia] had a postal card exhibition which vied with the Whistler picture show for public attention. These wares may be seen in New York on practically every street corner and most of the drug stores, cigar stands, hotels, barber shops, and department store gridirons are interested in their sale. Ten large factories are working overtime in this country to supply the demand, and many smaller ones are selling their output as fast as it is produced.

In many localities in the United States the post office facilities have been swamped by the excess of souvenir postals, while on the boardwalk at Atlantic City riots have been narrowly averted because the authorities had neglected to supply enough one cent stamps to meet the demand of the victims of Carditis Postale.

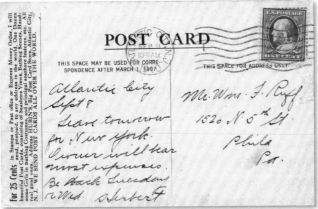

For 25 Cents in Stamps or Post office or Express Money Order, I will send, postpaid, to any address in the world, One Dozen beautiful Post Cards, consisting of Seashore Views, Bathing Scenes, Handsome Girls in Bathing Costumes, and principal seashore features, etc. All real good ones. Address HUBIN'S, Big Post Card Store, Atlantic City N.J. WE SEND POST CARDS ALL OVER THE WORLD.

In 1906 Hubin's Big Post Card Store in Atlantic City ordered a supply of cards with the Elephant Hotel, operated by John Gertzen. The hotel was an icon of that seaside resort. On the back the notation "This space may be used for correspondence after March 1, 1907" signaled the advent of the "divided back" era. This was at the height of postcard-collecting passion, and Hubin's offered a collection of a dozen view cards for 25¢. EF to Mint: $5–$9

On January 8, 1908, a Wisconsin postcard collector sent this RPPC to a collector friend in Lakewood, Ohio, with this message: "Interior of mailing division in Milwaukee Post Office. Thank you very much for pretty New Year greeting. Cross marks the sender. Puzzle: find him." (Hint: the X is in the center of the detail image; examining RPPCs in detail is an interesting pursuit.) EF to Mint: $60–$90

The preceding short version of Harrington's opinions saves the present reader from reading similar, but briefer, harangues against collecting other things, such as cigar bands, pewter mugs, minerals, souvenir spoons, meteorites, theater programs, antique violins, and even "arctic bugs." Ragtime music, all the rage in the first decade of the twentieth century, also had countless detractors.

Without credit to Harrington, the *Practical Druggist* and *Review of Reviews*, May 1906, each had its own "Postal Carditis" article, much briefer, but using some of the same examples, and concluding on an upbeat note with some money-making advice: "This trade is a very clean and simple one to handle, and druggists should take advantage of the various offers in our columns, to stock up with this profitable side line."

Postcards Made for Collectors
Artists' Cards

While scenic views were all the rage and RPPCs continued to be made depicting people and events, the passion for cards spawned many series especially made for collectors.

These included sets and runs of cards by artists such as Philip Boileau, Harrison Fisher, Ellen Clapsaddle, F. Earl Christy, and others. Some were sold in sets or small series, but most were available singly. Collectors endeavored to acquire one of each subject. Chapter 11 discusses these sets in detail.

"Sense of Smell, Falling in Love," Harrison Fisher. (Reinthal & Newman, Water Color Series No. 701.) EF to Mint: $10–$20

A Yale card by F. Earl Christy. (Raphael Tuck & Sons, London, "College Queens" Series No. 1767. Lithographed in Berlin.) EF to Mint: $10–$20

A Halloween card published by John Winsch. (Copyright 1913 by Winsch; printed in Germany.) EF to Mint: $150–$225

"At the Carnival, Music Hath Charms." (Raphael Tuck & Sons, Carnival Series No. 117; printed in Saxony.) EF to Mint: $10–$15

New Year Card, 1906. (No publisher; European back in multiple languages.) EF to Mint: $10–$15

Colorfully lithographed holiday cards were very popular. Most were issued singly and not in series. Collectors sought appealing images. Most were printed in Germany.

Other Series

Among many series made for collectors, the Roosevelt Bears were especially popular and consisted of color images of animated teddy bears going hither and yon on various adventures, with a cute rhyme below each image.

Zeno, a popular brand of chewing gum, issued many cards of city scenes, tourist attractions, and other views imprinted with the Zeno name on the front.

5A horse blankets were featured in an interesting series.

"No. 8. The Roosevelt Bears in the Department Store." / "It was worth a trip a mile to see / This paper package marked TEDDY-G." No. 8 in the first set of 16. EF to Mint: $10–$25

A postcard with "ZENO Means Good / CHEWING GUM" in the bottom border together with the title of the view (in this instance, "State House, Boston, Mass."). EF to Mint: $2–$3

"5A Plush Robe No. 1853." One of many cards advertising 5A horse blankets. EF to Mint: $6–$10

Many sets and series were produced in the first decade of the twentieth century, extending slightly into the 1910s. In addition to those made in America, series of cards were made in England, France, and Germany, some with American scenes (such as multiple series by Raphael Tuck in England) and others mainly circulated abroad. Among the latter were cards featuring the art of Alphonse Mucha (issued by Champenois in Paris) and Wiener Werkstätte cards produced in Vienna, eagerly sought by collectors today in Europe and, less so but significantly, in America. Sets and series are showcased in chapter 10.

While many sets have been documented in detail with titles, the extent of some other series is unknown, giving the opportunity for research and discovery today.

Into the 1910s
Transitions

From 1910 to 1914 massive quantities of high-quality postcards continued to be imported from Germany and, to a lesser extent, England. These included holiday greetings, scenes, and other subjects. After the World War started in Europe in July and August 1914, industry turned its attention to the conflict, which eventually expanded to include most of Europe. From 1915 onward many American companies supplied munitions and other supplies to England and France in their fight against the forces of Kaiser Wilhelm. America remained neutral, although most citizens sided with France and

In the Civic & Mercantile Parade held in Exeter, New Hampshire, on August 4, 1914, the Frank W. Swallow Postcard Co. of that town had a horse-drawn float carrying its employees. By this time the popular passion for collecting cards had passed, but Swallow's business remained strong as a regional supplier of view cards to general stores and small retail outlets in towns for which a wide selection of color-printed cards was not available. Most Swallow cards were black and white, but many were hand-colored, as seen here. EF to Mint: $20–$30

England. Some German-Americans hoped the German Empire would win. In the meantime, imports of all German goods diminished, marking the end of quantities of postcards from that region.

During this time, Detroit Publishing Company, Curt Teich, and many other printers and lithographers in America produced cards of high quality, often matching those from Germany. Most had a glossy surface, although there were many exceptions, those of Detroit Publishing being the most notable—not to overlook the Swallow Postcard Company, which hand-tinted its cards and mainly did business in the Northeast. White borders on cards increased in popularity and were almost universal on printed cards by the end of the decade.

Collecting Postcards

"Postal Carditis" had faded in popular accounts by 1910, and relatively little space was given to the hobby by newspapers and magazines. There were scattered exceptions, however.

The *Boston Globe*, July 13, 1910, published this note from "Traveling Kate": "I wish we could start a postcard club and send different members postcards as we travel along, don't you?"

The *Deseret Evening News*, published in Utah on July 30, 1910, included this news from the Xenia, Ohio, branch of the Mormon Church:

A lady with her postcard album in the early twentieth century.

By request of a Mormon girl in Utah the elders [in Xenia] called on a lady in Columbus and learned of the unusual way she became interested in the Gospel. Belonging to a postcard club she noticed the name of a Western girl and exchanged several cards before she was informed her correspondent was a Mormon. Doctrinal books followed, a ripe companionship developed, and the Columbus girl is now investigating the claims made by the Church of Jesus Christ of Latter-Day Saints.

Many "postcard clubs" of the era were commercial ventures that advertised widely in the classified sections of newspapers. They did not hold meetings but sold postcards through the mail. This is from the *Norwich Bulletin*, November 2, 1912:

WANTED: 10,000 people to join the Acme Postcard Club. Send for particulars and free postcards. Norton Publishing Co., Box 210, Norwich, Conn.

This similar commercial notice was printed in the *Oregon Daily Commercial Journal*, February 16, 1913, selling selections from the many cards printed in advance for the 1915 Panama-Pacific International Exposition:

10 POSTCARDS of California or 1915 Exposition buildings 10 cents. World's Fair Postcard Club, 1154 Market St., San Francisco, Cal.

Another of many examples, this is from the *Southern Democrat*, Oneonta, Alabama, March 11, 1915:

WANTED: You to join our postcard club. 10 swell postcards and list of members 10 cents. Superior Novelty Co., Island, Ky.

The postal rate for mailing a postcard from 1873 was 1¢, changed to 2¢ on November 2, 1917. It took time for the new rate to be widely observed, and "penny postcards" were the rule for many mailers. The post–World War years would bring more changes to American postcards and to the hobby.

POSTCARDS OF LATER YEARS

On July 1, 1919, the old rate of 1¢ to mail a postcard was resumed. On April 15, 1925, 2¢ became the official rate, continuing until July 1, 1928, when the 1¢ stamp again became official, continuing into the early 1950s. Relatively few people kept track of the changes, and many patrons used 1¢ stamps throughout the entire era, even when the rate was twice that.

By the late 1910s holiday greeting, comic postcards, and related issues gave way to printed, folded greeting cards mailed in envelopes. The issuance of postcard sets, such as signed artists, came to a near-conclusion by the end of this decade, as did the packaging of groups of cards for fairs and expositions.

This was the era of great popularity for the automobile, and it was common for automobilists to travel singly and, sometimes, in organized groups with an itinerary. At various stops, buying scenic postcards was the order of the day.

By 1920 most enthusiasts collected on their own as nonprofit postcard clubs were scarce. Sometimes they solicited friends for cards they received. Interest was concentrated on printed scenic cards. RPPCs were occasionally made for special events and happenings, but only at a tiny fraction of the output of the previous decade.

Postcards in the 1920s
Curt Teich Co.

The Curt Teich Company, founded in Chicago in 1898, was a major producer of view cards in later years, becoming especially important toward the end of the 1910s. After the Great War the firm printed more scenic cards than any other company in the world, continuing with large volume and without great competition into the 1930s. It remained in business until 1978. Later its archives formed the basis of the Lake County Discovery Museum, a local museum in northeastern Illinois. The collection was eventually moved to the Newberry Library in Chicago.

Curt Teich printed cards for many stationery stores, gift shops, and other local and regional sellers, adding their names along with Teich and, on the back of most cards, a Teich serial number. Research by the staff of the Lake County Discovery Museum using the Curt Teich archives has given this information of approximate serial numbers and dates:

Serial No.	Date Printed
28,000	1910
55,000	1915
80,000	1920
103,000	1925
124,181	December 1928

Starting in 1929 an alpha-numeric system was used, consisting of a letter followed by a number. In 1930 a formula including the date was launched. Numbers referred to the year in a decade, from 0 to 9. Decades were assigned letters:

Letter	Date Range
A	1930–1939
B	1940–1949
C	1950–1959
D	1960–1969
E	1970–1978

Thus, 4A means the card was printed in 1934. Then follows a dash, a letter referring to a specific printing process (for example, H is for Art Colortone) and the following number the sequence of a card for the year.

Accordingly, 6A-H1003 refers to a 1936 card of the Art Colortone process, the 1,003rd card variety issued that year. This system was not consistently followed, and many variations did occur.

Subjects and Styles

Most domestically printed cards after the mid-1910s and nearly all after the World War have white borders around the edge of the face. A description of the image was printed in black, usually, on the top and/or the bottom border. Stock numbers of cards were often printed on the front as well.

Postcards continued to be printed in large quantities, mostly of scenic views. In addition there were countless cards advertising products, giving notices of local events, and the like. Relatively few RPPCs were issued in the 1920s.

Postcard Clubs from the 1920s to Date

After the 1893 to 1918 Golden Age, many postcard clubs that advertised widely were commercial enterprises, not social gatherings of collectors. Notices for such appeared in many newspapers.

This in the *San Francisco Chronicle*, December 5, 1920, was of a specialized nature:

> JOIN our postcard club. Send for particulars. Object matrimony. Give age of correspondents desired and send for November list. Write for great special offer. Postcard collecting is not only a pleasant pastime but one of great educational values to people of all ages. Mrs. Frost, 1268 Eddy St., San Francisco.

Beyond these commercial ventures, in the 1920s many social postcard clubs met in various cities including Omaha, Nebraska; Evansville, Indiana; Minneapolis, Minnesota; Boise, Idaho; Trenton, New Jersey; and many other places. Brief notices of meeting times and places appeared in local papers, but feature articles on what happened at the meetings have not been found. No doubt many such clubs had newsletters and bulletins with information, but relatively few have survived because of their ephemeral nature.

Judging from inscriptions found on postally used cards from the 1920s to date, most club members collected scenic cards from different locations and older colorful holiday postcards from the Golden Age. Many of the new cards were posted on holiday trips and sent to friends back home.

Postcard clubs enjoyed dynamic growth in the late twentieth century with monthly meetings and, often, yearly shows. Anyone with a budget of two or three hundred dollars can spend an enjoyable day at any club show and go home with beautiful cards for their collections. No budget at all is necessary to attend and simply

A postcard for the Eastern States Postcard Exhibition, 1966.

The Metropolitan Postcard Club of New York City Collectors Exhibition, 1967.

Date	Rate
August 1, 1958	3¢
January 7, 1963	4¢
January 7, 1968	5¢
January 7, 1963	4¢
January 7, 1968	5¢
May 16, 1971	7¢
March 2, 1974	8¢
September 14, 1975	7¢
December 31, 1975	9¢
May 29, 1978	10¢
March 22, 1981	12¢
November 1, 1981	13¢
February 17, 1985	14¢
April 2, 1988	15¢
February 3, 1991	19¢
January 1, 1995	20¢
July 1, 2001	21¢
June 30, 2002	23¢
January 6, 2006	24¢
March 14, 2007	26¢
May 12, 2008	27¢
May 11, 2009	28¢
April 17, 2011	29¢
January 22, 2014	32¢
May 31, 2015	35¢
April 10, 2016	34¢
January 21, 2018	35¢

enjoy exploring the history and art on display in dealers' inventories. And of course a larger hobby budget opens the doors to countless treasures. The Metropolitan Postcard Club of New York City, founded in 1946, has drawn the largest gatherings at its annual shows and is a must-attend event for many hobbyists. It has done much research on postcards, including on American and foreign artists.

The late 1900s was also the beginning of the era for research and publication of information. Many talented researchers and writers began to produce reference books that have contributed greatly to the enjoyment of the hobby.

As of today, postcard clubs are dynamic. There are more than 100 active groups in the United States.

Barr's Postcard News & Ephemera is a national publication featuring much postcard information. *Picture Postcard Monthly*, published in England, is also a valuable resource. Many of the clubs have Internet sites. eBay has countless listings of postcards, but buyer beware of listings not by professional postcard dealers. Later chapters describe some of the potential dangers of the market.

Postcards in the Early 1930s

Most postcards of the 1930s continued the white-border style of the preceding decade. Curt Teich Co. remained the leading producer of cards, by far. Subjects were mostly scenic.

This was the era of the Great Depression, and money was scarce. Collecting and other inexpensive hobbies and pastimes came to the fore. Jigsaw puzzles became a national craze, and it was not unusual for a small town to have one or two puzzle shops that sold or rented them to enthusiasts. Crossword puzzles, which had become popular in the 1920s, became more so than ever. The stamp-collecting hobby expanded. President Franklin D. Roosevelt was a philatelist and he had Postmaster General James Farley produce many commemoratives and special issues for collectors.

Coin albums and "penny boards" also became popular, the latter launched in 1934 by Joseph Kent Post, a coin collector and engineer of Neenah, Wisconsin. His innovative product was acquired in 1935 by Whitman Publishing, which launched the Whitman line of coin boards, folders, albums, and numismatic reference books. Looking through coins in pocket change was a lot of fun, with certain rare coins worth several dollars or more—which was like a day's pay for the average working man.

The collecting of postcards expanded, mostly with enthusiasts acquiring scenic cards from friends and other sources and mounting them in albums with paper pages. However, information about postcards ranged from scarce to non-existent. Few details were known of the rarity or other aspects of earlier cards of the Golden Age, although collectors continued to desire them.

Postal Rates

The standard cost for a stamp to mail a postcard remained 1¢ until January 1, 1952, when the rate was raised to 2¢. As rates have increased over time, the propensity for a tourist to buy a large number of postcards has decreased. Later rate increases (and a few decreases) are listed on page 15.

The rationale for increases is that it costs the United States Postal Service nearly as much to handle a postcard as it does for a small envelope.

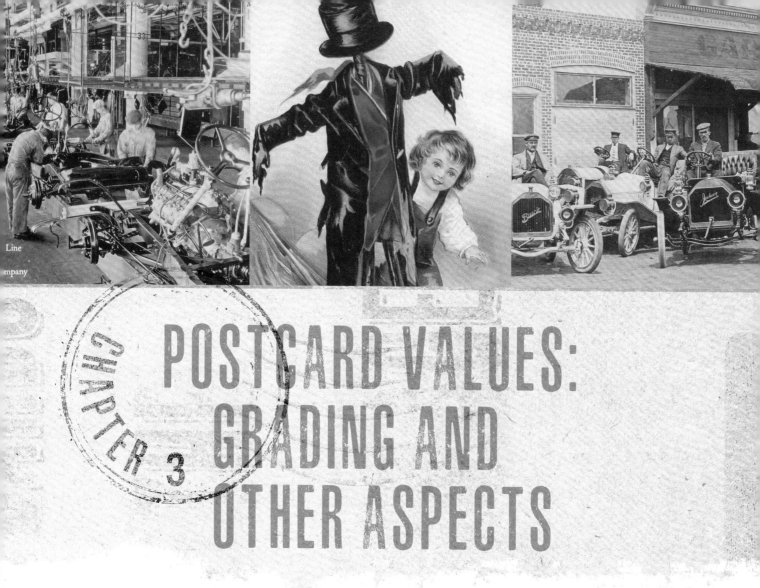

POSTCARD VALUES: GRADING AND OTHER ASPECTS

CHAPTER 3

Popularity, subject matter, image composition, rarity, grade, and many other factors can figure into the value of a collectible postcard. This chapter lays the foundation for your understanding of the market.

Things to consider include these:

Popularity

The more people who collect a postcard series or subject, the more valuable it will be.

Among holiday cards, those with Valentine's Day, Halloween (in particular), and Christmas scenes are more popular and sell for more than those for Saint Patrick's Day, Easter, or Independence Day. Labor Day cards are rare but were more eagerly sought a generation ago than they are today.

Among signed artist cards, those by Alphonse Mucha, F. Earl Christy, Raphael Kirchner, Philip Boileau, Harrison Fisher, Ellen Clapsaddle, and other well-known illustrators are collected more widely than are those by obscure or unknown artists.

Cards that are part of popular sets and series sell for more, the Roosevelt Bears being examples. In contrast, cards in the very extensive Zeno gum series are not widely collected, nor have they been studied or cataloged.

Popularity and subject matter (see below) are intertwined.

Subject

The subject of a card is often a key to its popularity. Among cards showing vehicles, those of early automobiles and trains are more popular than those of wagons or tractors. Santa Claus postcards are very popular, but ones showing Uncle Sam are less so. Comic cards of the Golden Age showing animals with human characteristics are a popular subject, while cards showing animals in farm scenes are not. Golden Age cards showing comic cats are more popular than are those with pigs. Cards showing train stations are more popular than those showing stretches of rail track. A street scene with vehicles and people is more desirable than one showing only buildings and no activity. Event and action cards are more desirable than those of inanimate scenes.

Among ships, sidewheel steamers on the Mississippi and Ohio rivers are more valuable than those showing rowboats, canoes, or fishing boats. Ocean liners are popular, including Art Deco types of the late 1920s through the 1930s.

This is a nice card of the Col. Clark E. Gale residence in Galesburg, Illinois, but it would draw no attention except from an intensely dedicated specialist in Galesburg scenes. EF to Mint: $4–$5

This "Typical Farm Scene Near Franklin, N.C." would not attract much interest at a postcard show or auction. EF to Mint: $5–$8

This RPPC showing the post office in Rock City Falls, New York, with a trolley car and people and postmarked (on the back) January 23, 1909, is a superb card that would attract many buyers. EF to Mint: $100+

"An Assembly Line of the Ford Motor Company," an RPPC made in quantity and showing the River Rouge plant, would appeal to many collectors. EF to Mint: $10–$20

Santa Claus, humorous animals, and Halloween are always popular subjects.

A Case Study of Image Compositions

"Dining Hall, Rocky Point, RI." (Charles H. Seddon, Providence, Rhode Island; 1919 postmark). This view devotes more space to a dirt road than to any other feature. Beyond that, collectors of amusement park images might collect this if they wanted one of each and every card from Rocky Point, but otherwise they would seek a card showing rides, a carousel, or other activity. EF to Mint: $6–$10

"Ferris Wheel, Rocky Point, R.I." In contrast to the "Dining Hall" card, this one would appeal to many buyers. (Robbins Bros., Boston; 1907 postmark). EF to Mint: $15–$25

"West Park St., Martinsburg, W. Va." This card, another with the image mainly composed of a dirt street and, beyond that, no people, vehicles, or signs of activity, is worth less than one with action. Its main appeal is for a specialist in this town. EF to Mint: $4–$7

"Main Street Looking North, Long Beach, Wash." This card, made from a photograph, has had its imagery strengthened and altered. A railroad locomotive (far too small!) has been added to the center of the street. Such a card would draw minimal interest. (Wesley Andrews, Baker, Oregon; Curt Teich. 1936 postmark.) EF to Mint: $7–$12

"Main Street, Balboa, Cal." shows many vehicles, people, and activity, making it a postcard with wide appeal. EF to Mint: $10–$20

Many collectors specialize in given subjects, such as train stations, commercial airliners, hotels and restaurants, and carousels—to mention just several of hundreds of collectible topics.

In nearly all instances, postcards of subjects from identifiable small towns and villages are worth more, often considerably more, than postcards from large towns and cities.

Image Composition

This is a very important aspect and one that is hard to define. Beauty is in the eye of the beholder. Take for example Main Street scenes. Several cards can show the same perspective. One that is a Real Photo Postcard with people, vehicles, and activity and in sharp focus is much more desirable than the same view that has been artistically altered by adding vehicles or using color that is not attractive. A printed panorama card can show interesting details such as buildings or an amusement park, or it can have the foreground composed of unattractive rooftops.

For signed artist cards, the treatment of the subject matter can vary. Women on such cards can be very appealing to view, or they can be over-colorized or unattractive.

There is no end of variations. The images and values given throughout as this book will provide much general information useful to collectors and sellers.

Rarity

Within a given popular subject or series, a rare card will sell for more than a common one of equally attractive composition and quality. An interesting aspect of postcards is that often the finest and most popular images were made in the largest quantities, making them quite affordable. By way of analogy, player piano rolls with popular tunes are more common and more desired today than those with obscure melodies.

This is not so for many other fields. For coins, tokens, medals, and paper money, many of the most popular and desired issues were made in small quantities. The same goes for stamps.

For any field, such rarity terms as *scarce, rare, common,* and the like do not have much helpful meaning. In numismatics (coin and paper-money collecting), such vague terms have been replaced by numerical scales.

The Universal Rarity Scale devised for coins in the 1990s follows a geometrical progression, with each level double that of the preceding. The use of the Universal Rarity Scale has been increasing in numismatics over the years and in time may be useful to postcard collecting. If adopted by postcard collectors and dealers, it will be a reference that is understandable to all.

The Universal Rarity Scale

URS-1 = 1 known, unique	URS-9 = 125 to 249
URS-2 = 2 known	URS-10 = 250 to 499
URS-3 = 3 or 4	URS-11 = 500 to 999
URS-4 = 5 to 8	URS-12 = 1,000 to 1,999
URS-5 = 9 to 16	URS-13 = 2,000 to 3,999
URS-6 = 17 to 32	URS-14 = 4,000 to 7,999
URS-7 = 33 to 64	URS-15 = 8,000 to 15,999
URS-8 = 65 to 124	URS-16 = 16,000 to 31,999

Certain rare RPPCs can be estimated as URS–1, 2, or 3. On the other hand, modern cards issued by Disney, airlines, and others can be estimated as URS-14 or higher.

In any event, rarity estimates are subject to change as new information emerges. If Mr. Jones attended a baseball game and was not seen by Mrs. Smith, he was still there. If on a walk through a forest you find no deer, there still may be some. Similarly, if today a card is estimated at, say, URS-4, if several more are found or if a hoard is located (as sometimes happens), the rating could be changed to URS–5 or 6.

Grade

The condition or grade of a postcard—a visual analysis of the amount of use and handling it has received—can affect its value, especially for printed cards. RPPCs are a separate and special case.

A Mint or New card as nice as when it was printed is usually more valuable than a damaged or worn one of the same type. Postally used cards can be very valuable in some instances, such as RPPCs, but postmarks and handwriting can detract from the value of an artist-signed card, for example. In any event, to achieve a high grade, a card's postal cancellations should not disfigure its image.

Numerical grading scales have been devised for numismatic items, sports cards, and even the restoration level of antique automobiles. The following standards may be of use if adopted by postcard collectors. In any event, the adjectives are already widely used, yet without precise definition.

Mint
Grade-10

Mint-10: Unused, in "as new" condition. Often called *New*. Such a postcard will have no cancellation, ink writing, or stray marks. The image will be as sharp as new, or only very slightly faded. There will be no scuffs, chips, or other evidence of handling or use.

Mint-10 is the grade most desired for signed artist cards, holiday and greeting cards, and sets and runs of advertising or other subjects.

Nearly Mint
Grade-9

Nearly Mint–9: Unused, but with some slight evidences of handling such as a minor abrasion, tiny points of discoloration, or hardly noticeable marks. Such a card cannot have creases, bends, chips, writing, or cancellations.

Extremely Fine (EF)
Grade-8

Extremely Fine–8: This is mainly used to describe a printed card or RPPC that has been used, has neat or small writing on the face (of pioneer and other undivided-back cards), and has a clear postmark and cancellation. Very minor abrasions are okay. The presence of the original cancelled stamp is desirable but not essential. Any writing on the back should be attractively done (not heavy pencil or scribbling, for example).

For *unused* cards, an Extremely Fine example can have some medium evidence of handling but no cancellations or ink marks (otherwise it would not be unused).

Many hobbyists consider this to be the minimum acceptable grade for linen and chrome cards.

Very Fine (VF)
Grade-7

Very Fine–7: This describes a card that is attractive overall but may have a few marks on the front, a few edge chips, or perhaps a light corner bend or some album-corner stains. Such a card should be attractive to view overall. This is the lowest generally collectible grade level for signed artist cards, greeting cards, and others with artistic images.

Fine (F or Fine)
Grade-6

Fine-6: This describes a card with problems such as medium marks on the face, edge chips, a couple corner folds, and overall evidence of extensive handling. Very rare printed view cards and RPPCs in this grade are desirable if better examples cannot be found.

Very Good (VG)
Grade-5

Very Good–5: This describes a card in lower condition than Fine, perhaps with a trimmed edge, very heavy cancellation, and/or unsightly writing on the back. Cards in Very Good and lower grades are seldom stocked by dealers or sought by advanced collectors.

Good (G)
Grade-4

Good-4: This grade describes a card with even more problems than one in Very Good condition, such as trimmed edges, small tears, scuffing, and the like.

Fair
Grade-3

Fair-3: This describes a card with many problems, including perhaps a missing corner or two, a heavy crease, or unattractive ink marks.

Poor
Grade-2

Poor-2: The design of a card in this grade is barely recognizable due to damage, fading, or discoloration.

Other Aspects of Price and Value

Postcards do not have standard values. Approximations such as those given in this book are useful, but in the marketplace prices can vary widely. If you are just beginning a collection, study the prices given here and also look on the Internet, such as on eBay, for more information. Spending a day or two at a postcard show can be like taking a seminar—a wonderful way to gain knowledge.

Most signed artist cards have market values within an approximate range. If a Harrison Fisher card has a general value of $10 to $15 in Mint condition, there is no need to pay $25 or $50. On the other hand, do not expect to buy a nice one for $5. A certain Alphonse Mucha card variety can be worth $300 Mint but less than $100 if Very Fine with multiple marks on the face.

A Case Study of Postcard Grades

(Mint-10) Postcard by Champenois of Paris, 1890s, with art by Alphonse Mucha. Mint: $800–$1,000

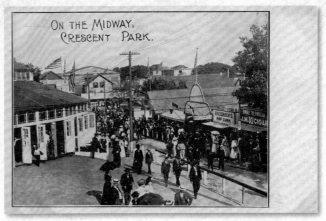

(VF-7) Album marks discolor the corners of this undated (circa 1905) card of Crescent Park. (No date, location, or publisher.) VF: $8–$15

(VG-5) The otherwise high value of this rare RPPC from the short-lived boom times of Goldfield, Nevada, is decreased considerably by the writing on the front, and there is no postmark to indicate the date (which was probably circa 1905). Furthermore, the buildings in the distance are not in sharp focus. VG: $150+

(Nearly Mint–9) RPPC of automobiles in Bushton, Kansas. A few spots are at the lower right, *1909* is penciled at the top (probably removable), and there is slight roughness on three corners. There are some marks on the back. As this is a very rare RPPC, the less-than-Mint grade does not affect the value. Nearly Mint: $150+

(Fair-3) This card of the carousel at Lakemont Park in Altoona, Pennsylvania, has the lower-right corner missing (the writing on the front is normal for a postally used undivided-back card). A carousel specialist might realize that this is a rare card and one that should be purchased regardless of its problems. (A.C. Bosselman & Co., New York.) Fair: $2–$4

Postmarks can add value. Among stamp collectors, there is a large collector base for cards and letters with postmarks from discontinued post offices, lists of which can be found on the Internet. Certain World's Fair postcards, if with a commemorative stamp and postmarked the first day of the fair, can be very valuable. Treasure-hunting for postmarks at postcard shows offers great possibilities, as few postcard collectors or dealers are aware of special dates and extra values.

By reviewing many prices, estimates, and images, including those in this book, you will gain knowledge. You will know that a Real Photo Postcard showing a sharp, close-up image of a trolley car and some storefronts is more likely to be worth $50 to $100, and at a postcard show you will not find one for $5 or $10. Similarly, you will know that a nice RPPC of the cemetery of the First Presbyterian Church without vehicles or people, or one showing a grove of trees or a pet dog, might not be worth more than a dollar or two at a postcard show or several dollars through the mail.

You will learn by doing. Experience will bring you knowledge.

In addition to the elements of postcard values given above, the expense of a dealer handling a card and/or creating an image of it to post online or in a print catalog will make it more costly, especially if purchased through the mail. On eBay it is not uncommon to add a few dollars for postage and handling. One Internet seller has a minimum of $9.95 for any card, to cover the costs of imaging, handling, and postage. However, at a postcard show the same card might cost just a dollar or two.

For rare and expensive cards, the Internet offers many opportunities as a few dollars charged for postage and handling is not important when purchasing an RPPC that is unique and valuable. However, a group of 100 common or unpopular cards is not worth $9.95 times 100, or $995, but might wholesale for less than $1 each, or might not be wanted at all. Generally, a group of cards gathered by an aunt during her twentieth-century travels is not worth much.

Similarly for coin collecting, *A Guide Book of United States Coins* lists 30¢ as the minimum price for a modern Lincoln cent in Mint State (Uncirculated). Buying a single modern cent through the mail in a separate transaction might cost a bit more. However, a roll of 50 new Lincoln cents is only worth face value plus a small handling charge. Coin shows and shops are the best places to buy common, cheap coins at reasonable prices. For rarities, the Internet, professional auctions, and other venues offer many opportunities.

On the Internet, much caution must be used. A Mucha card worth several hundred dollars offered for less than $10 is most certainly a modern replica. One dealer who was asked, "Why don't you say it is a reproduction?" replied, "Anyone will know that it is because of the price." We beg to differ. Many people just entering the field might be misled.

As is true for rare coins, stamps, and antiques, it is easier to buy a rare postcard than to sell one, especially for close to a retail price recently paid. Because of this, for postcards it is usually costly to buy a card in lower grade with the hope of finding a better one later. Except for certain RPPCs, it is far better to hold out until one in the right grade and price range is found.

In a phrase: go slowly and carefully and enjoy the experience.

(EF-8) The two postcards shown are examples of condition-acceptable handwriting and clear cancellation marking.

BUILDING A COLLECTION OF POSTCARDS

CHAPTER 4

A collection of postcards—old, new, or a mixture of different eras—can be a rich source of enjoyment and pleasure. Collectors and dealers can become fine friends in person or on the Internet.

Opportunities to buy are unlimited. The Internet offers eBay and other bidding sites as well as posted inventories of dealers, nearly always with images. Postcard shows and conventions are fun to attend and offer the opportunity to buy, sell, and learn.

There are no barriers to entry. You can have a modest budget or a generous one and either way build a fine collection. The key to involvement seems to be to have a collecting instinct combined with intellectual curiosity.

Postcards are a window on history, and nearly every aspect of the American scene from the 1890s to date has been memorialized. If you like history and enjoy collecting memorabilia, you've come to the right place!

Most collectors and dealers have great longevity in the hobby. Many people who helped with the present book were active a generation or two ago. If you get a modern case of Postal Carditis, chances are good that you will still be an enthusiastic collector a decade from now!

A modern postcard issued by Mary L. Martin, coauthor of this book.

Frank Pannill was one of a few collectors who issued his own postcards, including this one from the late twentieth century. EF to Mint: $10–$20

Observations and Commentary

To reiterate, the Internet in particular has made the collecting of older postcards more dynamic than ever, but caution is urged. Postcard shows are held regularly and allow visitors to spend a day or two looking through albums and boxes of cards to discover subjects of interest. The field is so varied that a hobbyist, traveler, or anyone interested in a special subject can always find a lot to collect.

As an example, a collection of automobile cards could contain many hundreds of cards from the turn of the twentieth century—the dawn of the automobile age in America—down to recent times. A collection of aviation cards can range from early biplanes to the various types of craft used by airlines into the present century, as well as advertising cards from many lines that no longer exist.

Collectors of Coca-Cola, Moxie, and other soft-drink memorabilia have added postcards to their collections, not only of a particular beverage but also of competitors. Postcards show signs for the products in stores, along the highway, and elsewhere.

Hometown cards are always favorites. A collection of fifty to a hundred cards from a small town will always

"Mount Ida, Easton, Pa." (Souvenir Post Card Co. 204,253; Valentine image. 1908 postmark.) Coca-Cola as advertised as part of a large group of billboards and posters at Mount Ida, Easton, Pennsylvania. While only a few varieties of advertising cards were issued by Coca-Cola in the early twentieth century, postcards showing signs as part of a view, as here, are avidly collected. EF to Mint: $12–$20

"Wilcox Flying Horses, Savin Rock, Conn." (E.P.J. Co. No. 1813. 1913 postmark.) This is a scenic card deluxe, circa 1910, showing a close-up of the carousel in motion with people riding and a clear view of the band organ that provided music. This card is worth multiples of what a view of a carousel at a distance and without people would bring. EF to Mint: $100+

evoke memories. Many, if not most, buildings and landmarks from generations ago are still there, and it is fun to compare what something looks like now to a view on a card postmarked, say, 1912. Scenic cards are frequently inexpensive—a few dollars on up for nice cards, perhaps $10 to $30 for subjects such as store interiors. Modern chrome cards often cost just a dollar or two at a postcard show (more if involving handling through the mail). Early twentieth-century cards of some towns that were small a century ago, but have large populations today, can be expensive—certain locations in Nevada, Arizona, and California are examples.

A collection of cards depicting Los Angeles, New York City, Chicago, or another metropolis could theoretically include multiple thousands. The Statue of Liberty in New York City and the Washington Monument in Washington, D.C., have been pictured on countless hundreds of different cards. Ditto for Niagara Falls, the Grand Canyon, and boats on the Mississippi River. The answer to this is to be selective—such as picking out several cards of Niagara Falls from different eras and perspectives.

On the other hand, there are thousands of small villages and towns in America for which relatively few cards have been published. An example is Honesdale, Pennsylvania, where coauthor Dave Bowers was born. A comprehensive collection of early twentieth-century Honesdale cards can take five or ten years to assemble and will include just a few hundred different subjects. A collection of cards from Unadilla, New York; Bath, New Hampshire; or Sumpter, Oregon, might include only a few dozen different subjects.

In an interview, coauthor Mary Martin was asked: "Suppose someone is from a hometown of, say, Peoria, Illinois. How many cards can they collect and how would you go about forming a collection of that particular place? What would you pick out if you were filling someone's request through the mail?"

She replied, "If someone wants to collect Peoria—perhaps they've just moved there, or have family in that place, or simply enjoy the history—they could come to my shop in Havre de Grace, Maryland, and probably see 150 early cards, say from 1900 to the 1930s. If they want modern cards, we have even more. The 'chrome' cards of the 1950s onward are very collectible. If they wanted to go into the 1970s to date, maybe 300 or so would be available."

Of course, the same seeker of Peoria cards can go to any postcard show and would be sure to get a good start.

Prices of older cards range from inexpensive (such as a card showing workers in a clothing shop) to tens of dollars (for a merry-go-round, a political rally, or other popular subjects for which cards are scarce). RPPCs printed from negatives in the early twentieth century are usually rarer and more valuable than are printed cards of the same subject. Some can run into the hundreds of dollars. The illustrations and price estimates given in this book demonstrate the wide range of prices.

"Signed artist" cards, as they are called, are printed in color and have the signatures of Harrison Fisher, Philip Boileau, F. Earl Christy, or another of the illustrators well known in the early twentieth century. These are very popular to collect in runs and sets. If a card is by Raphael Kirchner it can be worth hundreds of dollars, or if particularly rare and attractive it can challenge the thousand-dollar mark. On the other hand, dozens of different Fisher, Boileau, and Christy cards can be obtained, depending on condition, from slightly under $10 to about $20 or so.

With further regard to RPPCs, a lady pushing a baby carriage might be worth only a couple dollars, especially if there is no identification of the subject or location. On the other hand, an RPPC showing a schoolhouse interior with teacher and children and with identification as to time and place may command $15 to $25.

A few years ago at an auction by Lyn Knight, there was an RPPC of a tattoo artist that brought more than $4,000. Such cards illustrating events are very popular. One of "Teddy" Roosevelt speaking to an audience can cost in the tens of dollars. On the other hand, a Real Photo Postcard of a Ku Klux Klan march in a small town in Maine was recently valued at $400. A high-school band parade in the same town, had one occurred, would probably command only $20 or so. Again, values are hardly standard. This is quite unlike the market for rare coins or stamps, for which prices often fall within narrow guidelines for a specific item in a specific grade.

Most postcard collectors start by looking at a particular area. Often, they will say they want cards only from the early twentieth century—the Golden Age, so called. However, after they get quite a few of those, they will expand into the 1930s and later years. This is easy enough to do with hometown cards but also is popular with other subjects—such as automobiles, airplanes and airlines, political campaigns, and the like. Whether a card is from 1910 or 1960, it reflects what was going on at that particular time. An easy way to start is to buy modern cards and then go back in time.

Certain subjects reached a high of graphic and artistic excellence during the early twentieth century—such as Halloween scenes, Santa Claus, and the like. Later cards of the same subjects, such as those of the mid- to late twentieth century, draw little interest. Similarly, certain cards of the early 1900s advertising products ranging from farm equipment to automobiles to home products have more value than do similar cards from the 1930s to date.

An Art Nouveau card by Alphonse Mucha, printed in Paris, advertising American-made Waverley Cycles sold for $13,500 in 1999. However, most Golden Age advertising cards range from $5 or $10 up to $100, with only a few crossing that line. Some consumer products such as Zeno gum and 5A horse blankets issued multiple cards with different images that can be collected as a specialty.

In contrast, cards of amusement parks, hotels, entertainment, and some other subjects are popular from all eras. Among modern views, Disneyland (opened in 1955) and Walt Disney World (1971) cards are widely collected, as are cards of Universal City, Six Flags, and other amusement parks. An interesting display can be made of Holiday Inn postcards from modern decades.

If you are a specialty collector, and let's say you are collecting Santa Claus or Halloween cards, you will probably stay with the beautifully lithographed cards from the Golden Age. However, if you like billiards and billiard halls, then you would buy a nice card from 1908 or 1911, but also of interest would probably be an advertising card from maybe six years ago that has a famous pool player on it, such as featuring a certain type of cue. No two collectors are exactly alike—which contributes a lot to the interest and dynamics of the hobby.

Regarding modern postcards, in the earlier mentioned interview Mary Martin said:

When I visit different towns throughout the United States I always look for postcards when I go into drugstores, shops, or see a newsstand with them. I always ask the person, "Do you sell many of these?" They always tell me, "People will come in and buy one of every different view." Cards with views are very popular. Sending cards from far-away places remains very popular—for some a status symbol to send a card from the Broadmoor Resort in Colorado Springs or, until its recent closing, the Waldorf-Astoria in New York City.

There are many opportunities to buy older postcards as well as postally used modern cards. More than 500 dealers are known to the authors of this book, and if you count Internet sellers who do not go to shows, there are probably several thousand. This wide field offers many opportunities and spurs competition. Postcard shows enable visitors to quickly view countless cards, often in albums or boxes arranged by subject or location. Mary Martin estimates that what can be reviewed in a day at a show would take several weeks on the Internet. On the other hand, Internet surfing can be done from an easy chair at home and involves no travel. As a lot of people have time on their hands, this can be a pleasant way to spend it.

A fine collection of postcards can be easily displayed and stored. The most popular method is to put them into clear archival sleeves and keep them in a shoebox or similar container. Probably 95 percent of the collecting community does this. If you are a dealer, or if you want to show cards to other collectors, putting them into albums is the way to go. Hard plastic holders slightly larger than the card itself permit easy viewing and handling without risk of damage. The American Philatelic Society has information on its web site (www.stamps.org) about displaying postcards. Dave Bowers donated a collection of 17,000 New Hampshire cards in hard plastic holders to the Wolfeboro Public Library some years ago; ever since they have been a great resource for those interested in state history or desiring images.

How to Be a Smart Buyer

As you build your collection, time is on your side. With relatively few exceptions, such as for certain RPPCs, multiple copies exist of a given image. This is true in all areas—scenic, advertising, and signed artist postcards being examples. Over a long period of time most carefully acquired collections have held their value, and many have increased.

The concept of value for the price paid is important, even if your checkbook or credit card authorization is well fortified.

Here are some thoughts:
* Go slowly. Start by surfing the Internet or, better yet, by going to a postcard show. Meanwhile, read this book. An easy way to start is by collecting views of your hometown or, perhaps, a favorite summer-vacation place. You should be able to acquire a few dozen or more cards easily. When you have them in hand, study them under low magnification—including information about the publisher, the postmark, and the sharpness or other aspects of printing.
* Make quality your main guideline. For scenic cards, buy Extremely Fine or better, a nice card with a clear postmark and without marks on the front being ideal. For signed artist cards, buy Mint or nearly Mint. You will not run out of opportunities. If an offered card seems expensive, look on the Internet and elsewhere to see what comparable cards offered by professional dealers have sold for, and stay within that range. There is no sense in paying $150 for a $50 card. Examine every offered card carefully—in person at a show, or with a sharp image on the Internet. If you are buying an expensive card on the Internet, insist on a return privilege if it proves to be less than you expect, even if illustrated. Folds and defects often do not show in photographs and scans, and most Internet offerings do not show the back of a card, the condition of which can be important to its value. Once you have a card in hand, check the front, back, and edges. If there is the slightest problem, don't buy it.
* Explore. After you have gained experience and have purchased and examined many cards, explore other areas, possibly including rarer signed artist cards and RPPCs.

Caveat: Copies and reproductions have little value and are especially prevalent for RPPCs that are not postmarked. Many people who are not experienced dealers sell reproductions, sometimes unknowingly, but often with the knowledge that a beginner might think it to be an authentic bargain. If you are buying expensive cards, place your business with an established postcard dealer whenever possible.

A CLOSER VIEW OF POSTCARD PRODUCTION

This chapter gives additional details on the printing and distribution of postcards and aspects concerning their design and creation. It is for extra credit in knowledge, so to speak, and includes many technical aspects. You may wish to skip this chapter and return to it at a later time.

Black-and-White Printed Postcards

Postcards simply printed in black and white were the most frequently seen style in the late 1890s and early 1900s, before color cards became popular. Any print shop or newspaper could make them, usually from halftone plates similar to those used for newspaper illustrations (composed of tiny Ben-Day dots of varying size and spacing). As it was not until 1907 that messages could be written on the back of cards, nearly all of these early black-and-whites have a blank border or even a large space to the right and below the image on the face. Local and regional black-and-white cards continued to be popular into the 1910s. Postmark dates are not a

The Frank W. Swallow Postcard Co. used this "Main Street Looking West, Salem Depot, N.H." image to print an inexpensive black-and-white card as well as a fancier version with a printed "birch bark" border. (Border copyright 1907.) EF to Mint: $8–$15

reliable indicator of the publishing date, as many cards were kept on hand for years after they were printed. Most were made in smaller quantities than color cards, so some are scarce.

Hand-Colored Postcards

Black-and-white cards were often tinted by hand, using watercolors. Some cards that were carefully tinted were identified as such, as with the notation "Hand Colored," it was felt that such cards were artistic and especially desirable. More often there was no such notation, and the coloring was casual at best.

The preeminent New Hampshire publisher of hand-colored cards was Frank W. Swallow, of Exeter, who began business in 1904. Nearly all of his cards were printed (not lithographed) in black and white and were issued that way, or else hand-colored by local ladies who worked at home.

Black-and-White Lithographed Postcards

Cards lithographed in black and white or in variant tints (sepia was popular) were made in Germany before World War I, and to a lesser extent in the United States. Certain of these published by Rotograph, Albertype, and others, often with a local imprint added, are of exceedingly fine quality and reveal almost photographic details when viewed under magnification. Such cards bring a premium over ones of lesser printing quality.

In later times, from the 1920s onward and especially in the 1930s, Art Vue (New York City), Meriden Gravure Co. (Meriden, Connecticut), Dexter (West Nyack, New York), and others issued lithographed cards, but these generally lack the minute details of the earlier German issues.

Color Lithographed and Printed Postcards

Among lithographed and color printed cards, most of the early undivided-back view issues (March 31, 1907, and earlier), as well as most of the later cards to about 1914, were printed by large companies in major cities in the United States and in Europe (particularly in Germany) and were sold to publishers in American cities—examples being: Portland, Maine (Leighton and Morris); Boston (Chisholm and Metropolitan News); New York City (Rotograph, Albertype, American News, Langsdorf, and many more); and elsewhere. These major publishers took orders from sub-publishers in many

The Frank W. Swallow Postcard Co. kept a large stock of photographs on hand and used the same images over a long period of time. The black-and-white view is postmarked 1926, and the hand-colored one was mailed in 1911.
EF to Mint: $4–$7

A black-and-white lithographed postcard.

different towns and cities—sometimes even from individual stores—and added those imprints. "Publisher" on a card usually means distributor, not printer.

The original images used by the manufacturers came in several forms. Black-and-white photographs taken by a professional, with good composition of the subject and in sharp focus, were the best and constitute the majority of the pictures sent overseas by the leading American importers. Many other photographs were by amateurs and lack eye appeal or detail, or have other problems. Many printed cards were made by printing plates from RPPC images that had proved to be good sellers. Still others were second-generation reproductions from poorly printed black-and-white cards.

The major printer of postcards in the United States in the early twentieth century was also the largest publisher: Curt Teich Company of Chicago.

Color lithograph view cards made by the Curt Teich Co. in Chicago, by various lithographers in Germany for sale in America, and by others, were produced by colorizing black-and-white photographic prints. This was often done with a formula, as in the three California street scenes shown on page 31. Clouds and blue color were added to the sky, and in the distance a warm rosy glow simulated sunset or sundown.

The vast majority of color lithographed greeting and holiday cards printed before World War I (which

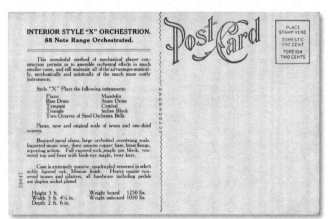

Production details as shown by the Commercial Colortype Co. for a postcard made for the Operators Piano Co. of Chicago, in the Octochrome series, No. 39647, indicating production in the year 1913. At least two types of backs were made: one showing printed details of the Style X Orchestrion and one with a blank space. EF to Mint: $50+

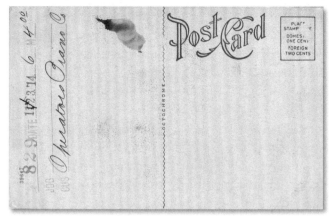

The back of another example of No. 39647, this being the factory record copy giving ordering details. This was reference 829, November 23, 1914, for 6,000 cards at $4 per thousand, placed by the Operators Piano Co. EF to Mint: $40+

Commercial Colortype Co. Octochrome card No. 40399, with multi-views of the Mobile (Alabama) Fire Department. Factory record card with information on the back (detail shown). This was reference 854, January 2, 1915, for 3,000 cards at $3.75 per thousand for the S.H. Kress Co. five-and-ten-cent store chain, and 3,000 for the L. Hammel Dry Goods Co. at $3.50 per thousand. EF to Mint: $25–$40

commenced in Europe in August 1914) were made in Germany and bear small imprints to this effect, as well as the names of importers, primarily in New York. After World War I nearly all color lithographed cards were produced in the United States, many by Curt Teich and the Commercial Colortype Company, both of Chicago, and E.C. Kropp of Milwaukee, and others, plus many whose cards are not identified.

Postcards for Anyone

Dozens of companies, mostly print shops and small publishers, offered to make short runs of 500 to 1,000 postcards. The procedure was simple: furnish a photograph or even another picture postcard (never mind the ethics of swiping someone else's image) and copies would be made.

In other instances, a company would solicit orders, work with a customer, and have the printing done by the Curt Teich Co. or another standard manufacturer. As one of many examples, the Nyce Manufacturing Co. of Vernfield, Pennsylvania, founded by Abraham H. Nyce, seems to have had a large business in this regard. Business was done in a three-story brick building that also accommodated the A.H. Nyce Clothing Factory. This firm issued "NYCE" (trade style used) generic cards with stock scenes, preprinted, to which a bottom line could be added on the front, such as "Greetings from No. Conway, N.H." The cards were made by the Curt Teich Co. and possibly others as well. Holiday and greeting cards were also sold this way. The company was active from the 1910s until the 1930s or later.

A circa-1930s advertisement printed in red on the back of a card (with an ink-bottle-and-pen logo at upper left) notes this, representative of the business of a small postcard manufacturer:

Sample of our Quality Line

GENERAL LANDSCAPE LOCALS

No. 941. 20 choice designs.

Fine selected Landscapes, Roadside and Woodland scenery. All scenes appropriate for any locality. Greetings from your town and state printed in brilliant red ink. 85¢ per 100, $4.00 per 500, or $7.90 per 1000 postpaid.

NYCE Manufacturing Co., Vernfield, Pa.

A fast seller for the summer trade. Preferred by many of our customers to local views made to order. The price is much lower and delivery is made in 48 hours. A large variety for your customers to select from.

Other Nyce series included:

No. 942 Boating and Water Scene Locals. 20 choice designs. Boating, moonlight, river, lake and general water scenes. All scenes appropriate for any locality. Greetings from your town and state printed in brilliant red ink. 85¢ per 100,

A Study of Color Lithographed Cards

"A business street, Marysville, Cal." (M. Rieder, Los Angeles. No. 8573. Circa 1910.) EF to Mint: $15–$25

"J Street. Fresno, Cal." (Newman Post Card Co., Los Angeles. No. 5702. Circa 1910.) EF to Mint: $10–$16

"Main Street north from Fifth Street, Los Angeles, Cal." (F.W. Woolworth Co. / Curt Teich Co., Chicago. No. a-33643. 1913.) EF to Mint: $8–$12

"NYCE" quality cards first picked from your racks.

No. 943 Farm and Country Scene Locals. 25 choice designs. Cattle, horses, sheep and general farm activities. A sure seller for all country towns. Greetings from your town and state printed in brilliant red ink. 85¢ per 100, $4.00 per 500, or $7.90 per 1000 postpaid. NYCE Manufacturing Co., Vernfield, Pa. The famous "NYCE" Quality Landscape Post Cards are recognized as the best on the market. We sell many millions each year and the demand this season is as big as ever. Display your cards well and your sales will increase.

No. 943 As preceding, but prices slightly cheaper: 85¢ per 100, $3.90 per 500, or $7.50 per 1000 postpaid.

No. 944 Auto and Road Scene Locals. 25 choice designs. Printed in nature's rich colors on fine double coated cardboard. All scenes appropriate for any locality. 85¢ per 100, $3.90 per 500, or $7.50 per 1000 postpaid. NYCE Manufacturing Co., Vernfield, Pa. This is the best quality Landscape Post Card for the price on the market. Notice the fine cardboard and high grade coloring used in these cards.

Over a period of time the prices and quantities were changed. In the early twentieth century there were hundreds of makers similar to NYCE, some larger but most smaller.

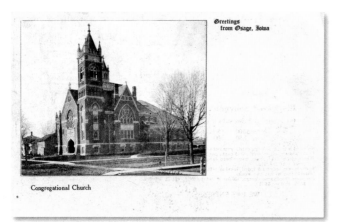

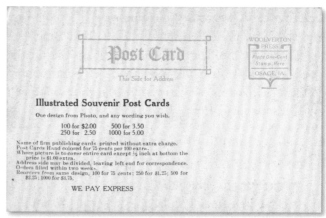

An early printer soliciting photographs from which postcards were made was the Woolverton Press in Osage, Iowa, circa 1904. EF to Mint: $7–$12

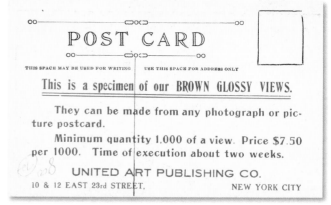

United Art Publishing Co. sent samples of its postcards, in this instance showing the post office in Salisbury, New Hampshire, to stores and other businesses, inviting them to have their own cards made from photographs or by sending in postcards to be copied. The sample card is cheap in its appearance, with some details such as edges and corners of objects strengthened. EF to Mint: $12–$18

The Auburn Post Card Manufacturing Co., a large-volume maker of inexpensive cards, issued this to solicit business. The addition of a blue tint to a black-and-white subject to create a cheap pseudo-color card was also done by Curt Teich, C.U. Williams, and others. EF to Mint: $6–$10

Manipulating Photographs

A given black-and-white photograph, professionally taken or otherwise, may have been manipulated to add color. In a printing plant in Leipzig, Saxony (Germany), or some other distant place, the artists had no idea if a building front was white, brown, yellow, or some other color, or if the structure was made of wood, brick, or some other material. As a result, color cards showing Main Street scenes, done by different manufacturers, often have the same subjects with different colors.

Upon request a business sign could be touched up or changed to reflect different information than on the original photograph. This was often done if a store changed hands or was given a new name after the picture was taken.

Many printers removed trolley cables and telephone poles and wires, deleted trash from the street, and in other ways improved the appearance of views. It was common practice to add an automobile or two, often brightly colored, to a street view that otherwise had only horse-drawn vehicles—showing that a community was modern and up-to-date. Adding trolley cars was often done, particularly for Main Street views of small communities. Likely for some the installation of such transportation had been envisioned by the town but not yet put in place (otherwise the cards would have been a farce).

If a moonlight or other night scene was desired, this was easily done by altering a daylight photograph. It was popular to have a bright moon illuminating puffy clouds. Manufacturers had teams of artists who could perform magic on about any image.

In addition, "stock" pictures were often given titles of locations other than where the photographs were taken. A merry-go-round picture titled for Luna Park, Hartford, Connecticut, was sold there, while an identical card bore a Coney Island inscription and was sold in New York. Country brooks, roadways, and the like, often captioned, "A Scene Near Wolfeboro, N.H.," "Haying in Kansas," or similar, might be made with dozens of different location imprints.

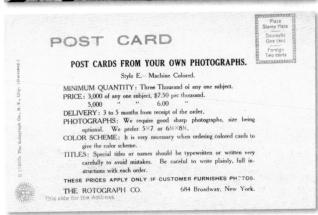

This Rotograph Co. card of about 1906 solicits orders. Customers were urged to send "good sharp photographs" of 5 x 7–inch or larger size. "It is very necessary when ordering colored cards to give the color scheme." The orders were sent to off to Germany, printed, and delivered three to five months later. While the German artists had no trouble making water blue, foliage green, and sand yellow, in the absence of detailed instructions (this usually being the case) they had to guess at the color of buildings and other man-made objects, often with inconsistent results. EF to Mint: $10–$20 with an advertisement; $1–$3 without

A Kropp "stock view" that could be sold almost anywhere, except in the middle of the Mojave Desert. Also shown is the advertisement on the back of the card. EF to Mint: $10–$18 with advertisement; $1–$3 without

A Curt Teich Co. "stock view" that could be ordered in small quantities with a generic caption, as illustrated. If the imprint of a specific town or other location was desired, the minimum quantity was 1,000. Unusual subjects such as that illustrated are worth much more than everyday subjects. EF to Mint: $20–$30 with advertisement; $12–$20 without

The original photograph for this panoramic view of Wilkes-Barre, Pennsylvania, must have been taken by an amateur, for clutter and a drab rooftop at the lower left occupy about 20 percent of the overall image. (Sabold-Herb Co., No. 41 / Curt Teich Co. No. R-77995. 1919.) EF to Mint: $5–$8

Oops! Norway, Iowa, did not have a trolley when this photograph was taken. The postcard producer added one, putting the new image partly over that of a carriage on the original! (No publisher. No. 17857. Circa 1910s.) EF to Mint: $15–$25

An automobile was added to this view of Redlands, California. Such alterations are very common. (M. Rieder. No. 219. Circa 1906.) EF to Mint: $2–$4

A man, two children, and a bright-red auto were added to this otherwise drab view of the William Galloway Plant in Waterloo, Iowa. (Acmegraph. No. 6228. Circa 1910.) EF to Mint: $6–$9

In Washington, D.C., this historic building has been a very popular subject for postcards. This and the following card were each made in the early twentieth century from the same black-and-white photograph. The printers had no idea as to the color of the structure, and each guessed differently. This one has a yellow-brown hue. (A.C. Bosselman & Co. No. 9740. Postmarked 1909.) EF to Mint: $2–$4

Several automobiles were added to this rather fuzzy street view of Webster City, Iowa. One auto has its license-plate identification removed, and drawings of people were added. (E.C. Kropp Co. No. 17969. Circa 1920s.) EF to Mint: $7–$12

Here we have a red-brick Ford's Theatre, the correct color, from the same image. (No publisher. No. 3012. Circa 1908.) EF to Mint: $2–$4

Three Versions of the Same Coney Island Scene

This card of Surf Avenue, Coney Island, New York, was printed on glossy stock by Davidson Brothers, New York and London, as Real Photographic Series 1032A. The original black-and-white photograph was reproduced with excellent fidelity and sharpness. (Postmarked 1909.) EF to Mint: $15–$25

The same photograph was colorized, had the overhead trolley lines removed, had clouds and dawn (presumably, as it is a view to the east) added, and the lettering on the Albemarle Hotel strengthened. This card was issued by another manufacturer as No. 52-S-16.
EF to Mint: $8–$12

Another publisher, not identified, did a different modification of the identical photograph by adding darkness punctuated by electric lights, adding different clouds and the moon, and adjusting other features.
EF to Mint: $8–$12

Universal City, the tourist attraction in Los Angeles opened in 1915, issued this as an RPPC made in quantity and titled "Showing how a movie is taken at Universal City, Cal."
EF to Mint: $20–$30

The same image was then used for a color printed card titled on the back, "Taking a movie from a beautiful spot at Universal City, Cal." (Cardinell-Vincent Co.)
EF to Mint: $12–$20

Multiple-View and Composite Cards

For the tourist who wanted to get a lot of coverage in a single card, the multi-view or composite postcard was ideal. These were made by arranging several printed postcards together, sometimes on an ornate or decorative background, and photographing the collage, after which a new card would be created. These were made in black-and-white as well as color versions.

Variations included "butterfly border" cards, which had four different views in panels of the wings in a butterfly outline, and "pansy border" cards with images in each part of the flower, usually made by photographing existing postcards. Such postcards were made for many different towns and cities. Although many are similar in appearance, they were made by various manufacturers in Europe, in addition to cards without imprints. "Large letters" cards featured scenes of a particular place, either taken from other postcards or from photographs, and cut out to form large, thick letters naming the city, town, or attraction.

A Gallery of Similar Coney Island Views

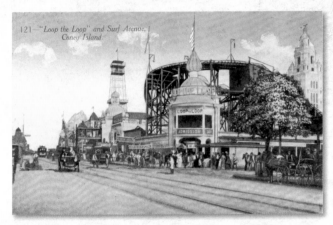

Cards of the "Loop the Loop" on Surf Avenue, Coney Island, show similar alterations to the Coney Island postcards on the previous page. This is a day view. (M. & Co., New York, No. 121. Circa 1907.) EF to Mint: $8–$12

The identical view, but at night. (Illustrated Post Card Co., New York. No. 176-21. Postmarked 1907.) EF to Mint: $8–$12

Riding an elephant at Luna Park, Coney Island, New York, made by altering a black-and-white photograph. This is a desirable view with patrons and an onlooker. (No publisher. Circa 1910.) EF to Mint: $10–$15

"Riding the Elephant" at Luna Park, Coney Island, New York. This is an art card adapted from the same illustration as the preceding. (J. Koehler, New York and Berlin, No. 1000. Postmarked 1912.) EF to Mint: $10–$20

Multiple-View Cards

A multi-view card showing tourist attractions of Nevada City, in the gold-rush area of California, high in the Sierra Nevadas. By the early twentieth century it had become a magnet for tourists. Printed in Austria. (J. Scheff & Brothers, San Francisco. Circa 1910s.) EF to Mint: $10–$15

One size fits all, so to speak. This Santa Barbara multi-view postcard is from the same publisher. EF to Mint: $8–$12

A Study of Lithographed Multiple-View Cards

Scenes of Webster, Massachusetts. (Austria.) EF to Mint: $20–$30

Scenes of Fort Wayne, Indiana. (PCK Series, Germany.) EF to Mint: $20–$30

Views of Meudon, France.
(France.) EF to Mint: $10–$20

Mistakes, Caption Revisions, and New Uses of the Old

Peach Trying, Fresno, Cal.

71838 No. 39 Publ Atlas Society 45 Perry Str. New York & C. H. Riege, Fresno, Cal. Made in Germany.

Printed in Germany, this card is imprinted "Peach Trying, Fresno, Cal." instead of "Peach Drying." Such errors were not infrequent as German makers sometimes misread written instructions and were not familiar enough with the English language to realize the error. (Atlas Society / C. H. Riege. 71838 No. 39. Circa 1906.) EF to Mint: $4–$7

Randsburg, Cal.
"The largest gold mining town on the great Mojave Desert." This is where my married daughter lives. M.L.H.

"Randsburg, Cal. The largest gold mining town on the great Mojave Desert." The unidentified German printing house that colorized a black-and-white picture to create this circa-1906 card was not aware that the Mojave Desert has very little greenery, so presented the view as a verdant landscape! Today, Randsburg is a ghost town. EF to Mint: $15–$25

Published by F. M. Ayer & Co.   Alton, N. H., in the Future

The Frank W. Swallow Postcard Co. of Exeter, New Hampshire, issued many different "In the Future" view cards of various towns, mostly in his home state. These were made by taking black-and-white views and pasting sketches or pictures of vehicles, aircraft, and other objects, then re-photographing the result. "Alton, N.H., in the Future," issued circa 1910, adds airships, a subway connecting to the city of Laconia, a trolley car, and an elevated railroad. EF to Mint: $8–$12

EVENTS AND TRANSITIONS ON POSTCARDS

Many postcards offer views of the passing parade of American life. The development of commercial districts from the horse-and-buggy era to the coming of automobiles can be traced on thousands of different street views from the turn of the twentieth century down to the latest models. In the twentieth century the rise of commercial airlines, from Ford Trimotor and Douglas DC-3 craft to transcontinental jets, can be viewed in great detail as most airlines issued postcards. Often an airport, Main Street, harbor, or other scene with activity will chronicle transitions very nicely.

Countless events are depicted on postcards. Fires, floods, parades, political rallies, celebrations, horse and car races, and other happenings can be found. A large percentage of these are on RPPCs, as such images needed to be published immediately while the event was still in the minds of postcard buyers. Many of these are very valuable.

Printed postcards were the usual venue for forthcoming conventions, anniversary celebrations, and situations publicized in advance. Event cards and cards showing the evolution of a Main Street from horses to automobiles are mostly collected by specialists focusing on a given town or state.

In most instances, the details on a card can lead to finding extensive historical information on the Internet. This can be an interesting pursuit. Selected examples are shown on the next page.

Detail of the Big Pool, Maryland, card on the next page.

A Selection of Events Shown in Postcards

"Cyclone taken at Kingsley, Ia., May 30, 1899—7:30 P.M. 3 miles away." This is an especially early RPPC. EF to Mint: $150+

The "Dog team en route Alaska to Washington" as it passed through Big Pool, Maryland, in March 1907. EF to Mint: $150+

Moving a house down a street in Catskill, New York, in June 1908. EF to Mint: $150+

A construction crew in Kalispell, Montana, depicted on a card postmarked June 8, 1908. "This is the way I appear when I am out working" is the message on the back, sent to Miss Bernice Smith of Greenfield, Illinois. EF to Mint: $150+

The first-ever balloon "point to point" race was held in North Adams, Massachusetts, on August 14, 1908. Contestants had to predict where they expected to land at a point at least 30 miles away. The closest landing was won by Arthur D. Potter, who came within five miles of the predicted destination in Haydenville. EF to Mint: $150+

The 1909 Hudson-Fulton was a short-lived fair with attractions on the water in New York City and nearby New Jersey. It lasted from September 25 to October 9 and celebrated Henry Hudson's voyage on the *Half Moon* and Robert Fulton's pioneer *Clermont* steamship. This RPPC shows the new *Clermont* in the foreground, a replica of the *Half Moon* in the distance. The message on the back reads: "Clermont, Half Moon, German cruiser, and Coney Island steamer all for a nickel. Have seen all. Also submarine, torpedo boat, dirigible, balloons, etc." EF to Mint: $20–$30

Election day in Newtown, Connecticut, June 1910.
EF to Mint: $100+

The Corn Carnival opened in Rock Falls, Illinois, on
September 28, 1910. Events included a mile-long auto race
on Main Street, various contests and exhibits, and a concert
by the Sterling Band. Thousands attended, according to an
article in the *Dixon Evening Telegraph*, September 29.
EF to Mint: $100+

An announcement for Carnival Bingo, Binghamton, New York,
September 28 and 29, 1910. This printed card has local
inscriptions and a Binghamton street scene on a generic
background. EF to Mint: $12–$20

The Tournament of Roses, 1911. Printed cards of forthcoming
events were often made in large quantities.
EF to Mint: $18–$25

"Walter Brookins in Wright Standard, San Francisco Aviation
Meet, Jan. 9-16-1911" is the caption on this card illustrating a
long-forgotten event. EF to Mint: $150+

Getting ready for the races at the Algona, Iowa, fairground on
July 21, 1912. (RPPC printed in multiples. American Post Card
Co., Mason City, Iowa.) EF to Mint: $150+

"Sharkey, the Famous Bucking Bull." A remarkably well-detailed fast-action scene taken at high speed. (Doubleday & Gustin, Pendleton, Oregon. No. 33. Circa 1913.) The copyright indicates this RPPC was made in quantity. These were probably taken on tour with the bull and sold in various locations. EF to Mint: $10–$15

A June 21, 1914, RPPC card showing Mount Lassen erupting in California. "Will and I saw the eruption of Lassen Sunday evening while out autoing five or six miles from Chico." On the back: "Mt. Lassen is causing considerable news for the newspapers." From 1914 to 1917 the volcano erupted more or less continuously, and on May 22, 1915, a spectacular explosion devastated the regional landscape and showered debris as far as 200 miles to the east. EF to Mint: $12–$18

Shortly after 5:00 in the afternoon of June 24, 1924, the worst tornado in Ohio history ravaged Lorain. Shown is the rubble of the State Theatre, where five people died.
EF to Mint: $6–$10

On March 10, 1933, the Lynwood Theatre in California was totally destroyed by an earthquake that did great damage in the area, especially in Long Beach. Organ pipes can be seen at the right of the image. EF to Mint: $15–$25

The solar eclipse of January 24, 1925, was memorialized on this RPPC. EF to Mint: $20–$30

"Dust cloud rolling over Western Kansas town. Feb. 21, '35." RPPC capturing the essence of the great Dust Bowl of the Depression era, a slice of American history. This is a generic card without a specific location and was probably made in multiples. EF to Mint: $10–$18

A Gallery of Fires

Fires were extensively reported in newspapers in the early twentieth century, often with low-resolution pictures. Postcards from the era are sharper and serve to record many such disasters.

"Bird's Eye View of Frisco fire when it Started." (H.G. Zimmerman & Co.) EF to Mint: $4–$7

The Kennard Block in Manchester, New Hampshire, was destroyed by fire on January 14, 1902. This color postcard was issued two or three years later. EF to Mint: $6–$10

"Golden Gate near Hyde St. Frisco. April 18th 06." (Douglass.) RPPCs of the San Francisco fire during its progress are rare. Most were made in small numbers. EF to Mint: $4–$7

Early in the morning of April 18, 1906, San Francisco was rocked by an earthquake. Fires broke out quickly, and by day's end much of the business center of the city was destroyed. Several hundred different varieties of printed postcards were issued. Collecting them can be a specialty in itself. This one is captioned "The burning Call Building, San Francisco, California. A magnificent spectacle of April 18–20, 1906." The flames and smoke were added by an artist, as was the case for nearly all others showing the fire in progress. (Britton & Rey. No 1108.) EF to Mint: $3–$6

"Lafayette Park, looking toward Market St., San Francisco, Cal., during fire, April 18, 1906." (Rieder-Cardinell Co. Postmarked May 22, 1906.) EF to Mint: $4–$7

Two views of the Boyertown, Pennsylvania, Opera House destroyed in January 1908. EF to Mint: $25–$40

The Lyric Theatre in Altoona, Pennsylvania, was gutted by fire on February 25, 1907. This is one of several varieties of postcards picturing the ruins. EF to Mint: $15–$25

"Aveline Hotel fire, Ft. Wayne, Ind., May 3rd, 1908." An Associated Press dispatch of the next day included this: "At an early hour today the death toll in the new Aveline Hotel, which was destroyed at an early hour Sunday morning by fire, stood at eleven, with several persons unaccounted for. . . . The fire, which had its origin near the elevator shaft on the first floor, was caused by defective wiring. It was discovered by a hotel employee at 3:10 o'clock, and the alarm was quickly spread throughout the hotel. Within five minutes, however, the interior of the hotel was a seething furnace, and many of the guests were caught in their rooms before they had time to get into the hallways and make their way to the fire escapes. . . ." (Long's Novelty House. No. 2+8.) EF to Mint: $30–$45

A Gallery of Floods

Floods caused much damage in the early twentieth century. In most towns photographers were on hand to capture images that were later reproduced on postcards.

There was a cloudburst in Jackson, Michigan, on July 18, 1908, as stated on this postcard. The image is fake, made by adding "water" to a normal street scene. (Drake Brothers, publisher) EF to Mint: $10–$15

State Street in Montpelier, Vermont, during the flood of November 4 and 5, 1927. EF to Mint: $15–$25

The flood in Herkimer, New York, March 1, 1910, did not amount to much, at least not on Mohawk Street, where the water was just a few inches deep. EF to Mint: $40–$75

"Morgan Street at Flood's Peak, Hartford, March 19, 1936." In 1927, 1936, and 1938 floods ravaged many New England towns. Many black-and-white cards were issued of these disasters. EF to Mint: $6–$10

Flood damage in Pueblo, Colorado, on a card postmarked June 3, 1921. EF to Mint: $60–$100

Extensive flood debris in Winchester, New Hampshire, March 21, 1936. EF to Mint: $8–$12

A Gallery of Wrecks

Wrecks of aircraft, ships, and trains were often captured on RPPCs. Today they provide an opportunity to learn about these unfortunate happenings—some with slight damage, others very serious—by searching on the Internet. Most were documented in newsprint.

In the summer of 1906 the 195-foot, three-masted schooner *Saranac* was wrecked against a pier. In 1907 it was purchased by George Tilyou and put on exhibit at Steeplechase Park at Coney Island. This postcard illustrates the vessel. (Rumford Press, Concord, New Hampshire.) EF to Mint: $8–$12

The wreck of a sidewheel steamship on the Ohio River, as depicted on a card postmarked March 20, 1913. "This is a picture of the Bedford that sank near the B[unclear] landing." EF to Mint: $30–$50

Wrecked locomotive cars, Canaan, New Hampshire, September 15, 1907. Four miles north of the station, the southbound Quebec to Boston Express, filled with visitors to the Sherbrooke (Ontario) Fair, collided head-on with a Boston & Maine freight train when a dispatcher's orders were confused. The accident killed 25 people and injured dozens of others. Several different RPPCs were issued showing the wreck from various perspectives. EF to Mint: $20–$45

A photographer captured this automobile wreck and captioned it, "Near Nashua NH June 26 1912 4 P.M." A covered bridge is in the distance. EF to Mint: $25–$45

A printed card of the September 25, 1907, Canaan wreck. EF to Mint: $10–$15

An August 19, 1912, wreck on the Boston & Maine Railroad, one mile south of The Weirs, a New Hampshire resort town on Lake Winnipesaukee. Several different RPPCs of the disaster were published. EF to Mint: $50–$75

Time-Lapse Views

The same scene recorded on postcards over a span of years often reveals many changes, some dramatic, and provides a window on changing technology and activities. Collecting these cards from a favorite town or city from the early days down to modern times is a very popular pursuit. A few of the endless possibilities are illustrated in the galleries that follow.

Downtown Wolfeboro, New Hampshire

The Town of Wolfeboro, New Hampshire, was incorporated in 1770. Located on Lake Winnipesaukee, it became a popular summer resort after the Pavilion, a grand hotel, was built in the 1850s. From the late 1890s to date, hundreds of different postcards have featured Wolfeboro scenes. Shown here are images of the central business district with the changing years well demonstrated by the evolution of the automobile. In contrast, views over a similar period of local forested areas and mountains would show little change.

This retro scene of downtown Wolfeboro in 1880 was published circa 1910. The wooden building at the extreme right is where the Peavey Block would be built in 1889. The red-brick building to the left was built for the Lake Bank in 1855. (Leighton 215856.) EF to Mint: $8–$12

Downtown Wolfeboro in 1905, with the three-story Peavey block to the right in the distance. EF to Mint: $8–$12

The Peavey Block and to its right the Goodwin Block in 1914. EF to Mint: $7–$10

The same buildings in the 1930s. EF to Mint: $5–$8

Downtown in the early 1950s. EF to Mint: $3–$5

Downtown in the 1960s, viewed looking in the direction opposite to the preceding images. EF to Mint: $3–$5

A Bank in Upstate New York

The First National Bank of Brewster, New York, was chartered in 1875, succeeding the private banking firm of Borden, Wells & Company. In 1914, slightly after the era of the postcards pictured here, the bank's capital was $100,000. Frank Wells was present and E.D. Stannard was cashier. It would be interesting to learn more about the transition.

The First National Bank of Brewster, New York—ivy-covered and in a setting with no nearby buildings. (ANC Litho-Chrome E4569. Postmarked 1912.) EF to Mint: $5–$8

The First National Bank in a new building of the same style as the old, but with different architectural details, located in the middle of downtown Brewster later in the decade. Ivy covering must have been a bank trademark.
EF to Mint: $10–$15

A New Hampshire Hotel Changes Names

Yesteryear and today it is not uncommon for hotels and other places of accommodation to change owners and names. These two cards show three name changes for the Ocean View House, a seaside resort hotel on the Atlantic Ocean at Rye North Beach, New Hampshire, which changed hands in 1910.

The new owners of the resort overprinted their supply of postcards by blanking out "View" and printing "Wave" above it, reflecting its new name. On the back, information was given concerning the transition and the amenities offered. (Moore & Gibson Co., No. 33234. Postmarked 1910.) EF to Mint: $10–$18

Years later the Ocean Wave House name was changed to The Harrington, and the new owner simply inked out the caption and added the new in ink. (Frank W. Swallow Postcard Co. Circa 1920s.) EF to Mint: $30–$45

What Might Have Been

Sometimes postcard subjects are ephemeral—here today and gone next year. Some show projects and structures that were envisioned but never came to pass, what might have been but wasn't, as illustrated by several examples here.

Having a grand structure towering over an exposition as a landmark spelled success for the Eiffel Tower built for the 1889 Exposition in Paris, and the same is true for the Ferris Wheel that dominated the World's Columbian Exposition in Chicago in 1893.

For the forthcoming Louisiana Purchase Exposition to be held in St. Louis in 1904, a local businessman, C.F. Blanke of the Blanke Coffee Company, proposed an even grander landmark, the Blanke Aerial Globe.

It was to be made of steel, 700 feet high from the cut stone base to the observation tower at the top. Within the globe would be many attractions including a German and an American restaurant, a menagerie, a two-ring circus, a palm garden, and a race track, according to an article in the *New York Times*, August 29, 1901.

Blanke issued related postcards by 1902, but that is as far as the project ever got.

In the same vein, another monumental globe was proposed: "New York will Soon Have the Highest Structure But One Ever Raised by Man," exclaimed the front page of the New York *Herald Tribune* on January 20, 1907. Occupying the rest of the page below the headline was an architectural rendering of the Friede Globe Tower. And what a glorious prospect it was. Opening was scheduled for a few months later, on May

15. Meanwhile, construction was underway, with concrete pilings set 30 feet into the sand to support the structure, and the foundation already taking shape.

At 700 feet in height, it would be second only to the 1,063-feet-high Eiffel Tower. But that Paris attraction was but a lacy open framework of iron and not much else. In contrast, the Friede Globe Tower was a city in the sky. Far above the ground a huge sphere would be divided into 11 floors providing ample room for the largest ballroom in the world, several restaurants (including one on the outside, rotating to permit a view of the landscape around in all directions), lavish gardens, and a super-circus with four rings of entertainment. A concert hall added to the list of wonders, not to overlook a bowling alley and a miniature railroad. There would be no need to go anywhere else. In fact, a hotel within the globe meant that visitors could stay several days if they wished. Including day-trippers, 50,000 people could be accommodated in the various interior attractions.

The entrepreneur who conceived the Tower was Samuel M. Friede, who had attended the 1904 Louisiana Purchase Exposition (St. Louis World's Fair) and had been impressed with the gigantic steel Ferris Wheel, earlier in use at the 1893 World's Columbian Exposition in Chicago, and by other buildings and attractions.

The Friede Globe Tower was never built.

In the meantime, at least several postcards had been issued of the Friede Globe Tower. These seem to have sold quite well, for examples are readily met with today.

The Blanke Aerial Globe—set to tower over the 1904 Louisiana Purchase Exposition. EF to Mint: $10–$15

An official Friede Globe Tower postcard issued by the promoters of the project, copyright 1906, and sold from an information stand at the base of the projected structure. EF to Mint: $8–$12

REAL PHOTO POSTCARDS (RPPCS)

CHAPTER 7

Postcards that were produced one at a time as contact prints, by transferring a camera photograph image from a negative to a postcard with a photo-sensitive face, are called "real photo" postcards, abbreviated as RPPCs.

As a class, RPPCs are the most valuable cards. They are also the most complex to understand and evaluate.

For the values of RPPCs you can learn by experience—that knowledge coming from reviewing the RPPCs in this and other chapters and reading our captions and prices. As you will see, for an RPPC there are many variables.

An RPPC can be identified in several ways. Held at an angle to the light, the face of the card will be glossy, like a photograph. Under magnification there will be no tiny dots as used in the halftone printing process. All RPPCs are black-and-white, although a few have been hand-tinted. Titles or identification of the cards are lettered, usually by hand, in the negative, and often rather crudely.

Although there were some large-scale producers, with the Eastern Illustrating Company of Belfast, Maine, being a prime example, most were produced by local photographers and small shops. As they were made individually, different examples of the same image can vary in lightness and darkness. Sometimes the negative used was larger than the face of the card, with the result that copies of the same image made in different runs can vary slightly in positioning.

The *Lewiston Evening Journal*, February 7, 1908, included this:

All the leading manufacturers of photographic supplies make blank postcards, sensitized so that photographic prints may be made upon them. These find a ready sale among amateurs who like to make their own cards. Many of the professional photographers find it profitable to use these photographic cards in their business. And, on the other hand, many first class photographers who had fair business in some small city or town have, since the card business reached its present proportions, closed or sold out their studios and now devote themselves exclusively to the work of making photographs for the souvenir card makers. In this they find a more lucrative employment than in the studio. In addition they are working in the open air and under far more healthful conditions. ...

Eastman Kodak conducted classes and also supplied stock RPPCs with printed backs for photographic studios to send out to local customers, encouraging them to make their own RPPCs on Kodak Velox postcard stock. Probably well over a thousand professional photographers and studios created RPPCs, and an even larger number of amateurs were active.

In imitation of RPPCs, some large companies made cards that resemble hand-made contact prints, but produced mechanically and in quantity. The Underwood & Underwood company, best known for its stereograph cards in the early days and news photographs at a later time, produced a line of postcards circa 1912 showing many buildings and other scenes from American cities and towns, large and small. These have white margins and printed borders and, while very desirable to collect, do not fall into the RPPC category. Other exceptions could be mentioned.

As most RPPCs were usually produced one at a time, and often in limited quantities, as a class they are scarce today. Those showing family scenes, pets, children, homes, parks, and the like have limited appeal to collectors today and have little demand. Robert Bogdan, in the *Real Photo Postcard Guide*, 2006, estimated that

What must be close to an ideal RPPC is this by the Eastern Illustrating Co., of Belfast, Maine, showing the Stafford, Connecticut, post office with the Eastern company truck in front, and nicely cancelled and postmarked by the same post office. It was the rule that in many small villages the general store housed the post office and the store owner was the postmaster. EF to Mint: $35–$50

among, say, 100 such cards taken from an old-time album rather than a collection, perhaps only 3 will be truly significant or valuable.

In the early twentieth century, continuing into the 1960s, relatively little attention was paid to RPPCs. Interest picked up in the 1970s, with Andreas ("Andy") Brown being one of the catalysts. As the proprietor of the Gotham Book Shop in New York City, each year prior to the Metropolitan New York postcard show he would mount an exhibit of his favorite cards. Among these were many RPPCs, a particular specialty. In 1981, with Hal Brown, he wrote *Prairie Fires and Paper Moons: The American Photographic Postcard 1900–1920*, published by D.R. Godine, of Boston. The reception in the postcard community was electric: countless collectors investigated these and quickly concluded that a selection of RPPCs, arranged with interesting captions, could be incredibly interesting. The die was cast, and RPPCs

An Underwood & Underwood RPPC made in quantity, showing Congress Street, Portsmouth, New Hampshire. 1912. EF to Mint: $15–$25

became a growing, then dynamic, category in the world of postcards. Since that time, other collectors have followed suit with books illustrated by such cards, some of which have been very well done. Numerous city and small-town history books have also been published using RPPCs as their main content, with captions providing narratives.

A.J. Schumann, a seller of printed postcards and maker of RPPCs in Chicago, Illinois, photographed this group of holiday cards, mostly German imports, circa 1910, and issued an RPPC to advertise them. EF to Mint: $60–$80

An Eastern Illustrating Co. card of the post office at East Thompson, Connecticut, and a detail from the card showing the EIC truck and people nearby. EF to Mint: $45–$75

Beginning around the turn of the century, the Eastman Kodak Company had an extensive promotion with photographic studios. Different cards showing vacationers and amateur photographers were made available to studios that produced RPPCs on Velox card stock. The face of this 1901 card gives information and has a Private Mailing Card back. Later promotional cards had printed messages and advertisements on the back. EF to Mint: $50–$75

In autumn 1911 W.S. Coyne produced this RPPC showing two friends, J.N. Kay and L.A. Combs (sitting on the cart, "the town bachelor"), in front of Coyne's photographic studio. EF to Mint: $175+

Another early card, enticing amateurs to get their own equipment to make RPPCs at home without the need of a laboratory. "Sample Velox Postal" imprint at the lower left. EF to Mint: $50–$75

Evaluating the desirability and price of an RPPC involves several different aspects. Two RPPCs of the same era and same subject can vary widely in quality. One can be a somewhat fuzzy second-generation print (see below), and another can be carefully focused and

As seen on the back of this RPPC, the Central Post Card Co., of Fort Scott, Kansas, solicited photographs and then sent them off to Chicago, where they were printed on postcard photo stock and then shipped to the customer, probably with a Central label. On the card the publisher is listed as the Pecos Valley Drug Co., probably the Scott customer. Depicted is the Princess Theatre, a nickelodeon in Roswell, New Mexico. Details reveal that *The Runaway* and *The Madcap of the Hills*, both June 1913 one-reel releases, were featured on this day, and that for three days there would also be vocal entertainment by tenor Carl W. Molter, with a change of program every other day. EF to Mint: $250+

Another RPPC in the Kodak Velox series, this one showing an amateur photographer developing her own film. Kodak did much to encourage the hobby of picture-taking. Enthusiasts made RPPC themselves or could have a local studio do that. This card has the imprint of W.H. Wheeler & Son, Springfield, Vermont. EF to Mint: $25–$50

"Thomson's Photos" offered by Thomson's Photo Studio at a fairground in Upstate New York. Other concessions included a Japanese Tea Set counter, "Railroad Station" (with a Hale's Tours car in which passengers sat to watch films, as if they were traveling: "Notice! All trips seen in this car taken from the end of a moving train"), and a stand for soft drinks and cigars. EF to Mint: $200+

In Augusta, Maine, the East Side Photo Studio advertised, "Postal Cards Finished while you wait. $1.00 Doz." (Circa 1910.) EF to Mint: $250+

printed from a negative with microscopic details. Although both might be described identically by a seller, the first card might be worth $10 and the second $100.

As baseball star and humorist Yogi Berra said, "You can see a lot by just looking." Thus it is with RPPCs. By viewing different examples in the marketplace you can gain appreciation for what is very desirable and what is ordinary or mediocre. This chapter, with estimated values attached to images of specific cards, will be a good guide.

RPPCs open the door to research on the Internet that can turn into a fascinating story. Take for example this card:

Post, Texas, in its entirety, as viewed through the entrance, circa 1910. At quick glance this is a card showing the entrance of a very small town on the prairie. The main street has a handful of buildings with a tree in the center. Some horses and wagons are seen in the distance. Value if the card were not identified as to location, EF to Mint: $10–$15. Value as identified and with its backstory, EF to Mint: $50–$75

Wikipedia reveals its history (excerpted):

Post, Texas

Post is located on the edge of the caprock escarpment of the Llano Estacado, the southeastern edge of the Great Plains. It is at the crossroads of U.S. Routes 84 and 380.

The land belonged to John Bunyan Slaughter, as it was on his U Lazy S Ranch. In 1906, Slaughter sold it to Charles William (C.W.) Post, the breakfast cereal manufacturer, who founded "Post City" as a utopian colonizing venture in 1907. Post devised the community as a model town.

He purchased 200,000 acres (810 square km) of ranchland and established the Double U

Company to manage the town's construction. The company built trim houses and numerous structures, which included the Algerita Hotel, a gin, and a textile plant. They planted trees along every street and prohibited alcoholic beverages and brothels. The Double U Company rented and sold farms and houses to settlers. A post office began in a tent during the year of Post City's founding, being established (with the name Post) July 18, 1907, with Frank L. Curtis as first postmaster.

Two years later, the town had a school, a bank, and a newspaper, the Post City Post. The railroad reached the town in 1910. The town changed its name to "Post" when it incorporated in 1914, the year of C. W. Post's death. By then, Post had a population of 1,000, 10 retail businesses, a dentist, a physician, a sanitarium, and Baptist, Methodist, and Presbyterian churches. Postex Cotton Mills began production in 1913 with 250 employees.

From 1910 to 1913, Post experimented with attempts at rainmaking. Explosives were detonated in the atmosphere at timed intervals. Precipitation records, however, showed that the efforts failed. The C. W. Post estate pledged $75,000 and the town raised $35,000 in 1916 to bid unsuccessfully to become the site of the proposed West Texas Agricultural and Mechanical College.

Beyond this chapter, various RPPCs are featured and discussed elsewhere in this book—under views by state, under transportation, and in other categories, including many RPPCs illustrated in the preceding chapter. The guidelines given here will be of use to you in those other collecting specialties.

Scenic Real Photo Postcards

The classic RPPCs were made mostly circa 1900 to 1930 but in the largest numbers from about 1905 to 1915, with the peak seemingly from about 1907 to 1910—as evidenced by postmarks on existing cards.

Most often RPPCs filled the need for general stores, newsstands, and the like to offer a selection of local views without having to order many hundreds or more printed cards. RPPCs could be made up a few at a time as needed. Popular subjects included Main Street scenes, municipal buildings, stores, post offices, banks, theaters, and parks. In some instances, Main Street views were altered before printing by adding tracks and a trolley car to make the place seem up-to-date, sometimes in anticipation that such transportation would be put in place, other times just for fun. Sometimes signs were blanked out and new lettering added to reflect a new store owner or other change.

In November 1911, Mrs. John Corkery, whose family owned the Spofford House, a New Hampshire summer hotel on Spofford Lake, took this RPPC and marked it up with ink, identifying the people. She mailed it to her son, J. Francis Corkery, a student at St. Anselm's College in Manchester, New Hampshire. "This card will make you feel good," she noted on the back. EF to Mint: $10–$15

"Drug and Grocery Stores, Main Street, Hammond, N.Y." This image invites research. On the left is a jewelry store (per the lettering on the front window) and on the right a drug store. The sign at the top of the jewelry store has been altered in the photograph to "GEORGE N. WYLLIE" in crude letters. A guess is that Wyllie was a grocer and later occupant of the store, which still had jewelry-store notices on the window. The sharp details of people and products add value. EF to Mint: $250+

In Ballston Spa, New York, the studio of J.S. Wooley published RPPCs of regional scenes. Shown here is Wilton Avenue in the summer, at "Lincoln Square," as it was called, the intersection with Washington Street. The awning at the left is on the front of the Wooley studio. (1906.) EF to Mint: $50–$80

In the depth of winter, the photographer took the same position and perspective. Such paired views are not common among RPPC and add much interest. (January 1907.) EF to Mint: $50–$80

A local stationer and postcard issuer created this multi-view RPPC by taking six RPPCs and placing them on an appropriate background and photographing the group. This was a very common way to create such views, both RPPC and printed types. Usually many cards were made. Today they have only modest values. (Wright, Barrett & Stillwell Co., circa 1910.) EF to Mint: $50–$75

An example of the Stadler Way of Reproducing Photographs.

The Stadler Photographing Co., with facilities in Chicago and New York City, was a major maker of RPPCs using Webster photo-printing machines. The firm made many advertising cards, usually second generation, by re-photographing a print and adding text at the bottom border. They also made many cards for individuals. EF to Mint: $40–$70

A postcard in the making: a Proof print sent by the Eastern Illustrating and Publishing Co. to a customer, showing the image reproduction on the face and, in pencil, the suggested caption, "Wharf and Anchorage from Hanly Boat Service, Falmouth Foreside, Me." EF to Mint: $20–$35

Scenic RPPCs depict American life as it was, unlike many printed cards that often had telephone poles brushed out, trash or anything unsightly removed, and people, automobiles, and other features added as a normal procedure. Some RPPCs were slightly altered, as noted above, but these are few and far between.

Collected from different eras, a group of RPPCs from a given town furnishes a record of change and progress.

Objects in motion, such as a car or wagon, are sometimes slightly blurred if the photographer used a slow shutter speed.

The same negative could be used over a period of years to turn out postcards as needed.

The vast majority of RPPCs in the marketplace today show outdoor scenes. Those depicting interiors required special flash or electric lighting, time exposures, or other special efforts, and are in the distinct minority except for studio pictures. Interior views were made of many stores, saloons, and other businesses. When these show interesting products and also depict people (usually posing near or behind a counter), they are especially desirable from a collecting viewpoint. The more identifiable signs and products that can be seen, the better. A Coca-Cola or Moxie sign in clear view can add considerably to the value of a card showing the interior of a general store. A saloon interior with people and a few slot machines can be worth several times the price of one that has none of these.

Most RPPCs are not identified on the face as to the photographer or issuer. On the back, nearly always white with black printing, photographic studios are sometimes mentioned, as are stores and other distributors.

As a rule of thumb, RPPCs are rare for large towns and cities, for the market was wide enough in such places that colorful printed cards could be ordered and sold in quantity. Accordingly, an RPPC of Broadway in New York City in 1912 would be a rarity, as dozens of varieties of cards in color were made in quantity, and less expensively. In contrast, an RPPC of the main thoroughfare in East Pharsalia, New York, would be expected, as there would have been little demand for a large quantity of printed cards in such a small village. There are many exceptions to this and other rules, but they apply in a general sense.

Picking up on the well-known comment, "there are three aspects to the value of real estate: location, location, and location," the same can be said for certain scenic cards. Generally, if today in the early twenty-first century a state, county, or town has a much larger population than it did a century ago, its cards are rare in proportion to the demand for them. A 1912-dated RPPC of a roadside store in a district of Los Angeles can be very valuable for this reason, whereas the same subject, but in Richmond Springs, New York, would engender only passing interest.

Topics and Specialties

While collecting RPPC views and scenes is very popular, many enthusiasts have opted to concentrate on a specialty. One of this book's authors, Dave Bowers, since the 1960s has collected RPPCs of nickelodeon theaters—these showing movie houses that typically charged 5¢ for admission. Some of the scenes are incredibly rustic—of storefronts with paper signs

"A busy place" is C.F. Stalcup's Blacksmith & Machine Shop, Gregory, South Dakota, as automobile enthusiasts gather in the front to be photographed. (1910.) EF to Mint: $125+

Similarly, automobiles stirred up a lot of interest in Lamar, Colorado, as owners posed for a photographer. (The Commercial Studio, Lamar, circa 1910s.) EF to Mint: $75–$125

advertising movie shows. In 50 years Bowers acquired hundreds of especially detailed views and many of a general nature (such as a nickelodeon among other businesses as part of a street scene). These were used to illustrate a popular Whitman Publishing book, *One Thousand Nights at the Movies: An Illustrated History of Motion Pictures, 1895–1915*. In the late 1970s and the 1980s his wife, collector Christine Bowers, gathered as many high-quality views as she could find of horse-drawn commercial vehicles, eventually collecting more than 500.

Circus, carnival, and vaudeville acts were the specialty of another collector. Robert Bogdan sought cards photographed by Henry M. Beach of Remsen, New York. Many other examples could be mentioned. Most collectors of specialty views seek printed cards as well as RPPCs.

The topics to be collected, apart from scenic views, are almost unlimited. The ultimate price and popularity of an RPPC is based on the popularity of its subject and how it is shown (sharply detailed, with interesting features, for example).

By fortuitous circumstance, the height of RPPC popularity coincided with the peak of interest in the automobile (dozens of new models were produced each year) and the popularity of the trolley car. Accordingly, each of these fields is rich with possibilities for a specialized collector. Airplanes were in use at the time but were not often seen at fairs or in visits to various towns until after 1910, after which time they became a popular RPPC subject, usually made in small quantities. As a class such cards are fairly scarce. In contrast, cars and trolleys were downtown and could be easily and frequently seen and photographed.

RPPCs of Commerce

RPPCs showing stores, factory interiors, automobile shops, candy stores, and the like are very popular and can have significant value. An RPPC of a saloon with slot machines on the bar and beer signs clearly readable is in great demand, and one showing the interior of a card parlor or gambling hall would be more valuable yet.

Interior views of general stores, drug stores, confectionery parlors, soda fountains, and grocery stores are widely collected and are of special interest if products are sharply defined enough to be clearly identified. Factory interiors showing people at work are desirable. Outside views of stores are in demand, especially if interesting signs are in view or the windows display merchandise. Horse-drawn ice wagons and delivery wagons are yet another category in demand.

Interesting signs and billboards add value to an RPPC if the details are sharp. Circuses that are coming to town, rodeos, store sales, and the like can be found, often as part of Main Street scenes.

On James Street in Columbus, Wisconsin, a brick wall was devoted to advertisements for local businesses (see the right side of the image). (Circa 1910.) EF to Mint: $60–$90

Aspects of Value for RPPCs

Relatively little has ever appeared in print or in Internet and other offerings concerning features that add to or detract from the value of an RPPC. The following thoughts are based upon the authors' considerable experience.

The originality of an RPPC card is vital to its value. Many modern copies exist of old RPPCs, and new versions of supposed RPPCs have been created by reproducing old photographs on postcard stock. There is no hard and fast rule to determine the age of a card, except that bright white cards are likely to be new, and ones toned to delicate off-white or light brown are more likely to be old. Experience, such as from viewing cards known to be old and noting their characteristics, is the best teacher. Like as not, a knowledgeable seller such as a professional dealer can offer specific information as well. A reproduction RPPC has no value.

Given a choice, most specialists in RPPCs would prefer one that has a clear postal cancel on the back, complete with part of the cancel on the stamp ("tied" to the stamp is the philatelic term). Although clever forgeries can be made, generally the cancel on a scenic or typical RPPC is authentic. Many have had their stamps soaked off or removed but leave the cancel with time,

place, and date. These are more desirable than RPPCs with a completely pristine, uncancelled back. Postal cancellations can be a two-edged sword: if there is a significant part of the cancellation or stray ink on the front of the card, distracting from the image, this detracts from the value.

The condition or grade of an RPPC is important. Ideal is a card in virtually new or "mint" condition, except for a pleasing postmark. However, such quality is not often possible. Many cards of Main Street scenes were kept as family favorites and have, perhaps, a light crease, a rounded corner, or some other problem. Such a card can still be desirable if it is the only choice you have. As an example, an RPPC of a 1907 scene in a gambling hall in Goldfield, Nevada, can be very valuable even if it has a slight tear or a nick on the edge. If a card is one of a kind, any condition can be accepted.

A damaged card: There is good news and bad news for this RPPC. The bad news first: two corners are missing, there is no identification as to the people or place, and it is not postally used. Any one of those factors would have added value. The good news is that it shows what must have been a very active shoe-repair shop, with four tradesmen working at a table with tools and shoe-making lasts. The focus is very sharp, and details show the calendar is dated February 1910 and was issued by the United States F [incomplete] Co. at 1128 Mission St., San Francisco, a dealer in "beer and air pumps," carbonic gas, and related items. The lettering on the window can be discerned to read "M.L. Jacobs." The wooden crate on the floor is lettered, "Grown and Packed by E.E. Taylor" and the notation "Cal." A directory check reveals that the Liquid Carbonic Co., maker of soda-fountain and related supplies, had a showroom at 1128 Mission Street in 1910. An unstudied town directory or newspaper advertisement could tell more about Jacobs. It would seem likely that he was located in California. The RPPC is probably one of a kind, or at least is extremely rare. If it could be identified as to location, it would have significant value, perhaps a quarter to a half of what an unimpaired card would bring. Good, impaired: $25–$40

Many RPPCs have faded, this being particularly true if they were not properly "fixed" chemically at the time they were made. Such a card will often be light sepia or brown, with little contrast, requiring a low-power magnifying glass to appreciate the subject. Unless a faded card is otherwise rare or important, it will have relatively low value.

Sharpness of the Image and Details

Clarity of the image is very important for RPPCs in which you wish to observe details. Accordingly, a card of Main Street in Boothbay Harbor, Maine, showing stores, people, and vehicles, will be much more valuable if under a low-power glass you can discern the lettering on signs and other details. If faces, signs, and other features show no improvement or are indistinct under low-power magnification, the card is not as desirable.

As a general rule, RPPCs printed directly by contact with the original negative are sharp if the image was well focused and sharp to begin with. Often, the maker of an RPPC would create a second-generation image by making a black-and-white print of the image, adding lettering, then re-photographing the whole. Nearly always, this resulted in a loss of detail. The subtle shades of contrast were often lost as well, eliminating continuous tone or gradation.

In many instances a local studio made a photographic copy of a printed card to add to its inventory and selection. In other instances groups of three, four, five, or more printed cards or RPPCs were arranged as a collage, then photographed to create a card with multiple views, as noted in chapter 5. Such photographic copies of other cards generally have lower market values, as do most other second-generation RPPCs.

The prominence of a desired topic has a great influence on the value. An RPPC showing the front of a traveling-show tent, with a barker addressing a crowd and gaudy signs describing attractions within, can be very desirable and expensive if this occupies the main part of the view. The exact same scene shown at a distance, across a field, and occupying just a small part of the view, would have much less appeal. A sparkling new roadster parked in a driveway with its proud owner at the wheel and with the license plate in view is very desirable if a close-up, but much less so if it is a small part of an overall view showing a house and lawn. A large Coca-Cola sign in the front of a store is more desirable than a tiny one barely visible at a counter in the back.

RPPC of the Bee Hive traveling sales wagon offering coffee, packaged seeds, and other items. Location unknown. (Circa 1910.) EF to Mint: $100+

East Madison Street, Waterloo, Wisconsin, as depicted on a sharply focused RPPC with a detail from the picture. Main Street views such as this are especially desirable if sharp, as many different products, signs, and the like can be studied and appreciated. (L.L. Cook, Lake Mills, Wisconsin. No. 106. Circa 1910s.) EF to Mint: $60–$90

Kellhofer's Mill in Chillicothe, Ohio, photographed on August 4, 1909. The RPPC has excellent detail, including interesting signs—always a plus for the value of an RPPC. EF to Mint: $100+

RPPC of the post office in Erin, New York, sharply detailed. A Model T Ford (with a 1914 New York license plate), people, horses and carriages, and many advertising signs add up to a great image. (Eastern Illustrating Co.) EF to Mint: $80–$150

The More Information the Better

If the photographer is identified on the front or back of the card, and there is collector interest in that particular person or studio, this can add value. Interesting messages and other notations on the back can be important if they impart information not otherwise known. As an example, "Train wreck near Canaan, New Hampshire, September 15, 1911," might give the card significant value, whereas the same card would be of relatively low interest if it had an obvious depiction of a smash-up but no indication of time or place. An RPPC of a burned-out building captioned to note it was taken after the April 1906 San Francisco earthquake and fire is highly collectible. The same subject without identification of time or location would be of very low value and interest. A view showing a horse with an unmarked wagon, or a picnic at the side of a lake, will likely remain unattributed forever.

For many cards that lack titles, other clues can be helpful in tracking down the location where the image was photographed. If a photographer or studio is imprinted, usually on the back, this can narrow the focus. A studio in Hayden, Idaho, likely issued cards relating to the immediate area, and not of Ohio, Kentucky, or Florida. With such information in hand, a researcher can examine the card for signs showing the names of businesses or other indications of the place where the picture was snapped. For many small towns, an Internet search can confirm, for example, that the picture was taken in Coeur d'Alene, Idaho (not far from Hayden, to continue this example).

A notation of "Opening day at the Bijou Theatre in Peoria on June 7, 1908," would make a card more valuable than one without such information. RPPCs of parades, carnivals, and other popular events are desirable if properly identified but are of much less interest if of an anonymous nature. Thanks to the Internet, sometimes signs, posters, and other details in a high-quality anonymous RPPC can be used to track down the place and/or time the picture was taken.

Postmarks can offer clues. Many cards have two postmarks—one from the sending post office and the other, often marked "RECD" or similar, from the receiving post office at a slightly later date. The latter usually is the same as that of the addressee of the card. The sending post office usually indicates the town or at least the general area of the subject.

As mentioned, chasing information on the Internet or elsewhere adds to the thrill of the hunt. By way of analogy, in numismatics there are many unattributed metal tokens of the early twentieth century, nicknamed "mavericks," that are published in the *Token and Medal Society Journal* (www.tokenandmedal.org) so historians can further research their origins. A token inscribed "Empire Saloon, 124 Main St.," has much more value if it can be attributed to, say, Cincinnati, and extremely more value if it is from a "Wild West" place such as Grass Valley, California. So it goes for RPPCs as well.

This RPPC has all of the information anyone could desire and, in addition, it is sharply focused and has interesting advertising posters to each side of the building. "Home of Savannah Poster Adv. Service. Pride and Mapes, owners. Savannah, Ga." The back identifies the maker: "Foltz Photographic Postals, 116 Bull St.—111 Whitaker St., Savannah, Ga." and is postmarked April 1, 1913. The signs include advertisements for, starting at the left, Anheuser-Busch ("Merry Christmas" with a parade), Snowdrift shortening, Peck's Clothes ("made in Syracuse"), Bijou Theatre (week of December 9, headlining Fennell & Tyson), Velvet tobacco, Prager's Laundry, Evansville Brewing Assn. Beer, Post Tavern Special ("made by Post at Battle Creek"), and Fatima cigarettes. An old faded sign above the two Peck's Clothes posters reads "Bernard Adv / Service," suggesting that the company may have been known under this name earlier. If it had automobiles, the value would be even greater. EF to Mint: $80+

This sharply focused and well-detailed RPPC is not identified as to location or maker of the card. As such it would be of relatively little value. The view includes the stores of Perry & Childs (with a Heinz Pure Vinegars banner), McClelland Meat Market, and the "Livery & Feed Barn." The horse-drawn vehicles suggest a date of about 1910. If these clues could be used to find the location, the card would immediately become highly collectible, and its value would multiply. EF to Mint: $15–$25

Rarity

In addition to the preceding, the rarity of a card is important to its value. C.W. Parker, the Abilene, Kansas, outfitter of circuses, carnivals, and amusement parks, had many RPPCs made in quantity—possibly by the many hundreds or even more—of merry-go-round models he had for sale in the 1920s and 1930s. Within the carousel specialty, such Parker cards are not rare, but the subject still gives them great interest and modest value. On the other hand, an RPPC showing a William Dentzel carousel, with crisp details and with date and place, has the potential of being very valuable.

Every now and then a hoard of RPPCs is found and comes on the market, such as cards of Gardner's Clothing Store in Sodus, New York. These were distributed in the 1970s, and at shows most dealers had at least one for sale.

As a general rule, an RPPC with a printed or hand-lettered caption on the front or a caption in dropout white within the image was made in multiples—perhaps dozens, perhaps hundreds, sometimes thousands. Hand-lettering was often done with black ink on the face of the negative, written backward so it would appear correct when printed. The art of writing backward or

Three cars are in front of the Davis City Garage in this RPPC, without a title on the face or imprint or postmark on the back. It is not known whether this is the City Garage in a place called Davis, or if it is in Davis City. A check revealed that there are a half dozen or more Davis towns and cities in America. An examination of a detail shows a West Virginia plate of 1914. A closer check suggests that Davis, West Virginia, also called Davis City, is the likely attribution. Now this card is well identified! Most of the value is due to the automobiles. EF to Mint: $250+

in mirror image required some practice, and it is common to see crude lettering and mistakes. In some instances a studio used the wrong side of the image, causing the view to appear backward—particularly noticeable if there are signs in the view.

An RPPC with a desirable subject but with no identification on the front and without a photo studio or photographer name printed on the back is likely an amateur effort, perhaps one of a kind, or in any event made in very small quantities. Accordingly, many of these range from unique to very rare. Because of this, grade takes a second seat to availability. Many of these have no message or other notation to identify the subjects. Again, in some instances detective work can be helpful—such as finding store names and doing a lot of searching on the Internet. Often, this spells success with sharply detailed Main Street views. For a card showing an automobile and its owner, or a drug store and pharmacist, you are usually out of luck. However, such cards may be of interest if classified by category—such as an REO automobile, Tufts soda fountain, or the like.

This RPPC from the Gardner's Clothing Store hoard would be worth more if rare. EF to Mint: $15–$45

Experience is needed to know what is rare and what is common, although the term "common" is relative (hoards of RPPCs are few and far between). Reproductions are plentiful, as are "RPPCs" made up on new stock by copying old images that were never used on cards in the early twentieth century. As noted, these have no collectible value. Postcard dealers and collectors are usually willing to share knowledge and can be very helpful. With some experience, including from examining cards at shows and on the Internet, you will be able to learn many things.

People at Home, Leisure Activities, Etc.

Many RPPCs were printed from amateur photographs taken of family, home, or other scenes that were important to the photographer at the time. A baby in a carriage, a young boy sitting on a porch with a dog, Father standing next to his new Ford Model T, a young girl dressed up for church—there is no end of such subjects. While the images were understandable to recipients at one time, today they are often unidentified as to people, time, or location. Photograph quality can range from quite good to poor and indistinct.

That said, a personal card with a notation, typically in pencil, on the back, saying, "Priscilla Jones and her new bicycle in Central Square, Keene, N.H., June 17, 1914," has more value and interest than would the same card absent any such information, the latter attracting little if any collector interest. Furthermore, value, sometimes substantial, can be added if there is something in the view that engenders collecting interest today. Thus, Father in front of his new Model T Ford would be a desirable subject, and Father in front of a sporty Stutz Bearcat would be better yet—assuming the image was

On rare occasions a studio created a double-fold RPPC, as seen here with the Main Street of Warsaw, New York. (No publisher, circa 1910.) EF to Mint: $60

in focus and pleasing. Best of all would be a Stutz Bearcat in a carnival midway or on a street with a penny arcade or nickelodeon theater.

Intended to amuse is this RPPC of three people posing in a field of weeds, with a carpet laid down, a table, and an Edison phonograph. On the back the participants are identified as Mr. and Mrs. W.H. Belchamber and Jennie Bledden. Some Internet searching found that Bledden was from Syracuse, New York, and the Belchambers were from Fulton in the same state. (Circa 1910s.) EF to Mint: $125+

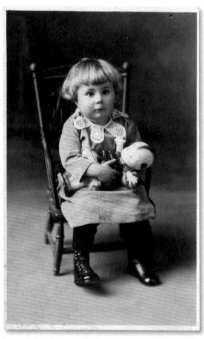

An RPPC of a little girl holding a doll, not identified as to person, place, or time. Sentimental, yes. Valuable, no. However, if the doll could be identified it would have value to a doll specialist. Such RPPCs are fairly plentiful, but most are not attributed. EF to Mint: $10–$15

This RPPC with a girl, at least five dolls, a copy of *Peter Rabbit,* and a decorated Christmas tree has value several times that of the average view without a child, an identifiable book, and dolls. EF to Mint: $20–$35

Residences, Cottages, Farms

RPPCs of houses, cottages, and the like are very common, as are scenes down home on the farm. If they are identified as to location, they gain value to collectors of a particular town or state. If the view is of the home of a president or other well-known public figure, it can have added value. The addition of people, as on a porch, or a vehicle parked out front, can add value. Few, however, have significant values.

"Mountain Hoosiers at Home" in their cabin in Terra Alta, West Virginia. This scene of rustic life in Appalachia has more value and interest than one of a regular home in a town or city. The term "Hoosier," usually applied to Indiana residents, was also used for folk who lived in the woods, who might holler "Who's there" if they heard a noise outside. EF to Mint: $60–$90

Mansions on Grymes Hill, Staten Island, New York City. (A. Loeffler. No. 832. Circa 1904.) EF to Mint: $30–$45

Studio RPPCs showing patrons "flying" in an airplane were done several ways, often by taking a photograph of a prop airplane, as here, and stripping in a studio portrait of the subject, then placing the result over a photograph of a landscape. Here an "Oklahoma" pennant is dangling downward to the left, a bit of added humor. The negative for this had been used a few too many times—there is a burn hole at the bottom, above the border below the pennant. (Circa 1910s.) EF to Mint: $30–$45

Posed Studio RPPCs

In the early twentieth century many amusement parks, vacation spots, and other locations with photo parlors offered scenic props, such as an automobile, crescent moon, hot-air balloon, locomotive cab, saloon back bar, or Wild West motif. Some were slightly naughty—what fun for a prim schoolteacher to be photographed in a saloon! Patrons would pose and have their pictures taken, sometimes in costumes—great fun to send back home. Countless varieties were made. An ideal card would be identified as to studio, location, and time (postmark), and perhaps with an interesting message. Not many fit that description.

RPPCs taken of people posed against a plain studio background or with a painted or furnished backdrop are usually of interest only if the people are identified by name and place, and even then only to a specialist seeking cards of a particular studio or town.

Aboard the "Express to Weirs N.H." The sign reflects that this RPPC was taken at one of New Hampshire's popular lake resorts. The little sign could be easily replaced with any other, should the photographer go to another location. Circa 1910s. EF to Mint: $15–$25+

Two cut-outs of "ladies of the evening" from the "Joy Parlor, Seattle" furnished a setting for this humorous studio photograph. (Circa 1910s.) EF to Mint: $20–$35

The paper moon was a fixture prop at many studios, and many variations were made. A young lad posed for this picture. (Circa 1910s.)
EF to Mint: $20–$35

The studio gave these girls each a pair of angel wings. (Circa 1910s.)
EF to Mint: $20–$35

While most paper-moon RPPCs feature children and women, occasionally men were photographed as well. The top of the crescent was a convenient place to hang a hat. (Circa 1910s.)
EF to Mint: $20–$35

Prop background of a "saloon," with misspelled signs offering booze, gambling, and other pleasures. The photo customer (left) stepped up to the "bar" and the photographer clicked his camera. (Sent from the tourist resort of Hot Springs, Arkansas, in 1921.) EF to Mint: $25–$40

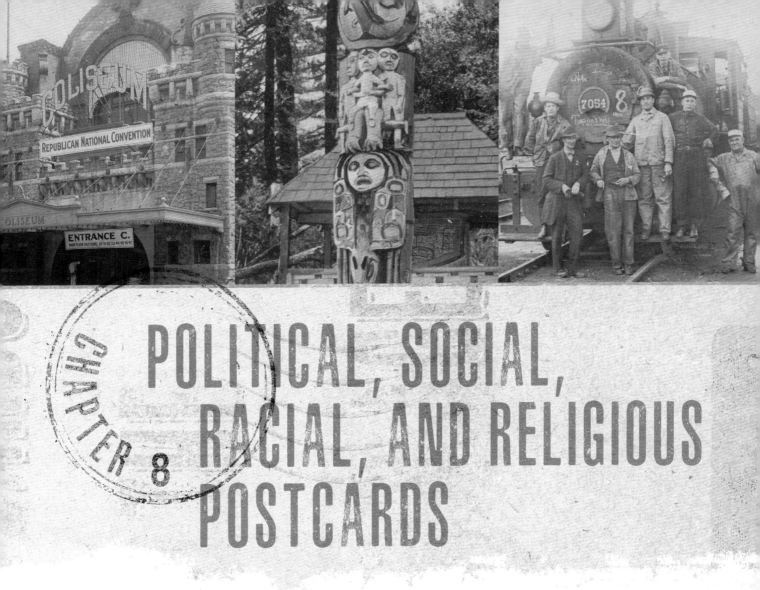

POLITICAL, SOCIAL, RACIAL, AND RELIGIOUS POSTCARDS

CHAPTER 8

Postcards that have to do with the mind—with thinking, with religion, with opinions, preferences and prejudices, with social movements and related topics that reflect the progress (or lack thereof) of American society—are very popular. American culture changes—illustrated, for example, by the treatment of minorities and women—and such changes can be explored by studying old postcards. With the exception of religious-oriented cards, most that deal with such cultural topics are in strong demand today.

Cards with political, social, and racial themes are often Real Photo Postcards and, with few exceptions, have strong values and enjoy a wide market. Relatively few were printed (as opposed to being produced one at a time, photographically).

Many depict events (and could just as easily be listed in chapter 6 or under the general RPPC commentary in chapter 7).

Views of churches were made in large quantities, are often exterior views, and rarely show people or vehicles. Related are views of cemeteries.

Price estimates given with the image captions in this chapter give ideas of values.

Presidential Elections and Politics

Printed cards showing the locations of nominating and other conventions are popular and in many instances range from scarce to rare. Cards showing political

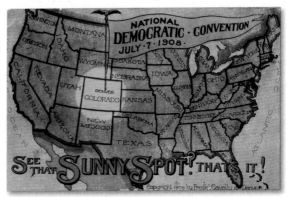

This postcard showcases Denver as the location of the 1908 Democratic party nominating convention. (Thayer Publishing Co., 1908.) EF to Mint: $15–$25

The Chicago Coliseum with a "Republican National Convention" sign. RPPC. (A.J. Schumann, Chicago. Postmarked June 16, 1908.) EF to Mint: $30–$50

Women's Suffrage and Rights

During the early twentieth century women did not have the right to vote in national elections, although the opportunity was available for state and local elections in some areas such as Wyoming.

Women in the workforce often put in long hours in factories. Management opportunities were rare. Cards showing women tending looms, running sewing machines in factories, and engaged in other such labor are very collectible. Many were issued by manufacturers to proudly show their workforce.

African Americans

Postcards showing African Americans and their lives and activities are very common. Many comic cards of the early twentieth century depict their subjects eating watermelons or engaging in mischief, stereotypical caricatures that some Americans found humorous at the time

candidates are mostly RPPCs. Those with local or regional candidates have nominal values and play to a limited audience. Those with presidential candidates start with Theodore Roosevelt's campaign of 1904, are often RPPCs produced in quantity, and are widely sought. Sharpness of the image and overall composition of the scene are important.

A Gallery of Women's Rights and Related Cards

Oklahoma schoolteacher and newspaper writer Kate Bernard was an advocate of women's rights, workers' rights, prison reform, and other movements in the early twentieth century. This RPPC shows her speaking at 2:30 in the afternoon of March 10, 1911, in Oklahoma City, with a crowd gathered in the street in front of the Huckins Hotel. EF to Mint: $200+

Advocates for women's suffrage, 1915, with oxen named after two recent presidents. (Postmarked Monticello, New York, September 23, 1915.) EF to Mint: $40–$70

"C.W. Klemm's Overall and Shirt Factory, Bloomington, Ill." (Postmarked 1909.) EF to Mint: $18–$30

"Section 2—Stitching room of Murphysboro plant, Brown Shoe Co., Inc." RPPC (postmarked 1914). EF to Mint: $70–$100

but which today are recognized as backward, marginalizing, and insulting.

Printed cards of African Americans at work in cotton fields and other labor exist in many forms and are in demand.

Some rare RPPCs depict violent and racist incidents such as lynchings and anti-black rallies, including Ku Klux Klan gatherings and parades. Some RPPCs show signs such as "White" and "Colored" in railroad stations and elsewhere.

Many other cards show studio portraits of black Americans and scenes of domestic life and family gatherings; these are popular.

African American–themed cards provide a window into how minority communities were viewed, from within and from outside, in the late 1800s and early 1900s. All except some of the early comic cards are in strong demand, not only by postcard collectors but also by historians.

A Gallery of African American and Related Cards

S. Langsdorf & Co., as part of its "alligator border" cards, printed and embossed in Germany, included a run of cards subtitled "Greetings from the Sunny South." (See chapter 10 for details.) African Americans were featured on some of these, as seen here: "A Watermelon Feast." EF to Mint: $75–$125

"Old Uncle Joe" on another Langsdorf card. EF to Mint: $75–$125

"In the Cotton Field" on another Langsdorf card. EF to Mint: $75–$125

"Way Down South in Dixie." Text on back: "A scene illustrating the real character of the Negroes living in and for the present and leaving the past be gone and the future to take care of itself, enjoying their recreation after daily labor in dance, song, and play. Usually such wild dances are witnessed in yards, alleys, and cabins, where crowds gather enjoying the delicacies of watermelons and performing wild dances by strands [sic] of accordions." (Illustrated Post Card Co. No. 815-1. Circa 1910.) EF to Mint: $20–$35

In January and February 1907, "Louis" visited Sugarland, Texas, a community with fields of sugar cane and a large processing mill. He mailed back more than a dozen RPPCs to Mrs. T.S. Jackson, of Utica, New York, each with a message or description on the front. This card, titled "Mexico, Sugarland, Tex.," noted: "This a row of houses or cabins that Negroes live in. They seem to call it Mexico because every payday night they have a dozen or so 'monte' games going. I guess Mexicans may have lived there once. They are all typical cabins anyway." EF to Mint: $75+

"A Young Preacher." EF to Mint: $15–$25

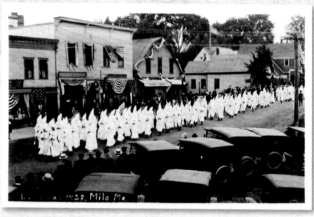

On Labor Day 1923 white-hooded Ku Klux Klan members paraded down the main street of Milo, Maine. After the release of the *Birth of a Nation* film in 1915, the semi-dormant KKK became very popular. In the Northeast it was viewed mostly as a patriotic "Yankee tradition" movement, not anti-black. EF to Mint: $200+

"The opening night of the Rex Theatre, Photo by Tomlinson, April 4, 1912, Hannibal, Mo." African American patrons were allowed only in the balcony seats. EF to Mint: $200+

A studio portrait of a lady scholar. RPPC. EF to Mint: $30+

A family posed on the porch of a home in Mound Bayou, Mississippi. (G.W. Burt. Burt moved to Mound Bayou in March 1900 and opened a portrait studio. Over a period of time he photographed many residents and issued a series of RPPCs, as seen here.) EF to Mint: $40+

Fun in the water in Greenville, Mississippi. This RPPC was postmarked 1909. EF to Mint: $50+

Native Americans

A wave of popular interest in Native Americans, universally designated as "Indians" in the early twentieth century, coincided with the Golden Age of the postcard. By the 1900–1910 decade the old American Indian way of life was fading, but there were still dozens of villages, settlements, and other communities in existence, mostly in the West.

By 1906 many different postcards had been produced by American publishers, including those printed in Germany, describing various Indian tribes and communities, and their settlers. Nearly all depicted people in a favorable light with rich costumes, ceremonial dances, festivals, and the like. The depiction of a man in ceremonial dress produced a very colorful card.

In 1906 financier J.P. Morgan commissioned photographer and researcher Edward Sheriff Curtis to travel West and create a series of magnificently illustrated volumes chronicling the life and activities of the North American Indian.

A selection of Curtis's own images appeared on an unnumbered group of cards, printed in sepia and not identified as to printer on the back. The names of the tribes and other captions were given prominently on the face, in artistic letters. Titles include "A Yakima," "Apache Girl," "Apache," "Apaches," "Blackfoot Encampment," "Chief Joseph," "Crow Eagle Blackfoot," "Hopi Girl," "Hopi Products," "Leschi Yakima," "Mohave Girl," "Navaho Boy," "Red Thunder Nez Perce," "Siwash Maid," "Zuni Girl," "Zuni Maid," and "Zuni Water Carriers," among others.

The Detroit Publishing Company, under its own name and also under the Fred Harvey name (Harvey ran a large string of restaurants and concessions, mainly at

A Gallery of Native American and Related Cards

An Edward S. Curtis card showing Red Thunder Nez Perce. (Curtis, 1906.) EF to Mint: $60+

"A row of Eskimo children, Alaska." (Portland Post Card Co. No. 90649. 1909.) EF to Mint: $3–$5

"Chiefs and totem poles, Kake, Alaska." (Lowman & Hanford Co., Seattle. Circa 1910.) EF to Mint: $3–$5

"Totem pole, Indian Cemetery, Ketchikan, Alaska." (Edward H. Mitchell. No. 1989. Circa 1910s.) EF to Mint: $3–$5

Some racism is evident in the banner at the top of this transcontinental rig, seemingly sponsored by Carter's Little Liver Pills and H.J. Heinz. Under magnification there is a line below "Ocean to Ocean" that reads: "In case we do wrong, correct us. Do not ball [sic] us like Indians. We are white." (RPPC, early twentieth century.) EF to Mint: $150+

"Indian Pony Race." EF to Mint: $8–$12

sometimes in groups. While some are generic, many are identified as to tribe and to the name of the portrait subject. Other cards show tribal life: scenes of teepees on the prairie, people at play or in recreation, and engaged in other day-to-day activity. The scarcer group depicts Native Americans in scenes involving the white man's civilization—visiting general stores, in town or city streets, attending races, or the like.

Alaskan natives, including Eskimos, are depicted on many postcards. Some of these also show ornately carved totem poles or, in some instances, totem poles alone, these being fairly scarce as a class.

Forming a collection of cards with American Indian motifs can be an interesting pursuit. While those signed by Curtis on the face have been highly desired and valuable for a long time, most of the others have slipped through the cracks in terms of market attention. By gathering them here and there, eventually you can form a fine collection. Or, a specialty can be made within a certain geographical area or perhaps concentrating on a publisher such as Detroit. Most are relatively inexpensive.

train stations), issued a particularly colorful and extensive group, not consistently numbered as part of any series, but collectible today with some patience. At the 1909 Alaska-Yukon-Pacific Exposition many cards were issued featuring native tribes, including indigenous people living in Alaska and northern Canada.

In general, the cards fall into several categories. Most prominent are those depicting portraits—usually full-face but sometimes side or angular views—of native men, women, and children, mostly singly, but

A Gallery of American Labor Cards

"State Constabulary on Duty—Bethlehem Steel Co. Strike." The back has a relevant message: "We are still holding our own. Most of the men have gone elsewhere to work. 18 of the strikers are on the city police force, including myself. It looks like a long strike. . . ." By the time the postcard was mailed, about 5,000 men had been on strike for nearly a month. The South Bethlehem (Pennsylvania) factory had lucrative government contracts for armor plate and other items, and the employees worked overtime, some of them 12 hours a day and seven days a week. However, the company refused their request to be paid at time-and-a-half rates for the overage. Charles M. Schwab, owner of the company, refused to bargain with the employees as a unit, and eventually most drifted back to work. (Conradi photo. Postmarked March 23, 1910.) EF to Mint: $150+

RPPC of downtown Columbus, Ohio, during the 1910 streetcar strike. The carmen, as they were called, wanted 27¢ per hour increase in wages, their union to be recognized by the management, and an arbitration clause in their employment agreement. Receiving no satisfaction, they voted to strike against the Columbus Railway & Light Co. Martial law was declared in July, with no end in sight. The state had 3,000 soldiers on watch there, trolley wires were cut, cars were destroyed, and other damage was done. On October 15 the standoff ended when the strikers decided further action would be futile. Most returned to work. (Myers Photo Co., Columbus, Ohio.) EF to Mint: $100+

RPPC captioned, "Oklahoma City Street Car Strike. Renewed March 9th 1911. Photo by That Man Stone." At 10 in the morning of March 5, the Street Railway Employees Union, Local 556, initiated a strike against the streetcar line, demanding that their union be recognized by management. In actuality, of the 300 employees of the company, only about a dozen were union members, but others wanted to be. Contemporary reports stated that "thugs" came from all directions to support the strikers, as did union workers from other industries, until there were an estimated 10,000 on the downtown streets. "I will throw over one of my lines into the ditch before I'll recognize the organization," stated Anton H. Classen, president of the Oklahoma Metropolitan Railway Co. The mayor rallied citizens, including 400 war veterans with guns, to end the matter, as most citizens resented the visiting strangers who were causing all of the trouble. In a matter of days, the situation returned to normal. EF to Mint: $150+

Railroad employees on strike in Bridgeport, Connecticut, in the summer of 1915, demanding an eight-hour work day and time-and-a-half overtime pay. EF to Mint: $150+

A San Francisco cable-car strike RPPC with the message, "Scene during street car strike in S.F. shows first cars run by the strike breakers, with police protection." There were several such strikes in the early twentieth century. (Miller, 1933 Divisadero St., San Francisco.) EF to Mint: $150+

"View of the N.Y. Mills strike. Started July 18th 1916. Benefit for the poor strikers." The Oswego *Daily Palladium*, August 19, 1916, carried this item, datelined Utica: "Defections in the ranks of the striking operatives of the New York Mills Company continue, several hundred having returned to the employment they left a number of weeks ago. The strikers claim that many of the Italian operatives are returning to work because of enmity toward the Polish strikers due to the war in Europe. The Polish people at the mills, who are striking for more pay, are said to be largely of Austrian or Prussian-Polish stock. These people are the enemies of the Italians in the European war, and this factor is said to influence the Italians in their attempt to cause a collapse of the strike. About 1,000 operatives continue on strike." (S. Kaczowka, Utica, New York.) EF to Mint: $75+

"Quilting Room, No. 11 Mill, Amoskeag Mfg. Co., Manchester, N.H." Most of the workers tending looms in New England textile factories in the early twentieth century were children and young women, with older men supervising each room. Quilting was dangerous work that required close attention. Injured workers were dismissed. (John B. Varick, Manchester; printed in Germany.) EF to Mint: $10–$15

Other Minorities

Other minorities, especially immigrants from Asia or from Europe, are depicted on many cards, usually printed. Many of these show ethnic districts of cities, such as Jewish streets in lower Manhattan and the large "Across the Rhine" German district in Cincinnati. Values depend on the composition and collectors' interest in the subject.

Labor History and Movements

Labor history overlaps with other subjects—often the rule, not the exception, among postcards. Women's rights and women's labor are parallel subjects.

Immigrants at work in factories are often in the same categories as ethnic minorities. Labor strikes and rallies are events and can be put in that category; most are RPPCs. All have strong value. Child labor, such as scenes of young people tending looms in textile mills, common in the early twentieth century, is a fairly rare postcard subject.

The Temperance Movement

Temperance was a leading social movement in America in the Golden Age of postcards, culminating with national Prohibition in 1920 (repealed in 1933). Postcard images include RPPCs showing protests at saloons,

A Gallery of Temperance Cards

"The Rum Room, City Hall, Portland, Me.," filled with bottles, distilling apparatus, signs, and, for good measure, playing cards. Maine in 1851 was the first "dry state." Many towns had a "rum room," as seen here. These were often burglarized, and mysterious disappearance of goods was also common. (Circa 1907.) EF to Mint: $10–$15

The divided city of Texarkana, with part in Arkansas, a "wet" area, and half in Texas, which was "dry," found the distinction interesting, as evidenced by the "Booze Line" on this card. (PCK No. 165917. Postmarked 1912.) EF to Mint: $12–$18

"Scott City, Kans. People Getting Ready to Finish a Joint." Temperance advocates with bottles of Jackson brand whiskey they have confiscated. EF to Mint: 150+

At the popular springs in West Baden, Indiana, many alcoholics took "the cure." Some of them posed on the Water Wagon prop to have their picture taken, as seen here. Being on the "water wagon" meant to be off of alcohol. (RPPC, circa 1910.) EF to Mint: $200+

parade banners, and the like. Printed cards are more limited but were issued in many states. Related in a way are advertising postcards for breweries, distilleries, and wine, beer, and liquor before Prohibition.

Religion, Churches, Worship, Sects

Countless churches, synagogues, and other houses of worship are depicted on postcards, mostly as printed views of exteriors. Interior views are scarcer. Only a few show vehicles or people. Values are very modest, often just a dollar or two each at postcard shows (more if purchased through the mail, due to handling and shipping).

The Shakers, a religious sect whose members practiced the simple life, did not marry, and spent much time with agriculture and crafts, established several communities. These were open to tourists and other visitors, who could buy furniture, baskets, and other products. Mount Lebanon, New York; Harvard, Massachusetts; and Canterbury, New Hampshire, were popular locations. Postcards exist of these venues. Jewish summer camps and vacation spots (such as in the Catskill Mountains in Upstate New York) can be found on many printed cards. Values for all such cards are modest.

RPPCs of camp meetings, church picnics, etc., exist for many events and usually are of nominal value.

A Gallery of Religious Cards

First Congregational Church, Los Angeles, California. (M. Rieder, Los Angeles. No. 8955. Circa 1910.) EF to Mint: $4–$7

Saint Joseph's Catholic Church in Mason City, Iowa. (Curt Teich Co. No. R-21857. 1910.) EF to Mint: $5–$8

The roof of the Mormon Tabernacle under construction in Salt Lake City, Utah, showing the complex roof trusses. (The Bureau, Salt Lake City. No. 455. Circa 1910s.) EF to Mint: $4–$7

A large outdoor assembly at the Church of God, Cleveland, Tennessee. (E.C. Kropp Co. No. 40-N/6. Postmarked 1933.) EF to Mint: $8–$12

"Mennonites from Colony Near Scotland S. Dak." An early twentieth-century RPPC. (Published by E.H. Treiber, Scotland, South Dakota.) EF to Mint: $75+

"No. 910. Group of Shakers, Mt. Lebanon, N.Y." A souvenir RPPC sold to tourists. (Made in Germany and published by the Gillett Post Card Co., Lebanon Springs, New York. Postmarked September 17, 1926.) EF to Mint: $30–$45

In the 1890s and early twentieth century evangelists Hart and Magan, based in St. Louis, Missouri, traveled extensively in the Midwest and staged revival meetings, reporting to newspapers how many people "professed" faith in Jesus Christ at each event. This amateur RPPC depicts their Union Revival, held each day at 2 and 7 p.m. EF to Mint: $75+

RPPC of the "Lebanon for Christ" revival meeting held in the Tabernacle at Lebanon, Missouri, by evangelists Hamilton and Hill, Sunday, August 20, 1911, at 11 a.m. EF to Mint: $125+

Representing the Massachusetts Bible Society, F.M. Robbins of Wilbraham traveled in this wagon. Lettering included, "Please Study John 3-18" and "Bibles 23¢." (Postmarked 1911.) EF to Mint: $125

HOLIDAY, GREETING, AND NOVELTY POSTCARDS

CHAPTER 9

Showcased in this chapter are artist-drawn and related postcards from the Golden Age of 1893 to 1918. This includes postcards covering holidays from New Year's Day to Christmas, cards with announcements and greetings, various comic cards with interesting characters and scenes, and novelty cards such as exaggerations or cards made in materials other than cardboard stock.

Aspects of Rarity, Price, and Collecting

Holiday, greeting, and novelty subjects are wide ranging and the cards are of various qualities, from well-done to crude. As beauty is in the eye of the beholder, value largely depends on how attractive a card is to a prospective buyer. No one has ever acquired an even nearly complete collection of any of these subjects, as thousands of different cards were made in America and Europe.

There is virtually no end to novelty cards. George and Dorothy Miller's *Picture Postcards in the United States 1893–1918* devotes a chapter to them.

In general, cards showing people or animals with human characteristics and cards with romantic scenes are the most popular and valuable. Cards with bright colors and a glossy finish, even better when embossed, are more valuable than ones flat-printed with subdued colors.

Holiday Postcards
New Year's Day

The vast majority of New Year's Day cards were printed in Europe. Raphael Tuck issued several series. German printers were the most prolific, and some cards were printed in France as well. Cards were made in flat-printed and embossed formats, the latter being most desirable. Many show Father Time, clocks, and even years, particularly 1907 and 1908. Cards that have comic scenes or show children or animals with human characteristics are worth slightly more than others.

German card with girl and holly, embossed. EF to Mint: $7–$12

German card with jester and banjo, embossed. EF to Mint: $10–$15

One of a series of this style by Paul Finkenrath, embossed. EF to Mint: $7–$12

New Year's Day Type	Value, EF to Mint
German, embossed, various	$3–$10
German, flat-printed, various	$3–$8
Paul Finkenrath, embossed	$5–$20
Paul Finkenrath, flat-printed	$3–$8
Tuck (several series), embossed	$5–$15
Tuck (several series), flat-printed	$3–$8

Tuck card from "New Year Greetings" series 600. EF to Mint: $3–$6

Card with lady and child, country of origin unknown (no location or company imprint on back; text all in English). EF to Mint: $3–$6

Groundhog Day

Groundhog Day is February 2, when a sleepy groundhog crawls out of his hole to see if his shadow is visible. If the day is bright, the critter is scared of his own shadow and goes back into hibernation for six more weeks, and the weather remains cold. If it is a cloudy day, all is well and groundhog believers expect that the next six weeks will be spring-like. In modern times a ceremony with "Punxsutawney Phil" has been held every year in Pennsylvania, with much media attention.

Among holiday cards, those of Groundhog Day (if it can be called a "holiday") are very rare. A set of four was issued by the Henderson Lithographing Co. of Cincinnati.

German card with French-language stamp on the front. EF to Mint: $8–$12

Groundhog Day card.

Groundhog Day Type	Value, EF to Mint
Henderson Lithographing Co.	$100–$150

Lincoln's Birthday

The birthday of Abraham Lincoln, born on February 12, 1809, was observed on many postcards. Today they are inexpensive and only mildly popular.

Celebrating Lincoln's Birthday. (International Art Publishing Co. Postmarked 1909.) EF to Mint: $4–$8

Lincoln's Birthday Type	Value, EF to Mint
Finkenrath	$5–$15
Sander	$3–$8
Shehan	$3–$8
Taggart	$3–$8
Various other cards	$3–$10+

Washington's Birthday

The birthday of George Washington on February 11, 1732 (Old Calendar), with February 22 (New Calendar) being the day later observed, was honored on many postcards.

Celebrating Washington's Birthday. (Winsch back; artist unknown.) EF to Mint: $4–$8

Washington's Birthday Type	Value, EF to Mint
A&S	$3–$5
International Art Co.	$3–$8
Nash	$3–$8
Sander	$3–$5
Taggart	$3–$5
Tuck	$4–$8
Various other cards	$3–$8+

Valentine's Day

Most Valentine's Day cards were printed in Germany and used in Europe, with many imported into America. Some, but not all, of the latter say PRINTED IN GERMANY. Countless American postmarks show that German cards without this imprint were widely used in America.

German printers were the most prolific. Cards were made flat-printed and in the more desirable and readily available embossed formats. Many show a boy, girl, and red heart. Cupids with wings or cherubs with one or more hearts were popular designs as well. Four-legged animals on cards are rare (but of no extra value). See the listing in chapter 11 for Winsch cards.

German card with two Cupids and hearts, a common theme. EF to Mint: $3–$6

Souvenir Post Card Co. series 102. German import with two cherubs and hearts. Embossed. EF to Mint: $3–$6

German card with young girl and doves, embossed. EF to Mint: $3–$6

Paul Finkenrath (PFB) card with cupids and heart, embossed. EF to Mint: $3–$6

German card with real cloth, part of a series. EF to Mint: $8–$12

German card with youngsters and an automobile, flat-printed. EF to Mint: $3–$6

Valentine's Day Type	Value, EF to Mint
German, embossed, various	$3–$10
German, flat-printed, various	$3–$8
German, with real cloth	$5–$15
Paul Finkenrath, embossed	$5–$12
Paul Finkenrath, flat-printed	$3–$8
Souvenir Post Card Co., embossed	$3–$8
Brown & Bigelow, February 1910 calendar card	$5–$10

St. Patrick's Day

Most St. Patrick's Day cards of the Golden Age were printed in Germany and used in Europe. Many were imported into the United States. Some, but not all, of those imports say PRINTED IN GERMANY. Cards were made in flat-printed and embossed formats. Green is the prevailing color on most St. Patrick's Day postcards, and shamrocks and mentions of Ireland are common. Some illustrate the friendship between Ireland and America. Most St. Patrick's Day cards are inexpensive. See the listing in chapter 11 for Winsch cards.

Tuck St. Patrick's Day card, series 106. EF to Mint: $10–$20

St. Patrick's Day Type	Value, EF to Mint
German, embossed, various	$10–$20
German, flat-printed, various	$10–$20
E. Nash, with H in a circle	$10–$20
Tuck	$10–$20
Various other cards	$10–$20

April Fool's Day

April Fool's Day, April 1, was featured on a number of cards. These are fairly scarce today. Most illustrate comic scenes.

April Fool's Day card.

April Fool's Day Type	Value, EF to Mint
French, various	$3–$10
Ullman	$3–$8
Paul C. Koeber	$3–$8

Easter

Most Easter cards of the Golden Age were printed in Germany and used in Europe. Many were imported into America and some of those have the notation PRINTED IN GERMANY.

Cards were made in flat-printed and embossed formats. Raphael Tuck, A.S.B., Finkenrath, Langsdorf, and others each issued sets. Cherubs, cupids, bunnies, and chickens with eggs are common motifs. Serious religious scenes are rare. Most Easter cards are inexpensive. Also see chapter 11 for Winsch cards.

Tuck card with chicken and eggs. EF to Mint: $3–$5

Mr. and Mrs. Rabbit card. Unidentified American issuer. EF to Mint: $6–$8

Finkenrath card with lambs and child, embossed. EF to Mint: $5–$7

International Art Publishing Co. German import card, flat-printed. EF to Mint: $3–$4

Curt Teich card. EF to Mint: $4–$8

Easter Type	Value, EF to Mint
A.S.B.	$3–$8
B.W.	$3–$8
Finkenrath, embossed	$5–$12
Finkenrath, flat-printed	$4–$8
German, embossed, various	$3–$8
German, flat-printed, various	$3–$5
Langsdorf	$5–$10
Teich	$4–$8
Tuck	$3–$15
Various other cards	$3–$10

Decoration Day / Memorial Day

Decoration Day (or Memorial Day), at the end of May, was observed on cards issued by many firms and also by Winsch (see chapter 11). Today they are a side interest within the larger hobby, with some active collectors.

Memorial Day card issued by M.W. Taggart, New York. Embossed. No German imprint. EF to Mint: $3–$5

Decoration Day card issued by E. Nash, New York. Embossed. No German imprint. EF to Mint: $3–$5

Decoration Day / Memorial Day Type	Value, EF to Mint
A.S.B.	$3–$8
Conwell	$3–$8
Samuel Gabriel	$5–$15
Nash	$3–$8
Santway	$3–$8
Taggart	$3–$8
Tuck	$5–$12
Various other cards	$3–$8+

Independence Day (Fourth of July)

In keeping with the general trend of Golden Age holiday postcards, most Fourth of July cards were printed in Germany in flat-printed and embossed formats. Raphael Tuck, A.S.B., Finkenrath, Langsdorf, and others each issued sets. Flags, firecrackers, cannon, and happy people are common motifs. Also see chapter 11 for Winsch cards.

E. Nash German Fourth of July card, embossed. EF to Mint: $5–$7

Fourth of July card printed in the United States. EF to Mint: $3–$5

Independence Day Type	Value, EF to Mint
German, embossed, various	$3–$8
German, flat-printed, various	$3–$6
Lounsbury	$5–$10
Nash	$3–$8
Tuck	$5–$12
Ullman	$5–$10
Various other cards	$3–$8+

Labor Day

Labor Day cards have always been the Holy Grail among cards of the significant holidays. E. Nash of New York City, the leading American importer of German-printed holiday cards, issued a pair of cards, illustrated below. Lounsbury Publishing issued a set of four cards, also printed in Germany.

"Labor Conquers Everything," sold by E. Nash. EF to Mint: $40–$50

"Service shall with steel sinews toil," sold by E. Nash. EF to Mint: $40–$50

Labor Day Type	Value, EF to Mint
Brown & Bigelow September calendar card	$10–$15
Lounsbury	$75–$100
Nash	$40–$50

Halloween

Halloween and Christmas postcards are the mostly widely collected of the holiday series. Most were printed in Germany, often with images by American artists. These were made in flat-printed and embossed formats, the latter being in the strongest demand among collectors and also the most readily available. For want of a better word, Halloween cards are a lot of *fun*. Pumpkins, witches, goblins, and happy children are common motifs. Artist-signed Halloween cards are the crème de la crème. Also see chapter 11 for Clapsaddle, Schmucker, and Winsch cards that are from some of the most popular artists for this type of card.

Halloween card with two witches, American. EF to Mint: $75–$125

Halloween card with 11 pumpkins. (M.L. Jackson. Postmarked 1910.) EF to Mint: $20–$30

Merry Halloween. (International Art Publishing Co., New York and Berlin.) EF to Mint: $15–$25

The highest expectations for Halloween. (Postcard Series No. 123. S. Garre, Germany. 1909.) EF to Mint: $20–$30

Halloween Type	Value, EF to Mint
Bien	$20–$25
German, embossed, various	$25–$30
German, flat-printed, various	$20–$30
International Art	$25–$50
Nash	$25–$50
Santway	$20–$30
Tuck	$20–$40
Various other cards	$15–$50+

Thanksgiving

Thanksgiving cards with the colorful hues of late autumn have always been popular. Most were printed in Germany, often with images by American artists, in flat-printed and the more desirable embossed formats. Turkeys and pumpkins are recurring motifs. Although Thanksgiving is strictly an American holiday, Raphael

Tuck in London produced at least 10 sets of related cards that were distributed through their New York City office. Cards distributed by John Winsch are particularly beautiful and desirable. Also see chapter 11 for signed artists' Thanksgiving cards.

Thanksgiving card from Raphael Tuck series 185. EF to Mint: $10–$20

German Thanksgiving card with Uncle Sam.

Thanksgiving Type	Value, EF to Mint
Finkenrath	$4–$10
Samuel Gabriel	$5–$15
German, embossed, various	$3–$8
German, flat-printed, various	$3–$5
Gottschalk	$3–$8
International Art	$3–$8
Nash	$3–$6
Sander	$3–$6
Taggart	$3–$8
Tuck	$3–$10
Various other cards	$3–$8

Christmas

Christmas postcards, especially those with colorful depictions of Santa Claus, are front-row-center with collectors. Most were printed in flat-printed or embossed formats in Germany, often with images by American artists. Motifs include Santa in various poses, reindeer, Christmas trees, gifts, and happy children. Many European cards show Santa dressed in other than a red suit. On the other hand, most cards printed in America or printed for America show jolly old Santa Claus in the mode of Clement Moore's *The Night Before Christmas*. Cards distributed by John Winsch are particularly beautiful and desirable. In all instances cards with Santa shown prominently in a bright red suit bring a sharp premium. Also see chapter 11 for signed artists' Christmas cards.

American Christmas card with Santa Claus in a traditional red suit. EF to Mint: $8–$10

Finkenrath German Christmas card with a dancing pig. EF to Mint: $4–$6

German Christmas card with Father Christmas. EF to Mint: $25–$40

Curt Teich Christmas card with a phonograph. EF to Mint: $5–$8

German Christmas card, embossed, with Santa Claus in his workshop. EF to Mint: $10–$15

German Christmas card signed by Jenny Nystrom. EF to Mint: $5–$8

Christmas Type	Value, EF to Mint
B.W.	$3–$10
E.A.S. (Schwerdtfeger)	$3–$10
Finkenrath	$5–$15
German, embossed, various	$4–$10
German, flat-printed, various	$3–$8
International Art	$3–$10
Langsdorf	$5–$15
Nash	$3–$10
Sander	$3–$8
Tuck	$5–$12
Various other cards	$3–$8

Greeting and Related Postcards
Special Occasions

Many special occasions were observed on postcards. Most greeting postcards had warm personal messages written on the back. These cards were extremely popular during the Golden Age but faded nearly completely from the market when greeting cards enclosed in envelopes became standard.

Birth-announcement cards were made in many designs, as were funeral announcement and condolence cards. These are not widely collected today. Other cards include congratulations for awards or accomplishments, graduation, entering military service, and other occasions.

Birthday cards, often sent to children, were the most numerous. Most of these are highly artistic, were made in Germany, and were embossed. Subjects are often young boys and/or girls with a pet, or riding in an automobile, or with flowers. At a quick glance many are similar to German Valentine's Day cards, minus the cupids and hearts.

Wedding postcards usually depict adults and flowers. Harrison Fisher cards have many romance and wedding subjects, as do Philip Boileau cards to a lesser extent (see chapter 11). Special occasion cards with people are more valuable than those without.

Special Occasions Type	Value, EF to Mint
Without people	$1–$5
With people, artistic	$2–$10

"With every good wish for your birthday."
(No imprint.) EF to Mint: $5–$8

"Happy may your birthday be." (No. 6894.) EF to Mint: $5–$8

Generic Greetings

Many postcards were made to use as greetings and for well-wishes, without mention of any particular special occasion. These often featured kittens, children, and other art. Most were imported from Germany.

"Best wishes" generic card. (Germany.) EF to Mint: $5–$8

"A token of esteem" generic card. (Germany.)
EF to Mint: $5–$8

"Heartiest congratulations" generic card.
(A.G. & Co., Germany.) EF to Mint: $5–$8

Generic postcard that could be filled out with any message on the front. (No imprint. Circa 1905.) EF to Mint: $3–$5

Generic Greetings Type	Value, EF to Mint
Without people	$1–$5
With people, artistic	$2–$10

"Best wishes" with sailor girl, generic card. (Series 748. Germany.) EF to Mint: $5–$8

Comic Postcards
Comic Art

Most cards with comic subjects were taken from panels in newspaper strips. Chapter 11, with artist-signed cards, discusses the work of many cartoonists, the prime example being R.F. Outcault's Buster Brown and the Yellow Kid. Many comic-art cards are collected as part of a series and are very popular.

Some comic cartoon-type cards are not from strips. Whether a card is from a strip is usually not mentioned on it. Happy, a comic character, appears on two sets of Tuck postcards. Many greeting cards and advertising cards have characters in mischievous or comic situations. These non-strip cards are usually collected one at a time based on their ability to cause a smile.

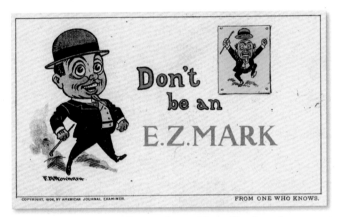

"From one who knows," a comic card from the *American Journal Examiner*, New York. Given free with the Sunday edition. EF to Mint: $8–$15

"This is so sudden," a comic card by Swinnerton from the *American Journal Examiner*, New York, 1906. Given free with the Sunday edition. EF to Mint: $5–$10

Comic Card Type	Value, EF to Mint
Not signed by artist; black-and-white or one color	$2–$10
Not signed by artist; color	$5–$15

Novelty Postcards
Hold-to-Light Cards

Hold-to-light cards, often abbreviated as HTL or H-T-L, were a popular novelty in the mid-1910s. One frequently seen type consisted of a front panel illustrated with a (usually) color image, with tiny holes machine-perforated at the windows of a building. The center panel is a thin transparent yellow sheet. The bottom or back panel has a matching set of perforations, and the back side is printed with regular postcard mailing information. The three sheets are sandwiched together with an adhesive. When viewed from the front with a light behind, the windows light up a bright yellow. The Samuel Cupples Envelope Co. of St. Louis, which had the franchise to sell official postcards of the 1904 Louisiana Purchase Exposition, published a series of hold-to-light cards with illuminated windows in the buildings. Joseph Koehler published a run of at least 113 cards featuring scenes of Atlantic City, Boston, Coney Island, New York City, and other popular tourist destinations. Other cards showed the sun, moon, stars, or a distant light.

Hold-to-light card with a lighthouse in Atlantic City. (No. 2200. L. Koehler, New York and Berlin, Germany.) EF to Mint: $25–$50

Hold-to-light card, "Bridge over Lagoon," from the 1904 Louisiana Purchase Exposition. (Samuel Cupples Envelope Co., St. Louis, Missouri; Germany.) EF to Mint: $20–$40

Hold-to-light card, "Happy New Year," 1908.
EF to Mint: $25–$50

Transparency Cards

Transparency postcards, another novelty type, were issued during the Golden Age. When viewed from the front in regular light, a scene is revealed. When the card is held up to a stronger light, a hidden scene, usually of a completely different subject or an alteration (such as changing a happy face to a sad face), becomes apparent. Transparency cards are very scarce.

Fred is fishing, and when the card is held to the light a hidden mermaid is seen at the lower left. (ShadowGraph, E.T.W. Dennis & Sons, London.) EF to Mint: $5–$8

When held to the light, a hidden wolf appears on this card. (Germany, no maker.) EF to Mint: $5–$8

Installment Cards

During the Golden Age several publishers in America and Europe issued installment cards. These usually consisted of a set of three to eight separate cards sold as a group. Each would be part of an image, usually comic. These would be mailed one at a time to a recipient, often over a period of days. The complete image would not be revealed until all cards were received and put in a certain order, such as left to right, up and down, or arranged in a rectangle. Publishers included Rose Postcard Company, Walter Wirth, Wildwood Postcard Co., Rotograph, and others, including various German firms. Huld issued various series called puzzle cards. Collecting such sets today is best done by waiting until all in a set can be purchased at one time. Attempting to complete a full set by purchasing stray cards usually is frustrating.

Santa Claus in four installment cards. (Hold's Puzzle Series No. 9. Frank Hold, New York.) EF to Mint: $200+

A pig in four installment cards. (Chain Series. Excelsior Post Card Co., New York, printed in Germany.) EF to Mint: $250+

Postcards with Attachments

For some Golden Age cards, pieces of cloth such as silk and linen were cut into various shapes (for example, resembling a woman's skirt) and glued to a postcard image. Many card faces featured simple cloth rectangles that could be detached by soaking and used to make a quilt or pillow. Colored feathers were attached to images of birds, often very realistically. Sequins, tinsel, metal cut into letters or other shapes, plant parts, buttons, sandpaper, and other items were used. Tuck issued cards with tiny phonograph records, perforated at the center, that could be played.

Wire-tail cards were made with two panels, front and back, with a wire attached with its thick end in the middle, then the panels were glued together. The protruding tail part was attached to the image of a dog, donkey, or other animal running—to imply speed. As the tails could damage other cards in the mail or injure postmen, they were mailed in envelopes. Democratic donkeys and Republican elephants with campaign messages were sometimes used.

Some cards were in the form of envelopes with flaps. Some were hinged and opened to reveal another image or a message. Postcards with absorbent fronts could be used as blotters.

A tickler with real feathers. EF to Mint: $8–$12

A lady with real hair attached. EF to Mint: $15–$25

A German card with a bird with real feathers. EF to Mint: $8–$12

A farm scene with a brass turkey attached. (Germany.) EF to Mint: $8–$15

A Christmas card with a brass ornament attached. (Winsch-type back, but not by Winsch. Germany.) EF to Mint: $5–$10

A Dutch-scene card with an automobile attached. (Germany.) EF to Mint: $8–$12

A 1908 William Jennings presidential campaign card with attached brass buttons. EF to Mint: $50+

A puzzle card with a protective envelope. (J. Tully, 1906.) EF to Mint: $14+

Many newspapers issued perforated sheets that could be torn apart to create multiple postcards. These were printed in black-and-white and usually showed local or regional scenes. Some cards would reveal hidden scenes and messages when heated with an iron.

Image-changing cards showed one scene when viewed from the left and another when viewed from the right. Mechanical cards, usually mailed in envelopes, had spring-actuated and other mechanisms.

Puzzle Postcards

Another type of puzzle card was made by H.C.J. Deeks & Co. of Paterson, New Jersey, with these instructions: "Look at this card sideways, first from one side and then from the other." When this is done, two completely different but related scenes can be seen.

Postcards with perforations were designed to be torn apart to make a puzzle that was a challenge to reassemble. These were mailed in envelopes to prevent their coming apart in transit.

A puzzle card with children in a rowboat. (AL Series Bh3. S. & M., New York and Berlin.) EF to Mint: $15+

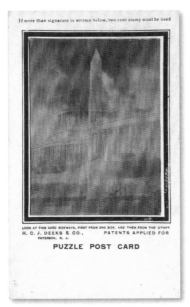

A Deeks puzzle card viewed head-on, showing traces of the two images on the card: the Washington Monument and the U.S. Capitol. EF to Mint: $30–$50

A Deeks puzzle card viewed head-on, showing traces of the two images on the card: Theodore Roosevelt and the White House. EF to Mint: $40–$65

Mechanical Postcards

Mechanical postcards show action. When the edge of a wheel is turned or a tab near the edge of the card is pulled, figures in the illustration move and legs, bicycle wheels, eyes, and other areas come to life. These cards were made in color and nearly all were imported from Germany during the Golden Age of postcards. All mechanical cards in nice condition have significant value.

When the white tab at the right is pulled, a leg on each dancer moves. EF to Mint: $100+

When the white tab at the bottom is pulled, the man's red tongue pops out. EF to Mint: $100+

When the edge of the wheel is turned at the top or the bottom, the interior part of each wing flashes, changing colors. EF to Mint: $40–$50

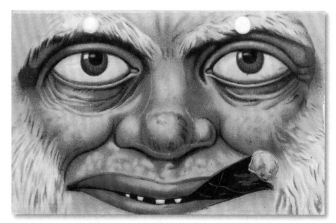

A face mask: hold to your face and look through the two holes. (Series 401. Unique Novelty Co., New York.) EF to Mint: $25–$40

A folding card issued by the Anderson-Dulin-Varnell Co., Knoxville, Kentucky, advertising Riker's Dresden Face Powder and showing Miss Hazel Dawn, who had the title role in *The Pink Lady*. EF to Mint: $6–$10

Squeeze the card and hear a whistle. (D.R.G.M. 336952; German patent.) EF to Mint: $50+

Folding Postcards

This type of postcard is hinged. When it is opened, another scene is shown on the back of the card's face and also on the front of the second panel—double width. Sometimes a hole in the face of the card permits a view of part of the interior.

Wooden, Leather, and Other Non-Cardboard Postcards

Postcards made of material other than cardboard were popular novelties and sold for more than the usual penny price. Wood was the most popular. A thin slice of wood could be easily printed and would stand up well through the mail. Farran Zerbe, who held the souvenir-coin franchise for the Louisiana Purchase Exposition in St. Louis in 1904, issued cards with a punning message and the illustration of coins, in at least two varieties. Several different types of wood were used by various manufacturers.

Thin leather panels, somewhat stiff but flexible, were used to make a wide variety of cards. Aluminum, celluloid, and copper were also used.

After the Treasury Department redeemed worn-out currency, it was heated and macerated into a pulp. This was made available to manufacturers, who molded it into figurines and other objects. Rolled into sheets and cut into rectangles, it was used to make many postcards.

A comic wooden (wood on cardboard) postcard: "You'll have to hurry in." (Burnt Wood Series. Tanner Souvenir Co., New York. 1906.) EF to Mint: $6–$8

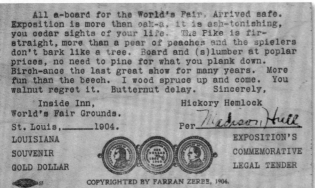

A wooden postcard issued by Farran Zerbe at the 1904 Louisiana Purchase Exposition. EF to Mint: $30–$50

A postcard made from macerated currency. EF to Mint: $100–$200

A comic wooden (wood on cardboard) postcard with an attached image. (Burnt Wood Series. Tanner Souvenir Co., New York. 1906.) EF to Mint: $8–$12

A postcard made from aluminum. (No imprint, "Bilhete Postal") EF to Mint: $20+

A comic postcard in leather. (M.T. Co., New York. Made in Japan.) EF to Mint: $5–$8

A leather card—a "Souvenir of the Catskill Mountains" with Rip Van Winkle. EF to Mint: $5–$8

Cherry Blossoms in Tokyo. Card covered with silk. (Made in Japan.) EF to Mint: $5–$8

Exaggeration Cards

What you see is what you don't get: exaggeration postcards. Very popular in the early twentieth century, exaggerations included views of anglers catching whale-size trout, farmers with ears of corn so large that one would fill a wagon, chickens laying huge eggs, and the like. Many of these were made by doctoring photographs.

"'Morning Exercises' at Poultry Farms, Rindge, N.H." shows a farmer bewildered by huge chickens and even larger eggs. By adding the Rindge town name, this card had local appeal. The same image could be imprinted with the name of any other location. (Frank W. Swallow Post Card Co., Inc. Copyright 1911.). EF to Mint: $6–$10

"Loading mammoth Washington corn." (Copyright 1909 by M.L. Oakes.) EF to Mint: $6–$10

"Potatoes grow big in our state." (Copyright 1908 by W.H. Martin.) EF to Mint: $10–$20

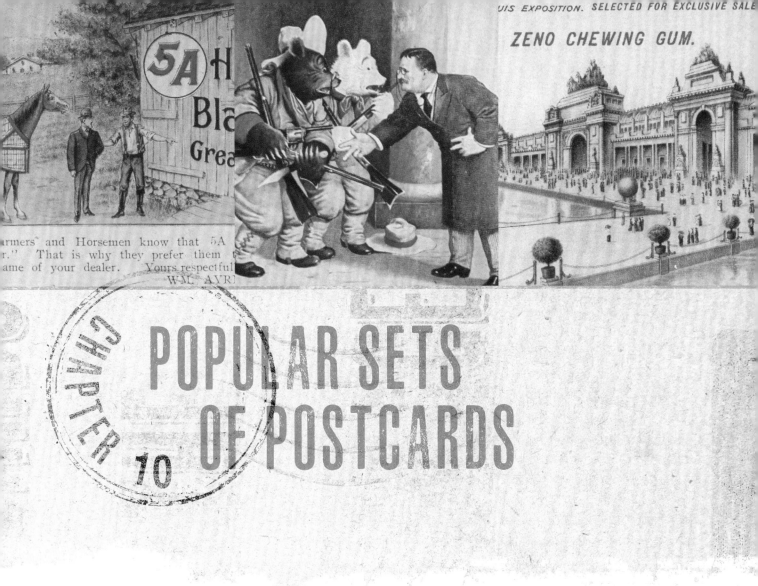

POPULAR SETS OF POSTCARDS

CHAPTER 10

Advertising, Non-signed Art

Sets were widely popular from about 1905 into the early 1910s, although some extended into the 1920s. The theory was that if a collector would buy one card of a teddy bear, he or she would be a candidate to buy a dozen or more as part of a set. Many sets were sold as such to collectors. The cards in other sets were distributed one at a time or in small groups, examples including 5A Horse Blanket and Langsdorf Alligator cards of Florida scenes. Several publishers issued multiple sets; Raphael Tuck of London, for example, offered many sets showing birds, animals, American scenes, and the like. Some sets were made just for collectors, such as the Roosevelt Bears; others were made to sell products, such as Bell telephones and Cracker Jack Bears; and others were made for tourists, such as the Alligator Border cards.

To give a full listing of popular sets with titles and information about the issuers would require a large separate book. To illustrate the concept of series, we give representative examples followed by a summary of many other popular sets as listed by George and Dorothy Miller in *Picture Postcards in the United States, 1893–1918*.

Sets with cards signed by artists are listed in chapter 11.

Bell Telephone

A collection of the Bell Telephone set of 12 numbered cards, published by the American Telephone & Telegraph Co. in the 1910s, can be completed without a great deal of effort. Each card reproduces a painting showing the telephone in use along with an appropriate caption, easily among the most effective advertising messages found on any Golden Age cards. The cards are colorful and attractive. The works are by several different artists. Most are unsigned.

Values for individual Bell Telephone cards in EF to Mint condition range from $2 to $10.

Each card has a hyphenated alphanumeric code, starting with R, on the lower-right margin of the face. The chart that follows can serve as a checklist while you complete your own collection.

A card from the Bell Telephone series.

	No.	Description	Collection Notes
☐	R-1	The Bell Telephone Announces Unexpected Guests	
☐	R-2	The Convenience of Marketing by Bell Telephone	
☐	R-3	The Bell Telephone Keeps the Traveler in Touch With Home	
☐	R-4	Into the Heart of Shopping District by Bell Telephone	
☐	R-5	Use the Bell Telephone When Servants Fail You	
☐	R-6	The Social Call by Bell Telephone	
☐	R-7	A Doctor Quick—By Bell Telephone	
☐	R-8	The Bell Telephone Guards the Home by Night As by Day	
☐	R-9	Use the Bell Telephone in Household Emergencies	
☐	R-10	The Bell Telephone Relieves Anxieties	
☐	R-11	The Bell Telephone Gives Instant Alarms	
☐	R-12	When the Elements Are Against You, the Bell Telephone is for You	

5A Horse Blankets

W.M. Ayres & Sons, whose factory was at 3rd and Cumberland streets, Philadelphia, produced a diverse line of horse blankets under the 5A label. Lap robes for carriage riders were also part of the line. These were advertised on a colorful series of postcards. Printing quality varied widely, even for the same subjects, resulting in variations in brightness and contrast. Connoisseurship is recommended to build a fine collection. Products included such items as 5A robes for yourself, 5A square blankets for the street, and 5A blankets for stable use. A typical slogan: "5A horse blankets will save you money. They wear the longest." Prior to this era, many 5A trade cards (not postcards) were issued, not relevant to the present text.

Individual 5A cards in EF to Mint condition are valued from $15 to $20.

The chart that follows (with cards listed alphabetically by title) can serve as a checklist while you complete your own collection.

"5A Fashion Square Blanket." EF to Mint: $15–$20

"Dear Sir." EF to Mint: $10–$20

	No.	Description	Collection Notes
❑	5A	Athol Blanket	
❑	5A	Bouncer Duck Stable Blanket	
❑	5A	Briar Burlap Stable Blanket	
❑	5A	Buster Burlap Stable Blanket	
❑	5A	Essex Square Blanket	
❑	5A	Fashion Square Blanket	
❑	5A	Myrtle Square Blanket	
❑	5A	Northwest Lumberman Blanket	
❑	5A	Paris Fawn Square Blanket	
❑	5A	Plush Robe No. 1300	
❑	5A	Plush Robe No. 1652	
❑	5A	Plush Robe No. 1853	
❑	5A	Storm King Square Blanket	
❑	5A	Stratton Duck Stable Blanket	

Alligator Border Cards (Langsdorf)

In the early twentieth century S.L. Langsdorf, of New York City, issued a series of "Alligator Border" postcards, serially numbered from S500 onward. Toward the end of the series many had "Greetings from the Sunny South" added as the first part of the captions. Although these cards were considered humorous in the early twentieth century, the stereotypes, language, and racial caricatures they depict are offensive today. The cards are high-quality embossed and lithographed, made in Germany. They do not seem to have been sold in complete sets, as the availability of various titles can vary widely. Presumably, most were sold as view cards, with certain specified locations (St. Augustine is an example) stocking extra supplies of views relating to those locations.

Values for individual Alligator Border cards in EF to Mint range from $25 to $100, with some commanding even higher prices.

Original Langsdorf serial numbers and card titles are below. The chart that follows can serve as a checklist while you complete your own collection.

S543, "Steamer Fred'k de Bary on St. John's River, Florida." EF to Mint: $100+

S511, "Portion of Key West, Florida." EF to Mint: $125+

Two Sunny South cards: S642, "Old Uncle Joe," and S652, "Horseless Carriage."

	No.	Description	Collection Notes
❏	S500	View of Miami, taken from Bay	
❏	S501	The Royal Palm & Miami River	
❏	S502	12th Street looking to East Miami	
❏	S503	Court House	
❏	S504	Reflections on Miami River	
❏	S505	S.S. Miami	
❏	S506	The Old Fort Dallas, Miami	
❏	S507	San Carlos Hotel, Miami	
❏	S508	Parade Grounds, U.S. Reservation, Key West	
❏	S509	Walking Dairy, Key West	
❏	S510	Wireless Telegraph Station, Key West	
❏	S511	Portion of Key West	
❏	S512	Ruth Hargrove Seminary, Key West	
❏	S513	Convent, Key West	
❏	S514	County Courthouse	
❏	S515	Tropical Street Scene, Key West	
❏	S516	Sand Key Lighthouse near Key West	
❏	S517	Lighthouse, Key West	
❏	S518	Royal Poinciana from across Lake Worth, Palm Beach	
❏	S519	Ocean Avenue, Palm Beach	
❏	S520	The Ramble and Cove, Palm Beach	
❏	S521	Palm Beach Hotel, Palm Beach	
❏	S522	Royal Poinciana and Gardens, Palm Beach	
❏	S523	View Toward West, Palm Beach	
❏	S524	White Hall South & East Views, Palm Beach	
❏	S525	Narcissus Street, West Palm Beach	
❏	S526	Garden and Veranda, Royal Poinciana	
❏	S527	Palm Walk, Palm Beach, Lake Worth	
❏	S528	Bethesda Church, Palm Beach	
❏	S529	Along the Lake, Palm Beach	
❏	S530	Gardens & Grounds of the Poinciana, Palm Beach	
❏	S531	Lake Front, Palm Beach	
❏	S532	Royal Palm Hotel & Brickell's Point	
❏	S533	Breiford's Cove, Lake Worth	
❏	S534	At the Wharf, Palatka	
❏	S535	Lemon Street, Palatka	
❏	S536	River Front looking toward Hart's Point across the St. John's River, Palatka	
❏	S537	Riverside, St. Johns River, Palatka	
❏	S538	City Hall, Palatka	
❏	S539	Scenery on the St. Johns River, Palatka	
❏	S540	The Crescent on the St. Johns River, Palatka	
❏	S541	On the Ocklawaha River	
❏	S542	Saratoga Hotel, Palatka	

	No.	Description	Collection Notes
❏	S543	Steamer Frederick de Bary on the St. Johns River	
❏	S544	The Plaza, St. Augustine	
❏	S545	Grounds of Hotel Alcazar, St. Augustine	
❏	S546	Outer Court, Hotel Ponce de Leon, St. Augustine	
❏	S547	The Cathedral and Plaza, St. Augustine	
❏	S548	Old City Gate, St. Augustine	
❏	S549	Entrance to Hotel Ponce de Leon, St. Augustine	
❏	S550	The Museum, St. Augustine	
❏	S551	Court Yard, Fort Marion, St. Augustine	
❏	S552	The Sea Wall and Bath House, St. Augustine	
❏	S553	The Outer Court Colonnades, Hotel Ponce de Leon, St. Augustine	
❏	S554	Old Watch Tower, Fort Marion, St. Augustine	
❏	S555	Memorial Presbyterian Church, St. Augustine	
❏	S556	The Court, Hotel Alcazar, St. Augustine	
❏	S557	Alcazar Hotel and Cordova Annex, St. Augustine	
❏	S558	Hotel Ponce de Leon, St. Augustine	
❏	S559	Middle Court, Hotel Alcazar	
❏	S560	Loading Phosphate at Port, Tampa	
❏	S561	Sulphur Springs, Tampa	
❏	S562	Palmetto Beach, Tampa	
❏	S563	Church of Sacred Heart	
❏	S564	Birds Eye View of Tampa	
❏	S565	U.S. Government Building & Post Office, Tampa	
❏	S566	Franklin Street Looking North, Tampa	
❏	S567	Waterfront, Tampa	
❏	S568	Ballast Point, Land View, Tampa	
❏	S569	Ballast Point, Water View, Tampa	
❏	S570	Six Mile Creek, Tampa	
❏	S571	Tampa Bay Hotel, Tampa	
❏	S572	Tampa Port and Inn, Tampa	
❏	S573	View in DeSoto Park, Tampa	
❏	S574	Old U.S. Garrison, Tampa	
❏	S575	Tampa Bay Hotel and Grounds, Tampa	
❏	S576	Veranda, Tampa Bay Hotel, Tampa	
❏	S577	Chinese Pavilion, Tampa	
❏	S578	On the Hillsboro River, Tampa	
❏	S579	Court House, Tampa	
❏	S580	Franklin Street, Tampa	
❏	S581	Hillsboro County School House, Tampa	
❏	S582	The Casino near Tampa	
❏	S583	River Front, Jacksonville	
❏	S584	Main Street, Jacksonville	

Chart continues on next page

	No.	Description	Collection Notes
❑	S585	Riverside Park, Jacksonville	
❑	S586	Riverside Park, Jacksonville	
❑	S587	Group of Ostriches at an Ostrich Farm	
❑	S588	Confederate Monument, Hemming Park, Jacksonville	
❑	S589	Hotel Windsor & Hemming Park, Jacksonville	
❑	S590	City Hall, Jacksonville	
❑	S591	Waterworks Park, Jacksonville	
❑	S592	Bird's Eye view of Jacksonville	
❑	S593	Riverside Park, Jacksonville	
❑	S594	Main Street, Jacksonville	
❑	S595	"Big Joe," Jacksonville	
❑	S596	Alligators, Native to Florida	
❑	S597	Hemming Park, Jacksonville	
❑	S598	Riverside Avenue, Jacksonville	
❑	S599	Riding bareback on an Ostrich at an Ostrich Farm	
❑	S600	Live Oak on St. Johns River	
❑	S601	The Everett, Bay St. East from Julia, Jacksonville	
❑	S602	Park Avenue, Jacksonville	
❑	S603	Bay Street West of Laura, Jacksonville	
❑	S604	Duval Hotel, Post Office, Castle Hall, National Bank of Jacksonville	
❑	S605	West Bay Street, Jacksonville	
❑	S606	First Presbyterian Church and Monroe St., Jacksonville	
❑	S607	Ruins of the Old Sugar Mill below Plantation, Ormond	
❑	S608	Buckhead Bluff on the Tomoka River	
❑	S609	Date Palms on the Banks of the Canal, Ormond	
❑	S610	Ormond Hotel, Ormond	
❑	S611	The Bostrom Oaks on the River Road, Ormond	
❑	S612	The Village Street, Ormond	
❑	S613	The Living Parade in Front of Hotel Ormond, Ormond	
❑	S614	Causeway, Ormond	
❑	S615	The Grand Canal by Santa Lucia Island, Ormond	
❑	S616	Canoeing on the upper Tomoka near Ormond	
❑	S617	Old Spanish Sugar House—Built 1705, Fort Orange near Daytona	
❑	S618	Triple Royal Palm, Ridgewood Ave, Daytona	
❑	S619	Ridgewood Ave and Ridgewood Hotel, Daytona	
❑	S620	Tree Branch Palmetto, Daytona	
❑	S621	Rapid Transit at Fort Pierce, Indian River	
❑	S622	Beach Street at Daytona, Indian River	
❑	S623	Beach Street at Indian River, Daytona	
❑	S624	Orange Street, Daytona	
❑	S625	Ruins of the old Sugar Mill, Daytona	
❑	S626	Big Tree near Daytona, Largest in Florida	
❑	S627	Canary Date Palm	

	No.	Description	Collection Notes
❏	S628	Grape Fruit Grove	
❏	S629	Picking Oranges	
❏	S630	Pineapple Grove	
❏	S631	Greetings from the Sunny South. Tobacco Prizing	
❏	S632	Greetings from the Sunny South. Picking Cotton	
❏	S633	Greetings from the Sunny South. Tobacco ready for Cutting	
❏	S634	Greetings from the Sunny South. Picking Tobacco	
❏	S635	Greetings from the Sunny South. Tobacco Sale	
❏	S636	Greetings from the Sunny South. Stemming Tobacco	
❏	S637	Greetings from the Sunny South. Tobacco Seed Bed	
❏	S638	Greetings from the Sunny South. The Smile that Won't Come Off	
❏	S639	Greetings from the Sunny South. At Leisure	
❏	S640	Greetings from the Sunny South. A Cotton Picker	
❏	S641	Greetings from the Sunny South. A Typical Southern Negro	
❏	S642	Greetings from the Sunny South. Old Uncle Joe	
❏	S643	Greetings from the Sunny South. When Melon is Ripe	
❏	S644	Greetings from the Sunny South. A Watermelon Feast	
❏	S645	Greetings from the Sunny South. Old Mammie	
❏	S646	Greetings from the Sunny South. Musical Coons	
❏	S647	Greetings from the Sunny South. Happy Coons	
❏	S648	Greetings from the Sunny South. Negroes Carrying Freight	
❏	S649	Greetings from the Sunny South. "Come seben, come eleben"	
❏	S650	Greetings from the Sunny South. Solid Comfort	
❏	S651	Greetings from the Sunny South. Negroes Scrambling for Money	
❏	S652	Greetings from the Sunny South. Horseless Carriage	
❏	S653	Greetings from the Sunny South. Cotton Compress	
❏	S654	Greetings from the Sunny South. In the Cotton Field	
❏	S655	Greetings from the Sunny South. A Cotton Field at Picking Time	
❏	S656	Greetings from the Sunny South. Transporting Cotton	
❏	S657	Greetings from the Sunny South. Where the Cotton Blossoms Grow	
❏	S658	Greetings from the Sunny South. Cotton Pickers	
❏	S659	Greetings from the Sunny South. Weighing Cotton	
❏	S660	Greetings from the Sunny South. The Latest Thing Out	
❏	S661	Sponge Fleet, Key West	
❏	S662	Sale of New Sponges, Key West	
❏	S663	A residence embowered in coconut trees, Key West	
❏	S664	Where many of the 'Maine' boys Rest, Key West	

Frog in Your Throat

In 1905 the Frog in Your Throat Company issued an illustrated set of 12 unsigned artist cards, most featuring an animated frog and a pretty lady to advertise their remedy. These measure 4 by 5-3/4 inches. A separate set of 10 are of much smaller size: 2-1/4 by 4-3/4 inches.

The frogs and ladies are lovable, making this a very popular collection.

The company was headquartered at 92 West Broadway, corner of Chambers Street, in New York City. On July 21, 1905, the firm registered 12 captions that were used on Mr. Frog postcards. Those printed subsequently had the notation on the front, "Copyright, 1905, Frog in Your Throat Company." Those with Private Mailing Card backs are found with or without this notice. Divided-back cards, first issued in 1907, seem to always have this notice. Within a given title there can be other printing variations, including the location of the copyright notice and slight differences regarding the advertising caption in relation to the lady.

Frog in Your Throat lozenges were advertised on billboards, using a painted display with frogs 20 feet high, on the well-traveled Pennsylvania Railroad line between New York and Philadelphia, in store fronts, and elsewhere. *The Adventures of Polly Wog and Taddy Pole* was copyrighted by the company in 1910. It seems that postcards continued to be issued for several years afterward. In this later era the New York office was closed and operations were concentrated in Philadelphia. Little was heard of the company after 1915.

Description		Collection Notes
	LARGE SIZE	
❑	A Favorite at All Times	
❑	A Social Success	
❑	A Universal Favorite	
❑	Don't Be Without It	
❑	For Everybody	
❑	For Singers	
❑	Frog in Your Throat?*	
❑	Innocent and Instantaneous	
❑	My Old Friend Dr. Frog	
❑	Needs No Introduction	
❑	Nothing Better	
❑	Pleasant to Take	
❑	Popular Everywhere	
	SMALL SIZE	
❑	Drives Away Cold Demons	
❑	Everybody's Taking Them	
❑	Fine for Smoker's Throat	
❑	Follow the Leader	
❑	For Dry Husky Throats	
❑	For Public Speakers	
❑	For that Tickling Sensation	
❑	Good in Stormy Weather	
❑	Renews the Voice for Singers	
❑	Stop Your Coughing	

* Advertising card with two frogs on a bench.

Individual Frog in Your Throat cards in EF to Mint condition are valued from $25 to $35 (for the large size) or $15 to $25 (for the small size).

The cards were not numbered. The chart at left can serve as a checklist while you complete your own collection.

A box of Frog in Your Throat lozenges (from an advertisement).

A Frog in Your Throat card. EF to Mint: $15–$25

Roosevelt Bears

In 1906 Edward Stern & Co., of Philadelphia, published a book titled *The Roosevelt Bears, Their Travels and Adventures*, by Seymour Eaton (nom de plume of Paul Piper). This told of the personified Teddy B and Teddy G and their exploits. Traveling on a hot-air balloon, they go to Harvard, visit New York City, call on Niagara Falls (where they are seen donning rubber suits under the falls, without the falls in view), land on an arctic iceberg, perform in a circus, and engage in other antics, all accompanied by rhyme.

The color illustrations by V. Floyd Campbell were soon published separately as the Roosevelt Bears set of 16 postcards, each with a serial number, title, and two lines of verse. This is called the "first set" of Roosevelt Bears. Campbell did not live to see the postcards.

The second set of 16 cards appeared in 1907 and had images from another Eaton book, *More About Teddy B and Teddy G*, with an advertisement for the book in multiple lines of red print below the serial number, title, and verse: "'More about the Roosevelt Bears.' The new Teddy Bear book for 1907, published September 1st, now ready at [name of local retailer printed here]." These were numbered from 17 to 32.

Beyond the above, other cards were made—some without numbers, others using numbers in the 17 to 32 range—without an advertising imprint and differing in titles. Some cards are without verses. It seems that the first set of Roosevelt Bears largely satisfied the demand,

for fewer were issued of the second set. Cards outside of these two sets are especially elusive.

The value of any particular Roosevelt Bear card generally depends on which set and printing it was issued in:

Roosevelt Bear Set	Description	Numbering	Value, EF to Mint
First set	Illustrated by V. Floyd Campbell	1 to 16 on the face, all vertically oriented	$10–$15
Second set, first printing	Illustrated by Richard Keith Culver; with red advertising imprint for *More About the Roosevelt Bears*	17 to 32 on the face, all vertically oriented	$20–$30
Second set, second printing	Four cards from the first printing; no advertising imprint, no titles, but with verses	Various (see below)	$20–$30
Second set, third printing	Certain cards with advertising imprint for *The Roosevelt Bears*, no titles, but with verses		$20–$30
Third set	Illustrated by Richard Keith Culver; with advertising imprint (in red, at the bottom) for *The Roosevelt Bears Abroad*; with titles, and verses	Not numbered	$50–$75
Others	See last chart in this section	See below	$15–$30

"No. 1. The Roosevelt Bears at Home." First card in the first set of 16.

"No.12. The Roosevelt Bears Take an Auto Ride." EF to Mint: $10–$15

"No. 14. The Roosevelt Bears on the Iceberg." EF to Mint: $10–$15

	Set	Printing	No.*	Description**	Collection Notes
❑	First	–	No. 1	The Roosevelt Bears at Home	
❑	First	–	No. 2	The Roosevelt Bears Go Aboard the Train	
❑	First	–	No. 3	The Roosevelt Bears in a Sleeping Car	
❑	First	–	No. 4	The Roosevelt Bears on a Farm	
❑	First	–	No. 5	The Roosevelt Bears at a Country School	
❑	First	–	No. 6	The Roosevelt Bears at the County Fair	
❑	First	–	No. 7	The Roosevelt Bears Leaving the Balloon	
❑	First	–	No. 8	The Roosevelt Bears at the Tailor's	
❑	First	–	No. 9	The Roosevelt Bears in the Department Store	
❑	First	–	No. 10	The Roosevelt Bears at Niagara Falls	
❑	First	–	No. 11	The Roosevelt Bears at the Boston Public Library	
❑	First	–	No. 12	The Roosevelt Bears Take an Auto Ride	
❑	First	–	No. 13	The Roosevelt Bears at Harvard	
❑	First	–	No. 14	The Roosevelt Bears on the Iceberg	
❑	First	–	No. 15	The Roosevelt Bears in New York City	
❑	First	–	No. 16	The Roosevelt Bears at the Circus	

* Numbered 1 to 16 on the face, vertically oriented. ** All illustrated by V. Floyd Campbell.
Chart continues on next page

"No. 22. The Roosevelt Bears in New York." Verse: "Teddy B threw the monkey and made him yell, / And caught him every time he fell."

"No. 32. The Roosevelt Bears at Washington." Verse: "With outstretched hand and smiling face, / He gave them welcome to the place." No. 32 in the second set of 16. President Theodore Roosevelt is depicted.

	Set	Printing	No.*	Description**	Collection Notes
❑	Second	First	No. 17	The Roosevelt Bears Out West	
❑	Second	First	No. 18	The Roosevelt Bears Put Out a Fire	
❑	Second	First	No. 19	The Roosevelt Bears at the Wax Museum	
❑	Second	First	No. 20	The Roosevelt Bears at West Point	
❑	Second	First	No. 21	The Roosevelt Bears as Cadets	
❑	Second	First	No. 22	The Roosevelt Bears in New York	
❑	Second	First	No. 23	The Roosevelt Bears in Philadelphia	
❑	Second	First	No. 24	The Roosevelt Bears at the Theatre	
❑	Second	First	No. 25	The Roosevelt Bears at Atlantic City†	
❑	Second	First	No. 26	The Roosevelt Bears at Independence Hall	
❑	Second	First	No. 27	The Roosevelt Bears Celebrate the Fourth	
❑	Second	First	No. 28	The Roosevelt Bears at the Zoo	
❑	Second	First	No. 29	The Roosevelt Bears Go Fishing	
❑	Second	First	No. 30	The Roosevelt Bears on a Pullman	
❑	Second	First	No. 31	The Roosevelt Bears as Hunters	
❑	Second	First	No. 32	The Roosevelt Bears at Washington	

* Numbered 17 to 32 on the face, vertically oriented. ** All illustrated by Richard Keith Culver. † Possible variant title, per Mashburn: The Roosevelt Bears Swimming.

	Set	Printing	No.*	Description**	Collection Notes
❑	Second	Second	No. 17	Same as No. 30 from the first printing; horizontal card	
❑	Second	Second	No. 18	Same as No. 31 from the first printing; vertical card	
❑	Second	Second	No. 19	Same as No. 26 from the first printing; horizontal card	
❑	Second	Second	No. 20	Same as No. 27 from the first printing; vertical card	

* Numbered on the face. ** No advertising imprint; no titles; but with verses.

	Set	Printing	No.*	Description**	Collection Notes
❑	Second	Third	No. 19	Same as No. 27 from the first printing; vertical card	
❑	Second	Third	No. 20	Same as No. 26 from the first printing; vertical card	

* Numbered on the face. ** With advertising imprint for *The Roosevelt Bears* (the first book); no titles, but with verses. An anomalous group of cards.

"The Roosevelt Bears Return from Abroad," an unnumbered card in the Third Set, with Uncle Sam. Verse: "His speech was short but generous, / We want you back, you belong to us."

	Set	Printing	No.*	Description**	Collection Notes
❑	Third	—	No. 101	"The Bears dressed up in kilts and plaid, / And everything the pipers had."	
❑	Third	—	No. 102	"We'll make steel fly and sabers clash, / And burst this old tower all to smash."	
❑	Third	—	No. 103	"Wishing for home and his mountain cave, / Where rocks and trees and the ground behave."	
❑	Third	—	No. 104	"Riding on trains quite new to bears, / And counting money to pay their fares."	
❑	Third	—	No. 105	"They strung it off at a lively rate, / And called it Shakespeare up-to-date."	
❑	Third	—	No. 106	"They laughed at jokes and spilled their tea, / And made a mess like you or me."	
❑	Third	—	No. 107	"But the Frenchman just excited grew, / For an English word he never knew."	
❑	Third	—	No. 108	"Next day these bears from Uncle Sam, / Met Dutchie Hans of Amsterdam."	
❑	Third	—	No. 109	"At a Custom House on a boundary line, / The Teddy Bears had to pay a fine."	
❑	Third	—	No. 110	"In a Russian jail with a window each, / Through which to coax or scold or teach."	
❑	Third	—	No. 111	The crowd of peasants cheered them well, / And said it equaled William Tell."	
❑	Third	—	No. 112	"Studying Latin and wasting time, / On Caesar's history or Virgil's rhyme."	
❑	Third	—	No. 113	"That water I swallowed just now, I say, / Tastes all the world like consommé."	
❑	Third	—	No. 114	"Show these Arabs that a Yankee bear, / Can make the sand fly anywhere."	
❑	Third	—	No. 115	"His speech was short but generous, / We want you back you belong to us."	
❑	Third	—	No. 116	"Next day the Bears went for a tramp, / With a snow-shoe club to a winter camp."	

* Numbers assigned by Q. David Bowers and Mary L. Martin. ** All illustrated by Richard Keith Culver; with advertisement for *The Roosevelt Bears Abroad* printed in red at the bottom; with titles and verses, but not numbered.

As mentioned above, several Roosevelt Bears cards require further study; these include cards with combinations of numbers and titles not in synchrony with the numbering systems in the sets already listed here. Some examples of this incongruity are listed on the next page:

	No.	Description	Collection Notes
❏	No. 11	The Roosevelt Bears in New York	
❏	No. 19	The Roosevelt Bears Celebrate 4th of July	
❏	No. 20	The Roosevelt Bears go to Atlantic City	
❏	No. 21	The Roosevelt Bears go Fishing	
❏	No. 22	The Roosevelt Bears go to the Zoo	
❏	No. 23	The Roosevelt Bears Ride the Train	
❏	No. 24	The Roosevelt Bears Visit West Point	
❏	No. 25	The Roosevelt Bears Attend the Theatre	
❏	No. 26	The Roosevelt Bears go to a Wax Museum	
❏	No. 27	The Roosevelt Bears go Hunting	
❏	No. 29	The Roosevelt Bears go to Philadelphia	
❏	No. 32	The Roosevelt Bears go to Washington*	

* Variant spelling in title.

Cracker Jack Bears

Cracker Jack Bears cards were issued in 1908 by the firm of Rueckheim Bros. and Eckstein, makers of the popular Cracker Jack popcorn-and-peanuts treat, and were given free in packages of the confection. Beyond that, a set could be obtained by mailing in labels. A complete set comprises 16 cards, each with bears from Chicago's Lincoln Zoo and a rhyme. These measure 5 by 3 inches, or slightly smaller than standard size. Many were postally used by their recipients. They were not titled, but a numbered list of subjects is given below.

This is a delightful comic series. In EF to Mint condition the cards are worth $10 to $25 each.

No. 1: Cracker Jack bears sailing away from the Lincoln Zoo. EF to Mint: $20

No. 15: Teddy Roosevelt has the bears up a tree. EF to Mint: $20

	No.	Description	Collection Notes
❏	No. 1	The Bears escape from the Lincoln Park Zoo by climbing a ladder to a balloon above	
❏	No. 2	On their way to adventure the Bears fly over the heads of children at the zoo and drop boxes of Cracker Jack to them	
❏	No. 3	One bear on a ladder dangling from an airship tries to save the other, who has just gone over the brink of Niagara Falls riding in a large Cracker Jack box	
❏	No. 4	The Bears climb on the top of the Statue of Liberty	
❏	No. 5	The Bears as vaudeville actors are on stage before an audience at Coney Island, "home of fun." One bear balances a box of the product on its nose	
❏	No. 6	In New York City, seemingly in Central Park, the bears "found each candy stand sold Cracker Jack on every hand"	

	No.	Description	Collection Notes
❑	No. 7	At the front of the White House, one Bear shakes President Roosevelt's hand, while the other looks on from the airship ladder	
❑	No. 8	Keeping up with the times, the Bears visit the Jamestown Tercentenary Exposition in Virginia	
❑	No. 9	The airship takes the Bears to the South, where they greet an African American man working in a peanut field	
❑	No. 10	Attending a husking bee, the Bears have a good time and see sacks of dried corn ready to be made into popcorn	
❑	No. 11	The Bears are with an elephant at the circus, one riding on its head and the other feeding it Cracker Jack	
❑	No. 12	With one at bat and the other as catcher, the Bears enjoy playing baseball	
❑	No. 13	The Bears in their airship hover near the five-story red brick building where Cracker Jack is made	
❑	No. 14	One bear stirs a large kettle while the other brings a heaping pan of popcorn to make Cracker Jack	
❑	No. 15	"Oh, Mr. Teddy, drop your gun," says a Bear as both are up a tree with the president standing menacingly below	
❑	No. 16	The Bears fly off to Mars, "and there they found a great demand / For Cracker Jack on every hand"	

The Thomas F. Schweitzer Series of Roosevelt Bears

This set of postcards featured certain illustrations from the Roosevelt Bears books. The cards that have been reported are listed here. More research will undoubtedly turn up information on others.

Individual cards are worth $15 to $20 in EF to Mint condition.

	No.	Description	Collection Notes
❑	No. 1		
❑	No. 2		
❑	No. 3		
❑	No. 4	The Roosevelt Bears leave their Mountain Home	
❑	No. 5	The Roosevelt Bears at the County Fair	
❑	No. 6	The Roosevelt Bears Arrive in Paris	
❑	No. 7	The Roosevelt Bears at Harvard	
❑	No. 8	The Roosevelt Bears in Paris	
❑	No. 9	The Roosevelt Bears see the Wax Musée: Roosevelt Bears, Buster Brown, and Tige	
❑	No. 10	The Roosevelt Bears see the Wax Musée: Buster Brown Resolution	

Sleepy Eye Flour Indian

The Sleepy Eye Flour Company issued a set of nine illustrated cards featuring various aspects of Indian life. These were printed in Milwaukee by Willman's Brothers. The set was available by mail for 10¢. Its fictitious emblem was Chief Old Sleepy Eye. The first Sleepy Eye flour mill was built in Sleepy Eye, Minnesota, in 1883. A second mill was built in the early 1900s. The large factory prospered and became well-known, and it earned a high prize at the 1904 Lewis and Clark Exposition. The business ran into financial problems in the late 1910s and closed in 1921.

The cards themselves were not numbered; the numbers listed here were assigned by authors Bowers and Martin for the convenience of collectors and historians.

Individual Sleepy Eye Flour Indian cards are valued at $15 to $25 in EF to Mint condition.

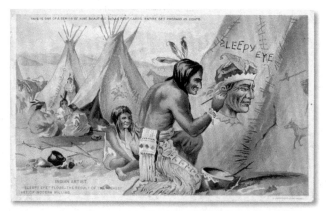

Sleepy Eye Flour card, "Indian Artist." EF to Mint: $25

	No.*	Description	Collection Notes
☐	1	A Mark of Quality	
☐	2	Chief Sleepy Eye Welcomes Whites	
☐	3	Indian Artist	
☐	4	Indian Canoeing	
☐	5	Indian Mode of Conveyance	
☐	6	Pipe of Peace	
☐	7	Sleepy Eye Mills	
☐	8	Sleepy Eye Monument	
☐	9	Sleepy Eye, The Meritorious Flour	

* These catalog numbers are not printed on the cards but are provided for convenience.

Zeno Gum Co.

The Zeno Gum Manufacturing Co. of Chicago offered several series of advertising cards. The earliest may have been those with "Illustrated Post Card Co., N.Y." and a serial number on the face, below a captioned scene in black and white. Some scenes have the imprint in the image noting they were copyrighted by A. Loeffler of Staten Island, New York.

Two main styles of Zeno postcards were issued in large quantities, each with scenic views. One has "ZENO MEANS GOOD CHEWING GUM" or a related inscription added by an artist to the scene. The other has "ZENO Means Good CHEWING GUM" in two lines in the bottom border. The subjects are as eclectic as can be and range from the Ivy Arch on Delaware Avenue in Buffalo, New York, to the United

Early Zeno advertising card, Illustrated Post Card Co. No. 1933, "Boat House, Central park, New York," from an image copyrighted by Loeffler in 1895. (Circa 1903–1905)

Post card with product name within the view, here "South Salina Street, Syracuse, N.Y.," with, in the distance, "ZENO MEANS GOOD CHEWING GUM" on the side of a building and to its right, on another building, "CHEW ZENO GUM DAILY."

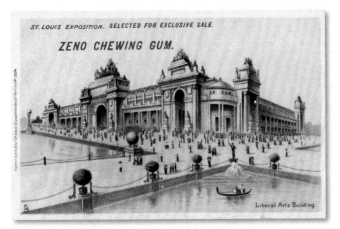

Zeno advertising card for the St. Louis Exposition (Louisiana Purchase Exposition 1904), "Liberal Arts Building," using a Tuck image and credited in the left margin; printed in America with a different back, and not by Tuck.

States Capitol. A few have been manipulated by adding Zeno advertising to the sides of buildings.

In addition there are other Zeno advertising cards, seemingly issued in smaller numbers, illustrating buildings at the 1904 Louisiana Purchase Exposition (using and crediting images from Tuck "St. Louis Exposition Series"). Further cards, not in extensive series, advertise Zeno Pepsin gum and for other topics.

Zeno cards are inexpensive and available with dozens of different scenes. No catalog of them has ever been made. This is an interesting specialty for anyone liking scenic views.

Card Type	Value, EF to Mint
Zeno postcard, typical scene	$3–$5
Zeno postcard, Illustrated Post Card Co.	$3–$5
Zeno postcard, St. Louis Exposition	$5–$8

Other Sets

The following sets include most of those listed by George and Dorothy Miller in *Picture Postcards in the United States*. Beyond these there are dozens of other series, particularly those advertising local or regional products or services. Except for cards issued by Tuck and other leading publishers, most of these series cards are very inexpensive. Good hunting grounds are postcard shows.

Examples of Bensdorp's, Doh-Wah-Jack, Kropp State Capitols, Langsdorf Fire Fighters, Mirror High Grade Candies, and Swift's Premium Butterine advertising cards.

Set	Value, EF to Mint
A.S.B. Virtues, series 178	$2–$5
Albastine Sanitary Wall Coating	$2–$10
American Fence Co.	$5–$12
American Line ships	$10–$15
Anheuser-Busch Brewing Association	$5–$15
Austin Busy Bears	$10–$15
Austin Famous Men	$5–$10
Austin World Rulers	$5–$10
Bamforth Songs	$2–$5
Bathing Girls colorful early lithographs	$10–$15
Bathing Girls, colorful embossed	$5–$10
Bathing Girls, flat printed	$2–$10
Bensdorp's Royal Dutch Cocoa, Amsterdam	$5–$9
Bergman Illustrated State Girls	$5–$10

Chart continues on next page

Examples of Swift's Premium Oleomargarine, Swift's Pride Soap and Washing Powder, Butter-Krust Bread, and Tuck Carnival advertising cards.

Set	Value, EF to Mint
Berry Brothers' Celebrated Varnishes	$5–$10
Bien "Want" series	$2–$10
Bosselman State Capitols	$2–$5
Boston Rubber Shoe Co.	$2–$10
Boston Sunday Post	$5–$15
Bristolboardline authors 574 and 583	$5–$15
Brooklyn Eagle (486 different black and white)	$5–$15
Brown's Bronchial Troches, Historical Boston	$5–$20
Buffalo Morning Express	$5–$10
Bull Durham Smoking Tobacco	$30–$50
Burlington Route Railroad	$2–$10
Clark, Rose-Busy Bears	$5–$10
Cleveland News Co. Presidents	$8–$12
Coins embossed (DRGM)	$15–$25
Coins embossed, foreign (DRGM)	$15–$25
Colonial Heroes	$10–$20
Cunningham Child's Prayer	$2–$8
Curtis Publishing Co.	$2–$10
Dam Family	$2–$8
Derby's Croup Mixture	$2–$10
Detroit 60,131 series art reproductions	$2–$5
Detroit 60,500 series art reproductions	$2–$5
Detroit Little Phostint Journeys	$2–$10
Detroit Miscellaneous Arts, Butterfly	$75–$125

Set	Value, EF to Mint
Detroit Miscellaneous Arts, Childhood Days	$100–$150
Detroit Miscellaneous Arts, Colorado Wild Flowers	$2–$5
Detroit Miscellaneous Arts, Fairy Queen	$125–$175
Doh-Wah-Jack Indian series (Beckwith Co., Round Oak Stoves, art by H.I. Saxton and Henry J. Soulen)	$5–$8
Donaldson Heroes	$3–$10
DuBois Brewing Co.	$3–$10
Dutch Masters Cigars	$5–$10
Eaton County Savings Bank (Charlotte, Michigan)	$4–$6
Evolution Comics (Moore and Gibson)	$8–$10
Ferloni Popes	$8–$10
Finkenrath 10 Commandments	$3–$5
Finkenrath Rosary	$3–$5
Flint-Bruce Furniture Co.	$6–$10
Ford Booster comics by Witt	$6–$8
Foster Brothers imprinted Detroit cards	$5–$8
Gold Dust Twins	$25–$30
Great Lakes Transportation Corporation ships	$6–$8
Guardian Angel series 250 and 636	$6–$12
Hamburg-Amerika Line	$10–$20
Harvey, Fred-Restaurants, views	$15–$30
Heal Bears	$6–$8

Set	Value, EF to Mint
Hearst newspaper cut-apart cards issued with papers	$8–$10
Hiram Walker & Sons	$5–$8
Holbrook Child's Prayer	$3–$5
Huld Flag and View	$3–$5
Huld State Girls	$12–$15
Illustrated Post Card Co. Presidents	$6–$10
International Harvester Farm Machines	$7–$12
Kornelia Kinks Jocular Jinks (Korn Kinks cereal)	$8–$20
Kropp State Capitols	$4–$6
Langsdorf Fire Fighters	$6–$8
Langsdorf Military Uniforms	$8–$10
Langsdorf State Capitols	$4–$6
Langsdorf State Girls	$15–$40
Langsdorf State Girls with Silk	$40–$60
Language of the Flowers	$3–$4
Leighton Governors	$3–$4
Leighton Presidents	$10–$15
Lincoln National Bank (Rochester, New York)	$4–$6
Lounsbury Fortune	$3–$5
Marks, J.T. Birth Month	$3–$5
McPhail Piano Co.	$3–$5
Metropolitan Life Insurance Co.	$2–$4
Mirror High Grade Candies, Navy ships	$8–$12
Mitchell Zodiac	$5–$8
Nash, E.-Gem Birthday	$3–$5
National Songs with "Winsch back"	$4–$6
National Souvenir Presidents	$4–$6
National State Girls by St. John	$8–$10
New York Central Railroad	$8+
Newspaper-issued cards, various	$7–$10
Nursery Rhymes (with spread-eagle trademark)	$10–$12
P.F.B. Comics	$6–$8
P.F.B. Lord's Prayer	$6–$8
Paul Revere's Ride	$3–$5
Peters Shoe Co., Weather Bird Shoes	$10–$15
Philadelphia Public Ledger	$5–$7
Pinkham, Lydia—College Campuses	$6–$8
Piso's Cure	$10–$12
Platinachrome State Girls	$10–$15
Prudential Insurance Co.	$6–$8
Red Star Line ships	$12+

Set	Value, EF to Mint
Riley Roses	$2–$3
Rose Co. 10 Commandments	$3–$5
Rose Co. Educational Series	$3–$5
Rost Famous Men (pioneer card reprints)	$3–$5
Rotograph "real photo" Presidents	$5–$10
Rotograph black and white presidents signed L.P. Spinner	$8–$12
Rotograph photoportraits	$3–$5
Ruhland Beer	$20+
Sander Prayer	$4–$6
Schlitz Beer	$15+
Sears Roebuck & Co.	$5+
Shehan Famous People	$3–$5
Shehan Poets and Homes	$3–$5
Shehan Your Fortune	$3–$5
Shorgi art reproductions, embossed	$2–$4
Shorgi art reproductions, flat printed	$1–$3
Southwick Birth Month	$2–$4
Souvenir Post Card Co. College Girls	$12+
Stamps embossed, foreign (O.Z.)	$10+
Stamps embossed, U.S. (O.Z.)	$10+
Stengel art reproductions	$1–$3
Stern, Edward-College Girls by R. Hill	$12+
Stroudsburg & Delaware Water Gap Scenic Railroad	$4+
Suggestions for Lovers from the Jungle	$5+
Swift's Premium Butterine, Aircraft of Nations	$3–$5
Swift's Premium Butterine, ethnic types (1908)	$7–$10
Swift's Premium Oleomargarine (1918)	$8–$10
Swift's Pride Soap & Washing Powder, "Me and My Shadow" series	$8–$10
Taggart 10 Commandments	$5–$7
Travelers Insurance Co.	$3–$5
Tower Bears	$5–$7
Tuck Animals and Birds (400, 401, 402)	$4–$7
Tuck Butterflies (403) advertising Butter-Krust Bread	$6–$8
Tuck Carnival series (117)	$10–$12

Chart continues on next page

Examples of Houses of the Presidents, Walk-Over Shoes, Woonsocket Rubber Co., and Zeno Gum advertising cards.

Set	Value, EF to Mint
Tuck Celebrated Posters series (1505)	$30+
Tuck Greetings from the Seaside	$6–$8
Tuck Heroes of the South	$8+
Tuck "Kyd" Dickens characters	$8+
Tuck Little Men and Women	$6+
Tuck Little Nursery Lovers	$6+
Tuck New England Colleges	$6+
Tuck Oilette Dickens by Copping	$6+
Tuck Oilette Dickens by Phiz	$6+
Tuck Oilette Houses of the Presidents	$6–$8
Tuck Oilette State Capitols	$4–$6
Tuck Oilette Virtues	$5–$8
Tuck Playtime series (550)	$8+
Tuck Presidents	$10+
Tuck Sentiments of the Month	$4–$6
Tuck U.S. Army and Navy (404, 405)	$5+
Tuck U.S. Battleships	$6+
Tuck Wagner	$6–$8
Tuck series, miscellaneous	$2+
U.S. Postcard Co. Governors	$5

Set	Value, EF to Mint
Ullman Busy Bears No. 49 by Wall	$5–$7
Ullman College Belles	$8–10
Union Pacific Railroad	$5+
Utopia Yarn, Dutch Children	$3–$5
Walk-Over Shoes American Scenes	$5–$6
Walk-Over Shoes Cartoons	$5–$6
Walk-Over Shoes, Famous Americans	$24
Walk-Over Shoes with small Afro-American figure	$6–$8
Wanamaker Indian Chiefs	$8–$10
Washington, Baltimore & Annapolis Electric Railroad	$8+
Webster Cigars	$10–$12
Westner News Co. presidents (flag and eagle)	$8–$10
Wheelock Presidents	$6–$8
Wheelock State Capitols	$3–$5
White Star Line ships	$20+
Women's World magazine	$5–$7
Woonsocket Rubber Co. Footwear of Nations	$8–$10

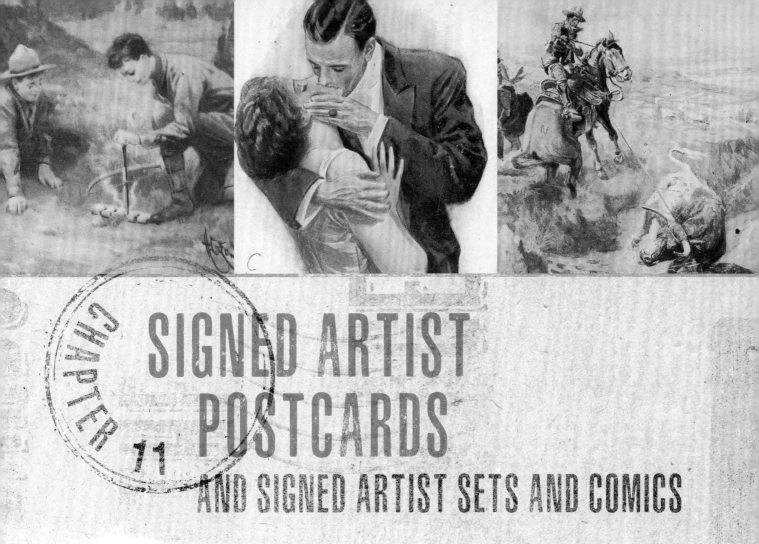

SIGNED ARTIST POSTCARDS

AND SIGNED ARTIST SETS AND COMICS

Signed artist cards, including those of Ellen Clapsaddle, Harrison Fisher, Philip Boileau, F. Earl Christy, Samuel L. Schmucker, and others, are listed alphabetically, first by selected American-born artists, then with selected foreign artists. A brief biography of each is given, followed by a list of readily collectible postcard types for several artists. If a list is not included, then artists and subjects are given, such as John O. Winsch and Clapsaddle cards. Some of the postcards bought and sold by dealers under the "signed artist" category are not signed at all, but are attributed to a specific artist based on his or her style or from the same image found on a signed poster, magazine cover, or other medium.

Picture Postcards in the United States 1893–1918 by George and Dorothy Miller lists many other artists, most of whom did limited work on postcards. Listed here are American and foreign cards that are popular today with American collectors. Important subjects in this category include pretty women, animals, children, and holidays.

The American Girl

Beginning in the 1890s, and reaching its stride in the early twentieth century, "the American Girl" was a category that attracted great public interest and was the most important single subject on signed artist cards. An ideal feminine figure was depicted in engravings, on magazine covers, and elsewhere—always beautiful and often engaged in romantic pursuits. The popularity of this character was launched by the Gibson Girl, created by Charles Dana Gibson in 1898 (see listing below). In some scenes she was aloof, unreachable, as exemplified in "The Eternal Question" (see page 136).

The concept of the American Girl caught on quickly, and by the early twentieth century, George Barr Mc-Cutcheon and a bevy of other authors were busily turning out cheap novels depicting her in various romantic circumstances. No doubt reading these accounts, such as McCutcheon's Beverly in the mythical kingdom of Graustark, provided a nice foil to everyday life, which for many consisted of cleaning house, working in a laundry, tending a loom in a mill, or picking crops in a

Pearle Fidler LeMunyan's American Girl. (American Girl No. 55, Edward Gross, New York.) EF to Mint: $15–$25

Pearle Fidler LeMunyan's American Girl. (American Girl No. 58, Edward Gross, New York.) EF to Mint: $15–$25

field. Such stories were an escape much as soap operas and tell-it-all magazines about actors and actresses would be to a later generation of radio, movie, and television consumers.

Beginning at the turn of the twentieth century, many other artists and illustrators took up the brush and created their versions of the American Girl. By the end of the 1910s she was well established on postcards. Pearle Fidler LeMunyan (see above) was one of many lesser-known artists.[2] In 1913 Philip Boileau, Harrison Fisher, and Penhryn Stanlaws were judges in a contest to find "America's most beautiful woman."[3]

With the coming of the World War in Europe in 1914 and America's serious involvement in 1917, emphasis changed, and in time the American Girl faded from the scene. Fisher continued his art, but in a sharply diminished fashion, with his portraits of women appearing on the cover of many Cosmopolitan magazines in the 1920s and 1930s. By that time, the era of "signed artist" postcards was history.

Reinthal & Newman

One of the leading publishers of artist-signed American Girl–style cards was Reinthal & Newman. A profile of the firm appeared in *The National Druggist*, April 1912:

Ten years ago practically all our picture postcards were imported from Europe. But today American cards set the standard for the world, and we are probably exporting to other countries a great many more than we import from them.

Among the publishers who have contributed to the attainment of this high standard and to whose enterprise is due the immense foreign business in American postcards is Reinthal & Newman, 106–110 W. 29th St., New York, N.Y. No firm anywhere can surpass the work of this excellent and reliable house. Their subjects are particularly well selected and comprise the best works of such artists as Harrison Fisher, Wiederseim, Philip Boileau, and others in their class. These works are reproduced in colors according to the highest standard of the printer's art. Reinthal & Newman, however, are not merely fine art printers. They are practical business men as well. They have studied thoroughly the tastes of the American people. They know what will sell best.

Druggists, therefore, can buy the cards of this house with the full assurance that they will not be left as dead stock on their shelves. The selling of postcards, as all dealers know, can only become profitable from a quick turn over. The subjects of the postcards of this firm are so well selected and the work is of so high a character that they are bound to be popular wherever they are displayed. They make none of the cheap, tawdry, inartistic goods that go begging at "bargain" prices. They do not seek the trade of dealers whose customers want stuff of that kind. Their goods are meritorious, artistic and sell well everywhere.

They publish a beautiful illustrated catalogue of some of their cards, and these are distributed to dealers only, free upon request. Druggists should write to this firm and see the handsome line of goods they put out. They draw the best class of customers—those who have money to spend and who can appreciate good things in art. Send for one of their catalogues and get acquainted with this firm.

Aspects of Rarity, Price, and Collecting

Signed artist cards printed in America are for the most part inexpensive and plentiful. Many different cards can be obtained in Mint condition for $10 to $20. Some titles are rarer than others but are not necessarily more expensive. Certain cards printed in Europe but popular with American collectors, such as those of Alphonse Mucha and the Weiner Werkstätte, run into the hundreds of dollars for Mint examples and enjoy a strong market on both sides of the Atlantic. Reproductions have been made of many cards and are often offered, especially on the Internet, without mention that they are such. Some specific postcard sites do the same and offer them at cheap prices, often under $10—an unfortunate practice that can mislead beginners. The best plan is to buy from an established postcard dealer with an impeccable reputation.

Most collectors pick one or several artists as a specialty and endeavor to acquire as many different titles as possible. Many of the Reinthal & Newman cards that were copied by foreign artists are usually of lower printed quality. Raphael Tuck in London issued many original, high-quality cards signed by American artists. A collector of Philip Boileau cards, for example, will typically desire one of each Reinthal & Newman and Tuck title and may add here and there some copies of R&N cards by European publishers.

Mint condition is the usual desired grade for signed artist cards, but cards with nice postal cancellations on the reverse, without any ink or marks on the face, are also very desirable.

Harrison Fisher took the American Girl one step further and introduced her to all sorts of romantic situations. In one scene she might be dancing with a man as handsome as a prince, in another she is at home cuddling her newborn baby with her proud husband in the offing, and in still another she is playing tennis. In other scenes she rides in an open-top automobile, spends a day on the lake in a canoe, or, perhaps, gazes upward at a sprig of mistletoe.

In contrast to Gibson's aloof, unobtainable American Girl, Fisher's lady was romantic at times and involved in everyday life in other instances; she was the ideal woman one might desire for a spouse or a daughter-in-law. The Fisher Girl would make a fine member of any family. Fisher went from one success to another. Without doubt he was far and away the most successful illustrator of the American Girl, with his images appearing on just about every medium imaginable. A collection of Harrison Fisher images was every woman's dream scrapbook—how a romance should be conducted, but probably wasn't conducted often in real life.

Artist Philip Boileau introduced Peggy, copyrighted in 1903 and widely published as a print in 1904. This initiated his version of the American Girl—usually as a portrait and with an especially alluring, indeed somewhat seductive, appearance. Many collectors consider Boileau cards to be among the most attractive of the genre.

The "Fisher Girl" (above) was drawn as a romantic figure in everyday life, while the "Gibson Girl" was more aloof.

AMERICAN-BORN ARTISTS
Bertha E. Blodgett

Bertha Eveleth Jones was born in 1866. She married Edward Dwight Blodgett, three years her senior, and spent most of her life in Cortland, New York. The couple had a son and a daughter. Under her married name, Bertha E. Blodgett, she became a prominent illustrator for many magazines and books. She was a latecomer to the postcard field as her first cards were for Easter 1910. Her specialty was nicely dressed children, often depicted on holiday cards. Her cards are signed B.E.B.

Bertha E. Blodgett died in Cortland in 1941.

Easter greetings with two ladies by Blodgett. (AMP Co.)

Easter greetings with a lady and two ducks by Blodgett. (AMP Co.)

Blodgett postcards	Value, EF to Mint
Children	$3–$12

Philip Boileau

The postcards of Philip Boileau, comprising over 200 different images, represent the American Girl in very appealing poses. In news articles and other contemporary publicity these were often called "ideal heads."

Most postcards show head or head-and-shoulders portraits, well done and colorful. Many portraits were also used elsewhere, such as for covers of *The Saturday Evening Post*. Philip Boileau's American Girl kept her life a secret, a mystery. She was pretty, but what she liked to do in her leisure time or whether she ever picnicked in a meadow or drove a fast convertible was left to the imagination. A study of many, if not most, of Boileau's images will reveal the lady in question typically depicted with the top part of her eyeballs not visible, hidden behind her eyelids. This is a "signature" of Boileau portraits, and to our knowledge was not used to any wide extent by anyone else. Perhaps this ocular treatment gives the ladies some of their charm and appeal.

Some cards show one or more other people, and a few show objects, but most are portraits. Reinthal & Newman, of New York City, was the main publisher of Boileau's cards, assigning them numbers that were not continuous, interspersed with numbers for other artists. In our listing we add publishers' inventory numbers, such as for Reinthal & Newman. Some Reinthal & Newman cards are in the so-called Water Color Series, intended to be artistic but actually less satisfactory in appearance than the regular printed versions.

Much more elusive are Boileau images on postcards by other publishers such as Raphael Tuck, Osborne Calendar Co., and KNG, to mention just three. Advertising postcards range from slightly scarce (such as for the Metropolitan Insurance Co.), to rare (Flood & Conklin), to very rare (President Suspenders).

Boileau studied art for four years at the Academy in Milan, Italy. His mother, Susan Taylor Benton, was the youngest daughter of Missouri Senator Thomas Hart Benton.[4] His father, Philip Gauldree de Boileau, was in the French diplomatic service. After studying art, Boileau seems to have traveled throughout Europe and also to South America. He married, but his first wife, a Russian singer, died. He later moved to Philadelphia for a short time, during which he met Emily Gilbert, who was to serve as the model for most of his pictures, including Peggy, copyrighted on November 11, 1903.[5] This motif was issued on various prints, less so on postcards, and was well reviewed, creating a sensation at the time. They married in New York on October 9, 1907, when she was 21 and he was 43. In 1910 he bought a home in Douglaston, Queens, where he did his art and enjoyed gardening.[6]

Among Boileau's earliest postcards were those for the National Art Company, portraying different seasons.

Over a period of time, Boileau copyrighted 141 images, giving him control of their use. Even so, many of his postcard designs were counterfeited or copied by European publishers and used on postcards, usually of poor quality. Boileau died at the age of 53 on January 18, 1917, after catching cold from walking out scantily clad in the yard of his Douglaston home. His postcards were showcased by Dorothy Ryan in her highly acclaimed 1981 book, *Philip Boileau: Painter of Fair Women*.

Values for individual Boileau cards have a wide range depending on the series. Original collections with card titles are below.

Reinthal & Newman 94 Series. Value, EF to Mint: $12–$20

Description
At the Opera
Peggy
Schooldays
Sweethearts
Thinking of You
Twins

Reinthal & Newman 95 Series. Value, EF to Mint: $12–$20

Description
A Mischiefmaker
Anticipation
Forever
Little Lady Demure My Chauffeur
Nocturne
Passing Shadow
Spring Song
Today
Tomorrow
Winter Whispers
Yesterday

Reinthal & Newman 109 Series. Value, EF to Mint: $12–$20

Description
Evening and You
Girl in Black
Her Soul With Purity Possessed
In Maiden Meditation
My Moonbeam
My One Rose
Ready for Mischief
The Secret of the Flowers
True as the Blue Above
Twixt Doubt and Hope
Waiting for You
With Care for None

Reinthal & Newman 200 Series. Value, EF to Mint: $12–$20

No.	Description
204	Rings on Her Fingers
205	Question
205	Chrysanthemums
206	The Enchantress
207	A Hundred Years Ago
208	Miss America
209	Youth
210	Joyful Calm
211	Chums
212	Sweet Lips of Coral Hue
213	His First Love
214	For Him
215	I Wonder
282	Ready for the Meeting
283	Miss Pat
284	Old Home Farewell
285	A Serious Thought
286	I Don't Care
287	The Eyes Say No, The Lips Say Yes
294	Blue Ribbons
295	A Little Devil
296	Once Upon a Time
297	My Big Brother
298	My Boy
299	Baby Mine

"Twixt Doubt and Hope." (Reinthal & Newman 159)

Philip Boileau continued on next page

Philip Boileau, continued from previous page

Reinthal & Newman Water Color 369–380 Series. Value, EF to Mint: $15–$25

No.	Description
369	Vanity
370	Haughtiness
371	Purity
372	Loneliness
373	Happiness
374	Queenliness
375	Whisperings of Love (Annunciation)
376	Fairy Tales (Girlhood)
377	Parting of the Ways (Maidenhood)
378	Here Comes Daddy
379	Lullaby (Motherhood)
380	Don't Wake the Baby

Reinthal & Newman 445 Series. Value, EF to Mint: $12–$20

Description
Spring Song
Today
Tomorrow
Forever
My Chauffeur
Nocturne

Reinthal & Newman 474 Series. Value, EF to Mint: $12–$20

Description
Spring Song
A Passing Shadow
A Mischiefmaker
Anticipating
Yesterday
Little Lady Demure

"In Confidence." (Reinthal & Newman 760)

Reinthal & Newman 700 Series. Value, EF to Mint: $12–$20

No.	Description
750	Be Prepared
751	Absence Cannot Hearts Divide
752	A Neutral
753	The Chrysalis
754	Pensive
755	The Girl of the Golden West
756	Pebbles on the Beach
757	Snowbirds
758	Boy Scout's Motto
759	The Flirt
760	In Confidence
761	The Coming Storm

Reinthal & Newman 800 Series. Value, EF to Mint: $12–$20

No.	Description
820	Devotion
821	Golden Dreams
822	Every Breeze Carries My Thoughts
823	Priscilla
824	Fruit of the Vine
825	Butterfly
826	When Dreams Come True
827	Sister's First Love
828	The Little Neighbors
829	Peach Blossoms
830	When His Ship Comes In
831	Need a Lassie Cry

"A Bit of Heaven." (Reinthal & Newman 936)

Reinthal & Newman Water Color 936-941 Series. Value, EF to Mint: $15–$25

No.	Description
936	A Bit of Heaven
937	Chic
938	Have a Care
939	Just a Wearying for You
940	Sunshine
941	Sincerely Yours

Reinthal & Newman 2000 Series. Value, EF to Mint: $12–$20

No.	Description
2052	Thinking of You
2063	Chums
2064	His First Love
2065	Question
2066	From Him
2067	The Enchantress
2068	Joyful Calm

Unnumbered Series

Description
The Dreamy Hour
Out for Fun

Reinthal & Newman Copyright. Distributed by Novitas. Value, EF to Mint: $12–$20

Description
A Mischiefmaker
A Passing Shadow
Anticipating
Forever
Little Lady Demure
My Chauffeur
Nocturne
Spring Song
Today
Tomorrow
Winter Whispers
Yesterday

Reinthal & Newman Copyright. Distributed by J. Beagles & Co., London. Value, EF to Mint: $12–$20

Description
Little Lady Demure
Nocturne
Winter Whispers

Osborne Calendar Co. Value, EF to Mint: $50–$75

No.	Description
459	Winifred
940	A Fair Debutante
941	The Blonde
942	Phyllis
943	Pansies
944	True Blue
945	Army Girl
946	Day Dreams
947	Passing Shadow
948	The Girl in Brown
949	Goodbye
950	Passing Glance
951	A Winter Girl
1459	Rhododendrons
1489	At Play
1738	Virginia
2076	Suzanne
3525	Autumn
3625	Chrysanthemums

Philip Boileau continued on next page

Philip Boileau, continued from previous page

"Spring." (National Art 17)

National Art Company. Value, EF to Mint: $15–$30

No.	Description
17	Spring
18	Summer
19	Autumn
20	Winter
150	The Debutantes
160	Summer
161	Autumn
162	Spring
163	Winter
230	Spring
231	Summer
232	Autumn
233	Winter

Flood & Conklin. Value, EF to Mint: $15–$30

Description
Girl in Blue
The Girl in Brown
His First Love

Taylor, Platt. Value, EF to Mint: $35–$50

Description
Chrysanthemums
Poppies
Violets
Wild Roses

Other American issuers of Philip Boileau

Publisher	Description	Value, EF to Mint
Soapine Advertising Card Sparks Tailoring R&N	Tomorrow	$15–$30
A.P. Co. Advertising Card Holland Magazine (Ad on back)	Miss Pat	$15–$30
A.P. Co. Advertising Card Holland Magazine (Ad on back)	Ready for the Meeting	$15–$30
Metropolitan Life Advertising		$15–$30
Will's Embassy Pipe Tobacco Mixtures	Nocturne	$15–$30
Worthmore Tay Tailors, Chicago	Ready for Mischief	$15–$30
First Nat. Bank, Cripple Creek, Colorado	Virginia	$15–$30
N. Snyder Art	Spring Song	$15–$30
S.E. Perlberg Co., Tailors (Ad on back)	My Moonbeam	$15–$30
S.E. Perlberg Co., Tailors (Ad on back)	My One Rose	$15–$30
S.E. Perlberg Co., Tailors (Ad on back)	Secret of the Flowers	$15–$30
S.E. Perlberg Co., Tailors (Ad on back)	True as the Blue Above	$15–$30
S.E. Perlberg Co., Tailors (Ad on back)	Twixt Doubt and Hope	$15–$30
Wolfe & Co	Fancy Free (Silk)	$15–$30
Unsigned, Unknown Publisher(s)	Chrysanthemums (To My Sweetheart)	$25–$50
Unsigned, Unknown Publisher(s)	Poppie (A Greeting from St. Valentine)	$25–$50
Unsigned, Unknown Publisher(s)	A Token of Love (2 types exist)	$25–$50
Unsigned, Unknown Publisher(s)	Violets (A Gift of Love)	$25–$50
Unsigned, Unknown Publisher(s)	Wild Roses (To My Valentine)	$25–$50

Foreign publishers of Philip Boileau

Publisher	Description	Value, EF to Mint
Raphael Tuck, Connoisseur Series 2819	At Home	$50–$75
Raphael Tuck, Connoisseur Series 2819	Au Revoir	$50–$75
Raphael Tuck, Connoisseur Series 2819	Fancy Free	$50–$75
Raphael Tuck, Connoisseur Series 2819	I Am Late	$50–$75
Raphael Tuck, Connoisseur Series 2819	Paying A Call	$50–$75
Raphael Tuck, Connoisseur Series 2819	Summer Breezes	$50–$75
H & S, Germany	Au Revoir	$50–$75
H & S, Germany	At Home (white border)	$50–$75
H & S, Germany	Fancy Free (white border)	$50–$75
H & S, Germany	Paying A Call (white border)	$50–$75
H & S, Germany	Paying A Call (No border, reverse image)	$50–$75
H & S, Germany	I Am Late (Unsigned blue reverse image)	$50–$75

KNG, Germany, Value, EF to Mint: $50–$75

Publisher	Description
Schöne Frauen Series 8010	I Am Late (no border)
Schöne Frauen Series 8010	Paying a Call (no border)
Schöne Frauen Series 8010	Summer Breezes (no border)
Schöne Frauen Series 8010	Fancy Free
Schöne Frauen Series 8010	Au Revoir
Schöne Frauen Series 8010	At Home
Schöne Frauen Series 8011	I Am Late
Schöne Frauen Series 8011	Fancy Free
Schöne Frauen Series 8011	Paying a Call (white border)
Schöne Frauen Series 8011	Summer Breezes (white border)
Schöne Frauen Series 8012	I Am Late (reversed image, unsigned, untitled)
Schöne Frauen Series 8012	Fancy Free
Schöne Frauen Series 8013	I Am Late (reversed image, unsigned)
Schöne Frauen Series 8013	Paying A Call (reversed image, unsigned)
Schöne Frauen Series 8013	Summer Breezes (blue reversed image)

"Studie." (Friedrich O. Wolter 1058)

An unauthorized postcard using a Boileau image. (No imprint)

Other foreign publishers of Philip Boileau include:

Publisher	Description	Value, EF to Mint
Apollon Sophia	My Big Brother (No. 21)	$20–$30
B.K.W.I, German	Ready for Mischief	$20–$30
B.K.W.I, German	June, Blessed June	$20–$30
Diefenthal, Amsterdam	The Enchantress	$20–$30
Diefenthal, Amsterdam	Question	$20–$30
Diefenthal, Amsterdam	A Hundred Years Ago	$20–$30
Diefenthal, Amsterdam	C'est Moi	$20–$30
MEU	Untitled woman/ dark hat dated 1905	$20–$30
Albert Schweitzer, Germany H. S. Speelman (probably Dutch)	Eva same as Peggy	$20–$30
A.V.N. Jones & Co., London distributed by B.K.W.I (Series 500)	Spring	$10–$20
A.V.N. Jones & Co., London distributed by B.K.W.I (Series 500)	Summer	$10–$20
A.V.N. Jones & Co., London distributed by B.K.W.I (Series 500)	Fall	$10–$20
A.V.N. Jones & Co., London distributed by B.K.W.I (Series 500)	Winter	$10–$20
K.K. Oy, Finland	Baby Mine	$20–$30
K.K. Oy, Finland	Sister's First Love	$20–$30
K.K. Oy, Finland	Snowbirds	$20–$30
K.K. Oy, Finland	Here Comes Daddy	$20–$30
Weinthal Co., Rotterdam, Friedrich O. Wolter, Berlin	1058 Studie	$20–$30
Russian	Various cards, most probably not authorized	$25–$50

Frances Brundage

Early undivided back with girl. (Little Sunbeam Series. Tuck)

Halloween Greetings. (Halloween Series 120. Samuel Gabriel & Sons, Germany)

Merry Christmas. (Christmas Series 108. Samuel Gariel & Sons, Germany)

Frances Isabelle Lockwood was born in Newark, New Jersey, on June 28, 1854. Her aptly-named father, Rembrandt Lockwood, was a talented artist. Frances developed talent in art under her father, who disappeared from his family when she was 17. At that time Frances began to make her living as a professional illustrator. Her first published works were book illustrations for Louisa May Alcott and Shakespeare plays. She eventually wrote and illustrated her own children's books. Throughout her career, her images, primarily of sweet-faced children, graced multiple media including paper dolls, valentines, calendars, trade cards, and books, in addition to her postcards.

At age 32, Frances married William Tyson Brundage, also an artist. They produced several illustrations and books together, some containing both signatures. They resided in Washington, D.C., during most of the year and at the seaside on Cape Ann, Massachusetts, in the summer. Later in life they moved to Brooklyn, New York. William died in 1923. Frances survived him and passed away on March 28, 1937.

Frances's postcards were issued during the Golden Age under her married name. In the first decade of the twentieth century she produced cards for Raphael Tuck and other publishers including TSN (Theo. Stroefer of Nuremburg), Nister, and Wexel & Naumann, starting with undivided backs. Most were in a soft chromolithographic style and are difficult to find today in good condition. Among the hardest-to-find items are her Tuck Postcard Painting books, seldom found intact, and her unsigned advertising series for Indian Corn Flakes. Later in her career, she worked for Samuel Gabriel & Sons Company. These cards are seen much more frequently. While some are still of great quality, most collectors feel that they were more mass produced and lack the warmth of her earlier works. The Halloween and better patriotic cards are the more difficult of Gabriel Art cards to find. Her works also included novelty postcards, including hold-to-lights, real hair attached, squeaker, and mechanical cards.

Today Frances Brundage postcards are very collectible. There is not an all-encompassing, comprehensive checklist of the 1,000+ postcards issued by numerous publishers, both signed and unsigned. Prices listed are for cards that are in excellent condition, with no writing or marks on the image. Unusually scarce images may range higher.

Brundage postcards	Value, EF to Mint
Early undivided backs—Tuck signed and unsigned	$30–$35+
Early undivided backs—Other publisher signed and unsigned	$25–$35
Early undivided backs—TSN, large young children unsigned	$35–$40+
Tuck divided back—Ever Welcome, Little Treasure, Maidens Sweet Series etc.	$20–$30
Hold-to-lights	$25–$35
Mechanicals	$25–$35
Real hair	$30–$40
Squeakers	$20–$30
Gabriel Art—Small images, linen type finish	$3–$8
Gabriel Art—Thanksgiving, Easter, Christmas, etc.	$5–$12
Gabriel Art New Year's Day, better children images, Patriotic, St. Patrick's Day	$15–$20
Tuck and Gabriel Art Halloween	$20–$35
Later unsigned miscellaneous publishers	$5–$15
Santa Claus	$20–$30

Harrison Cady

Walter Harrison Cady was born on June 17, 1877, in Gardner, Massachusetts. As a teenager he was apprenticed to local painter Parker Perkins. Cady's first art in print was in *Harper's Young People* in 1894 and was signed Walter H. Cady. His father died when he was 18 and Harrison and his mother moved to New York City, where he worked for the *Brooklyn Eagle* for four years.

Cady became well known as an illustrator and cartoonist, famously for Thornton Burgess's creation Peter Rabbit, a character Cady illustrated for 28 years. He illustrated hundreds of other stories by Burgess and his postcards illustrated Peter Rabbit. Some of those were related to the Quaddy Club started by Peter Rabbit for his friends, mentioned on the backs of some cards. After 75 years in art, Cady died in 1970.

Cady postcards	Value, EF to Mint
Peter Rabbit	$20–$30
Other cards	$10–$15

Eugene Carr

Gene Carr's comic, "King." (Rotograph. 1906)

"What are you laughing at?" Signed Gene Carr. (Rotograph)

F. Earl Christy

Harvard. (College Series No. 93. Ullman)

Cornell. (E.A. Schwerdtfeger, Berlin)

Eugene Carr was born in New York City on January 17, 1881. He became a successful artist as a teenager and pursued this for the rest of his life. He specialized in children enjoying themselves, in addition to comic adult characters.

His postcard publishers included Rotograph and Bergman Publishing, who issued various series. Carr died in 1959.

Carr postcards	Value, EF to Mint
Children's Games series, each card	$2–$10
Comic series, each card	$2–$10
Easter series, each card	$2–$10
Fourth of July series, each card	$5–$15
Mosquito series, each card	$5–$15
St. Patrick's Day series, each card	$5–$15
Other Carr cards	$2–$10

F. Earl Christy was born in Philadelphia on November 13, 1883. He studied at the Pennsylvania Academy of Fine Arts and in the early 1900s endeavored to gain income by becoming a commercial illustrator with the support of his father. Within just a few years he became widely known for his work in different media, including postcards. He created versions of the American Girl using upscale or Ivy League-type ladies, well dressed and engaged in tennis, golf, automobile rides, and other pastimes. His first cards with this theme were published in 1905 by the U.S.S. Postcard Company. In later life he illustrated magazine covers, package containers, posters, advertisements, and other media. Christy died in Freeport, New York, in 1961. He was of no relation to fellow illustrator Howard Chandler Christy.

Christy's College Kings and Queens and related college series, published by Raphael Tuck and others (including Bien, Illustrated Postal Card, Platinachrome, Reinthal & Newman, Schwerdtfeger, Souvenir Postal Card, and Ullman), are especially sought and depict mirrored images of men and women, with a K or Q in the corner and an appropriate club, spade, heart, or diamond. Others by various publishers were variations on the popular American Girl theme, nearly always visually appealing and therefore widely collected today. *American Belles: A Collector's Guide to Earl Christy*, by Norman I. Platnick and Audrey V. Buffington, gives extensive information.

F. Earl Christy postcards	Value, EF to Mint
College Kings (Tuck)	$75–$90
College Queens (Tuck)	$75–$90
College series (Ullman)	$30–$45
Good Luck series (Tuck)	$5–$15
Path of Love series (R&N)	$10–$15
University Girls (Tuck)	$15–$20
University Girls with silk (Tuck)	$20–$30
University Girls, Williston Seminary (Tuck)	$100–$125
Other Christy girls, various	$5–$15

Howard Chandler Christy

Howard Chandler Christy was born in Morgan County, Ohio, on January 10, 1872, and received early schooling in Duncan Falls. He showed an early aptitude for drawing and studied at the Art Students League in New York City from 1890 to 1891, then at the National Academy under William Merritt Chase at his New York City studio and at the summer gathering Chase held for artists at Shinnecock Hills in Long Island.

Christy's career as an artist included postcards as a footnote. For magazines, books, posters, and other printed media he painted scenes from the Spanish-American War of 1898, statesmen, military figures and scenes, and others. His versions of the American Girl, known as the Christy Girl, showed a lady with strength, confidence, and ability, not in the romantic scenarios of Fisher, Boileau, and some others. *The American Girl*, a book published in 1906 by Moffat, Yard and Co., and *The Christy Girl*, The Bobbs-Merrill Co. the same year, introduced her to a wide audience.

His first postcards titled "The Christy Postcard" were in black and white, had undivided backs, and were published in 1906. Beginning in 1908 Moffat, Yard & Co. published many color cards showing the Christy Girl as a lady who enjoyed elements of society and recreation.

Christy died of a heart attack on March 3, 1952. Today his murals are an attraction at the Café des Artistes in New York City.

"Excess Baggage." (Moffat, Yard & Co. 1908)

"The American Queen." (Moffat, Yard & Co. 1908)

"A Fisherman's Luck." (Moffat, Yard & Co. 1908)

Howard Chandler Christy postcards	Value, EF to Mint
Christy Girl	$8–$15

Ellen H. Clapsaddle

Christmas card by artist Ellen H. Clapsaddle, with Santa Claus. (International Art Publishing Co. New York and Germany; printed in Germany)

"The Highest Expectations for Halloween." (International Art Publishing Co. New York and Germany; printed in Germany)

Ellen Hattie Clapsaddle was born on January 8, 1863, in South Columbia, New York, about 200 miles from New York City.[7] She became one of the most widely published postcard artists. Her subjects included children, holiday scenes, animals, and more, often in soft colors. The International Art Publishing Co., of New York, produced her images on two postcards. These were an immediate success. She sold more to that company and moved to New York City to be closer to their activities.

In the early twentieth century she spent much time in Germany, the main center for printing art postcards, representing International Art and the related Wolf Publishing Company. She also did work for Raphael Tuck of London.

She invested in Wolf Publishing and other postcard activities, devoting her life to the business. When the World War started in Europe, she remained there. The business of German exports to the United States ceased and Clapsaddle lost direction, suffering a mental breakdown. In the 1920s she came back to America and was supported by the Wolf brothers, with whom she had earlier been associated in publishing. In 1932 she was admitted to the Peabody Home near New York City, where she died on January 7, 1934. She never married. Most of her original art was scattered and lost during the World War.

Today Clapsaddle postcards, numbering in the thousands of varieties, are widely collected. A large display could be made of Halloween cards alone, her favorite holiday. Prices of cards vary widely. A fine book on them was created by Ellen H. Budd, *Ellen H. Clapsaddle Signed Post Cards: An Illustrated Reference Guide*, 1989.

Clapsaddle postcards	Value, EF to Mint
Christmas with Santa Claus, mechanical airplane	$40–$50
Christmas with Santa Claus	$10–$25
Flowers, leaves, sleds, other inanimate items	$2–$5
Halloween (mechanical, with African American child)	$250–$300
Halloween (mechanical, with white child)	$100–$150
Halloween	$20–$75
Valentine's Day	$5–$10

John Cecil Clay

"The Poppy" by John Cecil Clay. (Rotograph)

Born on April 2, 1875, in Ronceverte, West Virginia, John Cecil Clay studied art under Henry Siddons Mowbray at the Art Students League. Success attended his efforts, and he became well known as an illustrator for magazines and other publications. Attractive young women were a favorite subject. Detroit Publishing, Rotograph, and others issued postcards with his work. A set of 12 cards featuring the faces of women in flower blossoms is especially desired by collectors. Clay died in 1930.

Clay postcards	Value, EF to Mint
Women	$25-40
Other subjects	$15-$30

Jay Norwood Darling

Jay Norwood Darling, known as "Ding" Darling, was born on October 21, 1876, in Norwood, Michigan, giving rise to his middle name. In 1886 his family moved to Sioux City, Iowa. He entered Yankton College in South Dakota in 1894 and transferred to Beloit College in Wisconsin a year later. There he became editor of the yearbook and produced art, signing it D'ing, a contraction of his last name.

In the early twentieth century he created cartoons for newspapers in Des Moines and New York City. In 1924 he won a Pulitzer prize. After he retired from art work, he became interested in ecology and conservation. Today a wildlife refuge on Sanibel Island in Florida bears his name, as does the Lake Darling State Park in Iowa. He died on February 12, 1962.

Certain of his early illustrations are reproduced on postcards and can be found today, typically signed J.N. Darling or J.N. Ding.

Darling postcards	Value, EF to Mint
Cartoons	$10-$20

William Wallace Denslow

William Wallace Denslow, usually in print as W.W. Denslow, was born on May 5, 1856, in Philadelphia. Largely self-taught, he studied art for brief periods in New York City at the National Academy of Design and the Cooper Union. He entered the profession by creating images for theater posters, advertising, and newspapers, plus work with the revivalist Roycroft Press. Most notably, he illustrated Frank Baum's *The Wonderful World of Oz* and others of Baum's books. He became a man of wealth and acquired Bluck's Island in Bermuda,

crowning himself as King Denslow I. His personal life, with three wives and a like number of divorces and other problems, was very confused. He died on March 29, 1915, one of the relatively few postcard artists to die before the Golden Age ended.

Certain of his postcards feature teddy bears and advertise Teddy Bear Bread, while others illustrate holidays and other subjects.

Denslow postcards	Value, EF to Mint
Teddy Bear bread 1 and 2	$15-$20
Teddy Bear bread 3 and 4	$35-$40
Thanksgiving	$10-$15

Clare Victor Dwiggins

"Smile in the rain and see the rainbow" Signed Dwig.
(Series No. 109 Smiles. Tuck)

"Help Wanted." Signed Dwig. (Germany)

Clare Victor Dwiggins, who signed his art as "Dwig," was born in Wilmington, Ohio, on June 16, 1874. He was set on a career in architecture but made sketches on the side. When his work was published in the St. Louis *Post-Dispatch* and the *New York World* in 1897, he decided to become a professional cartoonist. For many years he created strips with various titles, the longest-running (1918–1931) being "Tom Sawyer and Huck Finn," which used Mark Twain's characters but not the text. Another long-running theme was about school kids. He died in a rest home in North Hollywood on October 26, 1958.

His art was published on postcards by several firms including Henry T. Coates & Co., J. Marks, Raphael Tuck, and the Cardinell-Vincent Company. Some were issued in sets of 12 to 24 cards.

Dwiggins postcards	Value, EF to Mint
Coates & Co.	$30–$40
Halloween	$20–$40
Widow's Wisdom series, each card.	$50–$75
Zodiac set by Tuck, unsigned, each card	$20–$35
Comic, various	$4–$20

H.G. Edwards

Scout Gum card No. 3.

H.G. Edwards was born in 1846. He died in 1924. Edwards provided art for the Boy Scout Gum series of numbered cards issued by the Scout Gum Co. of Rochester, New York. Each showed a Scout activity on the face and a number and description of the activity on the back. These were issued in 1914.

Values for individual H.G. Edwards cards in EF to Mint range from $15 to $25. The cards themselves were not numbered; the numbers listed here were assigned by authors Bowers and Martin for the convenience of collectors and historians.

No.	Description
1	Bugle Calls
2	The Diving Board
3	The Building of a Fire Without Matches
4	Blazing a Trail
5	Signaling
6	Hiding a Trail
7	Vaulting a Stream
8	Loading a Canoe
9	Toting
10	First Aid
11	Flag Salute
12	The Camp Fire

Harrison Fisher

Born in New York City on July 27, 1875, Fisher became a newspaper illustrator and later the leading proponent of the American Girl in the early twentieth century. His subjects were depicted in various aspects of life: being entertained by men, engaging in sports, and a famous six-card set showing the progression of love, titled "The Proposal," "The Trousseau," "The Wedding," "The Honeymoon, "First Evening in Their Own Home," and "Their New Love." These were incredibly popular with the public. Fisher died in 1934.

His most famous card was "The Kiss," the best-seller of any Golden Age issue according to some experts. In addition to being published in America, many of his subjects were pirated in European countries, often with somewhat casual, if not downright poor, printing quality, but appealing to Fisher specialists because of their elusive nature.

Today Harrison Fisher postcards are the most available of the signed artist series. They are widely collected by series, the Reinthal & Newman cards being the most popular. The pricing of his cards is quite unusual, perhaps even unique among signed artists. For certain varieties there seem to be more cards than there are collectors for them. Other varieties range from scarce to rare, but no detailed study has been made of their availability. On eBay and elsewhere, some cards such as (presumably) unauthorized European issues have been listed for well over $100 each. Some Reinthal sets and series of six cards, framed, have been listed for $75 or $100 or so. We give a default price of $8 to $15 for authorized Fisher cards published by Reinthal & Newman, as when they are available, most can be purchased within this range from professional postcard dealers. However, in the wide marketplace many can be purchased singly for less. A plan might be to acquire choice common cards inexpensively and then purchase the scarcer ones from established dealers who guarantee quality and offer a return privilege. Also, beware so-called "modern" Fisher cards, reprints that are not always identified as such on the Internet.

Individual Fisher cards in EF to Mint condition usually range from $8 to $25, with foreign reprints reaching up to $100+.

Detroit Publishing Co.

No.	Description
14040	I suppose you lost...
14041	It's just horrid...
14042	Wasn't there...
14043	And shall we never...
14044	I fear there is no hope....

Book Advertising Cards: (G&D, Dodd-Mead, etc.)

Description
Bill Tippers
Featherbone Girl
54-40 or Fight
Half A Rogue
Hungry Heart
Jane Cable
Jewel Weed
Man from Brodney's
My Lady of Cleeve
Nedra
One Way Out
A Taste of Paradise
Title Market
To My Valentine
Goose Girl

Armour & Co.

Country	Description
U.S.	(B&W), narrow size
Germany	(B&W), narrow size

Reinthal & Newman Unnumbered Series

Description
After the Dance
Critical Moment
Motor Girl
Ready for the Run
Ruth
A Tennis Champion
Winter Girl

"The Kiss," likely the most widely distributed of all signed artist cards.

101 Series (12)

Description
American Beauties
Anticipation
Beauties
Danger
A Fair Driver
Odd Moments
Old Luck
He's Only Joking
His Gift
The Kiss
Lost?
Oh! Promise Me
Song of the Soul
Two Up

Harrison Fisher, continued on next page

Harrison Fisher, continued from previous page

123 Series (6)

Description
Making Hay
A Modern Eve
Taking Toll
You Will Marry a Dark Man
Fudge Party
In Clover

"The Rose." (No. 181)

180–191 Series

No.	Description
180	Well Protected
181	The Rose
182	Miss Santa Claus
183	Miss Knickerbocker
184	Following the Race
185	Naughty, Naughty!
186	Proposal
187	Trousseau
188	Wedding
189	Honeymoon
190	First Evening...
191	Their New Love

"Leisure Moments." (No. 199)

192–203 Series

No.	Description
192	Cherry Ripe
193	Undue Haste
194	Sweethearts
195	Vanity
196	Beauties
197	Lips for Kisses
198	Bewitching Maiden
199	Leisure Moments
200	And Yet Her Eyes...
201	Roses
202	In the Toils
203	Maid to Worship

"Good Night." (No. 259)

252–263 Series

No.	Description
252	Dreaming of You
253	Luxury
254	Pals
255	Homeward Bound
256	Preparing to Conquer
257	Love Lyrics
258	Tempting Lips
259	Good Night
260	Bows Attract Beaus
261	Girlie
262	Beauty and Value
263	A Prairie Belle

"Gathering Honey."
(Reinthal & Newman Water Color Series 392)

Water Color 381–392 Series

No.	Description
381	All's Well
382	Two Roses
383	Contentment
384	Not Yet – But Soon
385	Smile Even if it Hurts
386	Speak!
387	Welcome Home
388	A Helping Hand
389	Undecided
390	Well Guarded
391	My Lady Waits
392	Gathering Honey

"Behave!" (No. 302)

300 Series

No.	Description
300	Auto Kiss
301	Sweethearts Asleep
302	Behave!
303	All Mine!
304	Thoroughbreds
305	Laugh is on You

"All Mine!" (No. 303)

Harrison Fisher, continued on next page

Harrison Fisher, continued from previous page

400–423 Series

No.	Description
400	Looking Backward
401	Art and Beauty
402	Chief Interest
403	Passing Fancies
404	Pink of Perfection
405	He Won't Bite
406	Refreshments
407	Princess Pat
408	Fine Feathers
409	Isn't He Sweet?
410	Maid at Arms
411	He Cometh Not
412	Can't You Speak?
413	What Will She Say?
414	Music Hath Charm
415	Do I Intrude
416	My Queen
417	My Lady Drives
418	Ready and Waiting
419	Parasol
420	Tempting Lips
421	Mary
422	Courting Attention
423	My Pretty Neighbor

600–617 Series

No.	Description
600	Winter Sport
601	Winter Whispers
602	A Christmas Him
603	A Sprig of Holly
604	Snow Birds
605	A Christmas Belle
606	Serenade
607	Secret
608	Good Morning, Mama
609	A Passing Glance
610	A Fair Exhibitor
611	Paddling Their Own Canoe
612	Tea Time
613	Favorite Pillow
614	Don't Worry
615	June
616	Sketching
617	Chocolate

Water Color 700–705 Series, Senses

No.	Description
700	First Meeting
701	Falling In Love
702	Making Progress
703	Anxious Moments
704	To Love and Cherish
705	Greatest Joy Common Sense

"Looks good to me." (No. 765)

762–773 Series

No.	Description
762	Alone at Last
763	Alert
764	Close to Shore
765	Looks Good To Me
766	Passers By
767	At the Toilet
768	Drifting
769	Her Favorite Him
770	Third Party
771	Inspiration
772	Dangers of the Deep
773	Farewell

800 Series

No.	Description
819	Here's Happiness

"Over the Teacup." (No. 867)

No.	Description
832	Wireless
833	Neptune's Daughter
834	Her Only Pebble
839	A Love Score
840	Spring Business
841	King of Hearts
842	Fair and Warmer
843	Baby Mine
844	Compensation
845	Sparring for Time
846	Confidence
847	Her Future
848	Day Dreams
849	Muriel
856	Song of the Soul
860	By Right of Conquest
861	Evening Hour
862	Caught Napping
863	A Novice
864	Winners
865	A Midsummer Reverie
866	When the Leaves Turn
867	Over the Teacup
868	A Ripening Bud
869	I'm Ready
870	Reflections
871	Peggy
872	Penseroso
873	Girl He Left Behind
874	A Spring Blossom
875	A Study in Contentment
876	A Lucky Beggar
877	Roses

970–979 Series

No.	Description
970	Chums
971	Cynthia
972	A Forest Flower
973	Dancing Girl
974	Each Stitch a Prayer
975	Sailor Maid
976	My Man
977	My Hero
978	Her Heart's in the Service
979	Somewhere in France

Katharine Gassaway

"Mon dieu." (Rotograph)

Katharine Gassaway, after her marriage known in art as Miss Katharine Pierson, was born in Maryland circa 1873. She illustrated many books and created other art. She designed cards for Raphael Tuck (signed and unsigned), National Art, Rotograph, and Ullman Manufacturing Company in the early twentieth century. Most of her cards feature children with big, expressive eyes and round faces. In 1930 she had an art studio in Manhattan, went under the name of Miss Katharine Pierson, and was widowed. She had a daughter, Pauline.

Gassaway postcards	Value, EF to Mint
Children	$5–$10
Other cards	$2–$10

Charles Dana Gibson

"Helen." (Pictorial Comedy Series. James Henderson & Sons, London)

"The Eternal Question."

Charles Dana Gibson was born in Roxbury, Massachusetts, on September 14, 1867. When he was young, he moved with his family to Flushing, New York. After finishing school, he attended the Art Students League, where Frederick Remington was also enrolled. At the age of 19 he sold his first artwork to *Life* magazine, a journal of satire and society with no connection to the later photograph-filled magazine of the same name. In 1898 he created the "Gibson Girl" and became famous as a result. This gave rise to the popularity of the American Girl as later interpreted by many other artists.

Gibson's forte was pen and ink drawings. Typically, the Gibson Girl would be depicted as elegant and at the same time quite distant emotionally, while a swain in the background was doing his best to attract her attention or to have her accept some small favor or gift.

Later, he accepted an offer of $100,000 from *Collier's* magazine to create a thousand drawings in four years. His postcards are black-and-white images from *Life* magazine and were issued by Detroit Publishing in the 10,000 series beginning in 1901. James Henderson & Sons, London, published his postcards as well. Later, some cards featured images from *Collier's*. His work appeared in books, advertisements, and other media.

Gibson's sketches of the Gibson Girl were widely reproduced in magazines, on postcards, in prints, and in bound books. He seems to have hit his peak about 1907, by which time he had amassed a comfortable fortune and was a nationally known artist. Even today, the Gibson Girl is a familiar phrase. During the height of his career he lived in New Rochelle, New York, a suburban retreat for many artists, showmen, and others. He owned 700 Acre Island off the coast of Islesboro, Maine. Unfortunately, Gibson put his life savings in the Knickerbocker Trust Company, which failed in the financial panic of 1907, and he was wiped out. Although he created sketches for some years thereafter, he never regained his former popularity. Instead, the laurels had passed to others.

Gibson died in New York City on December 23, 1944.

Gibson postcards	Value, EF to Mint
Women and society	$8–$15

H.B. Griggs

"May the Easter Bunny bring you joy." Signed HBG. (L & E Series 254. Germany)

"May Your Blessings, Like Thanksgiving Turkeys, Come Home to Roost." Signed H.B. Griggs. (L & E Series 2233. Germany)

The biography of H.B. Griggs has not been located, and some authors (Miller and Nicholson) have wondered if Briggs is a man or a woman. What is known is that over 500 HBG and two H.B. Griggs signed cards were printed in Germany as early as 1907 and were published by Leubrie and Elkus of New York, including in series.

Griggs postcards	Value, EF to Mint
Suffrage	$30–$40
Holidays	$2–$10
Heart-design, African American children	$10–$20
Heart-design, white children	$5–$10
Other cards	$2–$10

Bessie Pease Gutmann

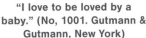

"I love to be loved by a baby." (No, 1001. Gutmann & Gutmann, New York)

"Rosebuds." (Gutmann & Gutmann, New York, 1911)

Bessie Collins Pease was born in Philadelphia on April 8, 1876. After graduating from high school she studied at the Philadelphia School of Design for Women, followed by the New York School of Art and the Art Students League, through about 1901. She illustrated children's books and other items, including work beginning in 1903 for Gutmann & Gutmann, Inc., New York art publishers. In 1906 she married Hellmuth Gutmann, a principal in the firm.

She became well known as an artist for magazine covers, books, and other publications, working in media including watercolor and oil. She specialized in infants and children, often modeled by her children: Alice, Lucille, and John. In the 1920s interest in those subjects faded, and she did other work until about 1947, when she retired due to failing eyesight. She died on September 29, 1960.

She created fewer than 100 postcards. Publishers included Reinthal & Newman (five sets of four cards), Brown & Bigelow (calendar cards), and American sellers of cards printed in Germany. Enough cards survive from this relatively small output that they are widely collected today.

Guttmann postcards	Value, EF to Mint
Infants and children, various	$10–$40

Margaret Gebbie Hays

"Wishing You a Merry Christmas."
(No publisher or country. Postmarked 1908)

Margaret Gebbie Hays was born in Philadelphia, the daughter of a highly successful art publisher. She was the older sister of Grace Gebbie Wiederseim Drayton (see Wiederseim listing). Margaret wrote the verses and texts for many of her sister's works. Margaret was schooled at home by governesses until she was 13, at which time she went to the Convent of Notre Dame boarding school in the same city. She married architect Frank Allison Hays. The couple had two children, Mary Anthony and William Anthony.

Margaret wrote and illustrated stories for children, including the Jennie and Jack, Kiddie Land, Kaptin Kiddo, Kido and Puppo, Polly Pig-tail, and other series; *Vegetable Verselets*; and more work for magazines and books, including toy books for E.P. Dutton & Co.

Hays postcards	Value, EF to Mint
Little children	$10–$15
Valentines	$10–$15
Other cards	$5–$10

Maud Humphrey

"Autumn" by Maud Humphrey.
(No. 595)

"May Time" by Maud Humphrey. (R.L. Conweil, New York)

Rally Day card attributed to Maud Humphrey. (Heidelberg Press)

Maud Humphrey was born in Rochester, New York, on March 30, 1868. She became interested in art at an early age, and she studied at the Art Students League in New York City and in Paris at the Académie Julian. In 1898 she married Dr. Belmont DeForest Bogart (1868–1934). The couple had one son and two daughters.

Maud won a Louis Prang & Co. competition for Christmas card designs, catalyzing her career as highly successful commercial artist and illustrator. She often used as a model her young son, who became famous as screen actor Humphrey Bogart. From the 1890s into the 1920s she illustrated many magazines, more than 20 books, and many calendars and cards. At one time she was earning over $50,000 a year. She was active in the suffrage movement. She died on November 22, 1940, and was interred at the Forest Lawn cemetery in Glendale, California.

Most of her postcards are unsigned. These were issued by various publishers and usually feature children. A professional postcard dealer is your best choice for this.

Humphrey postcards	Value, EF to Mint
Children, signed	$150–$200
Children, unsigned	$10–$25

Edwin H. Kiefer

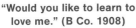

"Would you like to learn to love me." (B Co. 1908)

"When your heart aches, just think of me." (No. 125B. B Co., G. New York. 1909)

Edwin H. Kiefer was born in Port Huron, Michigan, on August 28, 1860. He studied at Berlin School of Design in Germany and in Paris. His postcards show the American Girl. Exhibitions of his work included at the Paris Salon in 1897 and 1898 and at the Detroit Institute of Arts in 1913. His art was varied and ranged from portraits to landscapes. Kiefer died in Detroit on April 24, 1931.

Kiefer postcards	Value, EF to Mint
Women	$10–$25

Alonzo Kimball

"Telltale lines" by Kimball. (Reinthal & Newman)

"A love knot" by Kimball. (Reinthal & Newman)

Alonzo Myron Kimball, known as Alonzo Kimball, was born in Green Bay, Wisconsin, in 1847. His art training included attending the Art Students League. As a commercial illustrator he created images for books and other publications. He died in Evanston, Illinois, in 1923. His postcards, published by Reinthal & Newman, bear a close resemblance to those of Harrison Fisher.

Kimball postcards	Value, EF to Mint
Miscellaneous	$5–$15

Hamilton King

Hamilton King's Cape May Girl.

Hamilton King was born in 1871. He is best remembered today for illustrating the "Coca-Cola Girls" calendars from 1910 to 1913. His Hamilton King Girls featured society women from different holiday locations such as Palm Beach, Bar Harbor, Cape May, and Manhattan Beach. King also illustrated many magazines, advertisements, calendars, candy boxes, motion picture and stage star publicity items, and other media and sheet music for Ziegfeld Follies, among other work. In 1903 he worked on a project to illustrate one girl from each of the states in the Union using living models. He spent much of his life in New York and Maine. King died in 1952.

King postcards	Value, EF to Mint
Coca-Cola Girl	$500+
Coca-Cola Motor Girl	$1,500–$2,000
Hamilton King Girl	$10–$20

Winsor McCay

"Valentine Greetings," a Little Nemo card by Winsor McCay. EF to Mint: $8+

Zenas Winsor McCay, who dropped his first name, may have been born in Spring Lake, Michigan, on September 26, 1869, but records are conflicting. He developed a talent for drawing and acting at an early age, and as a young man he made posters for shows and other events and acted on stage in Morton's Dime Museum. In 1903 he joined the *New York Herald*, after which he created comics for that paper and others. His most famous strip was "Little Nemo in Slumberland," which illustrated a young boy and the adventures he had in his dreams. Today he is best remembered for his animated silent film "Gertie the Dinosaur." His career in this and other films was important in that era. He would sit at the side of the stage during shows and in rapid succession make sketches of the action. His work with cartoon animation

was unmatched until the 1920s. He was a strong influence for Walt Disney. McCay died on July 26, 1934, with his wife Theresa, children, and son-in-law at his side.

Among American postcard illustrators, McCay's career was one of the most successful and diverse.

McCay postcards	Value, EF to Mint
Little Nemo (Tuck)	$20–$30
Valentines (Tuck)	$20–$30
Other cards	$10–$30

George McManus

A George McManus postcard featuring the Lexington Hotel. EF to Mint: $8+

George McManus was born in St. Louis on January 23, 1884. His talent as an artist was apparent at a young age. His first comic strip, "Alma and Oliver," was a great success. After winning $3,000 at a racetrack he headed for New York City, where he found ready employment in drawing comics. He was best known for his Jiggs and Maggie "Bringing Up Father" comic strip about Irish immigrants, a syndicated favorite for many years. He later moved to Hollywood, where he lived for the rest of his life. He died in Santa Monica on October 22, 1954, and was interred in Woodlawn Cemetery in the Bronx, New York City.

McManus postcards	Value, EF to Mint
Bringing Up Father card	$15–$25
Other cards	$8–$20

Rose O'Neill

"Love me and the world is mine!" Two Kewpies. (Klever Kard, Campbell Art Co., Elizabeth, New Jersey)

Traveling Kewpie. (Klever Kard, Campbell Art Co., Elizabeth, New Jersey)

Rose Cecil O'Neill was born on June 25, 1874, in Wilkes-Barre, Pennsylvania, a first cousin of Robert Robinson (see below listing). When she was three, the family moved to Nebraska, where she spent the rest of her youth and developed a talent for art. She took first prize in a drawing competition held by the *Omaha World* when she was 13. From that point she was successful in selling much of her art. Her father, a traveling bookseller who was experiencing hard times, took her to New York City, stopping at the World's Columbian Exposition on the way. In the city she lived in a convent, the Sisters of St. Regis. Her father returned to the Midwest and set up a homestead claim in Missouri.

In 1896 she married Gray Latham, who turned out to be a roving playboy. The couple divorced in 1901. The next year she married Harry Leon Wilson, an assistant editor at *Puck*, one of her art clients. She illustrated some of his novels and other works. They divorced in 1907.

Rose became famous in 1909 when her Kewpies cartoon characters made their debut in the *Ladies' Home Journal*. Kewpies were widely reproduced, including in prints, dolls, and postcards, and made her wealthy. O'Neill was the inspiration for the song, "The Rose of Washington Square." A millionaire, she led a bohemian lifestyle in New York City and had a residence there, one in Connecticut, one in Bonniebrook in Missouri, and another on a Caribbean island. Carabas Castle, her Connecticut mansion, had a boiler cast in the shape of a Kewpie. She also created Scootles and Kuddle Kewpie dolls and was important in the women's suffrage movement. After the World War she went to Paris, where she studied sculpture under Auguste Rodin and became well known in that field.

O'Neill returned to the United States in 1927 and set up a home in Missouri. During the Depression and the 1940s most of her money was dissipated by hangers-on, supporting other members of her family, and other incidents. There was no longer a market for her Kewpies and other work. She died of heart failure in Springfield, Missouri, on April 6, 1966.

O'Neill postcards	Value, EF to Mint
Advertising, miscellaneous	$75–$250
Birth announcement	$125–$150
African American characters (Tuck)	$30–$60
Ice cream	$125–$150
Kewpie Klever Kards	$35–$45
Kewpies, Gibson	$15–$25
Kewpies, Gross	$75–$100
Klever Kard, Miniature	$40–$50
Pickings from Puck	$85–$150
Suffrage Klever Kard	$100–$125
Suffrage, four babies	$150–$200
Suffrage, Spirit of '76	$125–$150

Frederick Burr Opper

"If mother could only see me now!" (Boston Sunday American)

"Happy Hooligan." (Valentine Post Card Series No. 11. Tuck)

Frederick Burr Opper, born in Madison, Ohio, in 1857, ranks as one of the oldest artists whose work was showcased on postcards of the Golden Age. He left school at age 14 to work for the local newspaper. When he was 19 he moved to New York City, where in time he created cartoons for many magazines. His most famous character, Happy Hooligan, was created in 1900. He illustrated books and magazines. Many of his various cartoons were published as postcards, often by newspapers. He suffered from failing eyesight in the 1930s and retired to his home in New Rochelle. His last work was done in 1934. Opper died on August 28, 1938.

Opper postcards	Value, EF to Mint
Happy Hooligan	$5–$10
Transformations	$2–$10
Other comic cards	$2–$10

Richard F. Outcault

"Buster Brown and His Bubble" "Black or White." No. 3 with the Yellow Kid and many African American characters depicted in stereotypes of the time. (Souvenir Post Card Co., New York, 1903)

"Buster Brown and His Bubble," No. 6 with the Yellow Kid. (Souvenir Post Card Co., New York, 1903)

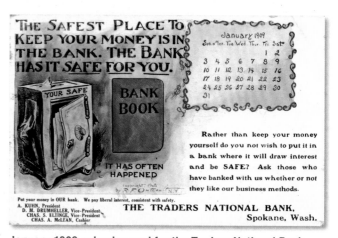

January 1909 calendar card for the Traders National Bank, Spokane, Washington.

October 1926 calendar card with Tige. Printing error showing the 1906 calendar; early undivided back.

October 1914 calendar card with Halloween motif.
(L. & E. Serie 2263)

Advertising postcard for Egg-O-See breakfast cereal.
(Kaufmann & Strauss, New York, 1903)

December 1909 calendar card with Santa Claus, for the
Rockford Watch Co.

"I have just been thinking" comic card with Tige. (Kaufmann
& Strauss, New York, 1904; issued by postcard club per right
border notation)

"There's no place like home" comic card. (J. Ottman, New York, 1905)

"The best of friends must part" comic card.
(J. Ottman, New York, 1906)

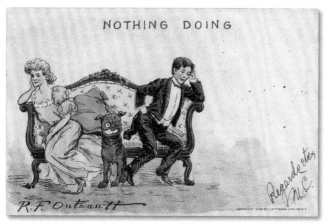

"Nothing Doing" comic card with Tige.
(J. Ottman, New York, 1906)

"Something Doing" comic card with Tige.
(J. Ottman, New York, 1906)

Valentine card by Outcault. (New Outcault Series Valentine Postcards No. 7. Tuck, London, 1908)

Richard Fenton Outcault was born on January 14, 1863, in Lancaster, Ohio. His birth last name was Outcalt; he later added a second u. From 1878 to 1881 he studied at McMicken University's School of Design in Cincinnati. After graduating he painted scenes on the front of safes for the Hall Safe & Lock Company. In the late 1880s he was employed by Thomas Edison to paint exhibits, including going to Paris in 1889 for the Exposition Universelle (famous for the Eiffel Tower).

He created humorous cartoons for *Judge* and *Life*, then Joseph Pulitzer's *New York World* newspaper. In the *World*, a single-panel cartoon, "Hogan's Alley," featured the Yellow Kid character. The term "yellow journalism" arose from this, meaning sensational and inaccurate reporting. Outcault and the Yellow Kid moved to William Randolph Hearst's *New York Journal*. He is best remembered for his Buster Brown character, a playful young lad, and his gruff-appearing dog Tige, introduced in 1902. The Buster Brown and His Bubble series was copyrighted in 1903 and is known with undivided and divided backs, indicating popularity over multiple years. In 1904 the Brown Shoe Co. of St. Louis arranged to use the Buster Brown name for a line of shoes introduced at the Louisiana Purchase Exposition that year. In this era Outcault licensed his characters to various companies and in 1905 reportedly earned $75,000 a year (more from royalties than from drawing) and had two secretaries to help with the business.

In 1906 Buster Brown calendar postcards were introduced and continued for a time. R.F. Outcault made calendar postcards for others as well, including many retailers and products. Most of these were in the cartoon style, but there were exceptions. Cards showing Buster Brown and Tige are sometimes titled, and the advertising message begins with, "Resolved that.…" Nearly all cards had a calendar panel for the month and year. These were issued by dozens of different firms. Other cards featured comic situations. His output was wonderfully diverse and often humorous and included cards for several holidays. Outcault's signature is very prominent on most of his cards.

Used or unused, most Outcault cards show signs of wear and handling today, reflecting that their early owners enjoyed viewing them many times. Typically they have the imprint of Outcault Advertising Co. Those issued for the Rockford Watch Company were made in particularly large quantities.

Outcault cards featuring Buster Brown and Tige are valued more highly across the board than his other cards. A wide selection of his cards is illustrated here.

Outcault postcards*	Value, EF to Mint
Buster Brown set for various firms each card	$30–$50
Buster Brown with the Yellow Kid	$50–$100
Rockford Watch Co. 1909–1910	$25–$50
Miscellaneous cards, mostly comic	$10–$50

* Add 50 percent for Santa Claus.

Robert Robinson

Baseball catcher. (Robert Robinson Series, Subject 210. Edward Gross Co.)

Boy with apples. (Robert Robinson Series, Subject 208. Edward Gross Co.)

Robert Bernard Robinson was born in Wilkes-Barre, Pennsylvania, on June 3, 1886. Rose O'Neill (see previous listing) was a first cousin. Early in his childhood he developed an interest in art, and by age 11 he was making sketches. Robinson secured a Bullseye camera outfit, took pictures, and developed film, creating some trick overlays and comic images. In the early twentieth century he got a job with Macy's and studied art under William Merritt Chase. He then studied at the Pennsylvania Academy of Fine Arts and, later, under Howard Pyle.

Robinson maintained a small studio in Wilkes-Barre, which he visited only occasionally. By 1908 he had sold art for magazine covers. From this point he did many magazine illustrations including for *Saturday Evening Post*, *American Druggist*, *Country Gentleman*, *Harper's Weekly*, *Leslie's*, *Farm Journal*, *Sea Stories*, *American Magazine*, *Adventure*, *Popular*, *Albatross*, *Life*, *Judge*, *Pictorial Review*, and *Motor*, among others. Having achieved financial comfort, he went to Europe for much of 1912 to 1914, where he studied in Paris at the École de Grande Chaumiere and Académie Moderne. In June 1914, two months before the outbreak of war in Europe, he returned to America and re-established his studio in Wilkes-Barre. On June 16, 1916, he married Ellen Scranton Stites. The union produced two children. After a highly successful career Robert Robinson passed away on December 6, 1952. In retrospect Robinson was one of the most consistently financially stable American illustrators and had a very fine personal life.

Twelve postcards of his art were published by Edward Gross and are fairly scarce today. The art was taken from *Saturday Evening Post* and *Sunday Magazine* covers. For reference see *Robert Robinson: American Illustrator*, Q. David and Christine Bowers, 1981. A set of 12 cards was advertised for $600 by Sandy Millns in 2018.

Robinson postcards	Value, EF to Mint
Magazine cover art card	$15–$30

Charles M. Russell

"Lassoing a bull." (W.T. Ridgley Press, Great Falls, Montana)

"Western stage coach." (No imprint)

Charles Marion Russell was born in Missouri on March 19, 1864. As a child he became interested in art and drew sketches and modeled animals in class. He also developed an interest in the Wild West, ranching, cowboy culture, and other aspects, which determined the course of his life. At age 16 he went to Montana to work on a sheep ranch. He remained in that state for the rest of his life, except for a brief return to his family in Missouri in 1882.

While not in the outdoors he spent time making watercolor paintings of ranch life, wild animals, and other topics of the area. In 1896 he married Nancy, age 18. She took a great interest in his art and was primarily responsible for the fame he acquired in the early twentieth century. The timing was perfect, for there was a great interest in the West, Indians, and related Western themes in books, magazines, posters, and films. He also developed close ties with Blackfoot Indians. During his career he produced about 4,000 works of art in watercolor, oil, and other media. Russell died on October 24, 1926.

Postcards of Russell's Western art were published by the regional firms of Glacier Stationery Co., Charles E. Morris, and W.T. Ridgley Press. Modern reproductions are common and of little value.

Russell postcards	Value, EF to Mint
Western scenes	$4–$12

Samuel L. Schmucker

Frog and gremlin attributed to Schmucker. (Detroit Publishing, 1907)

Lady in gown attributed to Schmucker. (Detroit Publishing)

Halloween card attributed to Schmucker. (John Winsch)

Halloween card with child, pumpkin, and cat attributed to Schmucker. (John Winsch)

Halloween Faces card attributed to Schmucker. (John Winsch)

Halloween Gambols card attributed to Schmucker. (John Winsch)

Samuel Loren Schmucker was born on February 20, 1879, in Reading, Pennsylvania. As a youth he contracted polio, which crippled his right arm for the rest of his life. He studied at the Pennsylvania Academy of Fine Arts from 1896 to 1899 and later under Howard Pyle until 1900. In the meantime, the Reading Art Club elected him as a director in January 1899. In December 1901 an exhibition of his work and three other students was held at the T-Square Club in Philadelphia. A report of the event noted: "Mr. Schmucker's talent takes a curative form. He has invented a very decorative means of expression in his burnt paper compositions with their rich tints and application of gold ornament. The young man also does book plates and illustrations with a fine fancifulness."[8]

In the early twentieth century he met and married Katharine Rice, then a student at the Pennsylvania Academy of Fine Arts. He later did a wide range of commercial art, including fashion illustrations. In 1907 he set up a studio at 737 Walnut Street in Philadelphia. The full extent of his postcard images is not known, as

most of his works were unsigned and some attributions are speculative. In the early 1910s he and his wife lived in Wilmington, Delaware, Katharine's home town. They then moved to New York City and lived at 129 West 45th Street.

He is thought to have produced many watercolor paintings for postcards for the Detroit Publishing Company circa 1907. His greatest fame came from the illustrious images published by John O. Winsch in the era from 1910 to 1915, with most cards issued early in this range. These are unsigned and by style are *attributed to Schmucker*. Some may be by other artists. Winsch copyrighted the designs. Other cards were signed with his name or with his initials, SLS. He also created designs for the National Art Company and Raphael Tuck, the extent of which is not known. On September 4, 1921, he died of heart failure in Southhold, New York. *Samuel L. Schmucker: The Discovery of His Lost Art*, by Dorothy Ryan and Jack Davis, 2005, includes much information about his life art.

Schmucker-attributed postcards published by Winsch*	Value, EF to Mint
Cards with full silk	$8–$30
Cards with silk inserts	$8–$20
Childhood Days	$60–$75
Drinkers	$125+
Halloween	$60–$400
Land Birds	$125+
Letters from Home	$40–$50
Mermaid's Lovers	$150+
Mottoes	$125+
New Year's Day	$5–$40
Smoker's Dreams	$125+
St. Patrick's Day	$8–$40
Winsch Girl	$10–$40
Other holidays	$6–75

* Also see John O. Winsch below.

Cobb Shinn

Hettie, by Cobb Shinn. (No imprint)

Shinn postcards	Value, EF to Mint
Charlie Chaplin card	$5–$8
Ford Motor Co. card	$5–$8
Riley Roses card	$5–$8
Sepia Wooden Shoe Dutch series card	$5–$8
Romantic subject	$5–$8
Tin Lizzie card	$5–$8
Other cards	$5–$25

Jessie Willcox Smith

"Among the Poppies." (Series 100. Reinthal & Newman)

Conrad Shinn, nicknamed Cobb, was born in Fillmore, Indiana, in 1887. He moved to Indianapolis, where he took art classes at the local YMCA. In 1907 he signed as a student in the John Herron School of Art and studied under William M. Allison and William Forsyth.

In his art career he created comic strips and other art, including for children's and other books, the latter notably including *Little Black Sambo*. In the 1920s he had an office at 23 Liberty Building in Indianapolis. Some art works were signed Cobb X. Shinn, Cobb X, or C.X.S. He also created what he called "freak photographs" not related to postcards, such as of a turtle drinking milk.

His work on postcards appeared as early as 1907 and in time included Riley Roses, Charlie Chaplin, and Tin Lizzie sets. A set of cards for the Ford Motor Co. was printed by the Commercial Colortype Co. His romantic subject cards are not as popular as those of most other artists. He also signed some postcards as "Tom Yad."

He served in the Army in France during the World War and returned to Indianapolis in 1919. By that time the market for original art on postcards was nearly extinct, so he illustrated books, clip art, and other products. Some of his art was used as fillers in newspapers nationwide and were listed in his "Stock Cutalog." In 1923 he married Ramona Dowlin. In the 1930s he photographed models for use in advertising illustrations. He died in Indianapolis in January 1951.

"Five o'clock tea." (Series 100. Reinthal & Newman)

Jessie Willcox Smith was born on September 6, 1863, in Philadelphia, the daughter of an investment banker. At age 16 she was sent to Cincinnati to complete her education while living with cousins. She studied to be a teacher but found that due to back ailments she had difficulty bending down to kindergarten children in her first class. She then attended art classes and realized that she had ambition and talent for this work.

Her next stop was to attend the Philadelphia School of Design for Women, followed by studies at the Pennsylvania Academy of the Fine Arts under Thomas Eakins and Thomas Anshutz. Soon she was illustrating for magazines and other publications while continuing her studies under Howard Pyle and others. In the late 1890s she shared a Philadelphia studio with two other artists, Elizabeth Shippen Green and Violet Oakley. In 1897 she and Oakley illustrated Longfellow's sensational best-seller *Evangeline*. To chronicle the rest of her illustrious career would take a book. She died on May 3, 1935, in the city of her birth.

Smith never created art specifically for postcards, but her illustrations from other works were used, most notably in "The Child in a Garden" six-card set by Reinthal & Newman.

Smith postcards	Value, EF to Mint
Child in a Garden card	$3–$15
Other cards	$3–$20

George Studdy

Bonzo and bee by George Studdy. (Bonzo Series. Valentine & Sons, London)

Bonzo with brush and palette. (A.R. & Cp. 1. B. 1521-3)

Bonzo celebrates New Year's in this card. The Dutch text on the card translates to "Happy New Year."

Born on June 23, 1878, George Studdy studied anatomy at Calderon's Animal School. Dogs were a special interest. In the meantime he developed his artistic talent and by the early 1910s had a good reputation as an illustrator and cartoonist. At the tail end of the Golden Age, Bonzo the cartoon dog was developed and became very popular. Postcards with this theme were made into the 1920s. Bonzo toys, books, and other items were produced.

Nearly a thousand different Bonzo postcards were made over the years. His character was copied by others. Today they are a minor entry among signed artist cards.

Studdy postcards	Value, EF to Mint
Bonzo, various	$3–$20
Bonzo with glass eyes	$10–$25
Bonzo cards not by Studdy	$3–$8

Charles H. Twelvetrees

Jilted boy. (Twelvetrees Series No. 70. Alpha Publishing Co., London)

Christmas card by Twelvetrees. (Gibson Art Co., Cincinnati, Ohio)

Charles Henry Twelvetrees was born in Utica, New York, in July 1872. Details of his life are sparse. He was married three times. Much of his illustration work was done with his father, Charles R. Twelvetrees (who is listed in some references as the person who created postcards). Over the years postcard art was just a small part of his output.

His postcards are signed C. Twelvetrees or C.T. In addition, many cards with his images were made without signatures. His postcard publishers included Bergman, Edward Gross Company, National Art, and Ullman. Many of his cards depict round-faced, happy children, often engaged in mischief.

Series No. 75 of 12 cards, "National Cupids," has dresses of as many nations. Series No. 77 of four cards, "Jungle Sports," shows large animals playing.

Some of his postcard images were used in magazines and cartoons. He worked in later years as an illustrator for many magazines and other publications. He seems to have lived in New York City for most if not all of his later life. On April 7, 1948, he died of natural causes while taking a bath in his room at the Hotel Le Marquis on 12 East 31st Street.

Twelvetrees postcards	Value, EF to Mint
African American characters	$20–$40
Children, various	$3–$10
Jungle Sports, each card	$3–$12
National Cupids, each card	$3–$12

Clarence F. Underwood

"Pretty—Cold" (Water Color Series 346. Reinthal & Newman)

**"Love me, love my horse." (F.A.S. Series 2.
Frederick A. Stokes Co. 1907)**

"Love on wings." (No. 642. M. Munk, Vienna, Austria)

Clarence Frederick Underwood was born in Jamestown, New York, on December 9, 1871. He enrolled in the Art Students League in New York City, studied in London, and in Paris studied with Laurens, Bougereau, Constant, and, starting in 1896, at the Académie Julian. He returned to America around the turn of the twentieth century.

His art was varied and ranged from romantic scenes to military posters, book and article illustrations, society settings, magazine covers, and more, including "American types" per some listings. Many of his illustrations other than postcards were scenic, border to border. In the early twentieth century he was a member of the

Society of Illustrators. In 1926 he was the first to picture a woman in American cigarette advertising (although they had been a staple in Europe in this regard for many years).

Postcard publishers included Max Munk, Reinthal & Newman, Frederick A. Stokes, and Raphael Tuck. These are not widely collected as a specialty, but collectors pick out favorite scenes, usually of romantic themes.

Underwood died in New York City on June 11, 1929, a few hours after he collapsed at his studio—an early passing among American postcard illustrators of the Golden Age. He was survived by his wife, a son, and two daughters.

Underwood postcards	Value, EF to Mint
Various	$5–$20

Florence Kate Upton

**Golliwogg Christmas card by Upton.
(Series 1791. Tuck Christmas Post Card)**

Florence Kate Upton was born on February 22, 1873, in Flushing, New York. Her parents were recent Jewish immigrants from England. Her father, Thomas, was with the American Exchange Bank in New York City. The family moved to Manhattan in 1884 so he would be closer to his work. The National Academy of Design was located nearby and offered free tuition to anyone who qualified. Florence at age 15 joined in evening classes.

In 1889 her father suddenly died, placing the family in a financial predicament. Her mother, who had been trained as a singer, gave voice lessons. Florence at age 16 became a professional illustrator, certainly one of the youngest of (later) postcard artists to enter the profession. Florence illustrated a number of novels and other books.

In 1893 the family went to the Hampstead district of London to visit relatives. Florence enjoyed the surroundings so much that she decided to stay. She quickly found employment with publishers and took further lessons in art. She came across a family toy in the attic that she named Golliwogg. This inspired her to write and illustrate *The Adventures of Two Dutch Dolls and A Golliwogg*, which was published in 1895.

After three years in London, by then being a lady of financial means, she returned to New York City and enrolled in the Art Students League. She then went to study in Paris and Holland, returning to London in 1906, where she lived for the rest of her life. The Golliwogg became extremely popular in Europe, a counterpart to Rose O'Neill's Kewpie in America. Upton did not copyright Golliwogg, resulting in countless unauthorized uses for dolls, books, and other objects, often spelled as Golliwog. James Robertson & Sons, a manufacturer of jams and jellies, used it as a mascot. All of this caused despair to its creator. She died in her London studio on October 16, 1922, following complications after surgery.

Upton Golliwogg postcards	Value, EF to Mint
With silver background	$15–$35
With Upton's signature	$15–$35

Walter Wellman

"Try Dan Cupid, M.D." (Wellman No. 1083. 1908)

"Recommending wife as secretaryess of war."
(Wellman No. 4001. 1909)

Walter Wellman was born in Dublin, New Hampshire, on May 25, 1879. As a young man he studied architecture at the Massachusetts Institute of Technology, where he was editor of the college newspaper. At the same time he created comics for the *Boston Globe*. After graduating in 1902 he moved to New York City, where he pursued a career in drawing comics, leaving architecture behind. His work included magazine covers, book illustrations, and pictorial puzzles.

Wellman's first postcards were copyrighted in 1906 and issued by himself. In the same year Rose Publishing Co. issued cards with his art. In 1907 a set of 12 calendar cards with a heart motif was issued. Other sets were made. In 1909 he incorporated the Walter Wellman Company. His last postcard designs were copyrighted in 1910. Later he worked in other fields, including as a secretary and a creator of crossword puzzles.

Wellman postcards	Value, EF to Mint
1907 Calendar set, each card	$5–$15
Hand series, each card	$5–$15
Last Will and Testament set, each card	$5–$15
Life's Little Tragedies set, each card	$5–$15
Merry Widow wiles set, each card	$5–$15
Need a Doctor? set, each card	$5–$15
Suffragette series, each card	$20–$45
Various other Wellman cards	$5–$45

G.G. Wiederseim (a.k.a. Viola Grace Drayton)

Girl with lamb. (No. 488. Reinthal & Newman)

Two girls and a puppy. (Set No. 10. Albert Schweitzer, Hamburg, Germany)

Campbell's Kids No. 1. (No imprint, circa 1905)

Viola Grace Gebbie was born in Darby, Pennsylvania, on October 14, 1877, daughter of George Gebbie, an art publisher. She engaged in art at an early age, often drawing children in different situations from happy to unhappy, in predicaments, and even in love. She studied at the Drexel Institution and the Philadelphia School of Design. While at the latter institution she was

Campbell's Soup Kid. (Campbell's Soups, Camden, New Jersey, 1913; part of a 1913 six-card set costing 6¢ in stamps)

influenced by a teacher, Robert Henri. In 1895 she became a freelance artist. She is considered to be one of the earliest female cartoonists. In 1904 she created the Campbell's Soup Kids with cheery round faces, rosy cheeks, and plump bodies—happy children who consumed the product. She also did comic strips and other commercial art.

Grace married Theodore E. Wiederseim in 1900, but she divorced him in 1911 to marry W. Heyward Drayton III, whom she divorced in 1923. Accordingly, her work can be found with three signatures, including Wiederseim and Drayton on postcards. Publishers included Quality Cards, Reinthal & Newman, Schweitzer, and Tuck. Her work with the Campbell's Soup Kids is particularly well known.

Wiederseim/Drayton postcards	Value, EF to Mint
Adam and Eve	$8–$25
Campbell's Soup Kids	$15–$250
Cunning Cupids (Tuck) card	$10–$30
Drayton Look-a-Likes	$3–$10
Halloween	$25–$50
Stages of Life series card	$8–$25
Swift's Pride Soap	$8–$25
Various advertising cards	$30–$100

John O. Winsch

Winsch Halloween card, artist unknown. Mint: $125–$200

Winsch Christmas card, artist unknown. Mint: $20–$50

John O. Winsch, a publisher and not an artist, lived in Stapleton, New York, and had an office in New York City at 147 Fifth Avenue. From 1910 to 1915 he issued and copyrighted greeting cards, many of which featured Halloween motifs. Judging from postmark dates, the height of his business seems to have been in 1911. Many, if not most, were printed in Germany.

Many of the finest cards used the art of Samuel L. Schmucker (see listing above), including many Halloween cards and "Winsch Girl" cards. Other Winsch artists located in over 3,000 copyright records studied by George and Dorothy Miller included Kathryn

Elliott, Jason Freixas, Fred Kolb, Charles Levi, and Helen P. Strong. Many cards were issued in sets of four or six.

Confirmed back design of a Winsch import with PRINTED IN GERMANY near the stamp box.

Winsch Backs: The authors believe that definite Winsch imports are cards with this design, with Winsch's imprint on the face and PRINTED IN GERMANY near the stamp box. Cards with this design but without the Winsch imprint and PRINTED IN GERMANY may or may not have been imported by Winsch. Certain of the latter were published by E. Nash, such as the National Songs series with Winsch backs.

Postcards published by Winsch, not including Schmucker*	Value, EF to Mint
Artists, various	$8–$15
Cards with silk	$10–$35
Children, various	$8–$30
Christmas with Santa	$15–$125
Christmas without Santa	$8–$30
Easter	$5–$25
Halloween (Freixas)	$60–$400
St. Patrick's Day	$8–$40
Valentine's Day (Freixas)	$8–$40
With Golly or Teddy	$8–$15

* For Schmucker, see above

FOREIGN-BORN ARTISTS

Postcards and series of foreign-born artists are desired by many American collectors today. Some foreign-born artists spent part of their lives in America. The interest of American collectors in cards never distributed in America—Mucha and Weiner Werkstätte—was largely catalyzed by members of the Metropolitan Postcard Club of New York City beginning in the 1960s and by books published about postcards from the late twentieth century to date.

Angelo Asti

"Irene" from a painting in the Paris Salon. (Tuck Connoisseur Series No. 2731.) EF to Mint: $5–$10

"Marguerite" from a painting in the Paris Salon. (Tuck Connoisseur Series No. 2731.) EF to Mint: $5–$10

"Portia" from a painting in the Paris Salon. (Tuck Connoisseur Series No. 2731.) EF to Mint: $5–$10

"Marguerite" (also found titled "Helena") from a painting in the Paris Salon. (Tuck Connoisseur Series No. 2731.) EF to Mint: $5–$10

Angelo Asti was born in Italy in 1847. He traveled widely during his life and at one time had a studio in Paris where most of his art was created. His subjects were diverse, but he is best known for his portraits of women, often with intense, heavy colors. These were formal and not at all suggestive. After his death in Mentone, France, in 1903, rights to his art passed to others and images were used without permission. Raphael Tuck and others produced postcards with his art, as Brown & Bigelow did on calendars.

Asti postcards	Value, EF to Mint
Women	$5–$10
Other subjects	$5–$25

Mabel Lucie Attwell

Two children by Mabel Lucie Attwell. (Valentine's Attwell Postcards, London.) EF to Mint: $8–$20

Child and dog by Mabel Lucie Attwell. (Valentine's Attwell Postcards, London.) EF to Mint: $8–$20

Mabel Lucie Attwell was born in London on June 4, 1879. She was educated privately and at the Coopers Company School and the Regent Street School. She learned art as a student at Heatherley's and the Saint Martin's School of Art. However, she developed her own style emphasizing imaginary subjects as well as sentimental illustrations of children, using her daughter Peggy as a model. Some included animals and some had wise sayings. Her commercial work included illustrations for many books, comics, and magazines. She died on November 5, 1964, outliving nearly all other artists from the Golden Age of postcards.

Most of her postcards featured happy children. Publishers included Raphael Tuck in England and Valentine & Sons in England and America.

Attwell postcards	Value, EF to Mint
Children (Tuck)	$8–$20
Children (Valentine)	$8–$20

Arpad Basch

Arpad Basch postcard in the Art Nouveau style after Mucha. Image dated 1900.

Zodiac by Arpad Basch. Image dated 1900. (No imprint)

Basch postcards	Value, EF to Mint
Zodiac series of women, art Nouveau card	$150–$200+
Military scenes	$75–$100+
Other cards	$75–$300

Thomas Browne

"My wife won't let me" by Thomas Browne. (Pictorial Post Cards from Originals by Thomas Browne, Serie 2606. Davidson Bros, London)

"Our servants" by Thomas Browne. (Pictorial Post Cards from Originals by Thomas Browne, Serie 2574-4. Davidson Bros, London)

"Volunteer v civilian" by Thomas Browne. (Pictorial Post Cards from Originals by Thomas Browne, "Sea-Side Flirtations." Davidson Bros, London)

Arpad Basch was born in Budapest on April 16, 1873. After studying metallurgy at the Staatliche Mittelschule for a year, he decided to become an artist. He studied art in Budapest under Bihan and Karlovsky, then in Munich with Simon Hollosy and in Paris with Drousset, Bonnat, and Laurens. He returned to Budapest in 1896. He did much work for almanacs, magazines, and other publications. Basch mastered an Art Nouveau style of portraits, notably of women in fancy dress, reproduced in elegant colors on postcards. In recent generations these have been popular with American collectors, although at the time of their issue they were not widely known in this country. He died in 1944.

Thomas Arthur Browne was born on December 8, 1870, in Nottingham, England. He became a popular cartoonist, illustrator, and painter in the late nineteenth and early twentieth centuries, drawing comics for newspapers and other publications. In 1908 he designed the monocled man featured on Johnnie Walker whiskey labels. Browne died on March 16, 1910, at Shooter's Hill, England.

Postcards featuring his art taken from other publications were published by Davidson Brothers, Raphael Tuck, Valentine, and others.

Browne postcards	Value, EF to Mint
Comic subjects	$5–$10
Sports subjects	$15–$25

Eva Daniell

Lady with bird.

Lady with beads.

Draped lady on bench.

Classic lady (not Art Nouveau).

Evangeline Mary Daniell, known professionally as Eva Daniell, was born in Ulverston, Lancashire, England, and was registered in early 1882.[9] She was the daughter of Charles Bampfylde Daniell and his wife Mary. Mrs. Mary Daniell was an accomplished artist whose works included portraits of high society. Their home was known as Morecambe Bank and was on Main Street in Ulverston.

Eva was recognized as an artist at a young age.

In 1896 she created the cover art for *The Seven Seas* by Rudyard Kipling, with her initials EMD at the bottom. On December 27, 1902, Daniell's booklet-style greeting card with the Fairy of Peace on the cover, published by Raphael Tuck, was distributed by Queen Alexandra (wife of King Edward VII) to Her Majesty's guests. Daniell's work has never been cataloged.

Around the turn of the twentieth century she created beautiful images in the Art Nouveau style that would have done credit to Alphonse Mucha. Perhaps best known are her cards for Raphael Tuck, including in the RTS "Art" Post Card Series 2524, "Modern Art" Series 2525, and "Artistic Series" (with RTS monogram in stamp box). Her life was very short, and she died in Fulham from consumption in early 1902. Few other details about her artistic career have been found.

Daniell postcards	Value, EF to Mint
Eva Daniell Art Nouveau postcard by Tuck, full-length figure	$125–$250
Eva Daniell Art Nouveau postcard, smaller image, often circular	$75–$150
Eva Daniell postcard in other style, full-length figure	$70–$150

Magnus Greiner

Comic card with running bear by Greiner.

Bear and three children by Greiner.

Magnus Greiner was born in Germany in May 1858. Images from *The Adventures of Molly and Teddy* were used on cards. Several other sets featured Dutch children against a blue tile background. He also created several sets for Tuck. His signature in script is often hidden in the design. Greiner died in Brooklyn, New York, on March 3, 1923.

Greiner postcards	Value, EF to Mint
Dutch children card	$4–$12
Black Americana cards	$15–$30
Molly and Teddy cards	$10–$15
Other cards	$2–$20

Archie Gunn

"Army, Navy and Reserve" by Gunn. (Series 1368. Illustrated Post Card Co., New York)

"Pals" by Gunn. (Series 1368. Illustrated Post Card Co., New York)

Archibald Gunn, who went by the name of Archie, was born on October 11, 1863, in Taunton, Somersetshire, England. His father, Archibald Aitken Gunn, was a professional painter and a member of the Royal Academy of Art. Archie learned painting from his father and from studies at Tottenham College and the Calderon Art Academy. As a teenager he was very accomplished and received commissions for society portraits. He also designed posters and costumes for stage productions, sometimes signing as "Chicot."

In December 1889 he sailed from England to New York aboard the S.S. *City of Chicago*. Success on this side of the Atlantic was assured, and he set up a studio in the Van Dyke Building at 939 Eighth Avenue. In ensuing years he designed many show posters, which were highly acclaimed, and also illustrated magazines and newspapers. In the early twentieth century certain of his art featuring attractive women was published on postcards. His favorite model was Mabel Andrews. In the 1910s he had a studio at 67 Madison Avenue. Gunn died on January 16, 1930.

Gunn postcards	Value, EF to Mint
Attractive women	$5–$15
Soldier/military World War	$5–$15
Soldier and attractive woman	$5–$15

Louis Icart

Louis Justin Laurent Icart was born on September 12, 1888, in Toulouse, France. As a young man who produced artistic sketches, he was introduced to the fashion world by an aunt. He became prominent in illustrations for the fashion press, including magazines and haute couture catalogs. During the World War he was an airplane pilot but continued drawing. In the 1920s his Art Deco depictions of fashionable women, some of which were semi-risqué, became famous in America and Europe. He left his wife and lived with his favorite model, Fanny Volmers, for over 35 years. Icart died in Paris in 1950.

His postcards of fashionable women are very popular. These are variously signed with his name or Helli, the latter approximating the sound of his initials L.I.

Icart postcards	Value, EF to Mint
Signed Helli	$70–$100 +
Signed Icart	$60–$100+

Raphael Kirchner

"Flowers" by Raphael Kirchner. EF to Mint: $175–$225

The spirit of Christmas. EF to Mint: $400+

Woman resting with snake. EF to Mint: $175–$225

Raphael Kirchner was born in Vienna on August 2, 1876. As a young man he attended the Academy of Fine Arts and worked as an artist, including painting portraits of members of Vienna society. He moved to Paris in 1900 and found employment as an artist for *La Vie Parisienne* and other publications. By 1901 his work appeared on postcards in Japanese style, later in the Art Nouveau style. They were often mildly erotic, suggestive, "semi-virgin," or depicted smoking, with most women modeled by his wife, Nina.

Reinthal & Newman published some of his images on postcards in the United States, including the Seven Deadly Sins; R&N cards are rare today. Most Kirchner cards were published in Europe. After the World War broke out in August 1914, his postcards and prints of women were very popular with the Allied troops. Not long afterward he moved to New York City. Kirchner died in 1917 and was survived by his wife. His postcards vary widely in price.

Kirchner postcards	Value, EF to Mint
Ladies in suggestive or romantic poses	$50–$800+

Catherine Klein

Letter S by Catherine Klein. EF to Mint: $15–$30

Letter X by Catherine Klein. EF to Mint: $45–$60

Catherina Klein, usually in print as Catherine Klein, was born in 1861 in Eylau in East Prussia. She spent most of her life in Germany. Beginning with the World War, she anglicized her name to Catherine.

She became well-known for oil and gouache paintings of flowers, some of which were reproduced on postcards published by International Art, Raphael Tuck, and others. One series featured letters of the alphabet decorated with flowers. Some letter cards are rarer than others. Catherine Klein died in 1929 in Berlin, Germany.

Klein postcards	Value, EF to Mint
Flowers	$3–$10
Letters except for below	$15–$20
Letters U, V, W, X, Y, Z	$20–$30

Mela Koehler

Lady in flowing purple dress by Mela Koehler. (B.K.W.I. 384-5, Austria.) EF to Mint: $75–$100

Lady at the shore by Mela Koehler. (B.K.W.I. 187-3, Austria.) EF to Mint: $75–$100

Mela Koehler, also known as Mela Koehler-Broman and Mela Leopoldina Köhler, was born in Vienna on November 18, 1885. She was a graphic designer and illustrator. Her images on postcards were published by Brother Kohn Wien (BKWI), Munk, and over 150 cards for the Wiener Werkstätte (see listing in this chapter). She died on December 15, 1960, in Stockholm.

Prices on Koehler postcards vary widely, many costing less than $50 and others costing $100 to $300.

Koehler postcards	Value, EF to Mint
Ladies and girls	$30–$300

Joseph C. Leyendecker

"Ace High."

Joseph Christian Leyendecker was born on March 23, 1874, in Germany. He developed an early interest in art, and by the time his family moved to Chicago in 1882 he had made many sketches. As a teenager he was apprenticed at J. Manz & Co. In the 1890s he studied at the Chicago Art Institute and in Paris at the Académie Julian, returning in 1899 to open an art studio. In 1900 he moved with his brother Frank and sister Mary to New York City.

His art was used by many magazines (including 322 covers for the *Saturday Evening Post*) and in other publications. His most famous illustration was of the "Arrow Shirt man," which was used in advertising for many years. He also made recruitment posters for both World Wars. In 1914 he built a 14-room mansion in New Rochelle, the getaway town "45 minutes from Broadway" for many artists and show folk. His younger

brother Frank was also a successful illustrator. He never married. Joseph C. Leyendecker died in 1951. His postcards are unsigned and advertise Chesterfield cigarettes. His original artwork is signed and enables this attribution.

Leyendecker postcards	Value, EF to Mint
Chesterfield cigarettes	$35–$50

Alphonse Mucha

Alphonse Maria Mucha, usually in print without his middle name, was born on July 24, 1860, in Ivančice, Moravia (today a region of the Czech Republic). Early in his career he was a singer, earning enough to continue through high school. His first love was drawing and painting. He worked on theatrical scenery in Moravia and in 1879 went to Vienna in the same pursuit. In 1881 he returned to Moravia, where Count Karl Khuen of Mikulov employed him to paint murals and decorate Hrušovany Emmahof and paid for his studies at the Munich Academy of Fine Arts.

His life changed dramatically when he moved to Paris in 1887 and continued his education at Académie Julian and Académie Colarossi, earning his way by creating commercial art. In 1894 he visited the Imprimeries Lemercier shop, which commissioned him to quickly create a poster for the famous actress Sarah Bernhardt in "Gismonda," a play at the Théâtre de la Renaissance. This was displayed on January 1, 1895. The play opened on January 4. The poster was an immediate sensation and became the definition of the Art Nouveau style. Poster collecting was at its height, and graphic works by Jules Chéret, Lucien Marie François Métivet, Eugène Grasset, and others found a ready sale in France and abroad. Imprimeries Lemercier produced over 8,000 copies of Gismonda during the next several years! Sarah Bernhardt signed Mucha to a six-year contract, during which time he produced many posters and other illustrated items. Mucha's images often featured attractive young women in flowing robes surrounded by vines and flowers, all in pastel colors that blended nicely.

In June 1897 Mucha held a one-man exhibit at the Salon des Cent gallery owned by *La Plume* magazine, where his art was already well known. His fame spread, and additional commissions were received. Soon the ever-innovative Champenois firm began publishing sets of postcards.

His murals were used to decorate several fairs including the International Exposition held in Paris in 1900.

In 1906 he married Maruška Chytilová, a union that produced a son and a daughter. He later moved to Czechoslovakia where he designed murals, stamps, and other art and became even more famous. He died of a lung infection in Prague on July 14, 1939. Today the Mucha Museum there features his art.

Among postcards, Mucha subjects have been the crème de la crème for a long time in America, Europe, and elsewhere. Exhibitions of Mucha cards at leading shows have invariably attracted attention, and the offering of a Mucha card or two in a postcard auction has marked the event as one of quality.

The various subjects were issued in sets as well as singly. Numbers given here are those assigned by Bowers and Martin in *The Postcards of Alphonse Mucha*.

Editions Cinos Series: Cards in the Cinos series, issued by F. Champenois circa 1898, are identified by a small circle enclosing an inscription which reads DESPOSE CINOS PARIS. This identification is printed twice on each card; on the front and on the back. Of the 36 or more cards in this series, five are by Mucha (see further information on Edition Cinos at the end of this chapter):

Gismonda. This is Mucha's most famous poster. (Editions Cinos No. 14)

No.	Description	Edition Cinos No.	Year	URS	Value, EF to Mint
102	La Dame aux Camélias	No. 15	1898	URS-7	$1,000–$1,200
103	Lorenzaccio	No. 12	1898	URS-5	$1,000–$1,200
104	La Samaritaine	No. 13	1898	URS-7	$1,000–$1,200

Waverley Cycles. (No. 36, Editions Cinos)

No.	Description	Edition Cinos No.	Year	URS	Value, EF to Mint
105	Waverley Cycles		1898	URS-4	$8,000–$12,000+

Among collectors this is the most famous single Mucha postcard. In 1984 Susan Nicholson sold one for $4,000. On April 7, 1990, J.W. Fairfield paid a record $13,500 for an example; at that time only two were known. Since then the number known has multiplied, but the postcard is still scarce. The present-day value is speculative.

Alphonse Mucha continued on next page

Alphonse Mucha, continued from previous page

Sarah Bernhardt's American tours postcards, single color, printed in America:

No.	Description	Year	URS	Value, EF to Mint
113	Hamlet. List of plays	1905–1906	URS-1	$7,000–$10,000
120	Hamlet. List of plays	1910–1911	URS-1	$8,000–$12,000
171	Job Calendar	1897. Circa 1905 postcard issue	URS-8	$900–$1,200

Horizontal format with image of woman with blonde hair (printed in rich gold ink) occupying nearly half of the left side of the card.

"Job." (No. 172 1909 calendar)

No.	Description	Year	URS	Value, EF to Mint
172	Job Calendar. Image as preceding. JOB Cigarettes JOB inscription in border above image, and with other inscriptions. BUREAU DE LONDRES.	1908 issue.	URS-6	$900–$1,100
173	Job Calendar. Image as preceding. Collection JOB inscription in border above image. Background of right side and margins consists of repeated JOB monograms in rhomboidal latticework.	1897. Circa 1911 issue.	URS-10	$200–$400
174	Job Calendar. Vertical format. Image similar to preceding. Image and inscriptions fill the entire front of the card. Divided back. 1897.	Circa 1914 issue.	URS-6	$900–$1,100
181	Job Poster. Horizontal format, with image of a woman with dark hair and pink gown occupying nearly half of the left side of the card.	1898. Circa 1911 issue.	URS-1	$300–$400
182	Job Poster. Vertical format, image similar to preceding. Image and inscription fill the entire front of the card. Divided back.	1898. Circa 1914 issue	URS-6	$900–$1,100
221	*Cocorico* magazine cover design. Image of Sarah Bernhardt holding a rooster at left side of card.	Circa 1900	URS-5	$1,200–$1,400

"Salome" card. (No. 448)

Moët & Chandon Menu Postcards. Set of ten menu cards, vertical orientation, face with Mucha design, postcard (instead of menu listing) backs; French and English versions. This is a very popular series.
301 to 310. Each R-9. EF to Mint: $550–$800

Collectors' Series Issued by F. Champenois

F. Champenois, the Paris publisher who issued nearly all of Mucha's graphic works in "le style Mucha" format, issued postcards for collectors around the turn of the century. Most of the subjects appeared earlier on decorative panels, calendars, periodical covers, or posters. There were some exceptions, including certain of the cards in the 3rd Series.

There are many color variations among the Champenois cards in these series, indicating that certain numbers were printed on several different occasions. Color intensities range from vivid for such series as the months of the year (Nos. 461 to 472) and times of the day (502-505) to muted pastels (all the cards in the 1st Series, 401-412, for example).

Originally, certain cards were sold in sets of 12 for 1 franc, 50 centimes (equal to about 30¢ U.S. funds at the time). Today, most cards are offered individually or in related pairs, groups of four, etc. Rarely is an intact set of 12 encountered.

Our grouping of cards into "sets" follows the format given by Jiri Mucha and Marina Henderson in *The Graphic Work of Alphonse Mucha* (Academy Editions, London, 1973). The same groupings were later used by Neudin in 1978. While many of the cards may have been issued as sets (Leonard A. Lauder reports the ownership of original envelopes for the first five sets, for example), it is probable that certain other cards were also issued individually, for the rarity of certain cards within some of the sets varies widely. In addition, some cards were distributed separately by la Belle Jardinière, a Paris department store with branches in Lyon and Bordeaux.

Although most postcard references have ascribed the dates 1900–1901 to the seven series, it is probable that certain of the later cards were sold for several years after that time. Building a full set of the seven series is a challenge that will be rewarded with a great amount of satisfaction. These form the core or essence of a specialized Mucha collection.

1st Champenois series. This first series of 12 cards comprises three groups of four cards each. The first is of the seasons (in French "saisons"): spring (printemps), summer (été), autumn (automne), and winter (hiver). These motifs were first published in 1897 and were distributed in the form of decorative panels. All cards in the 1st Series are rendered in soft pastel colors.

Adolescence. (No. 410)

Series	Description	URS	Value, EF to Mint
Seasons series (401–404)	Four cards. Printemps, été, automne, hiver	Each URS-11	$300–$400
Flowers (fleurs) series (405–408)	Titles in French and English with some variations	Each URS-11	$300–$400
Four ages series (409–412)	Titles in French and English with some variations: childhood (enfance), adolescence (adolescence), manhood (maturité), and old age (vieillesse)	Each URS-10	$400–$600

Alphonse Mucha continued on next page

Alphonse Mucha, continued from previous page

2nd Champenois series. The first cards in the series are two 1897 images of Byzantine heads (tête Byzantine), one a brunette and the other a blonde, the latter image inspired by a photographic portrait of actress Cora Laparcerie. The two Byzantine heads achieved wide recognition and were reproduced on decorative panels, plaques, jewelry, and other media. In postcard form each appears as a head surrounded by a circle, on the left side of the card. Apparently postcards were produced at different intervals, as examples seen today vary in the color intensity.

Zodiac. (No. 432)

Series	Description	URS	Value, EF to Mint
421	Byzantine Head, The Brunette. Woman's head facing right of card, surrounded by circle.	URS-10	$400–$500
422	Byzantine Head, The Blonde. Woman's head facing left of card, surrounded by circle.	URS-10	$400–$500
423	Spring (Printemps). Woman with blonde hair in pink dress.	URS-10	$300–$400
424	Summer (Été). Woman with red hair in white dress; body turned to the left of card.	URS-10	$300–$400
425	Autumn (Automne). Woman with brown hair in blue dress; facing to the right of card.	URS-10	$300–$400
426	Winter (Hiver). Woman in hooded white cloak.	URS-10	$300–$400
427	Painting (La Peinture). Woman in pink faces left of card. Crescent design surrounds.	URS-10	$400–$500
428	Dancing (La Danse). Woman in pink faces right of card. Crescent design surrounds.	URS-10	$400–$500
429	Poetry (La Poesie). Woman in blue faces right of card. Crescent design surrounds.	URS-10	$400–$500
430	Music (La Musique). Woman in blue with hands to her face. Crescent design surrounds.	URS-10	$400–$500
431	Reverie. Woman sits with an open book on her lap.	URS-8	$400–$500
432	Zodiac. Head and shoulders portrait of a woman facing left of the card.	URS-8	$450–$750

3rd Champenois series. The 12 cards in the third series, issued by Champenois circa 1900, consist of three vignette designs, another set of four seasons of different designs, and Salome, Crepuscule, Aurore, Primevere, and La Plume. The first three cards in the 3rd Series consist of untitled designs or vignettes for postcards. Each card is of the horizontal format with the image occupying about half of the front.

Design for a Postcard. (No. 443)

Series	Description	URS	Value, EF to Mint
441	Design for a Postcard. Woman with long red hair, dressed in white, reclines in seeming luxury. A vine curls at the top of the design. Issued without Mucha's signature.	URS-10	$400–$500
442	Design for a Postcard. Woman with long blonde hair, dressed in white, sits with elbows on knees and hands on chin.	URS-9	$400–$500
443	Design for a Postcard. Woman with blonde hair, dressed in green, faces right of card. Her hands touch flowers in her hair. Curved line frame ends with arabesques at lower left and right.	URS-9	$400–$650
444	Spring (Printemps). Woman with blonde hair in white dress. (This and the next three are different from earlier cards).	URS-9	$400–$500
445	Summer (Été). Woman with dark hair in yellow dress.	URS-9	$400–$500
446	Autumn (Automne). Woman with blonde hair in pink dress.	URS-9	$400–$500
447	Winter (Hiver). Woman in green.	URS-9	$400–$500
448	Salome	URS-9	$400–$650
449	Dawn (Aurore)	URS-9	$700–$900
450	Twilight (Crépuscule). Woman reclining, head to right, faces left with tree and sunset in the background.	URS-9	$700–$900
451	Primrose (Primevère). Also translated as Cowslip. Woman with flower in her hand faces right of card. A circle frames her head.	URS-9	$900–$1,100
452	The Feather (La Plume). Woman with quill in her hands faces left of card.	URS-9	$900–$1,100

4th Champenois series. Les Mois (The Months) series of 12 cards. This is far and away the most famous Mucha series. Titles are in French, but sometimes the title is omitted (these are rarer and very slightly more desirable). Each has a scene in a large circle at the left.

"Juillet." (Champenois)

Series	Description	URS	Value, EF to Mint
461 to 472	Janvier, Février, Mars, Avril, Mai, Juin, Juillet, Août, Septembre, Octobre, Novembre, Decembre	Each URS-9	$400–$500

Used cards with much writing on the face, often seen in the marketplace, are worth $100 to $150.

5th Champenois series. This series incorporates several single cards, a group of three covers for *Cocorico* magazine, and a group of menu designs. Generally, the cards in the 5th, 6th, and 7th series are scarcer than those in the preceding series, possibly because their "miscellaneous" nature did not prove as popular as the content of the earlier groups and also because of the declining novelty of Art Nouveau cards at the time.

Alphonse Mucha continued on next page

Alphonse Mucha, continued from previous page

Sarah Bernhardt. (No. 481 from *La Plume*)

One of the Flowers series of Mucha postcards. (No. 405)

Series	Description	URS	Value, EF to Mint
481	Sarah Bernhardt (from *La Plume*). Front-facing portrait of Bernhardt with circle and scallop design behind her head.	URS-7	$500–$900
482	Society for the Benefit of Austria-Hungary (Société de Bienfaisance Austro-Hongroise).	Above URS-7	$600–$800
483	*Cocorico* Cover Design. Woman believed to be Sarah Bernhardt, in pink dress, holds rooster.	URS-7	$900–$1,100
484	*Cocorico* Cover Design. Vertical format with woman dressed in white at top of card. A cluster of leaves in her hands. A decorative circle frames the portrait.	URS-9	$400–$500
485	*Cocorico* Cover Design. Vertical format with portrait in rectangle at upper two thirds of card, a striking image with almost a three-dimensional effect. Woman's face with hands close by; flowers in long brown hair.	URS-9	$500–$600
486	Banquet Menu. Vertical design occupies nearly the entire card. Woman in pink dress with hands in her lap sits in a large circle frame.	URS-7	$550–$700
487	Design for Menu. Woman in pink dress and green shawl rests chin on hands.	URS-9	$300–$400
488	Design for Menu. Woman in white dress and pink shawl holds plate of fruit.	URS-9	$300–$400
489	Design for Menu. Woman in white dress and pink shawl holds wine glass.	URS-9	$300–$400
490	Design for Menu. Woman in pink dress and green shawl holds plate of food.	URS-9	$300–$400
491	Design for a Fan. Vertical design of a circular fan and handle. The fan design is in the shape of a crescent with two women within.	URS-7	$550–$700
492	Paris Universal Exposition, 1900	URS-7	$700–$800

6th Champenois series. This series issued by Champenois contains 12 cards of various subjects, including a set of four illustrating the times of the day. The first is a design for a calendar or menu, a motif not related to any of the other cards in the 6th Series.

Series	Description	URS	Value, EF to Mint
501	Design for a Calendar or Menu. Vertical design fills most of card. Woman in gold dress with gilt arch in background.	URS-9	$350–$400

Champenois cards from 1899 decorative panels. Without question, these four cards are among the most beautiful in the entire Mucha series. Each card is of the vertical format with the design occupying more than half of the left side. The Gothic arch frame within a rectangle suggests a church window. Some sets were issued with advertising for La Belle Jardinière and other imprints.

Series	Description	URS	Value, EF to Mint
502 to 505	Awakening of Morning (Éveil du Matin), Brightness of Day (Éclat du Jour), Reverie of Evening (Rêverie du Soir), Repose of Night (Repos de la Nuit). R-4.	Each URS-9	$900–$1,000
506	Reverie (variant). Mucha's signature at lower left within image. Woman in green gown holding book from which pages are falling. Different from earlier card with the same title.	URS-9	$400–$500
506a	As above, but without Mucha's signature	URS-10	$350–$450
507	Design for a Soirée Program. Mucha's signature at lower left within image. Vertical design occupies about two-thirds of the card. Woman in green holding a stringed instrument. Crescent above. Occurs with and without signature.	URS-7	$600–$700
507a	As above, but without Mucha's signature	URS-7	$550–$650
508	Papeterie. Woman seated at table with pen and paper in hand, not in the Art Nouveau style.	URS-9	$500–$600
509	Spring (Printemps). Different from earlier card with the same title. Vertical design in poster style occupies the left two-thirds of the card. Woman in green gown holds a bouquet of flowers.	URS-7	$500–$600
510	Lady with a Pen. Vertical design occupies more than half of the card to the left. Close image of woman's face; long brown hair; pen held vertically in hand.	URS-7	$800–$900
511	Water Lily (Nenuphar). Often seen with La Belle Jardinière advertising imprint.	URS-7	$800–$900
512	Cherry Blossom (Fleur de Cerisier)	URS-7	$800–$900

7th Champenois series. This series, issued early in the twentieth century by Champenois, consists of 12 cards of varied character. While some of the cards may have been issued as part of sets of 12 cards each, others must have been issued singly, for the rarity ratings of cards in this series differ widely, and some are very hard to find.

Series	Description	URS	Value, EF to Mint
521	Autumn (Automne). Vertical design occupies about two-thirds of the card, with a margin to the right. Woman in yellow dress holds plate of fruit. Red shawl draped on chair. Decorative frame surrounds.	URS-7	$500–$600
522	Heather of the Bluff (Bruyere de Falaise)	URS-7	$800–$900
523	Thistle of the Shore (Chardon de Greves)	URS-7	$800–$900

Alphonse Mucha continued on next page

Alphonse Mucha, continued from previous page

Ivy (Lierre). (No. 524)

Topaz (Topaze). (No. 527)

Series	Description	URS	Value, EF to Mint
524	Ivy (Lierre)	URS-6	$900–$1,000
525	Laurel (Laurier)	URS-6	$900–$1,000
526	Lygie	URS-6	$800–$900
527	Topaz (Topaze)	URS-5	$1,000–$1,100
528	Emerald (Emeraude)	URS-6	$1,000–$1,100
529	Amethyst (Amethyste)	URS-6	$1,000–$1,100
530	Ruby (Rubis)	URS-6	$1,000–$1,100
531	The Fruit (Le Fruit). R-7.	URS-4	$1,000–$1,100
532	The Flower (Le Fleur)	URS-4	$1,000–$1,100

Miscellaneous Mucha cards

Series	Description	URS	Value, EF to Mint
550	Lygie (variation). Different from No. 526 with the same title. The central motif is a standing woman with her hands on her chin.	URS-4	$800–$900
601	Society for the Benefit of Austria-Hungary (Société de Bienfaisance Austro-Hongroise). Collection des Cent series.	URS-6	$700–$800
602	Peasant Girl. Not in the Art Nouveau style.	URS-2	$3,000–$4,000
650	Ricordo della Fiera di Beneficenza Bergamo Maggio 1900. Vertical. Standing three-quarter length figure of woman facing right of card. A postally used example sold for $2,242 at Jackson's International Auction, Cedar Falls, Iowa, in May 2007.	URS-2	$3,000–$5,000
651	Ricordo della Fiera di Beneficenza Bergamo Maggio 1900. Image as preceding, but reversed (mirror image) with figure facing in the opposite direction.	URS-1	$5,000–$8,000
704	Cognac Bisquit, German Agent	URS-2	$3.500–$5,000
705	Cognac Bisquit, Belgian Agent	URS-4	$3,000–$4,000
706	Cognac Bisquit. Vertical. Black and white. Image as foregoing, but larger and oriented vertically.	URS-2	$3,500–$5,000
720	Collection Lefevre-Utile	URS-6	$900–$1,000
750	La Revue du Bien	URS-6	$1,000–$1,200
760	Vin Mariani. Veiled and draped woman standing.	URS-4	$1,000–$1,200

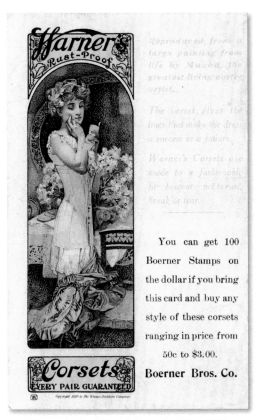

Warner's Rust-Proof Corsets. (No. 781)

Warner's Rust-Proof Corsets

Series	Description	Value, EF to Mint
780	No margin imprint	$800–$1,000
781	Three text paragraphs in margin	$800–$1,000
782	Four text paragraphs in margin	$800–$1,000

Postcards by various printers, later Slavic period, pre-1930. EF to Mint, depending on subject: $25–$100

Edmund H. Osthaus

DuPont Dog, Allambagh, Champion 1908.

DuPont Wild Game, Canvas Backs.

Edmund Henry Osthaus was born in Hildesheim, Germany, in 1858. As a youth in 1864 he traveled with his father and with Archduke Ferdinand Maximilian, who was to become emperor of Mexico during widespread civil disturbances in that country. Maximilian was executed, and the Osthauses escaped to the United States, then returned to Germany. After completing local studies Edmund studied at the Royal Academy of Arts in Dusseldorf.

His parents emigrated to America, and then in 1883 Edmund and his sister followed them. He was asked to become the principal of the new Toledo Academy of Fine Arts. In 1892 he married Charlotte Becker, with whom he raised a family.

A sportsman at heart, Edmund owned champion dogs. As a result, his most famous art is of sporting scenes and dogs. In 1893 he left the academy to devote his full time to art and to sporting, the latter including participation in national events. He opened a studio in Toledo and by 1911 he had opened a branch studio in the Walker Theater in Los Angeles. While dogs and sports were his favorite subjects, he also created cowboys and other characters and painted portraits, often including a pet dog or two. His art was widely published in magazines and elsewhere. In 1928 Osthaus died at his quail-hunting lodge in Marianna, Florida.

For the DuPont Company he created a popular series featuring dogs and another with wild game. The set of 13 featuring dogs was published in June 1916 and offered for 10 cents for a full set. Depicted were all of the Field Trial Championship winners from 1896 to 1910 (there was no trial in 1897; Sioux won in two years). The 12 wild game cards featured birds and animals.

Osthaus postcards	Value, EF to Mint
DuPont birds, each	$8–$12
DuPont dogs, each	$75–$100

Arthur Thiele

Four cats in a meadow. (T.S.N. Series No. 1671 of six designs.) EF to Mint: $25–$40

Photographing a group of cats. (Life in Catland Series 1, postcard 3434, Tuck Oilette.) EF to Mint: $25–$40

A mouse in the schoolroom. (T.S.N. Series 1423 of six designs.) EF to Mint: $25–$40

A cat enjoys tennis. (G.A. Novelty Art Series N, 851, 6 Des. Germany.) EF to Mint: $40–$60

A cat singer and his audience. (T.S.N. Series 1012 of six designs.) EF to Mint: $25–$40

Chickens and a passenger train. (Series 1376. C.W. Faulkner & Co., London.) EF to Mint: $35–$50

Photographing rabbits. (T.S.N. Series No. 1353 of four designs.) EF to Mint: $40–$60

Humans watch a zeppelin. (Adolph Klauss, Leipzig, Series 388.) EF to Mint: $25–$35

An unfortunate accident, crashing into an occupied privy. (Adolph Klauss, Leipzig.) EF to Mint: $25–$35

Carl Robert Arthur Thiele, whose first two names are usually dropped, was born in Leipzig, Germany, in 1860. As an artist he specialized in drawing cats, dogs, and other animals, giving them human expressions (also see Louis Wain below). Cats forming an orchestra, riding in a car that runs into an occupied privy, and related comic subjects were very popular. He also created

hybrid creatures such as a cat with butterfly wings. Other animals such as rabbits, monkeys, dogs, and chickens were illustrated. Some comic cards featured humans on vacation, bowling, in military dress, etc. Theo. Stroefer of Nuremburg (TSN) was his main publisher with cards numbered from 700 to 2500, but probably not continuously. Thiele died on June 18, 1936.

Nearly all of his cards are very humorous, especially those featuring several or more animals doing things.

Thiele postcards	Value, EF to Mint
Cats	$20–$35+
Chickens	$25–$40+
Dogs	$25–$40+
Humans	$20–$35+
Monkeys	$12–$20+
Pigs	$15–$25+
Rabbits	$25–$40+
Comic scenes	$20–$35+

Louis Wain

Louis Wain cats at the railway station, postmarked 1905. EF to Mint: $40–$60

Four cats having tea. (Series 549. Raphael Tuck, Paris office). EF to Mint: $40–$60

"The play's the thing." (Louis Wain Cats. Raphael Tuck, card No. 6444). EF to Mint: $40–$60

"Just a few words." (Write Away Post Card Series 539, R & S Artistic Series). EF to Mint: $40–$60

"Be careful." (No imprint). EF to Mint: $40–$60

Born in London, England, on August 4, 1860, Louis Wain had an aimless youth and was often truant from school. He developed a more realistic outlook as a teenager and studied at the West London School of Art and taught there for a short time.

At age 20 he was required to support his mother and resigned his teaching position. He became a freelance artist working for various magazines and journals, often drawing animals, farms, and country estates. At age 23 he married Emily Richardson, his sister's governess who was 10 years older, a union viewed as scandalous at the time. Emily developed breast cancer but was comforted by Peter, her pet cat. She passed away three years later.

Peter inspired Wain's later career of almost exclusively drawing cats and kittens with large eyes and emotional expressions such as laughter, sadness, and excitement. He often went to restaurants and other places to sketch humans, representing them in the form of cats. In 1907 he went to New York City and created some comic strips such as "Cats About Town" and "Grimalkin." He made it clear that he did not like city life there, attracting some unfavorable comments. He returned to England somewhat poorer as the result of a bad investment in an oil-lamp enterprise.

He produced more animated cat illustrations, many of which became popular on postcards during the Golden Age. Later he became mentally ill and was confined to an institution. Wain died on July 4, 1939.

Wain postcards	Value, EF to Mint
Typical cat postcard	$20–$50+
Santa Claus, Charlie Chaplin cat	$300–$400
Tuck paper doll Fairy Tale series of six cards, each card	$200–$300

Wiener Werkstätte

Established in 1903, the Wiener Werkstätte (Vienna Workshop) evolved from the Vienna Secession established in 1897 by a group of artists who sought new frontiers in design. Beginning in three rooms, the establishment grew to fill a three-story building with separate departments in bookbinding, ceramics, woodworking, leather, painting, and other elements of creative life. Its mission statement was that many ordinary items could be made to appear artistic. In 1905 about 100 people were at work, including over 35 recognized masters of particular trades. Nearly 1,000 postcards were issued with art by various members. The enterprise ended in 1932.

Prices vary widely from several tens of dollars into the low thousands. Many varieties were produced. Popular in Europe, Wiener Werkstätte cards attracted many American collectors when Leonard A. Lauder, Andreas Brown, and others, mainly of the Metropolitan Postcard Club of New York City, displayed them in the late twentieth century. Leonard A. Lauder donated his collection to the Neue Galerie in New York City, which mounted an exhibition from October 7, 2012, to January 17, 2013.

Wiener Werkstätte. Signed by Carl Krenck. (No. 908.) EF to Mint: $250–$300

Wiener Werkstätte. (No. 102.) EF to Mint: $250–$350

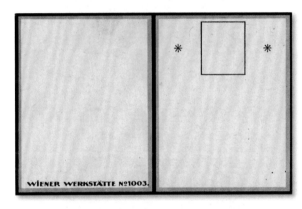

Wiener Werkstätte. (No. 214.) EF to Mint: $250–$300

Wiener Werkstätte. Signed by Kritzi. (No. 1003.) EF to Mint: $200–$250

Wiener Werkstätte postcard creator	Value, EF to Mint
Josef Hoffman	$1,500–$5,000
Moriz Jung	$400–$3,200
Mela Koehler	$300–$4,000
Oskar Kokoschka	$1,500–$6,000
Maria Likarz	$150–$1,400
Dagobert Peche	$500–$900
Egon Schiele	$3,500–$6,000
Jewish holidays	$75–$200
Other postcards	Prices vary widely from several tens of dollars into several thousands.

Lawson Wood

"You're a dear little beggar" by Lawson Wood. (Valentine's Lawson Wood Series. London.) Mint: $8–$12

Clarence Lawson Wood was born in London on August 23, 1878, the son of landscape artist Pinhom Wood. He studied at several art schools, after which he was employed by publisher C. Arthur Pearson, Ltd. Much of his art was humorous and featured animals, dinosaurs, policemen, and, especially, a chimpanzee named Gran'pop. He died in Devon, England, on October 26, 1957.

His postcards were published by several firms including International Art, Raphael Tuck, and Valentine.

Wood postcards	Value, EF to Mint
Comic animals	$5–$25
Other	$3–$20

ADDITIONAL ARTISTS

These lists include additional artists requested by customers of Mary L. Martin, Ltd. Of course there are many others whose postcards are asked for only at wide intervals. Additional artist are listed under "Two Popular French Series" below.

American Artists

- Rolf Armstrong (1889–1960). Born in Bay City, Michigan.
- Anna Whelan Betts (1873–1952). Born in Philadelphia, Pennsylvania.
- Ethel Franklin Betts (1878–1956). Born in Philadelphia, Pennsylvania.
- George Reiter Brill (1867–1918). Born in the United States.
- Nina K. Brisley (1888–1978). Born in the United States.
- Clara Miller Burd (1873–1933). Born in New York, New York.
- Frank Carson (1881–1968). Born in Waltham, Massachusetts.
- William Haskell Coffin (1877–1941). Born in Charleston, South Carolina.
- Henry H. Cross (1837–1918). Born in Flemingville, New York.
- Edward Cucuel (1875–1954). Born in San Francisco, California.
- Frederick Alexander Duncan (1881–?). Born in Texarkana, Arkansas.
- Rachael Robinson Elmer (1878–1919). Born in Ferrisburgh, Vermont.
- Louie Ewing (1908–1983). Born in the United States.
- Lyonel Feininger (1871–1956). Born in New York, New York.
- Alice Ercle Hunt (1848–1930). Born in the United States.
- Lillian Woolsey Hunter (1874–1926). Born in New York, New York.
- Zula Kenyon (1873–1947). Born in Deansville, Wisconsin.
- Lewis H. Larsen (1909–1997). Born near Moab, Utah.
- Louis Mayer (1869–1969). Born in Milwaukee, Wisconsin.
- Hilda T. Miller (1876–1939). Born in the United States.

- Earl Steffa Moran (1893–1984). Born in Belle Plaine, Iowa.
- Zoe Mozet (1907–1993). Born in Colorado Springs, Colorado.
- Clarence Coles Phillips (1880–1927). Born in Springfield, Ohio.
- Margaret Evans Price (1888–1973). Born in Chicago, Illinois.
- Ida Waugh (?–1919). Born in the United States.

Foreign-Born Artists

- Léon Bakst, name used by Leyb-Khaim Izrailevich Rosenberg (1866–1924). Born in Russia.
- Elisaveta Merkuryevna Bem (1843–1914). Born in Russia.
- Aurelio Bertiglia (1891–1973). Born in Italy.
- Maurice Boulanger (1909–?). Born in France.
- Sofia Chiostri (1898–1945). Born in Italy.
- Tito Corbella (1885–1966). Born in Italy.
- Luciano Achille Mauzan (1883–1952). Born in France.
- Henri Meunier (1873–1922). Born in France.
- Giovanni Nanni (1888–1969). Born in Italy.
- Margaret Winifred Tarrant (1888–1959). Born in England.
- Margaret Mary Tempest (1892–1982). Born in England.

TWO POPULAR FRENCH SERIES

Editions Cinos Series

The Editions Cinos postcards were published in Paris in 1898. They featured contemporary art as also used on posters of the era. Most depict dancing, music, and other entertainment just prior to the Paris Universal Exposition of 1900. These stand today among the most beautiful postcard series ever issued. The artists included Andreas, Barcet, Chéret, Duizolle, Grasset, Guillaume, Japhet, Metivet, Mucha (see four Art Nouveau postcards and the Waverley Cycles listings under the Mucha listing above), Meunier, Noury, Pal, Partridge, Redon, Tabouret, Toulouse-Lautrec, and Truchet. The Holy Grail card in the series is No. 33 by Toulouse-Lautrec.[10] Cards with extensive writing on the front are worth about half of the EF price.

No.	Description
No. 1	Chéret. Palais de Glace (couple).
No. 2	Chéret. Palais de Glace (Dame patinant).
No. 3	Chéret. Musée Grévin. Pantomimes lumineuses.
No. 4	Chéret. Musée Grévin. Les Dames hongroises.
No. 5	Chéret. Musée Grévin. Les Coulisses de l'Opéra.
No. 6	Chéret. Bal au Moulin Rouge.
No. 7	Chéret. Au Joyeux Moulin Rouge.
No. 8	Duizolle. Cirque d'Hiver.
No. 9	Grasset. The Century magazine. Napoléon Sur Son Cheval.
No. 10	Japhet. Le Pôle Nord.
No. 11	Métivet. The January Century.
No. 12	Mucha. Sarah Bernhardt. Lorenzaccio.
No. 13	Mucha. Sarah Bernhardt. La Samaritaine.
No. 14	Mucha. Sarah Bernhardt. Gismonda.
No. 15	Mucha. Sarah Bernhardt. La Dame aux Camélias.
No. 16	Noury. Pour les Pauvres de France.
No. 17	Pal. Casino de Paris.
No. 18	Partridge. Madame Sans Gêne.
No. 19	Partridge. Madame Sans Gêne.
No. 20	Georges Redon. Moulin de la Galette.
No. 21	Attributed to Redon. Souvenir du Moulin Rouge.
No. 22	Attributed to Redon. Souvenir d'une Visite à Trianon.
No. 23	Attributed to Tabouret. H. Fragson. Parisiana Concert.
No. 24	Chéret Casino de Paris.
No. 25	Unknown artist. La Goulue.
No. 26	Maurice Réalier-Dumas. Napoléon en Pied.
No. 27	Roedel. Moulin de la Galette.
No. 28	Andréas Les Chansonniers de Montmartre.
No. 29	Abel Truchet. Cabaret des Quat'z'Arts.
No. 30	Barcet. Théatre Pompadour.
No. 31	Guillaume. Le Pôle Nord.
No. 32	Grasset. The June Century. Napoléon in Egypt.
No. 33	Toulouse-Lautrec. Moulin Rouge. La Goulue.
No. 34	Roedel. Moulin de la Galette.
No. 35	Georges Meunier. Bal Bullier.
No. 36	Mucha. Waverley Cycles.

Palais de Glace by Chéret. (Cinos No. 2.)
EF to Mint: $250–$450

Moulin de la Galette, Montmartre, by Redon. (Cinos No. 20.)
EF to Mint: $250–$450

Pantomimes Lumineuses by Chéret. (Cinos No. 3.)
EF to Mint: $250–$450

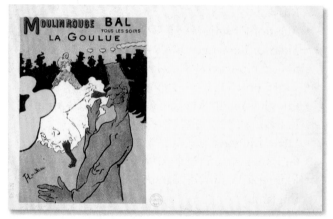

Moulin Rouge Bal by Toulouse-Lautrec. This is one of the most famous and desired cards in the series. (Cinos No. 33.)
EF to Mint: $5,000–$8,000

Collection des Cent Series

The Collection des Cent postcards were published in Paris at the turn of the century. The art, widely varied in style, is by nearly 100 artists who were said to be well-known at the time. The list includes: Auriol, Bac, Baer, Baschilec, Baudin, Bigot, Boiry, Bonnet, Borgex, Boutet, Burret, Cadel, Cadiou, Cappiello, Casse, Chantesais, Chapront, Chéret, Chivot, Conrad, D'Ache, De Barberies, Deavais, Delaw, Dinet Dola, Escudier, Espinasse, Fernel, Flament, Follot, Frog, Gambey, Gerbault, Giraldon, Girardot, Gorguet, Gose, Grasset, Gregoire, Grun, Guerin, Guignebault, Guillaume, Henrida, Heran, Herbinier, Huard, Ibels, Jossot, Jouve, Kauffmann, Kosa, Le Petit (A. and E.G.), Le Riverad, Leandre, Lebegue, Lelee, Lemm, Lewis, Malteste, Marodon, Merson, Metivet, Mirande, Morin, Mucha, Neunier, Noury, Orens, Paris, Paul, Pean, Ranft, Riom, Robida, Roubille, Steinlen, Tetevuide, Tild, Vallet, Vare, Verneuil, Villon, Vogel, Wely, Widhoft, and Willette.[11]

Napoléon by Grasset. (Cinos No. 9.) EF to Mint: $250–$450

Collection des Cent No. 16 by Grasset. EF to Mint: $75–$100

Collection des Cent No. 19 by J. Wely. EF to Mint: $100–$125

Collection des Cent No. 17 by F. Bac. EF to Mint: $200–$250

Collection des Cent No. 27 by R. Péan. EF to Mint: $175–$200

Collection des Cent No. 61 by Chivot. EF to Mint: $400–$500

ADVERTISING AND CALENDAR POSTCARDS

CHAPTER 12

Postcards advertising goods and services were very popular in the beginning of the twentieth century through the early 1930s. Cigarettes, household products, machines, and other items were featured on thousands of different subjects. As to pricing, the general rule is that if a card has children or adults with the product or has a scenic background, it is more desirable than one simply showing the product alone.

Some products were advertised on short series of monthly calendar postcards (see R.F. Outcault in chapter 11 for his series). Often a standard image was used by dozens of different banks or other entities. Most of these are very inexpensive in the marketplace unless signed by a well-known artist.

The following gallery of images and prices furnishes general information.

Printed Advertising Cards, National Advertisers, Singles, and Small Groups

This section includes products and services distributed over a wide geographical area. Many companies issued from one to a dozen or so advertising postcards, not part of numbered sets, but highly collectible as singles and small groups. Some companies offered a set of cards in exchange for labels, postage stamps, or small change. H.J. Heinz, Fisk tires, Kellogg breakfast cereals, and many different automobile manufacturers are examples. There were so many issued—some in large quantities, others with low print runs—that no complete listing will ever be made.

We include a wide selection of issues, many of the most popular among them. In many instances the values of related cards not described here can be estimated by using the values of those that are. As a general rule, early products and companies that are still familiar today have higher collector interest and values than those of businesses that ended long ago. Other factors helping to determine value include the appeal of the image and the item being shown.

Unlike view and most other postcard types, printers and publishers are not often noted on advertising cards.

American Wood Working Machine Co. card relating to Halley's Comet, which excited the world when it appeared in the sky in 1910. This card has significant added value because of this topic, with the depiction of its No. 77 machine less important. EF to Mint: $35–$60

Automatic Electric Washer and Wringer postcard. On the back is an advertising message to which is added the imprint of a local dealer. (Novelty Printing Co., Los Angeles, California.) EF to Mint: $75–$100

Bear Brand hosiery postcard. The depiction of a bear adds value. EF to Mint: $35–$60

Bevo, "The All-Year-Round Soft Drink," was made by Anheuser-Busch during Prohibition. Such cards were issued in large quantities and are seen with some frequency today. (Published by Anheuser-Busch.) EF to Mint: $60–$100

Buffalo Distilling Co. advertising postcard for Golden Grain Whiskey and Canadian Four-Cee Whiskey. Distributed widely, this card is easily found today. EF to Mint: $35–$60

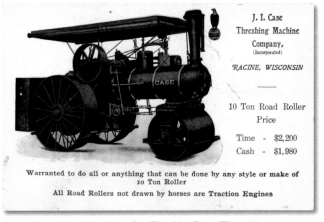

Case Threshing Machine Co. The J.L. Case Threshing Machine Co. used postcards effectively to advertise its line of machines, including the steam roller shown here. EF to Mint: $15–$30

"Case steam roller building country roads. (2,500,000 of this card were printed in November 1908, per back inscription.) EF to Mint: $7–$15

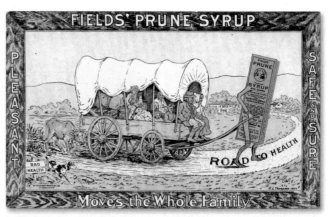

Fields' Prune Syrup laxative as advertised on a popular postcard, with the punning title, "Moves the Whole Family." EF to Mint: $25–$50

Case Threshing Machine Co. steam engine and steel separator. Many of these cards were issued. EF to Mint: $7–$15

Cherry Smash postcard featuring Mount Vernon, with George and Martha Washington at the lower left, taking a glass of the soda from a tray offered by a servant. EF to Mint: $15–$25

Fisk Tires "Time to Re-tire (Buy Fisk)" postcard, a popular image issued in several different imprint and border variations. A related version shows three of the same boy in a row and is much scarcer. EF to Mint: $20–$40

Advertising card by Norman Rockwell, 1924. Desirable due to the fame of the artist. EF to Mint: $15–$25

Flexible Flyer coaster sled advertised on a postcard. The action subject of children at play plus the scarcity of the card would make it a "find." EF to Mint: $25–$40

Gillette Safety Razor advertised on a widely circulated postcard with space for a dealer imprint at the bottom. EF to Mint: $10–$20

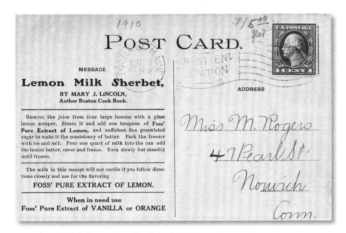

Foss Pure Extract of Lemon, one of two Foss products (the other was Orange) advertised in a large issuance of postcards. On the back were instructions for using. (Popular circa 1909–1912.) EF to Mint: $15–$25

Florodora Cigar label against a background of other cigar bands and labels. (Circa 1906.) EF to Mint: $15–$25

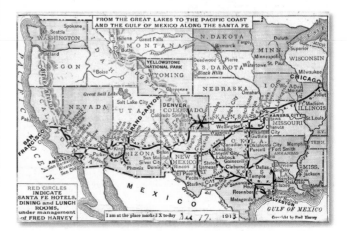

Fred Harvey, operator of lunch rooms and hotels on the Santa Fe Railroad route (and other routes) issued this map of the Santa Fe. Harvey issued many different postcards of views, Native Americans, and other subjects, many of which were made by the Detroit Photographic Co. (Postmarked La Junta, Colorado, 1913.) EF to Mint: $15–$25

Hubbard's Wire-Sewed Folding Delivery Boxes advertised with a view of the boxes full (top) and folded, in a wagon. Made by the Puffer-Hubbard Manufacturing Co., Minneapolis, Minnesota. (Postmarked 1909.) EF to Mint: $12–$15

Humphrey's Witch Hazel Oil advertised on a sign hanging from a biplane, in a time shortly after the airplane was invented. (Circa 1905.) EF to Mint: $10–$12

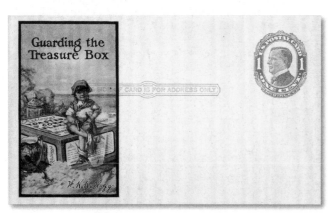

Heinz food products were advertised on many different cards, typically given away at fairs, exhibits, at the Heinz Pier in Atlantic City and elsewhere. They are colorful and attractive and comprise an interesting specialty. "Bottling Heinz Pickles" is the caption on this card. EF to Mint: $15–$20

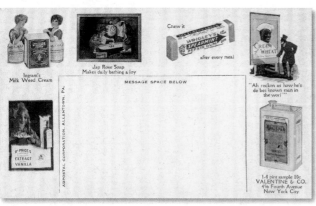

Kellogg's Toasted Corn Flakes are advertised on the front of this government postcard overprinted by the Adpostal Corporation of Allentown, Pennsylvania. The back advertises unrelated products, including Dr. Price's Extract of Vanilla, Ingram's Milk Weed Cream, Jap Rose Soap, Wrigley's Spearmint Gum, Cream of Wheat, and Valspar. Remainders (never used) are seen with frequency in the marketplace and are very popular. EF to Mint: $15–$25

Mecca Cigarettes, a popular early twentieth century brand. (Postmarked 1915.) EF to Mint: $15–$25

Moxie Boy advertising postcard from the 1910s. The Moxie Boy was widely featured in advertising and on signs. Grocery and fruit stand owners found that a Moxie Boy sign placed above items for sale reduced pilferage—as in a sense he was "watching." First formulated in 1885, Moxie grew to become one of America's favorite soft drinks. It is said that the beverage outsold Coca-Cola in New England in the early twentieth century. The drink is still formulated today and is sold in limited areas. The Moxie Company issued about a half dozen different advertising postcards, all of which are scarce and eagerly sought today. Scenic cards with Moxie signs are very popular as well. EF to Mint: $35–$60

Moxie Horsemobile, a vehicle combining an automobile chassis with a model of a horse. The driver straddled the horse and drove the Horsemobile via a small steering wheel. These were a sensation in parades and outdoor gatherings and were produced through the early 1930s. Just one original Horsemobile survives today. Postcards are scarce and are in strong demand. (Circa 1916.) EF to Mint: $45–$80

Moxie Bottle Wagon on a view card, "Entrance to Flag Staff park, Mauch Chunk, Pa." Popular from the turn of the twentieth century into the early 1910s, this consisted of a chassis in the form of a large Moxie bottle, actually a booth with an attendant inside who served Moxie through a window to visitors. Horse-drawn, the wagons were seen in streets, fairs, parades, and other outdoor locations. Although no Moxie Bottle Wagon advertising postcards are known, some view cards show one as part of other scenery. These are avidly collected. (Sexichrome No. 34667. Curt Teich Co., 1913.) EF to Mint: $25–$50

New Home, "The World's Greatest Sewing Machine" advertising cards. Postcards were a very effective medium for showcasing household items of all kinds. (Undivided back with illustration of machine and space for address. Circa 1905.) EF to Mint: $10–$15

St. Charles Milk, condensed and marketed for infants, advertised on a postcard. (Undivided back. Circa 1906.) EF to Mint: $20–$30

Swift's Premium Butterine card. One of a group with printed "handwritten" message on the back by Maud, this one: "I like the English Soldiers, they look so healthy with their bright red cheeks. I am sure that they eat Swift's Premium Butterine. Maud." (Circa 1910). EF to Mint: $10–$15

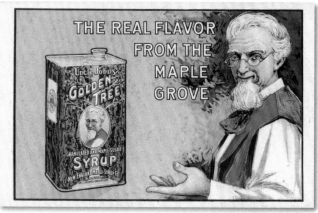

Uncle John's Golden Tree Granulated and Maple Sugar Syrup, New England Maple Syrup Co., Boston, was advertised on postcards. Widely distributed, these cards are easily found today. (Circa 1910s.) EF to Mint: $10–$15

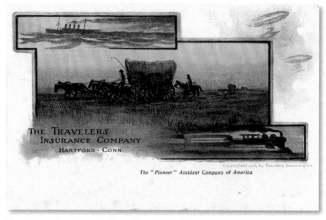

Travelers Insurance Co., Hartford, Connecticut, was a major user of postcards for advertising. This is one of several variations (with different illustrations at the upper left, here a steamship) featuring a Conestoga wagon, "The 'Pioneer' Accident Company of America." Other cards had different motifs. EF to Mint: $10–$15

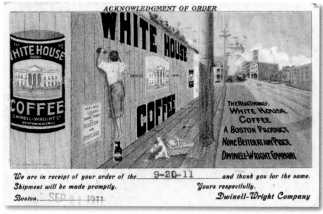

White House Coffee used a variant of an advertising postcard to acknowledge receipt of orders from customers. Many cards survive today. The back shows two cans of the product, "White House is the leading high grade coffee in the world." (Postmarked 1911.) EF to Mint: $15–$25

Twentieth Century No. 12 Fireman's (Acetyline) Hand Lantern advertisement created by overprinting a postcard otherwise issued as "Fire Scene, New York." EF to Mint: $5–$10

Allegheny Window Glass Co., Port Allegheny, Pennsylvania, issued a group of cards illustrating its activities. "Window Glass Blowing. Swinging & Turning Ball (reheated) to form Cylinder." (C.M. Williams, Port Allegheny. Circa 1906.) EF to Mint: $20–$30

Bekins Van and Storage postcard advertising an important California and Western company. A van is pulled by two elephants, a publicity stunt or parade scene. At the bottom is a Bekins building. (Benham Co. No. 2656 / Curt Teich Co. No. A-1846. Divided back. Circa 1907.) EF to Mint: $15–$25

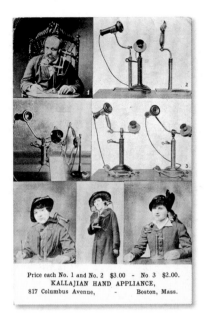

Kallajian Hand Appliance, made by L.S. Kallajian, of Boston, Massachusetts, was available in several different models. "Phone with both hands free," was printed on the back, with other information including, "Perhaps it will interest you to secure agencies in your locality." This is representative of many advertising postcards featuring obscure products, largely forgotten today. (Circa 1910s.) EF to Mint: $15–$25

Davis Standard Bread Co., Los Angeles, California. "Some of the Sixty Wagons Delivering Perfection Bread...." On the back: "If our bread and the service are satisfactory, tell others, if not, tell us." (Souvenir Publishing Co., San Francisco. Circa 1910s.) EF to Mint: $25–$35

Fuller's Floor Wax, made by W.P. Fuller & Co., was distributed on the West Coast. (Postmarked 1915.) EF to Mint: $15–$25

Delaware Coal Co. of Muncie, Indiana, issued these cards on a local basis. (Circa 1910.) EF to Mint: $25–$40

Laub Zink Furniture Co., New Albany, Indiana, advertised on a card with a boy and dog-drawn wagon. (No. R-35829. Curt Teich Co. 1913.) EF to Mint: $15–$25

Peoples Planing Mill, Hiram Reese proprietor, Punxsutawney, Pennsylvania, used postcards to advertise is business. Likely the Reese family is depicted in the image. (No. 11830. E.C. Kropp Co. Circa 1910s.) EF to Mint: $20–$30

Sterling Tires and their prices as featured on an advertising postcard. The maker, Rutherford Rubber Co., of Rutherford, New Jersey, had factory sales branches in New England and the mid-Atlantic states. (No. 4563. Chilton Co. Postmarked 1914.) EF to Mint: $25–$35

Real Photo (RPPC) Advertising Cards

Advertising RPPCs were issued by and for many companies, products, services, and events, national as well as local and regional. In nearly all instances original photographic prints were rephotographed, yielding second-generation quality without sharp details or nuances of shading. There were many exceptions, however.

The typical card was made by taking a picture of the product and placing it on a background to which lettering or art was added. Often an RPPC for a national product would bear the name of a local or regional distributor, who could then have them made on order as needed. The composition ranges from "down home" and amateur (for obscure products, inventions, and short-lived items) to professional. Many cards have additional information printed on the back.

Although the Rotograph Co. of New York City is best remembered for high-quality printed cards, it created many RPPC advertising cards as well. Most of these seem to be either lost to time or were issued without the Rotograph imprint, for identifiable Rotograph RPPCs are not easily found today.

Our presentation of advertising RPPCs is divided into two sections: (1) nationally important products or services, some with local or regional imprints, and (2) local or regional cards featuring services, inventions, and the like that are not of national recognition or importance. The delineation between the two classes is not sharply defined, but the distribution does include the majority of items in each category. No complete listing of advertising RPPCs will ever be compiled, as many of the thousands of different varieties are not known today.

Regarding values, products that are popular collecting specialties, such as liquor, automobiles, and certain other products, are in greater demand and thus higher priced than products that are largely forgotten today or that do not have a strong collector base.

A real photo advertising card for Crowley's Lion Brand Needles. This card was used by a local factory agent of the company.

A Selection of RPPC Advertising Cards

Rotograph card, not technically a postcard as the back is not so laid out, advertising its RPPC service circa the first decade of the twentieth century. EF to Mint: $5–$10

Born Steel Ranges, made by the Born Steel Range Co., of Cleveland, Ohio, had wide distribution in the early twentieth century, and it was said that in Utah alone 35,000 homes had them. The company seemed to appeal to a high level of customer, noting that in addition to homes, they were ideal for fine hotels, steamships, and railroads. This RPPC bears a reproduced handwritten message from "Gertrude," extolling the virtues of the product. (Postmarked 1909.) EF to Mint: $35–$50

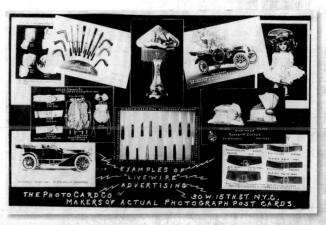

The Photo Card Co. of New York City issued this composite RPPC with photo cards of various products and scenes, noting, "Real Photo Cards Bring Orders." The cards shown, starting at upper left: Kunath & Kunath offering of New Aplik-Kraft Leather; panorama of Bay View development in Freeport, Long Island, offered by the Onslow-Moore Co. of Brooklyn; bronze statue; Weser Style C piano offered by Harry P. Bishop, Babylon, Long Island; Nathan Gold, manufacturer of neckwear, New York City; Moline 35 automobile for sale by the Delamater Byrnes Auto Co.; feather plumes by Charles J. Levy, New York City; skirt by Bert Salinger, New York City; and a delivery truck of the Ruppert Brewery, Westchester branch. EF to Mint: $60–$100

Another RPPC issued by the Photo Card Co. EF to Mint: $60–$100

Autocar, one of America's leading makes of trucks in the early twentieth century, used RPPCs, including, as here, multiple cards in a series issued by a regional distributor, the Autocar Sales and Service Co. of California, with branches in San Francisco, Oakland, Stockton, Sacramento, Los Angeles, Fresno, and San Diego. Photographs of trucks in use, as by the Crescent Creamery Co., were rephotographed, and on the back of each card a testimonial from the user was printed. EF to Mint: $150–$250

Beech-Nut Packing Co., maker and processor of food products, used this RPPC to showcase the cleanliness of its facilities. (Rotograph.) EF to Mint: $45–$80

Falstaff Beer, made by the Lemp Brewing Co. of St. Louis, Mo., advertised extensively on RPPCs. (Postmarked 1911.) EF to Mint: $100–$150

Another Falstaff Beer RPPC. (Circa 1910s.)
EF to Mint: $60–$85

Fleischmann Co., maker of Fleischmann Yeast, used this RPPC to show its fleet of delivery trucks. "In storm, in sunshine, rain, or sleet, You see our wagons on the street." EF to Mint: $45–$60

Franklin Motor Cars in the Glidden Tour were the subject of this RPPC, with a message on the back: "The Horseless Age in its report of the Glidden Tour says 'that air-cooling is a success has been fully proven by the performance of the Franklin cars. They were among the leaders at the night control each night.'" EF to Mint: $60–$90

Studebaker Junior wagon, made in South Bend, Indiana, advertised on an RPPC. The company went on to become a major manufacturer of automobiles. (Postmarked 1906.) EF to Mint: $25–$40

Great Western Champagne was used to christen this flying boat, providing the occasion for the Hammondsport (New York) company to rush out this RPPC. (Postmarked August 7, 1914.) EF to Mint: $60–$90

Kodak Velox advertising card, photographically printed face, large quantities made with various imprints of retailers. EF to Mint: $25–$50

Jeffrey Manufacturing Company, maker of mine hauling machines with a low profile, used this RPPC with reproduced handwriting to carry the advertising message. (Postmarked 1907.) EF to Mint: $50–$80

Mack trucks, made by the International Motor Co., were advertised on many different RPPCs. Typically, these showed a truck in use on the front and on the back a list of Mack owners. (H.P. Dutcher. Circa 1910s.) EF to Mint: $250–$350

A McCaffrey steel file held by a pretty girl resulted in an attractive RPPC. "Good luck and good temper" reads a lightly imprinted caption within the image at the lower right, hardly visible. (Circa 1909.) EF to Mint: $35–$45

Simplex Ironer made by the American Ironing Machine Co. of Chicago, Illinois. On the back: "The saving a Simplex will effect in your household, while it may by only a dollar a week, is quite a handsome sum by the end of the year.... Your ironing costs you that much more in time, labor, and fuel when done by the old laborious hand method...." EF to Mint: $35–$60

Monarch Typewriter featured on an RPPC. On the back is a hand-typed message relating to a recent event: "Let our local representative demonstrate the Monarch Expense Biller, Extract and Condensed Bill and Charge machine in your own office. Those who attended the Master Car Builders Convention at Atlantic City saw a demonstration of the above machines. All were convinced that the Monarch is the best." A nicely typed message directly related to the machine pictured on the front. (Postmarked 1910.) EF to Mint: $25–$45

An advertisement from The Snellenburg Clothing Co. asks readers for "A Moment's Reflection." EF to Mint: $15–$25

Kelly-Springfield Tires advertised on an RPPC. Made by the Consolidated Rubber Tire Co., New York City and Akron, Ohio. (Circa 1910s.) EF to Mint: $35–$50

The Philadelphia Lawn Mower "is the most popular mower made," notes the inscription on the back of this RPPC. A lady dressed in a flowing lace gown actually using a lawnmower, as here, is advertising license. EF to Mint: $35–$60

Standard Nine-Inch Fan mounted on a nearby table keeps mother, father, and daughter cool at mealtime. The Robbins & Myers Co., Springfield, Ohio, issued various RPPCs showing people in real-life situations, from public places to nurseries and hospitals, benefiting from the product. EF to Mint: $25–$40

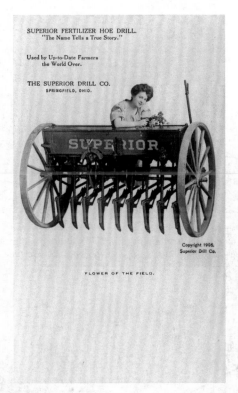

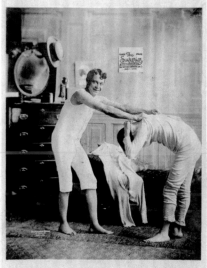

Superior Drills, for planting and farm work, made in Springfield, Ohio, were advertised on many different RPPCs, typically showing a lady sitting on or near a piece of equipment. EF to Mint: $30–$60

Superior Union Suit, a popular one-piece undergarment, as advertised by the maker, the H.S. Eaton Clothing Co., Westfield, Massachusetts. (Postmarked 1907.) EF to Mint: $35–$60

Advertising RPPCs of Local, Regional, and Short-Lived Products and Services

There is no end to the variety of local and regional RPPCs or those made for short-lived products, inventions, and the like. Many thousands of different cards were made. The following is a sampling to illustrate the diversity.

Fair Price Hat Co., 28-30 East 4th Street, New York City, illustrated and priced its styles on an RPPC. EF to Mint: $20–$35

G & J Tires, made in Indianapolis, Indiana, added a pretty girl to this scene, increasing interest in 1909 when this was posted and adding value today. Otherwise an RPPC of an auto tire would have little value. EF to Mint: $35–$45

Larrabee trucks: The Binghamton (New York) distributor for the Larrabee Speed Six Model 40 truck had this picture rephotographed with a typed label to create an RPPC to mail out to prospects. Message printed on the back: "May we have a representative call and consult with you on your transportation problems?" EF to Mint: $80–$120

Ideal Gas Engines were advertised on this RPPC. The message on the back: "We extend to you a cordial invitation to make our tent, while at the fair, your headquarters. We are looking for a dealer in your locality. Yours truly, Ideal Motor Co." EF to Mint: $150–$250

King Cornet RPPC. A pretty girl plus the product was always a winning formula to create an interesting card. EF to Mint: $35–$50

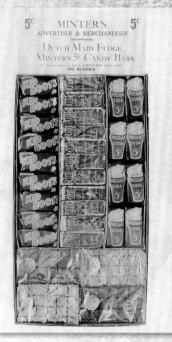

Minter's candies merchandising carton (Kid Boots, Choco Fudge, and Chocolate Soda brand candy bars) advertised on an RPPC. EF to Mint: $35–$50

Model Knitwear advertised on a hand-tinted RPPC. EF to Mint: $20–$30

May Brook whiskey advertised by an RPPC showing three children, one asleep, would not pass muster in an advertising agency today. (Postmarked 1907.) EF to Mint: $25–$45

Ohlen's Small Smithing Shop, conducted by the James Ohlen & Sons Saw Manufacturing Co., Columbus, Ohio, used this professionally made RPPC to advertise its services. (Postmarked 1906.) EF to Mint: $50–$80

Moonie's Taxi Cab as lettered on the side of the vehicle, variant spelling, Mooney & His Brother Taxi Service in the title, location not stated, but "Indiana" marked in pencil on the back. (Circa 1910s.) EF to Mint: $200–$300

Red "C" Oil for table lamps advertised on an RPPC that does not show the product, but describes its use. The warm glow of the lamp and the attractive girl make this a desirable card. EF to Mint: $20–$30

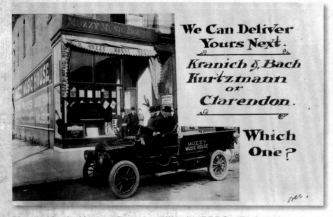

Muzzy Music House, Decatur, Illinois. RPPC offering three brands of pianos sold by the firm. Location not stated. (Circa 1910s.) EF to Mint: $200–$300

Reis Sunshine Homes issued this RPPC showing its brass band and showcasing the well-known brands of products used in construction. (Circa 1920s.) EF to Mint: $50–$80

Richards & Conover Hardware Co. used the pretty girl and product formula for this RPPC published in 1913. EF to Mint: $35–$60

Roberts Aero Motor, Model 4X, 40-60 H.P., made by the Roberts Motor Co., Sandusky, Ohio, advertised on an RPPC. (E.H. Schlessman, Commercial Photographer, Sandusky. Circa 1910s.) EF to Mint: $80–$120

Rider-Lewis Type 4 automobile advertised on an RPPC. "$1050. Anderson, Ind." This card, from circa 1910, was probably made by a local photographer for a product that had great expectations. The firm moved from Muncie, Indiana, to Anderson in 1909. By June 1910, production was about 30 to 40 cars per week. It ran into financial difficulties the same year and went into receivership, and the business ended in 1911. In this era there were dozens of start-up companies in the field. EF to Mint: $100–$200

Werner Brothers, Chicago movers and operators of a storage facility, advertised on an RPPC. (National Photograph Co., Chicago. Circa 1910s.) EF to Mint: $150–$250

Rock Island Sash & Door Works, Rock Island, Illinois, advertising RPPC. (No. 2. Photo Co. of America. Postmarked 1905.) EF to Mint: $45–$60

White Clover Butter featured on an RPPC issued by the Elgin (Illinois) Butter Co. EF to Mint: $60–$80

St. Louis Chocolate Co. "sales board" advertisement. These were punch boards with pretty ladies and other motifs. Patrons used a small metal rod to punch a slip of paper from a chosen spot. Boards were available with either 500 holes that patrons would pay 10¢ to punch, or 1,000 holes for 5¢. Each board had 42 winning holes, each yielding a box of "delicious golden brown chocolates." Each board cost $20, including 42 boxes of chocolates. "Big money for you by buying this wonderful Sales Board Candy Deal direct from the manufacturer. Board brings in $40, giving you $20 profit on a $20 investment." EF to Mint: $25–$40

Toledo Biscuits and related cookies, crackers, and goods, made in the Ohio city of that name, issued various RPPCs showing pretty girls and children with multiple boxes in view. On the back of this particular card a printed message stated that Toledo money should be kept in Toledo, "Do not send to Chicago and New York." Buying this hometown product would help with this campaign. (Postmarked 1909.) EF to Mint: $35–$45

Dr. Vance's Reducing Machine seemed to operate with a rotating drum that somehow benefited ladies pressing against it. A cheaply made RPPC with a second- or third-generation photograph showing little in the way of shading. EF to Mint: $20–$35

DR. VANCE'S REDUCING MACHINE

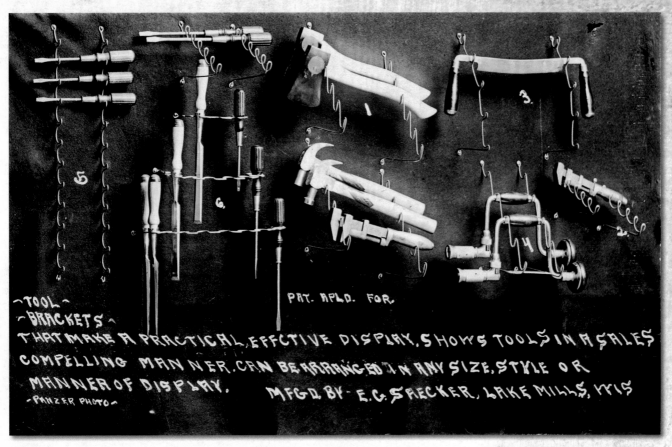

Saecker Tool Brackets made by E.C. Saecker, Lake Mills, Wisconsin. On the back, "Goods well displayed are half sold, and with the Brackets shown hereon you can arrange and show more tools more attractively than any other way, using less space and showing more goods. Nos. 1 to 5 sold at 20¢ per pair. No. 6, holding 27 tools, 35¢." (Panzer photo. Postmarked 1914.) EF to Mint: $60–$100

The Voss Swinging Wringer was to be demonstrated at the Sedalia (Missouri) Fair, August 9 to 16, 1919, in the Varied Industries Building, spaces 19 and 20, noted the message on the back of this RPPC. EF to Mint: $25–$35

Seipp [Conrad Seipp] Brewing Co., Chicago, RPPC showing the bottling production line. Conrad Seipp came to America from Germany and began brewing beer in Chicago in 1854. The Conrad Seipp Brewing Co., formed in 1872, became part of the City of Chicago Consolidated Brewing & Malting Co. in 1890, although the Seipp brand continued to be made and was one of the most important regional beers. (Circa 1910s.) EF to Mint: $150–$250

Calendar Advertising Cards, Printed

Printed advertising cards were issued by many firms. The most prominent was Brown & Bigelow of St. Paul, Minnesota. Many of their cards were perforated for hanging on a wall. Some are by well-known artists described in chapter 11. The Thomas D. Murphy Co. of Red Oak, Iowa, was probably the second-largest firm. Many of the images of the above two firms were also produced as blotters and as larger calendars. The same image and calendar was used on cards bearing the imprint of hundreds of different businesses. In 1908 the Wesley Art Advertising Co. of Chicago copyrighted a series of illustrations relating to banking, saving, thrift, and related subjects. These were made available to banks in 12-month runs through 1911.

Calendar Advertising RPPCs

RPPC calendar cards were usually made in large runs so that any given image is not rare today. Again, values depend on the appeal of the subject.

Brown & Bigelow artist James Arthur, Matinee Girl, calendar card. EF to Mint: $10–$15

Brown & Bigelow artist Stuart Travis, Deep Waters, calendar card. EF to Mint: $10–$15

Wesley Art Advertising Co. calendar card with the imprint of The Old National Bank of Grand Rapids, Michigan, issued in June 1910 with a June-related illustration and message. EF to Mint: $8–$12

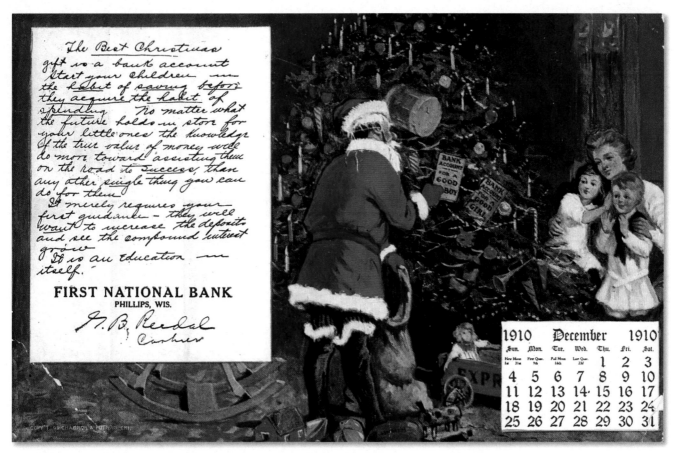

Champion & Putnam calendar card for the First National Bank of Phillips, Wisconsin, with Santa Claus. EF to Mint: $15–$20

California Almond Growers Exchange calendar postcard for July 1920, RPPC. EF to Mint: $30–$50

RESTAURANTS, ICE CREAM PARLORS, SALOONS, GAMBLING, PASTIMES, ETC.

CHAPTER 13

Eating, drinking, bowling, billiards, gambling, and other activities that involved going to a specific location were depicted on many postcards. These are widely collected today. Interior views are the most desirable. Prices vary and largely depend on the appeal of the image. Postcards showing people are more valuable.

Restaurants

Values are dependent on the appeal of the image. Cards showing people seated at counters or tables, a rare category, are worth more. Interiors that are colorful with art glass shades, plants, and the like are more desirable than ones that are plain.

Advertising card for The Edelweiss Restaurant, Chicago, early twentieth century, with images of players. EF to Mint: $10–$25

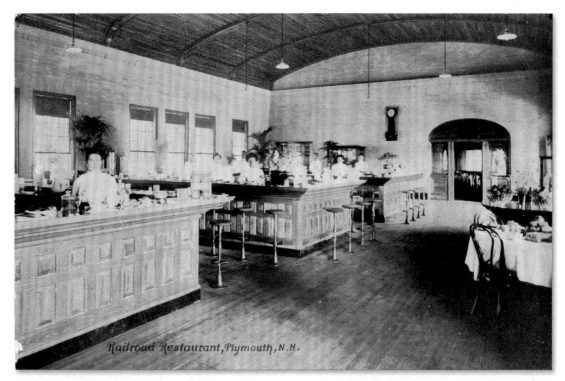

Railroad Restaurant, Plymouth, New Hampshire, circa 1910s. (G.W. Morris-314, German import). EF to Mint: $10–$25

Patterson's Restaurant, Ludlow, Vermont, snowed in, 1910. RPPC. EF to Mint: $50–$75

Restaurants	Value, EF to Mint
Interiors 1900–1930	$10–$50
Exteriors 1900–1930	$5–$40
Interiors, RPPC 1900–1920	$20+
Exteriors, RPPC 1900–1920	$20+

Ice Cream Parlors, Soda Parlors

Similar to restaurant cards, values are dependent on the appeal of the image. Cards showing people seated at counters or tables, a rare category, are worth more, as are colorfully decorated interiors.

Restaurant interior with staff at tables, Canobie Lake Park, New Hampshire, 1917. RPPC. EF to Mint: $25–$50

Donofrio's soda fountain and confectionery, Phoenix, Arizona. On the back, "A magic palace of deliciousness in a valley of perpetual sunshine." (No. R-66922. Curt Teich Co. 1916). EF to Mint: $15–$25

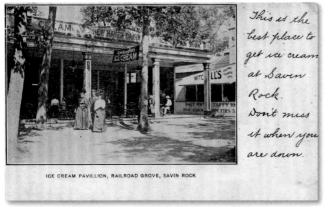

This is the best place to get ice cream at Savin Rock. Don't miss it when you are down.

ICE CREAM PAVILLION, RAILROAD GROVE, SAVIN ROCK

Ice Cream Pavillion, Savin Rock Park, Connecticut. (Postmarked 1906.) EF to Mint: $15–$25

J. Schrauth's Sons Ice Cream Parlor, Poughkeepsie, New York. A coin-operated Link orchestrion is under the banner on the far wall. EF to Mint: $20–$35

The Lake View Ice Cream Parlor in South Alburg, Vermont. A nicely detailed view that under magnification shows a sign with the Moxie Girl and other notices. RPPC. (Circa 1910s.) EF to Mint: $75+

Soda parlor, Warsaw, New York. RPPC. (Circa 1910s.) EF to Mint: $75+

Hastings Ice Cream Parlor, Hastings-on-Hudson, New York. RPPC. (Circa 1910s.) EF to Mint: $175+

Ice Cream Parlors, Soda Parlors	Value, EF to Mint
Interiors 1900–1930	$15–$60
Exteriors 1900–1930	$15–$40
Interiors, RPPC 1900–1920	$50+
Exteriors, RPPC 1900–1920	$50+

Cafes and Saloons

This is a very popular and expensive subject. Most valuable are cards that show people and/or slot machines and other devices. Many, if not most, cards of this type are RPPCs. The word *saloon* was often used to describe large gathering areas on ships and in halls, what we would call a *salon* today; those are not relevant to this category of postcard.

For many years Albert's Buckhorn Saloon in San Antonio, Texas, was one of the city's prime tourist attractions. Proprietor Albert Friedrich sold or gave away countless thousands of postcards and souvenir booklets showing the curiosities displayed on the various walls (west wall shown here). EF to Mint: $5–$10

Saloon RPPC, unknown location. EF to Mint: $75+

Saloon RPPC, unknown location, "Victor Zehnder 241" on back. EF to Mint: $30–$60

Saratoga Café, Pipestone, Minnesota. RPPC with slot machines and people. EF to Mint: $250+

Large café at Willow Grove Park, Philadelphia. EF to Mint: $4–$7

Rockingham Café at Rockingham Junction, New Hampshire. EF to Mint: $8–$12

Billiard games in progress at the Post Exchange, Marine Base, Norfolk, Virginia. Prominent Coca-Cola signs in the back of the room add to the value of this card. RPPC. (Postmarked 1910.) EF to Mint: $100+

The ornately decorated Franklin Café horse-drawn wagon, Worcester, Massachusetts. RPPC. (Circa 1910s). EF to Mint: $200+

Pool hall in Quincy, Illinois. RPPC with people and a Liberty Bell slot machine. On the back, John Wuehlmann Jr. writes to his father in Albany, New York, asking, "Do you see pool halls like this East" and says he is making $9 per day. (Postmarked 1911.) EF to Mint: $150+

Cafes and Saloons	Value, EF to Mint
Interiors 1900–1930	$5–$40
Exteriors 1900–1930	$4–$30
Interiors, RPPC 1900–1920	$20–$100+
Exteriors, RPPC 1900–1920	$20–$100+

Pool Halls, Billiard Parlors

Cards that show players in action are scarcer and more valuable. Exterior views are often part of street scenes.

Pool Halls, Billiard Parlors	Value, EF to Mint
Interiors 1900–1930	$10–$30
Exteriors 1900–1930	$5–$20
Interiors, RPPC 1900–1920	$25–$100+
Exteriors, RPPC 1900–1920	$35–$100+

Inscription on back of this RPPC: "This is a photo of Morley's Billiard Palace—the finest in the United States. 640 Broadway, Los Angeles, Cal." (Circa 1910s.) EF to Mint: $75+

Bowling Alleys

Cards that show bowlers in action are extremely rare and have additional value. Most interior views are from the back and have lanes in the foreground. Views of buildings have lesser value. Bowling was also known as boxball.

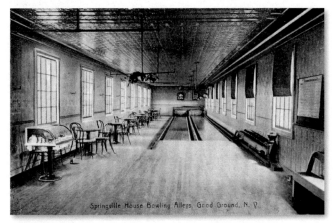

"Springville House Bowling Alleys, Good Ground, NY."
(German import. No. 57791. Postmarked 1909.)
EF to Mint: $10–$15

Boxball alleys at Bushkill Park, Easton, Pennsylvania.
(Germany. Circa 1906.) EF to Mint: $8–$12

"Bowling Alley, Waldameer Park, Erie, Pa." (No. 6626. Buffalo News Co. / ANC Litho-Chrome. Postmarked 1912.)
EF to Mint: $15–$25

Bowling lanes at Canobie Lake Park, New Hampshire.
EF to Mint: $15–$20

Crystal Maze and Bowling Alleys at Canobie Lake Park.
EF to Mint: $7–$10

Bowling comic card with embossed bumps on the edges. (J.B. & Co. Circa 1905.)
EF to Mint: $4–$8

Bowling Alleys	Value, EF to Mint
Interiors 1900–1930	$12–$40
Exteriors 1900–1930	$5–$20
Interiors, RPPC 1900–1920	$35–$100+
Exteriors, RPPC 1900–1920	$35–$100+
Bowling comic postcards: 1900–1930	$4–$20+

Gambling Parlors

This is a very popular and expensive specialty. Most cards are from the West. The more people in the scene, the more desirable a card is.

A busy roulette table in Rawhide, Nevada. RPPC. (By Osborn, photographer with G. & K. Drug Co., Rawhide. Circa 1915.) EF to Mint: $300+

Gambling parlor in Tonopah, Nevada, circa 1906. EF to Mint: $25–$40

A craps game in the West, no specific location. EF to Mint: $15–$25

"Cowboys shooting craps" (Detroit No. 235). EF to Mint: $5–$10

Gambling Parlors	Value, EF to Mint
Interiors 1900–1930	$10–$40+
Exteriors 1900–1930	$5–$20
Interiors, RPPC 1900–1920	$40–$150+
Exteriors, RPPC 1900–1920	$25–$100+

Games and Hobbies

Cards that depict games and their elements, such as chess, checkers, and recreational (not gambling) cards, comprise a fairly scarce category. Many are of a comic nature and were printed in Europe.

Comic chess card by J. Rotgans. (G.B. van Zoor Zonen, Gouda, Holland; part of a series.) EF to Mint: $20–$30

Comic chess card with animated players. Part of a series. (R. Schmidt, Homburg v.d. Höhe, Germany; distributed in Germany and France.) EF to Mint: $50–$100

"The Cardinal," a game of chess. (No. 85. S., New York, 1908.) EF to Mint: $12–$20

"A Game Answer" checkers comic card. (P. Sander. Postmarked 1911.) EF to Mint: $12–$20

Numismatics

Many postcards were issued in connection with numismatics—the collecting of coins, medals, tokens, and paper money. Most of these have to do with the production of coins at the several mints and the production of paper money at the Bureau of Engraving and Printing. In addition, sets of embossed postcards showing coins from different countries were made by Walter Erhard in Waldbitngen-Stuttgart, Germany, and others; certain varieties of these are very rare and were issued into the 1920s.

Carson City Mint. EF to Mint: $10–$30

Denver Mint. EF to Mint: $5–$15

Philadelphia Mint (closed in 1901) exterior. EF to Mint: $10–$20

Philadelphia Mint (third) exterior. EF to Mint: $5–$15

Philadelphia Mint interior. EF to Mint: $10–$25

Philadelphia Mint Cabinet. EF to Mint: $10–$20

Bureau of Engraving and Printing, old building. EF to Mint: $5–$10

BEP interior. EF to Mint: $12–$18

Bureau of Engraving and Printing, new building. EF to Mint: $3–$8

San Francisco Mint. EF to Mint: $5–$15

San Francisco Mint, 1906 earthquake. EF to Mint: $10–$25

10 Dollars	1 Dollar
41 Mark 98 Pfennig	4 M. 20 Pf.
41 Shillings 1¼ d (£ 2. 1. 1¼)	4 sh. 1⅓ d
51 Francs 83 Centimes	5 frs. 18 cts.
37 Kroner 31 Öre	3 Kr. 73 Öre
24 Gulden / Florins 88 Cents	2. fl. 49 cts.
19 Rubel / Roubles 43½ Kop.	1 R. 94 Kcp.
Wert in Gold. Valeur en or. Value in gold,	

1 Dollar ($) = 100 Cents.

Vereinigte Staaten von Amerika I.
United States of America I.   Etats-Unis d'Amérique I.
Estados Unidos de América I.

Embossed United States coin card made in Germany, latest coin dated 1914. EF to Mint: $15–$30

Embossed United States coin card made in Germany with some coins dated 1902. EF to Mint: $15–$30

Embossed Mexican coin card with Spanish inscription on the back. EF to Mint: $15–$25

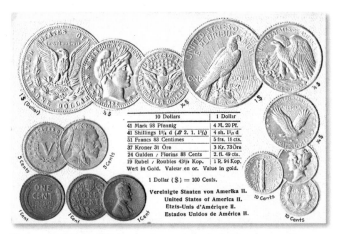

Embossed United States coin card made in Germany after the World War, showing the reverse of the Peace dollar introduced in 1921. EF to Mint: $15–$30

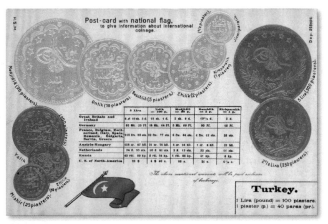

Embossed Turkish coin card made in Germany.
EF to Mint: $15–$25

BEP interior, stamps being produced. EF to Mint: $10–$20

Embossed Uruguay coin card made in Germany.
EF to Mint: $15–$25

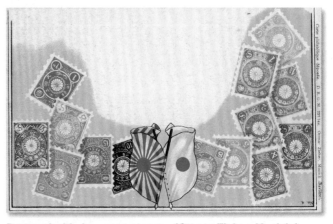

Postcard with United States stamps. (Ottmar Zieher, Munich.)
EF to Mint: $15–$30

Philatelics

Postcards depicting stamps mainly illustrate the Bureau of Engraving and Printing, where stamps are made. Post Offices are covered elsewhere in this book. In a related vein, postcards issued at expositions can have value if they have a commemorative stamp of the exposition and were postmarked on the opening day. The Scott specialized catalog of U.S. stamps gives first-day dates and values. For Bureau of Engraving and Printing postcards of buildings, see Numismatics, page 207.

Postcard with Japanese stamps. (Ottmar Zieher, Munich.)
EF to Mint: $15–$30

STORES, OFFICES, AND BANKS

CHAPTER 14

Stores, shops, offices, and related enterprises and their buildings form a very eclectic category. Specialties can be collected, such as five-and-ten-cent stores of F.W. Woolworth and others, a popular pursuit; gift shops; women's clothing shops; banks; and other views. Generally, interior views with interesting details are much more in demand than building exteriors of banks, department stores, and large businesses. Exterior views that include smaller shops, etc., with signs in front are popular as well. Small-town and village images can be worth more. The prices given in our tables are representative of establishments identifiable as to name and location. Others are worth much less.

A.C. Dietsche's Remembrance Shop in Detroit, Michigan. (No publisher. No. 218 B. Postmarked 1910.) EF to Mint: $15–$25

The front of Goodman's Bookstore, Manchester, New Hampshire. EF to Mint: $15-25

Clothing, bedding, and dry goods store front, Everett M. Staples, Biddeford, Maine. (Hugh C. Leighton. No. 3689. Postmarked 1908.) EF to Mint: $20–$30

Front of Euclid Tailor Parlors, Providence, Rhode Island. (No publisher. Circa 1910s.) EF to Mint: $20–$30

John Munroe's shoe store and repair shop in Stamford, New York. (No. 108917. Artino. Circa 1910s.) EF to Mint: $30–$45

Two rows of workers tend the pneumatic tube system of the Jordan Marsh department store in Boston. Cash and slips were sent in small containers to this basement facility, where change was made and returned to the sales clerk. (Circa 1910s.) EF to Mint: $10–$20

E.M. Mulliken hardware and furniture store, Humboldt, Illinois. (No. 5500.) EF to Mint: $25–$40

Salesroom, Central Supply Co. Steam, Gas, and Water Supplies. Worcester, Massachusetts. EF to Mint: $15–$25

The Groves-Stark Hardware Co. store, "Mantel and Fixture Department," Huntington, West Virginia. (No. R-47790. Curt Teich Co. 1914.) EF to Mint: $40–$60

C.E. Love, Furniture and Undertaking, Munnsville, New York. These two business specialties were a popular combination, with caskets being part of the inventory. RPPC. (Postmarked 1907.) EF to Mint: $150+

In Hood River, Oregon, near Mount Hood, Arthur Clark's small jewelry store offered a wide variety of jewelry, souvenir plates, clocks, and art objects to tourists, who were important to the area's economy. (Published by Clark. Postmarked 1914.) EF to Mint: $40–$60

Corner Hardware Store, New Hampton, Iowa, with a display of Monarch stoves and ranges for sale. (E.C. Kropp & Co. Circa 1910s.) EF to Mint: $35–$45

Sorenson Co. jewelry store in San Francisco, California, a large, brightly lighted emporium with merchandise in glass cases. (Richard Behrendt, San Francisco. Postmarked 1910.) EF to Mint: $25–$35

Exterior of the Jensen, Herzer & Jeck jewelry store in Nashville, Tennessee. Likely this building was in a commercial district with others to the right and left, removed from the negative by the postcard manufacturer. (No publisher. No. 17944. Circa 1910s.) EF to Mint: $30–$50

F.W. Woolworth store on Main Street, Concord, New Hampshire. (Leighton L1547. Germany. 1911.) EF to Mint: $6–$8

Interior of the Jensen, Herzer & Jeck jewelry store. (No publisher. Circa 1910s.) EF to Mint: $40–$60

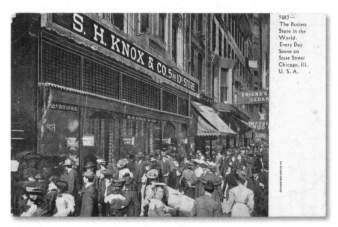

S.H. Knox & Co. store, Chicago, Illinois. (Souvenir Post Card Co., New York. Circa 1904.) EF to Mint: $4–$8

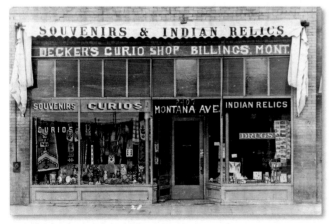

Decker's Curio Shop, Billings, Montana. RPPC altered by adding name of shop and address. Postcards are displayed in the right window. EF to Mint: $150–$200

F.W. Woolworth store on Main Street, Freeport, New York. (1920s.) EF to Mint: $8–$10

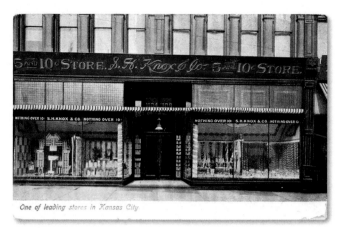

S.H. Knox & Co. store, Kansas City, Missouri.
(H.K. Knox & Co., Germany. 1906.) EF to Mint: $9–$12

Independent Store, Minneapolis, Minnesota. (Curt Teich Co.)
EF to Mint: $8–$10

Stores	Value, EF to Mint
Clothing, jewelry, and fashion shops, exteriors 1900 to 1930s	$10–$40+
Clothing, jewelry, and fashion shops, interiors 1900 to 1930s	$10–$50+
Clothing, etc. RPPC	$75–$200+
Five-and-ten cent stores, exteriors 1900 to 1930s	$10–$40+
Five-and-ten cent stores, interiors 1900 to 1930s	$10–$40+
Five-and-ten cent stores, interiors, RPPC 1900 to 1920s	$75–$200+
Flower, candy, gift shops, exteriors 1900 to 1930s	$10–$40+
Flower, candy, gift shops, interiors 1900 to 1930s	$10–$50+
Flower, candy, gift shops, interiors, RPPC 1900 to 1920s	$75–$200+
General commercial interiors 1900–1930s	$10–$50+
General commercial interiors RPPC 1900–1920s	$75–$200+
General commercial exteriors 1900–1930s	$10–$40+
General commercial exteriors RPPC 1900–1920s	$75–$200+

General Stores and Post Offices

In many small- and medium-size towns, a general store served the needs of people within walking or cycling distance. Relatively few people owned horses and carriages in the early twentieth century, as such required a stable, upkeep, and other expenses. Walking and bicycling were the usual ways to get around, unless there was a streetcar line nearby. A given town might have several general stores. These stocked groceries, hardware, clothing and other dry goods, and various necessities. Often the Post Office was within the store and was conducted by the proprietor—a satisfactory arrangement, as this brought patrons into the store regularly, often every day. Cards featuring general stores often included post offices, a two-for-one postcard. Cards of small rural post offices are more highly valued than those of large post offices.

Printed cards and RPPCs are widely available for these stores, most showing the exterior. Interior views are very desirable if the image is in sharp focus and the products can be identified. People add interest and value, as do vehicles in front. Post offices and general stores that have a "Post Office" sign have added interest if they bear the clear postmark of that office. Such cards are plentiful and are interesting to collect, but little additional value is usually attached. In many instances printed cards were ordered by the store and bear its imprint on the face or back.

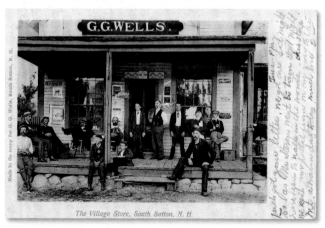

"The Village Store, South Sutton, N.H.," the general store of G.G. Wells. With many people in view and colorful advertising signs, this is a premium card among those of this type. (G.G. Wells. Postmarked 1906.) EF to Mint: $25–$40

"The Department Store" conducted by J. F. Molony at 1 Bluestone Boulevard, Mill Rift, Pennsylvania. A general store that had most anything needed by local customers. (Published by Molony, a German imported card. Postmarked 1909.) EF to Mint: $25–$40

General Stores and Post Offices	Value, EF to Mint
General store (some with post office) exteriors 1900–1930	$8–$20+
General store (some with post office) interiors 1900–1930	$12–$30+
General store (some with post office) exteriors, RPPC 1900–1920	$50–$125+
General store (some with post office) interiors, RPPC 1900–1920	$50–$175+
Post office exteriors 1900–1930	$4–$15
Post office interiors 1900–1930	$8–$30
Post office exteriors, RPPC 1900–1920	$15–$40+
Post office interiors, RPPC 1900–1920	$25–$100+

L.E. Culver's Store, Warners, New York. A sharply detailed RPPC with many different product signs readable. (H.A. Myer & Co. Postmarked 1909.) EF to Mint: $175+

Drug Stores

Drug stores are a niche postcard specialty. Small drug stores are more valuable than large drug stores. Exteriors are often found as part of street views.

Hand-colored printed card of Gilbert's Drug Store, Fort Collins, Colorado. (Albertype Co. Circa 1910s.) EF to Mint: $25–$40

S.H. Hallett's Store at Centerville, Massachusetts, a general store and Post Office. The horse-drawn truck of the Centerville and Craigville Variety Stores lends additional interest to this RPPC. (Postmarked 1908.) EF to Mint: $175+

Holt's Drug Store in West Point, Illinois, also specialized in postcards. RPPC. (Postmarked 1908.) EF to Mint: $200+

Kephart's Drug Store, Berrien Springs, Michigan. RPPC. (Postmarked 1908.) EF to Mint: $100+

Bowman's Pharmacy, Pine Plains, New York. (Great Britain.) EF to Mint: $25–$35

Drug Stores	Value, EF to Mint
Exteriors 1900–1930	$8–$20+
Interiors 1900–1930	$12–$30+
Exteriors, RPPC 1900–1920	$50–$125+
Drug store interiors, RPPC 1900–1920	$50–$175+

Food Stores, Stands, and Vendors

This is another varied specialty. Printed postcards of food stores in small towns are more desired than large stores, but both categories are very scarce. RPPCs are rare. Stands and vendors, usually seen on RPPCs, are highly desired and valuable.

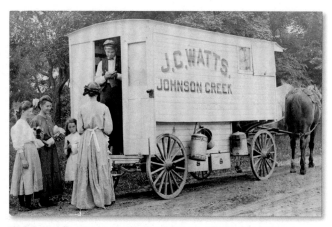

RPPC of J.C. Watts, of Johnson Creek, Wisconsin, whose horse-drawn delivery wagon filled with groceries called on various customers. A women and three young ladies hold cans and bottles, while Watts writes an invoice. (Circa 1910s.) EF to Mint: $150–$200

Grocery store interior, location unknown. RPPC. EF to Mint: $40–$50, this card would be valued at $125+ if identified

Macon Fish Co., Macon, Georgia. (Curt Teich Co.) EF to Mint: $35–$45

Grand Union store delivery wagon, Newburgh, New York. RPPC. EF to Mint: $200+

Grocery store interior, Jersey, Illinois. RPPC. (Postmarked 1911) EF to Mint: $125+

Grocery store and delivery wagon, Massillon, Ohio. RPPC. EF to Mint: $125+

Grocery store exterior, location unknown. RPPC. EF to Mint: $40–$60

Food Stores, Stands, and Vendors	Value, EF to Mint
Exteriors 1900–1930	$8–$20
Interiors 1900–1930	$12–$30
Exteriors, RPPC 1900–1920	$50–$125+
Interiors, RPPC 1900–1920	$50–$150+
Food vendors, mobile RPPC 1900–1920	$75–$200+
Food stands, RPPC 1900–1920	$75–$175+

Banks

Most postcards in this category are national banks. Such cards are often desired by numismatists who collect national bank notes. Nearly all are printed in color. RPPCs are rare but not expensive. Some years ago a collector acquired more than 4,000 different ones.

Cards of small banks are more valuable than those of banks in large city buildings.

Fourth National Bank of Atlanta, Georgia. EF to Mint: $5–$8

First National Bank of Douglas County, Castle Rock, Colorado, 1909. EF to Mint: $10–$15

Butler National Bank, New Jersey, 1907. EF to Mint: $10–$15

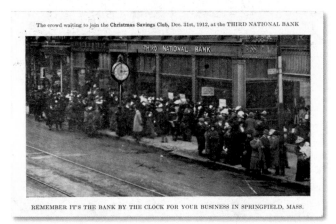

A crowd at the Third National Bank of Springfield, Massachusetts. This is an interesting social commentary of the time when banks offered savings clubs for $1 per week or another low amount. EF to Mint: $8–$12

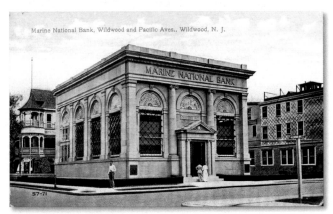

Marine National Bank, Wildwood, New Jersey. EF to Mint: $5–$10

First National Bank of Birmingham, Alabama, interior. EF to Mint: $12–$18

First National Bank of Muskogee, Oklahoma, interior.
EF to Mint: $10–$15

Wilkinsburg Bank, Wilkinsburg, Pennsylvania. (Valentine 212918). EF to Mint: $10–$15

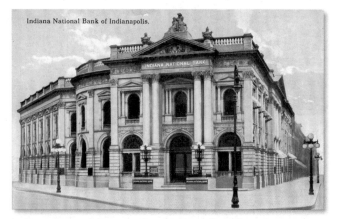

Indiana National Bank, Indianapolis, Indiana, exterior.
EF to Mint: $5–$10

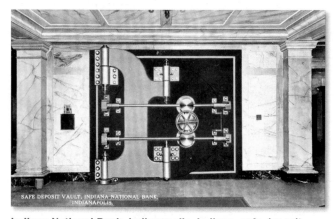

Indiana National Bank, Indianapolis, Indiana, safe deposit vault. (Curt Teich.) EF to Mint: $12–$18

Indiana National Bank, Indianapolis, Indiana, lobby. (Curt Teich.) EF to Mint: $8–$12

Indiana National Bank, Indianapolis, Indiana, directors' room.
EF to Mint: $12–$18

Banks	Value, EF to Mint
Exteriors 1900 to 1930s	$5–$15
Interiors 1900 to 1930s	$8–$20
Exteriors RPPC 1900 to 1920s	$8–$15
Interiors RPPC 1900 to 1920s	$10–$30

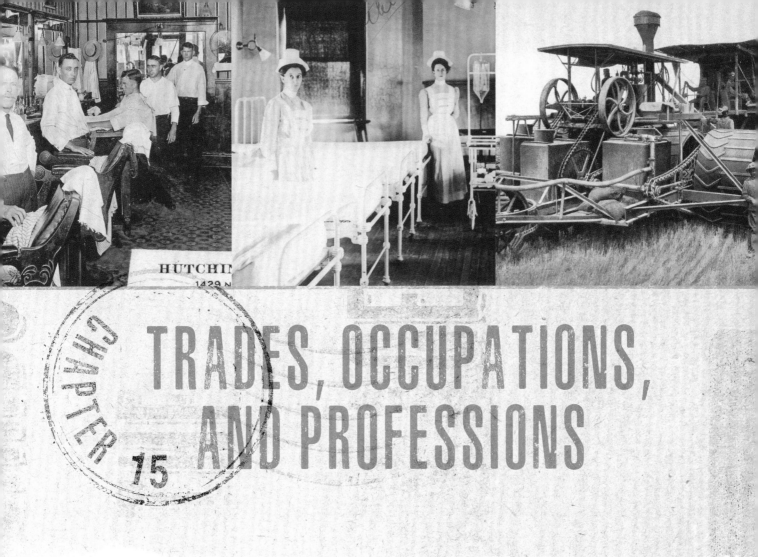

HUTCHIN
1429 N

TRADES, OCCUPATIONS, AND PROFESSIONS

CHAPTER 15

Various crafts, trades, occupations, and professions are depicted on countless different postcard scenes. Cards from the early years showing small offices, shops, construction projects, and the like are mostly RPPCs. Printed cards dominate for cards of the 1920s onward.

Such cards are often collected by category, such as medical and dental, construction, factory interiors, and the like. This is another varied and eclectic area; there is no end to the collecting possibilities. Except for some RPPCs, most are quite inexpensive.

Building, Craft, Mechanic, and Construction Trades

Manual arts, crafts, and trades range from sculpting to construction to road work. Cards, especially showing several people working, are windows on American life.

Surveying crew with a transit and stadia rods, Greenville, Pennsylvania. RPPC. This is a rare profession for card images. Surveyors were required to be licensed, but this did not apply to some helpers in the crew. (Postmarked 1908.) EF to Mint: $150+

Blacksmith shop in Windsorville, Maine, with horseshoeing sign. The sign reads, "C.E. Avery, Horse Shoeing and Repairing." RPPC. Many different images, mostly RPPCs, were made of such shops. (Postmarked 1912.) EF to Mint: $75+

Artistic and Specialty Trades

Painters, sculptors, watch and jewelry makers, and other trades involving skilled hand work and artistic ability can be collected across many categories.

Carver of stone monuments with his shop and products. RPPC postmarked Portland, Maine. Most medium-size and larger towns had one or more stone-carving shops. Not many were depicted on postcards. (Postmarked 1928.) EF to Mint: $40–$50

D.R. Nichols, watchmaker, in his office, 312 State Mutual Building, Worcester, Massachusetts. RPPC. (Postmarked 1908.) EF to Mint: $125

Edward V. Valentine, sculptor, of Richmond, Virginia. The back notes in part, "Is here shown in his studio, surrounded by models, casts, art works, etc. The bust in the foreground is a study of Robert E. Lee, executed in connection with the statue which Mr. Valentine designed for placement in Statuary Hall at Washington...." (No. A-5443. Curt Teich Co. Circa 1908.) EF to Mint: $25–$35

James Walter Folger, artist and woodcarver, Nantucket, Massachusetts. (No. 500. Henry S. Wyer, Nantucket. Circa 1910.) EF to Mint: $20–$30

Barber Shops, Beauty Salons, Shoe Parlors, Cobblers

These specialty businesses are featured on many cards, mostly RPPCs, and often have interesting personal messages. Barber shops are the most often encountered. Best are those with the name and location of the business stated.

Hutchings barber shop, Grand Rapids, Michigan. RPPC. Advertisements for local businesses are high on the left wall for customers to see. (Circa 1910s.) EF to Mint: $125+

Lawrence's Sanitary Barber Shop, apparently with the proprietor in front, on White Plains Road, Tuckahoe, New York. RPPC. (Circa 1908.) EF to Mint: $100+

E.G. Kimball's barber shop in Akron, Ohio. RPPC. (Postmarked 1918.) EF to Mint: $125+

A cobbler at work in Waitsfield, Vermont. RPPC. (Postmarked 1908.) EF to Mint: $125

Barber shop conducted by H.C. at 77 East Main St., Jamestown, New York, per the message on the back. The shelves display numbered shaving mugs for individual customers, a tradition at the time. A few have patrons' names (a more desirable type). RPPC. (Circa 1910s.) EF to Mint: $100+

Barber Shops, Shoe Parlors, etc.	Value, EF to Mint
Interiors 1900–1930	$15–$50+
Exteriors 1900–1930	$10–$40+
Interiors, RPPC 1900–1920	$60–$125+
Exteriors, RPPC 1900–1920	$40–$100+

Medical, Dental, Hospital, and Related Cards

Exterior views of hospitals and medical facilities are readily available on printed postcards, less so on RPPCs. Interior views on printed cards are extremely rare, and RPPCs are rare as well.

"Office of Chas. L. Buck, The Dentist, South Paris, Maine." Printed postcards with dentists and patients are very rare as a class. (Postmarked 1907.) EF to Mint: $25–$50

"Making X Ray Examinations, Sanitarium, Battle Creek, Mich. 14." One of a series of RPPCs featuring this well-known institution, early twentieth century. EF to Mint: $200+

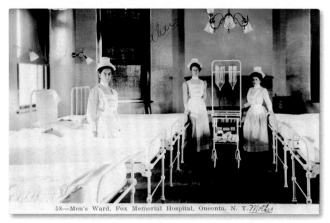

"Men's Ward, Fox Memorial Hospital, Oneonta, N.Y." (No. 58. Circa 1914.) EF to Mint: $20–$40

"Bangor [Maine] Jewelry and Optical Co.'s Model Examining Room" RPPC. Back text includes: "We have just finished remodeling our optical department and now have the finest equipped optical department in New England. Our examining room is equipped with all the latest instruments to make a scientific examination of the eye. We have two registered optometrists in attendance daily to attend to your optical needs. We grind all our lenses on the premises...." (Postmarked 1911.) EF to Mint: $125–$175+

Inventory cabinet of eyeglass lenses, frames, etc., of Dr. DeWitt B. Lewis, Bennington, Vermont. RPPC. (Circa 1910s.) EF to Mint: $125–$175

RPPC of a dentist with a patient in the chair. (Circa 1914.) EF to Mint: $125+

Agriculture, Dairy, Lumber, Ice, and Related

Farming, the raising of livestock and cattle, the harvesting of crops, lumber, and ice, and the use of land for related purposes has been essential to the American economy since the earliest days of the colonists. During the presidential campaign of 1896, William Jennings Bryan in his famous "Cross of Gold" speech said, "Burn down your cities and leave our farms, and your cities will spring up again as if by magic. But destroy our farms and the grass will grow in the streets of every city in the country."

During the early twentieth century, these activities furnished a rich opportunity for the issuance of postcards. Imported as well as domestic printed cards in color and black and white depicted a wide range of farming activities. Particularly popular were large steam-driven plows, harvesters, threshers, and the like. These expensive machines were the pride and joy of farm owners and were also featured on many RPPCs. Makers of such implements, from small devices and machines to huge plows and harvesters, used printed (mostly) postcards to advertise their products, often showing them in action.

While most agricultural subjects had to do with the harvesting of wheat and grain, others treated products such as alfalfa, walnuts, fruit, and related products.

Dairy farming, the tending of poultry, and other farmyard activities were also widely pictured on cards, often on RPPCs, less frequently on printed cards. However, many generic cards were made, using a scene of cows coming home in the evening or chickens in a yard, imprinted with the name of a particular town—never mind that the identical card was used for other towns as well. Exaggeration cards (see chapter 9) often featured agricultural and farmyard products—huge ears of corn, mammoth eggs, and the like, and oversized trophies such as huge fish. "Bigger is better" was the saying, and such cards were a lot of fun.

Logging, lumbering activities, sawmills, and the like were another popular topic, but not common on printed cards. RPPCs were made of many scenes, particularly logging sleds and trucks in rural areas, portable sawmills, river activities, and the like, usually by local photographers. An extensive specialized collection could be made of the lumber industry on its own. Ice harvesting, necessarily limited to the Northern states in wintertime, is a narrower topic, although hundreds of different cards were produced. These are a nice mixture of printed as well as RPPCs, usually showing the surface of a pond or lake and men with saws and other equipment harvesting ice, often placing it on a conveyor to be taken into a wooden warehouse nearby.

Certain of these cards are more available by region. For example, the harvesting of wheat and grain in large open areas is mainly found on cards of Oregon, Washington, and the prairie states. In the Pacific Northwest the harvesting and processing (packing in a factory) of fruit is depicted, while in California there were many crops, ranging from nuts and fruits to grain. In the prairie states, grains were important. In the lower part of the Central states, including Texas, sugar beets are on many postcards, while potatoes were a popular subject in New Jersey and cotton in the South. The possibilities are almost endless. The raising of livestock and poultry for meat is another aspect of agriculture widely depicted on both printed cards (mainly) and RPPCs.

Many of these cards are generic without specific location and furnish much information on labor and machinery of the times.

Agriculture

Harvesting grain in Eastern Oregon with horsepower in the literal sense. (No. 7721. Portland Post Card Co., Germany.) EF to Mint: $5–$7

"Steam Plow," with no information as to location, was a popular generic postcard that was sold widely in the West. (No. 8790. M. Rieder. Postmarked 1907.) EF to Mint: $8–$15

"Farming in the West—A seventeen furrow steam plough at work." (No. 786. Pacific Novelty Co. Circa 1910s.) EF to Mint: $6–$8

"Steam Harvester" illustrated a rig popular in the Midwest and West in large open fields of grain. (No. 5333. Spokane Post Card Co. Circa 1908.) EF to Mint: $8–$12

"The Tractor that made Charles City Famous, made by the Hart-Parr Co., Charles City, Iowa." (N.N. 2078/2. Circa 1908.) EF to Mint: $12–$20

"Modern Farm Horse Series No. 1, Hart-Parr Gas Tractor Breaking and Seeding, Beach, No. Dak." Advertising card for the equipment illustrated. "Photo only copyrighted 1909 by K.R. Smith Land Co., Beach, No. Dak." On the back: "Compliments of Hart-Parr Company, builders of The Modern Farm Horse, Charles City, Iowa. Watch for numbers 2, 3, and 4." (A-6710. Curt Teich Co. 1909.) EF to Mint: $10–$15

"Overflow of Wheat" evidencing a bountiful harvest. (No. 5398. Spokane Post Card Co. Postmarked 1911.) EF to Mint: $6–$10

"Bean Harvesting in California." (M. Rieder. Series 703. Circa 1910s.) EF to Mint: $5–$8

"Grading Walnuts in California." (M. Rieder, Series 703. Circa 1910s.) EF to Mint: $5–$8

"Roswell, N.M. Loading Alfalfa." (PCK No. 10808. Circa 1910s.) EF to Mint: $8–$12

"Golden Grains of the Flathead Valley, Kalispell, Mont." Message on the back: "You see these exhibitions in every town, even at railroad stations. They have glass cases with prize exhibits for advertising the place." (Thirl's Aerial View Service, View No. 10 / St. Paul Souvenir Co. No. 2016. Postmarked 1911.) EF to Mint: $25–$40

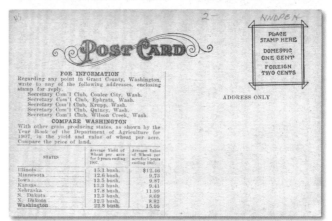

Grant County, Washington, issued a view card showing threshing activity as part of a campaign to attract more farmers to the area. The back of the card has 1907 farming statistics. EF to Mint: $8–$12

Harvesting grapes at Lake Keuka, near Penn Yan, New York. RPPC. (Harris Photo Post Card Co. Postmarked 1907.) EF to Mint: $25–$50

Pressing grapes at the Empire State Wine Co., Penn Yan, New York. RPPC. (Harris Photo Post Card Co. Postmarked 1907.) EF to Mint: $50–$100

Fresh produce for sale at the Woodside Farm on Howard St., Saugus, Massachusetts. RPPC. (Circa 1910.) EF to Mint: $75–$100+

"Potato Market at Elmer, N.J." RPPC. (Postmarked 1912.) EF to Mint: $125+

"Hauling Wool in the desert—a 20,000 pound load." (No publisher. Circa 1910s.) EF to Mint: $5–$8

Harvesting tobacco leaves near Turner's Falls, Massachusetts, 1915. RPPC. EF to Mint: $100+

"At the salmon cannery, Columbia River. Butchering Dept." RPPC. (Postmarked 1912.) EF to Mint: $75+

Harvesting at Roger's Island, Catskill, New York. (No. A-1005. Barton & Spooner Co., Cornwall-on-Hudson, New York. Printed in Germany.) EF to Mint: $10–$15

"Chase's Falls, Little Ossipee River, East Limington, Me." Lumbermen with pikes are standing on logs just below falls in the river, probably in early spring. (Postmarked 1910.) EF to Mint: $100+

Forestry and Lumber

Various aspects of forestry, the lumber industry, sawmills, lumberyards, and related activities are well represented on postcards. In particular, the field of RPPCs is rich with many views, mostly amateur or informal, but inevitably interesting.

Steam log haulers in Lincoln, Maine. A rare type of locomotive, shown with its operator. This card will attract a lot of attention. EF to Mint: $20–$40

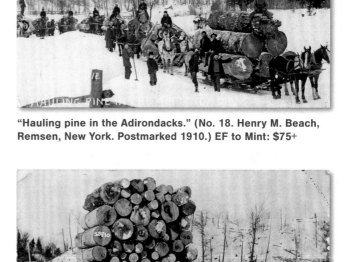

"Hauling pine in the Adirondacks." (No. 18. Henry M. Beach, Remsen, New York. Postmarked 1910.) EF to Mint: $75+

"Log Drivers at Work, Mississippi River, St. Cloud, Minn." RPPC (No. 526. Circa 1910s.) EF to Mint: $75–$100+

Horses haul a sled with a huge load of logs. Ladysmith, Wisconsin. Such scenes were photographed in various places as the lumbermen were proud of the feat. RPPC. (Circa 1910s.) EF to Mint: $50–$70

Workmen at a portable saw mill in Liberty, Maine. (F.W. Cunningham, photographer, Liberty, Maine. Circa 1910s.) EF to Mint: $100+

Harvesting ice on the Penobscot River in Brewer, Maine. RPPC. (Postmarked 1907.) EF to Mint: $125+

"Boiling sap, the way our grandfathers did it. Making maple sugar." (No. 11, "Making Maple Sugar Series." Green Mountain Card Co. Postmarked 1908.) EF to Mint: $10–$15

"A Vermont maple sugar camp." (No. 29052. Hugh C. Leighton. Postmarked 1910.) EF to Mint: $4–$8

"Grand Island Game Preserve, gathering maple sap." RPPC. (Garraway Co. Circa 1930s.) EF to Mint: $20–$30

TRANSPORTATION

Transportation postcards fall into several categories including horses and horse-drawn vehicles, automobiles, motorcycles, trucks and commercial vehicles, trains and stations, trolley and interurban cars, boats of all styles, and airships and airplanes.

These categories often include cards that are of interest to specialists in other categories. Cards with horses and automobiles also have interesting street scenes, and cards with horse-drawn or motorized fire engines are found among collections with horses and trucks. On many there are interesting background views of the American scene. Postcards with railroad, ship, and other transportation postmarks can be worth much more. In all categories in this book, postcards with postmarks of discontinued post offices are worth more.

Conversely, cards classified under other categories such as farming will often have horses or tractors, Main Street views will often have automobiles, and so on. Collecting transportation cards is very popular. Specialization is the order of the day. Someone seeking trains and railroad stations is not likely to look for ocean liners or automobiles. Most transportation card categories are virtually endless and furnish a great opportunity for exploring.

Horses, Horse-Drawn Vehicles, Livery Stables

From the 1890s through the early 1920s horses were an important part of commerce, pulling delivery wagons, rented out by livery stables, and the like. Transportation on roads was ruled by horsepower in the literal sense of the word.

Horse-drawn vehicles can be found in many Main Street and general views. When the horse and wagon comprise a major part of the image, the card is of greater interest to the specialist. The vast majority of close views of commercial wagons are RPPCs, of which many are identified as to place and date. Many carried food or dairy products. Sometimes the inscriptions on the wagon or details in the background can help place the card, in which instance it is significantly more valuable.

The Internet is a rich resource for such research as most of the larger firms advertised in newspapers. Stagecoaches for public transportation remained in use in the early twentieth century in some small towns and hilly areas not served by rail and comprise a fairly rare postcard category.

"Stage on the road to Middletown, Lake Co., California." (Richard Behrendt, San Francisco, published for Mrs. G. Barker, Middletown. Postmarked 1917.) EF to Mint: $30–$50

"Tally Ho Stage used only in the White Mountains of New Hampshire." These horse-drawn coaches, filled with passengers inside and sitting on top, were popular with tourists in the summer months. (No. 424555. Valentine. Circa 1910s.) EF to Mint: $15–$20

"Bartow and City Island Stage Coach Line." The venue was a district on the bay to the east of the northern tip of Manhattan. (No. 107440. Artino. Postmarked 1910.) EF to Mint: $40–$60

The Friendsville Stage at the Apalachin, New York, Post Office. (No. 938. Miller Bros., Apalachin. Circa 1908.) EF to Mint: $40–$60

"Market Square and Market House, Knoxville, Tenn." A Main Street postcard with a clear view of commercial horse-drawn wagons. Delivery wagons are a popular specialty. (Nos. 1148 and 598. International Post Card Co. Circa 1910s.) EF to Mint: $10–$15

Atlantic Tea Co. delivery wagon well photographed on an RPPC. Delivery wagons as the main subject of a card, as here, are especially scarce and desirable. Most are RPPC. (Postmarked Natick, Massachusetts, 1907.) EF to Mint: $100+

The Charles H. Dauchy paint and hardware store, Troy, New York, used a horse-drawn advertising rig with signs on both sides. (Postmarked 1908.) EF to Mint: $125+

The "Private Ambulance" (as lettered on the side), operated by H. Noble & Son, funeral directors, served equally well as a hearse. RPPC. (Circa 1910s.) EF to Mint: $125+

RPPC of "The Aero Wagon," operated by the Vacuum House Cleaning Co., of Hutchinson, Kansas, a licensee of the American Cleaning Co., Milwaukee. (Circa 1910s.) EF to Mint: $175+

A well-posed RPPC of the delivery wagon of Ormesby Farms Creamery, Pittsfield, Massachusetts. (Postmarked 1915.) EF to Mint: $150+

This holder of a franchise to sell Confers Remedies, Fine Extracts and Spices, as lettered on the wagon, used RPPCs to mail to customers to advise of the next time he would visit. (Postmarked Port Huron, Michigan, 1917.) EF to Mint: $150+

Horse-drawn wagon lettered "H.S. Souder / Excelsior / Cigar Box Manufacturer / Souderton, Pa." Seemingly a complete enterprise in one view: workers, factory, and delivery truck. (Circa 1910s.) EF to Mint: $75–$100+

"T.R. School" horse-drawn carriage with students lined up for the ride to school, holding lunch pails. RPPC. (Circa 1910.) EF to Mint: $75+

Popcorn and peanut wagon. This type of horse-drawn vehicle was very popular in the early twentieth century. Typically, they were positioned on a main street during the day, then taken away at night. Cast into part of the mechanism is "Made for E.M. Mudge." (Circa 1910.) EF to Mint: $250+

Transition in transportation: Oxen-drawn wagon and motor truck at the Clark Grain & Feed Co., Chippewa Falls, Wisconsin. (Postmarked 1912.) EF to Mint: $125+

Another transition in transportation card: Horse-drawn wagon and motor truck of the Schneider Brothers Home Baking Co., Cleveland, Ohio. (Circa 1910s.) EF to Mint: $150–$200

Automobiles and Related

The Golden Age of postcards in the early twentieth century coincided with the Golden Age of the automobile. By 1905 cars were in the forefront of interest everywhere, and during the next ten years dozens of different companies started in the business. At auto shows and elsewhere, some gave away beautifully lithographed advertising cards. Others distributed inexpensive black-and-white cards.

Early postcards of automobiles abound. The ownership of a new Ford, Mercer, Oakland, Oldsmobile, or other brand was a badge of accomplishment for many, and RPPCs were often made of vehicles and their proud owners. Other RPPCs show cars on streets, parked in front of buildings, and in other scenes and are of interest if the images are detailed. On some, the name of the car, the date, and the state of the license can be discerned. Early advertising cards for automobiles include printed cards for models sold in large quantities and RPPCs for many less popular models.

Filling stations, later called gasoline stations, were set up everywhere but were not the focus of printed cards at all and are usually found as part of street scenes. Automobile garage RPPCs are plentiful and are best when they show cars parked in the front.

As a general rule of thumb, for this specialty RPPCs offer a wider field of opportunity. Quality varies, as is typical of RPPCs. The best are well reproduced with detailed images and identified as to place, with a postmark indicating the date. Such cards are in the minority and are worth a premium. Happily, many other RPPCs showing garages are identified on the front caption. Automobile postcards after the Golden Age down to the latest chrome cards are eagerly sought.

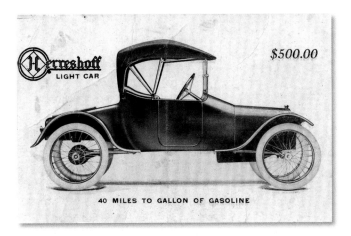

Advertising card for the "Locomobile 30 Roadster with Baby Tonneau. Shaft Drive. $3500. (Top Extra)." (No. 2795. Chilton Printing Co.) EF to Mint: $20–$40

The Herreshoff Light Car Co. advertised its $500 model on a card with specifications on the back. Although not marked "Post Card," the right side was obviously intended for an address. EF to Mint: $25–$50

A parade scene somewhere in Ohio with an elephant and automobile. RPPC. EF to Mint: $25–$40

Hupmobile advertising postcard showing two people enjoying themselves on a ride in Central Park, New York City. Colorfully lithographed and nicely postmarked Detroit, January 30, 1910, with the message stating this was obtained at the recent auto show there. An exceptional quality card worth a premium. (Chilton Publishing Co. 1910.) EF to Mint: $20–$40

An automobile rally in Lamar, Colorado. RPPC. EF to Mint: $75–$125+

Moyer automobile, new 1911 model, on an RPPC postmarked Syracuse, New York, where the Moyer factory was located. List price was about $2,200 or so. Features included a "Jericho horn." RPPC. (Herbert A. Myer & Co., Jordan, New York. September 19, 1910.) EF to Mint: $100+

The W.H. Norris Block in Epping, New Hampshire, with a gasoline filling facility in front next to the boy with bicycle. RPPC. (No. 696. Fletcher & Co. Circa 1912.) EF to Mint: $100+

The Westfield Garage, operated by G.C. Bennett in Westfield, Illinois, was a dealer in Maxwell and Cole automobiles in 1911. This RPPC with several automobiles, most with drivers, attributed as to time and place and with excellent detail, is a premium card. EF to Mint: $125+

RPPC of Hunt's Restaurant & Cabins, East Westmoreland, New Hampshire. Texaco gasoline was posted at 18¢ per gallon. (Eastern Illustrating Co. Circa 1920s.) EF to Mint: $25–$40

The building of Otto E. Scherer & Sons, Palmyra, Wisconsin, in the 1910s, with a lineup of Buick roadsters on display. The firm was the Buick distributor for southern Wisconsin. This RPPC has no date or location indicated, but research on the Internet quickly located the firm and information about it. A premium card. EF to Mint: $125+

Card's Garage in Edmeston, New York, as depicted on an RPPC. With a Texaco pump, two vehicles, an attendant, and several signs, this sharply focused image is an excellent example of its genre. (Circa 1910s.) EF to Mint: $100+

RPPC of the coach and driver on the Troy & Grafton (New York) Auto Line, E.L. Snyder, manager. The back carries this relevant message: "This auto came to Grafton Center for the first time April 10, 1910 with a load of passengers from Troy, and the picture was taken the same day near the Post Office or just below Will Wait's house, and Wait's house shows in the picture." EF to Mint: $75–$100

"Just before the first trip. Oct. 9, 1911." Seneca Falls & Ithaca Transfer Co. RPPC. EF to Mint: $50–$75

Motorcycles

Motorcycles were a favorite postcard subject, mostly RPPCs but with many printed cards as well. As a category such cards are quite scarce today. A given RPPC is usually unique. Motorcycles can be found on some cards showing service stations. Main Street scenes with a prominent motorcycle are rare.

Three young ladies enjoy a Harley-Davidson motorcycle in or near Dolgeville, New York. The one holding the handlebars is Florence Perkins. RPPC. (G.E. Perkins, Dolgeville. Circa 1910s.) EF to Mint: $125+

For this RPPC, Ernest (per back inscription) posed with his Indian motorcycle (made by the Hendee Manufacturing Co., Springfield, Massachusetts), to create a card to send to Miss Jennie Green at 218 South 5th Street West, Missoula, Montana. "I wish you were here. I would give you a ride on my motor." (Circa 1910s.) EF to Mint: $175

Two motorcycles in front of the Royal Oak, Michigan, Post Office. RPPC. No. 24 in a series published in Detroit. Dated 1910 on the back. Motorcycles are a fairly scarce subject on RPPC. EF to Mint: $100+

An Armac motor tricycle with a father (presumably) and three children as riders, photographed in Lincoln Park on July 4, 1910, and mailed from Covert, Michigan. EF to Mint: $150+

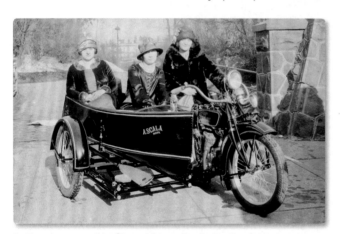

Indian motorcycle with a sidecar (by A. Scala, patent pending, per the inscription). RPPC. The female passengers and driver (dressed in velvet, satin, and fur) lend interest. (Circa 1910s.) EF to Mint: $250+

Indian motorcycles on display in a shop in Waterloo, Iowa. Sign on wall: "For sale or rent: Fishing tackle, guns, motorcycles, bicycles." Against the far wall is a player piano with rolls on top. RPPC. (Circa 1910s.) EF to Mint: $200+

Trucks and Other Motor Vehicles

Trucks with advertising are a popular postcard category. Availability ranges from scarce to rare, although a few,

such as printed cards, are common. Trucks with advertising on their sides are particularly desirable and are most often seen on cards from the 1920s onward.

Advertising and delivery truck of the Columbus Chemical Co., Columbus, Ohio, with signs for Quick Relief Balm. T.G. Coffey, proprietor and manager. RPPC. (Circa 1910s.) EF to Mint: $125+

Flat-bed truck operated by Rogers & Son, dealers in poultry. RPPC. (Circa 1910s.) EF to Mint: $100+

John F. Glenn, Urbana, Ohio, player piano delivery truck. RPPC. (Circa 1910s). EF to Mint: $125+

Motorized Book Wagon on Main Street, Provincetown, Massachusetts. RPPC. (Circa 1910s.) EF to Mint: $125

Fire Engines, Firefighting

Postcards depicting various aspects of municipal fire departments and firefighting are very popular and involve horse-drawn as well as motor units. Often, a horse-drawn Amoskeag steam pumper was an object of civic pride—showcased in parades and at other times watched in action as a team sped to a burning building.

A steam pumper was housed in a fire station at the entrance. The furnace under the boiler was kept burning day and night, banked to a low level, but ready to burst into an intense blaze as the unit was hitched behind a team of horses and dispatched to a fire. By the time it arrived, steam pressure was at a high level, and the unit was ready to suck water from a hydrant or other source and spray it at high volume.

Around the turn of the century self-propelled steam engines captured a small part of the market. Although horses were no longer needed, there was a delay in responding to a call, as the steam had to build up to a full head before the unit could move from the engine house. Then came motor trucks with gasoline motors to drive the pump.

While pumpers were usually the vehicles showcased in parades, several other types of equipment were in use and depicted on postcards. Hook-and-ladder wagons, at first horse-drawn, then succeeded by trucks, were an essential part of every department. Hose wagons and trucks were important as well. In addition, larger departments had a special wagon, later a special car, for the chief and his assistants. Large cities with multi-story buildings often had water towers, a ladder or crane-like device that was extended into the air, carrying a fire hose that could spray horizontally or at any angle as directed from the ground or by a fireman at the top.

Fire stations or houses were an important part of every town, medium-size on up to cities. Large cities had multiple stations, often over a dozen or more. Some stations were assigned specialties, such as Hose Company No. 3, Hook and Ladder Company No. 2, or Steam Company No. 1. While most fire stations were in separate buildings, some were located within city halls or other facilities.

During the Golden Age of postcards in the early twentieth century, fire equipment and stations furnished a rich opportunity for subjects, and many hundreds of different views were issued.

Printed generic postcards depicting firefighting were popular with young and old alike. Postcards of firefighting ranged widely in quality. In Washington, D.C., P.J. Plant issued a set of eight inexpensive sepia-printed cards showing the process from station to fire. S. Langsdorf & Co. published a beautiful set of deeply embossed, richly colored cards illustrating firemen in action in its "Fire Department Series P1400."

Postcards advertising equipment were published by different manufacturers and are rare and highly desirable today.

Printed cards are mostly attributed to location, showing various aspects of firefighting, including station interior (scarce) and exterior views, equipment on display and in use. Quality varies widely. Those with bright color and with good details and eye appeal are the most valuable.

"Propeller No. 4. Hartford Fire Dept." This was a chain-driven steam pumper, a rare type as they could not start quickly (see introductory text). Known as the "Pride of Hartford," this Amoskeag First Class Propeller No. 4 was the largest such unit in the world at the time. Advertising card issued by the Travelers Insurance Co. and distributed at the Automobile Show in New York City, January 24 to 31. This same card was imprinted for use in other venues as well. EF to Mint: $40–$60

A card with multiple appeals, this features the Milford (MA) National Bank decked out in patriotic bunting with an Amoskeag-type steam fire engine in the foreground. This would also be of interest to anyone collecting scenic cards of Milford or collecting banks. (No. S-871040. Annie Lawless, Milford. Circa 1907.) EF to Mint: $20–$25

"Our Noble Warriors," a card featuring a horse-drawn Amoskeag steam engine of the Findlay (Ohio) Fire Department. In their day such steam pumpers were a great attraction to the public. (No publisher. Postmarked 1909.) EF to Mint: $20–$30

Horse-drawn hose wagon in service with the Bristol (Tennessee) Fire Department. EF to Mint: $25–$30

"New Haven Fire Department, Engine No. 7 in action." Amoskeag-type steam pumper with hose drawing water into the unit and, in the distance, two hoses spraying water under high pressure. EF to Mint: $20–$30

"Water Tower on Parade, NY City," published by Rotograph from an image copyrighted in 1905 by De Witt C. Wheeler. An untinted (black and white) version was issued for the New York Underwriters series. (Rotograph No. G 132b.) EF to Mint: $8–$12

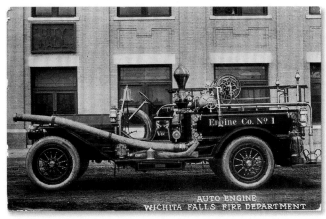

Motorized fire engine of the Wichita Falls (Texas) Fire
Department. (No publisher. Postmarked 1911.)
EF to Mint: $30–$40

"All Aboard, Fire Department, Janesville, Wis." Chief's motor
car and a hook and ladder truck. (Plate 175. E.C. Kropp Co.
Postmarked 1915.) EF to Mint: $20–$30

"Chemical Engine, Fire Department, Rogers, Ark." Motorized
vehicle. A particularly well composed card with the vehicle
and its personnel prominent. (Tom P. Morgan, Rogers / Curt
Teich Co. No. R-36013. 1913.) EF to Mint: $25–$35

Central Fire Station in New Bedford, Massachusetts, with a
combination of horse-drawn and motorized equipment.
EF to Mint: $10–$15

"New Chemical and Ladder Auto Truck No. 8. Manchester,
N.H." (Chamber of Commerce Series / Curt Teich Co. No.
R-38006. 1913.) EF to Mint: $10–$15

Continental fire truck with motorized pumps mounted in the
front. Made in Cincinnati. (Postmarked 1912.)
EF to Mint: $25–$35

Steam and Motorized Engines and Equipment

Coinciding with the Golden Age of postcards, in the early twentieth century through the beginning of the World War, much of the world was powered by steam. Such engines were used in boats, factories, locomotives, and other forms of transportation and equipment. Sights to behold included steam powered engines on the railroad tracks, hauling a thresher or combine across prairie land, carrying a pile of logs through the Maine woods, or smoothing out a street. Accordingly, such images were widely captured on postcards, both printed and RPPC.

From the 1920s continuing to modern times, most such engines and equipment have diesel or other combustion-type motors and are depicted on printed cards.

Steam engine-roller with smooth wheels for road work. "Town of McDonough" (Georgia) on side. RPPC. (Circa 1910s.) EF to Mint: $125+

"The New Huber Steam Road Roller." Advertising postcard from Huber, based in Marion, Ohio, a leading maker of road construction and maintenance equipment. EF to Mint: $20–$30

Team traction engine hauling a machine, by the Frick Co., Waynesboro, Pennsylvania. Several children pose aboard the rig along with adults. Such engines were always impressive to see. RPPC. (Circa 1910s.) EF to Mint: $75+

There was no better way to sell a piece of steam equipment than to show it off in front of a crowd. Here we have a Case steamer climbing a steep ramp. "Case Engines Are the Real Hill Climbers," two signs state. (Postmarked 1907.) EF to Mint: $15–$20

Trains and Stations

Since their invention, America has had a love affair with trains. Thousands of different images, mostly printed but many RPPCs of local scenes, have been issued over a long period of years. Particularly popular are railroad stations, often collected from as many towns as possible within a given state or other area of interest. If the image shows a train in the station or people on the platform, so much the better.

Marcellus & Otisco Lake Railroad Station in Marcellus, New York, on an ideal postcard: with a good view of the train, with train personnel present, with passengers and the station, and related to a very obscure rail line. (N.N. No. 1167. William Jubb, Syracuse. Postmarked 1910.) EF to Mint: $25–$35

"New Passenger Station, Naugatuck, Conn." (No. 35 1909 PM). Railroad stations are very popular. This one is a rather boring image without people, vehicles, or a train and is valued much less than if it had those features.
EF to Mint: $12–$25

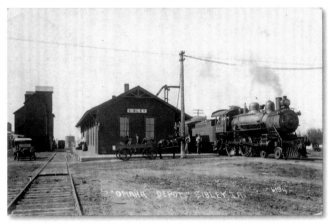

"Omaha Depot, Sibley, IA," No. 6194. RPPC showing C. St. P. M. & O. (Chicago, St. Paul, Minneapolis & Omaha Railroad) train, a horse-drawn wagon, and an automobile. ("Sterling Quality Photo Made by L.L. Cook, Lake Mills, Wis." Postmarked 1914.) EF to Mint: $100+

Laying new track in Uniontown, Kansas. RPPC. (Circa 1910s.) EF to Mint: $125+

"St. Joe G.I. & U.P. Station, Marysville, Kans. No. 22" reads the caption. A very nice image showing a stop for the St. Joseph and Grand Island Railroad and the Union Pacific Railroad. A locomotive is part of the scene, as are many people, contributing to the value of this card. RPPC. (Postmarked 1911.) EF to Mint: $100+

RPPC of "95 Ton Electric Locomotive at Official Test Nov. 12 '04." The message is addressed to a person who is said to know "most gentlemen around engine." Mailed on December 24, 1904, in an era in which messages could not be written on the back. Therefore, just about every empty space on the front is filled in with personal notes. This card is in low grade but is rare. Value if it were EF to Mint: $75+

Street Railroads and Interurban Cars

Horse-drawn street cars were an anachronism by the time the pictorial postcard became popular at the turn of the twentieth century. Most had long since been replaced by trolley cars. Still, in some American towns and cities they continued to be used, where they were often viewed as a curiosity, with postcards having tongue-in-cheek inscriptions such as "the latest." The number of postcards showing these is limited.

Trolley cars or street railways became a growth business in the late nineteenth century, and by 1900 most large cities were so equipped. These were often owned by local or regional power and light companies. Electricity was obtained by trolley wires strung above the street, with a contact rod and pulley extending from above the car to make a connection. A variation was the cable car, propelled by gripping a continuously running wire cable under the roadway and accessible via a slot. San Francisco cable cars, still in use today, are the most famous.

In the early twentieth century interurban rail lines were a dynamic industry. Rails were laid to connect towns and cities. Some interurbans were trolleys and others were motorized. At one time there were so many interconnecting lines that much of the Northeast along the coast could be traveled in this manner.

Postcards showing trolley cars are very plentiful, especially in views of downtown areas. A trolley adds interest to a Main Street view, enough that those showing a car in the distance are sometimes classified under the "trolley" category in collectors' listings. To be of the greatest interest to a specialist, such a postcard should feature the car or group of cars prominently, best if lettering and details can be seen. Cards that are devoted entirely to a car are somewhat scarce, but enough were made that a nice collection can be formed.[12] Many RPPCs were made showing trolleys. Often, special RPPCs were made to show the arrival of the first car in town. As mentioned earlier in the text, trolley cars and tracks were often added to RPPCs and printed cards by artistic manipulation.

Related to trolley car lines are amusement parks that were often built by the street railway companies (often called "traction companies") on the outskirts of towns or cities, accessed by the line and providing additional revenue in the summer (see chapter 19).

The Murphysboro (Illinois) Street Railway operated until 1908, when the Murphysboro Electric Railway & Light Co. installed a trolley line. The writing detracts, but the card is so rare that it would sell easily. (No publisher. Circa 1907.)
EF to Mint: $100+

Horse-drawn streetcar of the Cincinnati, Hamilton & Dayton Traction Co. The same line ran steam trains on other routes but used horse power in the streets of Middleton, Ohio, as shown here. This car was pulled by one horse or two, depending upon the passenger load. (Feicke-Desch Printing Co. Postmarked 1913.) EF to Mint: $25–$40

"Crosstown Rapid Transit 1905. N.Y. City." (A-1171. Rotograph. Postmarked 1909.) EF to Mint: $20–$30

Horse-drawn streetcar in Winfield, Kansas, comically titled "Electric Cars." Operated by the Union Street Railway Co. The sign on the side advertises the Winfield Chautauqua Assembly, June 18 to 28. (No. 10008. Garver Brothers. Postmarked 1908.) EF to Mint: $25–$40

"Limited Palace Car, F.J. and G.R.R., Gloversville, N.Y." Fonda, Johnstown & Gloversville Railroad. A very nice view card, but with some value deleted by the ink cancellation transfer marks at the upper left. (No. 201947. Valentine & Sons. Postmarked 1909.) EF to Mint: $10–$20

"Index Change for Cooperstown, Oneonta and Mohawk Valley Trolley." An ideal view card showing two trolley cars, a station and people. (No. D-89. American News Co. Photochrome. Postmarked 1909.) EF to Mint: $15–$20

High-quality view card of Herald Square, New York City, with a trolley car depicted; not the main part of the view, but significant enough that a trolley specialist would find this to be very desirable. (No. G-35b. Rotograph Co., Sol-Art Prints. Circa 1906.) EF to Mint: $5–$7

"Trolley Terminal and Hauser's, Delaware Water Gap, Pennsylvania." Hauser's window is filled with postcards. (Curt Teich Co.) EF to Mint: $20–$30

"Gasoline Electric Car on J.C. & L.E., Jamestown, N.Y." (No publisher. Postmarked 1914.) EF to Mint: $15–$25

Hartford & Springfield Street Railway trolley in a station.
EF to Mint: $15–$20

"Thomaston's First Trolley Car. Aug 3–1908." RPPC made by Van Griethuysen & Lowe in Ripley, Oklahoma.
EF to Mint: $100+

The Mount Lowe Railway, operated by the Pacific Electric Railway, climbed from near Pasadena (California) up a circuitous route to the summit, where refreshment and entertainment facilities beckoned. In the early twentieth century this was a very popular attraction. EF to Mint: $4–$7

Central Street in Marshfield, Wisconsin, did not have a streetcar. No matter, the photographic studio scribed some "wires" overhead and added a trolley. This was a very common thing for photography shops to do, and the same thing was done to add automobiles or airplanes. (Co-Mo Co., Minneapolis, "Genuine Photograph." Circa 1912.)
EF to Mint: $75+

Near Manchester, New Hampshire, the Uncanoonuc Incline Railway went from its base station in Goffstown up a steep grade to the top of Uncanoonuc Mountain, where a hotel, restaurant, and other amenities were available. This trolley line was very popular in its day. (No. 130800. John B. Varick Co. Postmarked 1909.) EF to Mint: $5–$7

"Building Trolley Line, Water St., Gardiner, Me. 10-17-'07." RPPC showing tracks being laid down the center of the business section of town, a rare postcard subject.
EF to Mint: $75

From Small Boats to Ocean Liners

Boats are a popular postcard subject. Many are pictured on scenic views of lakes and waterways. Hundreds of different cards show vessels on the Great Lakes, Hudson River, Lake Champlain, and at ports and docks inland as well as on the oceans. Sidewheel steamers on the Mississippi River can be collected on hundreds of different cards. Military vessels including battleships and submarines were depicted on many cards as well. Ocean liners running in and out of American ports are featured on many cards, including colorful advertising issues. Postcards with canoes, rowboats, and small vessels are usually inexpensive.

Return of the "Great White Fleet" sent around the world by President Theodore Roosevelt as a show of American military strength. (H.T. Cook, New York City. Circa 1909.) EF to Mint: $30–$50

"Kingston, N.Y. The chain ferry boat, Riverside Rondout to Port Ewen." (No. 12572. Kingston Souvenir Co. Circa 1910.) EF to Mint: $20–$25

The *Chief Wawatam*, an ice-breaker and railroad-car ferry, built in 1911 by the Toledo Shipbuilding Company, became a familiar sight in the Mackinac Straits of upper Michigan. The RPPC shows her in the ice, perhaps stuck, but not for long, as she went on to enjoy a long career on the Great Lakes. (Copyright by Clyde Johnson, Mackinaw, Michigan. Postmarked 1914.) EF to Mint: $50–$75

"Ferry Landing, Louisiana, Mo. 'The Dyke.'" A horse, wagon, and driver have just gone aboard at the town of Louisiana, about 90 miles upstream from St. Louis on the Mississippi River. RPPC. (W.J. Howden's Book Store. Postmarked 1908.) EF to Mint: $125+

Stern wheel steamboat *Captain Lewey* at Princeton, Maine. This vessel was built in 1853 and was a familiar sight on and near Grand Lake. RPPC. (Circa 1908.) EF to Mint: $100+

"Excursion on the 'Ticonderoga' at Plattsburgh, Lake Champlain." RPPC. EF to Mint: $75–$100

Based at Cape Vincent, New York, the *New Island Wanderer,* a 116-foot steamship built in 1884, offered tours of the Thousand Islands, a "Fifty Mile Ramble." RPPC. (Circa 1910s.) EF to Mint: $50–$75

Steamship *Connecticut* of the Providence Line at dock in Stonington, Connecticut. (G.A. Hyde, Stonington, Connecticut. Germany.) EF to Mint: $10–$12

Ship under construction in a yard in Boothbay Harbor, Maine. RPPC. (McDougall & Keefe, Boothbay Harbor. Circa 1910s.) EF to Mint: $25–$50

A Red Star Line advertising card showing a ship being towed into port to its wharf. EF to Mint: $15–$20

Alice Roosevelt, daughter of the president, aboard the USS *Logan* in the Philippine Islands. (No. 99 H.H. Co., New York. Germany.) EF to Mint: $15–$20

Aircraft, Planes, Balloons, Zeppelins

Aircraft of all kinds have been depicted on postcards. These range from RPPC views of the early twentieth century to printed cards distributed in quantity by modern airlines.

Cards prior to 1920 usually range from scarce to rare. Many RPPC cards are unique and show proud aviators and their biplanes, or accidents, or aircraft meets. Modern airline cards come in many varieties and most are inexpensive (see chapters 23 and 24). It is amazing how many airlines of the late twentieth century no longer exist.

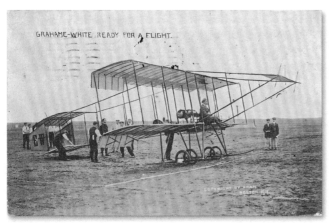

"Grahame-White ready for a flight." (Copyright by Aram, Boston. 1910.) EF to Mint: $15–$20

"Bleriot Speed Bird, Belmont Park, 1910." EF to Mint: $10–$20

Lieutenant James A. Whitted's Blue Bird seaplane in St. Petersburg, Florida. RPPC. (Circa 1910s.) EF to Mint: $75–$100

"This is one of the flying boats. It was at Michigan City on the shore just getting ready to leave there." RPPC. (Postmarked Ludington, Michigan, July 21, 1913.) EF to Mint: $75–$100

An RPPC card inscribed on the back, "Mr. Schmidt, the aviator, was killed Sept. 3 [sic], 1913. The one accompanying is lawyer Spellman." Probably snapped before the flight took off, this card shows both men smiling. The Lewiston (Maine) Daily Sun, September 2, 1913, carried this item, datelined Rutland, Vermont: "One man is dead and another is feared to be dying as the result of an aeroplane accident at the Rutland Fair late today. Five hundred men and women at the Fair saw the biplane of George Schmidt, carrying J. Dyer Spellman, assistant judge of the Municipal Court, as a passenger, turn turtle 200 feet in the air and fall like a plummet to the ground. As a result of his injuries Schmidt, who was 23 years of age, died at the local hospital tonight. Judge Spellman...is so badly burned that it is feared he may die...." EF to Mint: $125+

A hot air balloon launching at Edon, a town in northwest Ohio, July 31, 1909, with a crowd in attendance. EF to Mint: $100+

"U.S. Navy Hydro-Aeroplane." Could be launched from the deck of a battleship. (No. 14. American Colortype Co. Circa 1916.) EF to Mint: $6–$10

"Air Mail Hangar, Bellefonte, Pa." Biplane for airmail service. RPPC. (Circa 1910s.) EF to Mint: $40–$60

Charles Lindbergh and the Spirit of St. Louis, 1927. EF to Mint: $10–$20

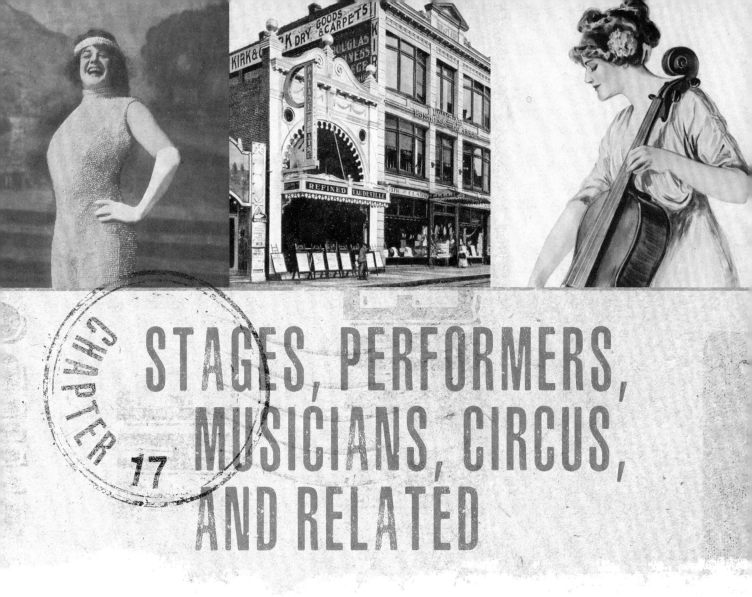

STAGES, PERFORMERS, MUSICIANS, CIRCUS, AND RELATED

During the Golden Age—before radio and television—most live entertainment was performed on stage, in carnivals, traveling shows, and other venues (films are treated in chapter 18). Singers, actors and actresses, high-wire aerialists, magicians, vaudeville troupes, and other skilled performers were highly admired in their day. It is a curious twist of history and collectibles that today the printed postcards of stage actors and actresses, being the most plentiful, are in very low demand. In contrast, silent-film and later movie stars are front and center in interest today.

Players and Plays on Stage

In the early twentieth century through the 1920s many different cards were issued depicting actors and actresses in stage performances, with the person as the subject or as part of a play scene. These were standard or stock cards and were distributed to theaters, which had local shops add their own imprint on the back, giving time and place. Sometimes unused cards from one venue simply had the theater address blanked out and another one printed in it. These were mailed to local patrons in some instances and in others were sold as souvenirs at the theater itself—remembrances of a performance. Other cards depicted an actor or actress and were generic, with no specific play mentioned.

These were widely collected in the early years, but after about 1910, when cards featuring motion picture players became available, most interest in stage actors and actresses dwindled. Today they are not widely collected and therefore are generally very inexpensive.

Surviving cards are typically in high grades—Extremely Fine or Mint, often not mailed, except for those sent out by theaters specifically named on the back. Vaudeville acts, traveling comics, burlesque, minstrel shows, and certain other subjects can be worth much more than those showing players from the legitimate stage.

Most printed cards are black and white with an added color. Multi-hued cards are a scarcer category. Add 50 percent if a theater location is given, add 75 percent if play title, place, and time are given. Many black-and-white cards have glossy surfaces and resemble RPPCs but were made in quantity.

For specialists in such cards, the Internet provides a rich source of data, as biographies or other information can be found concerning most players, and the same goes for popular plays.

Scene from **Mutt & Jeff** in "Panama"

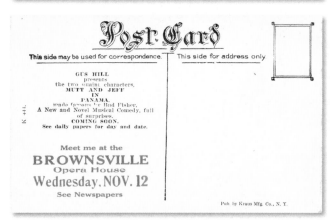

Mutt and Jeff in Panama, a comedy play advertised on a postcard. The back tells more about the play and is overprinted with a red notice stating a forthcoming engagement. A popular play prior to the 1914 opening of the Panama Canal. (Kraus Mfg. Co. 1913.) EF to Mint: $18–$25

Players in *Miss Patsy* at the Chicago Opera House. EF to Mint: $8–$12

Mary Ryan in *Ticey* at the Chicago Opera House. (Tokam Process Co., Chicago.) EF to Mint: $8–$12

Finale Act I.

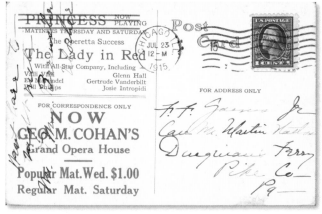

The Princess had a name change to Geo. M. Cohan's Grand Opera House. EF to Mint: $8–$12

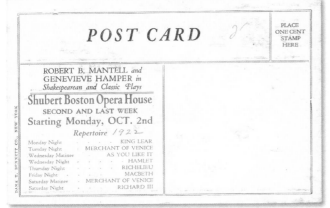

Program for the Shubert Boston Opera House.
EF to Mint: $8–$12

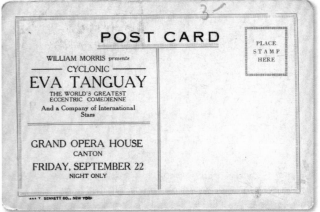

Eva Tanguay, the "I Don't Care Girl," would throw hundreds of Lincoln cents into the audience in one of her acts.
EF to Mint: $8–$12

Players and Plays on Stage	Value, EF to Mint
Before 1920	$5–$40
1920 to 1930s	$5–$25

Vaudeville

Every large city had one or more vaudeville theaters. The standard rate across the country was 10, 20, and 30 cents—spoken as ten, twent, and thirt—depending on the seat location. Up front near the orchestra was the most expensive, the balcony the least. Vaudeville acts included acrobatics, magic, ventriloquism, skits, music, and minstrelsy. The usual show had some of each, so as to satisfy all members of the audience. The typical vaudeville troupe went on the road from city to city and also to towns and villages. Related are melodramas presented by traveling companies, Wild West shows, and medicine shows.

Jules Murray and company in *The Mummy and the Humming Bird.*
EF to Mint: $12–$18

CC of C Minstrels, January 28–29, 1915. Minstrel shows were popular in their time, but the stereotypes and racial insensitivity they portrayed is recognized as wrong today. EF to Mint: $75–$125

Minstrel troupe on stage. RPPC. (H.F. Wilcox, Cuba, New York.) EF to Mint: $75–$125

Vaudeville	Value, EF to Mint
Before 1920	$6–$20
1920 to 1930s	$5–$15
RPPC	$6–$30

Chautauquas and Speakers

Starting in the 1890s at Lake Chautauqua near Jamestown, New York, the Chautauqua movement spread nationwide. The typical Chautauqua troupe stayed in a town for the best part of a week and was housed under a large tent or in an opera house. Programs were mostly serious, with talks on women's suffrage, science, religion, politics, and other topics, interspersed with music. Complementing these, many individuals went on the road to present lectures and lyceums illustrated with films, lantern slides, and handouts. Most of these were one-night engagements. Some towns erected Chautauqua buildings. The movement faded after the World War.

Postcards showing Chautauqua activities are scarce and collectors seeking them are scarce as well.

Chautauqua building in Boulder, Colorado. This still stands today. (Detroit #15257.) EF to Mint: $5–$10

Chautauquas and Speakers	Value, EF to Mint
Chautauqua scenes	$4–$18
Chautauqua scenes: RPPC	$12–$50+
Speakers and presenters: black and white.	$8–$20
Speakers and presenters: RPPC	$15–$40+

Stage and Vaudeville Theaters, Opera Houses

All across America, just about every medium-size town and every city had an opera house. The vast majority were built in the late nineteenth century. They provided a place for traveling shows, stage plays, concerts, and other activities intended to entertain and benefit a community. Often they were part of a city hall or municipal building, typically on the second floor. Other times they were in separate structures, again on the second floor, with the first floor devoted to stores and shops. In still other instances the entire building was devoted to entertainment. The term "opera house" was usually part of the title, although there were exceptions. When postcards began to be issued for stage performances and traveling shows in the early twentieth century, nearly all of these opera houses were still in use and provided a convenient venue. Postcards of opera houses nearly all show exterior views, with scattered exceptions. Many hundreds were depicted in the general period from 1900 through the 1920s.

In cities and larger towns there were often theaters set up by corporations, sometimes part of a chain such as the Orpheum circuit, Hippodrome circuit, Shubert circuit, and others. Orpheum, for example, had theaters in many different cities, in which they booked traveling companies and vaudeville shows on a rotating basis. In still other instances, theaters were not affiliated with any circuit but did their own booking or made arrangements through agents. These were a very popular subject for postcards, often with signs or lettering out front giving the name of the performance currently being shown. Again, exterior views are the rule and interior views the exception.

These are interesting to collect today but do not play to a wide audience, unless they are part of a Main Street scene or there is some particularly interesting activity depicted. Again, for many specific buildings the Internet offers historical information.

Most cards for opera houses and theaters are printed, the earlier ones in black and white, the later typically in color. Real Photo Post Cards (RPPCs) are not unusual for smaller towns and villages, but they are scarce for cities. Occasionally cards are found with messages on the back from players who are traveling, mentioning where they are at the time, or where they are headed next. Typically signed with first name only, few can be specifically identified as to the writer today, but they do lend interest, sometimes mentioning the popularity of a show and the attendance, or the local weather. Values

are for cards that have Opera House, Vaudeville Theatre, or related signs in prominent view, making up the main image on the card. Interior views are worth more.

Elks Opera House, Silver City, New Mexico, circa 1910.
EF to Mint: $12–$18

Dorris Opera House, Phoenix, Arizona, 1910s.
EF to Mint: $8–$12

Opera House, Lisbon, New Hampshire, circa 1908.
EF to Mint: $6–$8

Carroll Opera House, Carroll, Iowa. RPPC. Postmarked 1912. The sign in front says "A Married Bachelor" and "The Lion and the Mouse." EF to Mint: $30–$40

Miles Vaudeville Theatre. (Detroit News #237.)
EF to Mint: $10–$15

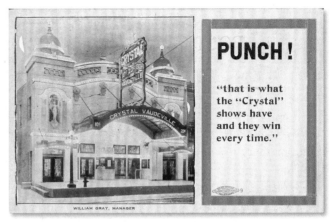

The Crystal Vaudeville Theatre, Milwaukee, Wisconsin.
EF to Mint: $15–$20

The Electric Theatre and the Palace Theatre, two vaudeville theaters side by side in Charleroi, Pennsylvania.
EF to Mint: $12–$18

The Museum Vaudeville Minstrels tent show RPPC, location unknown. (Published by M.F. Childs, Reading, Massachusetts.) EF to Mint: $65–$85

Two vaudeville theaters in Hastings, Michigan. RPPC. EF to Mint: $125+

Street fair, Monmouth, Illinois, RPPC postmarked October 14, 1908. Very elaborate show similar to a carnival, with concessions and acts, "Vodeville" and "Salome" show fronts. Excellent details, including acrobats in motion. An exceptional quality card. EF to Mint: $150+

Music and Musicians

The field of music is wonderfully varied and has been captured on countless different postcards. Their scenes range from solo players of instruments to bands and orchestras. Many postcards are artistic, with some of these being comic. The National Song Series, some with Winsch backs (see chapter 11), were copyrighted by E. Nash and, separately, by Charles Rose. Some cards of similar appearance have a European imprint. RPPCs are scarce except for parades and outdoor pictures.

Art card, lady with guitar, by F. Earl Christy. (Series No. 5 with 12 designs.) EF to Mint: $10–$15

In Columbus, Ohio, the Majestic Theatre, a vaudeville house, showed films. The title of *The Bishop's Carriage* is projected by a slide on the screen as an attraction, "Coming Monday." This was a five-reel Famous Players production filmed by Edwin S. Porter and with Mary Pickford in the cast. Released on October 4, 1913. EF to Mint: $8–$12

Stage and Vaudeville Theaters, Opera Houses	Value, EF to Mint
Opera houses: Large building	$5–$10
Opera houses: Small building, 1 to 3 floors	$7–$15
Opera houses: Small town RPPC	$20–$50+
Vaudeville theaters: Large building	$5–$20
Vaudeville theaters: Small building, 1 to 3 floors	$7–$30
Vaudeville theaters: RPPC	$25–$50+
Vaudeville tent shows: RPPC	$50–$150

"The largo," art card, lady with cello, by F. Earl Christy. (H Import No. 304-5. The Knapp Co, Inc., New York.) EF to Mint: $10–$15

257

"Tender memories," art card, lady playing the piano, by F. Earl Christy. (No. 217. Reinthal & Newman.)
EF to Mint: $10–$12

"At the Carnival. Music Hath Charms." Jester with mandolin. (Carnival Post Card Series No. 117. Raphael Tuck, London.)
EF to Mint: $10–$15

Christmas card with a child playing a set of orchestra bells. (Germany.) EF to Mint: $4–$6

A family band. (Albertype, Brooklyn, New York.)
EF to Mint: $8–$12

Old Fort Plain Band, Fort Plain, New York. (No. 27513. G.R. Chriss & Co., Fort Plain. Postmarked 1913.)
EF to Mint: $10–$20

"A Sunday afternoon concert in midwinter, Golden Gate Park, San Francisco." (Britton & Rey, San Francisco. Postmarked 1905.) EF to Mint: $4–$6

Advertising card for the Innes Orchestral Band appearance on May 11, 1904, at the Coliseum in Peoria, Illinois. EF to Mint: $12–$18

"A happy bunch on Sunday morning at Val's, Bristol, Ind." RPPC. EF to Mint: $50–$75+

DeRue Brothers Minstrels and Concert Band postcard advertising a coming appearance. (DeRue Brothers, Herkimer, New York. Postmarked 1910.) EF to Mint: $10–$20

"Sousa's Band and his audience." Willow Park, Pennsylvania, with 15,000 people at or near the Music Pavilion. (J.M. Canfield, Saxony.) EF to Mint: $10–$20

Holyoke, Massachusetts, marching band, 1914. RPPC. EF to Mint: $30–$50

Battle Hymn of the Republic, copyrighted by E. Nash, New York, 1909. Winsch back. EF to Mint: $4–$7

Nearer My God to Thee, copyrighted by Charles Rose, New York, 1908. EF to Mint: $4–$7

Comic card with a choir of cats. (T.S.N. Series 1012 of six designs). EF to Mint: $20–$25

Music and Musicians	Value, EF to Mint
Art card with musician and instrument prominent	$4–$12+
Card made from photograph with musician and instrument prominent	$8–$15+
Parades with music prominent	$8–$20+
Bands and orchestras	$8–$20+
Parades with music prominent	$8–20+
Concert, band, etc., advertising card	$10–$20+
Musician with instrument RPPC	$10–$20+
Parades with music prominent RPPC	$15–$30+
Bands and orchestras RPPC	$15–$30+
National song cards	$5–$10
Comic cards	$2–$8

Circuses and Carnivals

Postcards showing circuses and carnivals are very popular and can be expensive. Circuses usually set up under canvas in a large field. Carnivals did likewise, except for a few that were spread out on city streets. Postcards range from those printed in America in color to black-and-white printed cards to RPPCs. The most valuable are those that show interesting signs and tent fronts, performers in action, and rides. Values vary widely. The illustrated cards give a representation.

Starrett's Society Circus at an engagement at the Orange County Fair near Middletown, New York. RPPC postmarked September 8, 1906. Known also as Starrett's Society Shows, in 1906 an attraction was Charles Hopper, in his third season as a singing and talking clown (according to an item in *The New York Clipper*). Other entertainment included a band, solo musical performances, comedy acts, acrobats, and trained ponies. In 1910 the show became the first in America to tour in automobiles. EF to Mint: $50–$75

"Early morning along the upper Midway, Vermont State Fair." (No. 15. Vermont State Fair Series, Green Mountain Card Co. Circa 1910s.) EF to Mint: $15–$25

"Street in Huron during State Fair '07. J.M.H." RPPC from Huron, South Dakota, with excellent detail. Under magnification a horse-drawn popcorn wagon and a movable Ferris Wheel can be seen. Presumably, the main part of the fair was elsewhere. EF to Mint: $75–$100

"Midway from Ferris Wheel, White River Jct., Vt." RPPC postmarked September 14, 1914, from a concessionaire to a friend, a tale of woe: "We are here doing nothing today. Took in 40 cents, great day. Most people say that tomorrow will be a good day, but don't know. Couldn't get on the grounds until we paid all the rent—something that never happened before." This is probably a stock RPPC from an earlier fair, as the activity belies the message. EF to Mint: $50–$75

Live Fair at Waverly, Iowa, RPPC postmarked 1910. No. 114, apparently part of a large series of RPPC for this event. "1000 autos on grounds. 3rd day. Attendance 26032. Photo by F.W. Mueller." An excellent card with much detail, captioned, dated, and with photographer identified. The many automobiles may make this card of interest to a specialist in that area. EF to Mint: $50–$75

"Scenes at the Oshkosh Fair, Oshkosh, Wis." (Kropp 45/30477N. Circa 1920s.) EF to Mint: $10–$15

Willy Zimmerman's "Big Show" on the road. Signs promise "Moving Pictures," "Polite Vaudeville," Challence Orchestra," "Leo High Diving Dog Exhibition," "The Mer-Man," and more. Admission was 10¢. Zimmerman was a well-known vaudeville entertainer in the early twentieth century. Among his acts he impersonated musicians and other figures of present and past. RPPC. (Circa 1910s.) EF to Mint: $75–$100+

The Ketrow & Trover Western Comedy Show was operated by Ketrow & Trover's Western Dramatic Company. The show included a band and orchestra with lead singer Miss Flossie Warner. In this view it is seemingly about to set up with canvas on the ground. This troupe traveled from 1913 to 1916. RPPC. EF to Mint: $40–$50

"Manatee County Fair and Celery Exposition to be Held Feb. 25th to March 4th," the sign over the entryway states. Held in Manatee, Florida, on the Gulf Coast not far from Bradenton. Message: "This picture is looking east toward Manatee. This street is Florida Avenue... 85 degrees in the shade today." RPPC. (Potter photo. Postmarked March 25, 1916.) EF to Mint: $100+

Early Pictures and Studios

The first motion pictures were shown to paying audiences in 1895. From that time until the early twentieth century, nearly all films were short, lasting a minute to several minutes. Few were of 1,000-foot or 12-minute length when projected. Emphasis was on action: a gardener being squirted by a hose, a train coming down the tracks, and similar excitement. By 1910 one-reel pictures with stories—from comedy to documentary—were the rule, punctuated by some longer subjects up to several reels.

These movies were widely advertised on colorful posters and elsewhere, but the names of the players were hardly ever given. For actors and actresses, performing before the camera was everyday work, although dramatic talent was required. The star system had not yet been born. Edison, American Biograph, Vitagraph, Thanhouser, Independent Moving Pictures Co. (IMP), and other studios turned out hundreds of pictures. For example, a favorite lady was known as the "Biograph Girl,"

as her name was not listed in advertising, the credits, or anywhere else.

The various studios each had key players in their stock companies—men who would take heroic or romantic roles, women who would be subject to peril or would be pursued by suitors. Moviegoers began to recognize their faces and look for them in subsequent roles. By 1910 the growing desire of audiences to identify their favorite actors and actresses, and the usefulness of promoting the appearance of prominent film performers as a way to keep up frequent attendance, led nickelodeon managers to want to publicize leading players. Audiences and operators put increasing pressure on producers to identify and promote their performers.

Showcasing the identities of players was a two-edged sword for the film producers. On one hand, if Florence Lawrence (who had been identified as the "Biograph Girl" but had left that company), or Mary Pickford, or J. Warren Kerrigan became known and liked by audiences, a sign advertising "Little Mary (Pickford) Today" or "Home of Charlie Chaplin" would draw crowds. This was of obvious benefit to a studio. On the other hand, if the players realized that their acting was a drawing card contributing to profits, they were apt to demand higher salaries. Lawrence, Pickford, Chaplin, and some others were like bees in a flower garden, buzzing from one studio to another, with higher salaries each time. In time, Florence LaBadie, one of the Thanhouser Company's best-known personalities, gained acclaim for staying with that company as she emerged from obscurity and went on to become one of the most familiar personalities of her era.

Moving around could cause other problems, especially with publicity. Vitagraph's portrayal of *The Deerslayer* was filmed in 1911 but was delayed in its release. By the time it was on the screen, actress Florence Turner, famously known as the Vitagraph Girl, had departed to form her own studio, Turner Films, Ltd. Now the Vitagraph Girl was not with Vitagraph—a difficulty for promotion.

On February 11, 1911, J. Stuart Blackton of Vitagraph launched *Motion Picture Story Magazine*, which concentrated on Trust studios and players, giving names and illustrating scenes from the plays and storylines. Typical Trust production was seven to ten one- and two-reel pictures each month, giving the magazine a lot of potential editorial content. Eugene V. Brewster was editor. The initial print run was 50,000 copies, which vaulted to 300,000 within a short time.[13] This was the first of the "fan" magazines to catch hold. The earliest monthly editions had little other than scenarios and still pictures, plus a few advertisements geared to people who wanted to learn how to write short stories (or even movie scenarios). There was hardly any information about the performers or behind-the-scenes information at the studios. This changed, and quickly, as letters expressing curiosity about actors and actresses, and how movies were made, flooded in.

In July 1913 the First Annual Moving Picture Exposition was held at the Grand Central Palace in New York City. Exhibits were set up by sellers of theater equipment, ranging from projectors to automatic electric pianos. The various studios, still mostly located in the greater New York City area, sent players and offered souvenirs. Thousands attended to greet and mingle with the players, many of whom had never been to a publicity event before. The exposition was a smashing success for everyone concerned. Within the next several years, movie exhibitions and balls were held in many cities.

Movie Postcards

One way to appreciate the players and to preserve memories was to collect postcards. Advertisements in fan magazines offered groups of postcards showing actors and actresses from various studios. These were popular drawing cards and giveaways at the movies, and acquiring as many as possible became a popular passion. By 1915 there were thousands of different varieties of picture postcards depicting American movie actors and actresses and, in fewer numbers, cards showing scenes from serials (in particular) and other films. While most had postcard backs, some simply had plain backs and were designed to be passed out as souvenirs in theaters. Typically, the individual was shown in a photographic studio pose, portrait or full length, with a plain background.

The most prolific issuer seems to have been the Kraus Manufacturing Company of New York City, which produced cards printed in brown with a cream background to the border, giving the artist's name at the bottom and, often, the studio affiliation. The Commercial Colortype Company of Chicago produced color illustrations of artists in several different series and formats. At the time, viewers were accustomed to seeing their screen heroes in black and white, so color did not seem to have captured the fancy of the marketplace. The colors were made by tinting black-and-white photographs, not by color photography. The Kline Poster Company of Philadelphia issued a wide variety of color-tinted cards of good quality, with different poses.

Minor issuers of postcards in terms of output included Maurer, Schultz & Co. of Los Angeles; the Ess and Ess Photo Company of New York City; the Garraway Company in New Jersey; and the Photo-Player Publicity Company of Los Angeles. Butter Krust Bread in America, a division of General Baking Company, published cards showing stars. The General Baking Company issued a series of postcards with especially well-selected portraits. These bore an advertisement on the back: "Eat General Baking Company Butter Krust Bread."

In England (in particular), Germany, Scandinavia, and elsewhere, American films of the early twentieth century were very popular. Some studios had overseas branches such as Thanhouser Films, Ltd. Although there are exceptions, postcards produced overseas were often reproduced from photographic negatives, showing better details of the portraits than did their counterparts published in the United States. Many featured scenes of films, such as an entire series of Charlie Chaplin.

American-made postcards were distributed in a number of ways. Readers of fan magazines could order them by mail, striving to obtain as many different as possible. Over time the images used on Kraus cards, for example, did vary, and thus no two collections of cards would have the same set of pictures. Cards were also sold in theaters at the ticket office, at a separate counter, or by ushers. Many cards were simply mailed out with the name of the theater and the address rubber stamped on the back, often with something such as "See me at the Pastime," or "at the Gem March 23-27." Relatively few such postcards were ever used in correspondence between movie fans, an unusual situation. It seems that most who acquired cards simply kept them as souvenirs. Sometimes the period of issue of a card can be learned from the studio affiliation. As an example, Charlie Chaplin postcards that mention the Keystone Studio are circa 1914, and those mentioning the Essanay Studio (much more plentiful) can be attributed to 1915.

Postcards depicting players, scenes from specific movies, or showing the theater itself were a popular way to advertise. Cards were less than a cent each wholesale, and a stamp cost a cent. Generally, pictures of players were produced in immense quantities, and those showing scenes from or mentioning particular pictures were produced in smaller numbers, as they tended to become obsolete.

In the second decade of the twentieth century, most of the film industry, earlier centered in and around New York City, moved to California. Year-round pleasant weather and plenty of sunshine facilitated production. A prolific issuer of postcards was Universal City, opened in Los Angeles in 1915 by Carl Laemmle, a promoter par excellence. He started in the film exchange business and evolved to running the Independent Moving Pictures Company, then Universal. This attraction was open to tourists and proved to be very popular. Many varieties of cards were issued, showing buildings, scenes, and the like. Nearly all of these were printed.

The "Flying A" players in Southern California are depicted on a number of cards that resemble RPPCs but were printed in quantity. These typically show posed scenes with multiple players, often unidentified but no doubt well-known personalities in their time, gazing at the camera. RPPC cards were issued by some other studios as well. There is no particular premium attached to these, unless a specialist finds a subject to be rare.

In 1914 Henry Lang offered postcards of popular players of the day. This advertisement in a fan magazine suggested that readers might want to collect a complete set of "about 175." These were made by the Kraus Manufacturing Co. So far as is known, there is no complete listing of the subjects. (*Moving Picture Stories*, July 10, 1914.) EF to Mint: $8–$12

Likely, many of these RPPCs were simply made by the studios in their photographic departments, which could churn them out with little difficulty in response to whatever demand there might be from visitors and others. RPPCs of specific films being produced are a much rarer class and can have significant value if the names of players or the film are still recognized today.

As the vast majority of cards depicting Universal City and other studios were bought by film enthusiasts who kept them as souvenirs, the average grades tend to be quite high on surviving cards today. Pre-1912 cards showing studio scenes, usually in the East, are a rare class that has never been studied in detail.

As might be expected, cards of players whose names are more recognizable today—such as Mary Pickford and Charlie Chaplin—tend to be in greater demand and bring larger prices than do one-time stars who are not well known in the present day, such as John Bunny (a prominent comedian at Vitagraph), Florence LaBadie (a beautiful film star at Thanhouser, involved in many "action" pictures), and others. Relatively few present-day enthusiasts know much about Pearl White and the *Perils of Pauline* serial, with the actress involved in all sorts of scenarios certain to cause death, from which she miraculously escapes. However, such postcards are in greater demand than are cards from serials that were famous in their time and are little remembered today—such as the incredibly successful *Million Dollar Mystery*, *Dollie of the Dailies*, and the *Hazards of Helen*. It is a pleasurable pursuit to collect such cards and then seek information on them on the Internet. This element of postcard collecting research did not exist a generation ago and is of great benefit today.

Movie Actors and Actresses

Postcards issued in America depicting an actor or actress and giving the name of the studio (Kalem, Edison, Thanhouser, Paramount, etc.) are valued in grades of Very Fine and higher, as lower grades are seldom seen. Players whose names are still recognized today can sell for more. Cards imprinted on the back with a specific theater and location can be worth slightly more. "Autographed" cards were usually printed as such, or, if ink-signed, not by the person depicted. Prices are for cards with postcard backs. Cards with plain or other backs are worth much less. Many black-and-white cards have glossy surfaces and resemble RPPCs. These are worth no special premium.

Lillian Gish was perhaps director D.W. Griffith's favorite actress at Biograph. EF to Mint: $5–$8

Mary Pickford is the best-remembered actress from the silent film era. EF to Mint: $5–$8

Card No. 52 from Mack Sennett Comedies' "Bathing Beauties," featuring girls posed and in antics, black and white, RPPC-style but made in quantity. (Circa 1910s.) EF to Mint: $15–$20

Evelyn Nesbit, the femme fatale in Harry Thaw's shooting of Stanford White in Madison Square Garden in 1906, later went into films. EF to Mint: $5–$10

Florence LaBadie, leading lady with the Thanhouser Co., lead role in *The Million Dollar Mystery* serial. (Commercial Colortype Co. Circa 1914.) EF to Mint: $3–$5

"Two favorites." EF to Mint: $15–$30, as it includes auto advertising

Movie Actors and Actresses	Value, EF to Mint
Lesser known, early 1900s	$3–$5
Famous, early 1900s	$5–$10
Lesser known, black and white on glossy stock, foreign printed 1910–1920	$2–$4
Famous, black and white on glossy stock, foreign printed 1910–1920	$4–$8
Mack Sennett Comedies "Bathing Girls"	$10–$20

Scenes from Films

Postcards issued in America showing a scene from an identified film, the name of the studio, and, often, the lead player were used as handouts, for advertising, and other purposes. Some black-and-white cards have glossy surfaces and resemble RPPCs. Prices for RPPCs are for high-quality amateur views or low-quantity studio views; worth the most if the players and/or title are given.

RPPC issued for *Sapho* by the Atlas Mfg. Co. of St. Louis, one of many companies that endeavored to get into the film making or distribution business in the early twentieth century. This was an advertising card for the low-budget film. EF to Mint: $15–$25

Postcard with a scene from *An Unwilling Cowboy*, produced by Georges Méliès, Star Film Company, filmed in Texas in 1911. As is so often the case with cards of this type, it was viewed many times, probably by a movie fan, with the result that it is barely in Fine condition today. EF to Mint: $6–$10

Scene from the six part photo play "Arizona" produced under the personal direction of AUGUSTUS THOMAS, with CYRIL SCOTT in the leading role.

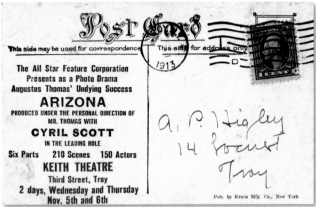

Postcard mailed by Keith's Theatre in Troy, New York, to advertise the film *Arizona*. (Kraus Manufacturing Co. Postmarked 1913.) EF to Mint: $6–$10

Advertising postcard with a dramatic scene from *Tracked by Wireless*, a Warner's Features three-reel film of 1912. This is one of several cards issued for the picture. The missing corner lowers its value considerably. (Kraus Mfg. Co.) EF to Mint: $10–$15

The Sheriff learns that Nat-u-rich killed Hawkins.—"THE SQUAW MAN"

Postcard issued for *The Squaw Man*, one of the most acclaimed films of its time. With rubber stamp on the back, applied by a theater showing it. EF to Mint: $6–$10

Rudolph (misspelled on the card as Rodolph) Valentino, Gloria Swanson, and Elinor Glyn. (California Postcard Co. 26633N.) EF to Mint: $8–$12

Scenes from Films	Value, EF to Mint
Lesser known players, black and white or single color, early 1900s	$3–$5
Famous players, early 1900s	$6–$15
Lesser known players, early 1900s	$4–$8

Studios, Film Production, Sets

Cards showing people on film sets, production in indoor or outdoor settings, groups of players identified by studio, etc., are very desirable and somewhat scarce. Most depict California studios after about 1912. Amateur or limited-quantity RPPCs are worth more, especially if identified as to players and/or title of film.

California Postcard Co. Series: In the early 1920s the California Postcard Company, Los Angeles, put out a unique set of cards, printed by Kropp of Milwaukee. These featured a wide selection of stars and studios—a movie fan's delight, as most showed behind-the-scenes action and were well composed. Issued in quantity, most of these are easily obtained today, but several are scarce. These are described here not because they are examples of great demand but rather as representative of available studio scenes. The titles are printed on the face of each card, plus the serial number of the card.

Serial No.	Name
26622	Clara Kimball Young, Garson Studios, Edendale
26623N	"Faking" a Snow Scene in Tropical California, Mack Sennett Studios, Edendale
26624	"Dr." Harold Lloyd and his patient, "Micky" Daniels (add 50 percent to value)
26625	An outdoor "Set" built in-doors, Christie Studios, Hollywood
26626	Resting between "Shots," Fine Arts Studios, Hollywood
26627	Building a "set" at the Metro Studios, Hollywood
26628	Charles Ray and Staff, The Charles Ray Productions, Hollywood
26631	"Shooting" a Chinatown scene, with Constance Talmadge at Hollywood
26632	Rupert Hughes directing one of his Stories, Goldwyn Studios, Culver City
26633	Rodolph [sic] Valentino, Gloria Swanson, and Elinor Glyn, Paramount Studios, Hollywood

Mary Pickford (California Postcard Co. No. 26634.)
EF to Mint: $10–$15

Buster Keaton (California Postcard Co. No. 26638N.)
EF to Mint: $10–$15

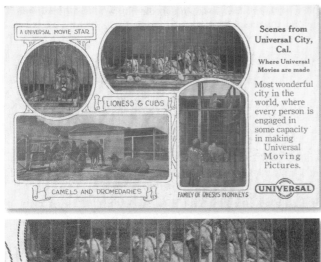

One of eight or more "Scenes of Universal City" cards issued
in 1915, the year the attraction opened. EF to Mint: $12–$18

Universal City, established in Los Angeles by Carl Laemmle
and his organization in 1915, issued large numbers of printed
postcards and RPPC. This is a panorama view of "The Capital
of Filmland." (No. 733. Van Ornum Colorprint Co. Circa 1916.)
EF to Mint: $8–$12

Visitors' entrance to Universal City. (No. 778. Van Ornum
Colorprint Co. Circa 1916.) EF to Mint: $10–$15

Laemmle Boulevard in Universal City, named after Universal's
founder, who began in the trade as a film distributor in Los
Angeles. (Julius J. Hecht / Curt Teich Co. No. 62,000. 1916.)
EF to Mint: $8–$12

"Scene seen behind the scenes. Universal City, Cal." RPPC. Circa late 1910s. EF to Mint: $20–$30

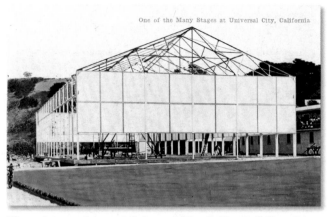

"One of many stages at Universal City, California." Circa late 1910s. (No. 780. Van Ornum Colorprint Co. Circa 1916.) EF to Mint: $8–$12

"An Old English street scene built for a movie at Universal City, Cal." RPPC. Circa late 1910s. EF to Mint: $25–$45

"This scene costing over $10,000 was built for Jules Verns [sic] 20,000 Leagues Under the Sea. Universal City, Cal." RPPC for a 1916 film. Carelessly photographed (slanting perspective to buildings and crudely lettered, not uncommon among Universal RPPCs). EF to Mint: $40–$50+

"Universal City, Cal. Main Stage. Taking the pictures." RPPC. Circa late 1910s. EF to Mint: $40–$50+

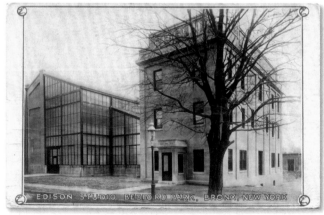

A glass studio operated by Edison in Bedford Park, Bronx, New York City. EF to Mint: $60+

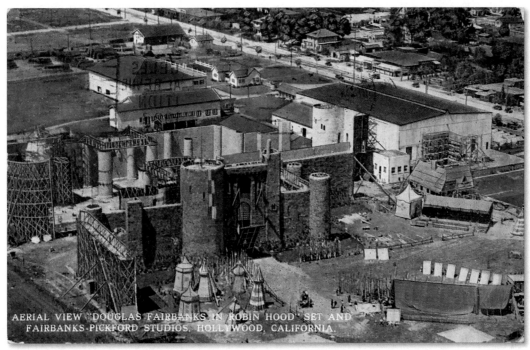

Aerial view of the Fairbanks-Pickford Studios in Hollywood when *Robin Hood* was in production. (No. A-69328. Curt Teich Co. 1916.) EF to Mint: $10–$15

American Film Co. studio in Santa Barbara, California, home of the "Flying A" pictures. (No. R-747898. Curt Teich Co. 1917.) EF to Mint: $8–$12

Mary Pickford Studios, Hollywood, California. (No. 101692. Curt Teich Co. 1924.) EF to Mint: $8–$12

Mack Sennett Studios in Los Angeles, the home of many comedy films. (Commercially produced RPPC.) EF to Mint: $40–$50

Garson Studio, Edendale, Los Angeles, printed card from an image earlier used for an RPPC. (No. 788. M. Kashower Co. Circa 1920.) EF to Mint: $8–$12

RPPC of the Charles Chaplin Studio, a view made in quantity. (1920s.) EF to Mint: $30–$40

Studios, Film Production, Sets	Value, EF to Mint
Studio action before 1930	$10–$20
Studio action, RPPC before 1920	$15–$50
Studio buildings before 1930	$8–$15
Studio buildings, RPPC before 1930	$20–$50+

Motion Picture Theaters

Motion pictures were first projected in opera houses, auditoriums, arcades, and the like during the late nineteenth century. By the time the era of postcard popularity came about, most motion picture shows were in their own buildings. Postcards depicting these locations date from about 1904 and 1905 and continue for decades afterward. The earliest cards, and the most desirable, are those from the "nickelodeon" era, the term being a combination of the word used for a five-cent coin and the French word for theater. A nickel was indeed a typical admission, sometimes a dime, but rarely higher in the earlier days. By about 1910 or so, as motion pictures changed to comedy and drama instead of just action and as movie stars came into prominence, admissions were raised so a quarter was typical for a night show. Some nickelodeons ran nonstop from morning until midnight, with patrons coming and going as they pleased, or else for shows lasting an hour, an hour-and-a-half, or two hours, sometimes spaced by an intermission.

Nickelodeons of the first decade of the twentieth century through about 1915 often had ornate facades, usually painted white, and were decorated with many electric bulbs. Many were depicted on postcards. Those showing people in the front or recognizable posters add interest and value. Many RPPCs were made, particularly of smaller theaters, and can be very valuable if with people and posters. Beautifully lithographed color cards made in Germany depict other nickelodeons, often as part of a street scene. Such a card is desirable to a collector of nickelodeon cards, especially if the theater occupies a prominent part of the image.

Traveling picture shows were part of the industry, and many itinerant exhibitors were featured on postcards, usually RPPCs. Well-focused cards with good content are very scarce and are a challenge to find. RPPCs with people and/or prominent posters out front are worth more.

After about 1915, ornate white theater fronts with countless electric bulbs gave way to more formal structures. From then through the early 1930s the "palace" theater became popular in larger cities, accommodating more than 1,000 people, with the interior a wonderland of painted scenes, ornate trim, and, often, films accompanied by a pipe organ. Large edifices were put up by Fox, Paramount, and other chains during the 1920s. Nearly all of these are depicted on printed cards, usually in color. The use of RPPCs faded. These theaters, too, were often shown as part of street scenes and can be collected as such, but the cards are most desired when the theater is prominent.

Dreamland Theatre, Catawissa, Pennsylvania, nickelodeon. EF to Mint: $100+

In Rockford, Illinois, a thriving manufacturing city, the Colonial Theatre offered Charlie Chaplin comedies for a nickel. Anyone passing could not help but notice that America's most famous comedian dominated the program. The bill included the Essanay films *Work* and *A Woman*, with Chaplin, and Kalem's two-reel *The Accomplice*. "Come in and See Great Pictures—Thousand Dollar Glass Curtain, the Only One in Rockford." RPPC. EF to Mint: $175+

The nickelodeon theater in the A. Tocce building with people and posters in the front. RPPC. EF to Mint: $125+

Bijou Theatre, Attica, New York, nickelodeon. EF to Mint: $20–$25

Happy Hour Theatre, Lestershire, New York. RPPC. EF to Mint: $125+

Dreamland Theatre, Livermore, Maine, nickelodeon. EF to Mint: $20–$25

The Bijou Dream nickelodeon in Rochester, New York.
EF to Mint: $50–$80

The Dixie nickelodeon in Manassas, Virginia. EF to Mint: $50+

The Hawes Moving Picture Company, a family operation, traveled from town to town, showing pictures in a black-lined tent. Shown is their setup in Skowhegan, Maine. Titles lettered on the "Picture Tonight" program board include *Isabella and Arragon* ("a very fine picture"), *The Tenderfoot, For His Sister's Honor, A New Burglar Alarm,* and *Mr. Brown Is Hustling* ("comedy"). The illustrated song was "Have a Drink to Yankee Land." EF to Mint: $50–$100+

The Bijou Dream nickelodeon in Pittsburgh, Pennsylvania. Face inscription: "Wurlitzer's wonderful electric organ, the finest musical instrument known to musical science. The most complete and finest picture theatre in Pittsburgh. Ceiling 75 feet high. Air ventilating domes. Electric fans. Coolest picture theatre in Pittsburgh." Back inscription: "Bijou Dream motion picture theatre. Illustrated songs and electric organ stands alone as the house of refined entertainment. 6021 Penn Avenue, East End. Change of program daily. 5 cts. Admission. 5 cts." (No. M-2687.) EF to Mint: $40–$80

Saenger Theatre, Hope, Arkansas. This was part of a Midwest chain of movie theaters. EF to Mint: $20–$25

Exterior street view and interior view of the Alamo Theatre, Louisville, Kentucky. EF to Mint: $8–$12

Atmospheric or scenic interior of Fox's Arlington Theatre, Santa Barbara, California. EF to Mint: $6–$8

Grauman's Chinese Theatre, Hollywood, Los Angeles, California. EF to Mint: $5–$8

Motion Picture Theaters	Value, EF to Mint
Nickelodeon, 1900–1915	$15–$25+
Nickelodeon, RPPC 1900–1915	$50–$200+
Nickelodeon interior, RPPC 1900–1915	$50–$200+
Traveling picture shows, 1900–1920	$50–$100+
Later theater exteriors, 1915–1930s	$3–$6+
Later theater interiors, 1915–1930s	$5–$10+
Later theater interiors, RPPC 1915–1930s	$30–$60+

AMUSEMENT PARKS

Amusement parks of the Golden Age of postcards are a popular collecting category of view cards. Many of these were operated by single corporations, while others, such as Venice (California), Coney Island (New York), and Bass Point (Massachusetts) were districts featuring attractions owned by many different interests. The very definition of amusement park is elusive. The authors consider such to be a commercially operated area (although a few were operated by municipalities) in a permanent location, constructed with multiple rides, concessions, and other attractions, including a carousel, Ferris Wheel, and scenic railroad (roller coaster), or at least two of these. Not included are nature parks, picnic parks, annual fairs, and traveling shows. As might be expected, there are scattered exceptions.

This ideal amusement park card was issued by G.A. Dentzel, Philadelphia maker of carousels, noting on the face that such rides were available in Atlantic City, New Jersey; Willow Grove, Pennsylvania; Woodside Park, Philadelphia, "and all other parks." EF to Mint: $75–$150

Depending upon the definition, close to 2,000 amusement parks and areas were established in the first three decades of the twentieth century, the general area emphasized here. Some operated for just a few years,

The Grove concession area in Savin Rock Park in Connecticut. Studying a card and then investigating its features is a pleasant pursuit. A large poster to the left advertises the film *The Unwritten Law*, a story of the Thaw-White murder trial centering on femme fatale Evelyn Nesbit. Released by Lubin in 1907, it dealt with Thaw's first court case, in which he was acquitted. The film showed the verdict as being on the grounds of justifiable homicide, with which many civic authorities disagreed, causing the film to be suppressed and thereby gaining much attention in the popular press. Due to the great controversy it stirred up, the picture remained popular for a number of years afterward—ideal as an evergreen title for an amusement park. (No. 253. Danziger & Berman, New London, Connecticut. Postmarked 1912.) EF to Mint: $15–$22

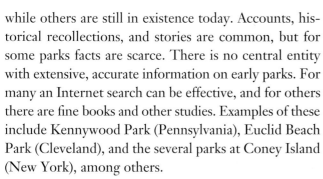

Panoramic view of Riverton Park, Portland, Maine, a smaller amusement park. (No. 22896. Metropolitan. Circa 1910s.) EF to Mint: $15–$20

Panorama of Ontario Beach Park, a very large facility also known as Charlotte Beach, in Rochester, New York. (Rochester News Co. / ANC Litho-Chrome. No. C-4930. Postmarked 1908.) EF to Mint: $12–$18

while others are still in existence today. Accounts, historical recollections, and stories are common, but for some parks facts are scarce. There is no central entity with extensive, accurate information on early parks. For many an Internet search can be effective, and for others there are fine books and other studies. Examples of these include Kennywood Park (Pennsylvania), Euclid Beach Park (Cleveland), and the several parks at Coney Island (New York), among others.

Amusement parks under a single ownership (such as a corporation) were created to have a special atmosphere, a "city" of entertainment delights not necessarily based on natural attractions or scenery, although beaches were a popular place to locate them. In America they were the evolution of pleasure gardens and other outdoor attractions, but with more features. It was not at all unusual for a park to have dozens of rides, galleries, concessions, and other places to spend time and money. In states in the Midwest and North, such parks were typically open only in "season"—the warmer months from late spring into autumn. In the South and in warmer climes, many were active all year.

Postcards of various rides and attractions are popular to collect. Johnstown Flood building, Paragon Park, Nantasket Beach, Massachusetts, re-enacted the May 31, 1889, disaster when a dam on Conemaugh Creek burst and drowned the city below it. Other parks had similar attractions. (No. 8791. Metropolitan News Co., Boston. Postmarked 1907.) EF to Mint: $10–$15

During the nineteenth century the outdoor amusement business evolved from traveling shows to permanent facilities near population centers. Many trolley car lines, known as street railways, were built in the 1880s and 1890s to provide inexpensive transportation within towns and cities, often connecting with other lines to provide a regional network. By the turn of the twentieth century, much of the East Coast was linked by such transportation, supplemented by interurban lines. Seeking additional revenue, many street railways constructed amusement parks on open land a few miles away from urban areas, generating passenger traffic on Saturdays and Sundays. In the trade these were known as "trolley parks."

The World's Columbian Exposition in Chicago in 1893, nicknamed the "White City," was a wonderland of exhibits, rides, and other attractions, brilliantly illuminated at night by electricity—a fairly new marvel in this context. After the fair closed, many existing amusement parks, as well as new ones, sought to emulate the Exposition by setting up buildings with themed rides and exhibits, some indeed called White City. The Coney Island district on the shore of the Atlantic Ocean in south Brooklyn, New York, was famous and served as a model for many parks, with more than a few copying such Coney names as Luna Park, Steeplechase, and Dreamland.

The typical small amusement park in the early twentieth century had several of the following: buildings with exhibits, a bandstand, a selection of rides, a carousel, a Ferris Wheel, a dozen or more concessions, a penny arcade, and a handful of other attractions. Larger parks

near big cities—Savin Rock near New Haven (Connecticut), several parks in Coney Island (New York), Euclid Beach Park (Cleveland), and White City (Chicago), for example—had more extensive facilities.

By the early twentieth century, when color lithographed postcards were starting to become popular in America, such shows in stand-alone buildings, as the Johnstown Flood, Rivers of Venice, Galveston Flood, Coal Mine, and Old Mill were favorites, usually charging a nickel or a dime for admission. Although there were variations, the Old Mill was often a water ride, a version of the "tunnel of love" in which patrons glided through a dark tunnel punctuated with occasional scenes and exhibits. Some romantic couples went through again and again! The Johnstown and Galveston shows had dioramas and exhibits relating to the disasters for which they were named. Many such attractions were ephemeral, and when their novelty faded, the names and themes were changed and the building became a new magnet for visitors.

Scenic railway rides came in many different forms with different themes. This card shows Pikes Peak Railway on Surf Avenue in Coney Island. (No. 5426. A.C. Bosselman & Co., New York. Circa 1908.) EF to Mint: $12–$18

The scenic railroad took several forms—a ride on rails through the Alps, or up Pikes Peak, or a trip back to ancient times, for instance—with painted panels and exhibits to be viewed along the way. These were often enclosed in buildings or within a framework representing a mountain. Open-air roller coasters took the place of scenic railroads as time went on, and by the 1910s and 1920s, most large parks had them. The larger the better, even more so if erected so it could be seen from a long distance away as a drawing card. In time, many parks were judged by the size of their coasters and the degree of fright they induced. In contrast, carousels and Ferris Wheels were taken for granted and rarely gained much special attention.[14] Today in the early twenty-first century, many amusement parks are famous for their roller coasters, but other attractions are not as well known. The iconic merry-go-round with its music provided by a band organ has evolved, now with composition plastic or related materials instead of carved wood horses and with amplified electronic music. The younger set does not know the difference. Later amusement park cards are discussed in chapters 23 and 24.

Shoot the Chutes at the Oaks in Portland, Oregon. (Louis Scheiner, Portland / Curt Teich Co. No. A-18367. Postmarked 1909.) EF to Mint: $8–$12

The Shoot the Chutes water ride, also called simply Chutes—a boat sliding on rails down a cascading ramp and splashing at high speed into a lagoon—was especially popular, as evidenced by the abundance of postcards showing them, often from various angles. In the early twentieth century, Chutes Park in San Francisco and similarly named attractions in Los Angeles and Chicago were popular.

Stage shows of short duration, circus acts, Japanese tea gardens, restaurants, miniature railroads, and more beckoned to visitors.[15] A strip or concourse with many small stands, concessions, and small attractions was designated as the midway, the zone, or some other term, drawing a continuing stream of visitors. A large park offered enough diversion to keep a patron entertained all day long, culminating with dancing or music in the evening.

Postcards

Most amusement parks are memorialized on postcards. In a few instances "official" cards were sold by the proprietors, but most were issued by postcard companies, vendors, and concessions. The more postcards mailed, the more free publicity there was for a park—so no restrictions were placed on their production or use.

Smaller parks might have a half dozen to a dozen or so views available at a given time, while larger layouts often had cards for each of the major attractions, sometimes multiple views of the same ride or show. At any given time hundreds of different views of Coney Island were available. Richard Snow's *Coney Island: A Postcard Journey to the Island of Fire*, published in 1989, is an example of the many books on American amusement parks that are illustrated with postcards.

Cards showing an electrically illuminated "wonderland" at night were made for many parks by taking daytime views and altering them in the graphics department of a manufacturer. In many instances, the identical view was used at first for an early black-and-white card, then in 1905 or later for a brightly colored depiction and also for an altered night time scene.

Composite or multi-view card of White City, Chicago. (No publisher. Postmarked 1909.) EF to Mint: $50–$75

Composite or multi-view card of Luna Park, Coney Island, New York made by photographing other cards. (Nos. E-1250 and 201457. No publisher. Circa 1910.) EF to Mint: $8–$12

For the visitor who just wanted to send a single card to a friend, a panoramic view of the park was ideal, or a composite card showing many little views (often a photographed montage of larger postcards) all at once. Alternatively, a card was picked of one of the more important attractions—such as Shoot the Chutes, a roller coaster, or an electrically illuminated tower.

Miniature Train, Elitch's Gardens, Denver, Colorado. (Souvenir Publishing and Mercantile Co., Denver. Circa 1905.)
EF to Mint: $8–$12

Souvenir stands that sold cards usually had stamps available as well. Cards could be addressed on the spot and mailed locally. Messages on such cards were nearly always brief, as the senders were busy having a good time. In contrast, a scenic view postcard sent from a grand hotel in the Adirondacks (New York) or White Mountains (New Hampshire) might have many sentences describing how the vacationer was doing—as more time was available to correspond. Most cards were mailed to local or regional recipients, with very few to distant places. This reflects that the majority of amusement park visitors were day-trippers, sharing their pleasures with family and friends.

More than just a few visitors to parks bought one each of a half dozen or more views to take home as sentimental souvenirs of a good time. Most of these cards were kept loose or in albums and never mailed.

"Dixieland Park at Night, Jacksonville, Fla." (Artistic Series No. 240. M. Mark, Jacksonville, Florida. Circa 1910.)
EF to Mint: $12–$18

Aspects of Rarity and Collecting

Amusement park postcards with the most popular rides or scenes were the most widely purchased and are easily found today. As an example, colorful cards showing Luna Park at night are among the most plentiful issued by any of the Coney Island attractions. Also easily available for most parks are cards showing promenades, towers, open areas with multiple features, and the most popular rides. This makes it a pleasant endeavor to assemble a representative collection of cards for a favorite park.

A multi-view card of the San Antonio Electric Park.
EF to Mint: $15–$20

On the scarce-to-rare side are rides and attractions that lasted for just a season, then closed. Small rides, exhibits, and features in a large park are often hard to find on postcards, as buyers who took home a dozen cards picked the more notable subjects, not minor rides or exhibits. Concessions and exhibits on a midway or in a zone are hardly ever located today, except as part of an overall scene showing a walkway or general area. Interior views are rare as a class. There are, however, many exceptions for specific parks.

Caterpillar ride at Old Orchard Beach. (No. 122733. Tichnor Bros. Circa 1920s.) EF to Mint: $15–$20

Peck's Prancing Ponies steeplechase ride at Old Orchard Beach. Only a few parks had rides of this type as complex mechanisms were needed. (No. A-45491. Curt Teich Co. 1913.) EF to Mint: $20–$30

Luna Park, Hartford, Connecticut. Panorama RPPC, one of various RPPCs issued for this attraction. RPPCs were made for relatively few parks. EF to Mint: $50–$75

Pioneer cards (before the Postal Act of May 19, 1898; see chapter 1) depicting amusement parks are rare as a class, but in black-and-white printed form often lack visual appeal. Accordingly, a dedicated specialist can acquire these now and again for reasonable prices. Black-and-white cards before about 1905 are common for many parks and vary in their eye appeal. These, too, are not widely sought and offer opportunities for the dedicated specialist. As examples, the apparently short-lived Mermaids and Stinger attractions in Savin Rock (Connecticut) can be found on black-and-white cards, but if they exist on color cards, extreme rarity is indicated. Some theme rides and exhibits are only found on these early cards, as they closed before the era in which color cards were popular. For attractions that remained popular into later years, the same images were used on color cards.

Real photo post cards are very rare for the larger and more popular parks, except for set-up scenes in photo-parlor concessions. A notable exception is Luna Park in West Hartford, Connecticut. For smaller parks, RPPCs showing activity—such as people enjoying themselves—are highly desirable and can be expensive, depending upon the eye appeal. Some cards are imprinted on the face with dates of a special "day" or event and are of interest to specialists. The same is true for some cards that have printed information about special events on the back.

Panorama of Paragon Park, Nantasket Beach, Massachusetts. Statistics printed in the right margin. (Metropolitan News Co., Boston. Postmarked 1906.) EF to Mint: $7–$12

Panorama of Wonderland, Revere Beach, Massachusetts. (No. 769. Metropolitan News Co. Postmarked 1906.) EF to Mint: $10–$15

A curiously slanted merry-go-round at Euclid Beach Park. (J. Sapirstein, Cleveland. Postmarked 1921.) EF to Mint: $20–$30

Within the general category of amusement and theme parks there are specialties that can be collected, such as carousels (merry-go-rounds), roller coasters, Ferris Wheels, restaurants, acrobatic acts, etc. Carousel cards in particular can be priced at multiples of the value of a panoramic or general scenic card.

Ideal amusement park cards are in Mint condition and without problems, or else Extremely Fine with a stamp and clear postal cancellation, postally used but without ink transfer or discoloration on the face of the card—depending on your preference. Probably, a dedicated specialist in amusement parks would prefer the latter.

There were many parks that left only a meager trail of postcards showcasing specific rides, although they may have had many visitors in their time. As an example, Whalom Park (Massachusetts) had several notable rides, but most extant postcards depict park (picnic settings, paths) and river scenes. While of interest to an amusement park historian, they are of limited appeal to a deltiologist. In contrast, cards of Savin Rock (Connecticut) are wonderfully diverse and show many attractions in close-up views. Such are exciting to collect.

The Bowery or general ride and concession area at Rockaway Beach, New York. The carousel building in the foreground adds to the value, as does the Ferris Wheel. EF to Mint: $18–$25

Mother Goose Shoe at Luna Park in Cleveland. To the right is Edisonia, a penny arcade. (No. 659. No publisher. Circa 1910.) EF to Mint: $8–$12

Otherwise, in the marketplace there are many cards that were never mailed, or else were postally used, that are in average Extremely Fine or so grade. Assuming there are no problems such as tears, discoloration, or ink transfers, a card in this category is highly collectible and represents the mainstream of interest among buyers.

Cards of small parks form a great challenge. Most of these were located outside of town and were set up by street railway companies to add revenue on weekends and evenings. Electric Park was a popular name, and this was used for at least a few dozen places. Trolley parks had a captive audience—local and regional citizens—and usually had relatively few rides. Postcards for many are hard to find, and for some, none have been found at all. Many such cards are panoramic—showing a view of multiple rides and attractions. While a postcard from

Monarch Park in Oil City, Pennsylvania, is scarce, its market value is typically less than that for a common card showing the Shoot the Chutes at Luna Park in Coney Island. It would seem that some of these smaller parks would be appealing to collect, in addition to the more famous ones.

"Joyride on the Mountain Scenic Railway, Willow Grove Park," Pennsylvania. (No. 404, J.M. Canfield. Detroit Publishing Co. "This is the only official postcard of Willow Grove Park." Circa 1910.) EF to Mint: $12–$18

Panorama of Cedar Point, Sandusky, Ohio. (Alexander Mfg. Co.) EF to Mint: $8–$12

Airships and the Mountain Scenic Railway at Willow Grove Park. (No publisher. Postmarked 1910.) EF to Mint: $10–$15

Market Values

Average market values are given for general subjects found on amusement park and related cards of the early twentieth century through the early 1930s. Those with unusual features, action scenes, specific timely events, and the like can be worth more, as can cards with excellent detail, such as by Rotograph, Albertype, and certain others. Cards that lack eye appeal or have low contrast can be worth less. For some scenes, night views with color illumination can be worth slightly more.

For specific rides, attractions, and the like, prices are for views that are close-ups or feature these as the main subject. Views that include them as part of a general background usually have lesser values. As an example, a scene showing a roller coaster in the distance is classified as part of a panorama, while a close-up view would be a highly desired subject. A card showing a carousel building, even if it is closed and the ride cannot be seen, can be worth multiples of what a panorama card showing the same structure would sell for.

In general, the most popular features of a large park were made in many versions. These can be reviewed so that one that is "just right" can be selected, unless you are a specialist and want as many different perspectives and angles as possible.

People in action can contribute greatly to the value of a card, especially if a particular building, ride, or other subject is usually without humans. A dance pavilion card with happy couples on the floor can be worth much more than a view of the same facility without a human being in sight, as "action" cards are scarce for this subject. The same is true for close-up views of carousels with riders. However, Shoot the Chutes rides typically show a sliding or splashing car and thus bring no special premium. Cards of miniature railroads, a popular amusement, usually show people.

Panorama of Rock Springs Park, Chester, West Virginia. (Bagley Co., East Liverpool, Ohio. / Hugh C. Leighton. No. 28030. Postmarked 1910.) EF to Mint: $15–$20

Another aerial view. (Souvenir Post Card Co. Postmarked 1913.) EF to Mint: $8–$12

Interior views are generally rarer than exteriors, with ballrooms and dance pavilions being exceptions.

The following categories are among those that are popular with collectors. No listing can ever be complete, as there were hundreds of different varieties of rides and attractions. For those, find an attraction that is somewhat similar in concept.

Most amusement park cards of the late nineteenth and early twentieth century are very inexpensive, no matter what the subject or category depicted is. *All prices in the following listing are for color printed cards. Black-and-white cards sell for less, RPPCs for more.*

Feltman's Restaurant on Surf Avenue, Coney Island, New York, issued many different cards: exterior, interior (various named rooms, without patrons), and lithographed cards advertising shore dinners. EF to Mint: $15–$20

Amusement Parks	Value, EF to Mint
Carousel close up with riders	$50–$150
Carousel in distance but very prominent	$20–$40
General view with people and various attractions	$8–$25+
Interior views of attractions	$20–$40+
Other rides close up	$10–$40+
Panorama of amusement park	$6–$100+
Roller coaster close up	$15–$40+
Roller coaster in distance but still prominent	$8–$20+
Other views, miscellaneous	$5–$100+

The Giant Racer, one of many roller coasters and related rides at Coney Island, was opposite Feltman's Restaurant on Surf Avenue. (No. R-3099. Curt Teich Co. Circa 1907.) EF to Mint: $15–$20

The Bowery, as described in text on the back of this card: "...is a narrow street running parallel with the beach. It is entirely occupied by moving picture shows, restaurants, and all kinds of amusement devices and is the most popular thoroughfare at this great resort." Most of the patrons in various Coney Island cards were adults. (Photo & Art Postal Art Co., New York / Curt Teich Co. No. A-70127.) EF to Mint: $12–$18

The entrance to Luna Park at night, colorized from a daytime view. (Illustrated Post Card Co. 1908.) EF to Mint: $8–$12

The ornate entrance to Dreamland on Surf Avenue, Coney Island, New York. The Creation tableau was circular, with seats in the middle, and depicted scenes from the biblical book of Genesis. (No. 102. M. & Co., New York. Postmarked 1911.) EF to Mint: $6–$10

Later entrance to Luna Park. (No. 211. UPPCo. Circa 1930.) EF to Mint: $10–$15

View in Dreamland, a promenade area. (No. 2104. S. Langsdorf & Co., New York. Circa 1906.) EF to Mint: $6–$10

Mountain Torrent ride at Luna Park was one of many scenic railway attractions at Coney Island. (A.C. Bosselman & Co., New York. Postmarked 1907.) EF to Mint: $12–$18

Atlantis, The Sunken City, at Steeplechase Park, an artistic rendering. (No publisher. Circa 1906.) EF to Mint: $8–$12

Virginia Reel, Luna Park. (No publisher. Postmarked 1911.) EF to Mint: $12–$18

The Human Roulette Wheel at Steeplechase Park was reported to have been purchased for $100,000. (Kraus Manufacturing Co., New York.) EF to Mint: $25–$35

The signature Steeplechase ride. (No. 1130. L. Stern, New York. Circa 1910.) EF to Mint: $5–$8

The El Dorado carousel. EF to Mint: $40–$70

Air Ship Tower at Steeplechase Park, a view exaggerating its height and the distance of the airships above the ground. (No publisher. Circa 1906.) EF to Mint: $5–$8

Early entrance to Steeplechase Park, Coney Island, New York. The "Steeplechase Funny Place" sign was the most familiar icon in all of Coney Island. (No publisher. Circa 1906.) EF to Mint: $12–$18

Noah's Ark, an attraction for the younger set at Steeplechase Park. (Manhattan Postcard Co. / Curt Teich Co. No. 109290. 1926.) EF to Mint: $8–$12

SPORTS AND RECREATION

Countless postcards were made of various sports and recreation activities. Except for baseball subjects, the typical cards from the Golden Age of postcards are modestly priced. Any activity cards that show players in action are more valuable than those that do not. Cards of stadiums and courts are more desirable if they show players, even at a distance

Comic cards were made for many activities, many in Germany during the Golden Era. These are interesting but of relatively modest values.

Baseball

Baseball, the great all-American sport, takes front row center when it comes to values of certain postcards. Those of the early twentieth century showing identified players in major-league team uniforms have brought very high prices at auction, sometimes into four figures. The buyers have not been postcard collectors but collectors of general sports memorabilia. The same specialists have paid in the hundreds of thousands of dollars

for Honus Wagner cigarette cards, and thousands of dollars for uniforms, signed baseballs, and other personal items. A printed baseball postcard with the verified ink signature of a player can be very valuable. On the other hand, postcards of minor leagues, school teams, and the like have relatively little value beyond sentimental and historical.

John A. Pfeister, pitcher for the Chicago Cubs. (A.C. Dietsche, Detroit, Michigan. Postmarked 1907.)
EF to Mint: $125–$175

American League Park, Washington, D.C., April 6, 1911.
RPPC. EF to Mint: $2,200+

William E. Donovan, pitcher for Detroit. Circa 1907 (A.C.
Dietsche, Detroit, Michigan.) EF to Mint: $125–$175

Washington Senators with pitcher Walter Johnson (standing,
third from right), 1918. RPPC. EF to Mint: $2,800+

Long Flat (New York) baseball team, 1908. RPPC.
EF to Mint: $20–$50+

Clarence Blair, Chicago Cubs 1929–1931. Autographed in ink.
RPPC. EF to Mint: $25–$35

Maranacook (Maine) baseball team, circa 1908. RPPC.
EF to Mint: $30–$50+

American League Ball Park, Cleveland. EF to Mint: $30–$60

Chicago vs. Cornell, 18-0 score, 1910. RPPC.
EF to Mint: $20–$40

Boston Braves stadium. (M. Abrams, Roxbury, Massachusetts.
Postmarked 1924.) EF to Mint: $20–$30

Polo Grounds, National League baseball park, New York City. (Success Postal Card Co., New York City.) EF to Mint: $15–$30

Yankee Stadium in the 1920s. (Haberman & Co., New York.) EF to Mint: $5–$10

"Delaying the game" comic card. (American circa 1910.) EF to Mint: $6–$12

Grade School and High School Sports

Cards in this category are mainly of interest to collectors of cards from specific schools or towns.

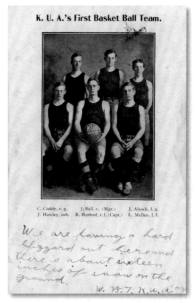

Kimball Union Academy basketball team, Meriden, New Hampshire. (Postmarked 1907.) EF to Mint: $15–$25

Valley City High School basketball team, Valley City, North Dakota. RPPC. EF to Mint: $20–$50

High school football game. (Postmarked 1909.) EF to Mint: $5–$10

Baseball	Value, EF to Mint
College and high school players in uniform	$12–$25+
Major league games in action	$20–$200+
Major league players in uniform	$20–$200+
Major league stadiums, outside view	$5–$200+
Major league stadiums, inside view	$10–$200+
Minor league games in action	$8–$75+
Minor league players in uniform	$15–$75+
College and high school players in uniform	$15–$75+
College and high school games in action	$5–$50+
Comic cards, black and white or one color	$5–$20
Comic cards, multi-colored	$8–$30

Golf

Most golf cards show courses, also called links. Most are of interest to collectors of specific locations.

Kingswood Club Golf Links, Wolfeboro, New Hampshire, 1923. (No. 865477. Curt Teich Co.) EF to Mint: $4–$8

Golfing at the Park Hill Inn, Hendersonville, North Carolina. (A 59823. Curt Teich Co.) EF to Mint: $8–$12

Bird's eye view of the golf links in Ormond, Florida. (A 67605. Curt Teich Co.) EF to Mint: $6–$8

Copyright, 1905, by U. Co., N. Y.
"GOLF."

Golf by F. Early Christy. (No. 501. U Co., 1905.) EF to Mint: $8–$12

Tennis

Cupid and lady in a tennis game. (Germany circa 1906.) EF to Mint: $4–$8

Field, Track, and Archery

Most field and track cards show competitive events and teams. Archery cards are varied.

"Or, what would you rather do?" (S.D.C., Canada.)
EF to Mint: $4–$7

University of Illinois track team, 1914. RPPC made in quantity.
EF to Mint: $40–$60

Tennis comic card. (Comic Series No. 710. Bamforth & Co., Yorkshire, England.) EF to Mint: $4–$7

"Indian bark house—practising shooting" with archer. RPPC made in quantity. (Martin Post Card Co. Circa 1909.)
EF to Mint: $30–$50

Archery comic card. EF to Mint: $4–$7

Aquatic Sports and Recreation

This category includes swimming, bathing, sailing, diving, surfboarding, and other aquatic sports and activities.

Bathers at Camp Wyanoke, Wolfeboro, New Hampshire, in 1924. EF to Mint: $5–$10

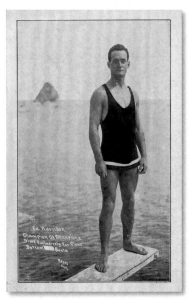

Ed. Harrison, "Champion Deep Sea Diver of America," Catalina Island, California. Record: 58 feet deep, 3 minutes, 48 seconds. EF to Mint: $5–$10

Canoe races in Alton Bay, New Hampshire, in the summer of 1910. RPPC. EF to Mint: $12–$18

Surfboarding in Honolulu. (Germany, circa 1906.) EF to Mint: $18–$30

Hawaii Mid Pacific Carnival, Honolulu, 1913. (Britton & Rey, San Francisco.) EF to Mint: $750+

Motorboat racing in Florida. (Hartman Card Co., Florida and Maine.) EF to Mint: $4–$7

Fencing, Swordsmanship

Many cards in this category were published in Germany. This field is lightly collected, resulting in low prices.

"Säbelmensur" (Swordsmen). (No. 9 in a series. Edm. Von König, Heidelberg.) EF to Mint: $8–$12

Hunting and Fishing

This category has many varied subjects and is popular with sports enthusiasts.

Two men with épées. (Heidelberg, Germany, circa 1905.) EF to Mint: $10–$15

Seabrook Fishing and Hunting Club, Houston, Texas. Circa 1908. EF to Mint: $8–$12

Swordsman in Wiesbaden, Germany, 1910. RPPC. EF to Mint: $8–$12

Sea lions killed by Indians, Alaska. (Central News Co., Tacoma, Washington. Postmarked 1911.) EF to Mint: $8–$12

A successful fox hunt. (Germany. Postmarked 1906.)
EF to Mint: $6–$10

The bear hunt. (George O. Restall, Los Angeles; printed in
Germany.) EF to Mint: $5–$8

Alpine hunter in France. (E. Reynaud, France.)
EF to Mint: $8–$12

"Hunters Dream" comic card. (Tichnor Brothers,
Boston.) EF to Mint: $2–$4

"A Fine String of Speckled Beauties, St. Petersburg, Fla."
(Tichnor, Curt Teich.) EF to Mint: $5–$8

"A few hours' catch of speckled trout on the Steinhatchee
River, Fla." (Asheville Post Card Co., Asheville, North
Carolina.) EF to Mint: $8–$12

Fishing in Phillips Lake, Lucerne-in-Maine. EF to Mint: $3–$5

Boxing and Wrestling

Cards in this category include many with unidentified athletes. Those showing famous boxing matches are more valuable.

Birosky the German boxer. RPPC made in quantity. (Lindstedt and Zimmerman, Coblenz am Rhein, Germany.) EF to Mint: $10–$15

Wrestling match, unknown location. RPPC printed in quantity. EF to Mint: $18–$20

Boxing match arena, Baltimore, 1912. RPPC printed in quantity. (Holmes & Bishop, Baltimore.) EF to Mint: $50–$75+

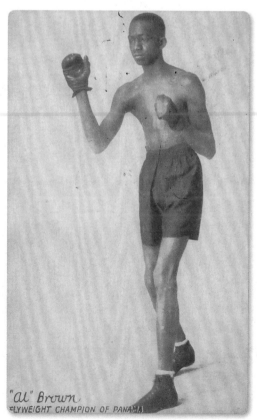

Al Brown, champion boxer. (Exhibit Supply Co., circa 1927.) EF to Mint: $18–$20

Ice Sports and Recreation

This category includes skating, sledding, skiing, and hockey. Most cards in this category are both scarce and inexpensive, a nice situation for a skating fan or other specialist.

Bobsled race at Huntington, New York. 1910. RPPC. EF to Mint: $75–$100+

Skating rink at the Shattuck Inn, Jaffrey, New Hampshire, 1912. RPPC. EF to Mint: $15–$20

Toboggan slide at Ben Riley's, Sarasota Springs, New York. EF to Mint: $8–$12

"Skating." (No. 164. K. Co., Inc., New York.) EF to Mint: $15–$20

"Ski jumper takes to the air from Olympic Ski Hill, Lake Placid, N.Y." (Curt Teich Co.) EF to Mint: $4–$7

Artist's drawing of a hockey player. (H-P, Prague.)
EF to Mint: $25–$35+

Horse Races and Rodeos

This is a fun topic with lots of action, a mixture of printed cards and RPPCs. In the early twentieth century many rodeo and cowboy "Wild West" troupes toured the country and performed at fairs and in theaters.

Horse racing at the Brockton, Massachusetts, Fair, 1905.
EF to Mint: $10–$15

Horse race, Stockman's Day, Rapid City, South Dakota, 1909.
EF to Mint: $100+

Hockey game in progress. (USSR) EF to Mint: $15–$20

Hockey game in progress. (February 1914 card with calendar and advertisement for Henry J. Tick, New Brunswick, New Jersey florist, on the back; copyright by Burgess, 1912.)
EF to Mint: $6–$10

Pyramid of six stunt riders on two horses, Sea Girt, New Jersey. RPPC. EF to Mint: $15–$25

Rodeo champion Bob Crosby receives the Roosevelt Trophy in 1917. RPPC. EF to Mint: $30–$40

Rodeo action in Pendleton, Oregon, 1915. RPPC made in quantity. EF to Mint: $8–$12

Rodeo action by a rider of the 101 Ranch, 1924. Based in Bliss, Oklahoma, the 101 Ranch troupes toured the Midwest with cowboy and Wild West programs. RPPC made in quantity. EF to Mint: $15–$25

Car and Motorcycle Races

This is a very popular category. Postcards with racing motorcycles are rare. Those with automobiles are fairly plentiful and are in strong demand.

Automobile and racer number 2 at Daytona Beach, Florida, early twentieth century. RPPC. EF to Mint: $100+

Automobile and racer number 7 at Daytona Beach, Florida, early twentieth century. RPPC. EF to Mint: $75+

New York to Paris Auto Race, 1908. EF to Mint: $20–$30

Automobile race at the New York State Fair, Syracuse. RPPC printed in quantity. EF to Mint: $25–$35

Cole Racer in Geneva, New York, 1910. RPPC, printed in quantity. EF to Mint: $75+

Cricket game in Worcester, England. (Photochrom Co., London.) EF to Mint: $6–$10

Other Sports and Recreational Activities

Other sports and recreational activities comprise many specialties including hiking, camping, football, pelote, ping pong, body strengthening, weight lifting, bicycling, and more. Most postcards are inexpensive. Most drawn by artists were published in Europe. Postcards issued in the United States and with identified participants and locations are more valuable, as are RPPCs. The challenge is finding them, not paying for them—as is true of many other specialized areas.

A Basque pelote game. (Part of a sports series published in Brussels, Belgium, by L. Pautauberge, a seller of patent medicines.) EF to Mint: $10–$15

Roller skaters. (Series No. 2748. The Rollers, Tuck.) EF to Mint: $8–$10

Bicycling in 1902. (No. 6097. PVK Z.) EF to Mint: $20–$40

Riding a bicycle. (Th. E. L Theochrom-Serie 1074.) EF to Mint: $20–$30

A game of shuffleboard on a ship deck. (N.G.I., Italy.) EF to Mint: $8–$12

Lacrosse team. (Postmarked Hoboken, New Jersey, 1907.) EF to Mint: $75+

Roller skating comic card. (Roller Skating Series No. 2. Postmarked 1907.) EF to Mint: $8–$12

Sumo wrestling in Yokohama, Japan. (Hermieu, Messageries Maritimes, Paris.) EF to Mint: $12–$18

Table tennis related to ping pong. (RS Artistic Series. England.) EF to Mint: $12–$18

Outdoor gymnastics. (No imprint.) EF to Mint: $10–$15

WORLD'S FAIRS AND RELATED EVENTS

CHAPTER 21

1893–1933

Expositions, some of which were designated as world's fairs, became popular in the nineteenth century, inaugurated in a significant way by the Great Exhibition of the Works of Industry of All Nations held at the Crystal Palace in London in 1851. Such events were usually characterized by the construction of special buildings, with the iconic Eiffel Tower for the 1889 Exposition Universelle in Paris being perhaps the most outstanding example. The similarly named 1900 Exposition Universelle held in the same city is especially remembered today as a showcase for the Art Nouveau movement, as epitomized by the work of Alphonse Mucha.

In 1853 in New York City, the Exhibition of the Industry of All Nations, copying the British event of

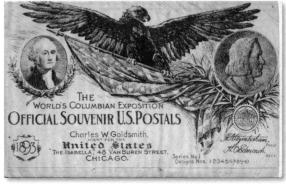

Series 1, design No. 2, one of a set of color postcards made by the American Lithographic Company, New York, for the World's Columbian Exposition held in Chicago in 1893. EF to Mint: $10–$20

1851, was opened in the Crystal Palace. This was not really a world's fair but rather a private enterprise for which the promoters solicited commercial and other exhibits. Showman P.T. Barnum was among those involved. After that time the American Institute and others held shows and displays at the Crystal Palace. In 1858 the structure, which had never earned a profit, burned to the ground.

The first world's fair held in America was the Centennial Exhibition in Philadelphia in 1876, celebrating the 100th anniversary of American independence. This was a grand affair and comprised many buildings and facilities in Fairmount Park. The event was highly successful. Regarding the issuance of postcards, the World's Columbian Exposition in Chicago in 1893 inaugurated the release of colorful cards illustrating the facilities. By that time many government postal cards had been imprinted with advertising and other notices, but the Columbian issues were the first to stand alone and require a separate stamp to be applied.

Important events included the Trans-Mississippi Exposition held in Omaha in 1898, the 1901 Pan-American Exposition in Buffalo (New York), the 1904 Louisiana Purchase Exposition (generally known as the St. Louis World's Fair), the Lewis and Clark Exhibition in Portland (Oregon) in 1905, the Jamestown (Virginia) Tercentenary Exposition of 1907, the 1909 Alaska-Yukon-Pacific Exposition in Seattle, the 1915 Panama-Pacific Exposition in San Francisco, and the 1926 Sesquicentennial of American Independence Exposition in Philadelphia.

Each of these events of the 1890s onward had officially appointed issuers of postcards, but beginning at the turn of the twentieth century, other publishers jumped into the fray, including makers of various cards showcasing products displayed at the fairs. Zeno chewing gum put out cards for the 1904 St. Louis Fair using images taken from a set of Tuck cards, but printed in America (instead of England) and of lesser quality. Typewriters, automobiles, patent medicines, and others were featured on advertising postcards, usually in color.

The largest and most successful of the early fairs were the 1893 Columbian, 1904 St. Louis, and the 1915 Panama-Pacific. Certain others did not live up to expectations. The 1901 Pan-American Exposition in Buffalo had trouble covering expenses, and the 1926 Sesquicentennial in Philadelphia lost money. Perhaps worthy of mention as a side note are the 1902 United States, Colonial, and International Exposition planned for New York City and, in the same year, the Ohio Centennial and Northwest Territory Exposition, neither of which was held.

Roster of World's Fairs

What does and does not constitute a world's fair has been a matter of opinion over the years. Can a fair be a world's fair because the sponsors call it one, or does it have to have recognition by an international body? That was a point of controversy with the 1964 World's Fair.

This list is from Wikipedia. Those with a bold date are official per the internationally recognized expositions listed by the Bureau International des Expositions. Those marked with an asterisk (*) had legal-tender commemorative coins issued in conjunction with them:

Pre-Postcard Era
- **1876** Centennial Exhibition, Philadelphia
- 1881 International Cotton Exposition, Atlanta
- 1883 American Exhibition of the Products, Arts, and Manufactures of Foreign Nations, Boston
- 1883 Southern Exposition, Louisville
- 1883 World's Fair (planned but never held), New York City
- 1884 World Cotton Centennial, a.k.a. New Orleans Universal Exposition and World's Fair, New Orleans
- 1887 Piedmont Exposition, Atlanta
- 1889 International Industrial Fair, Buffalo
- 1892 Exposition of the Three Americas (planned but not held), Washington, D.C.

1893 to 1933
The era studied in this chapter
- **1893** World's Columbian Exposition (planned for 1892, opened to the public in 1893), Chicago*
- 1893 World's Fair Prize Winners' Exposition, 1893
- 1894 California Midwinter Exposition of 1894, San Francisco
- 1895 Cotton states and International Exposition (a.k.a. Atlanta Exposition), Atlanta
- 1897 Tennessee Centennial and International Exposition, Nashville
- 1898 Trans-Mississippi Exposition, Omaha
- 1898 California Golden Jubilee, San Francisco
- 1899 National Export Exposition, Philadelphia
- 1901 Pan-American Exposition, Buffalo

- 1901 South Carolina Inter-State and West Indian Exposition, Charleston
- 1902 United States, Colonial, and International Exposition (planned but never held), New York City
- 1902 Ohio Centennial and Northwest Territory Exposition (planned but never held), Toledo
- **1904** Louisiana Purchase Exposition (a.k.a. Louisiana Purchase International Exposition and Olympic Games), St. Louis*
- 1905 Lewis & Clark Centennial Exposition*
- 1905 Irish Industrial Exposition, New York City
- 1907 World's Pure Food Exposition, Chicago
- 1907 Jamestown Tercentenary Exposition, Jamestown, Virginia
- 1908 International Mining Exposition, New York City
- 1909 Alaska-Yukon-Pacific Exposition, Seattle
- 1909 Portola Festival, San Francisco
- 1909 Hudson-Fulton Celebration, New York City
- 1911 International Mercantile Exhibition, New York City
- 1913 National Conservation Exposition, Knoxville
- 1914 National Star-Spangled Banner Centennial Celebration, Baltimore
- **1915** Panama-Pacific International Exposition, San Francisco*
- 1915 Negro Historical and Industrial Exposition, Richmond
- 1915 Lincoln Jubilee and Exposition, Chicago
- 1915–1916 Panama-California Exposition, San Diego
- 1917 Allied War Exposition, San Francisco
- 1918 Allied War Exposition, Chicago
- 1918 Bronx International Exposition of Science, Arts and Industries, New York City
- 1918 California Liberty Fair, Los Angeles
- 1923 American Historical Review and Motion Picture Review, Los Angeles
- 1924 French Exposition, 1924
- 1925 California Diamond Jubilee, San Francisco*
- 1926 Sesquicentennial Exposition, Philadelphia*
- 1928, Pacific Southwest Exposition, Long Beach
- **1933–1934** Century of Progress International Exposition, Chicago

1934 to Date
See chapters 23 and 24

- 1935–1936 California Pacific International Exposition, San Diego*
- 1936 Great Lakes Exposition, Cleveland*
- 1936 Texas Centennial Exposition, Dallas*
- 1937 Pan American Fair, Miami
- 1937 Greater Dallas & Pan American Exposition, Dallas
- **1939–1940**, 1939 World's Fair, New York City
- 1939–1940 Golden Gate International Exposition, San Francisco
- 1940 Pacific Mercado (planned but never held), Los Angeles
- 1942 Cabrillo Fair (planned but never held), Los Angeles
- 1953 (Exposition planned for the sesquicentennial of the Louisiana Purchase but never held), St. Louis
- **1962** Century 21 Exposition, Seattle
- 1964–1864 New York World's Fair (not officially sanctioned by the Bureau International des Expositions but popularly, if not correctly, considered a world's fair by most Americans), New York City
- **1968** HemisFair '68, San Antonio
- **1974** Expo '74 (a.k.a. International Exposition of the Environment), Spokane
- **1982** World's Fair (a.k.a. International Energy Exposition), Knoxville
- **1984** Louisiana World Exposition (a.k.a. 1984 World's Fair), New Orleans

Postcards of Fairs and Expositions
The Different Fairs

All cards for fairs and expositions are highly collectible. The larger the exposition, the more cards that were issued. The widest selections of colorful, artistic cards from the classic era are those of the 1904 Louisiana Purchase Exposition and 1915 Panama-Pacific International Exposition, although the 1905 Lewis & Clark Exposition, the 1907 Jamestown Tercentenary Exposition, and the 1909 Alaska-Yukon-Pacific Exposition each had their share.

The 1926 Sesquicentennial of American Independence Exposition produced many cards, mostly of the scenic type with white borders. Various other fairs issued cards as well.

The 1933 Century of Progress Exposition in Chicago created many cards featuring then-modern products. The 1939 World's Fair cards are a specialty with many collectors and are showcased in chapter 23. The fairs of the 1960s and 1970s generated many chrome cards discussed in chapter 24.

Aspects of Value and Collecting

The most popular cards are the colorfully lithographed cards from the 1890s through the 1915 Panama-Pacific International Exposition. Many of the most attractive cards were made in large quantities, with the result that they are inexpensive today.

Values of cards parallel those of amusement parks: those showing specific rides or interesting exhibits sell for more than panoramic and generic cards. Making a specialty of a given event can be done in the same manner as with amusement park cards by seeking one of each building, ride, or exhibit. For the expositions there is the added aspect of much art and statuary. Some buildings and exhibits were featured on multiple cards, often of varying quality. Picking out one or two attractive cards of each subject is a popular pursuit. Rarity does not count, and a very rare exposition card of average quality may have little demand.

To illustrate the variety of cards available, we give information on selected fairs. Extensive information about each can be found on the Internet and in many instances in books and guides.

Selected Expositions
World's Columbian Exposition, Chicago, 1893

In 1890 plans were made for America to celebrate the 400th anniversary of Columbus landing in the New World by holding an exposition in 1892. The 1876 Centennial Exhibition, held in Philadelphia, was a grand success a decade or so earlier and now it was intended to outdo this and any other fair ever held. St. Louis, New York City, Washington, D.C., and Chicago all competed for the honor to host the celebration. The choice was made by Congress, which passed an act on April 25, 1890, naming Chicago.

An undeveloped 686-acre site on the shore of Lake Michigan was selected for the Exposition grounds. In January 1891 a group of architects met in Chicago to plan the buildings, which were constructed mainly in the classical style reflecting Greek and Roman influences, with exteriors made of an artificial composition resembling marble, called "staff," giving rise to the name "White City" for the structures.

Work proceeded apace and the Exposition was dedicated on October 21, 1892, but as all exhibits were not yet in place, it was not possible to open the fair to the general public in the 400th anniversary year. Finally, at noon on May 1, 1893, President Grover Cleveland officiated at a ceremony that opened the Exposition grounds to the public. Strains of the "Hallelujah" chorus greeted the estimated 300,000 individuals who had come to attend the opening day festivities.

The Exposition was intended to showcase American progress in art, architecture, technology, science, agriculture, and other endeavors. No expense was spared to create a virtual city, complete with 160 buildings (many of which were connected by canals plied by gondolas and small steam-powered craft) and 65,000 exhibits devoted to commercial, national, artistic, and other subjects. Separate structures showcased the attractions and products of different states and a number of foreign countries. Sculptures and other works of art decorated many of the open spaces and building interiors. Ultimately the event cost an estimated $30 million to stage and attracted 28 million visitors. Attending the Exposition was the aim of citizens all across America, and to oblige them the various railroads ran special cars and excursions to Chicago. Many individuals made hometown newspaper headlines by walking or bicycling to the Exposition from distant locations.

Charles W. Goldsmith, of Chicago, was the official seller of postcards for the event. Printed by the American Lithographic Co. of New York, these featured color views of important buildings. Earlier, he sold four different types of Exposition cards printed on regular government postal card stock and sold at two for 5¢ in vending machines.

Series 1, No. 1. Naval Exhibit. (Goldsmith. American Lithographic Co.) EF to Mint: $8–$15

Fine Arts Building. (American Colortype Co.) EF to Mint: $12–$25

Manufacturers Building. (American Colortype Co.)
EF to Mint: $12–$25

Temple of Music Building at the Pan-American Exposition.
(Niagara Envelope Manufactory.) EF to Mint: $4–$7

Trans-Mississippi and International Exposition, Omaha, 1898

The Albertype Co., New York City, issued a set of 16 view cards for this event, a world's fair that attracted many people, primarily from the Midwest. The Chicago Colortype Co. printed an official set of 10 color cards, which were distributed with the imprint of the U.S. Postal Card Co. for 25¢ per set.

Pan-American Exposition, Buffalo, 1901

The Pan-American Exposition was the first in the twentieth century. Many different cards were issued, mostly unofficial. It was at this fair that President William McKinley was assassinated by an anarchist.

The Niagara Envelope Manufactory was the official postcard issuer with colorfully lithographed images. Arthur Livingston issued 18 black-and-white views of the Exposition. A set of 12 postcards was published by F.A. Busch. Wild & Pchellis published ten or more black-and-white cards relating to the event. Emil Pinkau published two or more color views, but without his imprint. The Albertype Co., New York, published several dozen different views. As a result cards, both common and rare, are inexpensive.

"Mines-Horticulture-Graphic Arts," a building with eclectic content at the Pan-American Exposition. (Niagara Envelope Manufactory.) EF to Mint: $4–$7

Postcard for the Smith-Corona typewriter issued for the Pan-American Exposition. EF to Mint: $45+

Louisiana Purchase Exposition, St. Louis, 1904

Panoramic view of the Exposition. EF to Mint: $8–$15

The Louisiana Purchase Exposition, popularly known as the St. Louis World's Fair, was intended to open in 1903 to commemorate the 100th anniversary of Thomas Jefferson's purchase of the territory in 1803, but delays postponed the opening of the event until April 30, 1904.

The fair continued until closing day on December 1 of the same year, by which time about 20 million people had attended, many of whom enjoyed humming or singing the popular song, "Meet Me In St. Louis."

The Exposition was situated on a 1,272-acre tract in Forest Park in St. Louis, one of the largest expanses of land ever allotted to an event of this type in the United States. Fifteen major buildings, including four art palaces (one of which exists today), formed the focus of the fairgrounds, with numerous smaller buildings, exhibit areas, fountains, gardens, and other attractions providing interest. Among the exhibits were many automobiles and other vehicles, demonstrations of wireless telegraphy, displays of the uses of electricity, and dirigibles. The Ferris Wheel from the World's Columbian Exposition was set up and towered above all else. Works of hundreds of different artists, mainly painters, were on display, but prominent sculptors were represented as well, including John Flanagan, Adolph A. Weinman, Evelyn Beatrice Longman, James Earle Fraser, Hermon A. MacNeil, and Daniel Chester French.

Samuel Cupples had the concession for 1904 St. Louis Fair cards as "sole World's Fair stationers." The Samuel Cupples Envelope Company issued hold-to-light cards featuring the Inside Inn and other buildings. Various other firms issued cards as well. Buxton and Skinner of St. Louis printed regular as well as silver background cards for Samuel Cupples to sell at the fair. E. Frey published 20 views numbered 58 to 67 and 196 to 205; these were imported from Germany. The American Colortype Company issued printed cards for the 1904 St. Louis Exposition, as did Adolph Selige, A. Kropp, and others. Wooden postcards issued by Farran Zerbe, who held the concession for commemorative coins at the fair, are scarce and widely sought (see chapter 9 for these).

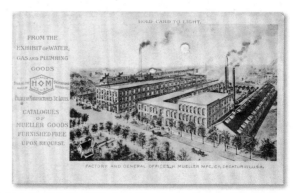

Hold-to-light advertising card for the H. Mueller Manufacturing Co. of Decatur, Illinois, an exhibitor at the Louisiana Purchase Exposition. EF to Mint: $20+

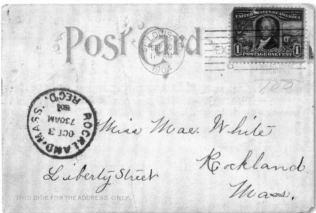

Postcard of the Ferris Wheel by Adolph Selige of St. Louis. This was a popular subject for several postcard makers. EF to Mint: $8–$15

The Inside Inn "Hold to Light" card by Cupples, mailed with a commemorative stamp of the Exposition. When held to the light, the windows in the building were illuminated. Postally used cards often had messages on the front, as here, as regulations did not permit such on the back. Hold-to-light cards issued for the Art Palace, Administration building, Cascade Gardens, and other places are popular and valuable today. EF to Mint: $100+

Administration Building card issued by Buxton & Skinner. EF to Mint: $7–$12

"Observation Wheel" (Ferris Wheel) by E.C. Kropp of Minneapolis. EF to Mint: $8–$15

Tyrolean Alps exhibit at the Louisiana Purchase Exposition. (Samuel Cupples.) EF to Mint: $3–$6

Lewis and Clark Exposition, Portland, 1905

Under the sponsorship of the American government, Captain Meriwether Lewis and William Clark sought to explore the upper reaches of the Missouri River to report on the land acquired in 1803 by the Louisiana Purchase. Departing from River Dubois, near St. Louis, on May 14, 1804, the party of several dozen men carried goods for trade and presentation to Indians. Supplies and provisions were carried in three large canoes and on packhorses. On March 23, 1806, they began their return trip, arriving in St. Louis on September 23, having traversed approximately 8,500 miles. Lewis and Clark were honored by Congress and given government offices in the West and tracts of land.

Held in 1905 in Portland, Oregon, the Lewis and Clark Exposition followed on the heels of the 1904 Louisiana Purchase Exposition and as a result did not draw much national attention, particularly as both expositions emphasized the same historical exploration. The event, held on a 406-acre site, attracted an estimated 2,500,000 visitors from opening day on June 1, 1905, until closing on October 14. Unlike the St. Louis fair of the preceding year, the Lewis and Clark Exposition was not designated by Congress as an international event, and no official government invitations were extended to foreign nations to exhibit. Notwithstanding this, 16 countries accepted offers from the Exposition itself.

Seven large buildings, many smaller ones, and the usual concessions and midway attractions entertained visitors. Exposition exhibits emphasized natural resources including fishing, mining, and forestry, but arts and manufacture were not neglected. The Forestry Building, measuring over 200 feet in length and constructed of native Oregon fir—including some logs of six or more feet in diameter—was a focal point of interest. After the Exposition closed, the structure was maintained as a museum of the lumber industry. In the annals of fairs in the United States, the Lewis and Clark Exposition is not one of the more memorable.

"Meet me on the Trail" at the 1905 Lewis and Clark Exposition. EF to Mint: $10–$15

Double-wide panorama card showing the 1905 Lewis and Clark Exposition. EF to Mint: $12–$20

The European Building. (B.B. Rich, official stationer.)
EF to Mint: $4–$7

Lakeview Terrace. Like most cards from the Lewis and Clark Exposition, the scene has been heavily retouched by an artist. Adding people was common practice as most cards for this and other fairs were prepared before the events were open to the public. (B.B. Rich.) EF to Mint: $5–$8

Panama-Pacific International Exposition, San Francisco, 1915

The 1915 Panama-Pacific International Exposition was planned to outdo all the other fairs that had been staged earlier. Foreign countries, domestic manufacturers, artists, concessionaires, and others were invited to become part of what eventually constituted a miniature city, whose sculptures and impressive architecture were intended to remind one of Rome or some other distant and romantic place, but which at night was more apt to resemble Coney Island. The object was to attract attention, draw visitors, make money, and enhance the glory of San Francisco, specifically to commemorate the rebuilding of the city after the 1906 earthquake and fire and to celebrate the 1914 opening of the Panama Canal.

The buildings of the Exposition were arranged in three areas. Festival Hall and several large exhibition "palaces" furnished the center of activity, flanked by buildings containing the exhibits of 44 states, several

U.S. territories, and 36 foreign nations; a racetrack; a livestock building; the amusement midway; and seemingly innumerable concessions.

Situated on 635 acres in Golden Gate Park in San Francisco, the Exposition cost about $50 million, opened on February 20, 1915, and closed on December 4, drawing an estimated 19 million visitors. The event was a smashing success by all standards. More than any other fair before or since, the fair was a showcase for the talents of American sculptors and artists.

The Panama-Pacific was the last truly large-scale exposition to be held in the United States until the 1933 Century of Progress Exposition in Chicago and the 1939 New York World's Fair.

Postcards from this event are extensive and include many issued in advance. In terms of beauty and variety, the classic era cards from this event are the most extensive. Many are invitations to the fair published before it opened, others show scenes, and some carry advertisements of products. A great collection can be formed of this event alone.

This card was prepared before the Panama-Pacific International Exposition was approved by Congress. (H.S. Crocker Co. San Francisco.) EF to Mint: $10–$12

Bird's eye view of the proposed Exposition grounds. (Exposition Publishing Co., San Francisco, a branch of Edward H. Mitchell.) EF to Mint: $15–$25

Card showing the personification of two continents, a theme also used on certain cards of the 1901 Pan-American Exposition. EF to Mint: $15–$25

Panama-Pacific card with bent corner and chipped edges sharply lowering its value. (Exposition Publishing Co.) EF to Mint: $10–$15

One of many welcoming cards. This one is postmarked August 14, 1914, and was sent by Thomas H. Cowens, who wrote to a friend in Los Angeles saying that he had visited the Exposition site to see the work in progress. He also had a "hot time in the old town" and would share the news when he returned home. Messages such as this can add interest to a postally used card. (Exposition Publishing Co.) EF to Mint: $12–$20

"Colonnades from the Court of the Universe." (Cardinell.) EF to Mint: $10–$15

The huge Inside Inn at the Exposition. People were added by an artist, per usual. (Cardinell.) EF to Mint: $6–$10

The Great Central Court. (Curt Teich Co.) EF to Mint: $4–$7

"On the Zone," the area with concessions and novelties. From a photograph taken at the Panama-Pacific International Exposition and showing people. (Ambrotype.) EF to Mint: $8–$12

The "End of the Trail" sculpture by James Earle Fraser. EF to Mint: $3–$5

The Submarines concession in the Zone. EF to Mint: $15–$25

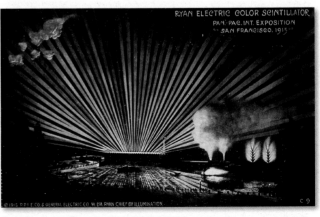

The General Electric Scintillator that cast colors on some of the buildings at night. (Cardinell.) EF to Mint: $12–$20

NIGHT ILLUMINATION PAN-PAC. INT. EXPOSITION SAN FRANCISCO, 1915

"Night Illumination." This card was probably made by colorizing a night photograph. (Cardinell.) EF to Mint: $3–$5

Palace of Fine Arts at night. This is the only PPIE building remaining today. (Bardell.) EF to Mint: $3–$5

Sesquicentennial of American Independence Exposition, Philadelphia, 1926

There is no doubt that the 150th anniversary of American independence, 1776–1926, was an event worthy of observing and a fitting successor to the Centennial Exhibition held in Philadelphia in 1876. The Exposition opened in Philadelphia on June 1, 1926, although many exhibits were not yet in place and much work remained unfinished, and continued until closing day on November 30. On view were many artistic, cultural, scientific, and commercial displays, partially financed by $5 million worth of bonds floated by the City of Philadelphia. The Palace of Agriculture and Food Products and the Palace of Liberal Arts were two of the larger structures.

As it did not attract national attention or support, the fair was a failure so far as commercial activities were concerned, and most firms reported that sales and publicity did not repay the expenses involved, although nearly six million people passed through the entrance gates. Postcards are mostly of the white-border style and heavily altered by artists. A group of several dozen can be gathered with ease. Most are inexpensive as this event has not had much collecting interest.

VIEW OF SESQUI-CENTENNIAL INTERNATIONAL EXPOSITION GROUNDS TAKEN FROM AIRPLANE.

SESQUI-CENTENNIAL INTERNATIONAL EXPOSITION, PHILADELPHIA, PA.

Bird's eye view of the Sesquicentennial Exposition, a colorized view of an artist's black-and-white conception. EF to Mint: $2–$4

Looking toward the entrance to the Sesquicentennial Exposition in the distance. EF to Mint: $2–$3

Boulevard at the Exposition, a card with many artistic additions. EF to Mint: $2–$4

Lighting effects were added by an artist to this card. EF to Mint: $2–$4

Lesser Fairs and Expositions

In addition to the foregoing, there were many other fairs, expositions, and notable events that attracted regional or national attention. A selection of postcards is given here.

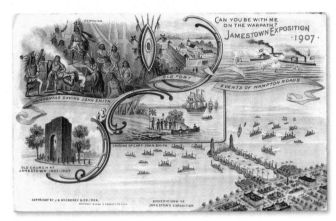

Multiple-scene card for the 1907 Jamestown Tercentenary Exposition. (Baltimore Badge & Novelty Co.) EF to Mint: $8–$12

Advertising card for the Pay Streak attraction at the forthcoming Alaska-Yukon-Pacific Exposition in Seattle, 1909. (Edward H. Mitchell, San Francisco.) EF to Mint: $8–$12

Yukon Avenue at the 1909 Alaska-Yukon-Pacific Exposition. The people and automobile have been added by an artist to a photograph taken before the gates of the Exposition were opened to the public. EF to Mint: $2–$4

1915 in advance: RPPC showing a fire engine at the groundbreaking celebration July 21, 1911, for the Panama-California Exposition to be held in San Diego in 1915 and 1916. By the time 1915 came around, the San Diego event was dwarfed by the Panama-Pacific International Exposition in San Francisco. EF to Mint: $100+

Panorama of the Panama-California Exposition in 1915. EF to Mint: $2–$4

View of at the 1933 Century of Progress Exposition in Chicago. Black-and-white card produced in quantity. (Gerson Bros, Chicago.) EF to Mint: $6–$10

Midway with concessions and exhibits at the 1933 Century of Progress Exposition. (Gerson Bros, Chicago.) EF to Mint: $3–$5

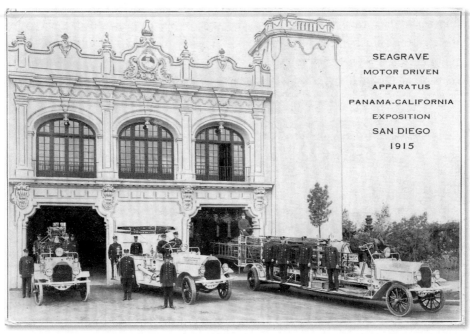

Seagrave fire engine advertising card from the Panama-California Exposition in 1915. EF to Mint: $20+

SCENIC AND VIEW POSTCARDS

CHAPTER 22

Color printed scenic cards without people or action necessarily cover some of the subjects discussed in earlier chapters. The pricing tables give a quick view of the values of many different categories. As a general rule, postcards from Alaska, Hawaii, Indian Territory (later Oklahoma), and territorial imprints pre-1912 on Arizona and New Mexico cards are worth slightly more.

Postcards of small towns are priced higher even if there is not a huge demand. Mary L. Martin comments:

"A small town such as Perryman, Maryland, card will sell for $100+ and I will actually pay that, but it might be only requested once every few years. Although I have millions of postcards in stock, including thousands of, say, New York City, to fill a request I could not find a single card from Phoenix, New York, a small upstate village. Accordingly, when I price I look at how small the town is, does it still exist, how many cards were printed of it and the era, condition and popularity. A postcard of a small town that no one has ever asked me for will still be priced higher than larger towns requested more often. When someone *does* ask me for it, I will be able to offer one. In time there are usually requests for any given small town or village. I do have many collectors that will collect small towns from the entire state. For instance, when I set up a display at a postcard show in Texas, collectors will ask for all small town views. Certainly main streets do not cost the same as cemeteries, but they will still buy them if they are a small town."

There are some general rules: views of towns and cities in the South are harder to find than those of the Northeast. Delaware, Alabama, Alaska, and Nevada are some of the hardest to find.

Within a given locality, postcards of churches, cemeteries, schools, colleges, residential districts, and public parks are much less expensive, unless they show people and action. A Harvard or Tufts graduate might want representative cards from those institutions but will not want every one of the hundreds of varieties—ranging from poorly printed black and white to glossy German imports from the Golden Age. National parks and national monuments are likewise soft. This is an advantage. A very large and comprehensive collection of national parks can be formed for only a few dollars per card.

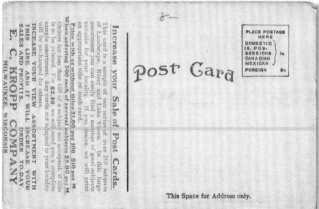

The E.C. Kropp Co. offered a large selection of generic views that could be imprinted with any desired location. EF to Mint: $5–$15

For the different states, subjects vary—with, for example, seacoast resorts being popular and common for New Jersey, as are farm scenes for Iowa. Mining is an important subject for Colorado but of little importance for Rhode Island. A postcard of a gold mine is worth more than one of a coal mine. Cards with "Wild West" aspects of some Rocky Mountain and mining towns make them favorites with collectors, while farm towns in Iowa or Pennsylvania generate little specialized interest.

Hometown views can be expensive for, say, Las Vegas, Nevada, in the early twentieth century but are cheap for most towns in the East and Midwest. In the Northeast many cards were issued with birch-bark borders, with simulated bark in black and white, or brown with a rectangular scene at the center.

Prices of view cards can vary widely. Postcards for many views can be bought for $2 to $5 each at postcard shows, or even $1 to $2 for subjects that are not widely collected. A majority of hometown views will sell for $4 to $20+ but many postcards will sell between $7 to $15. Pricing at $1 to $2 is rare unless it is a very common or modern view. At shows some dealers will have $1 boxes, but these will be filled with damaged cards, views of large cities, unsorted cards, and many modern linen and chrome cards. The entire view card field is very dynamic, and we estimate that at least 75 percent of all postcard transactions are in this category.

As noted, prices can vary, sometimes considerably. The following are generic prices for printed (not RPPC) scenic cards without action and without special human interest:

Card Type	Value, EF to Mint
Airports	$4–$20
Cemeteries	$3–$20
Churches	$4–$20

Statue of Liberty, New York City harbor.

Card Type	Value, EF to Mint
Civic statues and monuments, large and well-known	$3–$12
Civic statues and monuments, small	$4–$20

Vanderbilt Hall, Yale University, New Haven, Connecticut.

Card Type	Value, EF to Mint
Colleges and universities	$4–$15
Confederate monuments	$5–$20

"Cattle division, Union Stock Yards, South Omaha, Neb."

Card Type	Value, EF to Mint
Corrals and stockyards	$6–$15

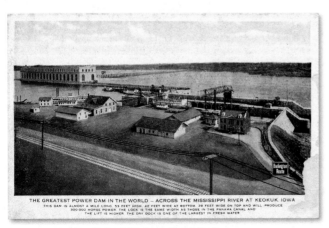

Dam on the Mississippi River at Keokuk, Iowa.

Card Type	Value, EF to Mint
Dams	$3–$15

The wharf at Douglas, Alaska.

Card Type	Value, EF to Mint
Docks and wharfs	$4–$25+

The Medicott factory in Windsor Locks, Connecticut, used water power to drive equipment.

Card Type	Value, EF to Mint
Factories, large	$5–$20

The Van Briggle art pottery factory in Colorado Springs, Colorado.

Card Type	Value, EF to Mint
Factories and shops, small	$8–$30+
Farms	$3–$15

Castle Geyser in Yellowstone National Park.

Card Type	Value, EF to Mint
Geysers	$2–$10

Searsport (Maine) High School.

Card Type	Value, EF to Mint
High schools and grade schools	$4–$20

Leaksville Hospital, Leaksville-Spray, North Carolina.

Card Type	Value, EF to Mint
Hospitals	$4–$20
Insane/State Hospitals	$5–$20
Hotels, interiors	$4–$20

The Willard Hotel near the White House in Washington, D.C.

Card Type	Value, EF to Mint
Hotels, large	$4–$10

The Golden Gate Hotel in Nome, Alaska.

Card Type	Value, EF to Mint
Hotels, small	$6–$20

The Cliff House, a seaside resort in San Francisco, was perhaps the most famous such establishment in the late nineteenth and early twentieth centuries, until it burned in 1907. Dozens of different postcard views of it were published.

The destruction of the Cliff House (flames added by an artist).

Card Type	Value, EF to Mint
Hotels, seaside resorts	$4–$50

Houses and an orange grove in Glendora, California.

Card Type	Value, EF to Mint
Houses and groups of houses	$4–$20

Library and Lyceum, Morristown, New Jersey.

Card Type	Value, EF to Mint
Libraries	$4–$20
Main Streets with few vehicles and no activity	$6–$30+

Main Street in St. Albans, Vermont.

Card Type	Value, EF to Mint
Main streets with activity	$8–$50+

Coal mine in Birmingham, Alabama.

Card Type	Value, EF to Mint
Mines, coal, copper, etc.	$6–$50+

Gold mine in Cripple Creek, Colorado.

Card Type	Value, EF to Mint
Mines, gold	$8–$60+

Altman, a small gold-mining town in the Cripple Creek District of Colorado.

Goldfield, Nevada, had a gold-mining boom in the early twentieth century. (Postmarked 1907.)

Card Type	Value, EF to Mint
Mining towns, old, of the West	$6–$50+
Municipal heating, water, other plants and facilities	$5–$15
National monument scenes	$2–$10

Grand Canyon, Arizona.

Card Type	Value, EF to Mint
National park scenes	$2–40+
Orchards	$2–$20

Panoramic view of Denver, Colorado.

Card Type	Value, EF to Mint
Panoramic views of cities	$4–$30

Panoramic view of Boothbay Harbor, Maine.

Panoramic View of Fort Dodge, Iowa.

Card Type	Value, EF to Mint
Panoramic views of small towns	$8–$50
Resort towns in the East and Midwest.	$3–$50
Resort towns in the West.	$5–$50

Panoramic view of Georgetown, Colorado.

The Boardwalk in Atlantic City, New Jersey.

Card Type	Value, EF to Mint
Resort towns, seaside	$3–$50
Synagogues	$10–$50+

Brewster Memorial Hall (Town Hall), Wolfeboro, New Hampshire.

Card Type	Value, EF to Mint
Town halls	$3–$15

Sulpho-Saline spa as advertised in 1930.

United States Capitol, Washington, D.C.

Card Type	Value, EF to Mint
Washington, D.C., federal buildings	$4–$8

Niagara Falls as viewed from the *Maid of the Mist* tourist ship.

Card Type	Value, EF to Mint
Springs and spas for health and recreation	$3–$20

Card Type	Value, EF to Mint
Waterfalls	$2–$10

LINEN AND OTHER POSTCARDS, 1930s TO 1950s

CHAPTER 23

So-called linen cards have no linen content but are printed on light cardboard stock with high rag content and a linen-texture front. Curt Teich (with the Colortone and other labels) was the originator of these, and other companies joined in as well, Tichnor Brothers being particularly prominent. E.J. Thomas of Cambridge, Massachusetts, called its linens "Teknitone" cards. MWM Color Litho, Nationwide Specialty Co., Eastern Photo Litho Co., Colourpicture (with Cambridge and Boston addresses), and others produced cards. Countless thousands of postcards with different names of issuers were actually made by Teich and not identified as such. Beyond that, there were hundreds of non-linen cards produced by local printers. Production overlapped with chrome cards and continued into the 1950s, with some stray issues after then.

Over a period of time the prices and quantities were changed. As an example, by the late 1930s the No. 944 cards issued by Nyce in Vernfield, Pennsylvania (see the history of the company in chapter 5), included 20 linen-type subjects priced at $1.15 per 100, $4.90 per 500, and $9.50 per 1,000.

Most linen cards were made from photographs that were heavily retouched in a manner that left little of the original photograph remaining. Bright colors were added, usually solid colors rather than the gradations of tone that would be seen in a photograph or in a later chrome card. Most linen cards have the images border to border, but quite a few have white edges.

In addition to linen cards, there are many printed with smooth surfaces on ordinary light postcard stock. RPPCs continued to be made, but in far lower quantities as the era of camera stores and photo studios issuing RPPCs on postcard stock was largely over.

Linen cards of scenic views are highly colorized and altered and do not compare in detail to earlier types. Large letter cards were made in hundreds of varieties with a city name, such as BUFFALO, in large letters across the front of the card, often at an angle, with the letters being composed of scenic elements. Advertising cards were made in countless varieties for products, amusement parks, hotels, restaurants, products, and services.

Many postcards of this era have significant values, making treasure hunting worthwhile among stacks of modern cards. Cards with recognizable automobiles are always worth more, as are those with activity; particularly choice scenes can multiply the price. For example, a store on a street may have little interest, but with a row of recognizable automobiles in front it can be quite valuable. An airport postcard with planes or a railroad station with passengers is more valuable than one without. Nearly all comic postcards of this and the following chrome types are not from comic strips but are usually separately created cartoons about the weather, personalities, etc. Categories and prices are given below, along with representative cards with values.

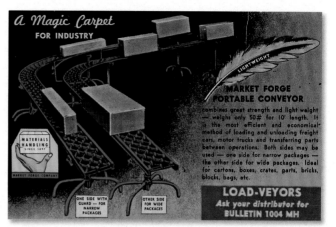

Load-Veyors made by the Market Forge Co. EF to Mint: $25–$35

Card Type	Value, EF to Mint
Advertising, miscellaneous (if not listed below)	$5–$200+

Otis Woven Awning Fabric. (Colourpicture, Boston.) EF to Mint: $15–$25

Eastern Airlines Lockheed Constellation. On back: "Hand to flight attendant for mailing." EF to Mint: $6–$10

Giant Underwood typewriter at the 1940 New York World's Fair. (Colourpicture, Cambridge.) EF to Mint: $6–$10

American Airlines Flagship. EF to Mint: $6–$10

Card Type	Value, EF to Mint
Airlines	$5–$40

Boeing B-17C Flying Fortress. (Longshaw Card Co., Los Angeles.) EF to Mint: $4–$6

Pan-American Airways Terminal in Miami, Florida. (Curt Teich Co.) EF to Mint: $6–$8

Card Type	Value, EF to Mint
Airports	$4–$25

Navy PBY Catalina (patrol planes, not bombers) in Florida. This card could just as well be collected in the military category. (Curt Teich Co.) EF to Mint: $5–$8

Amusement park and beach in Jacksonville, Florida. (Tichnor Brothers, Boston.) EF to Mint: $5–$7

Card Type	Value, EF to Mint
Airplane types	$4–$40+

Allentown-Bethlehem Airport in Pennsylvania. (Distributed by Mebane Greeting Card Co., Wilkes-Barre, Pennsylvania.) EF to Mint: $5–$8

Ocean View Park at night, Norfolk, Virginia. (Tichnor Brothers, Boston.) EF to Mint: $5–$7

Coney Island, Cincinnati, Ohio. (Tichnor Brothers, Boston.) EF to Mint: $8–$10

Card Type	Value, EF to Mint
Amusement parks	$5–$75+

1937 Dodge. "Smooth 87 H.P. engine, Hypoid rear axle, automatic choke, ride levelator and floating power." EF to Mint: $15–$25

Zell Motor Car Co., Packard dealer in Baltimore. EF to Mint: $50–$70

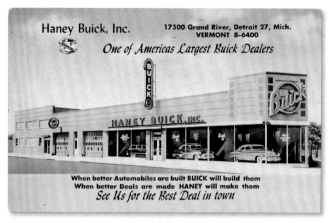

Haney Buick, Inc., Detroit, Michigan. EF to Mint: $50–$70

Roy Stauffer automobile centers in Pennsylvania. (Eastern Photo Litho Co.) EF to Mint: $50–$70

Lantern Brothers used cars, Brooklyn, New York. (Teknitone.) EF to Mint: $50–$60

Card Type	Value, EF to Mint
Automobile models, advertisements, and related	$5–$100+

329

Free Wheeling or Free Hugging comic card. (Auto Comics.) EF to Mint: $4–$6

"A scene along the road" comic card. (APCo.) EF to Mint: $2–$4

Dick Tracy comic card with spaces to fill in with writing. (Famous Artists Syndicate, 1942.) EF to Mint: $5–$8

Card Type	Value, EF to Mint
Comic postcards	$2–$20+

First Christian Church, Miami, Florida, interior view. (Curt Teich Co.) EF to Mint: $3–$5

Card Type	Value, EF to Mint
Churches	$3–$8
Synagogues	$6–$20
Cemeteries	$2–$8
Concerts	$3–$20

Triangle Diner, Folsom, New Jersey. EF to Mint: $40–$50

Clearview Diner, Pennsylvania. EF to Mint: $40–$50

Caldwell's Cafeteria, Columbia, South Carolina, with many automobiles. EF to Mint: $10–$15

Gold House Restaurants and locations. A later linen card judging from the station wagon. EF to Mint: $10–$15

Castagnola Brothers stall at Fishermen's Wharf, San Francisco. (Curt Teich Co.) EF to Mint: $5–$7

Pieroni's Sea Grill, Boston, Massachusetts. (Colourpicture, Boston.) EF to Mint: $6–$10

Trader Tom Steak House, New York City. (Teknitone.) EF to Mint: $5–$7

Card Type	Value, EF to Mint
Diners and restaurants	$5–$100+

Hollywood Bowl, Hollywood, California. (Curt Teich Co.) EF to Mint: $3–$5

Card Type	Value, EF to Mint
Events, concerts, tournaments, arenas, etc.	$4–$50
Factories, large buildings	$4–$12
Factories, small	$5–$20

Postcard from the 1935 California-Pacific Exposition in San Diego showing the tower that was central to the event. EF to Mint: $3–$5

Palace of Travel at the 1935 Exposition in California. EF to Mint: $3–$5

Multi-view card from the 1936 Texas Centennial Exposition. (E.C. Kropp, Milwaukee 21560N-1.) EF to Mint: $5–$7

Aerial view of the 1936 Great Lakes Exposition. EF to Mint: $5–$7

Entrance to the 1936 Great Lakes Exposition. EF to Mint: $2–$4

The Trylon and Perisphere, symbols of the 1939 World's Fair.
(Manhattan Postcard Publishing Co.) EF to Mint: $5–$7

General Motors Exhibit at the 1939 World's Fair. (Manhattan
Postcard Publishing Co.) EF to Mint: $5–$7

Schlitz Palm Garden at the 1939 World's Fair. (Curt Teich Co.)
EF to Mint: $5–$7

Card Type	Value, EF to Mint
Fairs and expositions	$3–$40

S.S. Kresge and Newberry 5- and 10-cent stores in Sioux Falls, South Dakota. (Curt Teich Co.) EF to Mint: $6–$9

Card Type	Value, EF to Mint
Five-and-ten cent stores	$4–$20

Johns Hopkins Hospital, Baltimore, Maryland. EF to Mint: $3–$5

Card Type	Value, EF to Mint
Hospitals	$3–$20

Travelers Motel, Columbia, South Carolina. (E.C. Kropp.) EF to Mint: $4–$6

Robert E. Lee Court, Richmond, Virginia. (MWM, Aurora, Missouri.) EF to Mint: $4–$6

Thompson's Cottage Court, Fayetteville, North Carolina. (Henry H. Ahrens, Charlotte, North Carolina.) EF to Mint: $4–$6

Card Type	Value, EF to Mint
Hotels, motels, inns, and motor courts	$4–$25
Lakes, forests, natural scenery	$2–$5

New Bedford, Massachusetts, large letters. (Curt Teich Co.) EF to Mint: $3–$5

Roanoke, Virginia, large letters. (E.C. Kropp.) EF to Mint: $3–$5

Card Type	Value, EF to Mint
Large letters cards	$2–$20

U.S. Army anti-aircraft gun crew. (E.C. Kropp.) EF to Mint: $3–$5

75 mm gun and crew. (E.C. Kropp.) EF to Mint: $3–$5

Card Type	Value, EF to Mint
Military except aircraft	$3–$20

Indian motorcycle. On the back: "See the six new Indian Arrow and Scout motorcycles." (Teknitone.) EF to Mint: $15–$25

Card Type	Value, EF to Mint
Motorcycles	$12–$60
Municipal buildings	$2–$4

Many Glacier Hotel, Glacier National Park. (Curt Teich Co.) EF to Mint: $2–$4

Crested Pool and Castle Geyser, Yellowstone National Park. (Curt Teich Co.) EF to Mint: $2–$4

"A hold up bear." Yellowstone National Park. (Johnston & Bordewyk, Rapid City, South Dakota.) EF to Mint: $2–$4

Mariposa Grove, Yosemite National Park. (Curt Teich Co.) EF to Mint: $2–$4

Card Type	Value, EF to Mint
National parks	$2–$6

"Souvenir record of Ft. Ticonderoga, N.Y." The record is transparent plastic on the front of the card and is not visible in the image. (Look & Listen series; Souvenirs, Inc., New York City.)

Card Type	Value, EF to Mint
Novelty and mechanical cards	$10–$15

President Franklin D. Roosevelt speaking at the dedication of the Great Smoky Mountains National Park. (Asheville Post Card Co., Asheville, North Carolina.) EF to Mint: $3–$5

The home of President Franklin D. Roosevelt in Hyde Park, New York. (Curt Teich Co.) EF to Mint: $2–$4

The Abilene, Kansas, home of Dwight D. Eisenhower's mother. (Woodgifts, Abilene, Kansas.) EF to Mint: $2–$4

"Motor boating over the sunny waters." (Colourpicture, Cambridge, Massachusetts.) EF to Mint: $2–$4

Card Type	Value, EF to Mint
Politics, candidates, elections	$2–$15+

Card Type	Value, EF to Mint
Racing and races	$2–$15

"The Break—West Flagler Dog Track Miami, Florida." West Flagler Kennel Club. (Tichnor Brothers.) EF to Mint: $2–$4

Pram racing in Clearwater Bay, Florida. (Hartford Litho Sales Co., Largo, Florida.) EF to Mint: $2–$4

"A Critical Point, a couple of Maine Yanks." Checkers game. (Meriden Gravure Co., Meriden, Connecticut. Postmarked 1946.) EF to Mint: $8–$15

Card Type	Value, EF to Mint
Recreation and games	$3–$20+

Father Borneman Parochial School, Reading, Pennsylvania. (Berkshire News Co.) EF to Mint: $2–$4

The Cunard Line's new *Queen Elizabeth* in the New York City harbor. (Curt Teich Co.) EF to Mint: $3–$5

Card Type	Value, EF to Mint
Schools	$2–$10

The S.S. *Boston* of the Eastern Steamship lines. (Union News Co.) EF to Mint: $3–$6

Sternwheel steam boat passing through locks near St. Louis, Missouri. (Tichnor Brothers.) EF to Mint: $4–$6

The Cunard Line's *Queen Mary* in the New York City harbor. (Colourpicture, Boston.) EF to Mint: $3–$5

U.S. Navy destroyer at sea. EF to Mint: $3–$5

Card Type	Value, EF to Mint
Ships, commercial and military	$3–$15

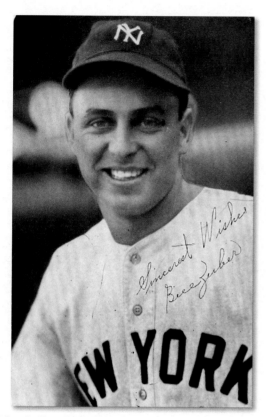

Bill Zuber in New York Yankees uniform; advertisement circa 1940s for his restaurant in Homestead, Iowa (per reverse inscription; not linen.) EF to Mint: $10–$20

Comiskey Park, Chicago, Illinois. EF to Mint: $8–$12

Ebbets Field, Brooklyn, New York. Part of a series. Not linen. EF to Mint: $8–$12

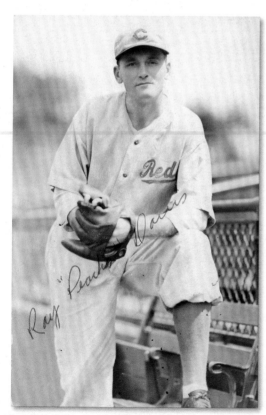

Ray Thomas Davis with the Cincinnati Reds, 1936–1939. Autographed in ink. (Regular printing, not linen.) EF to Mint: $20–$25

"World's Largest Football Player," Two Rivers, Wisconsin. (Curt Teich Co.) EF to Mint: $20–$25

Golfing at the Waynesville Country Club, Waynesville, North Carolina. (Asheville Post Card Co., Asheville, North Carolina.) EF to Mint: $4–$6

Game of polo. (Asheville Post Card Co., Asheville, North Carolina.) EF to Mint: $3–$5

Card Type	Value, EF to Mint
Sports and recreation	$3–$50+

The Naden Store, Camden, New Jersey. (Curt Teich Co.) EF to Mint: $10–$12

Clifton Park Clothes for Men factory outlet store. (Curt Teich Co.) EF to Mint: $30–$50

Madura Beach Business District, Florida. (Eastern Photo Litho Co.) EF to Mint: $15–$20

Lovelock Mercantile Co., Lovelock, Nevada. (Colourpicture, Boston.) EF to Mint: $10–$15

Marshall Field & Co., Chicago, Illinois. (Curt Teich Co.) EF to Mint: $4–$6

Globe Pottery, Springfield, Illinois. "12,000 square feet of beautiful art pottery and dinnerware. Imports, lamps, and garden pottery." (Nationwide Specialty Co.) EF to Mint: $12–$18

The Old Lady in the Shoe, "Most Interesting Place on the Coast of Maine." Perry's Tropical Nut House, East Belfast, Maine. (Colourpicture, Boston.) EF to Mint: $10–$12

Camera Center, Gatlinburg, Tennessee. EF to Mint: $10–$15

Card Type	Value, EF to Mint
Stores and shops	$5–$75+

Kates Brothers Shoes. EF to Mint: $60–$75

Santa Fe Super Chief locomotive and train. (Curt Teich Co.) EF to Mint: $8–$10

Speedy New York-Miami Streamliner. (Tichnor Brothers.) EF to Mint: $8–$10

Main Concourse, Pennsylvania Station, New York City (Colourpicture, Boston.) EF to Mint: $3–$5

Card Type	Value, EF to Mint
Trains and stations	$3–$30+

CHROME POSTCARDS, LATE 1930s TO DATE

Photochrome or chrome cards, made by chromo-lithography, have been made from the late 1930s to the present era. Sizes vary. Most have images out to the edge, but some have borders. Some cards have scalloped or serrated edges. These were made from printing plates using images from color photographs taken with Kodak, Ansco, and other brands of film. They are not RPPC cards and were not printed from negatives. Under magnification, microscopic color dots can be seen. A minority of cards have had the pictures retouched or altered. This is especially true of postcards advertising products or events.

Their popularity took a great leap forward after the Union Oil Company, based in California, made chrome cards starting in the late 1930s for use in its gasoline stations in the West. Mike Roberts of Lafayette, California, was a major producer of chrome cards starting soon after World War II, some under the Wesco label. Colourpicture Publishing of Boston made Plastichrome cards. Dexter Press of West Nyack, New York, was another major publisher. Most cards were issued by people and companies with no indication of where they were printed. Today as you read these words, chrome cards can be made to order by many firms, some of which advertise online. While chrome cards are dominant, many "plain" printed postcards have also been issued, as have some with slightly matte finishes.

Sizes of chrome cards varied over the years. In the late twentieth century many measured 4 x 6 inches, often called continental size, making this a standard format for easy display in sales racks. The typical chrome card has information concerning the publisher and a description of the scene on the left side of the back. Twenty-first-century postcards often have bar codes on the back.

Chrome postcards offer many opportunities for treasure hunting, as many cards that have value are not noticed. Automobile dealers are a possibility for finding postcards of past models and travel agencies may have airline, train, or steamship cards. Most chrome cards are worth very little on a wholesale basis and at shows can be bought for a dollar or two each or on the Internet for a few dollars (the price largely reflecting handling). However, there are many that are worth on the long side of $5 to $10.

The chrome era is the largest span of postcards produced over decades. Earlier chrome cards bring more than recent ones. Mary Martin has *paid* close to $100 for a particular RFK Stadium chrome. McDonald's cards are popular, and early ones can sell into two figures. As a general rule, most chrome cards sell for 25¢ to $5, depending on the subject. Chrome cards from the 1960s and 1970s have become popular in recent times as many collectors remember scenes from their childhood.

Rack cards, a modern category featuring advertising and other subjects, were free and placed on racks in stores, clubs, restaurants, bars, and other places. The two prime issuers were Max Racks and GoCard, with HotStamp coming in third. The last mainly distributed in college locations.[16]

Through the mail and online, all sell for more due to the time needed to describe and sometimes illustrate them and the cost of shipping and handling.

City and street views are inexpensive and popular. The same Main Street view from 1950 at intervals of several years down to today will reflect different automobile models and changing storefronts. There is a lot to like with chrome cards!

Kahlúa Coffee Liqueur. EF to Mint: $4–$8

Arrow shirts and ties. This card had different back imprints mailed out by various retailers. EF to Mint: $4–$8

Olympia model SG-3 typewriter. EF to Mint: $4–$8

Advertisement for Olympic Valley Cable Cardigans with stylish man holding a cigarette and with his Mercedes Benz convertible. (Mike Roberts.) EF to Mint: $8–$12

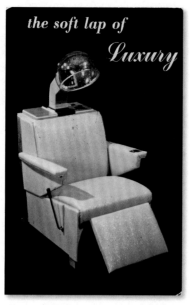

Bayette DeLite hair dryer. EF to Mint: $6–$10

TWA Convair-880 at the Kansas City Airport in April 1971. (Aviation World, Bethel, Connecticut.) EF to Mint: $1–$4

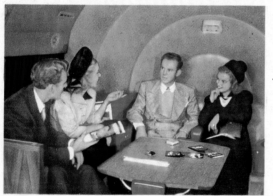

SKY LOUNGE in DC-6 Deltaliner has the luxurious appointments of an intimate club. Congenial groups gather here for cards, conversation, coffee, while the four-engined 58-passenger giant airliner carries them at more than 300 miles an hour between Chicago, Cincinnati, Atlanta, Jacksonville, Miami.

Delta DC-6 first-class cabin interior, 1950s. EF to Mint: $8–$12

Pan-American Airways Super 6 Clipper. EF to Mint: $1–$4

Card Type	Value, EF to Mint
Advertising, miscellaneous (if not listed below)	$3–$20+
Airlines	$1–$15+

Delta DC-9, Boeing 727, and Lockheed L–1011 aircraft. EF to Mint: $2–$5

Card Type	Value, EF to Mint
Airplane types	$1–$10+

the soft lap of *Luxury*

Continental Airlines jet at the Honolulu Airport. EF to Mint: $3–$5

Six Flags Over Texas, Confederate Section, Dallas–Fort Worth, Texas. (Colourpicture, Boston.) EF to Mint: $3–$5

Card Type	Value, EF to Mint
Airports	$1–$10+

Ocean View Amusement Park, Ocean View, Virginia. (Rowe Distributing Co., Norfolk, Virginia.) EF to Mint: $6–$10

Swimming pool, parachute jump, and Ferris Wheel in Steeplechase Park, Coney Island, New York. (No. 24. Acadia Card Co., New York City.) EF to Mint: $3–$5

Card Type	Value, EF to Mint
Amusement parks	$3–$15+

Brackenridge Park, San Antonio, Texas. (Curt Teich Co.) EF to Mint: $3–$5

1954 Ford automobile. EF to Mint: $6–$12

1956 Nash Statesman automobile. EF to Mint: $6–$12

1974 Cadillac. EF to Mint: $3–$6

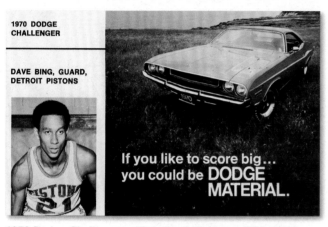

1970 Dodge Challenger with basketball player. EF to Mint: $10–$15

Ralph Oldsmobile agency, Smithtown, New York. EF to Mint: $12–$15

1974 Chevrolet trucks. EF to Mint: $4–$6

Advertisement for Jeep selective drive hubs and wheel covers. EF to Mint: $8–$10

Another BMW: the Bavarian Motor Wrecking, Rancho Cordova, California. (Albert L. Morse, Sausalito, California.) EF to Mint: $8–$12

Beachwagon Tropical Tape Tours, Honolulu, Hawaii. (Plastichrome by Colourpicture Publishing, Boston.) EF to Mint: $10–$15

Card Type	Value, EF to Mint
Automobiles and related motor vehicles	$1–$15+

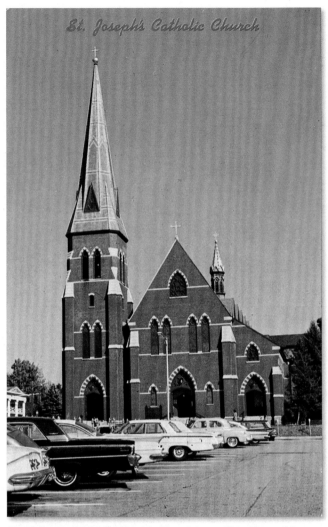

St. Joseph's Catholic Church, Manchester, New Hampshire. (Wakefield Trading Co., Wakefield, Massachusetts.) EF to Mint: $1–$2

Cemetery, Armenia, New York. (Colourpicture, Boston.) EF to Mint: $1–$2

Card Type	Value, EF to Mint
Churches, cemeteries	$1–$4

Confederate War Memorial, Warrenton, Virginia. (Dexter Press, West Nyack, New York) EF to Mint: $1–$2

Card Type	Value, EF to Mint
Civic monuments, statues, and related	$1–$2

Shipwrecked sailor comic card. (Baxter Lane Co., Amarillo, Texas.) EF to Mint: $1–$2

Card Type	Value, EF to Mint
Comic postcards	$1–$2

Hollywood Bowl, Hollywood, California. (Mike Roberts.) EF to Mint: $1–$2

Card Type	Value, EF to Mint
Concerts and venues	$1–$5+

Duff's Diner, Winchester, Virginia. (Walter H. Miller, Williamsburg, Virginia.) EF to Mint: $10–$15

Toffenetti Restaurant, New York City, a popular tourist stop. Card shows a bus (added to the image), theater marquee, and many people. (Published by Times Square Sightseeing Lines.) EF to Mint: $4–$6

Card Type	Value, EF to Mint
Diners, drive-thrus, and restaurants	$3–$20+

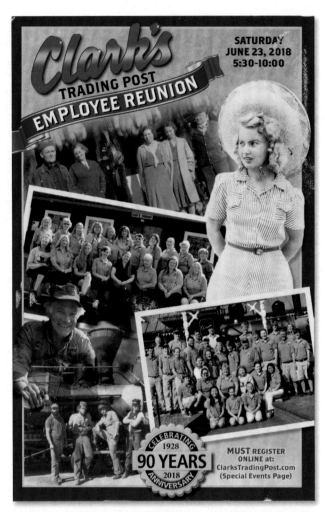

Clark's Trading Post reunion invitation card. EF to Mint: $0.50–$1

Card Type	Value, EF to Mint
Events, invitations, announcements, concerts, tournaments, etc.	$0.50–$8+

Richman's Country Fresh Ice Cream, Sharptown, New Jersey. Black-and-white card heavily retouched. EF to Mint: $6–$8

Card Type	Value, EF to Mint
Factories and plants	$2–$10+

The iconic Space Needle tower at the 1962 Seattle World's Fair. (Mike Roberts.) EF to Mint: $1–$2

Scene at the 1962 Seattle World's Fair. (C.P. Johnston Co., Seattle.) EF to Mint: $1–$2

1964–1965 New York World's Fair. (Dexter, West Nyack, New York.) EF to Mint: $1–$2

Scenes from the New York World's Fair. The Unisphere globe was the fair's main icon. (Dexter, West Nyack, New York.) EF to Mint: $1–$2

S.S. Kresge Co., Brockton, Massachusetts. EF to Mint: $2–$4

Card Type	Value, EF to Mint
Five-and-ten cent stores	$2–$5+
Hospitals	$1–$3

The AMF Monorail at the New York World's Fair. (Manhattan Post Card Co., New York.) EF to Mint: $1–$2

Bragg Motel, Fayetteville, North Carolina. (C.W. Ruth.) EF to Mint: $2–$4

Sunshine Bakers Exhibit at the 1964 New York World's Fair. EF to Mint: $2–$5

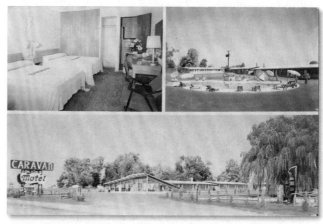

Caravan Motel, Dover, Delaware. (Dexter Press, West Nyack, New York.) EF to Mint: $2–$4

Card Type	Value, EF to Mint
Fairs and expositions	$1–$4+

Stevens Pass Summit Inn, Washington. (Ellis Post Card Co., Arlington, Washington.) EF to Mint: $2–$4

Conneaut, Ohio, large letters. (Tichnor Brothers, Boston.) EF to Mint: $1–$2

Beachcomber Oceanfront Inn, Daytona, Florida. (West Photography, South Daytona, Florida.) EF to Mint: $1–$3

Junction City, Kansas, large letters. (Curt Teich Co.) EF to Mint: $1–$2

Card Type	Value, EF to Mint
Large letters cards	$1–$6+

280 mm Atomic Cannon, Fort Bragg, North Carolina. (Colourpicture, Boston.) EF to Mint: $1–$3

Bush River Yacht Club (only card of this facility). EF to Mint: $8–$12

Card Type	Value, EF to Mint
Hotels and motels	$1–$5+
Lakes, forests, natural scenery	$1–$3

Sheppard Air Force Base, Texas. (Baxter Lane Postcard Co., Amarillo, Texas.) EF to Mint: $1–$3

1958 BMW R50 motorcycle with Watsonian sidecar. (Roaring Autos, Wall, New Jersey.) EF to Mint: $6–$8

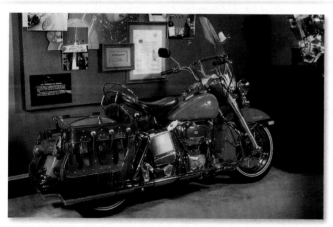

Hangars at Dover Air Force Base, Dover, Delaware. (Colourpicture, Boston.) EF to Mint: $1–$2

Card Type	Value, EF to Mint
Military	$1–$5+

Card Type	Value, EF to Mint
Motorcycles	$2–$10+
Municipal buildings	$1–$2

White Dome Geyser, Yellowstone National Park. (Curt Teich Co.) EF to Mint: $1–$2

Harley-Davidson FLH Heritage model. EF to Mint: $6–$8

Boat harbor in Colton Bay, Grand Teton National Park. (Mike Roberts.) EF to Mint: $1–$2

Card Type	Value, EF to Mint
National parks	$1–$3
Novelty and mechanical cards	$2–$5+

M/S *Grand Bahama* on the West Palm Beach-Grand Bahama route. EF to Mint: $2–$4

S.S. *Lurline*, Matson Lines luxury liner on the San Francisco to Honolulu route. EF to Mint: $2–$4

Card Type	Value, EF to Mint
Ocean liners and large boats	$1–$5+

Robert Dole campaign card. (Dole for Senate Committee.) EF to Mint: $2–$3

Card Type	Value, EF to Mint
Politics, candidates, elections	$1–$4+

Postcard show announcement. EF to Mint: $0.25–$0.50

Card Type	Value, EF to Mint
Postcard shows and events	$0.25–$2
Recreation and hobbies	$1–$5
Schools	$1–$3

Archery at Notre Dame Camp, Spofford, New Hampshire. EF to Mint: $3–$5

Fenway Park, Boston. EF to Mint: $3–$5

Chris Reynolds, New York Yankees. Printed signature. (Dormand Natural Color Baseball Series No. 109.) EF to Mint: $8–$12

University of Maryland basketball game at Cole Field House. EF to Mint: $5–$8

Little League baseball, Williamsport, Pennsylvania (Curt Teich Co.) EF to Mint: $4–$6

Surfers on Malibu Beach, California. (Plastichrome Colourpicture, Boston.) EF to Mint: $6–$8

Skiing at Cannon Mountain, New Hampshire. (Plastichrome Colourpicture, Boston.) EF to Mint: $1–$2

"There's good fishing here" inscription on back. (Nyce Manufacturing Co.) EF to Mint: $1

Golden Tornadoes 1960–1961 basketball team, Pompano Beach Senior High School, Pompano Beach, Florida. (Blackthorn.) EF to Mint: $4–$8

Hunter and dog. Advertisement for the Sport Shop, Caldwell, Idaho. (Noble, Colorado Springs, Colorado.) EF to Mint: $1–$2

Duck hunters. (Mirro-Chrome, H.S. Crocker, San Francisco.) EF to Mint: $1–$2

All American Soap Box Derby. (Dexter Press, West Nyack, New York.) EF to Mint: $2–$5

Card Type	Value, EF to Mint
Sports and recreation	$1–$10+

Interior of the Trading Post, Ketchikan, Alaska. (Lloyd's Studio, Ketchikan.) EF to Mint: $4–$6

Tri-Chem, a liquid embroidery product, as depicted on a chrome advertising card. EF to Mint: $3$5

Perry's Nut House, Belfast, Maine. (Sommerfeld Photo Film, Auburn, Massachusetts.) EF to Mint: $3–$5

A chrome advertising card for Storybook Shoe. EF to Mint: $3–$5

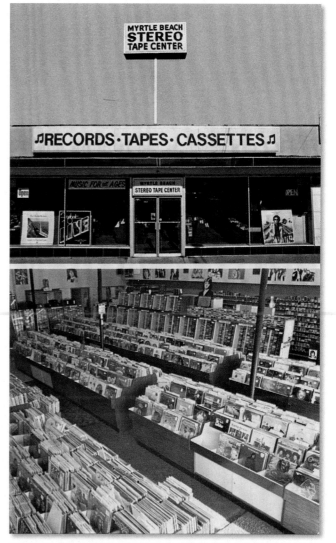

Myrtle Beach Stereo Tape Center, Myrtle Beach, South Carolina. (Wemett, Myrtle Beach.) EF to Mint: $6–$8

Card Type	Value, EF to Mint
Stores and shops	$2–$10+

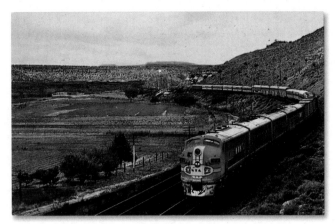

Santa Fe Railway's San Francisco Chief in the San Joaquin Valley, California. (Fred Harvey.) EF to Mint: $1–$2

Burlington Route Vista Dome Twin Zephyrs. EF to Mint: $2–$4

Card Type	Value, EF to Mint
Trains and stations	$1–$10+

A Selection of Rack Postcards

These cards have been distributed free in racks placed in stores, restaurants, colleges, theaters, and other locations. Values range from 25¢ to several dollars for most, plus handling and postage if ordered by mail. Those with social issues or current events sell for more. At postcard shows a box of these often appeals to the younger set familiar with many of the subjects featured. See introduction for more information.

Absolut Vodka, one of a series issued as rack cards. (GoCard.) EF to Mint: $3–$5

Rack card by Rizzoli Books advertising *Do You Remember?*, "a picture book that takes you back," featuring a McDonald's hamburger and advertising slogan. (Max Racks.) EF to Mint: $2–$3

This Rice Krispies card advertised a famous snack. (Supercards.) EF to Mint: $0.50–$1

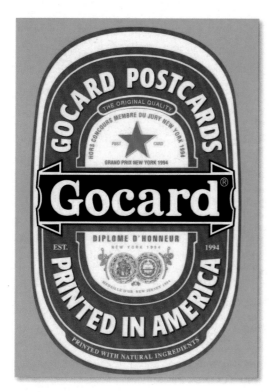

Dr. Martens boots, 1999. (HotStamp.) EF to Mint: $0.50–$1

A Selection of Modern Chrome Postcards

Purchased in 2018 from the large revolving rack of postcards at Black's Paper Store, Wolfeboro, New Hampshire, where author Q. David Bowers lives. Prices represent typical postcard show after-market values.

Self-advertising card. (GoCard.) EF to Mint: $1–$2

Pro–gay rights card. (GoCard.) EF to Mint: $5–$8

Black's Paper Store. (Scenic Art, Wolfeboro, New Hampshire.) EF to Mint: $1–$2

New England lobster cooking instructions. (Scenic Art, Wolfeboro, New Hampshire.) EF to Mint: $1

Wolfeboro, New Hampshire, waterfront from the Wolfeboro Bay shore. (Bromley & Co., Inc., Wolfeboro, New Hampshire.) EF to Mint: $1–$2

Generic autumn foliage. (Northeast Novelty and Gift Distributors, Orleans, Massachusetts.) EF to Mint: $1

M/S *Mount Washington*, Lake Winnipesaukee passenger cruise ship. (Scenic Art, Wolfeboro, New Hampshire.) EF to Mint: $1–$3

"Antler Envy" comic postcard. (Entertain Ya Mania, Westbrook, Maine.) EF to Mint: $1–$2

APPENDIX A
AMERICAN POSTCARD PRINTERS AND DISTRIBUTORS

Most twentieth-century postcards have the name of the printer (manufacturer) or distributor, and many have both. Curt Teich, the famous manufacturer in Chicago, distributed most of its cards through news companies, local and regional stores, and the like. Sometimes these are identified by the Curt Teich name (in various forms), the TCo logotype, or another way, often by a serial number such as A-00000. The Detroit Publishing Company usually printed its name on the face or back, often with the name of a distributor added.

The Toyland Post Cards & Novelties shop at Riverview Beach Park in Pennsville, New Jersey.

From the late 1890s until about 1914, untold millions of postcards were imported from Germany by Hugh C. Leighton, Valentine & Sons, S. Langsdorf & Co., Rotograph, and others, which gathered black-and-white photographs and shipped them overseas to be adjusted, colorized, and lithographed. These typically bear the name of the importer plus the name of the importer's customer, such as a store or news company. The Leighton company, for example, added its own serial number, but other serial numbers are sometimes found. Many German cards were imported with serial numbers but no other notation except "Printed in Germany," or similar.

Raphael Tuck & Sons, the London manufacturer of high-quality postcards, printed many subjects for distribution in the United States, including numbered sets for many towns and cities. These often had the name of a local or regional distributor added.

In many instances, monographs or notations were printed instead of a full name. The American News Company, for example, imported many cards from Germany and identified itself with ANC letters on a cloverleaf, with other notations such as Photo-Chrome, Mezzochrome, Newvochrome, etc., some of which referred to the appearance of the cards or the printing processes used to make them.

Photographic studios, photographers, and others issued large numbers of real photo postcards (RPPCs), using postcard stock supplied by Eastman Kodak or another source. Often the name of the issuer was imprinted vertically on the left side of the back. Some of these were very small operations, while others did a large business over an entire region. Likely, well over a thousand different issuers were active in the first several decades of the twentieth century.

In addition, many newspapers, insurance companies, railroads, hotels, steamship lines, airlines, department stores, general stores, news vendors, etc., issued postcards with their own imprints, usually self-explanatory. Many photographers and studios who issued RPPCs are listed as well, a sampling that includes most of the larger-volume publishers within this specialty.

For an index of printers and distributors by state and city, see page 417.

A

Abbe, James E. Newport News, VA. Published postcards in the early twentieth century.

Abell, A.H. Rochester, NY. Published RPPCs and postcards in the early twentieth century.

Abingdon Press. Cincinnati, OH. Publisher of postcards during the early twentieth century, including signed artists.

Abrams, M. Roxbury, MA. Published postcards in the early twentieth century.

Ackermann, Ed. New York, NY. Published a series of New York views prior to 1898.

Ackley, E.B. Sandusky, OH. Published postcards in the 1920s and 1930s, including from the Curt Teich Co.

Acme Art Store. Dubuque, IA. Published postcards in the early twentieth century.

Acme Greeting Card Co., also known as Acme Post Card Co. Cedar Rapids, IA. Published postcards in the early twentieth century.

Acmegraph Co. Chicago, IL. Located in Chicago, the Acmegraph Company published many high quality lithographed view cards in the first two decades of the twentieth century, closely resembling in style those printed nearby by the Curt Teich Company. Typically, serial numbers were printed on the upper front.

Adam, Meldrum & Anderson Co. Buffalo, NY; Chemnitz, Germany. Published view cards in the early twentieth century.

Adams, Arthur S. Worcester, MA. Photographed scenes and issued RPPCs during the early twentieth century.

Adams, John T. Marblehead, MA. Published view cards in the early twentieth century.

Adler, George. San Diego, CA. Published postcards in the early twentieth century.

Adpostal Corporation. Allentown, PA. Published postcards featuring commercial products, including multiple products on a standard government postal card.

Advocate Post Card Shop / Provincetown Advocate. Provincetown, MA. The *Advocate*, local newspaper, published view cards in the early twentieth century, including German imports and also domestic cards, the latter including those obtained from H.A. Dickerman & Son and printed by the Curt Teich Co. The Provincetown Advocate Post Card Shop had a large selection of postcards for sale. (Duplicate listing is under P)

Aerial Explorations, Inc. Made RPPCs in the mid-twentieth century.

Aerial Photo Co. San Francisco, CA. Published RPPCs in the early twentieth century.

Aero Distributing Co. Chicago, IL. Published postcards, in the late twentieth century, including Curt Teich Co. cards.

Ahrens, Henry M. Charlotte, NC. Distributor of view cards in the mid-twentieth century.

Alabama Post Card Co. Bessemer, AL. Published postcards in the late twentieth century.

Albany News Co. Albany, NY. Publisher of postcards, including German imports via American News Co. (ANC), in the early twentieth century.

Albertype Co. New York, NY. Postcards issued by the Albertype Company are nearly always of high quality with excellent definition of details. From the 1890s onward they were distributed by many news agencies, stores, and other publishers. The firm was active from 1887 until 1952 in Brooklyn and published thousands of different views. Many of its cards of the 1920s are particularly distinctive for their detail, in an era in which competitors' cards were not as sharply defined. Many are beautifully tinted with delicate colors. In 1952 the firm was sold to the Art Vue Post Card Company.

Alcan Moss Publishing Co. New York, NY. Publisher of postcards during the early twentieth century, including signed artists.

Alexander Manufacturing Co. Sandusky, OH. Alexander was a regional publisher of cards, circa 1900s and 1910s, using cards printed elsewhere, including German imports and from Metropolitan (Everett, MA).

Alexander, A.E. Published RPPCs in the early twentieth century.

Alexander, Jim A. El Paso, TX. Publisher of view cards during the early twentieth century, including cowboy and Wild West scenes.

Allard, N.J. Fitchburg and Leominster, MA. Published postcards in the early twentieth century.

Allen, B.E. Columbia Falls, ME. Published postcards in the early twentieth century.

Allen, W.I. Bridgeport, CT. Publisher of view postcards in the early twentieth century, including German imports.

Allis Press. Kansas City, MO. Published postcards in the early twentieth century.

All-Tom Corporation. Dallas and Fort Worth, TX. Published postcards in the late twentieth century, including cards from Colourpicture.

Alma Publishing Co. New York, NY (also see Alfred Mainzer, Inc., under M). Publisher of postcards during the early twentieth century, including signed artists.

American Art Post Card Co. New York, NY. Beginning about 1915, American Art published monotone and color view cards, continuing into the market for years afterward. Many were printed by the Curt Teich Co. Some were imprinted "H. Finkelstein & Son." Some regional views were copyrighted by Irving Underhill.

American Art Publishing Co. New York, NY. Starting business circa 1918, the company issued many view and other cards, most of which were supplied by the Curt Teich Co., The firm continued into the mid–1920s.

American Colortype Co. New York, NY; Chicago, IL. Active from about 1904, continuing for decades, American Colortype printed postcards in addition to many other paper items. These included greetings, views, holiday cards, and more. In 1956 the company merged with the Rapid Electrotype Co., of Cincinnati, and became known as Rapid American.

American Historical Art Publishing Co. New York, NY. This short-lived company was active during the middle of the first decade of the twentieth century. It published cards printed in Germany. The typical card depicted a scene from history.

American Import Co. Minneapolis, MN. In the early twentieth century the firm published monotone as well as color cards, including for the Northern Pacific Railroad, and also distributed German imports.

American Lithographic Co. New York, NY. Also known as ALCO, this company was a consolidation of several leading lithographers. In 1900 the Knapp Co., one of the original companies, became the art publishing arm and issued many postcards. The company printed cards for many distributors, including the official views of the World's Columbian Exposition, 1893, with the imprint of Charles W. Goldsmith.

American News Co. New York, NY. During the early twentieth century American News was one of the largest distributors of postcards in the country, through its kiosks, newsstands, and other outlets. It was generally given on postcards as ANC, with a letter on each of the three lobes of a clover leaf. Photo-Chrome was imprinted on many cards, along with other designations, most of which referred to a printing process or style, the details of most of which are unknown today. These included Newvochrome, Mezzochrome, etc. Many cards of the early twentieth century, until about 1914, bear the notations of Leipzig, Dresden, and Berlin, Germany, the location of factories from which cards were imported. Later cards were made elsewhere, including in France and, in particular, America. Certain of the added names on card are these:

- Americhrome: Color cards printed in America. Serial numbers with prefix M.

- Art Series: Color cards reproduced from art rather than photographs.

- Bromide-Chrome: Color lithographed cards with excellent detail, made in Germany. Serial numbers with prefix E. Not many were made with this imprint.

- Doubletone Delft: Blue-hued gravure cards, made in Germany. Not many were made with this imprint.

- Doubletone Sepia: Brown-hued gravure cards, made in Germany. Not many were made with this imprint.

- Druckchrome: Color cards printed in Germany. "Druck" means "print" in German. Not many were made with this imprint.

- Excelsior: High quality monotone, usually black and white, but some in blue or sepia, made in Germany. Some were hand-tinted. Serial numbers with prefix A, B, D, and F for black and white, prefix AA for colored cards.

- Helio Dore: Heliogravure printed in Germany. Not many were made with this imprint.

- Litho-Chrome: Color cards, made in Germany, often with another name (such as Mezzochrome) also added. Prefix letters A, B, C, D, E, G, and H. Monochrome cards marked Litho-Chrome have serial prefix B.

- Mezzochrome: Color cards made in Germany. Prefix letter D.

- Monotone: Black-and-white cards of medium quality. Not many were made with this imprint.

- Newvochrome: Color cards made in Germany. Prefix letters A to E.

- Octochrome: Color cards made in Germany. Prefix letters D and E.

- Photo Helio: Color cards made in Germany by the heliograph process. Not many were made with this imprint.

- Photo-Chrome: Color cards made in America. High quality with much detail. Prefix letters D, E, and M.

- Plenochrome: Color cards made in Germany, with a somewhat muted finish. Not many were made with this imprint.

- Poly-Chrome: Color cards made in Germany, with distinctive colors, often not blended together, giving more contrast. Prefix letter A for early cards, M for later white-border cards made in the United States.

- Quartochrome: Color cards made in Germany. Prefix letter E. Not many were made with this imprint.

- Rotochrome: Color cards made in Germany. Prefix letter D.

- Sextochrome: Color cards made in France in a six-step process. Prefix letter D. Produced beginning about 1917.

- Special Colored: Color cards printed in France but with German cities mentioned. A rare imprint.

- Steeldruckchrome: Brown gravure cards made in Germany. Not many were made with this imprint.

American Novelty Co. Pittsburgh, PA. Published printed and RPPCs during the early twentieth century.

American Photograph Co. New York, NY. Photographers, designers, engravers, and printers; issued postcards in the early twentieth century. Most were black-and-white views of the New York City area.

AMERICAN POST CARD COMPANY, MASON CITY, IOWA.

American Post Card Co. Mason City and Sioux City, IA. Publisher of RPPCs in the early twentieth century. No connection to the New York City firm.

American Post Card Co. New York, NY. In business from about 1903 to 1910, this company published many view cards in monotone, some with hand tinting. It also published holiday and greeting cards and selected other subjects. Important in its time.

American Post Card Company. Houston, TX. Published postcards in the mid-twentieth century, including cards by the Dexter Press.

American Publicity Company. Syracuse, NY. Published view cards in the early twentieth century.

American Souvenir Card Co. New York, NY. Active in the late 1890s, this company issued cards known as pioneer today. Most memorable are the 15 color Patriograph sets of 12 cards each. The quality was indifferent at best. Sets of 12 cards with tourist views were made of such locations as Alaska, Alabama, Baltimore, Boston, Chicago, Milwaukee, New York, Niagara Falls, Philadelphia, San Francisco, Staten Island, and Washington, as well as a voyage to Europe, and are desirable today. In 1898 remainder cards and some plates were acquired by Edward H. Mitchell of San Francisco, who later issued some of the same subjects. Mitchell went on to great prominence in the postcard field.

American Souvenir Co. Boston, MA. This firm issued colorfully lithographed cards printed by Armstrong & Co. of the same city, including a set of 12 regional subjects.

Ammann Advertising Co. Schulenburg, TX. Published postcards in the late twentieth century.

Anderson, Carl. Fort Collins, CO. Published postcards in the 1920s and 1930s.

Anderson's News Agency. Clarksville, TN. Published postcards in the early twentieth century.

Andover Bookstore. Andover, MA. Published postcards in the early twentieth century.

Andrews Book & Stationery Co. Chattanooga, TN. Published postcards in the early twentieth century, including those of the Curt Teich Co.

Andrews, C. Wesley. Baker and Portland, OR. Andrews was a professional photographer who issued RPPCs using his own images and also made them available to printers who created color cards from them. Most of his subjects were regional.

Anglo-American Publishing Co. / Anglo-American Post Card Co. New York, NY. In the first decade of the twentieth century, Anglo-American published color comic cards and black-and-white scenic subjects.

Anschutz, H.M. Keokuk, IA. Published postcards in the early twentieth century, including those obtained from Valentine Souvenir Co.

Arenson, Albert, Press (Albert Arenson Press). New York, NY. Publisher of postcards during the early twentieth century, including signed artists.

Aristophoto Co., The. New York, NY; Taucha, Saxony, Germany. Published view cards in the early twentieth century.

Armstrong, Albert. Ocean Park, ME. Published postcards in the early twentieth century, including German imports from the American News Co. (ANC).

Armstrong, J.B., News Agency. Winston-Salem, NC. Published view cards in the mid-twentieth century, including those of the Curt Teich Co.

Armstrong, W.L. Jacksonville, IL. Published postcards in the early twentieth century, including cards from Germany from American News Co. (ANC).

Arredondo, John. McAllen, TX. Published RPPCs in the early twentieth century.

Arrow Post Card Co. St. Louis, MO. Published postcards in the early twentieth century.

Art Association. Washington, D.C. Published postcards in the mid-twentieth century.

Art Lithography Co. San Francisco, CA. In the early twentieth century, until about 1915, this company issued many view cards, including color lithographic cards printed by Edward H. Mitchell.

Art Manufacturing Co. Amelia and Zanesville, OH. Art Manufacturing printed many cards, monotone and color, of a wide variety of categories and topics, which were marketed through various distributors.

Art Postcard & Novelty Co. Hoboken, NJ. In the 1910s this company published view cards, primarily of New Jersey and New York subjects.

Art Store. Winsted, CT. F.H. De Mars, proprietor. Published RPPCs in the early twentieth century.

Artino Post Card Co. / E.F. Branning's Artino Card. New York, NY. Artino, conducted by E.F. Branning, published many monotone and color cards printed in Germany, with scenic views of Eastern subjects being a specialty.

Arts Shop. Silver City, NM. Issued printed cards in the early twentieth century, some of which had cowboy and other Western themes.

Artvue. New York, NY. Artvue published monotone and color cards from the late 1940s onward. In 1952 the company acquired the remains of the Albertype Co.

Asheville Post Card Co. Asheville, NC. Published postcards in the mid- and late twentieth century, including cards from Metropolitan (of Everett, MA) and Curt Teich Co.

Astor House. New York, NY. This firm, taking its name from a well-known New York hotel, published postcards in the early twentieth century, including advertising, views, and other subjects.

Atherton, A.H. Jacksonville, IL. Published postcards in the early twentieth century

Atkinson News Co. Tilton, NH. Atkinson was a major regional publisher during the early twentieth century. Early cards included those imported from Germany, and many later ones were printed by the Curt Teich Co. "Naturkrom" was a name imprinted on the green backs of many cards.

Atlantic Post Card Co. Portland, ME; St. Petersburg, FL. Published postcards in the mid-twentieth century, including those printed by Kropp.

Atlas News Shop, The. Fort Worth, TX. Published postcards in the late twentieth century, including cards from E.C. Kropp Co.

Atlas Society. New York, NY. Publisher of cards during the early twentieth century, including German imports the firm distributed nationwide through sub-publishers.

Atlas Souvenir Card Co. New York, NY. Also known as the Atlas Society, this was a small firm in the industry. In the early twentieth century Atlas specialized in postcards made to order, such as scenic cards, issued under its own imprint as well as those of local and regional distributors. Some of their color cards were imported from Germany. A 1907 advertisement located the company at 10 East 23rd Street, New York City, offering "fancy post cards" and "view cards" in "almost any quantity."

Auburn Post Card Manufacturing Co. Auburn, NY. Auburn printed many cards and published those of other makers in 1913 (when its name was changed from the Witten-Dennison Post Card Co.) and extending into the late 1920s. Most were of medium quality, made for those desiring inexpensive cards. Some view cards.

Austen, J.I., Co. Chicago, IL. Publisher of postcards during the early twentieth century, including signed artists.

Austin & Sons. Utica, NY. Published view cards in the early twentieth century, including German imports.

Averill, D.M., & Co. Portland, OR. Averill published official cards for the Lewis & Clark Exposition held in Portland in 1905 and also sold commemorative gold dollars produced for the event. Later, the company published other subjects, including Native Americans.

B

B. & J. Sales. Abilene, TX. Published postcards in the late twentieth century, including cards from Dexter Press.

Babbitt Brothers Trading Co. Flagstaff, AZ. Published postcards in the mid-twentieth century, including those from the Curt Teich Co.

Babcock & Burrough. Albuquerque, NM. Publisher of postcards during the early twentieth century, including signed artists.

Bachelor Studios. Cincinnati, OH. Published postcards in the early twentieth century.

Bachman & Pickett. Commerce, TX. Maker of RPPCs including "Commercial Club Add [sic] Cards."

Bagley Co. East Liverpool, OH. Publisher of view cards in the early twentieth century, including German imports via Hugh C. Leighton.

Bagley, Roy A. Published postcards in the 1920s and 1930s.

Bain Candy Company. Lawrence, MA. Published postcards in the mid-twentieth century, including cards from Dexter Press.

Baker Brothers. Elmira, NY. Publisher of view postcards in the early twentieth century. Succeeded by the Owen Card Publishing Co. in the 1910s.

Baker Brothers Engraving Co. Omaha, NE. Published view cards in the early twentieth century, including those of the Curt Teich Co.

Baker, B.N., Dr. Rhinebeck, NY. Published view cards in the early twentieth century, including those made in Germany.

Baker, Milford. Bingham, ME. Issued RPPCs in the early twentieth century.

Baker, R.J. Honolulu, HI. Maker of RPPCs in the early twentieth century, including of native subjects. His cards are highly prized by deltiologists.

Balke, R.L., Indian Trading Company. Phoenix, AZ. Publisher of view cards in the early twentieth century.

Baltimore Badge & Novelty Co. Baltimore, MD. This company included postcards in its line of products and published the official cards for the 1907 Jamestown Tercentenary Exposition.

Baltimore Lithograph Co. Baltimore, MD. In the 1890s and early 1900s this company produced black-and-white cards advertising hotels and other businesses, some of which were hand-tinted.

Baltimore Stationery Co. Baltimore, MD. Beginning about 1908 this company published many view cards of regional scenes, including German imports.

Bamforth & Co., Ltd. Holmfirth, England. This well-known British publisher of postcards and other items opened a New York City office in 1906. Bamforth cards of many subjects are met with frequently today and are widely sought by American collectors.

Bamforth Co. Peekskill and New York, NY. American branch of British firm, sometimes with Ltd. after the name. Publisher of postcards during the early twentieth century, including signed artists.

Banks, Clyde. Bellingham, WA. Banks, a professional photographer, issued RPPC cards beginning about 1917 and also made his images available to printers of postcards who colorized them.

Banner Photo Co. Seattle, WA. Published postcards in the early twentieth century.

Bannister, C.M. Watertown, NY. Published view cards including German imports in the early twentieth century.

Barber Printing & Stationery Co. Winston-Salem, NC. Published view cards in the mid-twentieth century, including those of the Curt Teich Co.

Bardell & O'Neill / Bardell-O'Neill. San Francisco, CA. Published postcards in the early twentieth century. As seen, there are several variations with the Bardell name.

Bardell Art Co. / Bardell Art Printing Co. San Francisco, CA. Published view cards in the mid-twentieth century.

Bardell, J.C. San Francisco, CA. Published view cards in the mid-twentieth century.

Barkalow Brothers Co. Omaha, NE. In the early twentieth century, Barkalow published many printed items, including cards and other items for the Union Pacific Railroad headquartered in Omaha. Many were obtained from the Curt Teich Co.

Barnes, F.W. Uxbridge, MA. Published view cards in the early twentieth century, including German imports obtained from the American News Company (ANC).

Barnhill, Esmond. St. Petersburg, FL. A professional photographer, Barnhill published his own RPPCs, including hand-tinted subjects, and also made his images available to Albertype. His business began circa 1913.

Barnum, Harry. Averill Park, NY. Published view cards in the early twentieth century.

Barrera Publications. Laredo, TX. Published postcards in the late twentieth century, including cards from E.C. Kropp Co.

Bartlett and Baker. Greenfield, MA. Published view cards in the late twentieth century, including those made by Tichnor Brothers.

Barton & Spooner. Cornwall-on-Hudson, NY. This partnership published cards imported from Germany, on a wide variety of subjects including greetings, maps, holidays, regional views, and the "Foolish Question" series with Dutch girls.

Barton News Agency. Temple, TX. Published postcards in the late twentieth century, including cards from Colourchrome.

Barton-Cotton, Inc. Baltimore, MD. Publisher of postcards during the early twentieth century, including signed artists.

Bassett's Art Shop. Perry, NY. Published RPPCs in the early twentieth century.

Batsford, James E., & Son. Waterloo, NY. Published view cards in the early twentieth century, including German imports from the American News Company (ANC).

Baum, Otto M. Atlanta, GA. Published postcards for the Cotton States and International Exposition held in Atlanta in 1895.

Bawden Brothers. Clinton and Davenport, IA. Published postcards in the early twentieth century.

Baxter Lane Co. Amarillo, TX. Published postcards in the late twentieth century.

Baxtone. Amarillo, TX. Publisher of postcards during the early twentieth century, including signed artists.

Bay News Co. Ocean Park, CA. Publisher of view cards in the 1930s, including those made by H.C. Kropp.

Baylis Post Card Co. Cedar Rapids, IA. Conducted by William Baylis, publisher and landscape photographer; publisher of postcards in the early twentieth century.

Beach, Henry M. Remsen, NY. Beach, a professional photographer, issued many RPPCs, especially of upstate New York towns, with Main Streets and other popular views. Many are imprinted "Beach's Real Photo" on the back or "Beach-Series, Genuine Hand-Finished Photograph / B.S. Made From Any Photo at Remsen, N.Y."

Beals. Des Moines, IA. Manufactured "Glo Tone Color Postcards" in the early twentieth century.

Bean, O. Crosby. Bangor, ME. This publisher, also known as Bean's, distributed regional view cards during the early twentieth century, beginning about 1910. Early cards were printed in Germany.

Bear Photo Co. San Francisco, CA. Publisher of RPPCs from their own photographs and also sold printed cards, the most memorable of which show scenes from the 1906 San Francisco earthquake and fire. Other popular cards include views of Yosemite National Park.

Bearce, George M. San Antonio, TX. Published postcards in the early twentieth century, including German imports.

Beard, L. Atlantic City, NJ. published postcards in the early twentieth century.

Beatty, Edwin T. & Son. Published postcards in the mid-twentieth century, including from Curt Teich Co.

Beck Engraving Co. Philadelphia, PA. Printer and publisher of a postcard of Independence Hall, prior to 1898.

Becker, G.J. New York, NY. Published postcards in the 1920s and 1930s.

Beckett, Ward & Co. Clearwater, FL. Published postcards in the late twentieth century.

Beckley News Co. Beckley, WV. Published postcards in the 1920s and 1930s, including from the Curt Teich Co.

Beckwith & Beanchamp. Shenandoah, IA. Published postcards in the early twentieth century.

Beekwith, E.B. Chicago, IL. Publisher of postcards during the early twentieth century, including signed artists.

Behrendt, Richard. San Francisco, CA. Importer of various gift goods. He published many view cards beginning circa 1906, an early effort being views of the 1906 San Francisco earthquake and fire.

Bekudlingen Art Publishing Co. Denver, CO. Published postcards in the early twentieth century.

Belanger, Theodore. River Rouge, MI. Published view cards in the early twentieth century, including German imports obtained from the American News Company (ANC).

Belden, F.C. South Palm Beach, FL. Published postcards in the early twentieth century, including German imports.

Bell, J.P., Co. Lynchburg, VA. In the early twentieth century Bell was a publisher of books, postcards, and more, some of which they printed, others of which were imported, including from Raphael Tuck and Sons of England. Still others were acquired elsewhere, including from the Commercial Colortype Co.

Belmont Post Card Co. New York, NY. Beginning about 1910 and active for about five years, Belmont published many different types of color postcards.

Benham Co. Los Angeles, CA. In the early 1920s, Belmont, owned by L. Pepperman and H. and C. Rubin, published color postcards of regional views, many of which were imprinted "Made in California." A swastika was used as their logotype in an era in which this was a good luck sign.

Benham Indian Trading Company. Los Angeles, CA. A division of the above company. Issued view postcards, some depicting Native Americans.

Benjamin, E.A. Southbridge, MA. Published view cards in the early twentieth century, including some imported from Germany through the American News Co.

Benner, H.M. Hammondsport, NY. Published RPPCs in the early twentieth century.

Benson, E.A. Toledo, IA. Published postcards in the early twentieth century, including German imports.

Berdan Publishing Co. New York, NY. Publisher of postcards during the early twentieth century, including signed artists.

Berger Brothers. Newport and Providence, RI. Beginning circa 1910 and continuing for decades, Berger Brothers published black-and-white and color cards, mostly of regional views, and later printed chrome cards.

Bergman, S. New York, NY. In the 1910s Bergman published art cards with holiday, greeting, comic, and other subjects, nicely done and very colorful.

Berman, Morris. New Haven, CT. Berman published color view cards of regional scenes from about 1908 to the early 1920s.

Bernard's Studio. Wallace, ID. Published view cards in the early twentieth century, including those of the Curt Teich Company.

Bernstein, Max. Kansas City, MO. From about 1916 to the early 1930s, Bernstein published many cards, primarily views. The Curt Teich Co. was an important supplier.

Berry Paper Co. Lewiston, ME. For several years, from about 1907 to 1910, Berry published many monotone and color cards, mostly of regional views. Many were German imports.

Berryhill Co. Phoenix, AZ. Publisher of view cards in the early twentieth century.

Besaw Post Card Co. / Besaw's Studio / Western Post Card Co. Reedley, CA. Made RPPCs of Main Streets and various regional scenes. Conducted by George Besaw beginning in the 1910s, after he had served as a photographer for Edward H. Mitchell. Many Besaw cards are unsigned but can be identified by the hand-done block lettering in the negative captions. On some cards he signed his name in obscure places in the image.

Bey, George, Jr. Attica, NY. Published view cards in the early twentieth century, including German imports.

Bezant, M.R. Published postcards in the early and midtwentieth-twentieth century, including cards from the Curt Teich Co. Florida views were a specialty.

Bien, Julius, & Co. New York, NY. Bien published colorful art cards of comic, religious, greetings, and other subjects circa 1907–1909.

Binn Publishing Co. Baltimore, MD. Published view cards in the early twentieth century, including German imports.

Biren, A. New York, NY. In Brooklyn, New York City, Biren published mostly black-and-white scenic cards beginning circa 1912, later adding other subjects.

Bisbee Press. Lancaster, NH. Published view cards in the mid-twentieth century, primarily of regional scenes.

Black, Fred W., Co. Chicago, IL. Published postcards in the early twentieth century.

Blackney, R.U. Angola, NY. Published view cards in the early twentieth century.

Blanchard, I.H., Press Co. New York, NY. In the first decade of the twentieth century Blanchard published many colorful view cards.

Blanchard, Young & Co. Providence, RI. Beginning about 1906, this company published many regional view cards, first imported from Germany and England (including Valentine), then later printed in the United States, including by the Commercial Colortype Co.

Blanford, Paul G. Portsmouth, VA. Published postcards in the early twentieth century.

Bliss, E.A., Co. Meriden, CT. Published postcards in the early twentieth century.

Bliss, F.A. Warren, RI. Published postcards in the early twentieth century, including cards from Germany obtained from the American News Co. (ANC).

Blodget, E.H. North Hadley, MA. Published view cards in the early twentieth century.

Blood, G.C. Peterboro, NH. Produced RPPCs in the early twentieth century.

Bloom Brothers Co. Minneapolis, MN. Beginning circa 1907 this company published postcards, mostly of scenes of the Midwest and Rocky Mountains, including various Western themes. The company used several different logotypes over the years.

Bloom, J.W. Mount Vernon, IA. Published postcards in the early twentieth century, including cards from the Commercial Colortype Co.

Bluefield News Agency. Bluefield, WV. Published postcards in the 1920s and 1930s, including from the Curt Teich Co.

Boeckling, G.A., Co. Cedar Point, Sandusky, OH. Publisher of view cards in the early twentieth century, including Metrocraft / Metropolitan cards.

Boeres, A.O., Co. Phoenix, AZ. From about 1917, Boeres published regional view cards, most of which were printed by the Curt Teich Co.

Bonesteel, H.F., M.D. Sabael, NY. Published view cards in the early twentieth century.

Book & Tackle Shop. Watch Hill, RI. Publisher of postcards during the early twentieth century, including signed artists.

Bookshop, The. San Antonio, TX. Published postcards in the early twentieth century.

Bookstore, The. Davenport, WA. Published view cards in the early twentieth century, including those supplied by C.E. Wheelock & Co. Advertised to be "importers and publishers."

Bookstore, The. East Northfield, MA. Published view cards in the early twentieth century, including those made by Albertype.

A. C. Bosselman & Co., New York.

Bosselman, A.C., & Co. New York, NY. Bosselman was one of the most important New York City publishers in the early twentieth century. Beginning about 1901 and continuing for nearly two decades, the company issued views and other subjects, with early color cards important from Germany. Coney Island was a favorite topic.

Boston Post Card Co. Boston, MA. Starting about 1906 and continuing for about five years, this company published view cards, mostly black-and-white but with some amateurishly colored by hand. In a better vein the firm issued a set of black-and-white gravure cards of Boston with soft, artistic features, creating a memorable series.

Bottler Brothers. Houston, TX. Published postcards in the early twentieth century.

Boudreau, Joseph A. Fiskdale, MA. Published view cards in the early twentieth century, including those made by Mason Brothers.

Boughton-Robbins Co. Spokane, WA. Published view cards in the early twentieth century, including those of the Curt Teich Company. A very important West Coast publisher.

Boutelle, J.G. Toledo, OH. Publisher of view cards in the early twentieth century, including German imports.

Bowers, C.L. Somerset, MA. Produced RPPCs in the early twentieth century.

Boyer, Lynn H., Jr. Wildwood, NJ. Published postcards in the mid-twentieth century, including from the Curt Teich Co. Most were of mid-Atlantic subjects. Some were from Tichnor Brothers, late twentieth century.

Boyles Book Store. Towanda, PA. Issued postcards in the mid-twentieth century, including cards from the Curt Teich Co.

Brackett, Lorimer E. Monhegan Island, ME. From the late 1920s onward, Brackett published over 1,000 different RPPC views, many in large sets of 300. Most are of this island in the Atlantic off the coast of Maine, but others are of New Harbor and other mainland subjects.

Brackett, M.E. Peaks Island, ME. Published postcards in the early twentieth century.

Bradford & Co. St. Joseph, MI. Published cards in the early twentieth century.

Bradley, S.G. Newburgh, NY. Published view cards in the early twentieth century.

Brady Printing Co. Statesville, NC. Distributed view cards in the mid-twentieth century, including those of the Curt Teich Co.

Brainerd, J.M., and Co. Rome, NY. Published RPPCs in the early twentieth century.

Brakey, J.R. Ventura, CA. Postcard publisher in the early twentieth century.

Bramlee, M.E. Olean, NY. Published RPPCs in the 1930s.

Brandau's Studio. Hazelton, PA. Made RPPCs in the early twentieth century.

Branning, E.F. See Artino Post Card Co.

Braun Post Card Co. / Braun Art Publishing Co. Cleveland, OH. Braun was a publisher of regional view cards from about 1910 into the 1940s. Braun Art Publishing Co. was the later trade style. Most were printed by the Curt Teich Co. and Tichnor Brothers.

Briggs, E.E. Saunderstown, RI. Published postcards in the early twentieth century, including imports from Germany.

Briggs, L.E. Vineyard Haven, MA. Published cards in the early and mid-twentieth century, including those made by the Albertype Co.

Britton & Rey Lithographers. San Francisco, CA. Britton & Rey, with tradition dating back to the Gold Rush era, published postcards in the first two decades or so of the twentieth century. Many were of West Coast views and events.

Broatch, J.A. Middletown, CT. Published view cards in the early twentieth century, including German imports from H.C. Leighton and Rotograph.

Bromley and Co. Boston, MA. Published view cards in the late twentieth century, including those made by Mike Roberts. A large-volume issuer.

Brooke, Minnie E., Mrs. Chevy Chase, MD. Published postcards in the early twentieth century, including German imports.

Brooklyn Art Publishing Co. New York, NY. Brooklyn Art published regional view cards circa 1914 to 1917. The firm seems to have been affiliated with the Brooklyn Post Card Co.

Brooklyn Eagle Postcards. New York, NY. The Brooklyn Eagle, a popular newspaper, published sets of postcards from 1905 to 1907 with large-dot screened, black-and-white-views (newspaper format) of regional scenes, comprising 81 sets of six cards each, in addition to other subjects and views. These are of special historic interest today as many obscure subjects would not have been ordinarily depicted on cards.

Brooklyn Postcard Co., Inc. New York, NY. Issued view cards in the early twentieth century.

Brown & Bigelow, Inc. St. Paul, MN. Primarily known as a publisher of calendars and other advertising products, the company produced many color postcards, including calendar cards, during the early twentieth century. Most featured art.

Brown Book Co. Asheville, NC. Distributed postcards in the early twentieth century, including those of the Curt Teich Co.

Brown, F. Parkersburg, WV. Published postcards in the early twentieth century.

Brown, G.R. Co. Eau Claire, WI. Published view cards in the late twentieth century, including some using photographs supplied by the firm.

Brown, Harry G. Published postcards in the mid-twentieth century.

Brown, J.H., & Co. Atchison, KS. Publisher view cards, including German imports from American News Co. (ANC), in the early twentieth century.

Brown News Co. Kansas City, MO. Published postcards in the early twentieth century.

Brown, O.H., and Co. Publisher of view cards, including German imports, in the early twentieth century. Maine and New England scenes were a specialty.

Browning, Mrs. Robert. Charlestown, RI. Published postcards in the early twentieth century, including German imports through ANC.

Bryan Post Card Company, The. Bryan, OH. Published RPPCs in the early twentieth century.

Bryan, R.E. Tyler, TX. Published postcards in the early twentieth century, including cards from the Curt Teich Co.

Bryant Union Co. New York, NY. From about 1904 to 1912 the company published view and other cards printed by E.C. Kropp (Milwaukee) and others.

Buck, Charles E., Music House. Bath, NY. Published view cards in the early twentieth century.

Buck, Edith A. Concord, MA. Published postcards in the early twentieth century, including cards of American historical scenes.

Budow, H. San Antonio, TX. Published postcards in the early twentieth century.

Buettell Brothers Co. Dubuque, IA. Published postcards in the early twentieth century, including those of the Curt Teich Co.

Buffalo Morning Express. Buffalo, NY. Published black-and-white view cards in the early twentieth century, "Seeing Buffalo Series" and "Niagara Frontier Series," among others.

Buffalo News Co. Buffalo, NY. Published view cards in the early twentieth century, including German cards from the American News Co. Niagara Falls was a favorite subject.

Buffalo Paper and Postcard Co. Philadelphia, PA. Issued postcards in the mid-twentieth century.

Buffum, C.P. East Northfield, MA. Published postcards in the early twentieth century.

Bunting, C.M. Wilkinsburg, PA. Published view cards in the early twentieth century.

Burbank, A.S. Plymouth, MA. Publisher of postcards from the 1890s into the early twentieth century, some of the latter including Detroit Publishing Co. views and German imports obtained from the American News Company (ANC).

Burcham Paper Co. Colorado Springs, CO. Published postcards in the 1920s and 1930s, including those from the Curt Teich Co.

Burchards Studio. Denison, TX. Published postcards in the late twentieth century.

Burke, David. Binnewater, NY. Published view cards in the early twentieth century, including German imports.

Burnap, W.W. Fitchburg, MA. Published view cards in the early twentieth century, including those from the American News Co. (ANC).

Burrell, L.H. Elkhart, IN. Made RPPCs in the early twentieth century. Business sold to H. Whitneck.

Burroughs, O.F. Nassau, NY. Published view cards in the early twentieth century.

Burton & Skinner Printing and Stationery Co. / Burton & Skinner, Lithographers. St. Louis, MO. Published postcards in the early twentieth century.

Busch, F.A. Buffalo, NY. Publisher of postcards relating to the 1901 Pan-American Exposition in Buffalo, NY.

Butcher, S.D., & Son. Kearney, NE. Issued RPPCs in the early twentieth century, with many Main Streets of the Midwest.

Buxton & Skinner. St. Louis, MO. Well known lithographers, this company produced advertising and other postcards in the early twentieth century, including for the 1904 Louisiana Purchase Exposition.

B-W News Agency. Waco, TX. Published postcards in the mid-twentieth century, including cards from E.C. Kropp Co.

C

C.P.I. Washington, D.C. Issued view cards of Washington marked "published for the blind at the C.P.I. Washington, D.C."

Caldwell, M.S. Mechanicville, NY. Published view cards in the early twentieth century, including those of the Curt Teich Co.

Caldwell-Sites Co. Bristol, Roanoke, and Staunton, VA. Published postcards in the early twentieth century, including German imports.

California Art Card Co. San Francisco, CA. Publisher of postcards during the early twentieth century, including signed artists.

California Art Co. Santa Rosa and Monterey, CA. Publisher of black-and-white view cards in the early twentieth century when the firm was in Santa Rosa, later art cards when they relocated to Monterey. Most feature California subjects.

California Postcard Co. Los Angeles, CA. Early twentieth century publisher, including of cards supplied by Kropp. Some were of movie studios.

California Sales Co. San Francisco, CA. Publisher of postcards during the early twentieth century, including signed artists.

Calkins, F. Schenectady, NY. Publisher of RPPCs in the early twentieth century.

Cambridgeburg News Agency. Issued postcards in the mid-twentieth century, including from Tichnor Brothers.

Cameo Greeting Cards, Inc. Chicago, IL. Published cards in the late twentieth century, including those by Dexter Press.

Camera Shop. Woodstock, NY. Made RPPCs in the early twentieth century.

Campbell Art Company / Joseph Campbell. New York, NY. Publisher of postcards during the early twentieth century, including signed artists.

Campbell, Alf, Art Co. Elizabeth, NJ. Published postcards in the early twentieth century.

Campbell, Joseph. New York, NY; as Joseph Campbell and also as Campbell Art Co. Publisher of postcards during the early twentieth century, including signed artists.

Canedy, C.R. North Adams, MA. Published cards in the early twentieth century, including those of the Curt Teich Co.

Canfield, J.M. Willow Grove, PA. Publisher of view cards during the early twentieth century, including official cards for Willow Grove Park (although others published cards as well). Canfield sold products of various makers including Detroit Publishing.

Cantwell, T.A., & Co. Washington, D.C. Published postcards in the 1910s and 1920s, including those of the Curt Teich Co.

Cape Cod Photos. Orleans, MA. Published view cards in the late twentieth century.

Cape Shore Paper Co. South Portland, ME. Publisher of postcards during the early twentieth century, including signed artists.

Capital Engraving. Pequot Lakes, MN. Publisher of postcards during the early twentieth century, including signed artists.

Capitol News Co. Nashville, TN. Published postcards in the mid-twentieth century, including from the E.C. Kropp Co.

Capper, Arthur. Topeka, KS. Mainly a newspaper publisher, but also published art postcards during the early twentieth century, including signed artists.

Cappuyns, Pete. San Antonio, TX. Published postcards in the late twentieth century.

Cardinell, John D. San Francisco, CA. Publisher of postcards during the early twentieth century, including signed artists. Official distributor for postcards for the 1926 Sesquicentennial of American Independence.

Cardinell-Vincent Co. San Francisco, Oakland, and Los Angeles, CA (Seattle, WA, on some). Sometimes hyphenated, sometimes not. For about a decade, starting in the early twentieth century, the company published a wide selection of cards, the early ones mostly printed in Germany. The firm was the official supplier of postcards to the 1915 Panama-Pacific International Exposition in San Francisco.

Cargill Co. Grand Rapids, MI. Publishers of cards with comments and sayings accompanied by appropriate captions, suffragette cards, and advertising cards in the early twentieth century.

Carle, C.L. Ashtabula, OH. Published postcards in the 1920s and 1930s, including from the Curt Teich Co.

Caro, J.D. Juneau, AK. Published postcards in the early twentieth century, including those of the Curt Teich Co.

Carolina Card Co. Published view cards in the mid-twentieth century.

Carpenter Paper Co. Salt Lake City, UT. Early twentieth-twentieth century publisher of view cards and other subjects made by various printers.

Carpenter, L.H. Antrim, NH. Published postcards in the early twentieth century, including those imported from Germany.

Carqueville Lithographing Co. Chicago, IL. Successors to Shober & Carqueville. Printers of chromolithograph postcards in the early twentieth century until 1915.

Carroll Post Card Co. Carroll, IA. Made RPPCs in the early twentieth century and also published printed cards.

Carson-Harper Co. Denver, CO. Publisher of postcards from the 1890s through about 1915, including Pioneer-era cards and oversize cards. The Rocky Mt. Series included many subjects.

Cartagno, Bright & Gold, Printers. San Francisco, CA. Published postcards in the early twentieth century.

Cartee, C.H., & Co. Winston-Salem, NC. Distributed view cards in the early twentieth century, including those of the Curt Teich Co.

Carter & Gut. New York, NY. In the first decade of the twentieth century this firm published view cards in black and white and in color, typically of regional scenes.

Carter, A.E. San Mateo, CA. Published postcards in the early twentieth century.

Cartwright, Charles W. Chatham, MA. Published printed view cards in the late twentieth century, including some with his own photographs.

Case & Vaughan Art Co. Princeton, IL. Published postcards in the early twentieth century, including German imports.

Caulkins, Douglas. Pomona, CA. Published view cards in the mid-twentieth century.

Cawood Comic Card Co. Decatur, IL. Publisher of postcards during the early twentieth century, including signed artists.

C-B Co. Joliet, IL. Publisher of postcards during the early twentieth century, including signed artists.

CCCC. See Commercial Colortype Co., Chicago.

CCCP. Fort Scott, KS. Published postcards in the early twentieth century.

Cedar Rapids News Co. Cedar Rapids, IA. Published postcards in the early twentieth century.

Central News & Novelty Co. Phoenix, AZ. Published postcards in the mid-twentieth century, including those from the Curt Teich Co.

Central News Co. Phoenix, AZ; Akron, OH; Philadelphia, PA (main office); Tacoma, WA; Wheeling, WV. Publisher of view cards in the early twentieth century, primarily of regional scenes appropriate to the office or branch location.

Central Post Card Agency. Mount Pleasant, IA. Published postcards in the early twentieth century, including German imports.

Central Post Card Co. Fort Scott, KS. Publisher of RPPCs in the early twentieth century. The firm solicited photographs from a wide area and sent them to Chicago, where a third party printed and shipped them.

Century Post Card & Novelty Co. New York, NY. Publisher of regional view cards circa 1916–1919.

Century Post Card Co. Cleveland, OH. Publisher of regional view cards in the early twentieth century.

Chaffee & Co. Detroit, MI. Publisher of view cards in the early twentieth century, including those of Tichnor Brothers.

Chamberlain, J.N. Miami, FL; Oak Bluffs, MA. Chamberlain was a photographer and artist who began business in New England, then moved to Florida, but in the summer had an outlet in Massachusetts. His cards were printed in Germany and elsewhere, including Albertype and Curt Teich in the United States.

Champenois, F., & Co. Paris, France. Champenois was very important in the production and distribution of Art Nouveau postcards in the 1890s and early twentieth century, including many with the art of Alphonse Mucha. Although these were not distributed in the United States at the time, they are very popular with American collectors today.

Chandler's. Rocky Mount, NC. Published postcards in the 1920s and 1930s, including from the Curt Teich Co.

Chapin News Co. Hartford, CT. Published view cards in the early twentieth century, including German imports obtained from the American News Company (ANC).

Charlton, E.C., & Co. New Britain, CT; Berlin, Germany. Published view cards in the early twentieth century.

Charlton, E.P., & Co. East Los Angeles and San Francisco, CA. Publisher of cards in the early twentieth century, including views of the Lewis & Clark Exposition (Portland, 1905).

Chase, Clement. Omaha, NE. Published postcards in the early twentieth century.

Chicago Colortype Co. Chicago, IL. Printed postcards at the turn of the twentieth century, including for the 1898 Trans-Mississippi and International Exposition in Omaha.

Chicago Daily News. Chicago, IL. Newspaper publisher that also issued some black-and-white postcards in the early twentieth century.

Chicago Engraving Co. South Chicago, IL. Published postcards in the early twentieth century.

Childs, Charles R. Chicago, IL. Childs was a major producer and publisher of RPPCs, with thousands of regional subjects, many produced in quantity. "This is a real photograph...." printed in capital letters on the back of many cards.

Chilton Publishing Co. Philadelphia, PA. Large commercial publisher that also printed postcards, especially advertising cards, in the early twentieth century.

Chisholm Brothers. Portland, ME. The Chisholm company was one of New England's most important postcard publishers in the late nineteenth and early twentieth centuries, including color lithographed view cards from Germany circa 1905–1914.

Christian, Clarence. Portland, OR. Produced RPPCs of regional interest from the 1930s to the 1950s.

Christiance, H.L. San Diego, CA. Published cards in the early twentieth century, including those made by Albertype.

Cincinnati News Co. Cincinnati, OH. Publisher of regional view cards during the early twentieth century.

Cincinnati Postal Views Distributors. Cincinnati, OH. Publisher of regional view cards during the early twentieth century, including Tichnor Brothers cards.

City News Agency. Erie, PA. Issued postcards in the mid-twentieth century, including from Curt Teich and Co.

City News Agency. Rocky Mount, NC. Published postcards in the 1920s and 1930s, including from the Curt Teich Co.

Clarisse. New York, NY. Publisher of postcards during the early twentieth century, including signed artists.

Clark, C.H. West Brookfield, MA. Druggist who also published RPPCs, early twentieth century.

Clark, Frank A. East Derry, NH. Published postcards in the early twentieth century.

Clark, U.W. Danville, VA. Distributed natural-finish view cards in the mid-twentieth century.

Clarke, H.H. Oklahoma City, OK. Published postcards in the early twentieth century, including those from the Curt Teich Co.

Clemants, E.F. San Francisco, CA. Published cards in the late twentieth century, including Mike Roberts cards.

Cleveland News Co. Cleveland, OH. Publisher of regional view cards during the early twentieth century.

Cleveland Notion Co. Cleveland, OH. Published postcards in the 1920s and 1930s, including from the Curt Teich Co. Some of these had the trade style "Clenoco."

Cline, W.M. Co. Chattanooga, TN. Published modern view cards.

Clinton News Agency. Clinton, IA. Published postcards in the early twentieth century.

Clune, W.H. Los Angeles, CA. Publisher of view cards in the early twentieth century.

Cobb, Loyd M. Norwich, CT. Published postcards in the early twentieth century.

Cobb, W.F. Brunswick, ME. Published view cards in the early twentieth century.

Coburn, David Bugbee. Boston, MA. Published view cards in the early twentieth century.

Cochran, Myron J. Waverly, MA. Published postcards in the early twentieth century.

Cochrane Co. Palatka, FL. Published postcards in the early twentieth century, including cards from the Curt Teich Co.

Coffeen, Herbert A. Sheridan, WY. Publisher of monotone Western view cards and other topics in the second decade of the twentieth century, including from old images of the Custer battlefield in Montana.

Cogdell News Company. Abilene, TX. Published postcards in the mid-twentieth century.

Cohen, Jacob S., Co. Seattle, WA. Published postcards in the early twentieth century.

Cohn Brothers. Butte, MT. Published view cards in the early twentieth century, including those of the Curt Teich Co.

Cohn, Herman, News Agency. Muscatine, IA. Published postcards in the early twentieth century.

Coker, Gamble, Inc. (Gamble Coker, Inc.) Chicago, IL. Publisher of postcards during the early twentieth century, including signed artists.

Colby, Vincent V. Denver, CO. Publisher of postcards during the early twentieth century, including signed artists.

Coldeway, George. Springfield, IL. Published postcards in the early twentieth century.

Cole Book Co. Atlanta, GA. Published postcards in the early twentieth century.

Cole, F.P. Cole Farm, RI. Published postcards in the early twentieth century, including German imports.

Colesworthy Book Store. Boston, MA. Published postcards in the early twentieth century including those printed by the New England News Co.

Collier, Paul R. Plainfield, NJ. Published RPPCs in the early twentieth century.

Collins, D.F. Bloomingburg, NY. Published view cards in the early twentieth century.

Collotype Co. Elizabeth, NJ; New York City, NY. A major printing house, Collotype also printed view cards in the twentieth century, beginning about 1907 and continuing for decades afterward. Most of these were black and white.

Colonial Craftsmen. Cape May, NJ. Publisher of postcards during the early twentieth century, including signed artists.

Color Post Card Co. New York, NY. Printer of inexpensive color halftone cards, mostly views of regional interest, in the 1920s.

Colorado News Co. Denver, CO. Published postcards in the early twentieth century, including German imports through the American News Co. (ANC).

Colorado Selling Co. Denver, CO. Published postcards in the early twentieth century.

Colorcraft Art Co. Cambridge, MA. Publisher of postcards during the early twentieth century, including signed artists.

Colortype Engraving and Publishing Co. Omaha, NE. Published view cards in the early twentieth century.

Plastichrome® by COLOURPICTURE PUBLISHERS, INC., Boston 15, Mass., U.S.A.

Colourpicture Publishing, Inc. Boston and Cambridge, MA. Printer and publisher of linen and chrome cards from about 1938 through the 1960s, some later cards under the Plastichrome name.

Columbia Card Co. Portland, OR. Publisher of mainly view cards printed in Germany, circa 1910–1913.

Columbia Card Co. Washington, D.C. Published postcards in the early twentieth century, including German imports.

Columbia Publishing Co. Hollywood, CA. Publisher of postcards during the early twentieth century, including signed artists.

Comic Card Co. Minneapolis, MN. Published view cards in the early twentieth century. Saw a card with the comic logo on the back and the Minneapolis imprint on the front. Possibly affiliated with Pearson-Ullberg Co.

Comins & Cornack. Watertown, NY. Published view cards in the early twentieth century.

Commercial Art Post Card Co. New York (Brooklyn), NY. Publisher of view cards of regional interest, 1920s to the early 1930s.

Commercial Colortype Co., Chicago. Chicago, IL. This was a major printer and publisher of postcards from about 1904 to the 1920s. The company was affiliated in certain ways with the Curt Teich Co. Subjects included views, greetings, Native Americans, signed artists, and other subjects. In the 1920s advertised: "This card is produced in the Octochrome process by a photo-engraving concern that make a specialty of reproducing exterior and interior church views in their natural colors direct from photographs. Anyone desiring reproduction of this character or halftone or other plate work will receive special and prompt attention…" Produced Octochrome, Commercialchrome, and related cards, usually identified on the back by brown printing and by a serial number vertically at the lower left. Cards were sometime identified by a logotype with CCCC, with one C being for Chicago.

Commercial Photo Co. South Minneapolis, MN. Made RPPCs in the early twentieth century.

Commercial Printing House. Philadelphia, PA. Published postcards in the early twentieth century.

Commercial Sales Co. Pittsburgh, PA. Published postcards in the early twentieth century.

Commercial Studio. Lamar, CO. Issued RPPCs in the early twentieth century.

Commercialchrome Co. Cleveland, OH. Printer of color view cards in the 1910s. Midwest scenes were a specialty.

Co-Mo Co. Minneapolis, MN. Publisher of regional view postcards including some RPPCs.

Compton & Sons. St. Louis, MO. Published postcards in the early twentieth century.

Conklin, H.S. Patchogue, NY. Published view cards in the early twentieth century, including German imports.

Conover, Seely. Amsterdam, NY. Published view cards in the early twentieth century, including German imports.

Continental Art Co. Chicago, IL. Publisher of postcards during the early twentieth century, including signed artists.

Conwell, L.R., Co. New York, NY. Publisher of postcards during the early twentieth century, including signed artists.

Cook, A.T. Hyde Park, NY. Publisher of postcards during the early twentieth century, including signed artists.

Cook, H.T., Co. New York, NY. Published postcards in the early twentieth century, including of the Great White Fleet of battleships and signed artists.

Cook, L.L. Lake Mills, WI. Important large-volume publisher of regional interest RPPCs in the early twentieth century. Views included many Midwest towns.

Cook, M.A. Searsport, ME. Published postcards in the early twentieth century, including German imports through Reichner Brothers.

Coon, Walter. Canton, PA. Issued postcards in the mid-twentieth century.

Cooper, William B. Medford, NJ. Photographer and issuer of RPPCs in the early twentieth century.

Cooper's Book Store. Cleveland, TN. Published postcards in the early twentieth century.

Cooper's Photo. Great Falls, MT. Publisher of RPPCs during the early twentieth century.

Coppinger & Griel. Lancaster, PA. Publisher of postcards during the early twentieth century, including signed artists.

Corell. Titusville, PA. Photographer and maker of RPPCs in the early twentieth century.

Cornell, J.B. & J.M. New York, NY. Published postcards in the early twentieth century.

Cory Post Card Co. New York, NY. Publisher of view cards of regional interest, black and white and, later, in color, circa 1900–1912.

Cosby-Winter Co. San Francisco, CA. Published postcards in the early twentieth century.

Coster, P.R. Holland, MI. Issued RPPCs in the early twentieth century.

Cott Printing Co. Columbus, OH. Published postcards in the early twentieth century.

Cowens & Co. Denver, CO. Published postcards in the early twentieth century

Cowles & Casler. Gloversville, NY. Published view cards in the early twentieth century, including German imports.

Coyne, W.S. Ewing, NE. Made RPPCs in the early twentieth century.

Crescent Embossing Co. Plainfield, NJ. Publisher of colorfully lithographed cards by artists, patriotic subjects, and more, from the late 1890s into the early twentieth century. Many were copyrighted by Fred C. Lounsbury, the founder.

Crescent Photo Co. Minneapolis, MN. Maker of RPPCs in the early twentieth century.

Crocker, H.S., Co., Inc. San Francisco, CA. Important twentieth-century printer and publisher of view cards and other subjects, including in later years many for Disney.

Cross & Dimmitt. Portland, OR. Arthur B. Cross and Edward L. Dimmitt were photographers, printers, and publishers of RPPCs in the 1910s through the 1940s, mostly of regional scenes, and also a publisher of printed cards using their images. They issued a 20-card RPPC set, "Columbia River Highway."

Culbertson & Malcolm. Helena, MT. Published postcards in the early twentieth century.

Culbertson, S.J. Helena, MT. Published postcards in the early twentieth century, including those of the Curt Teich Co.

Cullen, Charles C., & Co. Knoxville, TN. Published postcards in the early twentieth century.

Cunningham, F.W. Liberty, ME. Photographer who issued RPPCs of regional interest.

Cupples, Samuel, Envelope Co. St. Louis, MO. Cupples was a very important producer of postcards from the late 1890s through the early twentieth century, including hold-to-light cards, Louisiana Purchase Exposition cards, and more.

Curhan Co. Gloucester, MA. Publisher of postcards during the early twentieth century, including signed artists.

Curt Teich Co. See entry under Teich, Curt.

Curtin, A.P. Helena, MT. A department store that published postcards of regional interest.

Curtis Publishing Co. Philadelphia, PA. Publisher of postcards during the early twentieth century, including signed artists such as Robert Robinson and W.L. Taylor. Best known as a publisher of magazines.

Curtis, Ashael, Photo Co. Tacoma, WA. Photographer Curtis made and published RPPCs from about 1911 to the early 1940s, emphasizing the state of Washington and regions to the north, including Alaska.

D

Dade County Newsdealers' Supply Company. Miami, FL. Published postcards in the early twentieth century.

Daferner, Charles. Galveston, TX. Published postcards in the early twentieth century, including German imports.

Dahrooge Post Card Co. San Antonio, TX. Publisher of color view cards circa 1907 to the late 1910s.

Dailey, Harry L. Parkersburg, WV. Published postcards in the 1920s and 1930s, including from the Curt Teich Co.

Dake Studio. Medford, OR. Issued RPPCs in the early twentieth century.

Damon, F.M., Curio Co. Scituate, MA. Published view cards in the early twentieth century.

Danborn, F.A. / F.A. Danborn's Variety Store. Madrid, IA. Published postcards in the early twentieth century, including those obtained from Zimmerman.

Danziger & Berman. New Haven, CT. This postcard publisher was very important in New York and New England in the first two decades of the twentieth century. Early cards were mostly German imports of very high quality, and later domestic cards were of a lower standard.

Darrough, C.H. Red Bluff, CA. Published view cards in the early twentieth century, including German imports via M. Rieder.

Dart, W.W. Belfast, NY. Published view cards in the early twentieth century, including German imports through American News Co.

Dattilo, S., & Co. New York, NY. Importers of German postcards during the early twentieth century. Typically with rust-colored printing on the back.

Daugherty, C.W. Huntington, MA. Published view cards in the early twentieth century, including German imports from the American News Company (ANC).

Davenport Post Card & Novelty Co. Davenport, IA. Published postcards in the early twentieth century, including from the Curt Teich Co.

David Lionel Press. Chicago, IL. Published "clear-vue" cards in the late twentieth century.

Davidson and Harper. Bath, NY. Published view cards in the early twentieth century including German imports from American News Co. (ANC).

Davidson Brothers. London, England; New York, NY. British publisher of lithographed cards with an office in New York. Topics included comics (including Tom Browne subjects), greetings, art, portraits, views, and more. Cards resembling RPPCs were made in quantity of view subjects, but not with sharp detail; many were labeled "Real Photographic Series."

Davie Printing Co. Nashville, TN. Published postcards in the early twentieth century, including those imported from Germany.

Davis News Co. Burlington, NC. Distributed view cards in the mid-twentieth century, including those of the Curt Teich Co.

Davis, A.M., & Co. London, England; Boston, MA. Producer and publisher of art cards, including greetings, artist-signed, etc., circa 1907–1916.

Davis, E.S. Seattle, WA. Published view cards in the early twentieth century.

Davis, J.P. Pascoag, RI. Published postcards in the early twentieth century, including cards from Germany obtained through the American News Co. (ANC).

Davis, R.S. Manitou, CO. Published postcards in the 1920s and 1930s, including those from the Curt Teich Co.

Dayton, C.S. Danielson, CT. Published view cards in the early twentieth century, including German imports by the American News Company (ANC).

De Mauro, P. New York, NY. Published postcards in the early twentieth century.

De Tartas Studios. Asbury Park and Long Branch, NJ. Made RPPCs in the early twentieth century.

Dean Color Service. Glens Falls, NY. Published view cards in the late twentieth century including Dexter Press cards.

Dean, Charles E. Arapaho, NE. Published view cards in the early twentieth century.

Deeks, H.C., Co. Paterson, NJ. Published the "Puzzle Post Card" with two different subjects if the image was viewed from different angles.

Deep South Specialties, Inc. Jackson, MS. Published postcards in the early twentieth century, including cards from H.S. Crocker Co., Inc.

deGroff, Edward. Sitka, AK. Published postcards in the early twentieth century, including those from ANC.

DeGroot & Drilsma. Guthrie, OK. Published postcards in the early twentieth century, including German imports obtained through the American News Co. (ANC).

Delaney, John T. Alexandria Bay, NY. Published view cards in the early twentieth century.

Denney, Oz, Advertising. St. Petersburg, FL. Published postcards in the late twentieth century, including cards from Dexter Press.

Denver Lithographing Co. Denver, CO. Published postcards in the early twentieth century.

Des Moines Postal Card Co. Des Moines, IA. Published postcards in the early twentieth century.

Detroit News Co. Detroit, MI. Published view cards in the early twentieth century, including German imports obtained from the American News Company (ANC).

Detroit Publishing Co. Detroit, MI. The Detroit Photographic Co., later known as the Detroit Publishing Co., was among the most important American printers and publishers of postcards. In 1897 the company licensed a Swiss photochrome lithographic process that Detroit later named Phostint. These color cards have excellent detail and somewhat muted, blended colors, quite unlike the color lithographed cards produced in Germany in the early twentieth century. William Henry Jackson, well-known photographer of the American West, was a partner and contributed many of his negatives. In the early twentieth century Detroit gathered thousands of photographs of local and regional views from all parts of the country, including small towns, creating an inventory unmatched by any other American postcard firm except the Curt Teich Co. Detroit Publishing Co. became bankrupt in 1924 and entered receivership, but they continued printing cards under contract until about 1932. Cards of this firm have been a focus of interest for many collectors and several researchers. The numbering system was sequential, but earlier numbers were sometimes used for later reprints, making it impossible for certain cards to be dated with accuracy. In general:

- 1898: Nos. F–1 to F–92, Detroit Photochrom Co. imprint. The first title: "Santa Barbara Mission — In the Garden."

- 1899: G–1 to G–35

- 1899 and 1900: 1 to 522, Detroit Photographic Co.

- 1901: 5000 to 5999, including reprints of earlier images. A few cards in this range were printed in Switzerland and have bright red titles on the face.

- 1902: 6000 to 6999. A few cards in this range were printed in Switzerland and have bright red titles on the face.

- 1903: 7000 to 7999

- 1904 and 1905: 9000 to 8999. After 8065 all were made slightly larger, to standard size.

- 1905 and 1906: 9000 to 9999

- 1905 to 1907: Images of art numbered 60000 to 60557

- 1906 and 1907: 10000 to 10999 "Phostint" imprint introduced.

- 1907: 14000 to 14751. Various subjects including old sketches and cartoons, art, portraits, etc.

- 1907: 14800 to 14999: Views

- 1908 and 1909: 12000 to 12999

- 1909 and 1910: 13000 to 13999

- 1910 to 1913: 70000 to 70999

- 1913 to 1919: 71000 to 71999. Printing date added on the back beginning in 1915.

- 1918 to 1932: 72000 to 72275

- Other sequences: Series 50000 to 59065, images published in various years, were produced as postcards and also as prints. Series 79000 to 79999, views made for other publishers, 1910 onward. Series 81000 to 81999 and 82,000 to 82,149, views for other publishers. H1199 to H4160 printed for Fred Harvey (operated restaurants and newsstands at railroad stations, etc.), 1901 to 1932.

Detweiler, I.C. Hatfield, PA. Published postcards in the early twentieth century, including German imports.

Devlin, B., & Co. Monticello, IA. Published postcards in the early twentieth century, including German imports.

Devlin, J.H. Valley Falls, RI. Published postcards in the early twentieth century, including German imports through ANC.

Dexter Photo Co. / J.C. Dexter Photo Co. Hartford, CT. Issued RPPCs in the early twentieth century.

Dexter, Thomas, Press / Dexter Press, Inc. West Nyack, NY. Dexter was a large-volume producer of view and other cards, linen and chrome.

Dezell, R.B. Canton, NY. Published postcards in the early twentieth century.

Dickerman, H.A., & Son. Taunton, MA. Publisher of regional view cards from circa 1907 to 1936.

Dickolph, J. Red Bank, NJ. Importer and publisher of German view cards, regional topics, in the first decade of the twentieth century.

Dietsche, A.C. Detroit, MI. Published view cards in the early twentieth century, including German imports.

Dimock & Sullivan. Sayre, PA. Publisher of view cards in the early twentieth century, including with the CCCC imprint.

Dio, Henry. Bristol, RI. Published postcards in the early twentieth century.

Dittmeyer, Walter E. Harper's Ferry, WV. Published view cards in the early twentieth century.

Dixie News Co. Charlotte, NC. Published postcards in the 1920s and 1930s, including those from Tichnor Brothers.

Dogwood Souvenirs. Palestine, TX. Published postcards in the late twentieth century.

Doherty, Dr. Neil. Holyoke, MA. Published postcards in the late twentieth century, including cards from Dexter Press, some featuring his own photography.

Dolice, Leon Louis. New York, NY. Publisher of postcards with etchings and art views of regional subjects, starting about 1920.

Donnelley, R.R., & Sons. Chicago, IL. Publisher of postcards, but primarily one of America's largest commercial printers, during the early twentieth century, including signed artists.

Donnelly, Reuben H., Corp. Chicago, IL. A subsidiary of the gigantic R.R. Donnelly & Sons publishing firm. Official publisher of postcards for the 1933 Century of Progress Exposition.

Doolittle & Kulling, Inc. Philadelphia, PA. Publisher of greeting and regional view cards circa 1908–1910.

Dorman Brothers. Rocky Ford, CO. Published RPPCs and view cards and other cards in the early twentieth century.

Dorsheimer, H.K. Elizabethtown, PA. Issued postcards in the mid-twentieth century, including those from Curt Teich Co.

Doubleday & Gustin / Doubleday. Pendleton, OR. Issued copyrighted "Wild West" RPPCs in the 1910s. Some are simply imprinted "Doubleday."

Doubleday-Foster Photo Co., Inc. Chicago, IL. Also known as D.F.P. Co., Inc. Publisher of postcards of rodeos, Western scenes, performers, etc., many RPPCs, others printed by the Curt Teich Co., etc.

Doucet Photo Co. Milton, MA. Produced RPPCs in the early twentieth century.

Dougherty, Frank. Albany, NY. Published postcards in the early twentieth century.

Douglas Publishing Co. Buffalo, NY. Published postcards in the early twentieth century.

Douglass Postcard Co. / Douglass Post Card & Machine Co. / Douglass Post Card Co. Philadelphia, PA. Published view cards, including of the San Francisco fire in 1906; undivided back, cards of signed artists, and other issues. Also published lithographic cards on heavy stock for dispensing in arcade machines. Some had postcard backs. Comic, risqué, etc., subjects popular in the first decade of the twentieth century.

Downham, Photographer. McDonald, PA. Produced RPPCs during the early twentieth century.

Downs, F.M., Co. Lincoln, NE. Published view cards in the early twentieth century, including German imports.

Draper, Frank V., Co. Des Moines, IA. Published postcards in the early twentieth century.

Drew, H. & W.B., Company. Jacksonville, FL. Published postcards in the early twentieth century, including cards imprinted "Florida Souvenir Post Card." Certain cards were from the Curt Teich Co.

Drysdale Co. Chicago, IL. Publisher of postcards during the early twentieth century, including signed artists.

Duclos Studio / Duclos Portrait Studio. Manchester, NH. Published RPPCs in the early twentieth century.

Duffy. Published postcards in the early twentieth century, including from Tichnor Brothers.

Duke & Ayres Nickel Store. Published postcards in the early twentieth century.

Dunbar & Williams. Paonia, CO. Published postcards in the early twentieth century, including German imports from the American News Co. (ANC).

Dunn Stationery and Supply Co. Titusville, PA. Issued postcards in the mid-twentieth century, including cards from the Curt Teich Co.

Durham Book and Stationery Co. Durham, NC. Published postcards in the 1920s and 1930s, including from the Curt Teich Co.

Dury, G.C., and Co. Nashville, TN. Published postcards in the early twentieth century, including Germany imports obtained from PCK.

Dutcher, H.P. Nyack, NY. Maker of RPPCs, including advertising cards, in the early twentieth century.

Dutton, E.P., & Co. New York, NY. This well-known book publisher also issued greeting and other postcards in the early twentieth century, mostly made in Europe.

Duval & Co. / Duval News Co. Jacksonville, FL. Similar to other "news companies," Duval distributed newspapers, magazines, and other printed material. Beginning in the first decade of the twentieth century, Duval published postcards emphasizing regional views, including cards from the Curt Teich Co.

Dye, M.E. Milton, IA. Published postcards in the early twentieth century.

E

E.P.J. Co. See Edward P. Judd Co. under J.

Eagle Post Card View Co. / Eagle Post Card Co. New York, NY. Publisher of inexpensive monotone and color cards, mostly of regional views.

Eagle, S.P. West Yellowstone, MT. Published postcards in the 1920s and 1930s, including from the Curt Teich Co.

Eastern Illustrating Co. / Eastern Illustrating and Publishing Co. Belfast, ME; Orange, MA; New London, NH. The Eastern Illustrating Co. (EIC; sometimes called Eastern Illustrating & Publishing Co.), based in Belfast, ME, with a factory in the nearby town of Camden, was the leading producer of these and created many different subjects. This studio, as it called itself, was founded in 1908 by Rudolph Herman Cassens, whose "Cassens" name appears on the face of some early cards. An EIC vehicle (there were several), with the company's name lettered on the sides, was occasionally captured in views of general stores and the like. EIC's trade was nearly completely in New England and some areas of eastern New York. At one time the company claimed to be the largest manufacturer of "photo cards" in the United States, which may have been true, for not many competitors were as prolific. Accordingly, with some effort it is possible to form an extensive collection of different towns in the Northeast, usually showing the Main Street or, more desirably, a general store or other place of business. EIC produced RPPCs into the 1950s, comprising over 30,000 different ones. Nearly all are well focused and well composed. Clearly, expert photographers were at work. Some EIC cards were issued with an Orange, MA, address (typically as Eastern Illustrating and Publishing Co.) Later, the company relocated to New London, NH, and published cards, including those supplied by the Dexter Press. R. Brewster Harding, a Maine collector and dealer, acquired many negatives, unsold cards, and other effects after the firm ceased operations and in 1982 created a book, *Roadside New England 1900–1955*.

Eastern News Co. Portland, ME. Publisher of view cards in the early twentieth century.

Eastman's Studio. Susanville, CA. Published chrome cards in the late twentieth century.

Eber, J.F. South Framingham, MA. Published view cards in the early twentieth century, including German imports.

Ebers, Paul. San Antonio, TX. Published postcards in the early twentieth century.

Ebers-White Co. San Antonio, TX. Published postcards in the early twentieth century, including German imports.

Eckert Litho. Co. Washington, D.C. Published postcards in the early twentieth century.

Economy Distributors, Inc. Worcester, MA. Published view cards in the mid-twentieth century.

Eddy, E.C. Distributor of postcards in the early twentieth century, including those made by Albertype.

Eddy's Studio. Southern Pines, NC. Published postcards in the early twentieth century.

Edney's Studio. Itasca, TX. Published postcards in the late twentieth century, including cards from Dexter Press.

Edwards & Deutsch Litho. Co. Chicago, IL. Publisher of postcards during the early twentieth century, including signed artists.

Edwards Post Card Co. Huntingdon, PA. Made RPPCs in the early twentieth century.

Egbert Photo Post Card Co. Atlantic, IA. Publisher of RPPCs in the early twentieth century.

Eggers-O'Flyng Co. Omaha, NE. Published postcards in the early twentieth century.

Eggleston, Lorin G. Fullerton, NY. A printer and publisher of view cards in the early twentieth century.

Eils Brothers. Pittsburgh, PA. Maker of RPPCs, marked "Photo Postals" on the back. Early twentieth century.

Eismann, Theodor. New York City, NY; Leipzig, Germany. From about 1908 to 1914 the New York office imported many fine German cards and had others printed in America. The "Th.E.L. Theochrome" imprint was used on some German issues.

Eldredge, W.F. Norwich, NY. Published view cards in the early twentieth century, including German imports by PCK (Paul C. Koeber & Co.).

Elite Post Card Co. Kansas City, MO. Publisher of view cards of regional interest in the early twentieth century, including many by Curt Teich Co.

Elkus, Edward. Los Angeles, CA. Published postcards in the early twentieth century.

Ellis, J. Boyd / Clifford Ellis. Arlington, WA. From 1920s to 1940s this father-and-son team produced about 5,000 RPPC subjects.

Elm City Post Card Co. New Haven, CT. Publisher of view cards in the early twentieth century.

Elson, A.W., & Co. Belmont, MA. Maker of art and other postcards, some of which were slightly smaller than regular size. Active in the early twentieth century.

Emerson, William A. Worcester, MA. Published Emerson's Old-Time Souvenir Postcards in the early twentieth century. These were printed in a sepia color.

Empire Art Co. Chicago, IL. Published postcards in the early twentieth century, including those of the Curt Teich Co.

Empire Gallery. Canton, OH. Published RPPCs in the early twentieth century.

Empire Publishing & Post Card Co. New York, NY. Published postcards in the early twentieth century.

Eno & Matteson. San Diego, CA. Publisher of view cards in the early twentieth century, including those of the Curt Teich Co.

Epstein, Charles, Co. Houston, TX. Published postcards in the mid-twentieth century, including cards from Tichnor Brothers.

Eskenasy, Paul. Kansas City, MO. Published view cards in the early twentieth century.

Es-N-Len Photos. Aurora, IL. Published view cards in the late twentieth century, including Mike Roberts cards.

Ess & Ess Photo Co. New York, NY. Active from the first decade of the twentieth century continuing through the 1920s. Published many view cards, including German imports in the early years.

Essinger & Cook. Nahant, MA. Publisher of view cards in the early twentieth century.

Etter, Samuel S. Published postcards in the mid-twentieth century, including from the Curt Teich Co.

Ettlinger, Max, & Co. London, England; New York City, NY. From about 1901 to 1916 the firm published a wide variety of cards, including hand-tinted RPPCs, printed art cards, and more, under such designations as Royal Series and, for the RPPCs, Lamanet, Photolet, and Photocolour.

Etz Studio & Camera Shop. Sweetwater, TX. Published postcards in the late twentieth century, including cards from Dexter Press.

Eureka Postcard Manufacturing Co. Wilmington, DE. Distributed postcards in the early twentieth century.

European Post Card Co. New York, NY. Publisher in the 1920s of views and other subjects.

Evans, J.K. Bloomingburg, NY. Published view cards in the early twentieth century.

Evans, Wilbur, Co. Cleveland, OH. Published postcards in the late twentieth century.

Evening and Sunday Star. Washington, D.C. Newspaper that issued cards imprinted "Souvenir postal card of Greater Washington, D.C." in the first decade of the twentieth century.

Exhibit Supply Co. Chicago, IL. Large-volume printer of cards on heavy stock for dispensing in arcade machines. Some cards of the 1920s have postcard backs but were not often mailed.

Exposition Publishing Co. San Francisco, CA. Operated by the Edward H. Mitchell Co. under license from the board of 1915 Panama-Pacific International Exposition. Issued postcards relating to the event.

F

F.E.C. News Co. West Palm Beach, FL. Published postcards in the mid-twentieth century, including cards from E.C. Kropp Co.

Faber, John T. Milwaukee, WI. Publisher of color halftone lithographed view cards of regional interest, including German imports.

Fagard, S.C. Niagara Falls, NY. Publisher of view cards, with Niagara Falls being the prime subject, in the first decade of the twentieth century.

Fairbanks & Son. MA. Published view cards in the early twentieth century, including Massachusetts scenes.

Fairbanks Card Co. Brookline and Holliston, MA. Publisher of view cards, late twentieth century.

Fairchild, A. Allen. Norfolk, VA. Published postcards in the early twentieth century.

Fairman Co. Cincinnati, OH; New York, NY. Publisher of postcards during the early twentieth century, including signed artists.

Farnham, Mrs. A.L. Angola, NY. Published view cards in the early twentieth century, including those from Leighton & Valentine.

Farwest Lithograph & Printing Co. Seattle, WA. Published postcards in the mid-twentieth century.

Faulk, D.W. Coatesville, PA. "Artistic photographer" who issued RPPCs in the early twentieth century.

Federal Engraving & Publishing Co. Boston, MA. Federal was a minor printer and publisher of view cards, typically of regional subjects, in the first decade of the twentieth century.

Feicke-Desch Printing Co. Cincinnati, OH. Printed and published view cards in the early twentieth century.

Fenberg, M. Cleveland, OH. Publisher of view cards in the early twentieth century.

Fergason Post Card Co. Waterloo, IA. Published postcards in the early twentieth century.

Festner, F.J. Phoenix, AZ. Published view cards in the late twentieth century.

Fetterly & Loree. Bound Brook, NJ. Publisher of postcards, including German imports via American News Co. (ANC).

Fine Arts Press. San Francisco, CA. Published postcards in the early twentieth century.

Finkelstein, H., & Son. New York, NY. Publisher of postcards, including some with American Art Post Card Co. imprint. Many were printed by the Curt Teich Co.

Finkenrath, Paul. Berlin, Germany. From about 1901 to 1910, Paul Finkenrath (often noted as PFB) produced many art and related cards for export to America.

Finn, William J. Boston, MA. Published postcards in the early twentieth century.

Finney, Ralph. New York, NY. Published postcards in the early twentieth century

Fish, Henry J., Advertising. Chicago, IL. Published postcards in the 1900s and 1910s, including of Native Americans.

Fisher and Co. Deadwood, SD. Distributors of postcards in the early twentieth century, including German imports.

Fisher, Charles F. Ashtabula, OH. Publisher of view cards in the early twentieth century, including some with the CCCC imprint.

Fisher, Elliott. Published view cards in the mid-twentieth century.

$5 Photo Co. Canton, NY. Dwight Church, a professional photographer, produced RPPCs beginning in 1933, continuing for years afterward. Most subjects were of regional interest. He died in 1973.

Flagler Fotoshop. Homestead, FL. Published postcards in the mid-twentieth century, including cards from Tichnor Brothers.

Flanagan Printing Co., Inc. Hendersonville, NC. Published view cards in the early twentieth century.

Fleetwood. Cheyenne, WY. Published postcards for collectors in the late twentieth century.

Fletcher & Co. Orleans, VT. In the second and third decades of the twentieth century Fletcher issued many RPPC cards, often defining landscape, Main Street, and related scenes of various towns, some quite small, with Vermont and New Hampshire being particular specialties. Those showing commercial scenes are most desired as they typically have exquisite details.

Flieg, W. Torrington, CT. Published RPPCs in the early twentieth century.

Florida Souvenir Co. St. Augustine, FL. Published postcards in the mid-twentieth century, including cards from E.C. Kropp Co.

Florida Speaks Corp. St. Petersburg, FL. Published postcards in the late twentieth century, including cards from Dexter Press.

Fluke, C.E. Chariton, IA. Sold view cards in the early twentieth century, including German imports.

Foltz Photographic Postals. Savannah, GA. Made RPPCs in the early twentieth century.

Foote, H.P. Canton Center, CT. Published view cards in the early twentieth century.

Forbes "The Kodak Man." Greenfield, MA. Published view cards in the early twentieth century, including German imports.

Fort Madison News Agency. Fort Madison, IA. Published postcards in the early twentieth century.

Fort Myers Studio Supply. Fort Myers, FL. Published postcards in the late twentieth century, including cards from Dexter Press.

Fort Wayne Printing Co. Fort Wayne, IN. Printed and published cards in the mid-twentieth century.

Forward's Color Productions, Inc. Manchester and Arlington, VT. Publisher of postcards during the early twentieth century, including signed artists and cards from E.C. Kropp Co.

Foster & Reynolds. Washington, D.C.; New York, NY. Publisher view cards of the region early in the twentieth century, later under the B.S. Reynolds imprint (see listing).

Foster, L.A., Photo Co. Glendive, MT; Kewanee, IL. Foster produced Main Street and other RPPC views in the early twentieth century.

Foster, Nathan H. Beverly, MA. Published postcards in the early twentieth century, including cards from the Curt Teich Co.

Fotofolio. New York, NY. Published portrait, art, and other cards, late twentieth century.

Francis, William M. Gloucester, MA. Published view cards in the late twentieth century, including those of the Plastichrome brand.

Frange, William. New York, NY. Made RPPCs in the mid-twentieth century.

Frank Book Printing Co. New York, NY. Publisher of postcards during the early twentieth century, including signed artists.

Frank, Abe. Austin, TX. Published postcards in the early twentieth century, including those of the Curt Teich Co.

Franklin Post Card Co. Chicago, IL. Publisher of many view cards, mainly German imports, in the first and second decades of the twentieth century.

Franklin's Studio. Gowanda, NY. Published view cards in the early twentieth century, including German imports.

Frasch, O.E. Seattle, WA. Published postcards in the early twentieth century.

Frasher's, Inc. / Frasher's Foto Co. Pomona, CA. Publisher of printed as well as RPPC cards, often of Western views, from the 1920s into the 1950s. Some glossy black-and-white views were in imitation of RPPCs.

Frederickson Co. Chicago, IL. Publisher of postcards during the early twentieth century, including signed artists.

Freede, W.J. Corpus Christi, TX. Published postcards in the early twentieth century, including those obtained from the H.H. Hamm Co.

Freeman Studios. Berrien Springs, MI. Published view cards in the late twentieth century.

Freeman, Jack, Inc. Longport, NJ. Published view cards in the late twentieth century, including Curt Teich Co. cards.

Freese, Mrs. John F. East Walpole, MA. Published view cards in the early twentieth century.

French, W.F. Milford, NH. Published postcards in the early twentieth century, including those imported from Austria.

Freter Brothers. Bridgeport, OH. Makers of RPPCs. "Famous Post Cards Made at Bridgeport, Ohio."

Frey Wholesale Postcard Co. Dallas, TX. Published postcards in the early twentieth century, including those of the Curt Teich Co.

Frey, E., & Co. New York, NY. Publisher of many view cards, mostly with East Coast subjects. Published a set of 20 cards for the 1904 Louisiana Purchase Exposition.

Fried, Julius. Butte, MT. Trading as "Julius Fried, Importer & Publisher." Published postcards in the early twentieth century, including cards imported from Germany.

Frye & Smith. San Diego, CA. Publisher of postcards during the early twentieth century, including signed artists.

Fryklund, Oscar. White River, SD. Published RPPCs in the early twentieth century, including of Native Americans.

Fullerton, Henry. Westfield, NJ. Published view cards in the late twentieth century, including those made by Dexter Press.

G

Gabriel, Sam. New York, NY. Publisher of postcards during the early twentieth century, including signed artists.

Gabriel-Mayerfeld Co. San Francisco, CA. Published postcards in the early twentieth century.

Galveston Wholesale News Co. Galveston, TX. Published postcards in the mid-twentieth century, including cards from Tichnor Brothers.

Garcia, Lawrence C. Lubbock, TX. Published postcards in the late twentieth century, including cards from Dexter Press.

Gardner, J.A., Importing Co. Tyrone, PA. Published postcards in the mid-twentieth century, including from the Curt Teich Co.

Gardner, Marshall. Nantucket, MA. Publisher of many black-and-white view cards printed from photographs he had taken. Most were of regional interest.

Gardner-Thompson Co. Los Angeles, CA. Published view cards in the mid-twentieth century.

Gardston Variety Store. IA. Published postcards in the early twentieth century.

Garraway Co. Rutherford, NJ. Maker of RPPCs cards for many stores and other outlets.

Garrison Toy & Novelty Co. Washington, D.C. Published postcards in the 1910s and 1920s, including those from E.C. Kropp Co.

Garrison, W.B. Published postcards in the early twentieth century.

Gartner & Bender. Chicago, IL. Publisher of many art cards. including greetings, comics, and likable characters, including Kewpie Angel and Dolly Dimples.

Garver Brothers. Winfield, KS. Published view cards in the early twentieth century.

Gatchel & Manning. Philadelphia, PA. Published postcards in the early twentieth century.

Gayden Brothers. Charleston and Columbia, SC. Published postcards in the early twentieth century, including those of the Curt Teich Co.

Gazette Publishing Co. Gastonia, NC. Published view cards in the mid-twentieth century, including those of the Curt Teich Co.

Gee, W.C. Atlantic City, NJ. Published postcards in the early twentieth century.

Gem City Postcard Co. Erie, PA. Issued postcards in the mid-twentieth century, including from the Curt Teich Co.

Gennawey, George H. Rocky Point, RI. Published postcards in the 1920s and 1930s, including those from Tichnor Brothers.

Genuine Photo Co. New York (Staten Island), NY. This firm made RPPC cards of regional interest, typically color tinted by hand.

George, P.A., & Co. Ronceverte, WV. Published postcards in the 1920s and 1930s, including from the Curt Teich Co.

Georgia News Co. Atlanta, GA. Distributor of many cards, including German imports, beginning about 1908. Some of these were acquired from the American News Co.

Gerlach, Barklow Co. Joliet, IL. Publisher of postcards during the early twentieth century, including signed artists.

German Novelty Co. Boston, MA. Published postcards in the early twentieth century.

German-American Novelty Art Co. New York, NY. Importer of view, artist-signed, and other cards from Germany, many of which were very attractive.

German-American Novelty Co. St. Louis, MO. Published postcards in the early twentieth century.

German-American Post Card Co. Cleveland, OH; New York, NY; Chicago, IL; Leipzig, Germany. Published postcards in the early twentieth century.

German-American Postcard Manufacturing Co. New York, NY. Publisher primarily of view cards of regional subjects. Early twentieth century.

Gerson Brothers. Chicago, IL. Published postcards in the early twentieth century.

Gerwig, H.L. South Bend, WA. Published view cards in the early twentieth century, including German imports.

Gibb, W.A. Bristol, CT. Published postcards in the early twentieth century.

Gibson Art Co. Cincinnati, OH. Publisher of postcards during the early twentieth century, including signed artists, but primarily of greeting cards.

Gibson Merchandise Co. St. Louis, MO. Published postcards in the mid-twentieth century, including those by the Curt Teich Co.

Gies & Co. Buffalo, NY. Published postcards in the early twentieth century.

Gifford, Benjamin Arthur. Portland and The Dalles, OR. Photographer and maker of RPPCs. His images were also used on printed cards.

Gildersleeve Studio. Huntington, NY. Published view cards in the early twentieth century.

Gill, J.K., Co. Portland, OR. Published postcards in the early twentieth century.

Gillett Post Card Co. Lebanon Springs, NY. Publisher of RPPCs, including for the nearby Mt. Lebanon Shaker village, in the early twentieth century.

Gillies' Sons, D. Wakefield, RI. Published postcards in the early twentieth century.

Gillin Printing Co. New York, NY. Published postcards in the early twentieth century.

Gilpin Publishing Co. Colorado Springs, CO. Published including of Native Americans, some of which were printed by the Meriden Gravure Co.

Givens, J.D. San Francisco, CA. Published RPPCs and other postcards in the early twentieth century.

Glasier, Herbert E., & Co. Boston, MA. Photographer and maker of RPPCs for various distributors. On the back, the stamp box typically is made up by repeating the words TRU VALU.

Glass & Prudhomme Co. Portland, OR. Published postcards in the early twentieth century.

Gleason, Fred C. Warren, NH. Published postcards in the early twentieth century, including those made in Germany.

Glenmere Co. Lynn, MA. Published view cards in the early twentieth century.

Globe Novelty Co. Los Angeles, CA. Published postcards in the early twentieth century.

Globe Photo. Jamestown, NY. Published RPPCs in the early twentieth century.

Globe Stamp Co. Stamford, CT. Published view cards in the early twentieth century.

Goeggel & Weidner. San Francisco, CA. Partners William Goeggel and Charles Weidner (see separate listing under W) issued 111 numbered postcards in 1903, of regional scenes.

Goerke, Curt. Published postcards in the 1920s and 1930s, including from the E.C. Kropp Co. Certain of his cards featured an icon titled "Balanced Rock," an attraction in Colorado Springs in Garden of the Gods.

Golden West. Long Beach, CA. Publisher of view cards in the mid-twentieth century. Some images were copyrighted by George E. Watson (whose GW initials were the same as used by the firm).

Goldsmith, Charles W. Chicago, IL. Sales agent for 1893 World's Columbian Exposition postcards printed by the American Lithographic Co.

Good Office Supply Co., The. Tiffin, OH. Published postcards in the 1920s and 1930s, including from the Curt Teich Co.

Goodridge Galleries. Boston, MA. Published postcards in the early twentieth century including art views of scenes.

Goodridge, L.T., & Co. Corning, NY. Published view cards in the early twentieth century, including German imports.

Goodwin, C.W. North Berwick, ME. Published postcards in the early twentieth century, including German imports.

Gordon, J.C. San Jose, CA. Commercial photographer who issued RPPCs in the early twentieth century.

Gottschalk, Dreyfuss & Davis. New York, NY. Publisher of German art cards with greetings, sentiments, etc., in the early twentieth century.

Gough Photo Services. Tulsa, OK. Published postcards in the mid-twentieth century, including postcards from Dexter Press.

Gove Photo Shop. Middlebury, VT. Published RPPCs in the early twentieth century.

Graf, Fred, Engraving Co. St. Louis, MO. Published postcards in the early twentieth century.

Graham, Charles R., Co. Springfield, IL. Issued postcards circa the 1920s and 1930s, including those of the Curt Teich Co.

Graham, John W. & Co. Spokane, WA. Published view cards in the mid-twentieth century.

Graham-Ilger Co. Mount Vernon, OH. Published postcards in the 1920s and 1930s, including from the Curt Teich Co.

Gramatan Art Co., Inc. Mount Vernon, NY. Published postcards in the late twentieth century.

Graphic Facts of America. Alamogordo, NM. Published postcards in the mid-twentieth century.

Graphic Postcard Co. New York, NY. Publisher of postcards during the early twentieth century, including signed artists.

Graves, George S. Springfield, MA; Harpswell and West Harpswell, ME. Photographer who published printed view cards using his images of regional subjects. Some printed cards were issued under the title of "Photo-Ty Post Card."

Gray & Thompson. Chapel Hill, NC. Distributed "natural-finish" view cards in the mid-twentieth century.

Gray News Co. Salt Lake City, UT. Published postcards in the early twentieth century, including from the Curt Teich Co.

Gray, D.E. Greeley, CO. Published postcards in the early twentieth century.

Graycraft Card Co. Danville, VA. Printed and published view cards in the mid-twentieth century.

Great Falls Kwality Co. Great Falls, MT. Published postcards in the early twentieth century, including those of the Curt Teich Co. Affiliated with the Charles E. Morris Co. of the same city.

Great Western Post Card & Novelty Co. Denver, CO. Publisher of view cards including German imports, 1900s and 1910s.

Greeley Printery of St. Louis. St. Louis, MO. Printer and publisher of postcards, various national subjects, in the early twentieth century.

Green Mountain Card Co. White River Junction, VT. Publisher of regional view cards in the early twentieth century, especially in the 1910s decade. Some pre–1915 cards were German imports. Some were issued in runs, such as the "Vermont State Fair Series."

Green's News Bazar. Peoria, IL. Publisher of view cards, including German imports, in the early twentieth century.

Greenberg, George & Son. Catskill, NY. Published view cards in the mid-twentieth century.

Greene Post Card Co. Camp Lewis, WA. Published view cards in the early twentieth century, including those from Albertype.

Greenman, A.A. Kingston, RI. Published postcards in the early twentieth century, including cards imported from Germany.

Greenwood Bookshop. Wilmington, DE. Publisher of postcards during the early twentieth century, including signed artists.

Greeting Card Manufacturing Co. New York, NY. Issued postcards in the early twentieth century.

Griffiths, C.A. Bellingham, WA. Published view cards in the early twentieth century.

Grimison, W.A. & Son. Huntingdon, PA. Published postcards in the mid-twentieth century, including from the Curt Teich Co.

Grimm, S.J. Published view cards in the early twentieth century.

Grogan Photo System, Inc. Milwaukee, WI. Maker of view cards of resorts, etc., including with a glossy finish in imitation of RPPCs. Did a nationwide business.

Grombach-Faisans Co., Ltd. New Orleans, LA. Published postcards in the early twentieth century, including German imports.

Gross, Edward. New York, NY. Publisher of books, also of postcards, including comic and artist-signed, such as the work of Rose O'Neill and C.H. Twelvetrees. Early twentieth century.

Grout, J.F. Rocky Point, RI. Published postcards in the early twentieth century, including German cards from ANC.

Guinnaud, Albert. White Sulphur Springs, WV. Published postcards in the 1920s and 1930s, including from the Curt Teich Co.

Gulf Coast Card Co., Inc. St. Petersburg, FL. Published postcards in the mid-twentieth century, including cards from the Curt Teich Co.

Gulf Stream Card & Distributing Co. Miami, FL. Published postcards in the late twentieth century, including Curt Teich cards.

Gulfport Printing Co. Gulfport, MS. Publisher of view and other cards, regionally important in the 1920s.

Gut & Steers. New York, NY. Publisher of view cards in the 1910s. Some are marked Photochrome or Polychrome.

Gutmann & Gutmann. New York, NY. Publisher of postcards during the early twentieth century, including signed artists.

H

Haenlein Brothers. Columbus, OH. Publishers of view cards, including those by Curt Teich Co., in the early twentieth century.

Hackney & Moale Co. Asheville, NC. Distributor of postcards in the early twentieth century, including German imports.

Hagar, Fred D. Peabody, MA. Produced RPPCs in the early twentieth century, and his name was often embossed rather than printed on the cards.

Hagelburg, Wolf. Berlin, Germany; New York, NY. Maker and publisher of color lithographed art cards, including hold-to-light cards. Early twentieth century.

Hagemeister, H., Co. New York, NY. Publisher of monotone and colored view cards printed in Germany. Active in the early twentieth century.

Hahn, Albert. New York, NY. Publisher of view cards printed in Germany. Scenes of New York state were a specialty. Active in the early twentieth century.

Hahn & Roberts. Utica, NY. Publisher of view cards in the late twentieth century.

Hahn, Harold, Co., Inc. New Haven, CT. Distributor of postcards, including from Metrocraft and the Curt Teich Co., mid- and late twentieth century.

Hale, Cushman & Flint. Boston, MA. Publisher of postcards during the early twentieth century, including signed artists.

Hale, W.B. Williamsville, MA. Published view cards in the early twentieth century, including German imports.

Hall Brothers. Kansas City, MO. Predecessor to the famous Hallmark Company. Published postcards in the early twentieth century.

Hall, George P., & Son. New York, NY. Publisher of marine and regional topics on postcards in the early twentieth century.

Hall, Ross. Sandpoint, ID. Issuer of RPPCs beginning in the late 1930s.

Hallam & Vesty. Alexandria Bay, NY. Published view cards in the mid-twentieth century, including those of the Curt Teich Co.

Hambro Novelty Co. New York, NY. Distributor of postcards, mid-twentieth century, including those by Tichnor Brothers.

Hamilton, J.M. Monmouth, IL. Published postcards in the early twentieth century, including German imports.

Hamlin & Moskowitz. New York, NY. Publishers of view cards, mostly German imports, in the early twentieth century, with many Coney Island, NY, subjects.

Hamm, Henry H. Erie, PA; Toledo, OH. Publisher of many regional view cards in the early twentieth century. A distinctive ham-shaped logotype was printed on many of their cards. An easel-shaped logotype was used on others. Most have the Erie address.

Hamm, M.E. Toledo, OH. Published view cards in the mid-twentieth century.

Hammon, V.O., Publishing Co. Chicago, IL; Minneapolis, MN. Important publisher of view cards of the upper Midwest. Early twentieth century to the early 1920s. Published cards for the 1904 Louisiana Purchase Exposition.

Hammond Printing Co. Fremont, NE. Published view cards in the early twentieth century.

Handy, W.C. Afton, NY. Published view cards in the early twentieth century, including German imports.

Hanna, A.E. Blair, NE. Published RPPCs in the early twentieth century.

Hardison & Bennett. Chattanooga, TN. Published postcards in the early twentieth century, including those from the Commercial Colortype Co.

Hardison, W.E. Published postcards in the early twentieth century, including those of the Curt Teich Co.

Harmonson. New Orleans, LA. Publisher of postcards during the early twentieth century, including signed artists.

Harpel's Art Studio / Harpel's Art Store / Harpel Stationer. Lebanon, PA. Published view cards in the early twentieth century, mostly of subjects of local and regional interest. Some were from the Curt Teich Co.

Harper, Samuel N. Bath, NY. Published view cards in the mid-twentieth century, including those made by Albertype.

Harriman, Alice, Co. Seattle, WA. Published postcards in the early twentieth century.

Harriman, S.F. Columbus, OH. Published postcards in the early twentieth century.

Harriman, W.S. Columbus, OH. Published postcards in the 1920s and 1930s, including from the Curt Teich Co.

Harris, William James. Pittston, PA; Lake Hopatcong, NJ; St. Augustine, FL. Photographer Harris made and issued many RPPCs of Florida and of New Jersey (where he summered) in the early twentieth century, some marketed under the name of the Acme View Co.

Harrisburg Specialty Co. Harrisburg, PA. Published view cards in the early twentieth century.

Hart & Houston. Johnson City, TN. Published postcards in the early twentieth century, including those from Germany through the American News Co. (ANC).

Hartford News Co. Hartford, CT. Early twentieth century distributor of postcards, including with the American News Co. (ANC) imprint.

Hartman Litho Sales, Inc. Largo, FL. Published postcards in the mid-twentieth century.

Hartman, J.V., & Co. Boston, MA. Publisher of view cards, early twentieth century.

Hart-Park Co. Charles City, IA. Published postcards in the early twentieth century.

Harvey, C.E. Boise, OH. Photographer who published view cards in the early twentieth century including German imports.

Harvey, Fred, Trading Co. Kansas City, MO. Operator of newsstands, restaurants, and kiosks, mainly in connection with railroads. Sold postcards printed by Detroit Publishing and Curt Teich. These usually depicted scenic views and other items of interest to tourists. From Detroit, Harvey obtained many different views of American Indians.

Harvey, W. Garden City, KS. Traded as the Post Office News Stand. Publisher of postcards in the early twentieth century, including German imports obtained from American News Co. (ANC).

Harwell-Evans Co. New York, NY. Published postcards in the early twentieth century.

Hathaway, H.J., & Co. Houlton, ME. Published postcards in the early twentieth century, including German imports through Reichner Brothers.

Hauck, S.W., & Sons. Erie, PA. Publisher of regional view cards, circa the second decade of the twentieth century.

Hauck, Tillie J. Erie, PA. Issued postcards in the mid-twentieth century, including from the Curt Teich Co.

Hayes. Southern Pines, NC. Distributor of postcards in the early twentieth century, including those made by Albertype.

Haynes, J.F., Photo Co. St. Paul, MN. Photographer and publisher of RPPCs and printed cards, most notably of Yellowstone National Park. Early twentieth century.

Hayward Photo. Charles Town, WV. Published postcards in the early twentieth century, including German imports.

Hearst, William Randolph. Various U.S. cities. Published black-and-white and color postcards in connection with Hearst newspapers. First decade of the twentieth century.

Heath, J., & Son Co. St. Petersburg, FL. Published postcards in the early twentieth century, including cards from Metropolitan, Everett, MA.

Hecht, Julius J. Los Angeles, CA. Published postcards in the early twentieth century, including those by the Curt Teich Co.

Heck, Rex, News Co. (Rex Heck News Co.) Clarksburg, WV. Published postcards in the 1920s and 1930s, including from the Curt Teich Co.

Hefton, W.M. Hanford, CA. Published postcards in the early twentieth century, including German imports supplied by publisher M. Rieder.

Heininger, Henry, Co. New York, NY. Publisher of printed cards, including comic, greeting, ethnic, signed artist, view (some misleadingly captioned "Fac-Simile Hand Painted Nature Views"), etc. Second and third decades of the twentieth century.

Heliotype Co. Boston, MA. Printer and publisher of many products, including postcards of regional scenes, in the early twentieth century. Not related to a Canadian firm of the same name.

Helmbright Brothers. Wheeling, WV. Published postcards in the early twentieth century, including from the Curt Teich Co.

Helme, Bernon E. Kingston, RI. Published view cards in the early twentieth century, including German cards from ANC.

Henderson Advertising Co. Johnstown, PA. Published postcards in the mid-twentieth century, including from the Curt Teich Co.

Hengerer, William, Co. Buffalo, NY. Published postcards in the early twentieth century.

Hennessy. Auburn, NY. Published view cards in the early twentieth century, including those made in Germany.

Henry, E.F. East Greenwich, RI. Published postcards in the early twentieth century, including cards imported from Germany.

Henry, L.E. Lake Pleasant, MA. Published view cards in the early twentieth century.

Hermitage Art Co. Chicago, IL. Published postcards in the mid-twentieth century.

Herrman, C.P.L. Hartford, CT. Published view cards in the early twentieth century.

Herz Brothers. Newport, RI. Published postcards in the early twentieth century.

Herz Post Cards. San Diego, CA. Harry Herz. Published view cards in the early twentieth century, including those of the Curt Teich Company.

Herz, Harry. Phoenix, AZ. Related to the preceding. Published view cards in the mid-twentieth century, including those of the Curt Teich Company.

Hesse Envelope Co. St. Louis, MO. Published postcards in the early twentieth century.

Heyboer Stationery Co. Grand Rapids, MI. Publisher of view cards during the early twentieth century, including those of Kropp.

H-H-T Co. See H.H. Tammen Curio Co. under T.

Hiawatha Card of Detroit. Ypsilanti, MI. Published view cards in the late twentieth century, including Plastichrome.

Hickey Brothers. Davenport, IA. Published postcards in the early twentieth century.

Highland Book Store. Fayetteville, NC. Published view cards in the mid-twentieth century, including those of the Curt Teich Co.

Higley, L.E. North Adams, MA. Published view cards in the early twentieth century.

Hildreth, E.G., Dr. Marlboro, NH. Published postcards in the early twentieth century, including those imported from Germany.

Hildreth, Frank and Carl. Longmont, CO. Photographers and publishers of RPPCs, some hand colored, in the early twentieth century. Mostly regional views.

Hileman, Tomer Jacob. Kalispell, MT. Photographer of the Rocky Mountains and related vistas and publisher of RPPCs, from about 1910 onward.

Hilig, Otto. Liberty, NY. Photographer whose views were issued on many printed postcards, regional scenes and views of people, early twentieth century.

Hillen, J.H. Pomona, CA. Published view cards of regional interest in the early twentieth century.

Hilton, Theara, & Co. Portland, ME. Published view cards in the early twentieth century, including German imports.

Himes, S.W., & Co. Phenix, RI. Published postcards in the early twentieth century, including German imports through ANC.

Hinds, L.E. South Orrington, ME. Published postcards in the early twentieth century, including German imports.

Hines, S.P. Rochester, NY. Published postcards in the early twentieth century.

Hirshberg, S. Rockaway Beach, NY. Publisher of view cards in the early twentieth century.

Hirth, Val. Issued postcards circa the 1920s and 1930s, including those of the Curt Teich Co. Advertised as Val Hirth Printing Service.

Hislop, F.L. Palmyra, NY. Published view cards in the early twentieth century, including those imported by American News Co.

Hivnor Card Co. Zanesville, OH. Published view cards in the late twentieth century.

Hodge Photo Art. Amarillo, TX. Published postcards in the late twentieth century, including cards from Dexter Press.

Hodl, Oscar. Juneau, AK. Publisher of art cards depicting animals in the 1930s, printed by Curt Teich.

Hoen, A. & Co. Baltimore, MD; Richmond, VA. Published postcards in the early twentieth century.

Hoffman, H.G. Huntington, WV. Published postcards in the early twentieth century, including those from the Curt Teich Co.

Hoffman, J.B. / J.B. Hoffman & Son. Harrisburg, PA. Issued postcards in the mid-twentieth century, including from the Curt Teich Co.

Hoffman, William G. Chicago, IL. Issued postcards circa the 1920s and 1930s, including those from Tichnor Brothers.

Holdsworth Distributing Co. Yarmouthport, MA. Published view cards in the late twentieth century.

Holland Brothers. Utica, NY. Published view cards in the early twentieth century, including German imports from the American News Company (ANC).

Hollander, Joseph. Norfolk, VA. Published postcards in the early twentieth century.

Hollingsworth, J.A. Narragansett Pier, RI. "Tourist photographer" who made RPPCs in the early twentieth century. He also did regional business and other work.

Holmboe Studio. Bismarck, ND. Made RPPCs in the second decade of the twentieth century.

Holmes the Newsman. Brockton, MA. Published view cards in the early twentieth century, including German imports obtained from the American News Company (ANC).

Holzman, Alfred, Co. Chicago, IL. Prominent printer and publisher of postcards in the early twentieth century, including hold-to-light cards.

Honolulu Paper Co. Honolulu, HI. Publisher of view cards from the second decade of the twentieth century onward.

Hooper, Lewis & Co. Boston, MA. Publisher of view and other postcards in the very early twentieth century, many of which were imported.

Hoover-Watson Printing. Indianapolis, IN. Published postcards in the early twentieth century.

Hopf Brothers Co. Seattle, WA. Published postcards in the early twentieth century, including German imports.

Hopf, V.O. Seattle, WA. Published view cards in the early twentieth century, including from Curt Teich Co.

Hopkins News Agency. San Diego, CA. Published view cards in the late twentieth century.

Horan, M. Wenatchee, WA. Published postcards in the early twentieth century.

Horne, Joseph, & Co. Pittsburgh, PA. Published postcards in the early twentieth century.

Horne, Walter H., Co. El Paso, TX. Prominent photographer and publisher of RPPC cards, including scenes of the Mexican Revolution, for a decade or so beginning about 1910.

Hornick, Hess & More. Sioux City, IA. Published postcards in the early twentieth century.

Hornick, More & Porterfield. Sioux City, IA. Published postcards in the early twentieth century.

Horning, A.A., & Co. McGregor, IA. Published postcards in the early twentieth century.

Hot Springs Novelty Co. Hot Springs, AR. Published postcards in the early twentieth century.

Houghtaling, Charles E. Albany, NY. Published view cards in the early twentieth century, including German imports.

Howe Press. Grantham, NH. Printed postcards in the early twentieth century.

Howe, Raymond. Chicago, IL. Publisher of colorful art postcards with greetings, holidays, comic scenes, etc., early twentieth century.

Howell's Photo Studio. Vineyard Haven, MA. Published postcards in the late twentieth century, including cards from Plastichrome.

Howes and Roote. Whately, MA. Published view cards in the early twentieth century, including German imports from American News Company (ANC).

Howland, M.W. Woodsville, NH. Published postcards in the early twentieth century, including those imported from Germany.

Hubermann, A.B. Omaha, NE. Published postcards in the early twentieth century.

Huckins, P.L. Chicago, IL. Publisher of RPPCs in the early twentieth century.

Huested Studios. Mannsville, NY. Early twentieth century publisher of RPPCs.

Huffman Pictures. Milestown, MT. Published postcards featuring Indians (Native Americans) in the early twentieth century.

Hughes, Charles W., & Co., Inc. Mechanicsville, NY. Publisher of regional views and other postcards from the 1910s onward, many of which were printed by Curt Teich Co.

Huld, Franz. New York, NY. Prominent publisher of printed postcards in the first decade of the twentieth century, with a wide variety of views including East Coast subjects, the 1906 San Francisco earthquake and fire, and installment sets. He filed for bankruptcy in 1914, by which time he had not published cards for several years.

Hulett, H.R. Ticonderoga, NY. Published view cards in the early twentieth century.

Humphreys, E.W. Woodstown, NJ. Photographer and merchant who distributed postcards, including of his own work, mostly made in Germany.

Humphries Co. El Paso, TX. Publisher of regional view postcards, including Mexican topics, in the first decade of the twentieth century.

Hunger's Office Supply. Punxsutawney, PA. Published postcards in the mid-twentieth century, including from the Curt Teich Co.

Hunt Brothers. North Adams, MA. Published view cards in the early twentieth century.

Hunt, E.P., and Co. Great Barrington, MA. Published postcards in the early twentieth century, including cards imported from England.

Hunt, Enos B., Jr. Des Moines, IA. Published postcards in the early twentieth century.

Hunt, George H., & Co. East Weymouth, MA. Publisher of view cards during the early twentieth century, mostly of regional subjects. Some were German imports. Also sold RPPCs.

Hunt, M.L., & Co. Weston, WV. Published postcards in the early twentieth century.

Hunt, P.S. Valdez, AK. Photographer and issuer of RPPCs of regional scenes in the early twentieth century.

Hunter Photo Co. Madison, CT. Publisher of cards, mostly imported from Germany, black and white and color, emphasizing regional views.

Huntington News Co., The. Huntington, WV. Published postcards in the 1920s and 1930s, including from Tichnor Brothers.

Huntley, M.E. Hamburg, CT. Published view cards in the early twentieth century, including those printed in Germany. He was the local postmaster.

Huntress, Louis Maynard. Osterville, MA. Photographer of regional scenes, issued as RPPCs and also printed, many of which were published by H.A. Dickerman.

Huston, James T. Clinton, IA. Published postcards in the early twentieth century, including German imports obtained from PCK.

Hutchinson, H.S., & Co. New Bedford, MA. Published view cards in the early twentieth century, including German imports.

Hyde Paper Co. Colorado Springs and Pueblo, CO. Published postcards in the early twentieth century, including from the Curt Teich Co.

Hyde Park Gift Shop. Hyde Park, NY. Publisher of postcards during the early twentieth century, including signed artists.

Hyman's News & Book Store. Des Moines, IA. Published postcards in the early twentieth century.

Hy-Sil Manufacturing Co. Boston, MA. Published postcards in the early twentieth century.

I

I.I.C. El Paso, TX. Published postcards in the mid-twentieth century, including cards from Colourpicture.

Illustrated Post Card Co. / Illustrated Postal Card & Novelty Co. New York, NY. "& Novelty" usually omitted on imprint. Sometimes as Illustrated Post Card Co. One of the more important publishers of color view and other cards, mostly printed by Emil Pinkau in Leipzig, Germany, in the early twentieth century. Art postcards printed in Dresden, Germany, were published as well in the early days. Later, the company printed its own cards. Many of their cards depicted an American eagle perched on a shield, facing to the right, with no printed information. A similarly named company was located in Montreal, Quebec, Canada.

Imperial Advertising Agency. Chattanooga, TN. Published postcards in the early twentieth century.

Imperial Greeting Card Co. Pittsburgh, PA. Published view cards in the late twentieth century including Plastichrome.

Import Postcard Co. Indianapolis, IN. Publisher of postcards during the early twentieth century, including signed artists.

Inbody, J. Elkhart, IN. Issued RPPCs in the early twentieth century.

Indian Arts and Crafts. Seattle, WA; Anchorage, AK. Publisher of postcards during the early twentieth century, including signed artists.

Indian Trading Co. Phoenix, AZ. Publisher of view cards in the early twentieth century.

Indiana News Co. Indianapolis, IN. Publisher of view cards, including German imports obtained from the American News Co. (ANC) and cards from the Curt Teich Co. Early twentieth century.

Ingersoll News Agency. Burlington, IA. Published postcards in the early twentieth century.

Inland Printing Co. Spokane, WA. Publisher of regional view cards and images of Native Americans, early twentieth century.

Interborough News Co. New York, NY. Distributed RPPCs in the mid-twentieth century.

Intermountain Tourist Supply, Inc. Salt Lake City, UT. Publisher of postcards during the early twentieth century, including signed artists.

International Drug Co. Nogales, AZ. Publisher of view cards in the early twentieth century, including those of the Curt Teich Company.

International Litho. Co. Rochester, NY. Published postcards in the early twentieth century.

International Novelty Co. San Francisco, CA. Published postcards in the early twentieth century.

International Post Card Co. New York, NY. Important publisher of view cards and other subjects, early twentieth century into the 1920s. Many if not most early cards were German imports.

International Postal Card Co. Chicago, IL. Publisher of a wide variety of view, art, comic, embossed, etc., postcards in the early twentieth century. Most were imported from Austria and Germany.

International Stereograph Co. Decatur, IL. Issued RPPCs in the early twentieth century. Some images were taken from half of a stereograph view.

Inter-State Postcard Co. Falls City, NE. Publisher of RPPCs in the early twentieth century.

Inverness Drug Co. Inverness, FL. Published postcards in the early twentieth century.

Iowa Post Card Co. Des Moines, IA. Published postcards in the early twentieth century, including German imports.

IS [logotype]. IS monogram over eagle, see Ignatz Stern under S.

Island Curio Co. Honolulu, HI. Publisher of view postcards and related subjects in the early twentieth century.

Island Heritage. Honolulu, HI. Publisher of postcards during the early twentieth century, including signed artists.

Ives Process Co. New York, NY. Published postcards in the early twentieth century.

J

Jackson, H.H. Bridgeport, CT. Published view cards in the early twentieth century, including German imports.

Jackson Photo Advertising Co. Chicago, IL. Published view cards in the early twentieth century, including from Curt Teich and Co.

Jaffe, Arthur, Inc. (Arthur Jaffe, Inc.) / Arthur Jaffe Heliochrome Co. New York, NY. Publisher of postcards made by Kunstanstalt Max Jaffé (Vienna, Austria), circa 1920s onward, and also cards from other sources.

Jamestown Amusement & Vending Co. Norfolk, VA. Publisher of postcards during the early twentieth century, including signed artists.

Jax News Co. Jacksonville, FL. Publisher of view cards in the early twentieth century.

Jennings & Graham. New York, NY; Cincinnati, OH. Publisher of postcards during the early twentieth century, including signed artists.

Jennings, W.N. Philadelphia, PA. Published postcards in the early twentieth century.

Jeweler Shaw. Putnam, CT. Published view cards in the early twentieth century.

Jewish Welfare Board. New York, NY. Publisher of postcards beginning in the First World War, continuing elsewhere. Many were made for American servicemen without regard to religion.

Johns-Byrne Co. Chicago, IL. Publisher of postcards during the early twentieth century, including signed artists.

Johnson Colburn Co. Southbridge, MA. Published view cards in the early twentieth century, including German imports.

Johnson News Agency. Big Springs, TX. Published postcards in the mid-twentieth century, including cards from Tichnor Brothers.

Johnson, C.T. East Jaffrey, NH. Published RPPCs of regional subjects in the early twentieth century.

Johnson, Frank. Key West, FL. Published postcards in the early twentieth century, including cards from the Curt Teich Co.

Johnson, J.W., & Son. Newport, NH. Published postcards in the early twentieth century, including those supplied by American News Co. (ANC).

Johnson, L.M. Chicago, IL. Publisher of postcards during the early twentieth century, including signed artists.

Johnson, S.A. Phillips, WI. Produced RPPCs in the early twentieth century.

Johnston, C.P., Co. Seattle, WA. Publisher of view cards featuring Pacific Northwest subjects, mostly printed by Curt Teich. Late 1920s onward.

Johnston's Art Stores. Niagara Falls, NY. Issued postcards in the first decade of the twentieth century, undivided backs, with its own imprint, of wide ranging subjects in the Eastern United States.

Jones, George W. Annapolis, MD. Publisher of regional view cards and other subjects, including those made by Raphael Tuck, in the early twentieth century.

Jones, H.L. Mahanoy City, PA. Published cards in the early twentieth century including those of the Curt Teich Company.

Jones, Keyser & Adams. New York, NY. Publisher of postcards during the early twentieth century, including signed artists.

Jones, L.E. Woodstock, NY. Photographer and issuer of RPPCs with regional views and topics, mainly in the 1920s.

Jones, Tom. Cincinnati, OH. Published postcards in the early twentieth century. Certain of his cards with blue tint were called "Delft." Some were printed by Curt Teich.

Jordan, E.C. Poland, ME. Published postcards in the early twentieth century.

Jordan, J. Murray. Philadelphia, PA. Publisher of view cards with East Coast subjects and also the Panama Canal, among other topics. Established the World Post Card Co. in 1903 but continued issuing cards under the J. Murray Jordan imprint.

Joske Brothers Co. San Antonio, TX. Published postcards in the early twentieth century.

Jubb, William, Co. Syracuse, NY. Publisher of view cards, mostly of regional interest, including German imports. Active in the early twentieth century.

Judd, Edward P., Co. New Haven, CT. Publisher of regional view cards in the first two decades of the twentieth century, including German imports. Sometimes as E.P.J. Co.

JV. Imprint in the image on the face of many Valentine cards, various related firms, see under V.

K

Kaber & Son. Cleveland, OH. Published postcards in the early twentieth century

Kackley, J.T., & Co. Maysville, KY. Published postcards in the early twentieth century.

Kaeser & Blair, Inc. Cincinnati, OH. Published postcards in the 1920s and 1930s, including those branded "Picto-Cards."

Kagan, A. Boston, MA. Publisher of view cards of regional interest. Active in the 1910s.

Kahill, J.B. Portland, ME. Publisher of view cards in the early twentieth century, including German imports.

Kansas Post Card Co. Salina, KS. Publisher of view and other cards in the early twentieth century, many of which were imported from Germany.

Kardmasters. Allentown, PA. Published view cards in the late twentieth century, including those made by E.C. Kropp Co.

Karl Brothers. Litchfield, CT. Published view cards in the early twentieth century, including German imports.

Kasell, Robert. Llano, TX. Published postcards in the late twentieth century, including cards from Dexter Press.

Kashower, M., Co. Los Angeles, CA. Publisher/distributor of view cards, some with this imprint alone, others with Van Ornum Colorprint Co.

Kaufmann & Strauss Co. New York, NY. Publisher of postcards during the early twentieth century, including signed artists.

Kaufmann, David. Baltimore, MD. Published postcards in the early twentieth century. Advertises "publishers of local views."

Kaufmann, Louis, & Sons. Baltimore, MD. Publisher of regional view cards, naval subjects, ethnic subjects, and other postcards, including many printed by Curt Teich. Active from the 1910s to the 1930s.

Kawin & Co. / K-win & Co. Chicago, IL. Published postcards in the early twentieth century.

Kayser, A. Oakland, CA. Pioneer publisher of postcards in the 1890s, sold out to Edward H. Mitchell in 1898. Cards feature California scenes, Yellowstone National Park, and advertising subjects.

Keane, Walter. New York, NY. Publisher of postcards during the early twentieth century, including signed artists.

Keck, J.H. Omaha, NE. Published view cards in the early twentieth century, including those of the Curt Teich Co. Some published with "The Burlington Series" imprint.

Keefe Brothers. Butte, MT. Published postcards in the early twentieth century.

Keenan News Agency. Spokane, WA. Published postcards in the mid-twentieth century.

Kelley Printing Co. Seattle, WA. Published postcards in the early twentieth century.

Kelley-Davis Co. Oakland, CA. Commercial printers who made and distributed view cards in the early twentieth century.

Kelliher, D. Exeter, NH. Published postcards in the early twentieth century, including those imported from Germany.

Kellogg Studios. Cuba, NY. Conducted by P.H. Kellogg, maintained studios in the towns of Cuba, Belmont, Fillmore, and Rushford, and issued RPPCs in the early twentieth century.

Kellogg, E.E. Fort Leyden, NY. Photographer and issuer of RPPCs in the early twentieth century.

Kemble-Cochran Co. Bristol, VA. Published postcards in the early twentieth century, including those from the Commercial Colortype Co.

Kempter, E.W. Galena, IL. Issued postcards circa the 1920s and 1930s, including those obtained from the E.C. Kropp Co.

Kenfield, Charles. Hastings, MI. Issued RPPCs in the early twentieth century.

Kenyon, Brewster C. Long Beach, CA. Published postcards in the early twentieth century.

Kenyon, Ida M. Usquepaugh, RI. Published postcards in the early twentieth century, including German imports.

Kenyon, O.P. Wakefield, RI. Published view cards in the early twentieth century.

Kerr & Larrabee. Presque Isle, ME. Published postcards in the early twentieth century, including German imports.

Ketcham, Charles A. Middletown, NY. Produced and distributed RPPCs in the first decade of the twentieth century for regional clients, including in New York City.

Ketchum, Everett H. Jamestown, NY. Published view cards in the early twentieth century, including those with undivided backs, but with ornate printing on the address side.

Ketterman, H.R. Published postcards in the mid-twentieth century, including some from the Dexter Press.

Keystone Photo View Co. Pittsburgh, PA. Publisher of RPPCs in the early twentieth century, some sold as "Crystaltypes."

Killough, G.W. Hummelstown, PA. Published view cards in the early twentieth century, including those from Valentine & Sons.

Kimmell, F.M. McCook, NE. Printer-stationer who distributed view cards in the early twentieth century.

Kingsbury, A.J. Antigo, WI. Made RPPCs, including of Native Americans.

Kingston News Service. Kingston, NY. Published view cards in the early twentieth century, including those made by Metropolitan.

Kingston Souvenir Co. Kingston, NY. Publisher of regional view cards in the early twentieth century. Some have a swastika (considered to be a good luck symbol before the Nazis used it in the 1930s) and K.S.C. on the back. Some cards were supplied by the Curt Teich Co.

Kirby, F.M. Wilkes-Barre, PA. Fred Morgan Kirby. Operator of five-and-ten cent stores who published postcards in the early twentieth century. Many were views of the East Coast and the South. Some postcards bear store addresses on the back, Providence, RI, being an example.

Kiser Photo Co. Portland, OR. Fred H. Kiser, a skilled photographer, captured many scenes of the Pacific Northwest that were published on printed cards in the early twentieth century. He established the Scenic America Publishing Co. in 1914.

Klein Brothers Paper & Twine Co. Allentown, PA. Issued postcards in the mid-twentieth century.

Klein, George R., News Co. Cleveland, OH. Published postcards in the 1920s and 1930s, including from the Tichnor Brothers.

Kline, J.B., &Son. Lambertville, NJ. Sold view cards during the early twentieth century, including those obtained from the American News Company (ANC).

Klein Postcard Service. Hyde Park, MA. Published postcards in the late twentieth century.

Kline Poster Co. Philadelphia, PA. Published postcards in the early twentieth century, including color cards depicting actors and actresses.

Knapp Co., Inc. New York, NY. Important early twentieth century publisher of art postcards, including artist-signed.

KNG. Germany. Imprint used on certain cards of American interest, including Philip Boileau portraits.

Knox, S.H., & Co. Buffalo, NY. This was one of several five-and-ten cent store chains that published postcards. Many bore the location of the distributing store. Active in the early twentieth century, until the stores were merged into F.W. Woolworth & Co.

Knoxville Engraving Co. Knoxville, TN. Published postcards in the early twentieth century, including some from Tichnor Brothers.

Koch, Peter. Alpine, TX. Published postcards in the late twentieth century, including cards from Dexter Press.

Koeber, Paul C., & Co. / PCK. New York, NY. In the early twentieth century Koeber imported many fine lithographed cards from Germany and sold them as the "PCK Series," using a peacock as part of his logotype. In most instances just the logo is shown, without mention of Koeber.

Koehler, Joseph. New York, NY. Very important publisher of German-made cards, often from original art and depicting many topics. Hold-to-light, mechanical, and other cards were sold, all being of very high quality and being favorites of deltiologists today. Some RPPCs were distributed as well.

Koelling & Klappenbach. Chicago, IL. Early twentieth century publisher of views and other postcards imported from Germany.

Kohle, Herman. New Brunswick, NJ. Publisher of regional view and other cards, circa late 1890s.

Kolb Brothers Studio. Grand Canyon, AZ. Publisher of RPPCs and printed cards of regional views, especially the Grand Canyon.

Koppel Color Cards. Hawthorne, NJ. Published postcards in the late twentieth century.

Korton, H.O. New York, NY. Publisher of regional view cards, including hand-colored images. First two decades of the twentieth century.

Kosmos Art Co. Boston, MA. Published view cards in the early twentieth century, including German imports.

Koster, Albert W. Stroudsburg, PA. Published postcards in the late twentieth century, including those by Dexter Press.

Kraemer Art Co. / A.O. Kraemer. Cincinnati, OH; Berlin, Germany. Publisher of view cards, including German imports in the early years.

Kraft, George, Co. Waterloo, IA. Published postcards in the early twentieth century.

Kraus Manufacturing Co. New York, NY. 1910s and 1920s publisher of halftone pictures of views, theater and film personalities, and other subjects.

Kregel Photo Parlors. St. Paul and Minneapolis, MN. Made RPPCs in the early twentieth century.

Kreh, C.F. Theodore. New York, NY. Publisher in the late 1890s of chromolithograph cards, mainly of New York City.

Kresge & Wilson. Detroit, MI. Published view cards in the early twentieth century, including German imports.

Kress, S.H., & Co. Nanticoke, PA. Operator of five-and-ten cent stores. Published cards made by various manufacturers, early twentieth century.

Krogstad, Chris N. Menominee, WI. Publisher of postcards during the early twentieth century, including signed artists.

Kropp, E.C., Co. Milwaukee, WI. Highly important maker of view and other cards for clients all across America. The letter N was often a part of the serial number. Active from 1896 through 1956. Founded by Emil C. Kropp. Trade style of E.C. Kropp Co. adopted in 1906, the same year Kropp died. Frederick M. Wilmanns took control of the company.

Kug-Art Photo Service. Glendale, CA. Put out RPPCs in the 1920s and 1930s.

Kurtz Stationery Store. Issued postcards in the mid-twentieth century.

K-win & Co / Kawin & Co. Chicago, IL. Published scenic postcards in the early twentieth century.

L

Labbie, J.A. Boothbay Harbor, ME. Photographer and publisher of RPPCs in the 1910s and 1920s

Lacik News Agency. Ardmore, OK. Published postcards in the 1920s and 1930s, including from the Curt Teich Co.

Lacy & Co. Monteagle, TN. Published postcards in the early twentieth century, including some from the Curt Teich Co.

Lagrange, R.E. Lyon Mountain, NY. Published view cards in the early twentieth century.

Lakeside Printing Co. / Lakeside Press. Portland, ME. In the early twentieth century, Lakeside was a firm of modest size, seemingly specializing in making small runs of printed cards to order. A circa-1910 advertisement noted: "Post Cards Made By Lakeside Printing Company, Portland, Maine. 1000 $5.50, 500 $4.25, 250 $3.25. Send Photographs." The request, "Send Photographs," is typical of that made by other post card issuers as well. Often, a favorite black-and-white photograph, or even an already existing postcard, was sent to the postcard printer and used— explaining why the same image sometimes is found with multiple imprints.

Lamb, C.M. Pleasant View, RI. Published postcards in the early twentieth century, including from Tichnor Brothers.

Lamb, William, & Co. Norfolk, VA. Published postcards in the early twentieth century.

Lamphere, George N. Palouse, WA. Published postcards in the early twentieth century, including German imports, acquired through M. Rieder.

Lampl, Albert A. Philadelphia, PA. Publisher of postcards during the early twentieth century, including signed artists.

Lamson Studio. Portland, ME. Publisher of RPPCs and printed cards (the latter made in Germany) in the 1900s.

Langdon, F. H., & Co. Denver, CO. Published postcards in the early twentieth century.

Langmead, C.J. Providence, RI. Published postcards in the early twentieth century.

Langsdorf, Samuel, & Co. New York, NY. Often as SL & Co. Major publisher of high-quality cards in the early twentieth century, mostly imported from Germany. These were in black and white and, mostly, high-quality color, many of the latter being deeply embossed. Their alligator border cards became collectors' favorites.

Larsen, L.H., Art Products. Kanab, UT. Publisher of postcards during the early twentieth century, including signed artists.

Larson, C.W., Co. / Press of C.W. Larson Co. Pittsburgh, PA. Printed postcards in the early twentieth century.

Lathrop, H.A. Sherburne, NY. Published view cards in the early twentieth century.

Lau, R.H. & Co. York, PA. Issued postcards in the early twentieth century, including those from Tichnor Brothers.

Law, J.H. Asheville, NC. Published view cards in the early twentieth century.

Lawless, Annie. Milford, MA. Published view cards in the early twentieth century, including those printed in Germany.

Layton Studio. Richmond, VA. Issued RPPCs in the early twentieth century, with subjects covering a wide geographical area.

Lazarus, J. Hyannis, MA. Published view cards, including some of his own copyrighted color photos, in the late twentieth century.

Leader, The. Lamoni, IA. Published postcards in the early twentieth century, including German imports obtained from C.E. Wheelock and Co.

Leading Novelty Co. New York, NY. Publisher of postcards at the turn of the twentieth century.

Leckie's. Matewan, WV. Published postcards in the 1920s and 1930s, including from the Curt Teich Co.

Lederle, Karl, Studio. Carthage and Lowville, NY. Issued RPPCs in the early twentieth century.

Leeland Art Co. Mitchell, SD. Publisher of RPPCs of regional views in the early twentieth century. Owned by Ole S. Leeland.

Leet Brothers. Washington, D.C. Publishers of local views, U.S. presidents, suffrage, and other topics. Many were printed in Great Britain. Active in the early twentieth century.

Legg, E. Pascoag, RI. Published postcards in the early twentieth century, including from the American Colortype Co.

Lehigh Variety Co. Allentown, PA. Issued postcards in the mid-twentieth century.

Leib, Frank H., Co. Salt Lake City, UT. Published postcards in the early twentieth century, including those obtained from the Commercial Colortype Co.

Leighton, Hugh C., Co. Portland, ME. Prominent publisher of view cards, mostly imported from Germany, in the first decade of the twentieth century. Merged with Valentine & Sons in 1908.

Leighton & Valentine. Portland, ME; New York (Brooklyn), NY; Dundee, Scotland. Successors in 1908 to the Hugh C. Leighton Co. Major publisher of view cards printed in England, later in the United States.

Lemon-Shepherd Co. Abilene, TX. Published postcards in the mid-twentieth century, including cards from Colourpicture.

Lenoir Drug Co. Lenoir City, TN. Published postcards in the early twentieth century, including some from the Curt Teich Co.

Lesesne, R.H. Daytona, FL. Traded as The Kodak Place and issued RPPCs in the early twentieth century. Some views were of early auto races on the Daytona beach.

Leubrie & Elkins. New York, NY. Publisher of greetings and other art postcards, early twentieth century.

Levering, A.R. East Northfield, MA. Published view cards in the early twentieth century.

Lewis Views. Reynoldsville, PA. Issued postcards in the early twentieth century.

Lewis, J.C. Nausauket, RI. Published postcards in the early twentieth century.

Lewis, J.J. Averill Park and Troy, NY. Published view cards in the early twentieth century.

Lewy, Ted -Arts (Ted Lewy-Arts). San Francisco, CA. Publisher of postcards during the early twentieth century, including signed artists.

Libby & Bowers. Penn-Mar, PA. Distributed view cards in the mid-twentieth century, including from Curt Teich Co.

Lillie, F.B., & Co. Guthrie, OK. Published postcards in the early twentieth century, including German imports.

Lincoln Supply Co. Waterloo, IA. Published postcards in the early twentieth century.

Lindsey, T.N. Louisville, KY. Published postcards in the early twentieth century.

Line & Co. Elizabeth, NJ. Published view cards, including German imports, in the early twentieth century.

Lionel, David, Press (David Lionel Press). Chicago, IL. Published "clear-vue" cards in the late twentieth century.

Lipscher Specialty Co. New Orleans, LA. Publisher of postcards of regional views in the first two decades of the twentieth century.

Lipscheutz & Katz. Portland, OR. Published view cards in the mid-twentieth century, including those from Curt Teich Co. Primarily regional views.

Little, Virginia Cleaves. Rockport, MA. Published view cards in the late twentieth century, including those made by E.C. Kropp Co.

Livermore & Knight. New York, NY. Publisher of novelty, greeting, and other art cards, active in the first decade of the twentieth century.

Livingston, Arthur. New York, NY. Publisher of comic, military, regional views and other subjects from the late 1890s into the first decade of the twentieth century.

383

LK Color Productions. Provincetown, MA. Published view cards in the mid-twentieth century.

Local View Printing Co. New York, NY. Printed view cards, some black and white with blue tint, for customers all over the country, including the West. Active in the 1900s and 1910s.

Loeffler, A. Tompkinsville, NY. Issued RPPCs in the early twentieth century, including views of regional interest, some including New York City.

Lollesgard Specialty Co. Tucson, AZ. Published view cards in the late twentieth century, including Curt Teich Co. cards.

Long Island News Co. Flushing and Long Island City, NY. Published view cards in the early twentieth century, including German imports obtained from the American News Co. (ANC).

Long Island Postal Card Co. Sea Cliff, NY. Published view cards at the turn of the twentieth century.

Longley, G.C., & Co. Athol, MA. Published cards in the early twentieth century, including those by the Curt Teich Co.

Longley, George S. North Anson, ME. Published postcards in the early twentieth century, including German imports.

Longshaw Card Co. Pasadena and Los Angeles, CA. Publisher of linen cards, with Southern California views and entertainment topics being specialties.

Lord, Robert H. Boston, MA. Publisher of art cards, usually with sentiments or sayings, in the 1910s.

Loring, Short & Harmon. Portland, ME. Published view cards in the mid-twentieth century.

Lorraine Manufacturing Co. Pawtucket, RI. Published postcards in the early twentieth century, including German imports through ANC.

Los Angeles Lithographic Co. Los Angeles, CA. Published postcards in the early twentieth century.

Los Angeles News Co. Los Angeles, CA. Published view cards in the early twentieth century, including German imports obtained from the American News Co. (ANC).

Louisiana News Co. New Orleans, LA. Published postcards in the mid-twentieth century, including cards from Metropolitan in Everett, MA.

Lounsbury, Fred C. NJ. Publisher of postcards during the early twentieth century, including signed artists.

Lowey, Edward. New York, NY. Publisher of colorful lithochrome postcards, late 1890s onward, imported from Germany, including some "Phönix Brand" lithographed scenic cards.

Lowman & Hanford Co. / Lowman & Hanford Stationery & Printing Co. Seattle, WA. Published view cards in the early twentieth century, including those of the Curt Teich Co. Many featured Native Americans.

Lumitone Press Photoprint. New York, NY. Publisher of color halftone pictures with muted hues, circa late 1920s to the 1950s.

Lund, Leland. Tacoma, WA. Published view cards in the early twentieth century, including those from Tichnor Brothers.

Lundborg, A.P. Worcester, MA. Published view cards in the early twentieth century, including those from Valentine and Son.

Lyman Press. Syracuse, NY. Publisher of postcards during the early twentieth century, including signed artists.

Lyon, William A. Norfolk, VA. Published postcards in the early twentieth century.

M

MacAusland, David B. San Anselmo, CA. Publisher of postcards during the early twentieth century, including signed artists.

MacDonald, D.L., Co. Lynn, MA. Published view cards in the mid-twentieth century, including those made by Tichnor Brothers.

MacFarlane, W.G., Publishing Co., Ltd. Toronto, Ontario, Canada; Buffalo, NY. Publisher of cards, mostly Canadian themes, but many United States topics; also Western and Native American subjects. American and well as German imports. First two decades of the twentieth century.

Macleith Photo System. Milwaukee, WI. Made RPPCs in the mid-twentieth century.

Maconi Service. Framingham, MA. Published view cards in the late twentieth century, including those published by Dexter Press.

Madciff, E. Hershey, PA. Published postcards in the mid-twentieth century, including from Curt Teich Co.

Madison News Agency. Madison, WI. Published view cards in the late twentieth century, including Curt Teich Co. cards.

Maether & Co. New York, NY; Berlin, Germany. Also imprinted as M. & Co. Publisher of view cards in the first two decades of the twentieth century.

Magee & Robinson Printers. Norfolk, VA. Published postcards in the early twentieth century.

Magee, J.D. Abilene, TX. Published postcards in the early twentieth century, including German imports obtained from S. Langsdorf & Co.

Maher, Mrs. S. Oakland Beach, RI. Published postcards in the early twentieth century, including German imports.

Mahoney News Agency. Muskogee, OK. Published postcards in the 1920s and 1930s, including from the Curt Teich Co.

Maine Farmer Publishing Co. Augusta, ME. Published postcards in the early twentieth century.

Mainzer, Alfred. Long Island City, NY. Publisher of linen and chrome view cards and, notably, "Dressed Cat" cards nicknamed "Mainzer Cats." Late 1930s onward.

Majestic Publishing Co. Indianapolis, IN. Publisher of postcards during the early twentieth century, including signed artists.

Mallison, H. Barryville, NY. Published view cards in the mid-twentieth century, including those made by Tichnor Brothers.

Malone, David. Euless, TX. Published postcards in the late twentieth century, including cards from E.C. Kropp Co.

Manchester New Hampshire Chamber of Commerce. Manchester, NH. Published a large series of view cards in the early twentieth century, including those made by Curt Teich.

Manhattan Post Card Co. New York, NY. Also operated as Manhattan Post Card Publishing Co. Publisher of color view postcards, mostly of regional interests, and signed artist cards, early twentieth century, many from Tichnor Brothers and Curt Teich Co.

Manz Engraving Co. Chicago, IL. Published postcards in the early twentieth century, including cards from the Curt Teich Co.

Marchant Commercial Photography. Hamlet, NC. Produced RPPCs in the early twentieth century.

Maring & Blake. Seattle, WA. Published postcards in the early twentieth century.

Mark, M. Jacksonville, FL. Publisher of view cards, including German imports, early twentieth century. Florida Artistic Series imprint on some.

Marken & Bielfield, Inc. Frederick, MD. Publisher of view cards of Mid-Atlantic states, 1920s to 1940s.

Markendorff, George. New York, NY. Publisher of postcards during the early twentieth century, including signed artists.

Markham, R.C. The Dalles, OR. Published RPPCs in the early twentieth century, with emphasis on Central Oregon scenes.

Marks, J.J. New York, NY. Publisher of art cards with holiday, comic, and other subjects, also signed artists, early twentieth century.

Marsh & Co. San Francisco, CA. Published postcards in the early twentieth century.

Marsh, A.F. Sangerville, ME. Published postcards in the early twentieth century, including German imports.

Martin News Agency. Dallas, TX. Published postcards in the mid-twentieth century, including cards from the Curt Teich Co.

Martin Post Card Co. Ottawa, KS. Issued RPPCs of Western and Native American scenes, some of which were copyrighted, in the first and second decade of the twentieth century. Some of their images were also issued by the North American Post Card Co. of Kansas City, Mo.

Martin, Harry N. Asheville, NC. Published postcards in the mid-twentieth century, including those by the Curt Teich Co.

Martin, J.H. Millville, NY. Published view cards in the early twentieth century.

Martin, William H. Ottawa, KS. Issuer of RPPCs and related cards of Western and regional scenes, including many interesting exaggerations, early twentieth century.

Martinson & Tiffany. New York, NY. Publisher of RPPCs with scenes of the First World War, including on the home front, late 1910s.

Maryland Litho. Co. Baltimore, MD. Published postcards in the mid-twentieth century.

Mason Brothers & Co. Boston, MA. Publisher of view cards, mostly of New England topics, many imported from Germany, early twentieth century. Later cards were made by E.C. Kropp and Curt Teich Co.

Mason City News Agency. Mason City, IA. Published postcards in the early twentieth century.

Mason, C.B. New Orleans, LA. Publisher of view cards of regional topics, early twentieth century to the late 1920s.

Maston & Hall. Wilmington, DE. Printers who produced black-and-white postcards in the early twentieth century.

Mather, G.G. Publisher of postcards during the early twentieth century, including signed artists.

Matteson, E.E. Apponaug, RI. Published postcards in the early twentieth century, including German cards obtained from ANC.

Matthews Northrup Co. Buffalo, NY. Engravers who printed and published postcards as early as 1893.

Mattingly, L.F. Lexington, KY. Published view cards in the mid-twentieth century, including those printed by the Curt Teich Co.

May Drug Co. Charles City, IA. Published postcards in the early twentieth century, including those of the Curt Teich Co.

Mayes, M.J. Glenwood Springs, CO. Published postcards in the early twentieth century, including German imports from the American News Co. (ANC).

Mayfair Photo Finishing Co. Brooklyn, NY. Published postcards in the late twentieth century.

Mayflower Sales Co. Provincetown, MA. Published view cards in the late twentieth century, including those made by Dexter Press.

Mayrose Co. Linden, NJ. Publisher of inexpensive view cards of regional topics, mostly in the 1940s.

McClure, A.C., & Co. Chicago, IL. Published postcards in the early twentieth century.

McConnell, E.W. Chicago, IL. Published postcards in the early twentieth century.

McConnell, H.C. Brush, CO. Published postcards in the early twentieth century.

McCormick-Armstrong Co. Wichita, KS. Publisher of art cards during the early twentieth century, including signed artists, but mainly a large commercial printer.

McCrory, J.G., & Co. New York, NY. Five-and-ten cent store chain that published postcards in the early twentieth century.

McCroskey, V.T., & Brothers. Colfax, WA. Published view cards in the early twentieth century.

McDaniel, George. Fort Recovery, OH. Photographer and publisher of RPPCs in the early twentieth century. Usually signed simply as McDaniel.

McDougall & Keefe. Boothbay Harbor, ME. Publisher of RPPC view cards of regional topics, 1910s to 1930s.

McElhinney, C.A. Washington, D.C. Published postcards in the early twentieth century.

McGee & Robinson. Norfolk, VA. Published postcards in the early twentieth century.

McGown-Silsbee Litho Co. New York, NY. Publisher of view cards, mostly of New York City subjects, 1910s.

McGrath, C.M. Sitka, AK. Published postcards in the early twentieth century, including those obtained from the American News Co. (ANC).

McGregor, H.R. Boothbay Harbor, ME. Publisher of RPPC view cards of regional topics in the 1930s.

McIntire, Edwin C. Gloucester, MA. Published view cards in the early twentieth century, including those from New England News Co.

McKay Art Co. Missoula, MT. Maker and publisher of RPPC regional views, 1920s to 1950s.

Merril, Harry. Newport, ME. Published postcards in the early twentieth century, including German imports.

Merrill, F.E. Freeport, ME. Published postcards in the early twentieth century, including German imports from the Hugh C. Leighton Co.

McKeague, George A., Co. Atlantic City, NJ. Publisher of RPPCs during the early twentieth century, including of images solicited from the public.

McKeough's Pharmacy. Gardner, MA. Published postcards in the early twentieth century.

McLaughlin & Barnhart. Omaha, NE. Published view cards in the early twentieth century, including those of the Curt Teich Co.

McLaughlin & Hotz. Omaha, NE. Published view cards in the early twentieth century, including those of the Curt Teich Co.

McLaughlin, J.F. Omaha, NE. Published postcards in the early twentieth century, including those of the Curt Teich Co.

McLauthlin, C.W. Green Harbor, MA. General store operator who published postcards of regional interest, early twentieth century.

McPhail's Colonial Shop. Orlando, FL. Published postcards in the mid-twentieth century, including cards from Dexter Press.

McQuiddy Printing Co. Nashville, TN. Published postcards in the early twentieth century, including some from E.C. Kropp.

Meadville News Co. Meadville, PA. Published postcards in the mid-twentieth century, including from the Curt Teich Co.

Medlar, Irvin A., Co. Omaha, NE. Distributed view cards in the early twentieth century.

Meeker, A.S. New York, NY. Publisher of art cards, including artist signed, some in series, with popular topics. Early twentieth century.

Meeker, Ezra. Seattle, WA. A traveler on the Oregon Trail in the mid–19th century, Meeker in the early twentieth century promoted its history and tradition, including publishing postcards with this theme.

- Meeker Series A: Oregon Trail, 16 subjects.

- Meeker Series B: Native Americans, etc, 16 subjects.

- Meeker Series C: Wagon travel, etc. 16 subjects.

Megathlin, C.W. Hyannis, MA. Publisher of view cards of regional topics, early twentieth century.

Megeath Stationery Co. Omaha, NE. Published view cards in the early twentieth century.

Mellinger Studios. Lancaster, PA. Published view cards in the late twentieth century.

Memphis Paper Co. Memphis, TN. Published postcards in the early twentieth century, including some from the E.C. Kropp Co.

Merchants Publishing Co. Lincoln, NE. Published view cards in the early twentieth century.

Meriden Gravure Co. Meriden, CT. Important printer of high-quality postcards, including black-and-white (mostly) views with excellent detail. The firm was also prominent in the production of prints, books, and other items.

Merrill, A.E. Damariscotta, ME. Photographer who issued RPPCs of regional scenes, 1910s and 1920s.

Merrill, Elbridge Warren. Sitka, AK. Photographer and publisher of RPPCs, early twentieth century. Merrill moved to Alaska from Massachusetts during the gold excitement of the turn of the century.

Merrill, F.E. Freeport, ME. Publisher of regional views, mostly German imports, most via the Hugh C. Leighton Co.

Merrimac & Monitor Postcard Co. Norfolk, VA. Published postcards in the early twentieth century.

Merrimack Picture Postcard Co. North Springfield, VT. Issued postcards in the mid-twentieth century.

Merrimack Post Card Co. Haverhill, MA. Distributed view cards in the mid- and late nineteenth century, covering a wide variety of Eastern topics.

Mertz, George. Anthony, RI. Published postcards in the early twentieth century, including cards printed in Germany.

Methodist Book Concern. Cincinnati, OH. Publisher of postcards during the early twentieth century, including signed artists.

Metrocraft / Metropolitan. Everett, MA. Printer of linen and chrome cards circa 1940s onward.

Metropolitan News Co. / Metropolitan News & Publishing Co. Boston, MA. Often with MNCo monogram, occasionally with Metropolitan News & Publishing Co. imprint. Important publisher of color view and other cards, most imported from Germany, later from American printers.

Meyers, J.C., & Co. Moundsville, WV. Published postcards in the early twentieth century.

Meyer, Leo. Easton, PA. Issued postcards in the mid-twentieth century, including from Curt Teich and Co.

Michigan Calendar Co. Detroit, MI. Published view cards in the early twentieth century.

Mid-Continent News Co. Oklahoma City, OK. Publisher of view cards, cowboy themes, etc., 1920s onward, including from the E.C. Kropp Co.

Midas, W. & L. New Haven, CT. Publisher of view cards, early twentieth century, some supplied by Tichnor Brothers.

Midland Publishing Co. New York, NY. Publisher of postcards during the early twentieth century, including signed artists.

Midwest Map Co. Aurora, MO. Printer and publisher of color cards, including comics. 1930s onward.

Midwest Novelty Co. Denver, CO. Published postcards in the 1920s and 1930s.

Millar, G.V., & Co. Scranton, PA. Publisher of regional views, including of coal mines, early twentieth century.

Miller Art Co. New York (Brooklyn), NY. Publisher of view cards. Logotype with M on flaming pot with handle. 1910s to 1940s. Issued many cards for the 1939 World's Fair.

Miller Brothers. Apalachin, NY. Published regional view cards in the early twentieth century.

Miller Studio. Peoria, IL. Maker of RPPCs. Advertised their RPPCs as collectible in sets. 1900s and 1910s.

Miller, Byron Y. Bethel, VT. Issued RPPCs of regional interest in the early twentieth century.

Miller, John A. Cairo, IL. Published postcards in the early twentieth century.

Miller, Ruth Murray. Philadelphia, PA. Publisher of postcards, mostly of East Coast scenes, in connection with the Art Advertising Service, late 1920s through 1930s.

Miller, Walter H. & Co., Inc. Williamsburg, VA. Published postcards in the early twentieth century, including cards from E.C. Kropp Co.

Milliken, E.W. Calais, ME. Published view cards in the early twentieth century, including some imprinted, "Made in Germany for E.W. Milliken, Calais, Maine," without mention of any intermediary firm.

Mills, J. Erskine. Middletown, NY. Published view cards in the early twentieth century, including those printed in Germany.

Milo, H.R., & Co. Nahant, MA; Norfolk, VA. Publisher of view cards in the early twentieth century.

Miner, George A., Co. San Francisco, CA. Produced postcards in the early twentieth century, including RPPCs featuring advertising and products.

Minnehaha Art and Publishing Co. Minneapolis, MN. Publisher of postcards in the early twentieth century.

Minnesota News Co. St. Paul, MN. Publisher of postcards, mostly regional views, early twentieth century. Many had American News Co. (ANC) imprints.

Minogue, D., Art. Seattle, WA. Published postcards in the early twentieth century.

Minsky Brothers & Co., Publishing Division. Pittsburgh, PA. Published postcards in the mid-twentieth century, including from the Curt Teich Co.

Miskinen, J.H. Glendive, MT. "Traded as J.H. Miskinen Importer & Publisher." Published postcards in the early twentieth century, including cards from C.E. Wheelock and Co., and imported by them from Germany.

Mitchell, A.B. Published postcards in the 1920s and 1930s.

Mitchell, Edward H., Co. San Francisco, CA. Major printer and publisher of postcards, mostly of Western subjects, and cards with exaggerations, flowers, and other subjects. Some early cards were imported from Germany and some were printed elsewhere, but most were manufactured by Mitchell, who also made cards for other firms. Many cards have muted colors with tints of brown. Active from the late 1890s to the early 1920s. Numbering of cards was often erratic, and many were published without numbers. Many monochrome cards are printed in heavy sepia on a cocoa-colored stock—not everyone's preference today in deltiology, but apparently considered artistic at the time. In connection with the 1915 Panama-Pacific International Exposition, Mitchell operated the Exposition Publishing Co., which issued postcards.

- Early monotone cards numbered 1 to 4999 plus some in the 8000 series; others bore no number.

- Early color cards with undivided backs, 1 to 999, plus cards without numbers.

- Divided back cards 1 to 3366 plus large quantities unnumbered cards, including many printed for other publishers.

Mitock & Sons. North Hollywood, CA. Published view cards in the late twentieth century, including Plastichrome.

Modern-Ad. Butler, PA. Published postcards in the late twentieth century.

Moebius, E., Phototyping. Camden, NJ. Published postcards in the early twentieth century.

Moehring & Groesbeck. Lynn, MA. Publishers of RPPCs of New England motifs, early twentieth century.

Moffat, Yard & Co. New York, NY. Publisher of lithographed cards with romantic and other scenes, also signed artists, early twentieth century to 1912, when the firm became part of the John Lane Co.

Mohr & Packer. San Francisco, CA. Published postcards in the early twentieth century.

Moll, J.B., Jr. Oxford, MD. Publisher of postcards during the early twentieth century, including signed artists.

Molony, J.F. Mill Rift, PA. Published cards in the early twentieth century, including German imports.

Moncier's, Inc. Knoxville, TN. Published view cards in the mid-twentieth century.

Monroe, George H. Jamestown, NY. Photographer and also a publisher of postcards, including those with his own images, printed in Germany in the early twentieth century.

Montana Post Card Co. Helena, MT. Published postcards in the early twentieth century, including from the Curt Teich Co.

Montana Souvenir Co. Missoula, MT. Publisher of regional view cards from the first decade of the twentieth century, continuing into the 1960s.

Montgomery, C.D. Chicago, IL. Publisher of postcards during the early twentieth century, including signed artists.

Montgomery, H. Hartford, WI. Published RPPCs of regional subjects in the early twentieth century.

Moore & Gibson Co. New York, NY. Published postcards in the early twentieth century, including German imports.

Moore, A. New York (Brooklyn), NY. Publisher of regional view postcards in the first decade of the twentieth century.

Moore, Clem. Richmond, MA. Published postcards in the late twentieth century, including cards from Dexter Press.

Moore, H.L., Co. West Yarmouth, MA. Published view cards in the late twentieth century, including those made by Tichnor Brothers.

Moore, S. Spencer, Co. Charleston, WV. Published postcards in the early twentieth century, including cards from the Curt Teich Co. Also appears in print as S. Spencer, Moore & Co. and, further, SS. Spencer-Moore Co.

Morgan Brothers. Portland, ME. Issued view cards in the early twentieth century, including German imports.

Morgan, H.C., & Co. Muskogee, OK. Published postcards in the early twentieth century, including German imports.

Morgan, Tom P. Rogers, AR. Published view cards in the early twentieth century, including those of the Curt Teich Co.

Morningside Printing Co. Sioux City, IA. Published postcards in the early twentieth century, including those of the Curt Teich Co.

Morrell, F.H. Irvington-On-Hudson, NY. Published view cards in the early twentieth century, including German imports from the American News Co.

Morrell, L.B. Lewiston, ME. Published postcards in the early twentieth century.

Morrill Press. Fulton, NY. Printed and published postcards, mostly view cards, in the early twentieth century.

Morris, Charles E., Co. Chinook and Great Falls, MT. Photographer of regional views that were printed and issued on postcards, including early imports from Germany, later cards by Curt Teich. "C E M Co. Kwality" logotype. Also produced RPPCs of regional scenes. Early twentieth century through the mid–1920s.

Morris, G.W. Portland, ME. Important publisher of view cards, mostly with East Coast topics, Maine to Florida, but with New England as a specialty. Early cards were German imports, later cards were made domestically by Curt Teich and others. Early twentieth century through early 1920s.

Morrison Brothers News Agency. Issued postcards in the mid-twentieth century, including cards of Curt Teich and Co.

Morse's Photo Service. Lake Wales, FL. Published postcards in the early twentieth century onward, including cards from Dexter Press, Curt Teich Company, and Albertype.

Moser, N. New York, NY. Photographer who issued many RPPCs, including aviation, naval, and military subjects, 1910s to 1930s.

Mosher Photo Service. Vineyard Haven, MA. Published view cards in the late twentieth century, including those made by the Transcolor Corporation.

Moss Photo Service, Inc. New York, NY. Publisher of inexpensive view cards, middle and late twentieth century, and RPPCs with advertising.

Moss, Alcan, Publishing Co. New York, NY. Publisher of postcards during the early twentieth century, including signed artists.

Moss, F.A. Denver, CO. Publisher of postcards during the early twentieth century, including signed artists.

Mothershed. San Benito, TX. Published postcards in the late twentieth century.

Moulin, Gabriel. San Francisco, CA. Published postcards in the early twentieth century.

Mound City Post Card Co. St. Louis, MO. Published postcards in the early twentieth century.

Mount Pleasant Mercantile & Supply Co. Mount Pleasant, IA. Published postcards in the early twentieth century, including those from the Albertype Co.

Mount Vernon Chapter of the Daughters of the American Republic. Washington, D.C. Published view cards relating to their organization in the early twentieth century, including German imports.

Moyland, Stephen, Press (Stephen Moyland Press). Whitford, PA. Publisher of postcards during the early twentieth century, including signed artists.

Mozert Studio and Camera Shop, The. Silver Springs, FL. Published postcards in the late twentieth century, including cards from Lusterchrome.

Muir & Co. Chicago, IL. Publisher of postcards during the early twentieth century, including signed artists.

Muller, Enrique and Robert. New York, NY. Photographers, especially of naval scenes, whose names are on many RPPCs. Early twentieth century.

Mullinix, L.M. Lookout Mountain, TN. Published postcards in the mid-twentieth century, including from the Curt Teich Co.

Murphy, John H., System. Minneapolis, MN. Traded as "John H. Murphy System." Published postcards in the early twentieth century.

Murphy, Thomas D., Co. Red Oak, IA. Publisher of postcards, many with advertising imprints, including signed artist cards, in the early twentieth century, this in addition to their main line of calendars (one of America's most extensive).

Musgrove, R.W. Bristol, NH. Published postcards in the early twentieth century.

Mutual Book Co. Boston, MA. Publisher of postcards during the early twentieth century, including signed artists.

MWM. Aurora, MO. Published "MRM Color Litho" postcards, late twentieth century.

Myer, Herbert A., & Co. Syracuse and Jordan (most imprints), NY. Photographer who made many RPPCs of regional views, prominent in the 1910s.

Myers Card Shop. Rock Island, IL. Published postcards in the early twentieth century, including those of the Curt Teich Co.

Myers Photo Co. Columbus, OH. Published RPPCs in the first two decades of the twentieth century.

Mynderse, J.F. Altamont, NY. Published view cards in the early twentieth century, including German imports from American News Co. (ANC).

N

N.E. Paper & Stationery Co. See New England Paper & Stationery Co.

Nash, A.N. Published postcards in the early twentieth century, including cards from Germany obtained from the American News Co. (ANC).

Nash, E. New York, NY. Publisher of colorful holiday, greeting, and other postcards, early twentieth century.

Nash, E.W. Damariscotta, ME. Published postcards in the early twentieth century, including those made by H.G. Zimmerman.

National Art Co. New York, NY. Publisher of view, comic, artist-signed, and other types of postcards, early twentieth century to about 1930. Archie Gunn was a popular artist whose works were used.

National Art Publishing Co. Elmira, NY. Published cards including printed greeting and other cards, in color with small real photographs affixed.

National Art Views Co. New York, NY. Early twentieth century publisher of high-quality view cards, mostly German imports, often with printed "frame" borders. Merged into the Rotograph Co. in 1904.

National Color Cards Co. Ridgefield Park, NJ. Published view cards in the late twentieth century, including those printed by Dexter Press.

National Colortype Co. Bellevue, KY. Printer and publisher of view cards covering a wide area of mid-America, circa 1900s to 1920s.

National News Co. New York, NY. Published view cards in the early twentieth century, including German imports from American News Company (ANC).

National Novelty Co. St. Louis, MO. Published postcards in the early twentieth century.

National Photograph Co. Chicago, IL. Made RPPCs, including advertising cards, in the early twentieth century. Its imprint was usually in the negative on the face.

National Photograph Co. Niskayuna, NY. Conducted by P. Goodfellow, produced RPPCs in the early twentieth century.

National Post Card Co. Philadelphia, PA; Atlantic City, NJ. Issued postcards in the mid-twentieth century.

National Studio. Oklahoma City, OK. Published postcards in the 1920s and 1930s, including from the Curt Teich Co. Managed by J. Thomas McHaney.

National Tribune. Washington, D.C. Published view cards in the early twentieth century for the general Washington area including Virginia, West Virginia, and Maryland.

National Woman Suffrage Publishing Co., Inc. Publisher of art cards of Rose O'Neill during the early twentieth century, including signed artists.

Nationwide Advertising Co. Tyler, TX. Published postcards in the mid-twentieth century.

Nationwide Postcard Co. Arlington, TX. Published postcards in the mid-twentieth century.

Navin, John. Williamstown, MA. Published postcards in the early twentieth century.

Nebraska Paper & Bag Co. Lincoln, NE. Published view cards in the early twentieth century, including those of the Curt Teich Co.

Neeley, J.L., Magazine Co. Memphis, TN. Published postcards in the early twentieth century, including some from Tichnor Brothers.

Neff Novelty Co. Cumberland, MD. Published postcards in the early twentieth century, including cards made by the Commercial Colortype Co.

Negler, A.C. Buffalo, NY. Published postcards in the early twentieth century.

Negus, N. Block Island, RI. Photographer and issuer of RPPCs as well as a distributor of printed cards. Early twentieth century. Some of his views were reproduced by American News Co. (ANC) in the Litho-Chrome series.

Neidlinger, W.J. Westbrook, CT. Published postcards in the early twentieth century, including German imports.

Nelson, C.M. Boston, MA. Photographer and maker of RPPC cards, including photographs with a birch-bark border surrounding. Printed cards were issued as well. Most were of Northeast views. Early twentieth century.

Nelson, Eric, News, Co. Omaha, NE. Distributed view cards in the mid-twentieth century, including those of the Curt Teich Co.

Nessiff, Minnie. Sistersville, WV. Published postcards in the early twentieth century, including those from H.G. Zimmerman.

Neuces News Agency. Corpus Christi, TX. Published postcards in the mid-twentieth century, including cards by E.C. Kropp Co.

Neuner Co. Los Angeles, CA. Publisher of colorfully lithographed cards. Featured the "Calitype Process."

Neunlist, J. Rudy. Pasadena, TX. Published postcards in the late twentieth century, including cards from Dexter Press.

Nevada Photo Co. Virginia City, NV. Issued RPPC cards in the early twentieth century, including of short-lived mining towns.

New England News Co. Boston, MA. Publisher of view and other cards in the early twentieth century, including German imports to about 1914 and domestic products after that. Many of their later view cards have somewhat muted colors. Most subjects are Northeastern views.

New England Paper & Stationery Co. Ayer, MA. Often as N.E. Paper and Stationery Co. Publisher of view cards of regional subjects, early twentieth century.

New England Printing Co. North Adams, MA. Printed view cards, including in color, in the early twentieth century.

New Era Printing Co. Parker, SD. Published postcards in the early twentieth century.

New Jersey Post Card Co. Newark, NJ. Publisher of view cards of regional scenes, most of which were printed by the Curt Teich Co. Second decade of the twentieth century.

New Orleans News Co. New Orleans, LA. Published postcards in the late twentieth century, including those by E.C. Kropp Co., and German imports via the American News Co. (ANC).

New York Gravure Co. New York, NY. Printer of high-quality black-and-white cards.

New York Postal Card Co. Chicago, IL. Published postcards in the early twentieth century.

Newberry, J.J., & Co. Stroudsburg, PA. Five-and-ten cent store chain that distributed postcards, 1910s onward.

Newcomb Publishing Co. New York, NY. Publisher of postcards during the early twentieth century, including signed artists.

Newman Post Card Co. / O. Newman Co. Los Angeles and San Francisco, CA. Oskar Newman, publisher of holiday, view, topical, and other cards in the 1900s and 1910s as O. Newman Co., 1910s to the 1960s as the Newman Post Card Co. Early subjects included the 1906 San Francisco earthquake and fire and the 1915 Panama-Pacific International Exposition.

News Stand Distributor. Los Angeles, CA. Published cards in the early twentieth century, including those by the Curt Teich Co.

News Tribune. Duluth, MN. Published postcards in the early twentieth century, including from the Acmegraph Co.

Neyhart, Frank A., & Co. Tacoma, WA. Published view cards in the early twentieth century, including those from Curt Teich Co.

Niagara Envelope Manufactory. Buffalo, NY. Niagara distributed many products including postcards for the 1901 Pan-American Exposition held in Buffalo, printed for them by Gies & Co.

Nichols, Charles F. Orono, ME. Published postcards in the early twentieth century.

Nickels, H.L., & Co. Nampa, ID. Published view cards in the early twentieth century, including those made by the E.C. Kropp Company.

Nicola & Harmon. Washington, IA. Published postcards in the early twentieth century, including German imports.

Nicoll's Art Store. Wheeling, WV. Published RPPCs in the early twentieth century.

Nobs, Fred. Brownwood, TX. Published postcards in the late twentieth century, including cards from Dexter Press.

Nolan and Prince. Mohawk, NY. Published view cards in the late twentieth century, including those made by Tichnor Brothers.

Nomis Manufacturing Co. New York, NY. Publisher of view (mostly) postcards with East Coast scenes, 1910s through 1930s. Some marked "hand colored."

Norfolk Printing Co. Norfolk, VA. Published postcards in the early twentieth century.

Norris, F.A. Eldora, IA. Published postcards in the early twentieth century, including those printed in Germany obtained from PCK.

North American Post Card Co. Kansas City, MO. Issuer of RPPC cards, 1910s and 1920s, with regional and Western scenes, many showing people, including Native Americans.

North Carolina News Co. Durham, NC. Distributed view cards in the mid-twentieth century, including those of the Curt Teich Co.

North Shore Novelty Co. Lynn, MA. Issued view cards in the early twentieth century.

North West Novelty Co. Seattle, WA. Issued view cards in the early twentieth century, including some imported from Germany.

Northwest Postcard & Souvenir Co. Butte, MT. Publisher of postcards during the early twentieth century, including signed artists.

Norton News Agency. Dubuque, IA. Published postcards in the early twentieth century.

Norwood Souvenir Co. Cincinnati, OH. Early twentieth century publisher of regional view postcards.

Novelti-Craft Co. Miami, FL. Published postcards in the mid-twentieth century, including cards from Colourpicture.

Novelty Post Card Co. Kansas City, MO. Published postcards in the early twentieth century, including German imports.

Novelty Post Card Studio. Seattle, WA. Published postcards in the early twentieth century.

Novelty Printing Co. Los Angeles, CA. Printed postcards including advertising postcards in the early twentieth century.

Novelty Store. Morristown, TN. Published postcards in the early twentieth century, including cards from the Curt Teich Co.

Nutter, H.H. Pittsfield, ME. Published postcards in the early twentieth century, including German imports and also made by the Curt Teich Co.

NYCE Manufacturing Co. Vernfield, PA. Sometimes as Nyce, but often as "NYCE" as a trademark or business style for the cards. This firm, founded by Abraham H. Nyce, issued generic cards with stock scenes, preprinted, to which on the front a bottom line could be added, such as "Greetings from No. Conway, N.H." The cards were made by Curt Teich (Chicago) and possibly others as well. Also issued signed artist cards.

Nye, Everett I. Wellfleet, MA. Publisher of regional view postcards, mostly in the 1910s.

O

O'Connell, J.P., and E. Boyle. Published postcards in the early twentieth century, including cards imported from Germany.

O'Neall Specialty Co. McAllen, TX. Published postcards in the mid-twentieth century, including cards from E.C. Kropp Co.

O'Neil, Garnet. Detroit, MI. Published postcards in the late twentieth century.

Oak Studio. Presque Isle, ME. Produced RPPCs in the early twentieth century. The firm's emblem was an oak leaf.

Oakes Photo Co. Seattle, WA. Made RPPCs and published printed cards in the early twentieth century.

Observer Printing House, Inc. Charlotte, NC. Distributed view cards in the mid-twentieth century.

Ocean News Co. Old Orchard Beach, ME. Publisher of view cards, including those of Tichnor Brothers, in the early twentieth century.

Oklahoma News Co. Tulsa, OK. Published postcards from the 1920s to the 1950s, including from the Curt Teich Co.

Olander, Emil, & Co. Primghar, IA. Published postcards in the early twentieth century, including German imports.

Oleogravure Co. New York, NY. Published postcards in the early twentieth century.

Oleson, C. Oscar, Photo Co. Lemmon, SD. Issuer of RPPCs in the early twentieth century.

Olmstead Brothers Co. Wheeling, WV. Published postcards in the early twentieth century.

Olson News Co. Sioux City, IA. Published postcards in the early twentieth century.

Olson's Book and News Store. Emporium, PA. Published postcards in the mid-twentieth century, including from the Curt Teich Co.

Olsson, J.F., & Co. Cambridge, MA. Published view cards of regional topics in the early twentieth century.

Omaha News Co. Omaha, NE. Publisher of postcards, early twentieth century, including German imprints via the American News Co. (ANC). Native Americans were a popular subject.

Oneonta Department Store. Oneonta, NY. Issued a very illustrious series of RPPCs in the early twentieth century, with interior and exterior views of buildings, events, people, and more. While they are not numbered as a series, in the aggregate they form a very diverse and interesting view of scenes in and around that town in Upstate New York.

Orcutt, J.C. & G.E. Lincoln, NE. Published view cards during the early twentieth century.

Oregon Art Co. Bend, OR. Issued RPPCs in the early twentieth century.

Oregon News Co. Portland, OR. Publisher of postcards, early twentieth century, including German imprints via the American News Co. (ANC) in the early years. twentieth century through the mid–1930s.

Orndorff Drug Store. El Paso, TX. Published postcards in the early twentieth century, including German imports via American News Company.

Oroszco, Ricardo J., Press. San Francisco, CA. Published postcards in the early twentieth century.

Osage Indian Curio Co. Tulsa, OK. Published postcards in the early twentieth century, including from the Commercial Colortype Co.

Osborne Calendar Co. Newark, NJ. Publisher of postcards, many with advertising imprints, including signed artist cards, in the early twentieth century.

Osborne, Ltd. New York, NY. Publisher of regional view cards, many imprinted "Made in America" and with a standing Indian.

Osborne, W.W. Santa Barbara, CA. Published view cards in the early twentieth century including those made by Albertype.

Osgood, H.W. Pittsfield, NH. Important regional publisher of RPPCs in the early twentieth century.

Ottenheimer, I. & M., Co. Baltimore, MD. Publisher of view cards with mid-Atlantic scenes, etc., early twentieth century onward.

Ottmann, J., Lithographic Co. New York, NY. Publisher of postcards during the early twentieth century, including signed artists.

Ottumwa News Agency. Ottumwa, IA. Published postcards in the early twentieth century.

Out West Photo. Denver, CO. Issued RPPCs in the 1920s and 1930s, including of rodeos and other Western subjects.

Ovren, O.C. Billings, MT. Traded as "O.C. Ovren Importer & Publisher." Published postcards in the early twentieth century.

Owen Art-Color. Newcastle, ME. Published postcards in the late twentieth century, including cards from E.C. Kropp Co.

Owen Card Publishing Co. Elmira, NY. Publisher of view, greetings, and other postcards in the 1910s and 1920s, following a line of earlier Baker Brothers imprints.

Owen, F.A., Co. Dansville, NY. Publisher of postcards during the early twentieth century, including signed artists.

Owens Brothers-Hillson Co. Boston, MA; Berlin and Leipzig, Germany. Published postcards in the early twentieth century.

P

Pacific Novelty Co. San Francisco, CA. Important publisher primarily of view postcards, mostly with California and West Coast subjects, early twentieth century onward. Many early cards were German imports.

Pacific Photo Co. Salem, OR. Issued RPPCs in the early twentieth century.

Pacific Stationery & Specialty Co. San Francisco, CA. Publisher of view cards in the early twentieth century, including those of the Curt Teich Co. "Super-Tone Quality Cards" was imprinted on some.

Paget Co. Chicago, IL. Published postcards in the early twentieth century.

Palmer Publishing Co. New York, NY. Publisher of postcards during the early twentieth century, including signed artists.

Palmer, Frank. Spokane, WA. Photographer and issuer of RPPCs, first two decades of the twentieth century.

Panama-Pacific International Exposition Novelty Co. San Francisco, CA. Published postcards relating to the Exposition.

Panama-Pacific International Exposition, Department of Fine Arts. San Francisco, CA. Published postcards relating to the Exposition.

Pan-American Publishing Corp. North Miami, FL. Published postcards in the late twentieth century.

Paper Products Co. Pueblo, CO. Published postcards in the 1920s and 1930s, including from the Curt Teich Co.

Park Manufacturing Co. St. Louis, MO. Published postcards in the early twentieth century.

Park, A.J. Seattle, WA. Published postcards in the early twentieth century.

Parke, W.T. Estes Park, CO. Published postcards in the early twentieth century.

Parker, Harold A. Pasadena, CA. Photographer and publisher of printed postcards, many hand-colored, some by the Albertype Co. Early twentieth century.

Parker, T.E., & Co. South New Berlin, NY. Published RPPCs in the early twentieth century.

Parkhurst Co. Oklahoma City, OK. Published postcards in the early twentieth century, including those from the Curt Teich Co.

Parkison, W.S. Glenwood Springs, CO. Published postcards in the early twentieth century.

Parlette-Wigger Co. Oklahoma City, OK. Published postcards in the 1920s and 1930s, including from the Curt Teich Co.

Parsons, F., & Co. Atlantic, IA. Published postcards in the early twentieth century, including those printed in Germany and obtained from PCK.

Parsons, Jack. Los Angeles, CA. Published view cards in Los Angeles in the early twentieth century. including those for the Pacific Electric interurban line.

Parsons, W.H. & Co. Roxbury Crossing, MA. Made RPPCs in the early twentieth century.

Pastime Novelty Co. New York, NY. Publisher of postcards including from sketches and other art. Early twentieth century.

Patterson, Frank. Medford, OR. Photographer who issued RPPCs, 1920s to early 1940s.

Patton Brothers & Cooke / Patton Post Card Co. / Post Card Studio. Salem, OR. Maker of RPPCs and publisher of printed cards in the early twentieth century.

Patton Postcard Co. Salem, OR. Published view cards in the early twentieth century.

Paul, Harry, & Associates. Boston, MA. Publisher of postcards during the early twentieth century, including signed artists.

Payne, T.H., & Co. Chattanooga, TN. Published postcards in the early twentieth century, including those from the Curt Teich Co. Products included the "Lookout Series" in various numbered sequences.

PCK. See entry under Koeber, Paul C., Co., under K. Peacock logotype.

Pearson-Ullberg Co. Minneapolis, MN. Published postcards in the early twentieth century.

Pease, C.H. (Press of C.H. Pease). Canaan, CT. Published view cards at the turn of the twentieth century.

Pease, L.F. Buffalo, NY. Publisher of postcards during the early twentieth century, including signed artists.

Pegley, H. Winslow. Reading, PA. Published postcards in the early twentieth century.

Peks China Store. Galesburg, IL. Published postcards in the early twentieth century, including cards made in Germany. Billed itself as "importers and publishers," but certain of their cards with this imprint were imported through G.C. Wheelock.

Pelicano, Rossie & Co. San Francisco, CA. Published postcards in the early twentieth century.

Pelton, Herbert W. Asheville, NC. Published postcards in the early and mid-twentieth century.

Pennington News Agency. Ponca City, OK. Published postcards in the 1920s and 1930s, including from the Curt Teich Co.

Pennsylvania News Co. Altoona, PA. Issued postcards in the mid-twentieth century, including from Tichnor Brothers. Also in print as Penn News Co.

Penobscot Studios. Stonington, ME. Issued RPPCs of regional subjects in the 1930s and 1940s.

Penrod Studio. Berrien Center, MI. Published view cards in the late twentieth century, including those made by Dexter Press.

Perkins & Butler, Inc. Worcester, MA. Publisher of postcards, including of Tichnor Brothers, early twentieth century.

Perkins, G.E. Dolgeville, NY. Published RPPCs in the early twentieth century.

Perkins, J.F. Damariscotta, ME. Published postcards in the early twentieth century.

Perkins, W.B. Black Hills (Lead), SD. Photographer who sold printed cards, including of his own images and of other subjects. Some early cards were German imports. Early twentieth century.

Perry & Perry. Published postcards in the early twentieth century, including German imports and cards obtained from S. Langsdorf and Co.

Perry Pictures Co. Malden, MA. Publishers of view cards, including of Provincetown, MA, in the early twentieth century.

Perry Studio. Armour, SD. Issued RPPCs in the early twentieth century.

Peterson, Martin. Algona, IA. Published postcards in the early twentieth century, including those obtained from Bloom Brothers.

Peterson, Paul C. Duxbury, MA. Published postcards in the early twentieth century, including cards from the Curt Teich Co.

Petley Studios / Bob Petley. Phoenix, AZ. Publisher of view cards in the mid- and late twentieth century.

Pettus, L.J. Chattanooga, TN. Published postcards in the early twentieth century, including those imported from Great Britain.

PFB. See listing under Paul Finkenrath, under F.

Pfeiffer Co. Cedar Falls, IA. Published postcards in the early twentieth century

THE ELITE SERIES
OF ORIGINAL
PHOTOGRAPHS
Made by C. H. PHELPS, SIDNEY, N. Y.

Phelps, C.H. Sidney, NY. Publisher of RPPCs in the early twentieth century, many sold as "The Elite Series."

Philadelphia Post Card Co. Philadelphia, PA. Publisher of postcards with views, stage personalities, etc., in the early twentieth century.

Phillips & Willson. Bozeman, MT. Published postcards in the early twentieth century.

Phillips, Augustus D., & Son. Northeast Harbor, ME. Published view cards in the early twentieth century.

Phillips, I. Denver, CO. Publisher of postcards during the early twentieth century, including signed artists.

Phillips, Luther S. Bangor, ME. Published view cards in the late twentieth century.

Photo & Art Postal Card Co. New York, NY. Publisher of color and monotone view cards of regional subjects, early twentieth century to the 1930s, including many by Curt Teich Co.

Photo Card Co. New York, NY. Maker of RPPC advertising and other cards, early twentieth century.

Photo Color Graph Co. New York, NY. Publisher of art cards with people, flowers, and other popular subjects. Early twentieth century.

Photochrome Process Co. Philadelphia, PA. Producer of color views organized by some employees of the defunct Detroit Publishing Co. Cards have a resemblance to the earlier Detroit Phostint cards, with somewhat subdued colors. Formed in the mid-1930s.

Photo-Electrotype Engraving Co. New York, NY. Printer of inexpensive halftone black-and-white and hand-colored cards in the early twentieth century.

Photograph Co. of America. Chicago, IL. Issued RPPCs in the early twentieth century, including those advertising products.

Photo-Ty Post Card Co. Philadelphia, PA. Printer of view and other cards, many with a glossy finish imitative of RPPCs. Early twentieth century into the 1930s.

Pictorial Card Co. New York, NY. Publisher of view cards of regional interest, early twentieth century.

Pictorial Center. Miami, FL. Published postcards in the early twentieth century.

Pieper, H.A. Troy, NY. Published view cards in the early twentieth century, including those obtained from the New England Printing Company.

Pierce, Jay M. Published postcards in the early twentieth century, including German imports.

Pierce, W.S., Illustrating Co. Welton, ME. Issued RPPCs in the early twentieth century.

Pike News Co. Clarksburg, WV. Published postcards in the early twentieth century.

Pillsbury Picture Co. / Pillsbury's Pictures, Inc. Oakland and San Francisco, CA. Photographer and large-volume issuer of RPPCs, including of the 1906 San Francisco earthquake and fire, Yosemite National Park, Main Streets of small towns, and other West Coast subjects. Early twentieth century into the 1940s.

Piltz, Stanley A., Co. San Francisco, CA. Publisher of view cards, including historical images, mainly of California, mostly printed by the Curt Teich Co. 1930s to 1950s.

Pinehurst, Inc. Pinehurst, NC. Distributed view cards in the early twentieth century, including those made by Albertype.

Pinkau, Emil, & Co. New York, NY; Leipzig, Germany. Published postcards in the early twentieth century.

Pinkussohn, J.S., Cigar Co. Jacksonville, FL. Published postcards in the early twentieth century.

Pinsker, William, Co. Coney Island, NY. Publisher of view cards, mid-twentieth century.

Pitkin, C.G. Whitehall, MI. Published view cards in the early twentieth century, including German imports.

Pitts (That Man Pitts). San Francisco, CA. Published postcards in the early twentieth century.

Plant, P.J. Washington, D.C. Publisher of art cards with sentimental descriptions, songs, romantic scenes, etc., first decade of the twentieth century. The Spirit-Graph novelty cards changed when a red film was placed over the image. Published a set of eight monochrome views of firemen in action.

Plastichrome. See Colourpicture Publishers, Inc.

Platinachrome Co. New York, NY. Publisher of postcards, including regional views, in the early twentieth century. New York City subjects were a specialty.

Pocket City Post Card Co. McGregor, IA. Published postcards in the early twentieth century.

Polychrome Co. San Francisco, CA. Printer of view postcards in the early twentieth century, including for various regional publishers.

Poole Brothers. Chicago, CA. Published postcards in the early twentieth century.

Porteous, Mitchell and Braun Co. Portland, ME. Published postcards in the early twentieth century, including from the Curt Teich Co.

Porter & Reynolds. Washington, D.C. Published postcards in the early twentieth century.

Porter, A.B. Waco, TX. Published postcards in the mid-twentieth century, including cards from E.C. Kropp Co.

Porter, A.V. Ellenville, NY. Published view cards in the early twentieth century, including those obtained from the Albertype Company.

Portland Candy Co. Portland, ME. Publisher of postcards, including those printed by the Dexter Press, late twentieth century.

Portland Post Card Co. Portland, OR. Publisher of view (mostly) postcards, emphasizing Pacific Northwest topics, including German imports. Official publisher of the 1909 Alaska-Yukon-Pacific Exposition cards.

Portsmouth News Agency. Portsmouth, OH. Published postcards in the 1920s and 1930s, including from the Curt Teich Co.

Pospeshil Card Service. Sioux City, IA. Publisher of postcards during the early twentieth century, including signed artists.

Post Card Distributing Co. Atlantic City, NJ; Philadelphia, PA. Issued postcards in the mid-twentieth century, including cards from the Curt Teich Co.

Post Card Exchange Publishers. Birmingham, AL. Publisher of view, greetings, and other postcards, early twentieth century to about 1920.

Post Card Shop. Seattle, WA. Published postcards in the early twentieth century.

Post Card Union of America. Philadelphia, PA. Publisher of postcards during the early twentieth century, including signed artists.

Power & Bloom. Mount Vernon, IA. Published postcards in the early twentieth century.

Powers, C.A. Moulton, IA. Published postcards in the early twentieth century, including German imports.

Powers, T.E., Novelty Co. San Francisco, CA. Published postcards in the early twentieth century.

Prang, Louis, & Co. (Louis Prang & Co.) Boston, MA. Publisher of art cards during the early twentieth century, including signed artists, famous as general lithographers.

Prann, Ernest L. Deep River, CT. Published postcards in the early twentieth century, including German imports.

Preedy, F.W. Portsmouth, VA. Published postcards in the early twentieth century.

Prescott Studio. Chicago, IL. Issued RPPCs in the early twentieth century.

Press of C.H. Pease. Canaan, CT. Published view cards at the turn of the twentieth century.

Press, The. Frederick, OK. Black-and-white postcards in the mid-twentieth century.

Price's Studio. Jacksboro, TX. Made regional RPPCs in the early twentieth century.

Pridgen's Studio. Orange, TX. Published postcards in the mid-twentieth century, including cards from Tichnor Brothers.

Prilay, W.M. Pittsfield, ME. Published postcards in the early twentieth century.

Prince, Henry M. Published view cards in the early twentieth century, including German imports.

Printline. New York, NY. Publisher of postcards during the early twentieth century, including signed artists.

Process Photo Studios. Chicago, IL. Mass-produced RPPCs in the early twentieth century.

Progress Corporation. Norfolk, VA. Published postcards in the early twentieth century.

Providence Novelty Co. Providence, RI. Publisher of postcards during the early twentieth century, including signed artists.

Provincetown Advocate Post Card Shop / Provincetown Advocate. Provincetown, MA. Published view cards in the early twentieth century, including German imports and also domestic cards, the latter including those obtained from H.A. Dickerman & Son and printed by the Curt Teich Co. The Gift Shop had a large selection of postcards for sale.

Pryse, Zack T. Mangum, OK. Published postcards in the early twentieth century, including German imports.

Publicaciones Barrera. Laredo, TX. Publisher of postcards during the early twentieth century, including signed artists.

Publicity Travel Bureau. Oswego, NY. Issued postcards in the mid-twentieth century.

Pudney, B.E. Sidney, NY. Published view cards in the early twentieth century, including German imports.

Pueblo Wholesale News Co. Pueblo, CO. Published postcards in the 1920s and 1930s, including from the Curt Teich Co.

Puget Sound News Co. Seattle, WA. Publisher of view (mainly) and other postcards, including German imports via the American News Co. Early twentieth century.

Pulman, O.S. Albany, NY. Published view cards in the mid-twentieth century.

Purdy, F.B. Belchertown, MA. Published view cards in the early twentieth century.

Purdy's Bookstore. Galveston, TX. Published postcards in the early twentieth century.

Puritan Art Co. Lynn, MA. Published view cards in the early twentieth century, including German imports.

Purvis, A.J. Utica, NY. Published view cards in the early twentieth century, including those made in Germany.

Putnam Art Co. Boston, MA. Distributor of view cards of regional interest, many of which were hand-colored. Flourished in the 1910s.

Putnam, E.D., & Sons. Antrim, NH. Photographers who issued RPPCs and distributed printed views of regional as well as national scenes, 1920s to 1940s.

Q

Quaddy Playthings Manufacturing Co. Kansas City, MO. Publisher of postcards during the early twentieth century, including signed artists.

Quadri-Color Co. New York, NY. Printer of color lithographic postcards in the early twentieth century.

Quimby, C.H. Wheeling, WV. Published postcards in the early twentieth century, including German imports.

Quinlan, B.A. Bennington, VT. Druggist who published a line of regional view cards in color, imported from Germany in the early twentieth century.

R

Rabe, S. San Antonio, TX. Published postcards in the early twentieth century, including cards from the H.H. Tammen Co.

Rabineau, G.T. Lake Placid, NY. Photographer of regional topics, some of whose works were issued as RPPCs. Flourished in the 1920s.

Radell, Louis A. Marblehead, MA. Published view cards in the early twentieth century, including those printed by the Curt Teich Co.

Raleigh News Agency. Raleigh, NC. Published view cards in the mid-twentieth century, including those made by E.C. Kropp Co.

Ranapar Studio. Tacoma, WA. Published RPPCs of regional interest, including Mount Rainier National Park. Some images were retouched or otherwise altered.

Range Land Publishing Co. Sheridan, WY. Publisher of postcards during the early twentieth century, including signed artists.

Rank, C.W. Virginia City, MT. Published postcards in the mid-twentieth century, including from the Albertype Co.

Rankin, A.L. Wells, ME. Published cards in the early twentieth century, including German imports.

Ransden, C.R. East Bridgewater, MA. Published RPPCs in the early twentieth century.

Read & White. Bloomington, IL. Published postcards in the early twentieth century, including from the Curt Teich Co.

Read House Cigar Co. Chattanooga, TN. Published postcards in the early twentieth century, including those of the Curt Teich Co.

Read, W.B. & Co. Bloomington, IL. Published postcards in the early twentieth century, including from the Curt Teich Co.

Red Farm Studio. Pawtucket, RI. Publisher of postcards during the early twentieth century, including signed artists.

Redfield Brothers, Inc. New York, NY. Published art postcards for the Hudson-Fulton Celebration in 1909.

Reed, Charles K. Worcester, MA. Publisher of postcards during the early twentieth century, including signed artists.

Reed, F.W.K. Bangor, ME. Published postcards in the early twentieth century, including from Curt Teich Co.

Reed, Harry. Moab, UT. Photographer who issued RPPCs of the Arches National Park and other views in the 1930s and 1940s.

Regensteiner Colortype. Chicago, IL. Published postcards in the early twentieth century.

Reichner Brothers. Boston, MA; Leipzig and Munich, Germany. Publisher of color view cards, mainly of Northeastern topics, printed in Germany. Their cards with added copper, such as in reflective windows, are of special interest.

Reid, Robert A. Seattle, WA. Published postcards in the early twentieth century.

Reinthal & Newman. New York, NY. Highly important publisher of artist-signed cards, including by Philip Boileau, F. Earl Christy, Harrison Fisher, and Jessie Wilcox Smith, and distributor of certain Raphael Kirchner cards. Most with American artists were printed in the United States. Most R&N cards were issued in large quantities, usually conveniently numbered, and are very popular with collectors today. Early twentieth century through the 1920s. See chapter 11 for much more information.

Reisenberg, A. New York, NY. Published view and art cards in the early twentieth century, including imports and animal subjects by Helena A. Maguire.

Renfro-Haven Co. San Bernardino, CA. Published postcards in the early twentieth century.

Reynolds, B.S. Washington, D.C. Publisher of art and view cards, many of Washington, D.C., being issued under the name of Foster & Reynolds (whose address is sometimes given as Washington, D.C.; other times as New York City); see listing above. A set depicts paintings displayed in D.C. Among their products was the "Beautiful Washington Quality Series" of views with a Capitol dome at the top of the back.

Rhode Island News Co. Providence, RI. Publisher of regional view postcards, including some German imports via the American News Co. (ANC).

Rialto Post Card Co. New York, NY. Publisher of postcards during the early twentieth century, including signed artists.

Rice & Hutchins. Boston, MA. Published postcards in the early twentieth century.

Rice, George, & Sons, Printers. Los Angeles, CA. Printers and publishers of postcards in the early twentieth century.

Rich, B.B. Portland, OR. Published postcards in the early twentieth century.

Richardson Studio. Chatham, MA. Issued RPPCs of regional interest in the early twentieth century.

Richardson, Henry Wendell. Newport, VT. Issued RPPCs of regional interest from the 1910s until after 1950.

Rick, F.F. Buffalo, NY. Published postcards in the early twentieth century.

Ricker, Hiram, & Sons. South Poland, ME. Published postcards in the early twentieth century, including those furnished by Hugh C. Leighton.

Ricker, W.A. Castine, ME. Published postcards in the early twentieth century, including German imports through PCK.

Ridgley, W.T., Calendar Co. Great Falls, MT. Published postcards with the art of Charles M. Russell and other western scenes, comics, etc. Early twentieth century into the 1940s.

Ridgway News Co. Ridgway, PA. Published postcards in the mid-twentieth century, including from the Curt Teich Co.

Rieder, M. Los Angeles, CA. Published view, Native American, and other postcard subjects, including German imports and those made by the Edward H. Mitchell Co. Important in the early twentieth century.

Rieder-Cardinell Co. Los Angeles and Oakland, CA. Published view cards in the first decade of the twentieth century, including of the 1906 San Francisco fire (also see Cardinell-Vincent).

Riege, C.H. Fresno, CA. Publisher of view cards in the early nineteenth century, including German imports obtained through the Atlas Society of New York City.

Published by Rieger, the California Perfumer.

Rieger, Paul. San Francisco, CA. Perfumer who published postcards of the 1906 earthquake and fire.

Riggins. Dayton, MT. Made RPPCs, including of Native Americans.

Rigo Chemical Co., Post Card Department. Nashville, TN. Published postcards in the early twentieth century, including those of the Curt Teich Co.

Rigot, Max, Selling Co. / Max Rigot. Chicago, IL. Publisher of view cards of regional interest, most printed by the Curt Teich Co., 1910s to the 1930s.

Ritchie Brothers. Centralia, IL. Makers of RPPCs, including holiday and greeting, wholesaler to dealers. Early twentieth century.

Riverside News Co. Riverside, RI. Published postcards in the 1920s and 1930s, including those from Tichnor Brothers.

Rizard, George. New York, NY. Published postcards in the early twentieth century.

Robbins Brothers Co. Boston, MA; Germany. Printer, importer, and publisher of art, view, and other postcards, including under their own imprint and for the Metropolitan News Co. (MNCo), early twentieth century.

Robbins, I., & Son / Robbins & Son. Pittsburgh, PA. Major distributor of view cards under the IRAS monogram, others with I.R.S. or an elliptical logotype. Many were printed by the Curt Teich Co. 1910s to 1940s. "Randson" was sometimes given as a trademark (R. and Son).

Robbins, J.L., Co. / Robbins-Tillquist Co. Spokane, WA. Publisher of scenic postcards of regional interest, 1920s and 1930s, most of which were printed by the Curt Teich Co.

Robbins, M.A. Bucksport, ME. Published view cards in the early twentieth century.

Roberts, Mike, Color Productions / Mike Roberts Studio. Berkeley and Oakland, CA. A highly important publisher and pioneer of photo-chrome color view cards widely distributed in North America. In 1996 the firm was moved to San Diego and named Scenic Art, Inc. Roberts operated from 1939 to 1996.

Roberts Variety Store. Mount Pleasant, IA. Published postcards in the early twentieth century, including German imports from S. Langsdorf and Co.

Robertson, C.B. Shawnee, OK. Published postcards in the early twentieth century, including those from the Curt Teich Co.

Robertson, Grant L. Metairie, LA. Published postcards in the late twentieth century, including cards of H.S. Crocker Co.

Robinson, Juan. South Hero, VT. Published postcards in the early twentieth century, including German imports.

Robison, E.C. St. Petersburg, FL. Published postcards in the mid-twentieth century, including cards from E.C. Kropp Co.

Robson & Adee. Saratoga Springs and Schenectady, NY. Published view cards in the early twentieth century, including German imports.

Rochester News Co. Rochester, NY. Publisher of regional view postcards, including some German imports via the American News Co. (ANC).

Rochester Photo Press. Rochester, NY. Maker of RPPCs, including advertising for clients all over the United States.

Rock Island Post Card Co. Rock Island, IL. Published postcards in the early twentieth century.

Rockmore Co. New York, NY. Publisher of postcards during the early twentieth century, including signed artists.

Rockport Photo Bureau. Rockport, MA. Published view cards, mostly monotone, of regional subjects, many of which were printed by the Albertype Co. Early twentieth century to the 1940s.

Rockport Post Card Co. Rockport, MA. Published view cards in the late twentieth century, including those made by Mike Roberts.

Rocky Mountain News / Denver Times. Denver, CO. Published postcards in the early twentieth century, mainly of scenic subjects.

Rocky Mountain Publishing Co. Denver, CO. Published postcards in the mid-twentieth century.

Rodionoff, S.S. Morrow Bay, CA. Publisher of postcards during the early twentieth century, including signed artists.

Roesch, Louis, Co. San Francisco, CA. Published postcards in the early twentieth century.

Rogero & Pomar. St. Augustine, FL. Publishers of view cards in the early twentieth century, including those of the Curt Teich Co.

Rogers, C.M. Austin, TX. Published postcards in the mid-twentieth century.

Rogers-Hoswell Co. Walla Walla, WA. Published view cards in the early twentieth century.

Rollins, R.F. Keokuk, IA. Published postcards in the early twentieth century, including German imports.

Romans Photographic Co. Seattle, WA. Published postcards in the early twentieth century.

Romer, G.W. Miami, FL. Published postcards in the mid-twentieth century.

Rooney, A. William / The Paper Store. Winchester, MA. Published view cards in the early twentieth century.

Root & Tinker. Buffalo and New York, NY. Published postcards in the early twentieth century.

Rosch. White Plains, NY. Publisher of postcards with topics of regional interest, early twentieth century.

Rose Agency, Inc. Durham, NC. Published postcards in the 1920s and 1930s, including those of the Curt Teich Co.

Rose Co. Philadelphia, PA. Publisher of postcards during the early twentieth century, including signed artists. Also listed as H.M. Rose Publishing Company and Charles Rose Co.

Rosenthall, Sam. San Antonio, TX. Published postcards in the early twentieth century.

Rosin & Co. Philadelphia, PA; New York, NY. Publisher of view cards in the early twentieth century, mostly German imports.

Rosser, H.H. Victor, CO. Published postcards in the early twentieth century. In 1901 he issued octagonal Lesher "souvenir dollars."

Rost, H.A., Printing & Publishing Co. / Ernst Rost. New York, NY. Printed and published postcards from at least 1897, continuing into the twentieth century.

Roth & Langley. New York (Brooklyn), NY. Publisher of postcards during the early twentieth century, including signed artists.

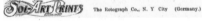

Rotograph Co. New York, NY. Important printer and publisher of high-quality cards in several different formats, first and second decades of the twentieth century. The company's view cards are among the finest of the era. Card categories include:

- Series A: Black-and-white images. A prefix plus number.

- Series B: Blue rotogravures, some not numbered, sometimes with a name such as "Marine Views Series." Also includes some RPPCs and novelty cards. A miscellaneous category.

- Series D: Printed in gray with a hint of blue.

- Series E: Color views with divided backs, 1907 and later. Within this series are some special views of Egypt.

- Series F: Color art cards, comics, etc., some with prefixes such as FD, FK, FL, and FR. Some with printed "frame" borders. Undivided (1907 and earlier) and divided (1907 and later) backs. Many variations.

- Series G: Color rotogravure cards, typically views, very high quality, among the best of the early view cards. For deltiologists these are especially appreciated, although some views are not necessarily rare.

- Series GL: Rotogravure, well detailed, but somewhat muted color.

- Series H: Hand-colored view cards of high quality. Also and somewhat unrelated, some cards with H prefix are lithographed greetings, including Dutch motifs; the H letter somewhat resembles an N.

- Series I and J: Japanese subjects. Colored.

- Series M: Color art painting reproductions. This series was later continued by Stengel.

- Series N: Night views in color, sometimes with bright windows, etc. (Night views can be found in some other series as well, such as B).

- Series NPG: Blue cards with Dutch scenes printed in Germany by the New Photographic Society.

- Series O: Resemble RPPC cards, made in quantity, tinted in color, made in England. Similar cards were made by the Davidson Brothers in London.

- Series P: Cards in the RPPC style in glossy paper with wide, embossed white borders. Made in England.

- Panorama Series: Cards with two, three, or four panels, fold-out, with views. P prefix for panorama and then a letter from one of the above series, such as PA, PD, PE, PG, PH.

- Series R: Images with embossed surfaces, red-letter titles, including images from other series. Made circa 1904 and 1905 with undivided backs.

- Series XS: Christmas greetings, monotone, on glossy paper.

- Series Z: Cards created for the New York Zoological Society, with no mention of the Rotograph name.

- Comic: Artist-signed cards with set numbers but not letter prefixes. Printed in Austria.

- RPPC: Advertising and other cards. Back imprinted: "This Card is a Real Photograph on Bromide Paper. The Rotograph Co., N.Y. City. (Printed in Germany)"

- Sol-Art Print: Logotype with this designation in at least two forms: circular and printed in red (usual), Sol-Art Prints horizontally with open centers to large S, A, and P letters. Includes some early National Art View images.

- Miscellaneous: Cuban views numbered within other series, but with titles in English and Spanish. G-prefix numbered cards are color halftones. Globe Trotter Series, numbered views of international topics issued in sets. Tinted views of the 1906 San Francisco earthquake and fire, from images provided by the San Francisco Ruins Publishing Co. Various hand-colored view cards not within a letter series.

Rowley, W.C., & Son. Utica, NY. Published view cards in the early twentieth century, including German imports.

Rowman, T.E. Durango, CO. Published postcards in the early twentieth century, including German imports from the American News Co. (ANC).

Royal Pictures. Colton, CA. Published chrome cards in the late twentieth century.

Ruben, J., Publishing Co. Newburgh, NY. Published view cards in early to mid-twentieth century, including those made by Tichnor Brothers and the Curt Teich Co.

Rucker, W.D. Amsterdam, NY. Published view cards in the early twentieth century, including those obtained from the American News Co.

Rugg, E.H. & F.A. Medford, MA. Published view cards in the early twentieth century.

Rumford Press. Concord, NH. Major commercial publisher who also printed a limited number of high-quality color postcards in the early twentieth century.

Runca Import Co. Rutherfordton, NC. Imported and distributed view cards in the mid-twentieth century.

Rusk, Samuel E. Haines Falls, NY. Photographer who published printed cards using his images, first decade of the twentieth century.

Russel & Wait. Glens Falls, NY. Published view cards in the early twentieth century, including German imports.

Russell, M.E. Sarasota, FL. Published view cards in the mid-twentieth century, including Curt Teich Co. cards.

Rust Craft Shop. Kansas City, MO. Publisher of artists signed postcards during the early twentieth century.

Rust, Fred Winslow / Rust Craft Publishing Co. Boston, MA. In the early twentieth century Rust published color greeting cards. This enterprise evolved into Rust Craft.

Ryans. Pawtucket, RI. Published postcards in the early twentieth century.

S

S.L. & Co. See Samuel Langsdorf & Co. under L.

Sabold-Herb Co. Philadelphia, PA. Published postcards in the early twentieth century, including from the Curt Teich Co.

Sackett & Wilhelms Corporation. New York, NY. Published postcards in the early twentieth century, including cards from the Valentine-Souvenir Co.

Sadler & Pennington. Oklahoma City, OK. Published postcards in the early twentieth century, including German imports (some through S. Langsdorf & Co.) and cards printed domestically by Curt Teich and others.

Saidy. Manitou, CO. Published postcards in the early twentieth century, including German imports.

Saidy, J.T. Okoboji, IA. Published postcards in the early twentieth century, including those of the Curt Teich Co.

Saint John's Publishing Co. St. John's, MI. Published view cards and RPPCs in the early twentieth century.

Saint Louis News Co. St. Louis, MO. Publisher of view cards in the early twentieth century, including German imports via the American News Co. (ANC).

Saint Louis Postcard Co. St. Louis, MO. Published postcards in the early twentieth century.

Saint Paul Souvenir Co. St. Paul, MN. Publisher of view cards of regional interest, early twentieth century, many imported from Germany. Maker of multi-view cards by assembling montages of RPPCs from various Midwest towns and rephotographing them.

Saint Petersburg News Co. St. Petersburg, FL. Published postcards in the mid-twentieth century.

Sakonnet Transportation Co. Sakonnet, RI. Published postcards in the early twentieth century, including cards from E.C. Kropp.

Sale Photographic Studio, Frederick. Published postcards in the early twentieth century, including those of the Curt Teich Co.

Saling, A. & Sons. Ligonier, PA. Published postcards in the mid-twentieth century, including from Tichnor Brothers.

Salomonsky, B.F. Norfolk, VA. Published postcards in the early twentieth century.

Saltzburg Merchandise Co. Atlantic City, NJ. Publishers of view cards in the early and mid-twentieth century.

Sampliner, H.S. Atlantic City, NJ. Published postcards in the mid-twentieth century, including Kropp cards.

Samson Brothers. New York, NY. Printer and publisher of art cards, greetings, Hudson-Fulton Celebration (1909), and many other topics. Early twentieth century.

Samuel Cupples Envelope Co. St. Louis, MO. Publisher of postcards during the early twentieth century, including signed artists.

San Antonio Card Co. San Antonio, TX. Published postcards in the mid-twentieth century, including cards from Metropolitan of Everett, MA.

San Francisco Litho. San Francisco, CA. Published postcards in the early twentieth century.

Sanborn Souvenir Co. Denver, CO. Maker of RPPC view cards, later distributed printed cards, 1920s into the 1970s.

Sanborn Vail & Co. San Francisco, CA, branches in Los Angeles, CA, and Portland, OR. Publisher of view cards, 1902 to 1920s.

Sander, P. New York, NY; Philadelphia, PA; Atlantic City, NJ. Publisher of postcards during the early twentieth century, including signed artists.

Sanders Manufacturing Co. Published postcards in the mid-twentieth century, including some from the Curt Teich Co.

Sanders, P. Philadelphia, PA. Publishers of view cards in the early and mid-twentieth century.

Sandhills Book Shop. Southern Pines, NC. Distributed postcards in the early twentieth century, including those made by Albertype.

Sandoval News Service. El Paso, TX. Published view cards in the late twentieth century, including those by the Curt Teich Co.

Sanford Card Co. Dansville, NY. Publisher of color holiday and greeting cards, early twentieth century.

POST CARD

Santway Photo-Craft Co. Star Lake, NY. Publishers of view cards in the early twentieth century, including by Curt Teich Co.

Sapirstein Greeting Card Co. Cleveland, OH. Publisher of view, greeting, etc., cards in the first decade of the twentieth century. In the 1930s the company printed cards, and in the same decade the firm became the American Greetings Publishers, later expanding to acquire other firms.

Sassara, Ralph N. Pittsburgh, PA. Distributed view cards in the mid-twentieth century, including from Dexter Press.

Saunders Bookstore. Benham, TX. Published postcards in the late twentieth century, including cards from Dexter Press.

Sauter & Kuehne. Austin, TX. Published postcards in the early twentieth century.

Savage, C.R., Co. Salt Lake City, UT. Published postcards in the early twentieth century.

Savage, G.W. North Anson, ME. Published postcards in the early twentieth century, including German imports from Hugh C. Leighton Co.

Sawyer Scenic Photo Co. Portland, OR. Publisher of RPPCs and printed cards, mostly views, 1920s to 1940s. In 1939 the company introduced the View Master hand-held stereo viewer, which became very popular.

Sawyer, Harold T., Photo and Art Shop. Chatham, MA. Photographer who published RPPCs and view cards of regional interest, including Albertype cards, in the early twentieth century through the 1940s.

Scates & Co. Caribou, ME. Published postcards in the early twentieth century

Scenic Art. Richmond, CA. Publisher of postcards during the early twentieth century, including signed artists.

Scenic Photo Publishing Co. Seattle, WA. Publisher of RPPCs covering views and many other topics in the 1920s.

Scenic View Card Co. San Francisco and Oakland, CA. Publisher of view cards, mid- and late twentieth century.

Schaaf, F.J. Albuquerque, NM. Published postcards in the late twentieth century.

Schaafsma, Harold F. Big Bend National Park, TX. Published postcards in the late twentieth century.

Schaefer, W.R. Philadelphia, PA. Publisher of postcards from 1897 into the twentieth century.

Schafer, H.A., News Co. Pittsburgh, PA. Published postcards in the early twentieth century.

Schaff, J., and Bros. San Francisco, CA. Published postcards in the early twentieth century, including imports from Austria.

Schallerer, Otto. Seward, AK. Photographer and issuer of RPPCs, circa 1910 to the 1960s.

Schanzer, Eda. Nantucket, MA. Published postcards in the early twentieth century.

Scheff, I., & Brothers. San Francisco, CA. Publisher of color view cards, including an extensive run for the 1906 earthquake and fire. Early twentieth century.

Scheff, I., Engraving Co., Inc. New York, NY. Printer of postcards from engraved steel plates, 1930s onward.

Scheiner, Louis. Portland, OR; Tacoma, WA. Distributed postcards in the early twentieth century, including those of the Curt Teich Co.

Scheller Co. Hackettstown, NJ. Published postcards in the late twentieth century.

Schickler, F.P. Aurora, IL. Published postcards in the early twentieth century, including cards imported from Germany.

Schlesinger Brothers. New York, NY. Photographers and publishers of greetings, cards with women, views, etc., Early twentieth century into the 1920s.

Schlessman, E.H. Sandusky, OH. Commercial photographer and issuer of RPPCs in the early twentieth century.

Schmidt, Arthur P., & Co. Chicago, IL; Boston, MA. Publisher of art postcards, sometimes with advertising on the back, early twentieth century.

Schmidt, H.R., & Co. Wichita, KS; Denver, CO. Published view cards in the early twentieth century, including many of Denver.

Schmidt, L. & L. / L. Schmidt Co. San Francisco, CA. Lithographer and publisher of postcards, including views for the 1893 California Midwinter International Exposition.

Schneider, C.R., Co. New York, NY. Publisher of postcards during the early twentieth century, including signed artists.

Schoenlein, M. Buffalo, NY. Published postcards in the early twentieth century.

Schofield, Oliver Carlton. Richmond, VA. Published postcards in the early twentieth century.

Schramel, Edward J. Del Rio, TX. Published postcards in the late twentieth century, including cards from Dexter Press.

Schulze Litho and Post Card Co. New York, NY. Printer of color postcards, early twentieth century.

Schumann, A.J. Chicago, IL. Issued RPPCs and regional views in the early twentieth century and also sold printing and greeting cards made by others.

Schwabe, E.J., Publishing Co. New York, NY. Publisher of view cards, historical scenes, etc., for depicting various American locations. Imported from Germany. First decade of the twentieth century.

Schwalbach, Lange B.L. Boston, MA. Publisher of view cards, the Colonial Heroes, and other series, imported from Germany. Early twentieth century.

Schwan's Studio. Mansfield, OH. Issued RPPCs in the early twentieth century.

MADE IN GERMANY "ALSA-NOVITAS" SCHWARZ & CO PUBL CHICAGO.

NOVITAS

Schwarz & Co. "Alsa-Novitas." Chicago, IL. Publishers of postcards during the early twentieth century, including German imports. Some marked "Alsa-Novitas" and/or with Alsa-Novitas logotype (in stamp box).

Scott Studio. Chicago, IL. Published RPPCs during the early twentieth century, including views of Chicago streets.

Scott, Ferris H. Santa Ana, CA. Published view cards in the late twentieth century, including those by H.S. Crocker.

Scrantom, Wetmore & Co. Rochester, NY. Publisher of view cards of regional interest, first two decades of the twentieth century.

Scranton News Co. Scranton, PA. Also S.N. Co. Publisher of view cards in the early twentieth century.

Scribner's, Charles, Sons (Charles Scribner's Sons). New York, NY. Publisher of art postcards during the early twentieth century, but primarily of magazines and books.

Seaich, Eric J., Co. Salt Lake City, UT. Published postcards in the late twentieth century.

Seat's Studio. Lebanon, TN. Published postcards in the early twentieth century, including some from the Curt Teich Co.

Seawall Specialty Co. Houston and Galveston, TX. Publisher of view cards in the early twentieth century.

Sebastian, B. Chicago, IL. Published postcards in the early twentieth century.

Seckel, M. New York, NY. Publisher of souvenir cards in the 1890s, most with regional topics.

Security Lithograph Co. San Francisco, CA. Printed chrome cards in the mid- and late twentieth century.

Seddon, J.L. & C.H. Providence, RI. Publisher of view cards during the early twentieth century, including German imports, some with the logotype of S. Langsdorf & Co.

Seeley, Alfred B. Angola, NY. Published view cards in the early twentieth century, including those from Leighton & Valentine.

Selige, Adolph. St. Louis, MO. Publisher of view, comic, Western theme, etc., cards, some marked Seliochrom and sold by others. His Northwestern Indian series featured numbered color cards. Early twentieth century.

Sellers, Elmo M. Los Angeles, CA. Published cards in the late twentieth century.

Ser Lithography Co. Rochester, NY. Printer of chromolithograph holiday, greeting, etc., cards in the early twentieth century. Merged with Karle & Co. in 1932.

Sersanti Brothers. New York, NY. Publisher of postcards during the early twentieth century, including signed artists.

Service News Co. New Bedford, MA. Published postcards in the early twentieth century, including cards from Tichnor Brothers.

Service News Co. Wilmington, NC. Published postcards in the mid-twentieth century, including from the Curt Teich Co.

Servis, G.O.W. Somerville, MA. Published view cards in the early twentieth century, including German imports obtained from the American News Company (ANC).

Settle, H.B. Published postcards in the mid-twentieth century, including from Curt Teich Co.

Setzer's Warehouse. Jacksonville, FL. Published postcards in the mid-twentieth century, including cards from Dexter Press.

Seward News Co. Seward, AK. Published postcards in the early twentieth century, including those of the Curt Teich Co.

Seyffarth, Fred. New York (Brooklyn), NY. Photographer, publisher of printed view cards of regional interest, early twentieth century.

Shambaugh, M.J. York, PA. Published postcards in the early twentieth century.

Shampang, G.A. Lake Odessa, MI. Publisher of RPPC postcards in the early twentieth century, some with embossed logotype.

Shattuck, R. Ukiah, CA. Produced RPPCs in the early twentieth century, including of Native Americans.

Shaver, E.B. Nassau, NY. Produced RPPCs in the early twentieth century.

Shaw & Borden Co. Spokane, WA. Published postcards in the early twentieth century.

Shaw, Jeweler (Jeweler Shaw). Putnam, CT. Published view cards in the early twentieth century.

Sheahan, M.T. Boston, MA. Printer and publisher of greetings, comic, animal, and general interest cards, early twentieth century.

Sheldon, George H. Wakefield, RI. Published postcards in the early twentieth century.

Shelton Color Corporation. Hackensack, NJ. Publisher of postcards during the early twentieth century, including signed artists.

Shenandoah Publishing Co. Strasburg, VA. Published postcards in the early twentieth century.

Sherman, W.H. Bar Harbor, ME. Publisher of regional view postcards, early twentieth century, including German imports via Reichner Brothers.

Shonkwiler, H.N. Springfield, IL. Issued postcards circa the 1920s and 1930s. Advertised as a distributing agency and news dealer.

Shoppers Guide Press. Alpine, TX. Published postcards in the late twentieth century, including cards from Dexter Press.

Shore, Rufus A. Winston-Salem, NC. Published postcards in the 1920s and 1930s.

Shorey Studio. Gorham, NH. Maker of RPPCs with regional views during the early mid-twentieth century.

Shoudy, William F. Syracuse, NY. Published view cards in the early twentieth century, including German imports.

Shumaker, J.L. Wray, CO. Published postcards in the early twentieth century, including cards imported from Belgium.

Shurtleff, Frank H. Gloucester, MA. Published view cards in the mid-twentieth century.

Shutterbug / R.H. Gobrecht. Mountainville, NY. R.H. Gobrecht Photography, using the name Shutterbug, made RPPCs in the mid-twentieth century.

Sidney Favorite Printing Co. Sidney, NY (presumably). Printed view cards in the early twentieth century. Styled itself as Commercial and Society Printers.

Sieburg, Dan. New London, NH. Published regional view cards in the late twentieth century, including Plastichrome cards by Colourpicture Publishers, Inc.

Sierra News Co. Reno, NV. Published postcards in the late twentieth century.

Simms Tobacco & Candy Co. Denison, TX. Published postcards in the mid-twentieth century.

Simon, A.M. / A.M.S. New York, NY. Publisher of view cards, black and white and color, including hand-colored. Early twentieth century.

Simons View Co. Moclips, WA. Published view cards in the early twentieth century, including German imports.

Simplicity Co. Chicago, IL; Grand Rapids, MI. Publisher of view, comic, greetings, and other cards, early twentieth century through the late 1920s.

Sims, J.A. Seattle, WA. Published postcards in the early twentieth century.

Sithens, W.C. / Sithens Post Card Co. / Virginia Postcard Co. Atlantic City, NJ. Published postcards in the early twentieth century, including Kropp cards.

Slack, C.C. Sioux Falls, SD. Produced RPPCs in the early twentieth century. Log with address of "Soo Falls, S.D."

Slate Co. Hyannis, MA. Published postcards in the late twentieth century, including those of the Plastichrome brand.

Sleight, W.F., Post Card Co. Mount Vernon, NY. Publisher of view cards of regional interest, early twentieth century.

Small, F.C. Buzzard's Bay, MA. Published view cards in the early twentieth century, including German imports.

Smiley, Alfred Fletcher. Lake Minniwaska, NY. Publisher of view cards of regional interest, 1940s and 1950s.

Smiling Cow. Boothbay Harbor and Camden, ME. Publisher of view cards of regional interest, 1930s onward.

Smith News Store. Plymouth, MA. Published cards in the early and mid-twentieth century, including those printed by Tichnor Brothers.

Smith Novelty Co. San Francisco, CA. Publisher of postcards during the early twentieth century, including signed artists.

Smith Syndicate. Excelsior Springs, MO. Published postcards in the early twentieth century, including those by the Curt Teich Co.

Smith Western, Inc. Portland, OR. Published view cards in the late twentieth century.

Smith, Charles H. West Roxbury, MA. Published view cards in the early twentieth century, including German imports from American News Co. (ANC).

Smith, F.H. Williston, ND. Made RPPCs in the early twentieth century including of Native Americans.

Smith, H. Tobey. Greenville, RI. Published postcards in the early twentieth century.

Smith, H.B. Atlantic City, NJ. Publisher of postcards during the early twentieth century, including signed artists.

Smith, H.T. Venice, CA. Publisher of view cards in the early twentieth century.

Smith, J. Homer. Yuma, AZ. Publisher of view cards in the early twentieth century.

Smith, J.D. Battle Creek, MI. Published view cards in the early twentieth century, including German imports.

Smith, W.H. Published postcards in the early twentieth century, including cards from Germany obtained from the American News Co. (ANC).

Smith's Book Store. Plymouth, MA. Published view cards in the early twentieth century, including those of the Curt Teich Co.

Smith's Photo Studio. Marysville, CA. Published RPPCs of regional subjects in the early twentieth century.

Smith's Scenic Views. Tacoma, WA. Published view cards in the late twentieth century.

Smith-Brooks Printing Co. Denver, CO. Published postcards in the early twentieth century.

Snow, James F. Brunswick, ME. Publisher of view cards, early twentieth century, including those printed by the Curt Teich Co. "Snow's Pine Tree State Post Cards."

Sohmer, Theo. Los Angeles, CA. Publisher of postcards, 1910s and 1920s, with Western Publishing and Novelty Co. imprint

Solomon, J., Inc. New London, CT. Publisher of regional interest view cards, many of which were from Tichnor Brothers. Early twentieth century.

Sommers, J.B. Miami, FL. Published postcards in the mid-twentieth century, including cards from Colourpicture.

Sonora News Co. Nogales, AZ. Publisher of view cards in the early twentieth century, including those of the Curt Teich Company.

Sooner News Co. Lawton, OK. Published postcards in the 1920s and 1930s, including from the Curt Teich Co.

South Shore Novelty Co. Hull, MA. Published view cards in the late twentieth century including those of the Curt Teich Co.

Souther-Mears Co. Boston, MA. Publisher of view cards of regional topics, early twentieth century.

Southern Bargain House. Richmond, VA. Published postcards during the early twentieth century, including those of the Curt Teich Co.

Southern Card & Novelty Co. Holly Hills, FL. Published view cards in the mid-twentieth century, including cards published by E.C. Kropp Co.

Southern Film Co. Gulfport, MS. Published postcards in the early twentieth century.

Southern Manufacturing Co. Richmond, VA. Published postcards in the early twentieth century.

Southern Post Card Co. Asheville, NC. Published view cards in the mid-twentieth century, including those of the Curt Teich Co.

Southwest News Co. Kansas City, MO. Sometimes as South-West News Co. Publisher of view cards, including German imports and others via American News Co. (ANC). Early twentieth century.

Southwest Post Card Co. Albuquerque, NM. Publisher of postcards with Western subjects, 1930s to 1950s.

Southwestern Engraving Co. Fort Worth, TX. Published postcards in the mid-twentieth century.

Southwick, A.Q. New York, NY. Publisher of high-quality color greetings, holiday, comic, and other postcards, early twentieth century.

Souvenir Novelty Co. Salt Lake City, UT. Publisher of view and other postcards, many of which were printed by the Curt Teich Co., early twentieth century into the 1920s.

Souvenir Post Card Co. New York, NY. Highly important publisher of view and other postcards printed by at least three manufacturers. Distinctive imprint with honeybee in the C of POST CARD on some cards, diamond logotype on others. "Souvo Chrome" name used on some lithographed cards. Active in the early twentieth century until merged into Valentine & Sons, later trading as the Valentine Souvenir Co. Series include:

- Serials 1 to 3099 and 12000 to 15000: Color cards, mostly views.

- Serials 5999 to 5999 and over 15000: Mostly views, black-and-white with greenish tint, some being the same subjects used on full color cards.

- Serials 6000 to 11999: Black-and-white postcards, mostly views.

Souvenir Post Card Exchange. Cleveland, OH. Publishers of view cards in the early twentieth century.

Souvenir Post Card Station. Davenport, OH. Published postcards in the early twentieth century.

Souvenir Postal Card Co. Albany, NY. Published view cards in the 1890s.

Souvenir Publishing & Mercantile Co. Denver, CO. Publisher of regional interest view cards, color halftones, often with an artificial aspect to the color. Early twentieth century.

Souvenir Publishing Co. Los Angeles and San Francisco, CA. Publisher of color cards, mostly views, early twentieth century. Some were deep sepia views on cocoa-color stock from or similar to E.H. Mitchell cards.

Spangenthal's Wholesale View Cards. Erie, PA. Issued postcards in the mid-twentieth century, including from the Curt Teich Co.

Sparrell Print. Boston, MA. Color view cards, including Boston scenes, in the first decade of the twentieth century.

Sparrow Press. Boston, MA. Printed and published color view cards in the first decade of the twentieth century.

Spaulding Card Co. Buffalo, NY. Published postcards in the early twentieth century.

Speights, Vergie. Hemphill, TX. Published postcards in the late twentieth century.

Spencer, J.R. Newport, ME. Published postcards in the early twentieth century, including German imports from Hugh C. Leighton Co.

Spiro & Lotz. Seattle, WA. Published postcards in the early twentieth century.

Spokane Post Card Co. Spokane, WA. Published postcards in the early twentieth century including imported German cards.

Spokane Publishing Co. Spokane, WA. Published postcards in the early twentieth century.

Springfield News Co. Springfield, MA. Publisher of view cards, including German imports via American News Co. (ANC). Early twentieth century.

Springfield Paper Co. Springfield, IL. Issued postcards circa the 1920s and 1930s.

Sprouse & Son. Tacoma, WA. Publishers of black-and-white and color view cards, mainly of regional interest, including German imports. Publishers also of exaggeration and novelty cards. Early twentieth century.

Stacy Studios. Sodus and Sodus Point, NY. Issued RPPCs in the early twentieth century.

Stadler Photographing Co. Chicago, IL; New York, NY. Produced RPPCs in the early twentieth century, including advertising cards. Invited customers to send negatives for printing.

Staeger Brothers. Chehalis, WA. Published view cards in the early twentieth century.

Stafford, Joseph M. Marietta, PA. Published postcards in the early twentieth century.

Standard Advertising and Printing Co. Fort Scott, KS. Produced Techni-chrome cards in the late twentieth century.

Standard Pictures Co. Plymouth, MA. Published view postcards in the early twentieth century.

Standard Postal Souvenir Card Co. New York, NY. Published view cards of local interest in the 1890s.

Standard Postcard and Novelty Co. / Standard Post Card Co. / Standard Postcard Co. Philadelphia, PA. Published postcards in the early twentieth century, including those from Tichnor Brothers.

Standard Supply Co. Otter Lake, NY. Published view cards in the late twentieth century.

Standish Photo Studio. Fort Wayne, IN. Made RPPCs in the early twentieth century

Star Post Card Co. Plainfield, NJ. Made RPPCs in the early twentieth century.

Star Stationery Co. Newark, NJ. Publisher of view cards, mostly linens, with regional including seashore topics, some printed by Tichnor Brothers. Late twentieth century.

Stead, C.A. Jacksonville, FL. Published postcards in the early twentieth century, including those by Tichnor Brothers.

Stecher Lithograph Co. Rochester, NY. Publisher of postcards during the early twentieth century, including signed artists.

Stedman & Lockwood. Lake Placid, NY. Made RPPCs in the early twentieth century.

Steinfeldt, I. Lancaster, PA. Published postcards in the mid-twentieth century, including from the Curt Teich Co.

Steinman, R., & Co. St. Paul, MN. Published postcards in the early twentieth century.

Stengel & Co. Dresden, Germany. Printer and publisher of art cards, including many distributed in the United States by Rotograph, which later turned over its own art card business to Stengel.

Stern, Edward, & Co. Philadelphia, PA. Printer and publisher of postcards in the early twentieth century, including signed artists and Roosevelt Bears. Many images were copyrighted by Rufus Hill and are so noted.

Stern, Ignatz. New York (Brooklyn), NY. Usually as I. Stern or simply an IS monogram with eagle. Publisher of view cards of regional and Eastern United States subjects, early twentieth century.

Stearns Fellbaum Photo. Cove, OR. Issuer of RPPCs in the early twentieth century.

Stevens & Hogan. Fort Dodge, IA. Published postcards in the early twentieth century.

Stichler & Co. Reading, PA. Published postcards in the early twentieth century, including from the Curt Teich Co.

Stiles Paper & Twine Co. Conneaut, OH. Published postcards in the 1920s and 1930s, including from the Curt Teich Co.

Stin Brothers Co. Hastings, NE. Published view cards during the early twentieth century, including German imports from American News Company (ANC).

Stobbs Press. Worcester, MA. Printer of inexpensive postcards, mostly color views, for much of the early twentieth century.

Stoddard Engraving Co. New Haven, CT. Published postcards in the early twentieth century.

Stokes, Frederick A., Co. New York, NY. Important printer and publisher of art cards of many genres, including comic, calendar, patriotic, reproduced paintings, signed artists (including R.F. Outcault), and more. Early twentieth century to the 1930s.

Stone & Barringer Co. Charlotte, NC. Published postcards in the early twentieth century, including German imports from S. Langsdorf & Co.

Stone Brothers. Charleston, WV. Published postcards in the early twentieth century.

Stone Brothers Co. Clarksburg, WV. Published postcards in the early twentieth century.

Storseth, Mollie. Chicago, IL. Published postcards in the early twentieth century.

Strate Half-Tone Process Co. New York, NY. Published postcards in the early twentieth century.

Stratton, H.H. Chattanooga, TN. Publisher of view cards with worldwide scenes, the "Great White Fleet" of the U.S. Navy, and other printed cards. Some view cards have backs imitative of those used on RPPCs. First two decades of the twentieth century.

Strauss, Arthur, Inc. New York City and Niagara Falls, NY. Printer of patriotic, political, view, and other cards, at first in black and white (sometimes with an eagle perched on a color shield added), later in color. Early twentieth century.

Strauss, Ferdinand, & Co. New York, NY. Publisher of pioneer cards in the 1890s, all of which are rare today. Known examples included three views of New York City, one of Lake George (NY), and four of Washington, D.C.

Strobridge Lithographers. Cincinnati, OH. Highly important poster and show printer for many years. Published many colorful postcards throughout the early twentieth century.

Stromberg & Penny. Galesburg, IL. Published postcards in the early twentieth century, including cards imported from Germany.

Strong, C.C. Waverly, NY. Published view cards in the early twentieth century, including German imports.

Strongin, Samuel. Savin Rock, CT. Publisher of postcards including those supplied by Metrocraft, mid-twentieth century.

Stroup, Walter M. Saratoga Springs, NY. Published view cards in the early twentieth century, including German imports.

Strykers' Western Photo Color. Fort Worth, TX. Published postcards in the late twentieth century. Some cards used images photographed by the firm.

Stuff Printing Concern. Seattle, WA. Published postcards in the early twentieth century.

Sturtevant, M.G. Great Barrington, MA. Published cards in the mid-twentieth century, including those made by Albertype.

Success Post Card Co. New York, NY. Publisher of view cards, including German imports (some via Valentine), in the early twentieth century.

Sudenfield, Jack. Old Orchard Beach, ME. Published postcards in the second half of the twentieth century.

Sugerman Brothers. Cleveland, OH. Published postcards in the 1920s and 1930s, including from the E.C. Kropp Co.

Suhling & Koehn Co. Chicago, IL. Published view cards in the early twentieth century, including German imports. Some branded as "Elite."

Sullivan, D.G. Watertown, CT. Published postcards in the early twentieth century, including German imports.

Sun Color Cards. Eau Claire, WI. Publisher of postcards during the early twentieth century, including signed artists.

Sun News Co. St. Petersburg, FL. Publisher of comic, greetings, view, and other postcards, 1940s onward.

Sunny Scenes, Inc. Winter Park, FL. Publisher of view cards, many hand-colored, of various locations, but mostly Florida, Hawaii, and California, reflective of the company's name. Active from the late 1920s into the late 1930s.

Sutherland, E.E. Moclips, WA. Published view cards in the early twentieth century.

Swallow, Frank W., Postcard Co. Exeter, NH. Frank W. Swallow, of Exeter, New Hampshire, entered the post card business in 1904 and remained in the trade until his death in 1927, after which his business was continued by his wife for several years. He produced cards for the upper New England region, with his output reaching many thousands of different views. He was a niche marketer, and tapped areas of revenue overlooked or considered insignificant by the mainstream publishers. Instead, Swallow emphasized country stores, churches, rural scenes, and other topics that were sold in the local areas depicted. As an example, the small New Hampshire town of Gilmanton Iron Works was a rich lode for Swallow, and over a period of years he issued dozens of different images and imprint variations. Presumably, many of these cards were ordered in small numbers by the general stores and others who sold them—perhaps only a few hundred cards at a time. Certain images became his stock-in-trade and over a period of time were reprinted and reprinted again, sometimes with different names of local merchants and other distributors. The vast majority of Swallow cards were printed in black and white with the benday process (with tiny black dots visible under magnification). Many of the early era cards and the majority of those made after about 1915 were hand-tinted with water colors.

Sometimes the coloring on extant cards shows great artistry and care, and other times the coloring is minimal at best and is limited to a few tree branches or rooftops. Circa 1906–1907, Swallow imported certain cards. An example is provided by a divided back card imprinted: "55934 Publ. For Frank W. Swallow, Exeter, N.H. by the Rotograph Co. (Germany)." The card, titled "Central Avenue Looking North from Franklin Square, Dover, N.H.," was a city view not much different in concept from those imported by G.W. Morris (Portland, Maine), Hugh C. Leighton (Portland), and others. An advertisement of the 1920s noted: "Established 1904, incorporated 1922." He presented his business as: "Manufacturers of Local View Post Cards in Hand Colored and Art Black. Jobbers of Holiday, Birthday and Miscellaneous Cards." In some instances the same image was circulated among various printers and publishers, with the result that a view appearing on a Swallow card printed in New Hampshire was also found on cards made in Germany. Around this time, "birch-bark border" cards became popular with different manufacturers. Swallow issued many printed versions. Today, view cards are very plentiful and serve to document many small Northern New England towns and villages in great detail.

Swenningsen, Jack. St. Petersburg, FL. Published postcards in the late twentieth century, including cards from E.C. Kropp Co.

Szalatany, Raf. D. New York, NY. Publisher of postcards during the early twentieth century, including signed artists.

T

Taber-Prang Art Co. Springfield, MA. Printer of view and art cards in the 1890s and early 1900s. Trade style adopted in 1897 when pioneer color lithographer Louis Prang retired.

Taggart, M.W. New York, NY. Publisher of art, patriotic, greeting, comic, etc. postcards, early twentieth century.

Tammen, H.H. Curio Co. / H-H-T Co. Denver, CO. Publisher of view, Western, and other cards, regional as well as national subjects, throughout much of the early twentieth century. H-H-T Co. imprint.

Tanner Souvenir Co. New York, NY. Published novelty, comic, and view cards in the early twentieth century, including German imports.

Tanner, K.S., Jr. Rutherfordton, NC. Distributor of view cards of American scenes imported from the Atelier Graphique H. Vontobel Switzerland, 1940s and 1950s.

Tanner, Mrs. G.N. / G.N. Tanner. Concord, MA. Published view cards in the mid-twentieth century.

Taylor Art Co. Philadelphia, PA. Printer of greetings, comic, art, and view cards, early twentieth century.

Taylor, Platt & Co. New York, NY. Publisher of postcards during the early twentieth century, including signed artists.

Ted Postcard & Novelty Co. Chicago, IL. Publishers of postcards, American-made, in the early twentieth century.

Teich, Curt, Co. Chicago, IL. The Curt Teich Co. was far and away the most important postcard printer and publisher in the United States. Curt Otto Teich came to American from Germany in 1896. Two years later he established the Curt Teich Co., in Chicago. By 1978 when it ceased business, it was the highest-volume postcard manufacturer in the world. Certain early cards were imported from Germany. In the early twentieth century, especially the years beginning about 1905, the quality of its color lithographed cards were on par with some of the finest makers in Germany, the center of the art. Its products evolved over the years, including the adding of white borders in the teen years, then in the 1930s the "linen" card (in which style Curt Teich was dominant), then chrome cards—with other variations. The company published cards in different levels of price and quality. For example, Sky-tint cards of the 1930s were inexpensive black-and-white cards with blue tinting. Fortunately for the postcard collecting community, the Curt Teich Archives are preserved by the Lake County Discovery Museum, Wauconda, IL, under an appreciative and talented curatorial staff. Many interesting exhibits are on view.[17] Early cards of the era up to 1908 were identified by numbers only, without a prefix letter. Numbers ran from 1 to 14989. Copyright dates on certain cards indicate production years, but surviving records are incomplete. From 1908 onward, prefixes A (usually) and R were used on cards, these being numbered up to 124180 in 1928. Certain other letters were used from time to time, such as W (for Woolworth), BS, DT, RG, and RT. Production numbers from 1908 to 1913, given below, are from the Archives. As production dates are not known with certainty, the ranges are approximate. After 1913 dates were added now and then to production ledgers, making the record

clearer. From 1922 onward the production numbers were well documented. After about 1924 prefix letters were omitted for most cards. Teich was connected in a way with the Commercial Colortype Co. of Chicago, particularly in the production of certain Commercialchrome, Octochrome, and related postcards.

Curt Teich 1900 to 1929 Serial Numbers:

Year	Serial Number
1900–1928	1 to 14989 (no prefix)
1908–1910	A1 upward
1910	A19922 upward
1911	A22998 upward
1912	A32000 upward
1913	A32236 to A45599
1914	A45600 to A53999
1915	A54000 to A61999
1916	A62000 to A71999
1917	A72000 to A77320
1918	A77321 to A77481
1919	A77482 to A81999
1920	A82000 to A83599
1921	A83600 to A87975
1922	A87976 to A92873
1923	A92874 to A96826
1924	A96827 to A102410
1925	A102411 to A107826
1926	A107827 to A112867
1927	A112868 to A118311
1928	A118312 to A124180

Curt Teich 1929 and 1930 Serial Numbers:

In 1929 and 1930 a revised system was devised in which the number of the card was followed by two digits indicating the year.

Year	Serial Number
1929	Example 6262-29; this was card 6262 issued in 1929.
1930	Example 2934-30; this was card 2934 issued in 1930, actually the last in this system.

Curt Teich 1930 to 1978 Serial Numbers:

Partway through 1930 the numbering system was again revised. A letter was used to indicate the decade, as: A for the 1930s, B for the 1940s, C for the 1950s, D for the 1960s, and E for the 1970s. A digit preceding the letter indicates the year within that decade, as 0A for 1930, 1A for 1931, etc. The transition from the old style to the new saw the last card in the old system, 2934 to 30, followed by the first in the new system, 0A2935.

In 1931 "linen" cards were introduced. Cards of this style, called the Art Colortone Method, had an H added after the decade letter, as in 1AH followed by a serial number. In the late 1940s when the chrome printing process was introduced the letter K was put after the decade letter.

Under the new processes we have the following numbers.

Year	Serial Number
1930	0A2935 to 0A5363
1931	1A1 to 1A3637 + linen 1AH1 to 1AH565
1932	2A1 to 2A1562 + linen 2AH1 to 2AH1082
1933	3A1 to 3A552 + linen 3AH1 to 3AH1656
1934	4A1 to 4A654 + linen 4AH1 to 4AH2223
1935	5A1 to 5A650 + linen 5AH1 to 5AH270
1936	5A1 to 5A668 + linen 5AH1 to 5AH2913
1937	7A1 to 7A710 + linen 7AH1 to 7AH3989
1938	8A1 to 8A923 + linen 8AH1 to 8AH3291
1939	9A1 to 9A982 + linen 9AH1 to 9AH2637
1940	0B1 to OB996 + linen 0BH1 to 0BH2755
1941	1B1 to 1B954 + linen 1BH1 to 1BH2693
1942	2B1 to 2B545 + linen 2BH1 to 2BH1581
1943	3B1 to 3B432 + linen 3BH1 to 3BH1722
1944	4B1 to 4B436 + linen 4BH1 to 4BH1657
1945	5B1 to 5B510 + linen 5BH1 to 5BH1509
1946	6B1 to 6B721 + linen 6BH1 to 6BH2667

Year	Serial Number
1947	7B1 to 7B561 + linen 7BH1 to 7BH2149
1948	8B1 to 8B791 + linen 8BH1 to 8BH1993
1949	9B1 to 9B782 + linen 9BH1 to 9BH1904 + chrome 9BK1 to 9BK129
1950	0C1 to 0C700 + linen 0CH1 to 0CH2125 + chrome 0CK1 to 0CK448
1951	1C1 to 1C653 + linen 1CH1 to 1CH1937 + chrome 1CK1 to 1CK305 1CP1450 to 1CP2030 + The P indicates the C.T. Photochrom process. Most of the cards printed with this new process were reprints of cards the Teich Company produced in other styles.
1952	2C1 to 2C564 + linen 2CH1 to 2CH1680 + chrome 2CK1 to 2CK401 2CP2001 to 2CP2638
1953	3C1 to 3C494 + linen 3CH1 to 3CH1433 + chrome 3CK1 to 3CK1548 3CP2001 to 3CP2254
1954	4C1 to 4C420 + linen 4CH1 to 4CH909 + chrome 4CK1 to 4CK2194 4CP2001 to 2CP2109
1955	5C1 to 5C230 + linen 5CH1 to 5CH705 + chrome 5CK1 to 5CK3091 5CP2001 to 5CP2049
1956	6C1 to 6C100 + linen 6CH1 to 6CH228 + chrome 6CK1 to 6CK3110 6CP2001 to 6CP2022
1957	7C1 to 7C8 + linen 7CH1 to 7CH92 + chrome 7CK1 to 7CK3151
1958	linen 8CH1 to 8CH62 + chrome 8CK1 to 8CK3280
1959	linen 9CH1 to 9CH6 + chrome 9CK1 to 9CK3023
1960	chrome 0DK1 to 0DK2443
1961	chrome 1DK1 to 1DK2385
1962	chrome 2DK1 to 2DK2073
1963	chrome 3DK1 to 3DK2035
1964	chrome 4DK1 to 4DK1936

Year	Serial Number
1965	chrome 5DK1 to 5DK2006
1966	chrome 6DK1 to 6DK1957
1967	chrome 7DK1 to 7DK1795
1968	chrome 8DK1 to 8DK1477
1969	chrome 9DK1 to 9DK1330
1970	chrome 0EK1 to 0EK885
1971	chrome 1EK1 to 1EK785
1972	chrome 2EK1 to 2EK699
1973	chrome 3EK1 to 3EK561
1974	chrome 4EK1 to 4EK392 4ED1 to 4ED558 +

In 1974 the Teich Company was sold to Regensteiner Publishers also in Chicago. The Teich Company continued to operate in the same building and continued printing Teich postcards until 1978 when the plant closed. The 'ED' series postcards are Curteichcolor 3-D natural color reproduction and are international size.

Year	Serial Number
1975	chrome 5EK1 to 5EK537 + 3-D international 5ED1 to 5ED981
1976	chrome 6EK1 to 6EK689 + 3-D international 6ED1 to 6ED954
1977	chrome 7EK1 to 7EK454 + 3-D international 7ED1 to 7ED368
1978	chrome 8EK1 to 8EK116 + 3-D international 8ED1 to 8ED187

Curt Teich Duotone Series Serial Numbers:

In 1929 the Duotone or D Series was launched, including postcards among the early numbers, but mostly devoted to blotters, souvenir booklets, brochures, leaflets, fold-out postcards, and advertising items. The company continued printing D cards after it was sold in 1974, but the new orders were not written in the company books. The last D card printed before the plant closed in 1978 was D20363.

Year	Serial Number
1929	D1 to D558
1930	D559 to D1100
1931	D1101 to D1720
1932	D1721 to D2400

Chart continues on next page

Year	Serial Number
1933	D2401 to D3200
1934	D3201 to D3650
1935	D3651 to D4200
1936	D4201 to D4750
1937	D4751 to D5200
1938	D5201 to D5700
1939	D5701 to D6200
1940	D6201 to D6470
1941	D6471 to D6790
1942	D6791 to D7090
1943	D7091 to D7435
1944	D7436 to D7685
1945	D7686 to D8000
1946	D8001 to D8492
1947	D8493 to D8741
1948	D8742 to D9105
1949	D9106 to D9450
1950	D9451 to D9725
1951	D9726 to D9971
1952	D9972 to D10203
1953	D10204 to D10431
1954	D10432 to D10713
1955	D10714 to D11134
1956	D11135 to D11600
1957	D11601 to D11935
1958	D11936 to D12352
1959	D12353 to D12772
1960	D12773 to D13075
1961	D13076 to D13355
1962	D13356 to D13612
1963	D13613 to D13822
1964	D13823 to D14095
1965	D14096 to D14390
1966	D14391 to D14796
1967	D14797 to D15261
1968	D15262 to D15684
1969	D15685 to D16231
1970	D16232 to D17000
1971	D17001 to D17770
1972	D17771 to D18600
1973	D18601 to D19325
1974–1978	D19326 to D20363

Curt Teich RC Series Serial Numbers:

The RC series was made from 1912 to 1915. Company records are incomplete as most numbers were not entered. This listing must be viewed as approximate.

Year	Serial Number
1912	RC1 to RC360
1913	RC361 to RC1800
1914	RC1801 to RC4500
1915	RC4501 to RC6680
1916	RC6681 to RC8842
1917	RC8843 to RC10193
1918	RC10194 to RC10566
1919	RC10567 to RC12318
1920–1922	unknown number ranges
1923	RC12637 to RC14175
1924	RC14176 to RC14528
1925	RC14529 to RC14804

Curt Teich addenda:

Certain small series were made by Teich with other prefixes, with two letters before the serial number. It is thought that the second letter indicated the printing or finish process. Such prefixes are thought to include AD, AC, AH, AP, AS, RC, RD, RH, RP, RS, WC, OR, and WP. Little is known about them.

The website for the Curt Teich Archives notes this: "The series of cards known as C cards were printed approximately between 1905 and 1926. Not much is known about this series because many numbers were not entered in the company records and few were recorded with a date. Many of the cards in the files are printer's proofs—not finished cards. Many of the backs of the finished cards are printed with a brown (sepia) tone. There are a number of different styles in this series, which include: Octochrome, Commercialchrome, and Sky-tint, but there may be others. In some cases, the C or even a CC may follow the production number or may not be present at all."

Some L-prefix cards were made for the Hugh C. Leighton Co., Portland, Maine. Some miniature view cards, usually sold in packets, have B or E prefixes. Teich printed many view cards for V.O. Hammon.

Temme, F.G., Co. Orange, NJ. Publisher of view cards, mostly German imports, early twentieth century.

Tengg, Nic. San Antonio, TX. Published postcards in the mid-twentieth century, including cards from the Curt Teich Co.

Tetirick, James. Kansas City, MO. Published postcards in the late twentieth century.

Texacolor Card Co. Dallas, TX. Published postcards in the late twentieth century.

Texarkana Books, Inc. Texarkana, TX. Published postcards in the late twentieth century, including cards from Dexter Press.

That Man Pitts. San Francisco, CA. Published postcards in the early twentieth century.

Thayer, Frank S., Publishing Co. / Thayer Publishing Co. Denver, CO. Publisher of Western topics and views on postcards, first two decades of the twentieth century.

Thayer, Porter C. Williamsville, VT. Made RPPCs in the early twentieth century.

Thiem, James E. Raleigh, NC. Published view cards in the early twentieth century, including those of the Curt Teich Co.

Thomas, E.B. Cambridge, MA. Published view cards in the mid-twentieth century.

Thompson & Thompson. Boston, MA. Important regional publisher of view postcards, including those from Valentine & Sons and imports from France. Early twentieth century through the late 1920s.

Thompson Souvenir Station. Albany, NY. Published RPPCs in the early twentieth century.

Thompson, C.L. Monmouth, ME. Published postcards in the early twentieth century, including German imports through Hugh C. Leighton Co.

Thompson, D.C. Vineyard Haven, MA. Published view cards in the late twentieth century, including those of the Plastichrome type.

Thompson, Franklin E.S., Studio. Marblehead, MA. Photographer who published printed views, mostly of regional interest, including many German imports, in the early twentieth century.

Thompson, G.L. New York, NY. Publisher of view and topical cards with emphasis on regional military installations and fortifications, early twentieth century.

Thompson, Nyla. Austin, TX. Publisher of postcards during the early twentieth century, including signed artists.

Thompson, W.M. Saunderstown, RI. Published postcards in the 1920s and 1930s.

Thompson's Book Store. Carlisle, PA. Issued postcards in the mid-twentieth century, including from the Curt Teich Co.

Thomsen-Ellis Co. Baltimore, MD. Created "Typogravure" postcards in the early twentieth century.

Thomson & Thomson. Boston, MA. Printed view cards in the early twentieth century, including those imported from Great Britain.

Thorner, Leonard P. Marblehead, MA. Published postcards, including German imports, in the early twentieth century.

Thwaites, John E. Ketchikan, AK. Photographer and issuer of RPPCs, early twentieth century. Sold his business to Otto Schallerer in 1932.

Tichenor & Rudolph. Middletown, NY. Publisher of view cards of regional interest, early twentieth century onward, including Germany imports in earlier times.

Tichnor Art Co. Los Angeles, CA. Published postcards in the 1930s.

Tichnor Brothers. Cambridge and Boston, MA; Los Angeles, CA. Major national publisher of postcards with emphasis on views, early twentieth century, continuing into the 1980s. Most activities were in Massachusetts. Some were imprinted Lusterchrome or Tichnor Gloss.

Tilton Postcard Co. Tilton, NH. Published postcards in the early twentieth century, including those imported from Germany.

Tilton's. North Adams, MA. Published view cards in the early twentieth century

Tingle Printing Co. Pittsville, MD. Published modern postcards, including Plastichrome.

Tipton, W.H., & Co. Gettysburg, PA. Photographer who published printed view cards, especially of the Gettysburg battlefield and park, early twentieth century.

Titlebaum, Nat., & Co. Boston, MA. Issued view cards in the early twentieth century, including those made in Austria.

Toland & Little. Battle Creek, MI. Published RPPCs in the early twentieth century. Their business name was arranged to create the borders of the stamp box.

Tomlin Art Co. Babylon, NY. Published view cards beginning in the mid-twentieth century.

Tothaker, Edgar R. Phillips, ME. Published postcards in the early twentieth century, including from the Curt Teich Co.

Tower Manufacturing and Novelty Co. New York, NY. Publisher of monotone gravure cards, mostly views and mostly published in Germany. Issued a set of cards illustrating the 1906 San Francisco earthquake and fire.

Townsend, Charles A. Belfast, ME. Photographer who issued many RPPCs, especially of Maine coastal subjects, 1910s to 1930s.

Transcolor Corporation. New York, NY. Published view cards in the late twentieth century.

Traub, D.E. Baltimore, MD. Published view cards in the late twentieth century including Plastichrome cards.

Treiber E.H. Scotland, SD. Published RPPCs in the early twentieth century.

Tuck, Raphael, & Sons. London, England; New York, NY. Raphael Tuck & Sons was the most important European postcard publisher with distribution in America, in terms of sales and variety of subjects. The firm's products were of uniformly high quality. Founded in 1866, the firm began printing postcards in the 1890s, continuing for decades afterward. In 1900 Tuck opened a branch at 122 Fifth Avenue, New York City. Many different printers were used over a long period of years, mostly in England, Germany, and Holland. The numbering of Tuck cards was erratic and sometimes duplicated. Tuck cards are listed elsewhere in the present work, including some of the following:

Early view cards of American interest include these Private Mailing Cards, 1898 and later, in three sets:

Serial No.	Location
3000 to 3009	Washington, D.C.
5010 to 5010	Boston, MA
5020 to 5029	Philadelphia, PA

Chromolithographic Private Mailing Cards, color and signed by artists, include:

Serial No.	Location
5051 to 5070	New York, NY
5071 to 5080	Atlantic City, NJ
5081 to 5090	Hudson River, NY
6000 to 6011	Chicago, IL
6012 to 6023	New York, NY

Lithochrome cards, sometimes called photochrome, of the early twentieth century were made of dozens of different American cities and towns. These were usually sold in packets of six cards, each with the same series number. Most were printed in Germany and were of high quality.

Oilette cards reproduced art in color and were very popular, including in the Wide World Series. Some were made of American views, mostly of the New York City area, and include Greater New York (Series 1038), Cosmopolitan New York—Ghetto (Series 1012), Cosmopolitan New York—Little Italy (Series 1014), and Cosmopolitan New York—Chinatown (Series 1068), Many other topics, including comic, novelty, etc., postcards were published with the Oilette designation.

Raphotype color view cards were printed in Holland, numbered 5000 consecutively to 6100, and mainly comprise American views.

Tucker, C.O. Boston, MA. Publisher of regional and nautical views, including U.S. Life Saving Service topics, in the first two decades of the twentieth century. Published RPPCs.

Tucker, H.D. Lake Placid, NY. Published postcards in the early twentieth century, including German imports.

Tucker, K.V., Mrs. Amsterdam, NY. Published view cards in the early twentieth century, including German imports.

Tuppen Co. Studio. Syracuse, NY. Made RPPCs in the early twentieth century.

Turlington, H.A. Published view cards in the mid-twentieth century, particularly of military installations. He was a technical sergeant.

Turner, S.B., and Son. Norfolk, VA. Published postcards in the early twentieth century.

Tygert, George F. Oneida, NY. Published view cards in the early twentieth century, including those printed in Germany.

U

Ullman Manufacturing Co. New York, NY. Important regional printer and publisher of postcards of many topics, including greetings and views, first two decades of the twentieth century. Many imprinted "American Post Cards" in an era when German imports were all the rage. Their Gold Border cards are distinctive. Color cards issued from about 1907 to 1910, numbered 501 to 599, are mostly signed by artists.

Underwood & Underwood. New York, NY. One of the most important American makers of stereograph cards, the company published many postcards in the early twentieth century, most notably circa 1911–1912, these imitative of RPPCs and covering many subjects. These are of very high quality. The company was sold to the Keystone View Co., of Meadville, PA, in 1921.

Union Lithograph Co. San Francisco, CA. Published postcards in the early twentieth century.

Union News Co. New York, NY. Union, a subsidiary of the American News Co. (ANC), operated newsstands in cities, hotels, railroad stations, and elsewhere, and published postcards for sale there, from the early twentieth century onward.

Union Oil Co. CA. Published the numbered series, "Union Oil Co.'s Natural Color Photographic Scenes of the West," mid-twentieth century.

Union Photo Engraving Co. San Francisco, CA. Sometimes published as Photoengraving. Printed postcards for the California Midwinter International Exposition in San Francisco, 1894.

United Art Co. Boston, MA. Publisher of view cards of regional interest, 1930s onward.

United Art Publishing Co. New York, NY. Publisher of postcards of various topics, including views. Many were German imports. Active in the first two decades of the twentieth century.

United Lithographing and Printing Co. Rochester, NY. Published postcards in the early twentieth century.

United Post Card & Novelty Co. Chicago, IL. Published postcards in the early twentieth century.

United States Postal Card Co. Omaha, NE. Distributed official cards for the 1898 Trans-Mississippi and International Exposition, Omaha, 1898, and its successor, Greater American Exposition in Omaha, 1899. The cards were printed by the Chicago Colortype Co.

United States Postcard Co. Wilmington, DE. Published postcards in the early twentieth century.

United View Co. Newark, DE. Publisher of view cards with topics relating to the mid-Atlantic states.

Universal Postal Card Co. New York, NY. Publisher of scenic and historical postcards, including of the Spanish-American War (1898). Active from 1897 through the next decade.

Unusual Photographs Reproduction Co. New York, NY. Published regional interest postcards resembling RPPCs, most of which were imported. Active in the 1930s and 1940s.

Upper Michigan Card Co. Manistique, MI. Published view cards in the late twentieth century.

Utica Paper Co. Utica and Verona, NY. Publisher of regional interest view cards in the first two decades of the twentieth century.

Utley, H.D. New London, CT. Published view cards in the early twentieth century.

V

Valence Color Studios. Miami, FL. Published view cards in the late twentieth century, including those from Dexter Press.

Valentine & Sons Co. New York, NY; Boston, MA. In 1907, Valentine's, an important publisher of postcards in Scotland with affiliates in the British Empire, opened an office in New York City, soon followed by one in Boston. The company published many different view cards, often with the serial numbers in script in the face plate. In 1909 it merged with the Hugh C. Leighton Co., of Portland, ME, to form Leighton & Valentine. The latter firm merged with the Souvenir Post Card Co. in 1913 to become the Valentine Souvenir Co. (see below).

Valentine Souvenir Co. New York, NY. Formed in 1914 by a merger of Leighton & Valentine and the Souvenir Post Card Co., this company operated for about a decade and was well known for its colored view cards.

Valley News Service. Parkersburg, WV. Published postcards in the 1920s and 1930s, including from the Curt Teich Co.

Van Griethuysen & Lowe. Perkins and Ripley, OK. Published RPPCs in the early twentieth century.

Van Noy-Interstate Co. Kansas City, MO. Published postcards in the mid-twentieth century, including cards from Albertype.

Van Ornum Colorprint Co. Los Angeles, CA. Publisher of color view cards in the early twentieth century, through about 1921. Some have M. Kashower Co. distributor imprint.

Van Tyne, R.T. Fishkill Landing, NY. Publisher of color view cards, including from Leighton & Valentine.

Vancard. Los Angeles (Hollywood), CA. Publisher of postcards, including reproductions of watercolor views of New York by Marcus A. Van Der Hope.

Varick, John B., Co. Manchester, NH. Published postcards in the early twentieth century, including those imported from Germany by Reichner Brothers. Postcards were a small part of a business that sold many things, including hardware.

Vickery & Hill Publishing Co. Augusta, ME. Publisher of postcards, including American and international views. Formed by P.O. Vickery and Dr. John Fremont Hill, this company was prominent in the publishing industry. Postcards were a specialty from the early 1900s to the early 1940s.

Vienna Post Card Co. New York, NY. Publisher of regional interest view cards. Active in the 1910s.

Virginia Postcard Co./ W.C. Sithens. Atlantic City, NJ. Published postcards in the early twentieth century, including E.C. Kropp Co. cards.

Vogel, Paul R., Co. Chicago, IL. Published postcards in the early twentieth century, including those of the Curt Teich Co.

Voigt, John C., Post Card Co. Jersey City, NJ. Published postcards in the first two decades of the twentieth century, specializing in regional views.

Volland, P.F., & Co. Chicago and Joliet, IL. Established by Paul Frederick Volland, this company printed many things, including art, view, and other postcards in the early twentieth century, into the 1950s. Certain artist-signed cards and Arts and Crafts style cards are especially popular. The company merged with Gerlach-Barklow and moved to Joliet in the 1920s.

Von Bardelben, F. New York, NY. Cards printed in Germany were marketed by von Bardelben. Views included monotone images of New York City historical scenes.

Voorhees, D.J. Valley Forge, PA. Issued postcards in the mid-twentieth century, including cards from the Curt Teich Co.

Voris Printing Co. Waterloo, IA. Publisher of postcards during the early twentieth century, including signed artists.

W

Waddey, Everett, Printing & Stationery Co. Richmond, VA. Published many postcards in black-and-white gravure, some titled Copper Plate Etching. Colonial Williamsburg views were a specialty. Active in the early twentieth century into the 1930s.

Wagner, Charles T. Susquehanna, PA. Issued postcards in the mid-twentieth century, including those of the Curt Teich Co.

Wakefield Trading Co. Wakefield, MA. Published cards in the late twentieth century including those from Tichnor Brothers.

Walcott and Sons. San Angelo, TX. Published postcards in the late twentieth century, including cards from E.C. Kropp Co.

Walcott, Charles R. San Benito, TX. Photographer and a publisher of printed view cards. "Hill Country Fotocolor Artist." Second half of the twentieth century.

Walford, D.N. Washington, D.C. Published postcards in the early twentieth century, including cards printed in England.

Walker's Postcard Shop. Publisher of postcards during the early twentieth century, including signed artists.

Wall, Nichols & Co. Honolulu, HI. Publisher of postcards beginning with Spanish-American War scenes in 1898, continuing into the 1910s. Cards were printed by various mainland companies.

Wallace, Alvis W. Pennsville, NJ. Publisher of view cards, including of Curt Teich Co., early twentieth century.

Wallace, J.N. Guthrie, OK. Published postcards in the early twentieth century.

Wallick & Flater. Iowa City, IA. Published postcards in the early twentieth century.

Walmer, J.P. Harrisburg, PA. Issued postcards in the mid-twentieth century, including cards from the Curt Teich Co.

Walraven Brothers, Inc. Dallas, TX. Published postcards in the 1920s and 1930s.

Walsh, John F. Oakland Beach, RI. Published postcards in the early twentieth century, including from the Commercial Colortype Co.

Wanamaker, John (John Wanamaker Department Store). Philadelphia, PA. Published postcards in the early twentieth century, including views of Native Americans from the Wanamaker Historical Expedition.

Ward, Jay. Mitiwanga, OH. Published postcards in the 1920s and 1930s, including from Metropolitan (from Everett, MA).

Warne, F.W., & Co. London, England; New York, NY. Publisher of postcards with children's themes, circa 1914, later reprinted.

Warner Photo Shop. New Castle, PA. Published postcards in the mid-twentieth century, including from the Curt Teich Co.

Warriner, Mrs. Nellie E. Adams, NY. Published view cards in the early twentieth century.

Washington News Co. Washington, D.C. Published postcards in the early twentieth century, including cards imported from Germany by the American News Co. (ANC).

Washington Souvenir Co. Washington, D.C. Publisher of Private Mailing Cards in sets with Washington and patriotic scenes at the turn of the twentieth century.

Waterloo News Agency. Waterloo, IA. Published postcards in the early twentieth century.

Waterman, L.E., Co. New York, NY. Published postcards in the early twentieth century.

Watt, Alexander. Albion, NY. Published view cards in the early twentieth century, including German imports from the American News Co. (ANC).

Wayley, Frank, Post Cards. Corpus Christi, TX. Published postcards in the late twentieth century, including cards from Dexter Press.

Wayne Paper Box & Printing Co. Fort Wayne, IN. Maker of "Clear View" postcards in the mid-twentieth century.

Wayside Industries. South Sudbury, MA. Published postcards in the mid-twentieth century.

Weaver-Fagerstrom, Inc. Pueblo, CO. Published postcards in the 1920s and 1930s, including from the Curt Teich Co.

Weaver-Gibbs Co. Pueblo, CO. Published postcards in the 1920s and 1930s, including from the Curt Teich Co.

Webb Cut Rate Drug Co. St. Petersburg, FL. Published postcards in the mid-twentieth century.

Webb-Freyschlag Mercantile Co. Kansas City, MO. Published postcards in the early twentieth century.

Wegler, L.C., Lithographers. Buffalo, NY. Published postcards in the early twentieth century.

Weidner, Charles. San Francisco, CA. Photographer who published RPPCs and printed postcards, including German imports. Views of the 1915 Panama-Pacific International Exposition were popular. Weidner began publishing postcards under his own name, shortly following cards issued under the imprint of Goeggel & Weidner, with partner William Goeggel. Some later reprints continue this name. Charles Weidner was active through the 1910s, save for the publishing of a few black-and-white cards later.

Weill, D.R., Co. Chattanooga, TN. Published postcards in the early twentieth century, including cards from E.C. Kropp Co.

Weiner News Co. San Antonio, TX. Published postcards in the mid-twentieth century.

Weit News Co. Ephrata, PA. Published postcards in the mid-twentieth century, including from the Curt Teich Co.

Well Novelty Co. New Haven, CT. Published view cards in the early twentieth century.

Weller, H. Dunkirk, NY. Published view cards in the early twentieth century, including German imports.

Wells, Edward. Dumont, NJ. Published view cards in the late twentieth century, including those printed by Dexter Press.

Wend, Lewis. Nelsonville, OH. Published postcards in the 1920s and 1930s.

Wentworth, Stacy H. Chatham, MA. Publisher of regional view postcards. Active in the 1920s.

Werst, Platt O. Easton, PA. Published view cards in the early twentieth century, including German imports.

Wesley Advertising Co. Chicago, IL. Published postcards in the early twentieth century, including advertising calendar cards.

Wesley Andrews Co. Portland, OR. Published view cards in the early twentieth century.

Wessa, W.H. Antigo, WI. Publisher of RPPCs in the early twentieth century, including of Native Americans.

West, E.D., Co. South Yarmouth, MA. Publisher of regional view postcards from the 1910s to the 1950s.

West, Thomas H. Miami, FL. Published postcards in the early twentieth century, including cards from the Curt Teich Co.

Western Lithographing Co. Los Angeles, CA. Published postcards in the early twentieth century.

Western News Co. Chicago, IL. Publisher of postcards during the early twentieth century, including signed artists and cards imported from Germany through American News Co. (ANC).

Western Post Card Co. / Western Card Co. / Besaw's Studio / Besaw Card Co. Reedley, CA. Made RPPCs of Main Streets and various regional scenes. Conducted by George Besaw beginning in the 1910s, after he had served as a photographer for Edward H. Mitchell.

Western Printing and Lithographing Co. Racine, WI. Publisher of postcards during the early twentieth century, including signed artists.

Western Publishing & Novelty Co. Los Angeles, CA. Publisher of view and other postcards, early twentieth century onward. Cards printed by Tichnor Brothers, Curt Teich Co., and others.

Western Resort Publications. Santa Ana, CA. Published chrome view cards in the late twentieth century.

Western Souvenirs, Inc. Spokane, WA. Published view cards in the mid-twentieth century

Westminster Press. Philadelphia, PA. Publisher of postcards during the early twentieth century, including signed artists.

Weynant, C.J. Fort Montgomery, NY. Published view cards in the early twentieth century, including those made by Albertype.

Wheeler, E.S. Binghamton, NY. Made RPPCs in the early twentieth century.

Wheelock, C.E., Co. Peoria, IL. Publisher of postcards, mostly views, primarily imported from Germany along with other souvenir items, later published Commercial Colortype Co. cards. The company logotype, combining a wheel and a padlock, is usually in the stamp box.

Whitcomb Summit Co. North Adams, MA. Published view cards in the mid-twentieth century, including those of the Curt Teich Co.

White Advertising Bureau, Inc. Seattle, WA. Published view cards in the early twentieth century.

White City Art Co. Chicago, IL. Publisher of postcards of various types, active from the turn of the century to about 1910. Certain views were from William Henry Jackson photographs. Some cards were printed by R.R. Donnelly & sons.

White, James R. Kalispell, MT. Published postcards in the early twentieth century.

White, T.J. (Tommy). Buchanan Dam, TX. Published postcards in the late twentieth century, including cards from Plastichrome.

White, W.R. Providence, RI. Published postcards in the early twentieth century, including cards imported from Germany.

Whiting, Frank E. Plainville, MA. Published view cards, including German imports, in the early twentieth century.

Whitmore, R.D. Published view cards in the early twentieth century, including those made in Germany

Whitneck, H. Elkhart, IN. Made RPPCs in the early twentieth century.

Whitney Valentine Co. Worcester, MA. This company, with an interest in Valentine's Day cards, made postcards from the turn of the century into the early 1940s, including mechanical, greetings, holidays, sentimental, and other topics.

Whitten & Dennison. West Bethel, ME. Makers of printed RPPCs from negatives supplied by clients; early twentieth century.

Whittenboch Drug Co. Harlingen, TX. Published postcards in the mid-twentieth century, including cards from Dexter Press.

Wienecke, H.C. Iowa City, IA. Published postcards in the early twentieth century.

Wiener Werkstätte. Vienna, Austria. Established in 1903 by Josef Hofmann and Koloman Moser, the "Vienna Workshop" was a focal point for artists of the era, a group sometimes referred to as "secessionists." The work of Gustav Klimpt, Oskar Kokoschka, Egon Schiele, and others was reproduced on postcards, often in bright colors. These and others of the early era are in great demand today and are often very expensive. The facility operated until 1932.

Wier, Bob, Photocards. Old Adelphi, NY. Distributed RPPCs in the mid-twentieth century.

Wiese Studio. Ridgway, PA. Produced RPPCs during the early twentieth century.

Wilcox, H.F. Cuba, NY. Produced RPPCs in the early twentieth century.

Wild & Pchellas. Buffalo, NY. Published postcards in the early twentieth century.

Wilkerson, Thaddeus. New York, NY. Photographer who issued RPPCs and also published printed scenes of regional interest in the first two decades of the twentieth century.

Wilkes-Barre News Agency. Wilkes-Barre, PA. Issued postcards in the mid-twentieth century, including those from Tichnor Brothers.

Willard, Stephen H. Palm Springs, CA. Artist who published art and view cards, circa 1910s into the second half of the twentieth century. Many were printed by the Curt Teich Co.

Williams, Alfred, & Co. Raleigh, NC. Distributed view cards in the early and mid-twentieth century, including those made by the E.C. Kropp Company.

Williams, C.M. Port Allegheny, PA. Printed and published postcards in the first decade of the twentieth century.

Williams, C.U. / Photoette. Bloomington, IL. Major publisher of regional view cards during the early twentieth century. Many had a blue tint over the black-and-white image on the face. Titles were often hand-lettered with heavy "blobs" at the lower part of the letters, a distinctive feature making such cards instantly identifiable as Williams products by looking at the title. Most bore the Photoette trade style in addition to Williams' name. Identification on the back was usually within the stamp box.

Williams, J.I. Worcester, MA. Important publisher of view cards of regional interest.

Williams Photo Co. Hastings, NE. Published view cards during the early twentieth century, including those of the Curt Teich Co.

Williams, W.W. IA. Published postcards in the early twentieth century, including German imports, obtained from A.M. Simon.

Williams, William. Jamestown, RI. Printed view cards in the early twentieth century, including German imports.

Williamson-Haffner Co. Denver, CO. Early twentieth century printer and publisher of view, comic, and other postcards. Color is sometimes exaggerated on early view cards.

Williamsport Paper Co. Williamsport, PA. Published postcards in the early twentieth century, including distribution in the West.

Willis Book and Stationery Co. Greensboro, NC. Published postcards in the early twentieth century, including from the Curt Teich Co.

Willis, J.R. Albuquerque, NM. Published postcards in the mid-twentieth century, including those from the Curt Teich Co.

Willis, Jimmie. Waco, TX. Published postcards in the late twentieth century, including cards made from his own photographs.

Wills, E.S. Distributed postcards in the early twentieth century, including those printed in Germany and obtained from PCK.

Wilsher, J. Weston, WV. Published postcards in the early twentieth century, including those from the Commercial Colortype Co.

Wilson and Judd. Palmer Lake, CO. Published postcards in the early twentieth century.

Wilson, Albert M. Buffalo, NY. Publisher of view cards, mostly of regional interest but also some of Palestine. Comic and greeting postcards were sold as well. Active in the first two decades of the twentieth century.

Wilson, D.C. Sabbathday Lake, ME. Published postcards in the early twentieth century, including those made by Tichnor Brothers.

Wilson, Edward L. Philadelphia, PA. Published postcards in the early twentieth century.

Wilson, H.H., Co. Minneapolis, MN. Publisher of view cards of regional interest in the early twentieth century.

Wilt, W.W. Conneaut Lake Park, PA. Issued postcards in the mid-twentieth century, including from Curt Teich and Co.

Wiltzius, M.H., Co. Milwaukee, WI. Published postcards in the early twentieth century.

Winchell, E.E. New York, NY. Published postcards in the early twentieth century.

Wines, F.B., Co. Tacoma, WA. Published view cards in the mid-twentieth century.

Winsch, John O. Stapleton, NY. Highly important publisher of artist-signed, holiday, and related art cards, most of which were printed in Germany but some domestically. The art of Samuel L. Schmucker is the best known. Winsch cards are highly sought today for their excellent art and bright colors, with holiday cards being favorites. Active in the first two decades of the twentieth century.

Winter Art Litho. Chicago, IL. Published postcards in the early twentieth century.

Winter, Lloyd Valentine, and Edwin Percy Pond. Juneau, AK. Professional photographers who operated a shop. Among their products were RPPC regional views. Some images were reproduced on printed cards as well. Early twentieth century.

Wiseman. Hico, TX. Issued RPPCs in the early twentieth century.

Wisner, J. Published postcards in the early twentieth century, including German imports.

Witt Brothers. Atlanta, GA. Publisher of postcards, including German imports, early twentieth century.

Witt, Eli, Cigar & Tobacco Co. Miami, FL. Published postcards in the mid-twentieth century, including cards from Colourpicture.

Witten-Dennison Post Card Co. Auburn, IN. Founded in Maine, the company moved to Auburn, Indiana, in 1910 and in 1913 became known as the Auburn Post Card Manufacturing Co. (see listing). Cards under the Witten-Dennison name, greetings and views, were published up to that time.

Woehler, H.L. Buffalo, NY; Dresden, Germany. Printer, publisher, and importer of holiday, greeting, and view cards in the early twentieth century.

Wolf Co. Philadelphia, PA. Also Wolf & Co. A division of the International Art Publishing Co., Wolf published holiday, greeting, and artist-signed cards in the 1910s and 1920s.

Wolte, Friedrich O. Berlin, Germany. Publisher of postcards, including some with American art, such as portraits by Philip Boileau.

Wonday Film Service, Inc. Wilkinsburg, PA. Published view cards in the mid-twentieth century, including Dexter Press cards.

Wood, Elmer, Co. Moulton, IA. Published postcards in the early twentieth century, including German imports.

Wood, W.E. Greenfield, MA. Published view cards in the early twentieth century, including German imports from the American News Company (ANC).

Wood, W.H. Haverhill, MA. Published postcards in the early twentieth century, including imported cards obtained from Hugh C. Leighton.

Wood's. Orange, TX. Published postcards in the late twentieth century.

Wood's, Inc. / Wood's Post Card, Inc. Los Angeles, CA. Publisher of view cards in the early twentieth century, including in dark sepia from or similar to E.H. Mitchell cards.

Woodward & Tiernan Printing Co. St. Louis, MO. Maker of private mailing cards, advertising cards, and other issues from the 1890s to the 1910s. Some cards copyrighted 1908 have undivided backs.

Wooley, Jesse Sumner. Ballston Spa, NY. Photographer and issuer of RPPCs and publisher of printed cards using his images. Active in the early twentieth century.

Woolson Co. Mount Vernon, OH. Published postcards in the 1920s and 1930s, including from the Curt Teich Co.

Woolverton Press. Osage, IA. Printed postcards from pictures supplied by customers, early twentieth century.

Woolworth, C.S., & Co. Portland, ME. Published postcards in the early twentieth century, including German imports from S. Langsdorf and Co.

Woolworth, F.W., Co. New York, NY. The largest of the five-and-ten cent store chains, Woolworth published many cards in the early twentieth century, with the Curt Teich Co. being an important supplier. These usually had the letter W within a diamond-shaped frame.

Wootton, Bayard. Jamestown, VA. Published postcards in the early twentieth century.

World Post Card Co. New York, NY; Philadelphia, PA. Publisher of black-and-white and color view cards in the first two decades of the twentieth century. Established by J. Murray Jordan (see listing above), whose name appears as publisher on many cards.

Worth, Walter. New York, NY. Published postcards in the 1890s.

Wright, Barrett & Stilwell Co. St. Paul, MN. Published postcards in the early twentieth century.

Wright, T.A., Photography. Sulphur Springs, TX. Published postcards in the late twentieth century, including cards from E.C. Kropp Co.

Wright-Harris Grocer Co. Mineral Wells, TX. Published postcards in the early twentieth century, including cards from the Curt Teich Co.

Wyanoak Publishing Co. New York, NY. Publisher of theater scene and other cards, early twentieth century.

WYCO Products. Jenkintown, PA. Published view cards in the late twentieth century.

Wyer, Henry S. Nantucket, MA. Photographer and publisher of printed postcards, early twentieth century, the latter including German imprints.

Wyn-Kraft Co. Boston, MA. Published postcards in the early twentieth century.

Y

Yankee Colour Corp. Southboro, MA. Published view cards in the late twentieth century.

Ye Postte Cardde Shoppe. Block Island, RI. Publisher of view cards of local interest. Active in the 1910s.

York Litho. Miami, FL. Published postcards in the late twentieth century.

York News Agency. York, PA. Issued postcards in the mid-twentieth century, including from the Curt Teich Co.

Young & Carl. Cincinnati, OH. Publisher of postcards, including views of regional interest, many of which were imported from France. Active in the first two decades of the twentieth century.

Young, Leonard & Harrall Co. Providence, RI. Published postcards in the early twentieth century.

Young, Ralph. Canton, OH. Published postcards in the 1920s and 1930s, including from the Curt Teich Co.

Yukon Postcard Co. Seattle, WA. Published postcards in the early twentieth century.

Z

Zan of Tamalpais. Mill Valley, CA. Publisher of RPPCs with California and other Western views from the 1920s into the early 1950s. Most were photographed by Alexander ("Zan") J. Stark.

Zaytoun News Agency. New Bern, NC. Distributed view cards in the mid-twentieth century, including from the Curt Teich Co.

Zeese, A., Engraving Co. Dallas, TX. Published postcards in the early twentieth century.

Zeese, I., and Co. Chicago, IL. Published postcards in the early twentieth century.

Zerbe, Farran. Tyrone, PA. Numismatist who published postcards in connection with expositions in the early twentieth century.

Zercher, M.L., Book and Stationery Co. Topeka, KS. Manufactured (per their imprint) regular cards and RPPCs during the early twentieth century.

Zibart Brothers. Nashville, TN. Published postcards in the early twentieth century, including cards from the Curt Teich Co.

Ziff, S.N., Paper Co. Worcester, MA. Published color view cards in the late twentieth century, including some of those made by Dexter Press.

Zimmerman, H.G., & Co. Chicago, IL. Under the ZIM trademark this firm published view cards of national interest in the first two decades of the twentieth century.

APPENDIX B
U.S. POSTCARD CLUBS

Club contact details can change regularly; please check online for the latest information. If your postcard club isn't listed, send us the club's details and contact information and we will update in the next edition.

California

San Francisco Bay Area Post Card Club
320 B Monterey Blvd.
San Francisco, CA 94131
www.postcard.org

San Jose Postcard Club
P.O. Box 23115
San Jose, CA 95153
Contact: shavlavigne@yahoo.com

Colorado

Denver Postcard Club
2038 S Pontiac Way
Denver, CO 80224
www.denverpostcardclub.org

Florida

Sunshine Post Card Club
www.facebook.com/Sunshine-Post-Card-Club-Tampa-Florida-240273249329625
Contact: LeahCard@aol.com

Tropical Postcard Club
tropicalpostcardclub.com

Georgia

Georgia Postcard Club
c/o Kenneth H. Thomas Jr.
P.O. Box 901
Decatur, GA 30031
www.facebook.com/groups/458667644214264
Contact: Ken Thomas, ktomjr@aol.com

Idaho

Eagle Stamp and Postcard Club
P.O. Box 731
Meridian, ID 83680
eaglestampandpostcardclub.com

Maryland

Capitol-Beltway Postcard Club
Includes Maryland, Virginia, and Washington, D.C. areas.
www.facebook.com/groups/CBPCclub
Contact: silverh01@comcast.net

Massachusetts

Bay State Postcard Collectors Club
www.ludix.com/bspcc/index.html
Contact: Arthur Bennett, arthurbennett@comcast.net

Michigan

Southwest Michigan Post Card Club
7265 West Main Street
Kalamazoo, MI 49009
www.facebook.com/swmpcc

Minnesota

Twin City Postcard Club
twincitypostcardclub.com
Contact: Dianne Lamb, dvlamb@hotmail.com

New Jersey

Garden State Postcard Club
686 River Road
Fair Haven, NJ 07704
www.seocom.com/gspcc/index.html

New York

Buffalo Postcard Club
4774 Union Road
Cheektowaga, NY 14225
www.facebook.com/thebuffalopostcardclub

Metropolitan Postcard Club of New York City
219 West 16 Street #2B
New York, NY 10011
metropolitanpostcardclub.com/
Contact: stadiatins@earthlink.net

Upstate New York Post Card Club (Gansevoort)
www.facebook.com/Upstate-New-York-Post-Card-Club-108660657178665/

Western New York Postcard Club
WNY Postcard Club
c/o Michael Bloch
P.O. Box 555
Penfield, NY 14526
wnypostcardclub.com

Ohio

Firelands Postcard Club
Sandusky, OH
Contact: firelandspostcards@yahoo.com

Heart of Ohio Postcard Club
www.judnick.com/Judnick/HeartOfOhioPostcardClub.htm
postcard@judnick.com

Oregon

Webfooters Post Card Club
P.O. Box 17240
Portland, OR 97217
www.thewebfooters.com

Pennsylvania

Institute of American Deltiology
300 West Main Avenue
Myerstown, PA 17067
Contact: broiad@comcast.net

Lancaster County Postcard Club
www.facebook.com/LCPClub
sfg47@comcast.net

Susquehanna Valley Stamp and Postcard Club
classic.stamps.org/SVSPC
Contact: Michael Hengst, susquehanna.valley@yahoo.com

Washington Crossing Card Collectors Club
P.O. Box 39
Washington Crossing, PA 18977
wc4postcards.org

Rhode Island

Rhode Island Post Card Club
P.O. Box 2032
Woonsocket, RI 02895
ripcc.org
Contact: ripostcardclub@yahoo.com

Texas

Capital of Texas Postcard Club
ctxpc.org
Contact: ctxpc@ctxpc.org

Dallas Metroplex Postcard Club
801 W. Ave. B
Garland, TX 75040
dallaspostcardclub.com/welcome.html
Contact: htick3@verizon.net

Houston Area Postcard Club
sites.google.com/view/hapc/home
Contact: houstonpostcard@gmail.com

Tomball Postcard Club
17415 Walnut Lane
Magnolia, TX 77355
www.facebook.com/TomballPostcardClub
Contact: humrbird@juno.com

Virginia

Old Dominion Postcard Club
Richmond, VA
www.facebook.com/pg/odpcc

Washington

Pacific Northwest Postcard Club (Seattle)
www.pnwpostcard.org
Contact: pnpcc.board@gmail.com

Wisconsin

Monroe Stamp and Postcard Club
Contact: rdriese@tds.net

Four Lakes Postcard Club
P.O. Box 259085
Madison, WI 53725
www.facebook.com/Four-Lakes-Postcard-
Club-1622988998018286

There are many postcard collecting groups and communities on social media sites like Instagram and Facebook. Search for "postcard club" and similar terms to find a group. Here are a few of the groups that were active at the time of publication:

50 States Postcard Club
www.facebook.com/
groups/50StatesPostcardClub

DelMarVa Postcard Club
www.facebook.com/
groups/1475466289438757

Gateway Postcard Club St. Louis
www.facebook.com/
groups/701173233664295

Indianapolis Postcard Club
www.facebook.com/Indianapolis-Postcard-
Club-1122130561254206

Lehigh Valley Postcard Club
www.facebook.com/
LehighValleyPostcardClub

Postcard collectors
www.facebook.com/groups/
Keeperofpostcards1971

Space Coast Postcard Club
www.facebook.com/
Postcardspacecoastclub

Twin City Postcard Club
www.facebook.com/
groups/239283426226028

West Michigan Post Card Club
www.facebook.com/
westmichiganpostcardclub

Wichita Postcard Club
www.facebook.com/WichitaPostcardClub

NOTES

Chapter 1

1. These are smaller and are called trade cards, not mailable. The typical card had a color subject on the face, made by a drawing or painting (not by colorizing a photograph), and on the back an advertisement for a product or service.

Chapter 11

2. Her sister Alice Fidler Person also contributed as an artist to the American Girl series by Edward Gross.

3. Robert Grau. *The Theatre of Science*, 1914, pp. 154–155.

4. A sister, Jessie, married John C. Fremont, "the American Pathfinder," who was the Republican presidential candidate in 1856. Senator Benton, nicknamed "Old Bullion," was one of the most powerful politicians of his era.

5. High quality lithograph prints of Peggy were widely sold in 1904. These closely resemble original art, and today many offerings of such prints are thus described incorrectly.

6. In 1981 one of the authors (Bowers) visited the former Boileau home on Arleigh Road (less well known as 35th Avenue) in Douglaston. The house, owned by Brice Rae, was for sale. His granddaughter gave a nice tour of the premises. Interestingly, postcard artist Robert Robinson's former home was but a short distance away in the same town.

7. Her birth year is given erroneously as 1865 in some texts.

8. *Philadelphia Inquirer*, December 15, 1901.

9. Research by Julia Casey.

10. The cards were not numbered. The numbers here originated in L'Officiel International des Cartes Postales by Jöelle and Gérard Neudin, modified and updated in the June 1910 issue of Mannekin Pis Club Edition Speciale, Associan Cartophile de Bruxelles.

11. *Ibid.*

Chapter 16

12. Several decades ago a Connecticut postcard dealer specialized in trolley car cards. With a manual typewriter she added the name and location to the top part of the view, a practice which, she said, libraries appreciated. However, for collectors this was a negative. In some instances, especially for RPPCs, the typewriter ink could be removed by careful use of a gum eraser.

Chapter 18

13. Marian Blackton Trimble, *J. Stuart Blackton: A Personal Biography by His Daughter*, p. 54.

Chapter 19

14. In the late twentieth century roller coasters became a nationwide passion, and much publicity was given to them in new theme parks. A large hobbyist and historical interest developed as well. Due to the cost of construction, carousels became less ornate as time went on, and those built after the 1920s tended to be simple in their construction. A wide circle of friends of carousels developed and today many hobbyists and historical groups preserve certain of these, and their history has been the subject of much excellent research. Ferris Wheels have garnered less specific interest other than in connection with amusement parks in general.

15. Japanese themes were very popular, but, for some reason, Chinese-based attractions were few.

Chapter 24

16. See postcard.com for more information.

Appendix

17. Certain information was provided by Christine A. Pyle, curator of the Curt Teich Archives.

GLOSSARY

GLOSSARY OF POSTCARD TERMS

chrome postcard • Modern glossy postcard usually made from a color photograph. The most popular modern format.

deltiology • The hobby, art, and science of collecting and studying postcards.

divided back • American postcard after the mid–1910s with the back divided with a vertical line, with a space for the message to the left and for the address to the right.

hold-to-light postcard • Early twentieth-century postcard made in Germany, with three layers: front and back with tiny circular holes punched on parts of the illustrated subject, such as windows in a building; with a red (usually) thin, transparent inner layer. When the postcard is viewed from the front in a bright room, the windows or other areas are illuminated in color.

linen postcard • Matte-surface card with artist-added color, popularized from the 1930s onward by Curt Teich.

pioneer postcard • A postcard from the nineteenth century.

postal • Another term for postcard.

real photo postcard • Postcard hand-printed on photographic stock from a negative. Especially popular for limited-runs of cards by local or regional photograph parlors and related shops.

RPPC • Abbreviation for real photo postcard.

signed artist postcard • Printed postcard bearing on the face the printed signature of the artist.

undivided back • American postcard issued in the early twentieth century with the back entirely devoted to the address. Any personal messages were placed on a white space at the bottom of the front of the card.

white border postcard • Postcard from the 1910s onward with the image framed with a white border. Especially popular in the 1920s and 1930s.

BIBLIOGRAPHY

Baeder, John. *Diners. New York, NY: Henry N. Abrams, 1981.*

Baeder, John. *Gas, Food, and Lodging.* New York, NY: Abbeville Press, Inc., 1982.

Bogdan, Robert, and Todd Weseloh. *Real Photo Postcard Guide: The People's Photography.* Syracuse, NY: Syracuse University Press, 2006.

Bowers, Q. David, and Ellen H. Budd. *Harrison Fisher.* Cincinnati, OH: Ellen H. Budd, 1984

Bowers, Q. David, and Mary L. Martin. *The Postcards of Alphonse Mucha.* Perryville, MD: Mary L. Martin, 1980 and 2015.

Budd, Ellen H. *Ellen H. Clapsaddle Signed Post Cards.* Cincinnati, OH: Ellen H. Budd, 1989.

Goldsack, Robert. *A Century of Fun: A Pictorial History of New England Amusement Parks.* Nashua, NH; Midway Museum Publications, 1993.

Kyriazi, Gary. *The Great American Amusement Parks.* Secaucus, NJ: Citadel Press, 1976.

Metropolitan Postcard Club of New York City website. metropolitanpostcardclub.com.

Miller, Dorothy. *Philip Boileau: Painter of Fair Women.* New York, NY: Gotham Book Mart, 1981.

Miller, George and Dorothy. *Picture Postcards of the United States 1893–1918.* New York, NY: Clarkson N. Potter, Inc., 1982.

Miller, George, and Dorothy. *Picture Postcards of the United States 1893–1918.* New York, NY: Clarkson N. Potter, Inc., 1976. Succeeded by revised edition by Dorothy Ryan (see listing).

New York State Library: "Lyall D. Sqair Theodore Roosevelt Postcard Collection." 742 items. Listing on the Internet at NYSED.gov.

Nicholson, Susan Brown. The Encyclopedia of Antique Postcards. Radnor, PA: The Wallace-Homestead Book Company, 1994.

Stanton, Jeffrey. "Coney Island—Independent Rides." Internet listing, copyright 1997.

Stechshutte, Nancy Stickels. *The Detroit Publishing Company Postcards.* Big Rapids, MI: Published by the author, 1994.

ABOUT THE AUTHORS

Q. David Bowers: Dave has collected, studied, and written about postcards for many years. He is a numismatist, writer, and historian by profession and is the author of more than 60 books on various subjects.

Mary L. Martin: Mary, with the same name as her late mother, grew up in the postcard business when her parents were among the nation's leading dealers. She conducts Mary L. Martin Ltd. with her son Joe Russell, buying and selling postcards and also holding postcard shows. Find her on Facebook at facebook.com/marymartinpostcards and on Instagram @marymartinpostcards.

CREDITS AND ACKNOWLEDGEMENTS

The authors express appreciation to the following for information, images, answers to queries, and other help from the late twentieth century to date:

Black's Paper Store, Christine Bowers, Andreas Brown, Ellen Budd, Julia Casey, eBay, Leonard Lauder, Bob Leonard, Metropolitan Postcard Club of New York City, Joseph Russell, Dorothy Ryan.

The postcards of Phoenix, New York, pictured in the publisher's preface are courtesy of Gail Gleason and Pamela Ruetsch English. All other postcard images in this book are from the collections and archives of the authors. The publisher would like to thank Leonard A. Lauder for writing the foreword.

INDEX

INDEX OF AMERICAN POSTCARD PRINTERS AND DISTRIBUTORS BY LOCATION

Refer to the appendix (page 361) for historical information on each printer and distributor.

Alabama

Bessemer: Alabama Post Card Co.

Birmingham: Post Card Exchange Publishers

Alaska

Anchorage: Indian Arts and Crafts (also see Seattle)

Juneau: J.D. Caro; Oscar Hold; Lloyd Valentine Winter and Edwin Percy Pond

Ketchikan: John E. Thwaites

Seward: Otto Schallerer; Seward News Co.

Sitka: Edward DeGroff; C.M. McGrath; Elbridge Warren Merrill

Valdez: P.S. Hunt

Arizona

Flagstaff: Babbitt Brothers Trading Co.

Grand Canyon: Kolb Brothers Studio

Nogales: International Drug Co.; Sonora News Co.

Phoenix: R.L. Balke Indian Trading Company; Berryhill Co.; A. O. Boeres Co.; Central News & Novelty Co.; Central News Co (also see Akron, Ohio; Philadelphia; Tacoma, Washington; and Wheeling, West Virginia); F.J. Festner; Harry Herz; Indian Trading Co.; Petley Studios

Tucson: Lollesgard Specialty Co.

Yuma: J. Homer Smith

Arkansas

Hot Springs: Hot Springs Novelty Co.

Rogers: Tom P. Morgan

California

Berkeley: Mike Roberts Color Productions (also see Oakland)

Chicago: Poole Brothers

Colton: Royal Pictures

Fresno: C.H. Riege

Glendale: Kug-Art Photo Service

Hanford: W.M. Hefton

Hollywood: Columbia Publishing Co.; Mitock & Sons; Vancard

Long Beach: Golden West; Brewster C. Kenyon

Los Angeles: Benham Co.; Benham Indian Trading Company; California Postcard Co.; Cardinell-Vincent Co. (also see Los Angeles, Oakland, and Seattle); E.P. Charlton & Co. (also see San Francisco); W.H. Clune; Edward Elkus; Gardner-Thompson Co.; Globe Novelty Co.; Julius J. Hecht; M. Kashower Co.; Longshaw Card Co. (also see Pasadena); Los Angeles Lithographic Co.; Los Angeles News Co.; Neuner Co.; Newman Post Card Co. (also see San Francisco); News Stand Distributor; Novelty Printing Co.; Jack Parsons; George Rice & Sons, Printers; M. Rieder; Rieder-Cardinell Co. (also see Oakland); Sanborn Vail & Co. (also see San Francisco and Portland, Oregon); Elmo M. Sellers; Theo. Sohmer; Souvenir Publishing Co. (also see San Francisco); Tichnor Art Co.; Tichnor Brothers (also see Boston and Cambridge, Massachusetts); Van Ornum Colorprint Co.; Western Lithographing Co.; Western Publishing & Novelty Co.; Wood's, Inc.

Marysville: Smith's Photo Studio

Mill Valley: Zan of Tamalpais

Monterey: California Art Co. (also see Santa Rosa)

Morrow Bay: S.S. Rodionoff

Oakland: Cardinell-Vincent Co. (also see Los Angeles, San Francisco, and Seattle); A. Kayser; Kelley-Davis Co.; Pillsbury Picture Co. (also see San Francisco); Rieder-Cardinell Co. (also see Los Angeles); Mike Roberts Color Productions (also see Berkeley); Scenic View Card Co. (also see San Francisco)

Ocean Park: Bay News Co.

Palm Springs: Stephen H. Willard

Pasadena: Longshaw Card Co. (also see Los Angeles); Harold A. Parker

Pomona: Douglas Caulkins; Frasher's, Inc.; J.H. Hillen

Red Bluff: C.H. Darrough

Reedley: Besaw Post Card Co. / Western Post Card Co.

Richmond: Scenic Art

San Anselmo: David B. MacAusland

San Bernardino: Renfro-Haven Co.

San Diego: George Adler; H.L. Christiance; Eno & Matteson; Frye & Smith; Herz Post Cards; Hopkins News Agency

San Francisco: Aerial Photo Co.; Art Lithography Co.; Bardell & O'Neill; Bardell Art Co.; J.C. Bardell; Bear Photo Co.; Richard Behrendt; Britton & Rey Lithographers; California Art Card Co.; California Sales Co.; John D. Cardinell; Cardinell-Vincent Co. (also see Los Angeles, Oakland, and Seattle); Cartagno, Bright & Gold, Printers; E.P. Charlton & Co. (also see Los Angeles); E.F. Clemants; Cosby-Winter Co.; H.S. Crocker Co., Inc.; Exposition Publishing Co.; Fine Arts Press; Gabriel-Mayerfeld Co.; J.D. Givens; Goeggel & Weidner; International Novelty Co.; Ted Lewy-Arts; Marsh & Co.; George A. Miner Co.; Edward H. Mitchell Co.; Mohr & Packer; Gabriel Moulin; Newman Post Card Co. (also see Los Angeles); Ricardo J. Oroszco Press; Pacific Novelty Co.; Pacific Stationery & Specialty Co.; Panama-Pacific International Exposition Novelty Co.; Panama-Pacific International Exposition, Department of Fine Arts; Pelicano, Rossie & Co.; Pillsbury Picture Co. (also see Oakland); Stanley A. Plitz Co.; Pitts (That Man Pitts); Polychrome Co.; T.E. Powers Novelty Co.; Paul Rieger; Louis Roesch Co.; San Francisco Litho.; Sanborn Vail & Co. (also see Los Angeles and Portland, Oregon); Scenic View Card Co. (also see Oakland); J. Schaff and Bros.; I. Scheff & Brothers; L. & L. Schmidt; Security Lithograph Co.; Smith Novelty Co.; Souvenir Publishing Co. (also see Los Angeles); Union Lithograph Co.; Union Photo Engraving Co.; Charles Weidner

San Jose: J.C. Gordon

San Mateo: A.E. Carter

Santa Ana: Ferris H. Scott; Western Resort Publications

Santa Barbara: W.W. Osborne

Santa Rosa: California Art Co. (also see Monterey)

Susanville: Eastman's Studio

Ukiah: R. Shattuck

Venice: H.T. Smith

Ventura: J.R. Brakey

Colorado

Brush: H.C. McConnell

Colorado Springs: Burcham Paper Co.; Gilpin Publishing Co.; Hyde Paper Co. (also see Pueblo)

Denver: Bekudlingen Art Publishing Co.; Carson-Harper Co.; Vincent V. Colby; Colorado News Co.; Colorado Selling Co.; Cowens & Co.; Great Western Post Card & Novelty Co.; F.H. Langdon & Co.; Midwest Novelty Co.; F.A. Moss; Out West Photo; I. Phillips; Rocky Mountain News (Denver Times); Rocky Mountain Publishing Co.; Sanborn Souvenir Co.; H.R. Schmidt & Co. (also see Wichita, Kansas); Smith-Brooks Printing Co.; Souvenir Publishing & Mercantile Co.; H.H. Tammen Curio Co.; Frank S. Thayer Publishing Co.; Williamson-Haffner Co.

Durango: T.E. Rowman

Estes Park: W.T. Parke

Fort Collins: Carl Anderson

Glenwood Springs: M.J. Mayes; W.S. Parkison

Greeley: D.E. Gray

Lamar: Commercial Studio

Longmont: Frank and Carl Hildreth

Manitou: R.S. Davis; Saidy

Palmer Lake: Wilson and Judd

Paonia: Dunbar & Williams

Pueblo: Hyde Paper Co. (also see Colorado Springs); Paper Products Co.; Pueblo Wholesale News Co.; Weaver-Fagerstrom, Inc.; Weaver-Gibbs Co.

Rocky Ford: Dorman Brothers

Victor: H.H. Rosser

Wray: J.L. Shumaker

Connecticut

Bridgeport: W.I. Allen; H.H. Jackson

Bristol: W.A. Gibb

Canaan: C.H. Pease

Canton Center: H.P. Foote

Danielson: C.S. Dayton

Deep River: Ernest L. Prann

Hamburg: M.E. Huntley

Hartford: Chapin News Co.; Dexter Photo Co.; Hartford News Co.; C.P.L. Herrman

Litchfield: Karl Brothers

Madison: Hunter Photo Co.

Meriden: E.A. Bliss Co.; Meriden Gravure Co.

Middletown: J.A. Broatch

New Britain: E.C. Charlton & Co.

New Haven: Morris Berman; Danziger & Berman, Elm City Post Card Co.; Harold Hahn Co., Inc.; Edward P. Judd Co.; W. & L. Midas; Stoddard Engraving Co.; Well Novelty Co.

New London: J. Solomon, Inc.; H.D. Utley

Norwich: Loyd M. Cobb

Putnam: Jeweler Shaw; Jeweler Shaw

Savin Rock: Samuel Strongin

Stamford: Globe Stamp Co.

Torrington: W. Flieg

Westbrook: W. J. Neidlinger

Winsted: Art Store

Watertown: D.G. Sullivan

Delaware

Newark: United View Co.

Wilmington: Eureka Postcard Manufacturing Co.; Greenwood Bookshop; Maston & Hall; United States Postcard Co.

Georgia

Atlanta: Otto M. Baum; Cole Book Co.; Georgia News Co.; Witt Brothers

Savannah: Foltz Photographic Postals

Florida

Clearwater: Beckett, Ward & Co.

Daytona: R.H. Lesesne

Fort Myers: Fort Myers Studio Supply

Holly Hills: Southern Card & Novelty Co.

Homestead: Flagler Fotoshop

Inverness: Inverness Drug Co.

Jacksonville: H. & W.B. Drew Company; Duval & Co.; Jax News Co.; M. Mark; J.S. Pinkussohn Cigar Co.; Setzer's Warehouse; C.A. Stead

Key West: Frank Johnson

Lake Wales: Morse's Photo Service

Largo: Hartman Litho Sales, Inc.

Miami: J.N. Chamberlain (also see Oak Bluffs, Massachusetts); Dade County Newsdealers' Supply Company; Gulf Stream Card & Distributing Co.; Novelti-Craft Co.; Pan-American Publishing Corp.; Pictorial Center; G.W. Romer; J.B. Sommers; Valence Color Studios; Thomas H. West; Eli Witt Cigar & Tobacco Co.; York Litho

Orlando: McPhail's Colonial Shop

Palatka: Cochrane Co.

Sarasota: M.E. Russell

Silver Springs: The Mozert Studio and Camera Shop

South Palm Beach: F.C. Belden

St. Augustine: Florida Souvenir Co.; William James Harris (also see Lake Hopatcong, New Jersey, and Pittston, Pennsylvania); Rogero & Pomar

St. Petersburg: Atlantic Post Card Co. (also see Portland, Maine); Esmond Barnhill; Oz Denney Advertising; Florida Speaks Corp.; Gulf Coast Card Co., Inc.; J. Heath & Son Co.; E.C. Robison; Saint Petersburg News Co.; Sun News Co.; Jack Swenningsen; Webb Cut Rate Drug Co.

West Palm Beach: F.E.C. News Co.

Winter Park: Sunny Scenes, Inc.

Hawaii

Honolulu: R.J. Baker; Honolulu Paper Co.; Island Curio Co.; Island Heritage; Wall, Nichols & Co.

Idaho

Nampa: H.L. Nickels & Co.

Sandpoint: Ross Hall

Wallace: Bernard's Studio

Illinois

Aurora: Es-N-Len Photos; F. P. Schickler

Bloomington: Read & White; W.B. Read & Co.; C.U. Williams / Photoette

Cairo: John A. Miller

Centralia: Ritchie Brothers.

Chicago: Acmegraph Co.; Aero Distributing Co.; American Colortype Co. (also see New York City); J.I. Austen Co.; E.B. Beekwith; Fred W. Black Co.; Cameo Greeting Cards, Inc.; Carqueville Lithographing Co.; Chicago Colortype Co.; Chicago Daily News; Chicago Engraving Co.; Charles R. Childs; Gamble Coker, Inc.; Commercial Colortype Co.; Continental Art Co.; David Lionel Press; R.R. Donnelley & Sons; Reuben H. Donnelly Corp.; Doubleday-Foster Photo Co., Inc.; Drysdale Co.; Edwards & Deutsch Litho. Co.; Empire Art Co.; Exhibit Supply Co.; Henry J. Fish Advertising; Franklin Post Card Co.; W.J. Freede; Gartner & Bender; German-American Post Card Co. (also see Cleveland, Ohio, and New York City); Gerson Brothers; Charles W. Goldsmith; V.O. Hammon Publishing Co. (also see Minneapolis); Hermitage Art Co.; William G. Hoffman; Alfred Holzman Co.; Raymond Howe; P.L. Huckins; International Postal Card Co.; Jackson Photo Advertising Co.; Johns-Byrne Co.; L.M. Johnson; Kawin & Co.; Koelling & Klappenbach; David Lionel Press; Manz Engraving Co.; A.C. McClure & Co.; E.W. McConnell; C.D. Montgomery; Muir & Co.; National Photograph Co.; New York Postal Card Co.; Paget Co.; Prescott Studio; Process Photo Studios; Regensteiner Colortype; Max Rigot Selling Co.; Arthur P. Schmidt & Co. (also see Boston); A.J. Schuman; Schwarz & Co. "Alsa-Novitas"; Scott Studio; B. Sebastian; Simplicity Co. (also see Grand Rapids, Michigan); Stadler Photographing Co. (also see New York City); Mollie Storseth; Suhling & Koehn Co.; Ted Postcard & Novelty Co.; Curt Teich Co.; United Post Card & Novelty Co.; Paul R. Vogel Co.; P.F. Volland & Co. (also see Joliet); Wesley Advertising Co.; Western News Co.; White City Art Co.; Winter Art Litho.; I. Zeese and Co.; H.G Zimmerman & Co.

Decatur: Cawood Comic Card Co.; International Stereograph Co.

Galena: E.W. Kempter

Galesburg: Peks China Store; Stromberg & Penny

Kewanee: L.A. Foster Photo Co. (also see Glendive, Montana)

Jacksonville: W.L. Armstrong; A.H. Atherton

Joliet: C-B Co.; Gerlach, Barklow Co.; P.F. Volland & Co. (also see Chicago)

Monmouth: J.M. Hamilton

Peoria: Green's News Bazar; Miller Studio; C.E. Wheelock Co.

Princeton: Case & Vaughan Art Co.

Rock Island: Myers Card Shop; Rock Island Post Card Co.

Springfield: George Coldeway; Charles R. Graham Co.; H.N. Shonkwiler; Springfield Paper Co.

Indiana

Auburn: Witten-Dennison Post Card Co.

Elkhart: L.H. Burrell; J. Inbody; H. Whitneck

Fort Wayne: Fort Wayne Printing Co.; Standish Photo Studio; Wayne Paper Box & Printing Co.

Indianapolis: Hoover-Watson Printing; Import Postcard Co.; Indiana News Co.; Majestic Publishing Co.

Iowa

Algona: Martin Peterson

Atlantic: Egbert Photo Post Card Co.; F. Parsons & Co.

Burlington: Ingersoll News Co.

Carroll: Carroll Post Card Co.

Cedar Falls: Pfeiffer Co.

Cedar Rapids: Acme Greeting Card Co.; Baylis Post Card Co.; Cedar Rapids News Co.

Chariton: C.E. Fluke

Charles City: Hart-Park Co.; May Drug Co.

Clinton: Bawden Brothers (also see Davenport); Clinton News Agency; James T. Huston

Davenport: Bawden Brothers (also see Clinton); Davenport Post Card & Novelty Co.; Hickey Brothers

Des Moines: Beals; Des Moines Postal Card Co.; Frank V. Draper Co.; Enos B. Hunt Jr.; Hyman's News & Book Store; Iowa Post Card Co.

Dubuque: Acme Art Store; Buettell Brothers Co.; Norton News Agency

Eldora: F.A. Norris

Fort Dodge: Stevens & Hogan

Fort Madison: Fort Madison News Agency

Iowa City: Wallick & Flater; H.C. Wienecke

Keokuk: H.M. Anschutz; R.F. Rollins

Lamoni: The Leader

Madrid: F.A. Danborn

Mason City: American Post Card Co. (also see Sioux City); Mason City News Agency

McGregor: A.A. Horning & Co.; Pocket City Post Card Co.

Milton: M.E. Dye

Monticello: B. Devlin & Co.

Moulton: C.A. Powers; Elmer Wood Co.

Mount Pleasant: Central Post Card Agency; Mount Pleasant Mercantile & Supply Co.; Roberts Variety Store

Mount Vernon: J.W. Bloom; Power & Bloom

Muscatine: Herman Cohn News Agency

Okoboji: J.T. Saidy

Osage: Woolverton Press

Ottumwa: Ottumwa News Agency

Primghar: Emil Olander & Co.

Red Oak: Thomas D. Murphy Co.

Shenandoah: Beckwith & Beanchamp

Sioux City: American Post Card Co. (also see Mason City); Hornick, Hess & More; Hornick, More & Porterfield; Morningside Printing Co.; Olson News Co.; Pospeshil Card Service

Toledo: E.A. Benson

Washington: Nicola & Harmon

Waterloo: Fergason Post Card Co.; George Kraft Co.; Lincoln Supply Co.; Voris Printing Co.; Waterloo News Agency

Kansas

Atchison: J.H. Brown & Co.

Fort Scott: CCCP; Central Post Card Co.; Standard Advertising and Printing Co.

Garden City: W. Harvey

Ottawa: Martin Post Card Co., William H. Martin

Salina: Kansas Post Card Co.

Topeka: Arthur Capper; M.L. Zercher Book and Stationery Co.

Wichita: McCormick-Armstrong Co.; H.R. Schmidt & Co. (also see Denver)

Winfield: Garver Brothers

Kentucky

Bellevue: National Colortype Co.

Lexington: L.F. Mattingly

Louisville: T.N. Lindsey

Maysville: J.T. Kackley & Co.

Louisiana

Metairie: Grant L. Robertson

New Orleans: Grombach-Faisans Co., Ltd.; Harmonson; Lipscher Specialty Co.; Louisiana News Co.; C.B. Mason; New Orleans News Co.

Maine

Augusta: Maine Farmer Publishing Co.; Vickery & Hill Publishing Co.

Bangor: O. Crosby Bean; Luther S. Phillips; F.W.K. Reed

Bar Harbor: W.H. Sherman

Belfast: Eastern Illustrating Co. (also see Orange, Massachusetts and New London, New Hampshire); Charles A. Townsend

Bingham: Milford Baker

Boothbay Harbor: J.A. Labbie; McDougall & Keefe; H.R. McGregor; Smiling Cow (also see Camden)

Brunswick: W.F. Cobb; James F. Snow

Calais: E.W. Milliken

Camden: Smiling Cow (also see Boothbay Harbor)

Caribou: Scates & Co.

Castine: W.A. Ricker

Columbia Falls: B.E. Allen

Damariscotta: A.E. Merrill; E.W. Nash; J.F. Perkins

Freeport: F.E. Merrill; F.E. Merrill

Harpswell: George S. Graves (also see Springfield, Massachusetts)

Houlton: H.J. Hathaway & Co.

Lewiston: Berry Paper Co.; L.B. Morrell

Liberty: F.W. Cunningham

Monhegan Island: Lorimer E. Brackett

Monmouth: C.L. Thompson

Newcastle: Owen Art-Color

Newport: Harry Merril; J.R. Spencer

North Anson: George S. Longley; G.W. Savage

North Berwick: C.W. Goodwin

Northeast Harbor: Augustus D. Phillips & Son

Ocean Park: Albert Armstrong

Old Orchard Beach: Ocean News Co.; Jack Sudenfield

Orono: Charles F. Nichols

Peaks Island: M.E. Brackett

Phillips: Edgar R. Tothaker

Pittsfield: H.H. Nutter; W.M. Prilay

Poland: E.C. Jordan; Hiram Ricker & Sons

Portland: Atlantic Post Card Co. (also see St. Petersburg, Florida); Chisholm Brothers; Eastern News Co.; Theara Hilton & Co.; J.B. Kahill; Lakeside Printing Co.; Lamson Studio; Hugh C. Leighton Co.; Leighton & Valentine (also see New York City); Loring, Short & Harmon; Morgan Brothers; G.W. Morris; Porteous, Mitchell and Braun Co.; Portland Candy Co.; C.S. Woolworth & Co.

Presque Isle: Kerr & Larrabee; Oak Studio

Sabbathday Lake: D.C. Wilson

Sangerville: A.F. Marsh

Searsport: M.A. Cook

South Orrington: L.E. Hinds

South Portland: Cape Shore Paper Co.

Stonington: Penobscot Studios

Wells: A.L. Rankin

Welton: W.S. Pierce Illustrating Co.

West Bethel: Whitten & Dennison

Maryland

Annapolis: George W. Jones

Baltimore: Baltimore Badge & Novelty Co.; Baltimore Lithograph Co.; Baltimore Stationery Co.; Barton-Cotton, Inc.; Binn Publishing Co.; A. Hoehn & Co. (also see Richmond, Virginia); David Kauffman; Kauffman, Louis & Sons; Maryland Litho. Co.; I. & M. Ottenheimer Co.; Thomsen-Ellis Co.; D.E. Traub

Chevy Chase: Mrs. Minnie E. Brooke

Cumberland: Neff Novelty Co.

Frederick: Marken & Bielfield, Inc.

Oxford: J.B. Moll Jr.

Pittsville: Tingle Printing Co.

Massachusetts

Andover: Andover Bookstore

Athol: G.C. Longley & Co.

Ayer: New England Paper & Stationery Co.

Belchertown: F.B. Purdy

Belmont: A.W. Elson & Co.

Beverly: Nathan H. Foster

Boston: American Souvenir Co.; Boston Post Card Co.; Bromley and Co.; David Bugbee Coburn; Colesworthy Book Store; Colourpicture Publishing, Inc. (also see Cambridge); A.M. Davis &Co.; Federal Engraving & Publishing Co.; William J. Finn; German Novelty Co.; Herbert E. Glasier & Co.; Goodridge Galleries; Hale, Cushman & Flint; J.V. Hartman &

Co.; Heliotype Co.; Lewis Hooper & Co.; Hy-Sil Manufacturing Co.; A. Kagan; Kosmos Art Co.; Robert H. Lord; Mason Brothers & Co.; Metropolitan News Co.; Mutual Book Co.; C.M. Nelson; New England News Co.; Owens Brothers-Hillson Co.; Harry Paul & Associates; Louis Prang & Co.; Putnam Art Co.; Reichner Brothers; Rice & Hutchins; Robbins Brothers Co.; Fred Winslow Rust; Arthur P. Schmidt & Co. (also see Chicago); Lange B.L. Schwalbach; M.T. Sheahan; Southern-Mears Co.; Sparrell Print; Sparrow Press; Thompson & Thompson; Thomson & Thomson; Tichnor Brothers (also see Cambridge, Massachusetts, and Los Angeles); Nat. Titlebaum & Co.; C.O. Tucker; United Art Co.; Valentine & Sons Co. (also see New York City); Wyn-Kraft

Brockton: Holmes the Newsman

Brookline: Fairbanks Card Co. (also see Holliston)

Buzzard's Bay: F.C. Small

Cambridge: Colorcraft Art Co.; Colourpicture Publishing, Inc. (also see Boston); J.F. Olsson & Co.; E.B. Thomas; Tichnor Brothers (also see Boston and Los Angeles)

Chatham: Charles W. Cartwright; Richardson Studio; Harold T. Sawyer Photo and Art Shop; Stacy H. Wentworth

Concord: Edith A. Buck; Mrs. G.N. Tanner

Duxbury: Paul C. Peterson

East Bridgewater: C.R. Ransden

East Northfield: The Bookstore; C.P. Buffum; A.R. Levering

East Walpole: Mrs. John F. Freese

East Weymouth: George H. Hunt & Co.

Everett: Metrocraft

Fiskdale: Joseph A. Boudreau

Fitchburg: N.J. Allard (also see Leominster); W.W. Burnap

Framingham: Maconi Service

Gardner: McKeough's Pharmacy

Gloucester: Curhan Co.; William M. Francis; Edwin C. McIntire; Frank H. Shurtleff

Great Barrington: E.P. Hunt & Co.; M.G. Sturtevant

Green Harbor: C.W. McLauthlin

Greenfield: Bartlett and Baker; Forbes "The Kodak Man"; W.E. Wood

Haverhill: Merrimack Post Card Co.; W.H. Wood

Holliston: Fairbanks Card Co. (also see Brookline)

Holyoke: Dr. Neil Doherty

Hull: South Shore Novelty Co.

Huntington: C.W. Daugherty

Hyannis: J. Lazarus; C.W. Megathlin; Slate Co.

Hyde Park: Klein Postcard Service

Lake Pleasant: L.E. Henry

Lawrence: Bain Candy Company

Leominster: N.J. Allard (also see Fitchburg)

Lynn: Glenmere Co.; D.K. MacDonald Co.; Moehring & Groesbeck; North Shore Novelty Co.; Puritan Art Co.

Malden: Perry Pictures Co.

Marblehead: John T. Adams; Louis A. Radell; Franklin E.S. Thompson Studio; Leonard P. Thorner

Medford: E.H. & F.A. Rugg

Milford: Annie Lawless

Milton: Doucet Photo Co.

Nahant: Essinger & Cook; H.R. Milo & Co. (also see Norfolk, Virginia)

Nantucket: Marshall Gardner; Eda Schanzer; Henry S. Wyer

New Bedford: H.S. Hutchinson; Service News Co.

North Adams: C.R. Canedy; L.E. Higley; Hunt Brothers; New England Printing Co.; Tilton's; Whitcomb Summit Co.

North Hadley: E.H. Blodget

Oak Bluffs: J.N. Chamberlain (also see Miami)

Orange: Eastern Illustrating Co. (also see Belfast, Maine and New London, New Hampshire)

Orleans: Cape Cod Photos

Osterville: Louis Maynard Huntress

Peabody: Fred D. Hager

Plainville: Frank E. Whiting

Plymouth: A.S. Burbank; Smith News Store; Smith's Book Store; Standard Pictures Co.

Provincetown: Advocate Post Card Shop; LK Color Productions; Mayflower Sales Co.; Provincetown Advocate Postcard Shop

Richmond: Clem Moore

Rockport: Virginia Cleaves Little; Rockport Photo Bureau; Rockport Post Card Co.

Roxbury: M. Abrams

Roxbury Crossing: W.H. Parsons & Co.

Scituate: F.M. Damon Curio Co.

Somerset: C.L. Bowers

Somerville: G.O.W. Servis

South Framingham: J.F. Eber

South Sudbury: Wayside Industries

South Yarmouth: E.D. West Co.

Southboro: Yankee Colour Corp.

Southbridge: E.A. Benjamin; Johnson Colburn Co.

Springfield: George S. Graves (also see Harpswell, Maine); Springfield News Co.; Taber-Prang Art Co.

Taunton: H.A. Dickerman & Son

Uxbridge: F.W. Barnes

Vineyard Haven: L.E. Briggs; Howell's Photo Studio; Mosher Photo Service; D.C. Thompson

Wakefield: Wakefield Trading Co.

Waverly: Myron J. Cochran

Wellfleet: Everett I. Nye

West Brookfield: C.H. Clark

West Roxbury: Charles H. Smith

West Yarmouth: H.L. Moore Co.

Whately: Hows and Roote

Williamstown: John Navin

Williamsville: W.B. Hale

Winchester: A. William Rooney

Worcester: Arthur S. Adams; Economy Distributors Inc.; William A. Emerson; A.P. Lundborg; Perkins & Butler, Inc.; Charles K. Reed; Stobbs Press; Whitney Valentine Co.; J.I. Williams; S.N. Ziff Paper Co.

Yarmouthport: Holdsworth Distributing Co.

Michigan

Battle Creek: J.D. Smith; Toland & Little

Berrien Springs: Freeman Studios; Penrod Studio

Detroit: Chaffee & Co.; Detroit News Co.; Detroit Publishing Co.; A.C. Dietsche; Kresge & Wilson; Michigan Calendar Co.; Garnet O'Neil

Hastings: Charless Kenfield

Holland: P.R. Coster

Grand Rapids: Cargill Co.; Heyboer Stationery Co.; Simplicity Co. (also see Chicago)

Lake Odessa: G.A. Shampang

Manistique: Upper Michigan Card Co.

River Rouge: Theodore Belanger

St. John's: Saint John's Publishing Co.

St. Joseph: Bradford & Co.

Whitehall: C.G. Pitkin

Ypsilanti: Hiawatha Card of Detroit

Minnesota

Duluth: News Tribune

Minneapolis: American Import Co.; Bloom Brothers Co.; Comic Card Co.; Commercial Photo Co.; Co-Mo Co.; Crescent Photo Co.; V.O. Hammon Publishing Co. (also see Chicago); Kregel Photo Parlors (also see Minneapolis); Minnehaha Art and Publishing Co.; John H. Murphy System; Pearson-Ullberg Co.; H.H. Wilson Co.

Pequot Lakes: Capital Engraving

St. Paul: Brown & Bigelow, Inc.; J.F. Haynes Photo Co.; Kregel Photo Parlors (also see Minneapolis); Minnesota News Co.; Saint Paul Souvenir Co.; R. Steinman & Co.; Wright, Barrett & Stilwell Co.

Mississippi

Gulfport: Gulfport Printing Co.; Southern Film Co.

Jackson: Deep South Specialties, Inc.

Missouri

Aurora: Midwest Map Co.; MWM

Excelsior Springs: Smith Syndicate

Kansas City: Allis Press; Max Bernstein; Brown News Co.; Elite Post Card Co.; Paul Eskenasy; Hall Brothers; Fred Harvey Trading Co.; North American Post Card Co.; Novelty Post Card Co.; Quaddy Playthings Manufacturing Co.; Rust Craft Shop; Southwest News Co.; James Tetirick; Van Noy-Interstate Co.; Webb-Freyschlag Mercantile Co.

St. Louis: Arrow Post Card Co.; Burton & Skinner Printing and Stationery Co.; Buxton & Skinner; Compton & Sons; Samuel Cupples Envelope Co.; German-American Novelty Co.; Gibson Merchandise Co.; Fred Graf Engraving Co.; Greeley Printery of St. Louis; Hesse Envelope Co.; Mound City Post

Card Co.; National Novelty Co.; Park Manufacturing Co.; Saint Louis News Co.; Saint Louis Postcard Co.; Samuel Cupples Envelope Co.; Adolph Selige; Woodward & Tiernan Printing Co.

Montana

Billings: O.C. Ovren

Bozeman: Phillips & Willson

Butte: Cohn Brothers; Julius Fried; Keefe Brothers; Northwest Postcard & Souvenir Co.

Chinook: Charles E. Morris Co. (also see Great Falls)

Dayton: Riggins

Glendive: L.A. Foster Photo Co. (also see Kewanee, Illinois); J.H. Miskinen

Great Falls: Cooper's Photo; Great Falls Kwality Co.; Charles E. Morris Co. (also see Chinook); W.T. Ridgley Calendar Co.

Helena: Culbertson & Malcolm; S.J. Culbertson; A.P. Curtin; Montana Post Card Co.

Kalispell: Tomer Jacob Hileman; James R. White

Milestown: Huffman Pictures

Missoula: McKay Art Co.; Montana Souvenir Co.

Virginia City: C.W. Rank

West Yellowstone: S.P. Eagle

Nebraska

Arapaho: Charles E. Dean

Blair: A.E. Hanna

Ewing: W.S. Coyne

Falls City: Inter-State Postcard Co.

Fremont: Hammond Printing Co.

Hastings: Stin Brothers Co.; Williams Photo Co.

Kearney: S.D. Butcher & Son

Lincoln: F.M. Downs Co.; Merchants Publishing Co.; Nebraska Paper & Bag Co.; J.C. & G.E. Orcutt

McCook: F.M. Kimmell

Omaha: Baker Brothers Engraving Co.; Barkalow Brothers Co.; Clement Chase; Colortype Engraving and Publishing Co.; Eggers-O'Flyng Co.; A.B. Hubermann; J.H. Keck; McLaughlin & Barnhart; McLaughlin & Hotz; J.F. McLaughlin; Irvin A. Medlar Co.; Megeath Stationery Co.; Eric Nelson News Co.; Omaha News Co.; United States Postal Card Co.

Nevada

Reno: Sierra News Co.

Virginia City: Nevada Photo Co.

New Hampshire

Antrim: L.H. Carpenter; E.D. Putnam & Sons

Bristol: R.W. Musgrove

Concord: Rumford Press

East Derry: Frank A. Clark

East Jaffrey: C.T. Johnson

Exeter: D. Kelliher; Frank W. Swallow Postcard Co.

Gorham: Shorey Studio

Grantham: Howe Press

Lancaster: Bisbee Press

Manchester: Duclos Studio; Manchester New Hampshire Chamber of Commerce; John B. Varick Co.

Marlboro: Dr. E.G. Hildreth

Milford: W.F. French

New London: Eastern Illustrating Co. (also see Belfast, Maine and Orange, Massachusetts); Dan Sieburg

Newport: J.W. Johnson & Son

Peterboro: G.C. Blood

Pittsfield: H.W. Osgood

Tilton: Atkinson News Co.

Warren: Fred C. Gleason

Woodsville: M.W. Howland

New Jersey

Asbury Park: De Tartas Studios (also see Long Branch)

Atlantic City: L. Beard; W.C. Gee; George A. McKeague Co.; National Post Card Co. (also see Philadelphia); Post Card Distributing Co. (also see Philadelphia); Saltzburg Merchandise Co.; H.S. Sampliner; P. Sander (also see New York City and Philadelphia); W.C. Sithens (Virginia Postcard Co.); H.B. Smith;

Bound Brook: Fetterly & Loree

Camden: E. Moebius Phototyping

Cape May: Colonial Craftsmen

Dumont: Edward Wells

Elizabeth: Alf Campbell Art Co.; Collotype Co. (also see New York City); Line & Co.

Hackensack: Shelton Color Corporation

Hackettstown: Scheller Co.

Hawthorne: Koppel Color Cards

Hoboken: Art Postcard & Novelty Co.

Jersey City: John C. Voigt Post Card Co.

Lake Hopatcong: William James Harris (also see Pittston, Pennsylvania, and St. Augustine, Florida)

Lambertville: J.B. Kline & Son

Linden: Mayrose Co.

Long Branch: De Tartas Studios (also see Asbury Park)

Longport: Jack Freeman, Inc.

Medford: William B. Cooper

New Brunswick: Herman Kohle

Newark: New Jersey Post Card Co.; Osborne Calendar Co.; Star Stationery Co.

Orange: F.G. Temme Co.

Paterson: H.C. Deeks Co.

Pennsville: Alvis W. Wallace

Plainfield: Paul R. Collier; Crescent Embossing Co.; Star Post Card Co.

Red Bank: J. Dickolph

Ridgefield Park: National Color Cards Co.

Rutherford: Garraway Co.

Tilton: Tilton Postcard Co.

Westfield: Henry Fullerton

Wildwood: Lynn H. Boyer Jr.

Woodstown: E.W. Humphreys

New Mexico

Alamogordo: Graphic Facts of America

Albuquerque: Babcock & Burrough; F.J. Schaaf; Southwest Post Card Co.; J.R. Willis

Silver City: Arts Shop

New York

Adams: Mrs. Nellie E. Warriner

Afton: W.C. Handy

Albany: Albany News Co.; Frank Dougherty; Charles E. Houghtaling; O.S. Pulman; Souvenir Postal Card Co.; Thompson Souvenir Station

Albion: Alexander Watt

Alexandria Bay: John T. Delaney; Hallam & Vesty

Altamont: J.F. Mynderse

Amenia: J.J. Capron

Amsterdam: Seely Conover; W.D. Rucker; Mrs. K.V. Tucker

Angola: R. U. Blackney; Mrs. A.L. Farnham; Alfred B. Seeley

Apalachin: Miller Brothers

Attica: George Bey Jr.

Auburn: Auburn Post Card Manufacturing Co.; Hennessy

Averill Park: Harry Barnum; J.J. Lewis (also see Troy)

Babylon: Tomlin Art Co.

Ballston Spa: Jesse Sumner Wooley

Barryville: H. Mallison

Bath: Charles E. Buck Music House; Davidson and Harper; Samuel N. Harper

Belfast: W.W. Dart

Binnewater: David Burke

Binghamton: E.S. Wheeler

Bloomingburg: D.F. Collins; J.K. Evans

Buffalo: Adam, Meldrum & Anderson Co.; Buffalo Morning Express; Buffalo News Co.; F.A. Busch; Douglas Postcard Co.; Gies & Co.; William Hengerer Co., Ltd.; S.H. Knox & Co.; W.G. MacFarlane Publishing Co., Ltd.; Matthews Northrup Co.; A.C. Negler; Niagara Envelope Manufactory; L.F. Pease; F.F. Rick; Root & Tinker (also see New York City); M. Schoenlein; Spaulding Card Co.; L.C. Wegler Lithographers; Wild & Pchellas; Albert M. Wilson; H.L. Woehler

Canton: R.B. Dezell; $5 Photo Co.

Carthage: Karl Lederle Studio (also see Lowville)

Catskill: George Greenberg & Son

Corning: L.T. Goodridge & Co.

Cornwall-on-Hudson: Barton & Spooner

Cuba: Kellogg Studios; H.F. Wilcox

Dansville: F.A. Owen Co.; Sanford Card Co.

Dolgeville: G.E. Perkins

Dunkirk: H. Weller

Ellenville: A.V. Porter

Elmira: Baker Brothers; National Art Publishing Co.; Owen Card Publishing Co.

Fishkill Landing: R.T. Van Tyne

Flushing: Long Island News Co. (also see Long Island City)

Fort Leyden: E.E. Kellogg

Fort Montgomery: C.J. Weynant

Fullerton: Lorin G. Eggleston

Fulton: Morrill Press

Glens Falls: Dean Color Service; Russel & Wait

Gloversville: Cowles & Casler

Gowanda: Franklin's Studio

Haines Falls: Samuel E. Rusk

Hammondsport: H.M. Benner

Hyde Park: A. T. Cook; Hyde Park Gift Shop

Irvington-on-Hudson: F.H. Morrell

Jamestown: Globe Photo; Everett H. Ketchum; George H. Monroe

Jordan: Herbert A. Myer & Co. (also see Syracuse)

Kingston: Kingston News Service; Kingston Souvenir Co.

Lake Minniwaska: Alfred Fletcher Smiley

Lake Placid: G.T. Rabineau; Stedman & Lockwood; H.D. Tucker

Lebanon Springs: Gillett Post Card Co.

Liberty: Otto Hilig

Long Island City: Long Island News Co. (also see Flushing); Alfred Mainzer

Lowville: Karl Lederle Studio (also see Carthage)

Lyon Mountain: R.E. Lagrange

Mannsville: Huested Studios

Mechanicsville: Charles W. Hughes & Co., Inc.

Middletown: Charles A. Ketcham; J. Erskine Mills; Tichenor & Rudolph

Millville: J.H. Martin

Mohawk: Nolan & Prince

Mount Vernon: Gramatan Art Co., Inc.; W.F. Sleight Post Card Co.

Mountainville: Shutterbug / R.C. Gobrecht

Nassau: O.F. Burroughs; E.B. Shaver

New York City: Ed Ackermann; Albert Arenson Press; Albertype Co.; Alcan Moss Publishing Co.; Alma Publishing Co.; American Art Post Card Co.; American Art Publishing Co.; American Colortype Co. (also see Chicago); American Historical Art Publishing Co.; American Lithographic Co.; American News Co.; American Photograph Co.; American Postcard Co.; American Souvenir Card Co.; Anglo-American Publishing Co.; The Aristophoto Co.; Artino Post Card Co.; Artvue; Astor House; Atlas Society; Atlas Souvenir Card Co.; Bamforth Co. (also see Peekskill); G.J. Becker; Belmont Post Card Co.; Berdan Publishing Co.; S. Bergman; Julius Bien & Co.; A. Biren; I. H. Blanchard Press Co.; A.C. Bosselman & Co.; Brooklyn Art Publishing Co.; Brooklyn Eagle Postcards; Brooklyn Postcard Co., Inc.; Bryant Union Co.; Campbell Art Company; Joseph Campbell; Carter & Gut; Century Post Card & Novelty Co.; Clarisse; Collotype Co. (also see Elizabeth, New Jersey); Color Post Card Co.; Commercial Art Post Card Co.; L.R. Conwell Co., H.T. Cook Co.; J.B. & J.M. Cornell; Cory Post Card Co.; S. Dattilo & Co.; Davidson Brothers; P. De Mauro; Leon Louis Dolice; E.P. Dutton & Co.; Eagle Post Card View Co.; Theodor Eismann; Empire Publishing & Post Card Co.; Ess & Ess Photo Co.; Max Ettlinger & Co.; European Post Card Co.; Fairman Co. (also see Cincinnati); H. Finkelstein & Son; Ralph Finney; Foster & Reynolds (also see Washington, D.C.); William Frange; Frank Book Printing Co.; E. Frey & Co.; Sam Gabriel; Genuine Photo Co.; German-American Post Card Co. (also see Chicago and Cleveland, Ohio); German-American Postcard Manufacturing Co.; Gillin Printing Co.; Gottschalk, Dreyfuss & Davis; Graphic Postcard Co.; Greeting Card Manufacturing Co.; Edward Gross; Gut & Steers; Gutmann & Gutmann; Wolf Hagelburg; H. Hagemeister Co., Albert Hahn; George P. Hall & Son, Hambro Novelty Co.; Hamlin & Moskowitz; Harwell Evans Co.; Henry Heininger Co.; Franz Huld; Illustrated Post Card Co.; Interborough News Co.; International Post Card Co.; Ives Process Co.; Arthur Jaffe, Inc.; Jennings & Graham (also see Cincinnati); Jewish Welfare Board; Jones, Keyser & Adams; Kauffman & Strauss Co.; Walter Keane; Knapp Co., Inc.; Paul C. Koeber & Co.; Joseph Koehler; H.O. Korton; Kraus

Manufacturing Co.; C.F. Theodore Kreh; Samuel Langsdorf & Co.; Leading Novelty Co.; Leighton & Valentine (also see Portland, Maine); Leubrie & Elkins; Livermore & Knight; Arthur Livingston; Local View Printing Co.; Edward Lowey; Lumitone Press Photoprint; Maether & Co.; Manhattan Post Card Co.; George Markendorff; J.J. Marks; Martinson & Tiffany; Mayfair Photo Finishing Co.; J.G. McCrory & Co.; McGown-Silsbee Litho Co.; A.S. Meeker; Midland Publishing Co.; Miller Art Co.; Moffat, Yard & Co.; Moore & Gibson Co.; A. Moore; N. Moser; Moss Photo Service, Inc.; Alcan Moss Publishing Co.; Enrique & Robert Muller; E. Nash; National Art Co.; National Art Views Co.; National news Co.; New York Gravure Co.; Newcomb Publishing Co.; Nomis Manufacturing Co.; Oleogravure Co.; Osborne, Ltd.; J. Ottmann Lithographic Co.; Palmer Publishing Co.; Pastime Novelty Co.; Photo & Art Postal Card Co.; Photo Card Co.; Photo Color Graph Co.; Photo-Electrotype Engraving Co.; Pictorial Card Co.; Emil Pinkau & Co.; William Pinsker Co.; Platinachrome Co.; Printline; Quadri-Color Co.; Redfield Brothers, Inc.; Reinthal & Newman; A. Reisenberg; Rialto Post Card Co.; George Rizard; Rockmore Co.; Root & Tinker (also see Buffalo); Rosin & Co. (also see Philadelphia); H.A. Rost Printing & Publishing Co.; Roth & Langley; Rotograph Co.; Sackett & Wilhelms Corporation; Samson Brothers; P. Sander (also see Atlantic City and Philadelphia); I. Scheff Engraving Co., Inc.; Schlesinger Brothers; C.R. Schneider Co.; Schulze Litho and Post Card Co.; E.J. Schwabe Publishing Co.; Charles Scribner's Sons; M. Seckel; Sersanti Brothers; Fred Seyffarth; A.M. Simon; A.Q. Southwick; Souvenir Post Card Co.; Stadler Photographing Co. (also see Chicago); Standard Postal Souvenir Card Co.; Ignatz Stern; Frederick A. Stokes Co.; Strate Half-Tone Process Co.; Arthur Strauss Inc. (also see Niagara Falls); Ferdinand Strauss & Co.; Success Post Card Co.; Raf D. Szalatany; M.W. Taggart; Tanner Souvenir Co.; Taylor, Platt & Co.; G.L. Thompson; Tower Manufacturing & Novelty Co.; Transcolor Corporation; Raphael Tuck & Sons; Ullman Manufacturing Co.; Underwood & Underwood; Union News Co.; United Art Publishing Co.; Universal Postal Card Co.; Unusual Photographs Reproduction Co.; Valentine & Sons Co. (also see Boston); Valentine Souvenir Co.; Vienna Post Card Co.; F. Von Bardelben; F.W. Warne & Co.; L.E. Waterman Co.; Thaddeus Wilkerson; E.E. Winchell; F.W. Woolworth Co.; World Post Card Co. (also see Philadelphia); Walter Worth; Wyanoak Publishing Co.

Newburgh: S.G. Bradley; J. Ruben Publishing Co.

Niagara Falls: S.C. Fagard; Johnston's Art Stores; Arthur Strauss Inc. (also see New York City)

Niscayuna: National Photograph Co.

Norwich: W.F. Eldredge

Nyack: H.P. Dutcher

Old Adelphi: Bob Wier Photocards

Olean: M.E. Bramlee

Oneida: George F. Tygert

Oneonta: Oneonta Department Store

Oswego: Publicity Travel Bureau

Otter Lake: Standard Supply Co.

Palmyra: F.L. Hislo

Patchogue: H.S. Conklin

Peekskill: Bamforth Co. (also see New York City)

Perry: Bassett's Art Shop

Remsen: Henry M. Beach

Rhinebeck: Dr. B.N. Baker

Rockaway Beach: S. Hirshberg

Rochester: A.H. Abell; S.P. Hines; International Litho. Co.; Rochester News Co.; Rochester Photo Press; Scrantom, Wetmore & Co.; Ser Lithography Co.; Stecher Lithograph Co.; United Lithographing and Printing Co.

Rome: J.M. Brainerd and Co.

Sabael: H.F. Bonesteel, M.D.

Saratoga Springs: Robson & Adee (also see Schenectady); Walter M. Stroup

Sea Cliff: Long Island Postal Card Co.

Schenectady: F. Calkins; Robson & Adee (also see Saratoga Springs)

Sherburne: H.A. Lathrop

Sidney: C.H. Phelps; B.E. Pudney; Sidney Favorite Printing Co.

Sodus: Stacy Studios

South New Berlin: T.E. Parker & Co.

Stapleton: John O. Winsch

Star Lake: Santway Photo-Craft Co.

Syracuse: American Publicity Company; William Jubb Co.; Lyman Press; Herbert A. Myer & Co. (also see Jordan); William F. Shoudy; Tuppen Co. Studio

Ticonderoga: H.R. Hulett

Tompkinsville: A. Loeffler

Troy: J.J. Lewis (also see Averill Park); H.A. Pieper

Utica: Austin & Sons; Hahn & Roberts; Holland Brothers; A.J. Purvis; W.C. Rowley & Son; Utica Paper Co. (also see Verona)

Verona: Utica Paper Co. (also see Utica)

Waterloo: James E. Batsford & Son

Watertown: C.M. Bannister; Comins & Cornack

Waverly: C.C. Strong

West Nyack: Thomas Dexter Press

White Plains: Rosch

Woodstock: Camera Shop; L.E. Jones

North Carolina

Asheville: Asheville Post Card Co.; Brown Book Co.; Hackney & Moale Co.; J.H. Law; Harry N. Martin; Herbert W. Pelton; Southern Post Card Co.

Burlington: Davis News Co.

Chapel Hill: Gray & Thompson

Charlotte: Henry M. Ahrens; Dixie News Co.; Observer Printing House, Inc.; Stone & Barringer Co.

Durham: Durham Book and Stationery Co.; North Carolina News Co.; Rose Agency, Inc.

Fayetteville: Highland Book Store

Gastonia: Gazette Publishing Co.

Greensboro: Willis Book and Stationery Co.

Hamlet: Marchant Commercial Photography

Hendersonville: Flanagan Printing Co., Inc.

New Bern: Zaytoun News Agency

Pinehurst: Pinehurst, Inc.

Raleigh: Raleigh News Agencyc; James E. Thiem; Alfred Williams & Co.

Rocky Mount: Chandler's; City News Agency

Rutherfordton: Runca Import Co.; K.S. Tanner Jr.

Southern Pines: Eddy's Studio; Hayes; Sandhills Book Shop

Statesville: Brady Printing Co.

Wilmington: Service News Co.

Winston-Salem: J.B. Armstrong News Agency; Barber Printing & Stationery Co.; C.H. Cartee & Co.; Rufus A. Shore

North Dakota

Bismarck: Holmboe Studio

Williston: F.H. Smith

Ohio

Akron: Central News Co (also see Phoenix, Arizona; Philadelphia; Tacoma, Washington; and Wheeling, West Virginia)

Amelia: Art Manufacturing Co.

Ashtabula: C.L. Carle; Charles F. Fisher

Boise: C.E. Harvey

Bridgeport: Freter Brothers

Bryan: The Bryan Post Card Company

Canton: Empire Gallery; Ralph Young

Cedar Point: G.A. Boeckling Co. (also see Sandusky)

Cincinnati: Abingdon Press; Bachelor Studios; Cincinnati News Co.; Cincinnati Postal Views Distributors; Fairman Co. (also see New York City); Feicke-Desch Printing Co.; Gibson Art Co.; Jennings & Graham (also see New York City); Tom Jones; Kaeser & Blair Inc.; Kraemer Art Co.; Methodist Book Concern; Norwood Souvenir Co.; Strobridge Lithographers

Cleveland: Braun Post Card Co.; Century Post Card Co.; Cleveland News Co.; Cleveland Notion Co.; Commercialchrome Co.; Wilbur Evans Co.; M. Fenberg; German-American Post Card Co. (also see Chicago and New York City); Kaber & Son; George R. Klein News Co.; Sapirstein Greeting Card Co.; Souvenir Post Card Exchange; Sugerman Brothers

Columbus: Cott Printing Co.; Haenlein Brothers; S.F. Harriman; W.S. Harriman; Myers Photo Co.

Conneaut: Stiles Paper & Twine Co.

Davenport: Souvenir Post Card Station

East Liverpool: Bagley Co.

Fort Recovery: George McDaniel

Mansfield: Schwan's Studio

Mitiwanga: Jay Ward

Mount Vernon: Graham-Ilger Co.; Woolson Co.

Nelsonville: Lewis Wend

Portsmouth: Portsmouth News Agency

Sandusky: E.B. Ackley; Alexander Manufacturing Co.; G.A. Boeckling Co. (also see Cedar Point); E.H. Schlessman

Toledo: J.G. Boutelle; Henry H. Hamm (also see Erie, Pennsylvania); M.E. Hamm

Zanesville: Art Manufacturing Co.; Hivnor Card Co.

Oklahoma

Ardmore: Lacik News Agency

Frederick: The Press

Guthrie: DeGroot & Drilsma; F.B. Lillie & Co.; J.N. Wallace

Lawton: Sooner News Co.

Mangum: Zack T. Pryse

Muskogee: Mahoney News Agency; H.C. Morgan & Co.

Oklahoma City: H.H. Clarke; Mid-Continent News Co.; National Studio; Parkhurst Co.; Parlette-Wigger Co.; Salder & Pennington

Perkins: Van Griethuysen & Lowe (also see Ripley)

Ponca City: Pennington News Agency

Ripley: Van Griethuysen & Lowe (also see Perkins)

Shawnee: C.B. Robertson

Tulsa: Gough Photo Services; Oklahoma News Co.; Osage Indian Curio Co.

Oregon

Baker: C. Wesley Andrews (also see Portland)

Bend: Oregon Art Co.

Cove: Stearns Fellbaum Photo

Medford: Dake Studio; Frank Patterson

Pendleton: Doubleday & Gustin

Portland: C. Wesley Andrews (also see Baker); D.M. Averill & Co.; Clarence Christian; Columbia Card Co.; Cross & Dimmitt; Benjamin Arthur Gifford (also see The Dalles); J.K. Gill Co.; Glass & Prudhomme Co.; Kiser Photo Co.; Lipscheutz & Katz; Oregon News Co.; Portland Post Card Co.; B.B. Rich; Sanborn Vail & Co. (also see Los Angeles and San Francisco); Sawyer Scenic Photo Co.; Louis Scheiner (also see Tacoma, Washington); Smith Western, Inc.; Wesley Andrews Co.

Salem: Pacific Photo Co.; Patton Brothers & Cooke; Patton Postcard Co.

The Dalles: Benjamin Arthur Gifford (also see Portland); R.C. Markham

Pennsylvania

Allentown: Adpostal Corporation; Kardmasters; Klein Brothers Paper & Twine Co.; Lehigh Variety Co.

Butler: Modern-Ad

Canton: Walter Coon

Carlisle: Thompson's Book Store

Conneaut Lake Park: W.W. Wilk

Easton: Leo Meyer; Platt O. Werst

Elizabethtown: H.K. Dorsheimer

Emporium: Olson's Book and news Store

Erie: City News Agency; Gem City Postcard Co.; Henry H. Hamm (also see Toledo, Ohio); S.W. Hauck & Sons; Tillie J. Hauck; Spangenthal's Wholesale View Cards

Gettysburg: W.H. Tipton & Co.

Harrisburg: Harrisburg Specialty Co.; J.B. Hoffman; J.P. Walmer

Hatfield: I.C. Detweiler

Hazelton: Brandau's Studio

Hershey: E. Madciff

Hummelstown: G.W. Killough

Huntingdon: Edwards Post Card Co.; W.A. Grimison & Son

Jenkintown: WYCO Products

Johnstown: Henderson Advertising Co.

Lancaster: Coppinger & Griel; Mellinger Studios; I. Steinfeldt

Lebanon: Harpel's Art Studio

Ligonier: A. Saling & Sons

Mahanoy City: H.L. Jones

Marietta: Joseph M. Stafford

McDonald: Downham

Meadville: Meadville News Co.

Mill Rift: J.F. Molony

Nanticoke: S.H. Kress & Co.

New Castle: Warner Photo Shop

Penn-Mar: Libby & Bowers

Philadelphia: Beck Engraving Co.; Buffalo Paper & Postcard Co.; Central News Co (also see Akron, Ohio; Phoenix, Arizona; Tacoma, Washington; and Wheeling, West Virginia); Chilton Publishing Co.; Commercial Printing House; Curtis Publishing Co.; Doolittle & Kulling, Inc.; Douglass Postcard Co.; Gatchel & Manning; W.N. Jennings; J. Murray Jordan; Kline Poster Co.; Albert A. Lampl; Ruth Murray Miller; National Post Card Co. (also see Atlantic City); Philadelphia Post Card Co.; Photochrome Process Co.; Photo-Ty Post Card Co.; Post Card Distributing Co. (also see Atlantic City); Post Card Union of America; Rose Co.; Rosin & Co. (also see New York City); Sabold-Herb Co.; P. Sander (also see Atlantic City and New York City); P. Sanders; W.R. Schaefer; Standard Postcard and Novelty Co.; Edward Stern & Co.; Taylor Art Co.; John Wanamaker Department Store; Westminster Press; Edward L. Wilson; Wolf Co.; World Post Card Co. (also see New York City)

Pittsburgh: American Novelty Co.; Commercial Sales Co.; Eils Brothers; Joseph Horne & Co.; Imperial Greeting Card Co.; Keystone Photo View Co.; C.W. Larson Co.; Minsky Brothers & Co., Publishing Division; I. Robbins & Son; Ralph N. Sassara; H.A. Schafer News Co.

Pittston: William James Harris (also see Lake Hopatcong, New Jersey, and St. Augustine, Florida)

Port Allegheny: C.M. Williams

Punxsutawney: Hunger's Office Supply

Reading: H. Winslow Pegley; Stichler & Co.

Reynoldsville: Lewis Views

Ridgway: Ridgway News Co.: Wiese Studio

Sayre: Dimock & Sullivan

Scranton: G.V. Millar & Co.; Scranton News Co.

Stroudsburg: Albert W. Koster; J.J. Newberry & Co.

Susquehanna: Charles T. Wagner

Titusville: Corell; Dunn Stationery and Supply Co.

Towanda: Boyles Book Store

Tyrone: J.A. Gardner Importing Co.; Farran Zerbe

Valley Forge: D.J. Voorhees

Vernfield: NYCE Manufacturing Co.

Whitford: Stephen Moyland Press

Wilkes-Barre: F.M. Kirby; Wilkes-Barre News Agency

Wilkinsburg: C.M. Bunting; Wonday Film Service, Inc.

Williamsport: Williamsport Paper Co.

Willow Grove: J.M. Canfield

York: R.H. Lau & Co.; M.J. Shambaugh; York News Agency

Rhode Island

Anthony: George Mertz

Apponaug: E.E. Matteson

Block Island: N. Negus; Ye Postte Cardde Shoppe

Bristol: Henry Dio

Charlestown: Mrs. Robert Browning

Cole Farm: F.P. Cole

East Greenwich: E.F. Henry

Greenville: H. Tobey Smith

Jamestown: William Williams

Kingston: A.A. Greenman; Bernon E. Helme

Narragansett Pier: J.A. Hollingsworth

Nausauket: J.C. Lewis

Newport: Berger Brothers (also see Providence); Herz Brothers

Oakland Beach: Mrs. S. Maher; John F. Walsh

Pascoag: J.P. Davis; E. Legg

Pawtucket: Lorraine Manufacturing Co.; Red Farm Studio; Ryans

Phenix: S.W. Himes & Co.

Pleasant View: C.M. Lamb

Providence: Berger Brothers (also see Newport); Blanchard, Young & Co.; C.J. Langmead; Providence Novelty Co.; Rhode Island News Co.; J.L. & C.H. Seddon; W.R. White; Young, Leonard & Harrall Co.

Riverside: Riverside News Co.

Rocky Point: George H. Gennaway; J.F. Grout

Sakonnet: Sakonnet Transportation Co.

Saunderstown: E.E. Briggs; W.M. Thompson

Usquepaugh: Ida M. Kenyon

Valley Falls: J.H. Devlin

Wakefield: D. Gillies' Sons; O.P. Kenyon; George H. Sheldon

Warren: F.A. Bliss

Watch Hill: Book & Tackle Shop

South Carolina

Charleston: Gayden Brothers (also see Columbia)

Columbia: Gayden Brothers (also see Charleston)

South Dakota

Armour: Perry Studio

Black Hills: W.B. Perkins

Deadwood: Fisher and Co.

Lemmon: C. Oscar Oleson Photo Co.

Mitchell: Leeland Art. Co.

Parker: New Era Printing Co.

Scotland: E.H. Treiber

Sioux Falls: C.C. Slack

White River: Oscar Fryklund

Tennessee

Chattanooga: Andrews Book & Stationery Co.; W.M. Cline Co.; Hardison & Bennett; Imperial Advertising Agency; T.H. Payne & Co.; L.J. Pettus; Read House Cigar Co.; H.H. Stratton; D.R. Weill Co.

Clarksville: Anderson's News Agency

Cleveland: Coopers Book Store

Johnson City: Hart & Houston

Knoxville: Charles C. Cullen & Co.; Knoxville Engraving Co.; Moncier's, Inc.

Lebanon: Seat's Studio

Lenoir City: Lenoir Drug Co.

Memphis: Memphis Paper Co.; J.L. Neeley Magazine Co.

Monteagle: Lacy & Co.

Morristown: Novelty Store

Nashville: Capitol News Co.; Davie Printing Co.; G.C. Dury and Co.; McQuiddy Printing Co.; Rigo Chemical Co., Post Card Department; Zibart Brothers

Texas

Abilene: B. & J. Sales; Cogdell News Co.; Lemon-Shepherd Co.; J.D. Magee

Alpine: Peter Koch; Shoppers Guide Press

Amarillo: Baxter Lane Co.; Baxtone; Hodge Photo Art

Arlington: Nationwide Postcard Co.

Austin: Abe Frank; C.M. Rogers; Sauter & Kuehne; Nyla Thompson

Benham: Saunders Bookstore

Big Bend National Park: Harold F. Schaafsma

Big Springs: Johnson News Agency

Brownwood: Fred Nobs

Buchanan Dam: T.J. White

Commerce: Bachman & Pickett

Corpus Christi: W.J. Freede; Neuces News Agency; Frank Wayley Post Cards

Dallas: All-Tom Corporation (also see Fort Worth); Frey Wholesale Postcard Co.; Martin News Agency; Texacolor Card Co.; Walraven Brothers, Inc.; A. Zeese Engraving Co.

Del Rio: Edward J. Schramel

Denison: Burchards Studio; Simms Tobacco & Candy Co.

El Paso: Jim A. Alexander; Walter H. Horne Co.; Humphries Co.; I.I.C.; Orndorff Drug Store; Sandoval News Service

Euless: David Malone

Fort Worth: All-Tom Corporation (also see Dallas); The Atlas News Shop; Southwestern Engraving Co.; Strykers' Western Photo Color

Galveston: Charles Daferner; Galveston Wholesale News Co.; Purdy's Bookstore; Seawall Specialty Co. (also see Houston)

Harlingen: Whittenboch Drug Co.

Hemphill: Vergie Speights

Hico: Wiseman

Houston: American Post Card Company; Bottler Brothers; Charles Epstein Co.; Seawall Specialty Co. (also see Galveston)

Itasca: Edney's Studio

Jacksboro: Price's Studio

Laredo: Barrera Publications; Publicaciones Barrera

Llano: Robert Kasell

Lookout Mountain: L.M. Mullinix

Lubbock: Lawrence C. Garcia

McAllen: John Arredondo; O'Neall Specialty Co.

Mechanicville: M.S. Caldwell

Mineral Wells: Wright-Harris Grocer Co.

Orange: Pridgen's Studio; Wood's

Palestine: Dogwood Souvenirs

Pasadena: J. Rudy Neunlist

San Angelo: Walcott & Sons

San Antonio: George M. Bearce; The Bookshop; H. Budow; Pete Cappuyns; Dahrooge Post Card Co.; Paul Ebers; Ebers-White Co.; Joske Brothers Co.; S. Rabe; Sam Rosenthall; San Antonio Card Co.; Nic Tengg; Weiner News Co.

San Benito: Mothershed; Charles R. Walcott

Schulenburg: Ammann Advertising Co.

Sulphur Springs: T.A. Wright Photography

Sweetwater: Etz Studio & Camera Shop

Temple: Barton News Agency

Texarkana: Texarkana Books, Inc.

Tyler: R.E. Bryan; Nationwide Advertising Co.

Waco: B-W News Agency; A.B. Porter; Jimmie Willis

Utah

Kanab: L.H. Larsen Art Products

Moab: Harry Reed

Salt Lake City: Carpenter Paper Co.; Gray News Co.; Intermountain Tourist Supply, Inc.; Frank H. Leib Co.; C.R. Savage Co.; Eric J. Seaich Co.; Souvenir Novelty Co.

Vermont

Arlington: Forward's Color Productions, Inc. (also see Manchester)

Bennington: B.A. Quinlan

Bethel: Byron Y. Miller

Manchester: Forward's Color Productions, Inc. (also see Arlington)

Middlebury: Gove Photo Shop

Newport: Henry Wendell Richardson

North Springfield: Merrimack Picture Postcard Co.

Orleans: Fletcher & Co.

South Hero: Juan Robinson

Williamsville: Porter C. Thayer

Virginia

Bristol: Caldwell-Sites Co. (also see Roanoke and Staunton); Kemble-Cochran Co.

Danville: U.W. Clark; Graycraft Card Co.

Jamestown: Bayard Wootton

Lynchburg: J.P. Bell Co.

Newport News: James E. Abbe

Norfolk: A. Allen Fairchild; Joseph Hollander; Jamestown Amusement & Vending Co.; William Lamb & Co.; William A. Lyon; Magee & Robinson Printers; McGee & Robinson; Merrimac & Monitor Postcard Co.; H.R. Milo & Co. (also see Nahant, Massachusetts); Norfolk Printing Co.; Progress corporation; B.F. Salomonsky' S.B. Turner & Son

Portsmouth: Paul G. Blanford; F.W. Preedy

Richmond: A. Hoehn & Co. (also see Baltimore); Layton Studio; Oliver Carlton Schofield; Southern Bargain House; Southern Manufacturing Co.; Everett Waddey Printing & Stationery Co.

Roanoke: Caldwell-Sites Co. (also see Bristol and Staunton)

Staunton: Caldwell-Sites Co. (also see Bristol and Roanoke)

Strasburg: Shenandoah Publishing Co.

Williamsburg: Walter H. Miller & Co., Inc.

Washington

Arlington: J. Boyd Ellis

Bellingham: Clyde Banks; C.A. Griffiths

Camp Lewis: Greene Post Card Co.

Chehalis: Staeger Brothers

Colfax: V.T. McCroskey & Brothers

Davenport: The Bookstore

Moclips: Simons View Co.; E.E. Sutherland

Palouse: George N. Lamphere

Seattle: Banner Photo Co.; Cardinell-Vincent Co. (also see Los Angeles, Oakland, and San Francisco); Jacob S. Cohen; E.S. Davis; Farwest Lithograph & Printing Co.; O.E. Frasch; Alice Harriman Co.; Hopf Brothers Co.; V.O. Hopf; Indian Arts and Crafts (also see Anchorage, Alaska); C.P. Johnson Co.; Kelley Printing Co.; Lowman & Hanford Co.; Ezra Meeker; D. Minogue Art; North West Novelty Co.; Novelty Post Card Co.; Oakes Photo Co.; Post Card Shop; Puget Sound News Co.; Robert A. Reid; Romans

Photographic Co.; Scenic Photo Publishing Co.; J.A. Sims; Spiro & Lotz; Stuff Printing Concern; White Advertising Bureau, Inc.; Yukon Postcard Co.

South Bend: H.L. Gerwig; A.J. Park

Spokane: Boughton-Robbins Co.; John W. Graham & Co.; Inland Printing Co.; Keenan News Agency; Frank Palmer; J.L. Robbins Co.; Shaw & Borden Co.; Spokane Post Card Co.; Spokane Publishing Co.; Western Souvenirs, Inc.

Tacoma: Central News Co (also see Akron, Ohio; Phoenix, Arizona; Philadelphia; and Wheeling, West Virginia); Ashael Curtis Photo Co.; Leland Lund; Frank A. Neyhart & Co.; Ranapar Studio; Louis Scheiner (also see Portland, Oregon); Smith's Scenic Views; Sprouse & Son; F.B. Wines Co.

Walla Walla: Rogers-Hoswell Co.

Wenatchee: M. Horan

Washington, D.C.:
Art Association; C.P.I.; T.A. Cantwell & Co.; Columbia Card Co.; Eckert Litho. Co.; Evening and Sunday Star; Foster & Reynolds (also see New York City); Garrison Toy & Novelty Co.; Leet Brothers; C.A. McElhinney; Mount Vernon Chapter of the Daughters of the American Republic; National Tribune; P.J. Plant; Porter & Reynolds; B.S. Reynolds; D.N. Walford; Washington News Co.; Washington Souvenir Co.

West Virginia

Beckley: Beckley News Co.

Bluefield: Bluefield News Agency

Charles Town: Hayward Photo

Charleston: S. Spencer Moore Co.; Stone Brothers

Clarksburg: Rex Heck News Co.; Pike News Co.; Stone Brothers Co.

Harper's Ferry: Walter E. Dittmeyer

Huntington: H.G. Hoffman; The Huntington News Co.

Matewan: Leckie's

Moundsville: J.C. Meyers & Co.

Parkersburg: F. Brown; Harry L. Dailey; Valley News Service

Ronceverte: P.A. George & Co.

Sistersville: Minnie Nessiff

Weston: M.L. Hunt & Co.; J. Wilsher

Wheeling: Central News Co (also see Akron, Ohio; Phoenix, Arizona; Philadelphia; and Tacoma, Washington); Helmbright Brothers; Nicoll's Art Store; Olmstead Brothers Co.; C.H. Quimby

Wisconsin

Antigo: A.J. Kingsbury; W.H. Wessa

Eau Claire: G.R. Brown Co.; Sun Color Cards

Hartford: H. Montgomery

Lake Mills: L.L. Cook

Madison: Madison News Agency

Menominee: Chris N. Krogstad

Milwaukee: John T. Faber; Grogan Photo System, Inc.; E.C. Kropp Co.; Macleith Photo System; M.H. Wiltzius Co.

Phillips: S.A. Johnson

Racine: Western Printing and Lithographing Co.

Wyoming

Cheyenne: Fleetwood

Sheridan: Herbert A. Coffeen; Range Land Publishing Co.